HANDBOOK OF EMPIRICAL
SOCIAL WORK PRACTICE

HANDBOOK OF EMPIRICAL SOCIAL WORK PRACTICE

Volume 1 ————————————

Mental Disorders

Edited by
Bruce A. Thyer and John S. Wodarski

John Wiley & Sons, Inc.
New York • Chichester • Weinheim • Brisbane • Singapore • Toronto

Library of Congress Cataloging-in-Publication Data:
Handbook of empirical social work practice / edited by Bruce A. Thyer
    and John S. Wodarski.
        p.   cm.
    Includes bibliographical references and index.
    Contents: v. 1. Mental disorders—v. 2. Social problems and
practice issues.
    ISBN 0-471-15361-3 (cloth : alk. paper).—ISBN 0-471-15363-X
(set : alk. paper)
    1. Social case work.   2. Psychiatric social work.   I. Thyer,
Bruce A.   II. Wodarski, John S.
HV43.H316   1998
361.3′2—dc21   97-15312
                                                          CIP

Printed in the United States of America
10 9 8 7 6 5 4 3 2 1

Contributors ————————————————————

KIA J. BENTLEY, MSW, PhD
School of Social Work
Virginia Commonwealth University
Richmond, Virginia

JUDITH R. BORDNICK, MSW
Private Practice
Houston, Texas

PATRICK S. BORDNICK, MSW, PhD
Department of Psychiatry
University of Texas
Health Science Center
CLEAR
Houston, Texas

JOEL BREGMAN, MD
Institute Medical Group
Hartford, Connecticut

BRUCE BROTTER, MSW, PhD
New York Hospital
Cornell Medical Center
White Plains, New York

JOHN F. BUTLER, MSW, PhD
Col, USAF, BSC
Sheppard AFB
Wichita Falls, Texas

RICK L. CAMPISE, PhD
Maj, USAF, BSC
Malcolm Grow USAF Medical Center
Andrews AFB, Maryland

DANIEL CARPENTER, PhD
New York Hospital
Cornell Medical Center
White Plains, New York

JOHN F. CLARKIN, PhD
New York Hospital
Cornell Medical Center
White Plains, New York

IRIS COHEN, MSW
School of Social Work
Boston University
Boston, Massachusetts

RICHARD F. DANGEL, PhD
Graduate School of Social Work
University of Texas
Arlington, Texas

TONI M. DiDONA, MSW, PhD
Program Director
Alternate Family Care
Plantation, Florida

CHERYL DAVENPORT DOZIER, DSW
School of Social Work
University of Georgia
Athens, Georgia

CATHERINE N. DULMUS, MSW
School of Social Work
State University of New York
Buffalo, New York

SOPHIA F. DZIEGIELEWSKI, MSW, PhD
School of Social Work
University of Central Florida
Orlando, Florida

ROSEMARY L. FARMER, MSW, PhD
School of Social Work
Virginia Commonwealth University
Richmond, Virginia

DANIEL J. FISCHER, MSW
Department of Psychiatry
University of Michigan Medical Center
Ann Arbor, Michigan

JOHN GERDTZ, MSW, PhD
Spectrum Center
Berkeley, California

JOSEPH A. HIMLE, MSW, PhD
Anxiety Disorders Program
Department of Psychiatry
University of Michigan Medical Center
Ann Arbor, Michigan

ANDRÉ IVANOFF, MSW, PhD
School of Social Work
Columbia University
New York, New York

J. AARON JOHNSON, MA
Department of Sociology
University of Georgia
Athens, Georgia

MARYLOUISE E. KERWIN, PhD
Department of Psychology
Bowan College
Glassboro, New Jersey

PETER LEHMANN, DSW
Graduate School of Social Work
University of Texas
Arlington, Texas

MARSHA M. LINEHAN, PhD
Department of Psychology
University of Washington
Seattle, Washington

MARTHA J. MARKWARD, MSW, PhD
School of Social Work
University of Georgia
Athens, Georgia

ROBERT W. McLELLARN, PhD
Private Practice
Portland, Oregon

LAURA L. MYERS, MSW
School of Social Work
University of Georgia
Athens, Georgia

JOSEPH J. PLAUD, PhD
Department of Psychology
University of North Dakota
Grand Forks, North Dakota

LISA A. RAPP, MSW
School of Social Work
State University of New York
Buffalo, New York

KARRIE L. RECKNOR, M.A.
Department of Psychology
University of Washington
Seattle, Washington

CHERYL RESNICK, MSW, DSW
Department of Social Work
Georgian Court College
Lakewood, New Jersey

JULIE ROSENZWEIG, MSW, PhD
Graduate School of Social Work
Portland State University
Portland, Oregon

JOY SCHMITZ, PhD
Substance Abuse Research Center
University of Texas
Health Science Center
Houston, Texas

NANCY HALE SILLS, MSS
Children's Seashore House
Philadelphia, Pennsylvania

NANCY J. SMYTH, MSW, PhD
School of Social Work and
Research Institute on Addictions
State University of New York
Buffalo, New York

KAREN P. SOWERS-HOAG, MSW, PhD
College of Social Work
University of Tennessee
Knoxville, Tennessee

GAIL STEKETEE, MSW, PhD
School of Social Work
Boston University
Boston, Massachusetts

BRUCE A. THYER, MSW, PhD
School of Social Work
University of Georgia
Athens, Georgia

KEITH G. VAVROVSKY, BSSW
North Dakota Developmental Center
Grafton, North Dakota

M. ELIZABETH VONK, MSW, PhD
College of Social Work
Ohio State University
Columbus, Ohio

JOSEPH WALSH, MSW, PhD
School of Social Work
Virginia Commonwealth University
Richmond, Virginia

JOHN S. WODARSKI, MSW, PhD
School of Social Work
State University of New York
Buffalo, New York

BONNIE L. YEGIDIS, MSW, PhD
School of Social Work
University of Georgia
Athens, Georgia

Preface

Noting the tremendous progress in clinical research over the last two decades, we conceived of preparing this two-volume *Handbook of Empirical Social Work Practice.* We obtained commitments from a number of eminent social workers and other human service professionals to prepare chapters. Some two years later, with a sigh of relief, we passed the edited manuscripts on to our capable editor at Wiley, Kelly Franklin. The result is before you, the first compilation of empirical research findings with direct relevance to practice, developed exclusively by and for the profession of social work.

Similar works have been prepared by the professions of psychiatry (American Psychiatric Association, 1989), clinical psychology (Hayes, Follette, Dawes, & Grady, 1995), and the general field of psychotherapy (Ammerman, Last, & Hersen, 1993; Giles, 1993), with the aim of communicating to practitioners in those arenas the latest findings derived from empirically based research pertaining to the assessment of, and intervention with, selected problems or disorders. Like these related books, our handbook takes a problem-focused approach, as we believe that this affords greater utility for social work practitioners. Clients present with problems, which they would like some assistance in resolving. Clinicians need a convenient compendium of practice guidelines that provide some clear and concise directions about how to assess and what to do. Other books in this field have used a *theory-based* structure (e.g., Roberts & Nee, 1970; Dorfman, 1988; Turner, 1986; Brandell, 1997), in that individual chapters describe the approach taken by a given *theory* to deal with generic or particular problems. We believe that although such books may be well suited for the needs of academic social workers charged with teaching survey courses on practice methods, they are of little utility to practitioners, who are not concerned so much with what Theory X has to say about helping a client with Problem Y, but who are interested in finding the best supported methods of *helping* clients with problem Y, irrespective of theory. This latter need dictated the problem-focused approach of the present book.

Given that social workers constitute the largest group of providers of psychotherapy services in the United States, and that clinical social work in the field of mental health employs more professional social workers than any other area of practice, we decided that Volume 1 should focus on the so-called mental disorders, as currently conceptualized in the fourth edition of the *Diagnostic and Statistical Manual of Mental Disorders* (*DSM-IV;* American Psychiatric Association, 1994).

Although controversy continues to rage regarding the strengths and weaknesses of *DSM-IV* as a diagnostic tool and its role in a complete social work assessment, it is undeniable that this one work remains the most influential book in contemporary mental health practice. We cannot conceive of a well-trained clinical social worker who is not thoroughly conversant with the use of *DSM-IV* (and aware of its problems).

Accordingly, Volume 1 follows the diagnostic outline found in *DSM-IV.* After an introductory chapter entitled "First Principles of Empirical Social Work Practice," which establishes the conceptual underpinnings of the book, each of the remaining 22 chapters deals with one (sometimes two) of the major so-called mental disorders found in *DSM-IV.* We hope that this will facilitate its use as a reference tool. Does the client meet *DSM-IV* criteria for Panic Disorder with Agoraphobia? If so, turn to Chapter 15 to learn the best methods to complete your assessment and to develop a treatment plan. Is Bulimia Nervosa a part of the picture? Then Chapter 22 will prove useful for the same purposes.

We are acutely aware of the limitations of this approach. Clients and their families are more than sets of diagnostic criteria. The so-called mental disorders (which really should be labeled *behavioral, affective, and intellectual disorders,* to avoid an unwarranted etiological inference, in our opinion) exist within a complex system of the client's biological structure (the body) and physical and psychosocial worlds, and the interactions among these entities. A prescriptive approach to treatment, which is encouraged by the *DSM-IV* framework, can discourage, to some extent, a thorough functional analysis of a problem in situation. In particular, marital and family dynamics are not usually well developed using the *DSM-IV* system. This is why we believe that an accurate *DSM-IV* diagnosis is a part of a, but is not a complete, social work assessment. Make no mistake, the blind application of particular interventions—no matter how well supported by empirical research—is never a part of the picture of professional social work practice. Empirical research *informs,* it does not dictate; it supplements, not replaces, clinical judgment. Social work is not yet a well developed interventive science, and art alone is an insufficient foundation on which to base one's professional practice. Rather, it is the judicious integration of both science and art that we believe should characterize contemporary empirical social work practice.

DSM-IV presently contains several hundred formal diagnoses. Space limitations prevent us from including more than two dozen of those most commonly encountered in contemporary clinical social work practice. We apologize for those omitted and promise to partially rectify the situation should we be so fortunate as to succeed to a second edition. We welcome constructive suggestions from readers to improve the work in the future.

Of course, social work practice encompasses far more than treating individual clients suffering from one or more of the *DSM-IV* disorders. Many psychosocial problems experienced by individuals do not lend themselves to the *DSM-IV* format, and many problems transcend practice with individuals and entail organizational, institutional, or community-level interventions. Thus, Volume 2 of this *Handbook of Empirical Social Work Practice,* subtitled *Social Problems and Practice Issues,* addresses additional selected areas of social work practice. Again, there are far more problems than we could possibly include, so we winnowed out topics on the basis of the amount of empirical research that is presently available to guide practice. Some very important areas are quite undeveloped in this respect, such as community organization and policy practice; therefore, we were unable to address them. As scientific foundations for practice emerge in these fields, our hope is to include them in future editions, as well.

We gratefully acknowledge the valuable lessons taught to us by our clients, students, peers, and families, which have helped to shape our views regarding the immense constructive contributions of empirical research to social work practice. In particular we recognize those voices in the early years of the development of the social work profession that called for the accurate measurement of social problems, for proceduralized interventions that could be taught to others, and for the ongoing evaluation of social work services at all levels. Only now is their vision becoming fulfilled. It is to these little-recognized pioneers of empirical social work practice that we respectfully dedicate this book.

Bruce A. Thyer
Athens, Georgia

John S. Wodarski
Buffalo, New York

REFERENCES

American Psychiatric Association. (1989). *Treatments of psychiatric disorders.* Washington, DC: Author.

American Psychiatric Association. (1994). *Diagnostic and statistical manual of mental disorders* (4th ed.). Washington, DC: Author.

Ammerman, R. T., Last, C. G., & Hersen, M. (Eds.). (1993). *Handbook of prescriptive treatments for children and adolescents.* Boston: Allyn & Bacon.

Brandell, J. (1997). *Theory and practice in clinical social work.* New York: Free Press.

Dorfman, R. (Ed.) (1988). *Paradigms of clinical social work.* New York: Brunner/Mazel.

Giles, T. R. (Ed.) (1993). *Handbook of effective psychotherapy.* New York: Plenum Press.

Hayes, S. C., Follette, V. M., Dawes, R. M., & Grady, K. E. (Eds.) (1995). *Scientific standards of psychological practice: Issues and recommendations.* Reno, NV: Context Press.

Roberts, R., & Nee, R. (Eds.) (1970). *Theories of social casework.* Chicago: University of Chicago Press.

Turner, F. (Ed.) (1986). *Social work treatment* (3d ed.). New York: Free Press.

Contents

Chapter 1

FIRST PRINCIPLES OF EMPIRICAL SOCIAL WORK PRACTICE

Bruce A. Thyer
John S. Wodarski

OVERVIEW

The focus of this book is empirical research that has direct applications to social work practice. It is always useful to begin by defining one's terms, and in turning to the *Social Work Dictionary* (Barker, 1995, p. 119), we find that the word *empirical* means "based on direct observation or experience" and that *empirically based practice* is defined as:

> A type of *intervention* in which the professional social worker uses research as a practice and problem-solving tool; collects data systematically to monitor the intervention; specifies problems, techniques, and outcomes in measurable terms; and systematically evaluates the effectiveness of the intervention used.

On the face of it, this description seems quite reasonable. Indeed, should it not be characteristic of *all* of social work practice? Well, the issues are more complicated. For example, some areas of social work practice suffer from a lack of ways to measure the phenomena of interest (which makes data gathering problematic). Others are more value-based, such as the advocacy of "pro-choice" laws pertaining to abortion rights or of the rights of gays and lesbians to legally marry. Empirical research is not a particularly salient argument in such discussions.

Even more fundamentally, the very term *empirical* has been subjected to differing interpretations. For some, it means something to the effect of, "If I can see it, it is real." Hence, if I can see improvement in my clients, then I can be pretty sure they are indeed getting better, and you should take my word for this. A problem with this approach is that sometimes individuals (e.g., social work practitioners, and even clients) can be deceived. The history of quack medicine and the explanations of

1

ghosts, crop circles, flying saucers, and extrasensory perception inform us of how easy it is for well-educated, informed, and even skeptical persons to unintentionally deceive themselves or to be intentionally deceived by the unscrupulous. And, to be fair, so does the history of science—witness the discovery in 1989 of so-called cold fusion. Additional safeguards are necessary, beyond the level of personal observation, for a finding to be considered to be empirical. For example, Arkava and Lane (1983, p. 11) claim:

> Empiricism is the process of using evidence rooted in objective reality and gathered systematically as a basis for generating human knowledge. . . .

Here the key word is *systematic,* which implies a method of observation that can be reliably communicated to others who, in turn, can undertake essentially the same method of observation.

Grinnell (1993, p. 442) adds another dimension to the definition:

> *Empirical*—knowledge derived from observation, experience, or experiment.

As does a common dictionary (Berube, 1991, p. 449):

> *Empirical*—a. relying upon or derived from observation or experiment, b. capable of proof or verification by means of observation or experiment.

These latter definitions indicate that there is more to empiricism than simply relying upon the evidence of the senses. For an observation to be called empirical it should also be obtained through *systematic* observations capable of being *replicated* (i.e., verified) by other individuals, and subject to some evidentiary standards of *proof.*

Empirical methods are also founded on several other not unreasonable philosophical assumptions, such as *realism,* which maintains "that the world has independent or objective existence apart from the perception of an observer" (Chapin, 1975, p. 443), and *naturalism,* "the point of view which regards mental processes, attitudes, and other psychological processes as part of the system of natural phenomena and therefore interpretable according to natural laws" (Chapin, p. 335). Under empiricism, explanations for phenomena are first sought via material causes which do not rely upon supernatural or metaphysical mechanisms. This perspective is the point of view known as *positivism,* "a philosophical and scientific position which holds that knowledge is limited to experience and to observed facts and that metaphysical questions concerning the nature of ultimate reality are outside the scope of science or philosophy" (Chapin, p. 397).

To reiterate, empiricism implies more than data obtained by the senses.

If experience is a necessary ingredient of social work methods, then one must find means of discovering whether that experience is valid; whether the interaction with another did, in fact, lead to desired changes in that person's behavior, attitudes, and so forth; whether the methods are sound; and whether the theories that inform the methods are sound. (Williams, 1995, p. 881)

Now, what does all this philosophy have to do with social work? Very much, as so ably articulated by Reamer (1993, 1994). Certain philosophical positions are intimately linked with the profession's values and ethics. Among these are the valuing of the methods of science and of empirically based methods. More on this later. The balance of this chapter offers an overview and positive presentation of the fundamental principles of empirically based social work practice. Beginning with selected philosophical assumptions, initially touched on in the preceding, this chapter will proceed to show how these apply to all areas of practice in the field of social work. Along the way, certain misconceptions about empirical social work practice will be addressed and corrected.

FIRST PRINCIPLES

There Is an Objective Reality

Apart from accepting this as a philosophical assumption (assumptions are accepted as true, by their very definition as assumptions), there are strong logical and practice grounds supporting this principle. Millions of years ago, sentient beings called dinosaurs roamed the earth. These animals were aware of their surroundings; they ate, slept, procreated, and hunted—in other words, they *lived*. Now dinosaurs are no more, but the world continues on unabated—a changed world, granted, lacking dinosaurs, but its essential nature continues. In the future, should human beings become extinct, perhaps as the victims of some lethal viral plague, it seems reasonable that the physical structure of the world would similarly not be changed. It would continue its existence, independent of the perceptions of human beings. The dark side of the moon was unobserved by humans until a few decades ago. Did we doubt its existence then? Of course not.

The opposite of realism is *constructivism,* which has been defined as "the view that 'reality' or what we 'know' about the world and our experience of it, is a product of our own mental processes rather than something that actually exists" (Gallant, 1994, p. 119). Constructivism itself is simply a reworking of the point of view known as *solipsism* (see Thyer, 1995a), "whatever exists is a product of will" (Wolman, 1973, p. 352), and solipsism is itself derivative of a much earlier Greek philosophical school.

Although these two perspectives are often seen as antithetical, they need not be. To accept realism is *not* to deny the possible merits of those who support the solipsistic perspective. To state that the world has an independent or objective existence is not, on the face of it, to contend that subjective elements are irrelevant. Realism need not imply that the *only* reality is that which is objective and material, just that there *is* such a reality. Realism simply states that an objective and material reality is a very important piece of our universe. To claim, as do the constructivists, that the world is a social construction is certainly acceptable, as long as the position is that social constructivism may be *a part* of the universe, not the whole thing. To accept realism is not to deny the role of subjective elements as a part of the world. To accept constructivism need not be to deny the existence of an objective reality—witness the reaction of the constructivist who receives a speeding ticket while driving to the meeting of the Solipsism Society!

Those who label themselves as empiricists, realists, or positivists delimit the scope of their inquiry to the material, the objective, to that which has an independent existence. To the extent that the problems addressed by social work practitioners contain a realistic, material, and objective reality, an empirical perspective is a useful one. Conversely, empirical research has little to say about those aspects of the world that are wholly subjective, immaterial, or supernatural. The study of these areas is the subject matter of other disciplines, such as philosophy and religion.

Psychosocial Phenomena Are a Part of That Reality

As a practical matter, social workers accept this principle without too much debate. Few doubt that unemployment really exists out there in the world, that HIV disease is killing thousands, that spouses are being battered, and that children are being sexually assaulted. The phenomena labeled *bipolar disorder* are real (regardless of the current fad in diagnostic criteria) and exert their deleterious influences on the lives of clients and their families. Of course, there are gray areas—the validity of *repressed memory syndrome, multiple personality disorder,* and *late luteal phase dysphoric disorder* are a few examples. But schizophrenia was similarly gray 100 years ago, and the widespread prevalence of child abuse and incest was barely guessed at then. Like the maps of Africa and Asia of 100 years ago, the gray areas of social work practice are slowly being pushed back. Preliminary work gives way to more detailed investigations; initial impressions are corroborated or disconfirmed, new questions arise, and more accurate answers slowly emerge.

While these gray areas are being sorted out, the profession of social work is hard at work on those that are fairly unambiguous—working to eliminate racial discrimination and poverty, to promote economic self-sufficiency, to reduce the deleterious effects of so-called mental illnesses, and to deter domestic and community violence. Indeed, the empirical social worker can reasonably contend that virtually the entire focus of our discipline is on the objective reality of deleterious psychosocial environments and of people's reactions to those circumstances. Our field is charged with discovering not the *meaning* of homelessness or of being abused, but, rather, what can be done to *eliminate* homelessness and to prevent abuse.

One of the seminal figures in social work practice and education had this to say on the matter:

> At first glance it seems unnecessary to state that, if we believe in a *noncapricious and objectively reliable universe,* [italics added] such belief also includes social and economic forces with which we can cooperate. Actually, we constantly deny this reliance on objective reality in favor of subjective fantasies. (Reynolds, 1963/ 1991, p. 315)

And,

> A second characteristic of scientifically oriented social work is that *it accepts the objective reality of forces outside itself* [italics added] with which it must cooperate. (Reynolds, 1942, p. 24)

Here, Bertha Capen Reynolds is unambiguously asserting that the universe is lawful (noncapricious) and does have its own existence apart from social constructions. The implications of this position are not trivial. A lawful universe contains the potential for meaningful and effective social work intervention. A capricious one holds little hope for the value of structured social work interventions at the level of micro- or macropractice. If the objective realities of poverty are either denied or seen as unimportant, then the focus of social work is on changing the *perceptions* of clients about the world in which they live. If the material world is seen as real and important, then the focus of intervention is most fruitfully seen as improving the objective circumstances of people's lives—for example, housing, nutrition, employment, and safety—as opposed to their *perceptions* of these matters. Gutheil (1992) provides a nice summary on the importance of the physical realities of life in social work assessment and intervention which does not discount the psychological ones.

Knowledge of Psychosocial Phenomena Can Be Arrived At

In support of this principle, we can again cite Reynolds' common-sense views:

> I believe that it is possible to understand scientifically the movement of social and economic forces and to apply our strength in cooperation with them. (Reynolds, 1963/1991, p. 315)

And well before her, we can turn to the proceedings of the National Conference on Charities from more than 100 years ago:

> Most of the leaders of the conference accepted the implications of a scientific approach to social work problems. They acted on the tacit assumption that human ills—sickness, insanity, crime, poverty—could be subjected to study and methods of treatment. . . . This attitude raised these problems out of the realm of mysticism into that of a science. . . . As a result of the adoption of this scientific attitude, conference speakers and programs looked forward towards progress. . . . They believed in the future; that it was possible by patient, careful study and experimentation to create a society much better than the one they lived in. (Bruno, 1964, pp. 26–27)

However, the subject matter for the professional social worker is perhaps more complex than that for any other discipline. We envy the chemist, who mixes uncontaminated chemicals in a flask and always finds the same result; the experimental physicist, who turns on the apparatus and obtains replicable observations; and the rocket scientist charged with designing a spacecraft to fly to Mars, who, perhaps after some initial failures, finally lands a probe on the surface of another planet. Such problems, daunting though they may be, pale in comparison to the prospects of finding a sufficiency of families to adopt orphans, of eliminating drug abuse, or of making the inner cities safer places to live. Try developing an *effective* program to ensure that the maximum number of persons with chronic mental illness can live independent lives; to encourage single mothers to get off welfare when there are no jobs to be had; or even to do something *simple*—like prevent high school drop outs! Ours is far and away the more difficult challenge!

Nevertheless, the complexity of our field does not shake the calm, confident belief that the phenomena with which we deal are grounded in a physical reality, are potentially capable of being understood, and are based on natural laws governing human behavior and biology. Arthur Todd's (1920, p. 73) prescient book, *The Scientific Spirit and Social Work,* had this to say on the matter: "It (science) does not deny that a thing exists merely because it is not easily seen." The empiricist sees no need to invoke metaphysical variables in the face of our current lack of understanding. We recognize that it is better to withhold judgment than to seize upon spurious explanations. Outside of the laboratory, the physicist cannot predict where Forrest Gump's feather will fall, but this inability does not cause him or her to rush around invoking spirit entities or thought forces to explain what happens. Present difficulties in explanation or prediction do not shake the faith (so to speak) that viable causal accounts are potentially achievable for even the most intractable intrapersonal and social problems our field deals with. Again, turning to Todd (p. 71):

> Science does not claim to have complete knowledge of the truth or to have established perfect order out of chaos in this world. It is less an accomplished fact than an attitude.

We can point to the considerable progress that has been made already. We now know much more than we did 50 years ago about the etiology of alcoholism, of the consequences of sexual trauma, and of the prevalence of domestic violence. And we now know much more than before about effective psychosocial interventions (see following).

Mary Richmond (1917, p. 53) asserted, "Thoughts and events are facts. The question whether a thing be fact or not is the question whether or not it can be affirmed with certainty." Richmond believed that some degree of certainty, and hence fact, *could* be arrived at. In fact, her entire text *Social Diagnosis* is an attempt to teach social workers a methodology to obtain as many facts in a case as possible, and to make correct inferences from those facts. She lamented that:

> No considerable group of social case workers . . . seem to have grasped that the *reliability* of the evidence on which they base their decisions should be no less rigidly scrutinized than is that of legal evidence by opposing counsel. (Richmond, 1917, p. 39)

To rectify this, she devoted chapter after chapter to such relevant topics as the nature and use of social evidence, bias in testimony, and making reasonable inferences, all operating on the assumption that objective knowledge of psychosocial phenomena is possible.

The opposite of this principle is *nihilism*—"a doctrine that all values are baseless and that nothing is knowable or can be communicated" (Berube, 1991, p. 842). The very existence of the methods of science and of social work's application of these tools to make useful discoveries is a repudiation of this view.

It is often maintained that since research is conducted by human beings, who themselves hold values and beliefs, then by necessity the entire scientific enterprise is suspect (see Witkin, 1991, for one example of this position). This misses the point that science itself is intensely self-critical and has devoted extensive work to this very problem (e.g., Rudner, 1953). The answer lies in the ability of empirical findings to be effectively transmitted and replicated by others. As Gorenstein (1986, p. 589) noted:

> It makes no sense to reject the potential scientific import of a construct simply because social values may have played some role in its formulation. The question of whether a construct has any scientific import is an empirical one. It has to do with whether the construct exhibits lawful properties.

In science, the culture, politics, religion, race, or gender of the investigator have little to do with the merits of what his or her research uncovers (although how this is used is another matter). This is actually a great strength of the empiricist position. Entertain the opposite stance, and you have the Nazis burning the books of Einstein because he was Jewish; racists denigrating the agricultural research of George Washington Carver because he was Black; and chauvinists dismissing the findings of Marie Curie because of her gender. Social work professor Leon Williams summed this principle up well:

Social work must assume, for the sake of epistemology, that the field can attain certain, if not valid, knowledge about the human condition. To settle for something equal to or less than probable knowledge is to settle for knowledge dictated by dogma and naive belief, and that appears untenable in an applied discipline. (Williams, 1995, p. 881)

Scientific Inquiry: The Most Reliable Way to Arrive at Such Knowledge

The previous sections have intimated at this principle, but it is worthy of being explicitly stated. Although the word *science* is barely 150 years old, the methodological tools of empirical science have proven to be an extremely valuable method for discovering facts about the world. Conventional scientific inquiry covers a multitude of methodologies, including both qualitative and quantitative approaches. Science is intensely self-critical and is constantly evolving, incorporating new methods and discarding outmoded ones:

> Science always moves on. The charitable methods of twenty years ago may be utterly obsolete now. Our methods, even the most scientific, may be the laughing stock of our descendants in the twenty-first century. (Todd, 1920, p. 85)

Field research, naturalistic observations, participant observational studies, correlational investigations, surveys, longitudinal studies, quasi-experiments, single-system research designs, and classical experimental analyses are all subsumed under the rubric of empirically based science. No subject or problem within social work is inherently excluded from scientific analysis, although some things are certainly more difficult to investigate than others. The edifice of conventional, empirical science employs a multitude of methods, qualitative and quantitative—those which investigate linear, simple, causal phenomena, and those which are applicable to the analysis of complex, multiply determined interactive psychosocial systems. As long as the phenomena in question is seen as occurring (at least in part) in the material, physical world in which we live, then science can investigate it. As long as the methodology is systematic and replicable, and possesses verifiable standards of proof, it is a welcome member of the community of scientific methods. It only took Jane Goodall seeing *one* chimpanzee eating meat in the wild to disconfirm the then-current hypothesis that chimps are naturally exclusively vegetarian. Such field observational studies are a valuable tool in science. When others see the same thing in different settings, or when videotapes can be made of the event, naturalistic observational studies are granted even stronger credence. At the other end of the hierarchy (or rainbow, if you prefer) of scientific research methods is the multinational randomized controlled clinical trial, conducted by diverse investigators with disparate clients (e.g., with respect to such characteristics as race, gender, and age), which obtains replicated results.

All are not given equal credence, however. Evidence obtained from a well-conducted randomized controlled clinical trial is seen as more persuasive than an individual case history presented narratively. Studies with long-term follow-ups are seen as better tests of a treatment's efficacy than those that assess clients only immediately posttreatment. Correlational studies with thousands of respondents are seen as more credible than those using only ten people, and replicated studies are seen as more reliable than unreplicated ones (see Thyer, 1989, 1991). Both qualitative and quantitative research methods have a valuable function in mainstream science. In general, qualitative methods are very useful for learning about a specific problem area or clientele, and for generating hypotheses or meaningful questions. Quantitative methods are, in turn, most useful for developing *answers* to questions once they have been formulated, but they are not particularly strong for originating theory or generating hypotheses.

No methodology is without its problems. In 1925, anthropology student Margaret Mead traveled to Samoa to learn something of the realities of adolescent life there. Using a qualitative participant observation methodology and two key informants during her long-term stay, Mead came away with a view of Samoan adolescence characterized as being sexually uninhibited, anxiety-free, and generally without stress. Her work culminated in the popular book *Coming of Age in Samoa*. It was not until the 1980s that it emerged that Mead had been hoaxed by her informants—who had decided to play a trick on her and basically told her what they thought she wanted to know—and that quantitative data (e.g., statistics on juvenile crimes) failed to corroborate Mead's "findings" (see Gardner, 1993).

In 1989, chemists in Utah announced the discovery of cold fusion, a potential source of limitless energy. Within a few weeks, leading research laboratories across the world announced their replication of the cold fusion phenomenon. Unfortunately, a few nay-saying voices emerged, claiming alternative explanations for the chemical phenomenon in question. Over several months, it slowly became clear that the detractors were correct. The claims of cold fusion were erroneous (see Rothman, 1990).

One would have hoped that the length of Mead's stay in Samoa would have revealed the truth to her, and that their detailed knowledge of the laws of physics would have deterred Pons and Flieschmann from making premature claims about their new energy source—but such are the vagaries of science, no matter what method is employed, whether the anthropologist's field study or the chemist's laboratory experiment. The process of scientific inquiry, though, tends to preclude errors from being perpetuated in the long run, and allows the truth to emerge. This self-corrective feature is not characteristic of other ways of knowing, such as divine inspiration, reliance on prior authorities, intuition, or even practice wisdom. Science provides a manner—empirical research—to resolve conflicting views; revelation and other approaches to discovery do not. This is a distinctive strength of scientific inquiry.

The field of social work has long recognized this. So much so, that the *Code of Ethics* of the National Association of Social Workers (NASW) clearly states that "Social workers should base practice on recognized knowledge, *including empirically-based knowledge,* relevant to social work practice" (NASW, 1996, p. 20). The *Curriculum Policy Statement* of the Council on Social Work Education (CSWE) mandates that "Every part of the professional foundation curriculum should . . . help bring students to an understanding and appreciation of a scientific, analytic approach to knowledge building at practice. The ethical use of scientific inquiry should be emphasized throughout" (CSWE, 1982, p. 10).

One of the seven original organizations that formed the NASW was the *Social Work Research Group* (SWRG; itself established in 1949), which had adopted the positivist philosophy of science as its guiding research paradigm (see Tyson, 1992, p. 542). When the NASW was founded in 1955 (incorporating the SWRG as its Research Section), the new organization's bylaws proclaimed that one of its three major purposes was "to expand through research the knowledge necessary to define and attain these goals" (e.g., to improve conditions of life; NASW, 1955, p. 3). Numerous early articles and books in social work valued the methods of science and the potential that empirical research possessed to be of benefit to the field and to society (e.g., Gordon, 1956; Preston & Mudd, 1956; Todd, 1920; see Zimbalist, 1977, for a summary). In 1880, Charles D. Kellogg of the Philadelphia Charity Organization believed that "Charity is a science, the science of social therapeutics, and has laws like all other sciences" (Germain, 1970, p. 9). While perhaps an overstatement, Kellogg's sentiment expresses the optimistic empiricist *zeitgeist* surrounding the establishment of the social work profession.

To reiterate, to claim that empirical methods have much to contribute to developing advances in knowledge and practice in social work intervention is not to automatically deny the role of alternative ways of knowing. Rather, it is for the advocates of methods of discovery that are apart from mainstream science to demonstrate the value of those other approaches. Neither does science inherently claim that issues which fall outside its purview are unimportant or meaningless to others. Love, altruism, faith, beauty, commitment, courage, and hope are all of vital significance to humanity. For science to state that it does not address such topics is not to say that they are insignificant. Thyer stated it this way:

> Many questions of great importance to our profession, such as the value base of social work, are simply outside the purview of scientific inquiry and other standards apply to the discussion of such topics apart from the conventional rules of scientific inference, standards such as those pertaining to religious beliefs, morality, and other philosophical convictions. Logical positivists are fully aware that many significant areas of our professional and personal lives should not be scrutinized through the lenses of science, but when the issues relate to social work theory and the evaluation of our practice methods, the role of controlled scientific investigations . . . becomes a relevant factor. (Thyer, 1994, p. 6)

Measuring Psychosocial Phenomena: Some Good Methods

Bloom, Fischer, and Orme have done us a service by uncovering an important quote from Dr. Richard Cabot, who addressed a national social work convention in 1931:

> I appeal to you. . . . Measure, evaluate, estimate, appraise your results, in some form, in any terms, that rest on something beyond faith, assertion, and "illustrative cases." (Bloom et al., 1995, p. xiii)

A major obstacle to the conduct of quality empirical research in social work was the lack of suitable measures. Preston and Mudd (1956, p. 36) asked (and answered):

> What is preventing progress in the identification of factors contributing to positive movement (results) in social casework? First is the fact that movement indices, while reliable, have not yet been shown to be valid.

A problem similarly noted by Gordon:

> Social workers have . . . felt the lack of more systematic and objective means of making these observations . . . and with methods that make them more than individual impressions. (Gordon, 1956, p. 82)

Mary Richmond (1917/1935, p. 362) provided one partial solution to this problem: "To state that we think our client is mentally deranged is futile; to state the observations that have created this impression is a possible help." In other words, be parsimonious in description, keep unwarranted inferences to a minimum, and note what actually occurs, as opposed to interpreting what is seen.

As it happens, considerable progress has been achieved in developing both reliable and valid measures of client progress. Fischer and Corcoran's (1994) source contains several hundred rapid assessment measures covering the panoply of fields of clinical practice—children, adults, families and couples. Many of these reliable and valid instruments are of great value in supplementing clinical judgment in social work assessment and in monitoring change during the course of intervention. An increasing number of similarly constructed sources is available to agencies and practitioners (e.g., Sederer & Dickey, 1996; Wetzler, 1989; National Institute on Drug Abuse, 1994). Apart from formal pencil-and-paper, client-reported rapid assessment instruments, corresponding advances have been made in systematizing the direct observation of behavior in its natural contexts (e.g., Polster & Collins, 1993).

Occasionally, one encounters a colleague who asserts, "Well, you just can't measure problem *X*!" Smile upon hearing remarks like this and inquire, "Well, do you mean that *X* can't *ever* be measured, by anyone? Or do you mean that *you* do not know how to measure *X* now?" Modesty usually compels the naysayer to back up a bit and acknowledge that the latter position is what was really meant. In point of fact, most of the psychosocial problems dealt with by social workers *have* had some form of reliable and valid method of assessment developed. Perhaps these methods do not cover every area, or are not evenly distributed across fields of practice. Depression, for example, enjoys a much richer assessment literature than does, say, multiple personality disorder; and clinical social work practice has a more developed empirical assessment methodology than does community organization. But an operating assumption of the empirical social worker is that if a problem (or strength) exists in the real world, it is potentially measurable. And if it is measurable, we are in a better position to offer interventive services and to see if we are helping the client-in-situation.

This does not disregard the unfortunate fact that our measures are often imperfect and require improvement. The national census undercounts illegal immigrants, racial minorities, and the homeless. However, what alternatives are there to the census? What other database shall we rely upon to estimate the numbers and characteristics of the citizenry? Clearly, the answer is to improve the technology for taking the census, not to stop counting people. Similarly, ways to measure unemployment, the rate of inflation, the cost of living, or the quantity and quality of a client's affective disorder suffer from varying degrees of imperfection. Like astronomers' calculations of the mass of the universe, the social work–related disciplines are getting better and better at assessing the psychosocial problems of clients. The measurement of clinical anxiety is considerably advanced over the techniques of two decades ago. Similar progress has been made in the analysis of social support, expressed emotion, caregiver burden, quality of life, and degree of independent living. Can these constructs be measured perfectly, in a manner completely isomorphic with nature's reality? Probably not. Are we coming progressively closer to capturing nature's reality? Most definitely!

Some Empirically Supported Interventions

This is a really exciting area of social work practice: The development of psychosocial treatments that have been shown, through credible scientific tests, to *really* be of help to clients. Perhaps not to every client with a particular difficulty, and perhaps not to the point of complete resolution or cure, but for many problems we are in a position to offer professional social work services that are quite likely to benefit a significant proportion of our clients to a clinically meaningful extent. Indeed, the balance of this text provides summaries of this practice-research literature, so the point will not be belabored here. Rather, note that the American Psychiatric Association (APA, 1995), the American Psychological Association (Chambless et al., 1996; Task Force, 1995), and the NASW are at work developing practice guidelines as to what treatments are first indicated for particular problems. Within the American Psychological Association, careful compilations are being made of psychosocial interventions that work for particular disorders (see Sanderson & Woody, 1995), and this information will have an increasing influence on the conduct of practice.

Within all the human services, it is becoming increasingly evident that some psychosocial treatments are effective for particular problems and some are not. A number of recent books summarize these findings, such as Giles (1993); Ammerman, Last, and Hersen (1993); and the Institute of Medicine (1989); as do some recent articles within social work, notably Gorey (1996); MacDonald, Sheldon, and Gillespie (1992); Rubin (1985); Thomlison (1984); Thyer (1995b); Gorey, Thyer, and Pawluck (in press); and Reid and Hanrahan (1982). This is delightful news which should be shouted from the rooftops. Contrary to the nihilistic view that "virtually any intervention can be justified on the grounds that it has as much support as alternative methods" (Witkin, 1991, p. 158), numerous outcomes studies comparing various forms of psychosocial treatment find that some types of interventions work better than others for particular problems. Consult any recent issue of *Research on Social Work Practice,* the *Journal of Consulting and Clinical Psychology,* or the *Archives of General Psychiatry* for evidence of this contention.

Our Obligation to Apply This Knowledge

Once the preceding principles have been established, it follows quite naturally that we should be obliged to apply this knowledge. Indeed, it would be premature to assert it had the appropriate empirical foundations not been established. Now that our field has sufficiently progressed, the following position is a reasonable one:

> The clinician would first be interested in using an intervention strategy that has been successful in the past. . . . When established techniques are available, they should be used, but they should be based on objective evaluation rather than subjective feeling. (Jayaratne & Levy, 1979, p. 7)

Although, in Corcoran's (in press) analysis, jurisprudence has not yet established that social work clients have a legal right to effective treatment, Myers and Thyer (1997) argue that the ethical right certainly does already exist. Note that the principle is *not* that clients are guaranteed to benefit from social work intervention, but is rather the more limited concept that they have the right to *receive* treatment with some credible degree of support as a first-choice therapy, whenever such is available.

The right to receive effective treatment is being convincingly argued in a number of human service disciplines. In psychiatry, Klerman (1990, p. 417) states that:

> The psychiatrist has a responsibility to use effective treatment. The patient has a right to proper treatment. Proper treatment involves those treatments for which there is substantial evidence.

This view has come to be known as *evidence-based psychiatry* (see Goldner & Bilsker, 1995).

In behavior analysis it is asserted that "the individual has the right to the most effective treatment procedures available" (Van Houten et al., 1988, p. 113), and an organization called the International Association for the Right to Effective Treatment has been formed. In clinical psychology, Chambless et al. (1996, p. 10) claim that:

> Whatever interventions that mysticism, authority, commercialism, politics, custom, convenience, or carelessness might dictate, clinical psychologists focus on what works. They bear a fundamental ethical responsibility to use where possible interventions that work and to subject any intervention they use to scientific scrutiny.

And in social work, Tutty (1990, p. 13) suggests that:

> It is important to provide the most effective treatment available. This entails professionals keeping current on the research on treatment effectiveness for their particular client populations.

While it would have been premature to assert this principle some 10 to 20 years ago, each new advance in clinical-research knowledge adds weight to the argument in favor of the right to effective treatment. This view is consistent with practice wisdom, with the NASW *Code of Ethics,* and with the accreditation standards of the CSWE. What are the merits of the alternative perspective?

Evaluating the Outcomes of Our Interventions

The need for social workers to regularly evaluate the outcomes of practice at all levels has long been recognized within the profession. This principle is codified in the NASW's *Code of Ethics,* which states:

> Social workers should monitor and evaluate policies, the implementation of programs, and practice interventions. (NASW, 1996, p. 20, section 5.02 [a])

In the furtherance of this principle, the CSWE's *Curriculum Policy Statement* mandates that:

> The content on research should impart scientific methods of building knowledge and of evaluating service delivery in all areas of practice. It should include quantitative and qualitative research methodologies; designs for the systematic evaluation of the student's own practice; and the critical appreciation and use of research and of program evaluation. (CSWE, 1982, p. 11)

The lack of research designs appropriate for clinical and program evaluations was keenly felt in our profession's early years. Preston and Mudd (1956, p. 36) noted in the inaugural issue of *Social Work* (NASW's flagship journal): "Much technical work remains to be done before even the most elementary of experimental designs can be applied." Field research on naturalistic social work services does not lend itself to the strictures of classical experimental research designs. It is almost always impossible to randomly *select* a sample of clients from the larger population of those with a particular psychosocial problem; and random *assignment* to treatment and no-treatment or placebo-control groups is equally problematic. Obtaining enough clients to allow for sufficient statistical power of inferential tests is also a difficulty.

To some extent, these problems have been dealt with pragmatically. For example, if we scale back our expectations and standards so that we limit initial investigations to answering the question, "Did our clients get better after receiving social work services?," then nonexperimental designs such as pre- and posttest group studies on convenience samples of individuals are quite adequate to the task. Asking practitioners to provide credible answers to the question, "Did social work intervention *cause* your clients to improve?" requires the imposition of rigorous experimental designs, and is most often an impractical endeavor. Asking the less rigorous but still important question, Did they get better?, is a far more feasible endeavor.

The development and application of single-system research designs (SSRDs) is another major positive development. About a dozen social work books have been published on the topic in the past two decades, as well as several hundred journal articles discussing and applying the approach (see Thyer & Thyer, 1992). Social work generalist research texts now regularly include one or more chapters on the conduct of SSRDs, and evaluation research making use of this methodology, representing a variety of practice and theoretical orientations, has appeared in all the major social work professional journals.

Concommitant advances have been made in the design and conduct of group research designs. The number of such published studies is growing exponentially. In Gorey's (1996) review, over 85 outcome studies on social work practice appeared in print from 1990 to 1994. Contrast this to the *total* of 17 found by Fischer (1976) that appeared prior to 1972. More sophisticated statistical procedures such as meta-analysis permit the aggregation of group outcome studies, enhancing the power to detect changes in client functioning (see Gorey, 1996; Gorey et al., in press).

Conducting evaluation research in social work is perhaps our field's most challenging endeavor (Harrison & Thyer, 1988). However, students and practitioners are now being exposed to the practical tools necessary to undertake such evaluations (they weren't before), and the profession's code of ethics mandates such work (previously it did not). Outcome studies can be profitably undertaken by individual clinicians focused on individual clients, by administrators supporting program evaluations of the results of particular agency-based services, and by policymakers and legislators expecting some evidence of effectiveness. Soon, it is to be hoped, a stronger standard will be adopted by the profession, one which reads something like this:

tifiable—respect for the individual, a concomitant focus on individually based and societally directed interventions, and the promotion of self-determination and social justice (Thyer, 1996b).

One of the best tools to promote the values of the profession is empirical social work practice. Telling the truth is one of those values (Reamer, 1995, p. 897), and discovering the truth is something that empirical research is very good at. The balance of this book presents credible reviews of contemporary empirical literature pertaining to selected behavioral, affective, and intellectual disorders, and their psychosocial assessment and treatment. That such a book is now possible is a striking affirmation of the merits of the approach to social work called *empirical clinical practice.*

REFERENCES

American Psychiatric Association. (1995). *Practice guidelines for the treatment of patients with substance abuse disorders.* Washington, DC: Author.

Ammerman, R. T., Last, C. G., & Hersen, M. (Eds.). (1993). *Handbook of prescriptive treatments for children and adolescents.* Boston: Allyn & Bacon.

Arkava, M. I., & Lane, T. A. (1983). *Beginning social work research.* Boston: Allyn & Bacon.

Barker, R. L. (Ed.). (1995). *The social work dictionary* (3rd ed.). Washington, DC: NASW Press.

Berube, M. (Ed.). (1991). *The American heritage dictionary* (2nd college ed.). New York: Houghton Mifflin.

Bloom, M., Fischer, J., & Orme, J. (1995). *Evaluating practice.* Boston: Allyn & Bacon.

Bruno, F. J. (1964). *Trends in social work: 1874–1956.* New York: Columbia University Press.

Chambless, D., Sanderson, W., Shoham, V., Johnson, S., Pope, K., Crits-Crisotph, P., Baker, M., Johnson, B., Woody, S., Sue, S., Beutler, L., Williams, D., & McCurry, S. (1996). An update on empirically validated therapies. *The Clinical Psychologist, 49*(2), 5–18.

Chapin, J. P. (1975). *Dictionary of psychology.* New York: Dell.

Corcoran, K. J. (in press). Clients without a cause: Is there a legal right to effective treatment in clinical social work? *Research on Social Work Practice.*

Council on Social Work Education. (1982). Curriculum policy for the master's degree and baccalaureate degree programs in social work education. *Social Work Education Reporter, 30*(3), 5–12.

Ewalt, P. L. (1995). Clinical practice guidelines: Their impact on social work in health. *Social Work, 40,* 293.

Fischer, J. (1976). *The effectiveness of social casework.* Springfield, IL: Charles C Thomas.

Fischer, J., & Corcoran, K. (1994). *Measures for clinical practice.* New York: Free Press.

Gallant, J. P. (1994). New ideas for the school social worker in the counseling of children and families. *Social Work in Education, 15,* 119–128.

Gardner, M. (1993). The great Samoan hoax. *Skeptical Inquirer, 17*(winter), 131–135.

Germain, C. (1970). Casework and science: A historical encounter. In R. Roberts & R. Nee (Eds.), *Theories of social casework* (pp. 3–32). Chicago: University of Chicago Press.

Giles, R. R. (Ed.). (1993). *Handbook of effective psychotherapy.* New York: Plenum Press.

Goldner, E. M., & Bilsker, D. (1995). Evidence-based psychiatry. *Canadian Journal of Psychiatry, 40,* 97–101.

Gordon, W. E. (1956). The challenge of research to today's medical social worker. *Social Work, 1*(1), 81–87.

Gorenstein, E. E. (1986). On the distinction between science and valuation in the mental health field (letter). *American Psychologist, 41,* 588–590.

Gorey, K. (1996). Effectiveness of social work intervention research: Internal versus external evaluations. *Social Work Research, 20,* 119–128.

Gorey, K., Thyer, B. A., & Pawluck, D. (in press). The differential effectiveness of social work interventions: A meta-analysis. *Social Work.*

Grinnell, R. M., Jr. (Ed.). (1993). *Social work research and evaluation* (4th ed.). Itasca, IL: F. E. Peacock.

Gutheil, I. A. (1992). Considering the physical environment: An essential component of good practice. *Social Work, 37,* 391–396.

Harrison, D. F., & Thyer, B. A. (1988). Doctoral research on social work practice: A proposed agenda. *Journal of Social Work Education, 24,* 107–114.

Institute of Medicine. (1989). *Research on children with mental, behavioral, and developmental disorders.* Washington, DC: National Academy Press.

Jayaratne, S., & Levy, R. L. (1979). *Empirical clinical practice.* New York: Columbia University Press.

Klerman, G. (1990). The psychiatric patient's right to effective treatment: Implications of *Osheroff v. Chestnut Lodge. American Journal of Psychiatry, 147,* 409–418.

MacDonald, G., Sheldon, B., & Gillespie, J. (1992). Contemporary studies of the effectiveness of social work. *British Journal of Social Work, 22,* 615–643.

Myers, L. L. & Thyer, B. A. (1997). Should social work clients have the right to effective treatment? *Social Work, 42,* 288–298.

National Association of Social Workers. (1955). *Bylaws of the National Association of Social Workers.* New York: Author.

National Association of Social Workers. (1996, November). The National Association of Social Workers Code of Ethics. *NASW News,* 17–20.

National Association of Social Workers' National Committee on Lesbian and Gay Issues. (1992). *Position statement—"Reparative" or "conversion" therapies for lesbians and gay men.* Washington, DC: NASW Press.

National Institute on Drug Abuse. (1994). *Mental health assessment and diagnosis of substance abusers* (NIH Publication No. 94-3846). Washington, DC: Author.

Polster, R. A., & Collins, D. (1993). Structured observation. In R. M. Grinnell (Ed.), *Social work research and evaluation* (pp. 244–261). Itasca, IL: F. E. Peacock.

Preston, M. G., & Mudd, E. H. (1956). Research and service in social work: Conditions for a stable union. *Social Work, 1*(1), 34–40.

Reamer, F. G. (1993). *The philosophical foundations of social work.* New York: Columbia University Press.

Reamer, F. G. (1994). *The foundations of social work knowledge.* New York: Columbia University Press.

Reamer, F. G. (1995). Ethics and values. In R. L. Edwards (Ed.), *Encyclopedia of social work* (19th ed., pp. 893–902). Washington, DC: National Association of Social Workers.

Reid, W. J., & Hanrahan, P. (1992). Recent evaluations of social work: Grounds for optimism. *Social Work, 27,* 328–340.

Reynolds, B. C. (1942). *Learning and teaching in the practice of social work.* New York: Farrar & Reinhart.

Reynolds, B. C. (1963/1991). *An uncharted journey.* Silver Spring, MD: NASW Press.

Richmond, M. (1917/1935). *Social diagnosis.* New York: Russell Sage.

Rothman, M. A. (1990). Cold fusion: A case history in "wishful science"? *Skeptical Inquirer, 14*(Winter), 161–170.

Rubin, A. (1985). Practice effectiveness: More grounds for optimism. *Social Work, 30,* 469–476.

Rudner, R. (1953). The scientist *qua* scientist makes value judgements. *Philosophy of Science, 20,* 1–6.

Sanderson, W. C., & Woody, S. (1995). Manual for empirically validated treatments: A project of the Task Force on Psychological Intervention, Division of Clinical Psychology, American Psychological Association. *The Clinical Psychologist, 48*(4), 7–11.

Sederer, L. I., & Dickey, B. (1996). *Outcomes assessment in clinical practice.* Baltimore: Williams & Wilkins.

Syers, M. (1995). Abraham Flexner. In R. L. Edwards (Ed.), *Encyclopedia of social work* (19th ed., pp. 2584–2585). Washington, DC: National Association of Social Workers.

Task Force on Promotion and Dissemination of Psychological Procedures. (1995). Training in and dissemination of empirically-validated psychological treatments: Report and recommendations. *The Clinical Psychologist, 48*(1), 2–23.

Thomlison, R. J. (1984). Something works: Evidence from practice effectiveness studies. *Social Work, 19,* 51–57.

Thyer, B. A. (1989). First principles of practice research. *British Journal of Social Work, 19,* 309–323.

Thyer, B. A. (1991). Guidelines for evaluating outcome studies on social work practice. *Research on Social Work Practice, 1,* 76–91.

Thyer, B. A. (1994). Social work theory and practice research: The approach of logical positivism. *Social Work and Social Services Review, 4,* 5–26.

Thyer, B. A. (1995a). Constructivism and solipsism: Old wine in new bottles? *Social Work in Education, 17,* 63–64.

Thyer, B. A. (1995b). Effective psychosocial treatments for children and adolescents: A selected review. *Early Child Development and Care, 106,* 137–147.

Thyer, B. A. (1995c). Promoting an empiricist agenda in the human services: An ethical and humanistic imperative. *Journal of Behavior Therapy and Experimental Psychiatry, 26,* 93–98.

Thyer, B. A. (1996a). Guidelines for applying the empirical clinical practice model to social work. *Journal of Applied Social Sciences, 20,* 121–127.

Thyer, B. A. (1996b). Forty years of progress toward empirical clinical practice? *Social Work Research, 20,* 77–81.

Thyer, B. A., & Thyer, K. B. (1992). Single-system research designs in social work practice: A bibliography from 1965–1990. *Research on Social Work Practice, 2,* 99–116.

Todd, A. J. (1920). *The scientific spirit and social work.* New York: Macmillan.

Tutty, L. (1990). The response of community mental health professionals to client's rights: A review and suggestions. *Canadian Journal of Community Mental Health, 9,* 1–24.

Tyson, K. B. (1992). A new approach to relevant scientific research for practitioners: The heuristic paradigm. *Social Work, 37,* 541–556.

Van Houten, R., Axelrod, S., Bailey, J., Favell, J. E., Fixx, R. M., Iwata, B. A., & Lovaas, O. I. (1988). The right to effective behavioral treatment. *The Behavior Analyst, 11,* 111–114.

Wetzler, S. (Ed.). (1989). *Measuring mental illness: Psychometric assessment for clinicians.* Washington, DC: American Psychiatric Press.

Williams, L. F. (1995). Epistemology. In R. L. Edwards (Ed.), *Encyclopedia of social work* (19th ed., pp. 872–883). Washington, DC: National Association of Social Workers.

Witkin, S. (1991). Empirical clinical practice: A critical analysis. *Social Work, 36,* 158–163.

Wolman, B. B. (Ed.) (1973). *Dictionary of behavioral science.* New York: Van Nostrand Reinhold.

Zimbalist, S. E. (1977). *Historic themes and landmarks in social welfare research.* New York: Harper and Row.

PART I ——————————————

Disorders Usually First Diagnosed in Infancy, Childhood, or Adolescence

Chapter 2

MENTAL RETARDATION

John Gerdtz
Joel Bregman

OVERVIEW

Is the social work profession interested in mental retardation? Although individual social workers have served persons with mental retardation and their families for many years, the evidence from the professional social work literature is not encouraging. Almost 20 years ago, Horejsi (1979) noted that the professional social work literature contained very few articles on mental retardation or other developmental disabilities. A search of the more recent social work literature indicates that the situation has not changed much since Horejsi's article was published. Very few articles on mental retardation or developmental disabilities were published in social work journals, and there has been an almost complete absence of articles on empirically based interventions in the field of mental retardation in the social work literature. There has, however, been a slight increase in the number of empirically based interventions by social workers published in the specialized literature devoted to mental retardation and other developmental disabilities.

Do social workers have useful and empirically based interventions available to help persons with mental retardation and their families? There has certainly been an enormous increase in the number of empirically based articles relating to persons with mental retardation and their families, and this literature will be reviewed later in the chapter. As the mental retardation service system slowly changes to a program of individualized supports for children and adults with disabilities (Schalock & Genung, 1993; Stoneman & Malone, 1995), the knowledge and skills of the professional social worker are, at least potentially, very important to this system. But this potential will only be recognized if social workers deliver services that are appropriate, clinically useful, and have at least some empirical evidence of effectiveness. A review of the recent professional literature in preparation for writing this chapter, both the social work literature and the mental retardation/developmental disabilities literature, indicated an almost complete absence of empirically based interventions involving social workers, with a few notable exceptions.

This chapter reviews the characteristics and diagnosis of mental retardation, the nature and costs of programs providing services to individuals with mental retardation in the United States, the role of social work in this service sector, and an overview of the interventions available to social workers who serve persons with mental retardation and their families. All of the interventions reviewed in this chapter have some empirical evidence of effectiveness, although the quality and nature of this evidence varies greatly. To be included in this chapter, these interventions—and the evidence of their effectiveness—must have been published in a professional journal or book and been subject to peer review before publication.

WHAT IS MENTAL RETARDATION?

Mental retardation is a condition with three major characteristics. The first characteristic involves a significant deficit in intellectual or cognitive functioning. The second characteristic involves a significant deficit in adaptive behavior (that is, those skills required to meet the daily requirements of life). Third, these deficits were manifest during the developmental period, prior to age 18. The fourth edition of the *Diagnostic and Statistical Manual of Mental Disorders* (*DSM-IV;* American Psychiatric Association [APA], 1994) requires these three criteria for the diagnosis of mental retardation.

A significant deficit in cognitive or intellectual functioning is identified by the results of a standardized test of intelligence. The scores obtained from these tests are often referred to as an *Intelligence Quotient* or *IQ score.* According to *DSM-IV* (APA, 1994, pp. 39–40), a significant deficit in cognitive function is defined as an IQ score of two standard deviations below the mean score for the standardized test. For most tests, an IQ of 70 or below meets this criterion. It is important that the diagnosis of mental retardation not be made simply on the basis of the IQ score.

As noted in *DSM-IV* (APA, 1994), a diagnosis of mental retardation is made only if the IQ score is 70 or below *and* there are also significant deficits in adaptive behavior. *Adaptive behaviors* are those skills needed to cope with the everyday demands of life that are commonly faced by persons of the individual's chronological age. An individual's level of adaptive skill is influenced by a variety of factors which should be considered when assessing IQ and adaptive behavior. There are a number of standardized instruments available to assess adaptive behavior, and some of these instruments have summary scores that indicate whether a particular score lies within the range of mental retardation in the general population. Once again, as with intelligence tests, it is essential that the appropriate standardized test of adaptive behavior be used with each individual, that test scores be interpreted with due consideration for the validity and reliability of the measure, and that all scores be interpreted within the context of the complete clinical situation presented by the individual. Birth, medical, developmental, and educational histories are important in assessing adaptive behavior. These histories should also, whenever possible, be collected from a number of independent sources, including family members, members of the community, teachers, physicians, social workers, and other professionals (APA, 1994).

As a developmental condition, mental retardation must be present before an individual reaches age 18. An individual over age 18 could receive a diagnosis of mental retardation as long as significant deficits in intellectual functioning and adaptive behavior were present before the individual reached age 18 (APA, 1994).

DSM-IV (APA, 1994, pp. 40–42) identifies levels of severity of mental retardation based on ranges of IQ scores. Mild Mental Retardation (with an IQ range from 50–55 to approximately 70) is most common, accounting for about 85% of those persons diagnosed with mental retardation. Moderate Mental Retardation (with an IQ range from 35–40 to 50–55) is the next level of severity representing about 10% of persons with mental retardation. Severe Mental Retardation (with an IQ range of 20–25 to 35–40) is the next level of severity and accounts for approximately 3% to 4% of persons with mental retardation. Finally, Profound Mental Retardation covers the range of IQ scores below 25 or 20; approximately 1% to 2% of persons with mental retardation function in this IQ range. *DSM-IV* also permits a diagnosis of Mental Retardation, Severity Unspecified (APA, 1994, p. 40) when there is good reason to presume a diagnosis of mental retardation but it is not possible to assess the individual using standardized tests.

Mental retardation can also be diagnosed using criteria and categories not contained in *DSM-IV*. The most common alternative to *DSM-IV* is the diagnostic manual developed by the American Association on Mental Retardation (AAMR; Luckasson et al., 1992). The AAMR diagnostic system relies on criteria that are similar to those of *DSM-IV*—that is, significant deficits in cognitive and adaptive living skills—but it uses a different approach to diagnosis and to classification of severity. The AAMR system requires similar levels of significant deficit in IQ as does *DSM-IV*, but it also requires significant deficits in at least two of the ten identified areas of adaptive behavior. Rather than define levels of severity by IQ score, as in *DSM-IV*, the AAMR system identifies levels of support needed by the person with mental retardation, with the support levels ranging from Intermittent to Pervasive. The AAMR system specifically rejects IQ scores alone as a means of determining support levels or levels of severity (for more details, see Luckasson et al., 1992), as does *DSM-IV*.

Some educational systems and programs may use other methods to identify mental retardation for purposes of classification or eligibility for services. In the United States, however, most clinicians use either *DSM-IV* or the AAMR system to diagnose and classify mental retardation.

Persons with mental retardation constitute a very diverse population with a large variety of etiologies or causes for their condition. Even when extensive assessments are used, it may not be possible to identify the causes of mental retardation in 30% to 40% of the cases evaluated (APA, 1994). The most common identifiable causes of mental retardation appear to be environmental factors, such as general lack of appropriate nutrition and of physical, language, social, and educational stimulation. Together these factors probably account for 15% to 20% of the identifiable cases (APA, 1994). Other causative factors include a variety of genetic conditions (such as Down syndrome, fragile X syndrome, and tuberous sclerosis) which may account for 5% of the cases. Insults during the development of the embryo, including the effects of consumption of alcohol or other substances during pregnancy, may account for about 30% of the cases. Other difficulties during pregnancy or at birth, including trauma, infection, and prematurity, account for about 10% of the cases. Last, medical problems during infancy or childhood, such as injury or exposure to lead or other toxic substances, account for about 5% of the cases (APA, 1994). For more information on the etiology of mental retardation and medical and psychiatric issues related to mental retardation, see Bregman and Harris (1995).

Estimates of the prevalence of mental retardation in the general population have varied from study to study. The average prevalence rate across studies in the United States is about 1.26% of the general population (Luckasson, Schalock, Snell, & Spitalnick, 1996). Bregman and Harris (1995) have a more detailed discussion of the epidemiology of mental retardation, including a review of a number of interesting European studies, several of which place the prevalence at approximately 2% of the general population.

Community studies found that children and adults with mental retardation are significantly more likely to suffer from a variety of psychiatric disorders than are comparison groups of persons without mental retardation (Bregman, 1991). The psychiatric disorders identified in the mentally retarded population include such conditions as Depression, Bipolar Disorder, Schizophrenia, Obsessive-Compulsive Disorder, and a number of other conditions (see Bregman, 1991, pp. 861–863). Persons with mental retardation may have difficulty in gaining access to mental health services and treatment programs for their psychiatric problems because mental health professionals may not have the training or experience to serve individuals with mental retardation (Torrey, 1993).

Programs in the United States designed specifically to serve persons with mental retardation have been identified by historians as far back as 1751 (see Scheerenberger, 1983, pp. 91–105). The costs and complexity of programs designed to provide services to children and adults with mental retardation have grown steadily, with the federal government assuming an increasing role in funding and mandating services (Braddock, 1987). Combined federal and state expenditures on programs for persons with mental retardation and developmental disabilities, adjusted for inflation, increased 18% from 1980 to 1984, 25% from 1984 to 1988, and 28% from 1988 to 1992 (Braddock, Hemp, Lakin, & Smith, 1994).

More recently, the federal government has been reducing its role in funding local services for persons with mental retardation, resulting in increased costs for state and local governments and, in some cases, reduction or elimination of services (Braddock & Hemp, 1996). Even with this reduction in funding, considerable resources are still devoted to programs for persons with mental retardation. State and federal expenditures on the Medicaid program for persons with mental retardation and other developmental disabilities totaled almost $15 billion in 1995 (Braddock & Hemp, 1996). It is important to keep these numbers in context. Medicaid and Medicare together were less than 20% of the total federal budget in 1996. In addition, there are about 60,000 persons with mental retardation and other developmental disabilities on waiting lists for community residences and family support services in the United States (Braddock & Hemp, 1996, p. 13).

SOCIAL WORK AND MENTAL RETARDATION

How important is the profession of social work to services for persons with mental retardation? There is certainly a perception that social workers have a peripheral role in programs serving individuals with mental retardation (Hanley & Parkinson, 1994). Specific social work interventions listed as appropriate for social workers in mental retardation service programs include counseling and emotional support for individuals and families, especially those in crisis; assisting individuals and families in gaining access to community resources and programs (case management and advocacy); teaching skills related to parenting, social interaction, and problem solving; and assessing individuals and families to assist in diagnosis and in determining eligibility for programs (Hanley & Parkinson, 1994; Levy, 1995).

Do social workers receive information about mental retardation and related disabilities as part of their training? The results of a recent survey of social work training programs (both undergraduate and graduate programs were included) by DePoy and Miller (1996) were not encouraging. Even interpreting the results with the limitations of survey research in mind, the outcomes reported by DePoy and Miller were disturbing. Only about 20% of social work programs responding to the survey offered course work in mental retardation and developmental disabilities, although almost 90% of the programs had field assignments available in developmental disabilities. When social work courses in developmental disabilities were offered, they were often taught by professionals who were not social workers.

The challenge facing the social work profession is that services provided by social workers are important and valuable to persons with mental retardation and their families. Such services are becoming more focused on individual supports in community settings (Schalock & Genung, 1993; Stoneman & Malone, 1995), making the social work skills of assessment and intervention increasingly important. As noted in the next section of this chapter, a number of empirically based interventions appropriate for use by social workers in the mental retardation service system have been developed (usually by members of other professions). A number of questions remain. Will social workers in training learn about these interventions and apply them in practice? Will social workers develop empirically based interventions of their own and publish their results in the social work and other professional literature? Will social workers who work in the mental retardation service system still find little interest in developmental disabilities in the social work literature 20 years from now?

ASSESSMENT METHODS

Social work assessment serves a number of important functions: (a) assistance in diagnosis and determining eligibility for services; (b) assistance in planning clinical interventions with individuals, families, or groups; and (c) less frequently, assistance in research or other data collection purposes. This section focuses on social work assessment in mental retardation for purposes of diagnosis and for planning and implementing clinical interventions.

The diagnosis of mental retardation involves an assessment of cognitive or intellectual functioning, as well as an assessment of an individual's adaptive behavior skills. Most social workers are not trained or licensed to administer IQ tests, and there will be no further discussion of these tests in this chapter. However, an assessment of adaptive behavior is as important as cognitive testing in accurately diagnosing mental retardation. There are a number of standardized assessments of adaptive behavior, and social workers are qualified to administer these assessments.

The standardized assessments of adaptive behavior—including the Vineland Adaptive Behavior Scales, the American Association on Mental Retardation Adaptive Behavior Scale, and the Woodcock-Johnson Scales of Independent Behavior—are administered to informants (parents, teachers, or staff) who know an individual well. The published scales have generally good reliability and validity, and some (including the three listed here) have computer scoring programs available. In many clinical and educational programs for persons with mental retardation, it is often the social worker's responsibility to administer assessments of adaptive behavior and to obtain medical and developmental histories and general family information.

A comprehensive medical and developmental history, as well as an assessment of the family situation and the current status of the individual (commonly called a *psychosocial assessment*), are important components of a social work assessment for diagnosis and clinical planning. The history is most commonly obtained from family members or other informants, and is often supplemented by a review of the available records. There is a tendency to view the psychosocial assessment as of secondary importance to the results of standardized testing in diagnosis and planning for clinical intervention. However, an accurate and comprehensive history is an essential component of the process of diagnosing mental retardation, especially for cases in which standardized testing is not possible (APA, 1994). Comprehensive psychosocial assessments are also important for planning and implementing clinical interventions in mental retardation. For example, Herzog and Money (1993) reported a case in which a comprehensive record review by a social worker indicated the presence of a previously undiagnosed genetic condition (Klinefelter syndrome) in an adult man with mental retardation. Social workers are usually well trained and experienced in the development of psychosocial assessments.

As noted previously, children and adults with mental retardation are more likely to develop a variety of mental health problems than are persons who do not have mental retardation. Therefore, an assessment of mental health problems and behavioral difficulties is important for diagnosis and for planning clinical interventions. A number of standardized checklists of symptoms and behaviors associated with various mental health problems have recently been developed, and some of these checklists are appropriate for use with persons with mental retardation. Checklists such as the Child Behavior Profile, Reiss Screen for Maladaptive Behavior, Psychopathology Inventory for Mentally Retarded Adults (PIMRA), and the Aberrant Behavior Checklist (ABC) have generally acceptable reliability and validity (Bregman, 1995), and could be administered by a social worker familiar with the instrument. Most of these instruments also rely on information provided about an individual by knowledgeable informants. See Bregman (1995) for a more comprehensive discussion of these symptom checklists; Aman, Burrow, and Wolford (1995) for validity data on the revised version of the Aberrant Behavior Checklist; and Sturmey and Bertman (1994) for validity data on the Reiss Screen for Maladaptive Behavior. The Aberrant Behavior Checklist has been used successfully in research to track the effects of medication (Bregman, 1995), and would be a good resource for a social worker monitoring medications for the prescribing physician or for an interdisciplinary team.

An assessment of maladaptive or problem behaviors may also be necessary. Studies estimate that 14% to 38% of students with mental retardation enrolled in public school programs engage in aggressive or destructive behaviors, and 6% to 40% of these students engage in self-injurious behaviors (Repp & Karsh, 1990, p. 331). The symptom checklists previously described may provide some information about problem behavior. In cases of severe or prolonged maladaptive behavior, a functional analysis of the behavior is often necessary. *Functional analysis* refers to a process of assessing problem behavior to determine the function (or the gain) of the behavior for the individual; identify situations, circumstances, and environments that make the problem behavior more or less likely to occur; and produce an evaluation of the circumstances and skill acquisition for the individual that would make the problem behavior significantly less likely to occur. Functional analyses are usually conducted by psychologists or special educators with intensive training in applied behavior analysis. The actual process of functional analysis involves interviews of informants, direct observations of the individual in a variety of situations and environments, and, sometimes, direct manipulations of environments and situations to determine the effects on the problem behavior (called *analog situations*). The scatter plot technique developed by Touchette, MacDonald, and Langer (1985) is an efficient and effective data collection system for functional analysis, and social workers with appropriate training can make use of scatter plots in assessing problem behaviors. The use of scatter plots and other data collection systems as part of a functional analysis can provide the clinician with important, and sometimes unexpected, information about seemingly straightforward behaviors.

Functional analyses can be complicated and, in certain circumstances, can have undesired side effects (Iwata, Vollmer, & Zarcone, 1990), so it is important that the professional conducting the analysis be appropriately trained in applied behavior analysis and be supervised by an experienced behavior analyst. Functional analysis procedures can be used to design effective treatment programs, do not necessarily take excessive periods of time and resources (Wacker et al., 1990), and can be carried out effectively in outpatient clinics (Wacker et al., 1990), classrooms (Munk & Repp, 1994) and other clinical settings.

Although functional analyses are typically conducted by special educators and psychologists, there is no reason why they could not be carried out by a trained social worker. Readers seeking more information about functional analysis assessment should see Iwata et al. (1990), Munk and Repp (1994), and Repp and Karsh (1990). Information and guidelines for conducting functional analysis assessments in clinical and community settings can be found in O'Neill, Horner, Albin, Storey, & Sprague (1990). The clinical application of functional analysis assessments is discussed in the "Social Work Interventions" section of this chapter.

Assessment of the families of persons with mental retardation is also important. Standardized scales have been developed to assess family functioning and needs, and these scales may be helpful as part of a comprehensive psychosocial assessment. Virtually all the scales to assess family functioning are self-report instruments to be completed by one or both parents.

The Family Environment Scale has been used by clinical social workers, and may be appropriate for use with families of children or adults with mental retardation (see Reichertz & Frankel, 1993, for a discussion of the clinical use of the Family Environment Scale). The Family Environment Scale has been used in research on families of children with mental retardation (e.g., Dyson, 1993), and appears to be a valid measure of various aspects of the lives of these families (Nihira, Weisner, & Bernheimer, 1994).

The Questionnaire on Resources and Stress (QRS) is often used in clinical work (Levy, 1995), and also in research on families with a child with mental retardation (e.g., Dyson, 1993). The QRS was originally developed in 1974, and was revised several times in order to make it briefer and to increase its reliability and validity (Clayton, Glidden, & Kiphart, 1994). The QRS, in its shortened form, consists of 52 items with factor scores for parent and family problems, optimism and pessimism, child characteristics, and physical incapacitation (of the child with disabilities). A total score is given that indicates the level of parental stress (higher scores indicating greater stress). Although the QRS has been popular in research and in clinical work with families, there are important questions regarding the validity of some aspects of the instrument (see Clayton, et al., 1994, for a good discussion), and judgment is necessary when interpreting the QRS scores.

In their research on families of infants and toddlers with developmental delays (including mental retardation), Dunst, Trivette, and Deal (1988) developed a series of checklists and interview schedules that can enhance some psychosocial assessments. The instruments have acceptable reliability and validity, although the data on these instruments have been derived only from families with preschool children. A variety of measures were developed, including interviews assessing family strengths, needs, functioning style, and sources of both informal and formal support. Copies of the instruments, scoring information, and reliability and validity data are available in Dunst et al. (1988).

Other scales that may be useful in the assessment of families of persons with mental retardation include the Beck Depression Inventory, which has been used for clinical assessment (Levy, 1995) and in evaluations of family support programs (Irvin, 1989). Observational scales, such as the Home Observation for the Measurement of Environment (HOME), have been developed to assess the home and family environments of young children with disabilities (Nihira et al., 1994). These scales may be useful as part of a comprehensive assessment of family functioning.

As with psychosocial assessments, standardized scales can be helpful in the assessment of families of individuals with mental retardation if the appropriate instruments are chosen, individual family factors are considered, and the reliability and validity of the particular instrument are kept in mind. No scale is likely to take the place of a comprehensive and sympathetic clinical interview in the process of family assessment.

EFFECTIVE INTERVENTIONS

As noted at the beginning of this chapter, the criteria for choosing the interventions listed in the following include the appropriateness for use by a properly trained and supervised social worker, empirical evidence of the effectiveness of the intervention, publication in a peer-reviewed book or journal, and, in most cases, publication within the past 5 years. Some articles that were published more than 5 years ago, but were considered especially interesting or important, were included in this section. The articles were identified by computer searches of databases devoted to social work and to developmental disabilities, as well as hand searches of the major journals in developmental disabilities.

Individual and family interventions are described separately. Group interventions are addressed under either individual or family interventions, according to the focus of the group.

Interventions with Individuals

Individual counseling has been identified as an appropriate intervention for social workers to provide to persons with mental retardation (e.g., Hanley & Parkinson, 1994; Levy, 1995). Psychiatrists also recommend individual counseling or therapy for some individuals with mental retardation (Bregman & Harris, 1995; Torrey, 1993). Although there are useful guidelines and recommendations available for individual counseling with individuals with mental retardation (e.g., Ryan, 1993; Torrey, 1993), no articles with empirical outcomes of individual counseling in mental retardation were identified by the data search done in preparation for this chapter.

However, there is related evidence that supports the potential effectiveness of individual counseling with some persons with mental retardation. For example, Rockland (1993) found evidence for the effectiveness of supportive psychotherapy with a number of psychiatric populations. *Supportive psychotherapy* is generally a directive, concrete approach to counseling with a focus on present difficulties and adjustment to the environment. It is likely that supportive psychotherapy would be effective for some persons with mental retardation; more research is needed.

The primary mode of clinical intervention in the field of mental retardation is *applied behavior analysis* or *behavior modification.* Much of the behavioral intervention research in mental retardation is based on the principles of operant conditioning. *Operant conditioning* procedures focus on the relationship between a specific behavior, the contexts (including environmental context) in which the behavior does and does not occur, and the consequences of the behavior for the individual. The goal of operant behavior therapists is to describe and modify the contexts and consequences of associated behaviors such that the frequency and severity of maladaptive behaviors decrease. Behavior therapists generally aim for specific and measurable outcomes of their treatment, and claim success when they have data to indicate that salient parameters of the targeted behavior are changed by systematic manipulations of the contexts and consequences of that behavior. Another form of behavior therapy is called *respondent* or *classical conditioning* and is best represented by the work of the eminent Russian physiologist Ivan Pavlov. In respondent conditioning, an unconditioned stimulus (in Pavlov's work, the presentation of food) results in an unconditioned response (again in Pavlov's work, a dog salivating when the food is presented). Systematic pairings over time of the unconditioned stimulus with conditioned stimuli (for example, a tone) will result in the conditioned stimuli eliciting an unrelated conditioned response (salivation without the presentation of the food). Because respondent conditioning is usually concerned with reflexive behaviors (or behaviors of the autonomic nervous system) the clinical application of this type of conditioning is usually found in programs involving relaxation, stress management and anger control, and desensitization of phobias. The relatively small literature on respondent conditioning procedures in mental retardation is discussed later in this section. Readers interested in more detailed discussion of the various types of behavior modification and applied behavior analysis should consult Alberto and Troutman (1990, pp. 3–38).

There is a large and growing literature on empirically based behavioral interventions for children and adults with mental retardation. Many of the teaching techniques now used in special education programs for students with mental retardation are based on the principles and procedures of applied behavior analysis. Behavioral interventions vary in effectiveness with certain problem behaviors (Bregman & Harris, 1995; Konarski, Favell, & Favell, 1992), and the published behavioral literature in mental retardation does not document very well the generalization (that is, therapeutic benefit outside the immediate treatment setting) or the maintenance (long-term effectiveness) of the interventions (Scotti, Evans, Meyer, & Walker, 1991). Even when effective interventions are documented, they may not be appropriately implemented in clinical or educational programs (Peterson & Martens, 1995). The professional behavioral journals are addressing some of these problems by requiring the documentation of generalization and maintenance of interventions, and also of the social validity (or acceptability) of the interventions to family members, other members of the clinical team, and persons in the community (e.g., Sundel, 1994). Clinical programs developed to address problems of maintenance and generalization and have proven to be effective (e.g., Jauss, Wacker, Berg, Flynn, & Hurd, 1994). Behavioral interventions are likely to remain the most common type of clinical programming in the field of mental retardation in the future.

Behavioral procedures are often used to treat severe problem behaviors such as aggression and self-injury. Although a review of the literature is beyond the scope of this chapter, general issues regarding this topic are discussed. As noted previously, there are very few documented treatment interventions for problem behaviors in mental retardation reported by social workers; however, there are several exceptions (Figueroa, Thyer, & Thyer, 1992; Underwood, Figueroa, Thyer, & Nzeocha, 1989). The knowledge and competencies needed to design behavioral treatment strategies have been summarized by Green (1990), and are available to the social worker who wishes to gain the appropriate training and supervision. The social workers involved in the Figueroa et al. and Underwood et al. studies described in the preceding were able to design effective behavioral interventions for severe aggressive behaviors. A number of useful treatment manuals are available for professionals (e.g., Konarski et al., 1992; Meyer & Evans, 1989), and there are helpful guidelines available for incorporating the results of functional analysis assessment into a treatment plan (O'Neill et al., 1990, pp. 56–60; Munk & Repp, 1994).

Articles that outline the translation of the findings of functional assessment to the development of specific behavioral interventions can be especially helpful. For example, Umbreit (1996) conducted an elegant functional assessment of the disruptive behavior of a preschool child with mental retardation and, based on the assessment, implemented an effective treatment plan for the behavior. Readers who wish to review other examples of clinical programs to treat behavior problems of persons with mental retardation should consult recent issues of such journals as the *Journal of Applied Behavior Analysis, Behavior Modification,* the *American Journal on Mental Retardation,* and *Mental Retardation.*

A number of examples from the behavioral literature indicate that behavioral procedures can be implemented in conjunction with medications and other interventions (Bregman & Harris, 1995). Bregman and Gerdtz (1995) reported on the collaboration between a psychiatrist and a social worker in the development of a treatment program that included medication and behavioral interventions to address the aggressive behavior of a young adult with mental retardation and autism. Jackson and Altman (1996) reported on the successful treatment of aggression and other problem behaviors exhibited by a man with mild mental retardation. The authors used a number of behavioral techniques and cognitive-behavioral techniques (self-management and role playing) and developed a collaborative relationship with the man's family and the staff of his vocational program. All these factors were important in the success of their intervention program.

Learning new skills is also of benefit to persons with mental retardation. As illustrated by Jackson and Altman in the preceding, the development of new competencies can assume a central position in a comprehensive program designed to treat severe behavioral disturbances (O'Neill et al., 1990). Learning new skills is obviously also important for the majority of children and adults with mental retardation who do not exhibit severe problem behaviors. Special educators are usually the lead professionals involved in teaching new skills; however, social workers can also play an important role in teaching social skills, problem solving, and general coping skills, especially in community settings. Social workers can also be instrumental in coordinating education programs between school and home environments, and in training parents in basic teaching techniques. Coordination with families and parent training are addressed later in this chapter.

Despite the potential importance of social workers in teaching new skills to those with developmental disabilities (Hanley & Parkinson, 1994), only two published articles were identified in the review of the literature that included empirically based methods (Maeser & Thyer, 1990; Sundel, 1994). This is the case despite the fact that the techniques needed to teach these skills effectively in the community can be mastered by social workers with appropriate training. A number of effective teaching programs that are appropriate for trained social workers to implement with children or adults with mental retardation are reviewed in the following.

As previously noted, a small number of empirically based interventions based on respondent or classical conditioning are available. Classical conditioning techniques are often used together with operant procedures and other interventions in a clinical program (e.g., Singer, Irvin, & Hawkins, 1988). Relaxation procedures are the most commonly implemented respondent conditioning techniques among persons with mental retardation. A study comparing the effectiveness of two relaxation programs for adults with moderate to severe mental retardation found that a relatively simple program (Behavioral Relaxation Training) was as effective as a more complex program, both of which were superior to the outcome of a control group (Lindsay, Baty, Michie, & Richardson, 1989). The Lindsay et al. article is especially noteworthy because of its relatively sophisticated research design (including a control group and a large sample size of 50 subjects) and its clear discussion of both the benefits and the shortcomings of the relaxation procedures. In a later study, Lindsay, Fee, Michie, and Heap (1994) confirmed the effectiveness of Behavioral Relaxation Training with a smaller sample of adults with severe mental retardation. Gross (1994) developed a very creative treatment plan for the temper tantrums of a young boy with mental retardation who was also deaf and blind by using classical conditioning procedures. The temper tantrums (involving biting, hitting, kicking, and scratching) were severe enough to interfere with the boy's educational program. Gross identified those periods of the day during which the boy appeared happiest and most relaxed. She then gradually introduced an odor (spearmint) that the boy seemed to find pleasant; over time, the odor of spearmint was paired with behaviors indicating happiness and relaxation. The spearmint was then introduced during times of the day when problem behaviors were most likely to occur, and also when tantrums started. Although tantrums were not eliminated, the frequency and severity of the tantrum behaviors declined significantly.

Classical or respondent conditioning procedures offer the clinician a number of potentially powerful and useful interventions, although these procedures may have to be combined with other interventions to be fully effective. More research is needed to assess the effectiveness of respondent procedures with a wider variety of problem behaviors (see Mirenda, 1986, for a review).

Teaching social skills (skills needed to behave appropriately during interpersonal interactions) is an intervention that receives considerable attention in the mental retardation literature. Although there are a number of published behavioral interventions available, many of these studies lack sufficient evidence of the generalization (the use of skills in settings other than the training setting) and maintenance (long-term effectiveness) of the social skills training programs (Gumpel, 1994). A meta-analysis of the research on teaching social skills to persons with moderate to severe mental retardation by Soto, Toro-Zambrana, and Belfiore (1994) revealed problems with generalization and maintenance. Soto et al. (1994)

also found that combining social skills training with cognitive procedures (such as self-instruction and self-management) improved generalization and maintenance.

There are social skills training programs with impressive documentation of maintenance and generalization. For example, Foxx and his colleagues developed a social skills training program in a board game format for adults with mild mental retardation. An assessment 8 years after the initial training revealed that many of the adults maintained the social skills they were taught in the program (Foxx & Faw, 1992). There is additional research evidence supporting the effectiveness of the social skills training program used by Foxx and Faw for high school students with mild mental retardation (Langone, Clees, Oxford, Malone, & Ross, 1995).

In an empirical study by a social worker, Sundel (1994) developed a list of job-related social skills for adults with mental retardation through a literature review and interviews with professionals involved in vocational training programs. Sundel then taught the relevant skills in a group format to 6 adults with mental retardation by role playing activities and videotaped feedback for the participants. Independent judges rated the social skills of the participants as improved at the conclusion of the training program. O'Reilly and Glynn (1995) used similar role-playing and systematic feedback strategies to teach social skills to high school students with mild mental retardation; these authors also used 2 other students with mental retardation as peer tutors to teach and assess the new social skills in a variety of settings other than the classroom.

There has also been a growing interest in social skills programs relating to dating and sexuality for persons with mental retardation. Mueser, Valenti-Hein, and Yarnold (1987) compared the effectiveness of a dating skills problem solving program, a relaxation training program, and a control group of subjects. The researchers randomly assigned subjects to treatment and control groups, and found that the dating social skills program was more effective than relaxation training. Both treatment groups had better outcomes than the control group. A follow-up study that also used a control group (Valenti-Hein, Yarnold, & Mueser, 1994) confirmed the effectiveness of the dating skills training program. The authors found that skills gained during the program began to fade about 2 months after the study's conclusion unless review and reinforcement were provided. The authors developed a training manual, the Dating Skills Program (Valenti-Hein & Mueser, 1990), which is an excellent resource for social workers providing services to adults with mental retardation. An important issue related to social skills training involves teaching sexually active adults with mental retardation about the risks of AIDS. Such programs have only recently been developed for persons with mental retardation and other developmental disabilities. Scotti, Masia, Boggess, Speaks, and Drabman (1996) developed an educational program about AIDS for adults with mild and moderate mental retardation. Posttest evaluations indicated that a significant increase in knowledge about the risk factors associated with AIDS was gained by most participants. However, an evaluation conducted 5 weeks after the end of training indicated that the persons with mild mental retardation retained the information, but those with moderate mental retardation did not. Clearly, more research is needed in this area. However, based on research with other populations, it seems that knowledge about the risk factors for AIDS does not necessarily reduce sexually dangerous behaviors, and this may also be true for programs for adults with mental retardation (Scotti et al., 1996).

Generalization and maintenance of social skills is enhanced by support from members of the general public. For example, Gaylord-Ross, Park, Johnston, Lee, and Goetz (1995) provided a social skills training program and the assistance of a coworker on the job site to 2 adults with mental retardation and sensory impairment (blind and deaf). The authors found that the most effective sequence of interventions involved social skills training followed by the intervention of a coworker.

Programs have also been developed for specific social skills. For example, Sievert, Cuvo, and Davis (1988) developed a program to teach self-advocacy skills to a group of adults with mild mental retardation and other disabilities. Using videotape role playing and rehearsal, the authors trained the adults to recognize and respond appropriately to violations of personal, community, human services, and consumer rights. Follow-up role plays in community settings indicated that the adults had mastered the advocacy skills; however, long-term generalization and maintenance were not assessed. Another important social skill is the ability to make choices and to understand the consequences of those choices. Foxx, Faw, Taylor, Davis, and Fulia (1993) helped 6 adults with mild mental retardation assess their own preferences for community living, obtain information about the options available to them in the community, and match their preferences with the available options. The adults engaged in a group process of identifying their individual preferences, reviewing community residences and other relevant options, and rehearsing information-gathering strategies regarding the living arrangements. Sequential photographs placed in albums were used to help the adults remember the specific questions they needed to ask. All clients maintained their skills in simulations after the training, and 5 of the 6 adults participated in actual interviews and tours to select their own community residences. In a later study using a similar intervention with 4 adults with mild mental retardation, Faw, Davis, and Peck (1996) also obtained positive outcomes, with skills maintained at a 1 month follow-up. Unfortunately, the authors noted that due to the shortage of community living opportunities, adults with mental retardation often have to take available openings rather than engage in the process of evaluating a variety of options.

An issue related to the expression of preference for a particular residential option is the ability of an adult with mental retardation to give informed consent to living in a residence or participating in a program. Many adults with mental retardation are in legal or quasi-legal guardianships, with other designated persons giving consent for residences and programs. Lindsey (1994) developed the Consent Screening Interview (CSI) to assess the ability of an adult with mental retardation

Professionals who provide successful support services for families possess the ability to assess and deal with a complex matrix of individual and family variables, as well as cultural and ethnic differences (Harry, 1992; Heller, Markwardt, Rowitz, & Farber, 1994). In some families, increased professional involvement may be perceived as adding to the burden of care rather than assisting the family (e.g., Heller et al., 1994, p. 298). In spite of these complexities, effective programs for parents are available. Psychoeducational group treatment approaches have proven effective in helping parents cope with the stress and responsibilities of caring for a child with mental retardation. Singer et al. (1988) combined a number of cognitive behavioral interventions, including cognitive reframing, self-monitoring, relaxation training, and coping skills instruction for parents of children with severe disabilities. Parents were assigned randomly to a treatment group or a waiting list control group. Posttest measures of depression and anxiety indicated significant improvement for the parents in the treatment group, although no long-term follow-ups were conducted. In a similar project, Nixon and Singer (1993) used the same research design of random assignment to treatment and control groups to evaluate the effectiveness of a cognitive behavioral treatment program for parents of children with severe disabilities. The parents in this study exhibited what was considered excessive self-blame and guilt. Outcome measures, such as the Beck Depression Inventory and the Situation Guilt Scale, indicated significant improvement for the treatment group versus the control group. Even though long-term follow-ups were not carried out, the random assignment to treatment and control groups provides strong preliminary evidence of the effectiveness of these interventions with parents.

Smith, Majeski, and McClenny (1996) developed a psychoeducational support group for aging parents (over age 50) of individuals with mental retardation. Parents whose children lived at home with them, and those whose children lived away from home, were included in the study. The group met weekly for 6 weeks and included information about services, planning, dealing with crisis, etc., as well as training in problem-solving and relaxation. Posttest evaluations by the group participants were positive, but long-term follow-up was not conducted. A study by Kirkham (1993) reported on the 2-year outcomes of a psychoeducational group for mothers of children with mental retardation and other developmental disabilities. The intervention was based on a cognitive behavioral model with emphasis on building the mothers' problem solving, stress management, and communication abilities. There was random assignment to either the skills-building group previously described or to a parent support group. Outcome measures obtained immediately at the conclusion of the intervention and at a 20- to 26-month follow-up indicated that the mothers in the skills group developed and maintained significant coping behaviors over time as compared with the mothers in the control group. The outcome measures used in this study included the Questionnaire on Resources and Stress (QRS) and the Beck Depression Inventory.

There have been concerns from some parent advocates that teaching parents skills, especially skills related to dealing with the behavior or education of their child with mental retardation, may do little more than add to the caregiving burden experienced by many families. Baker (1989) and his colleagues, who developed the Parents as Teachers Training Program, evaluated the long-term effectiveness and the degree of caretaking burden resulting from their program. This study (Baker, Landen, & Kashima, 1991) measured parental teaching skills, as well as parental depression and anxiety and family cohesion. Outcomes were measured immediately after training and at 1-year follow-up. Families reported positive outcomes and most families were using the teaching techniques 1 year after training. There was no evidence of increased family stress as the result of this training, although families already under stress at the beginning of training were less likely to implement the teaching techniques at home. The authors recommended that increased attention may have to be directed to stress management and to increasing marital communication and satisfaction for some families before specific skills training can be effective. The Support and Education for Families Model (SAEF) developed by Singer, Irvine, and Irvin (1989) attempted to address these issues by combining two interventions, teaching parents specific behavioral intervention skills for their children and cognitive behavioral skills to reduce stress and enhance problem solving for themselves. At a 1-year follow-up, a group of 25 parents was selected from the original group; 1 year after training, a majority of this subgroup of participating parents maintained their teaching skills and problem-solving and stress management capabilities.

Kashima, Baker, and Landen (1988) assessed the effectiveness of the video versus the live presentation formats of the Parents as Teachers Training Program. The authors randomly assigned parents to media (video), live presenter, and control groups (parents who would be trained later). Parents from both the video and live groups significantly increased their skills and knowledge compared to the control group. The outcomes for the live presenter and video groups were similar, suggesting that the less expensive video presentation format may be appropriate for many families. Many of the teaching programs from the Parents as Teachers Program are available in Baker and Brightman (1989) and are appropriate for use by social workers.

Collaboration between home and school is an important issue for many parents and teachers. A number of demonstration programs have been designed to encourage and assist parent involvement in the education of children with disabilities, and also to help schools better meet the needs of parents. Some of these programs have good outcome data. Goetz, Anderson, and Laten (1989) described the Parents as Effective Partners (PEP) program in the metropolitan Chicago area, which involved information groups with a focus on special education, the IEP process, role playing and rehearsal, stress management, and general discussion. The groups were co-led by a parent and a professional. Follow-ups as long as 2 years following the conclusion of the group indicated that, compared to pretest scores, parents had improved and retained knowledge of special education laws and practices and had maintained good relations with special education staff. Walker (1989) developed a comprehensive program to enhance communication between teachers and parents through a psychoeducational group approach in which parents and teachers were trained in the techniques of effective written and verbal communication, dispute resolution, problem solving, and positive reinforcement. Outcomes assessed by pre- and posttest skill scores indicated that both parents and teachers increased their skills and reported using the skills regularly after the group concluded. Long-term outcomes were not assessed. Kohr, Parrish, Neef, Driessen, and Hallinan (1988) also trained a group of mothers of children with developmental disabilities in the skills needed to communicate effectively with professionals. Posttest outcome assessments by independent raters indicated that the mothers developed improved communication skills. There was no long-term evaluation of this outcome.

Training parents to teach skills to other parents is another intervention that has some empirical support in the mental retardation literature. A number of parent and family support programs have used the *train the trainer* model (Goetz et al., 1989). Hester, Kaiser, Alpert, and Whiteman (1996) taught a group of 3 professionals the skills needed to be effective trainers of parents (coaching, providing positive examples, giving specific instructions and specific feedback on performance). The professionals trained 3 parents, and the trained parents then trained a group of other parents. The focus of the training was to have parents implement basic language programs in the home. The outcome data indicated that trainer and trainee parents acquired the necessary skills, and the targeted children increased their language abilities. Although effective training of trainers requires specific skills and can be time-consuming, this type of intervention can be implemented by a social worker with the necessary experience.

Behavioral interventions and skill development training conducted within the family home represent effective interventions in selected cases. Irvine, Singer, Erickson, and Stahlberg (1992) developed a coordinated program to teach high school students with moderate to severe mental retardation the skills needed to follow a picture schedule both in the classroom and in the home. All the students learned the skills in both settings and were using the schedules at home at 4-month follow-up. Project Ecosystems in California provided home and community-based skills training for children with mental retardation and other disabilities who were at risk for out-of-home placement. Their parents received training in stress reduction and problem solving (Lutzker, Campbell, Newman, & Harrold, 1989). Preliminary outcome data (primarily rereferrals and the number of placements out-of-home) have been positive for Project Ecosystems. In-home and in-community support services for persons with mental retardation in crisis have been shown to reduce the need for residential placement (Colond and Wieseler, 1995). However, in-home services can also be effective for people who are not in crisis situations. In one interesting study, Swenson-Pierce, Kohl, and Egel (1987) trained a group of 3 children to teach their younger siblings with mental retardation basic domestic and self-care activities. The intervention was successful for 2 of the 3 children participating in the study. The authors cautioned that care must be taken in the selection of siblings for this type of intervention so that the training program is perceived as positive by both children. See Swenson-Pierce et al. for further discussion.

Case management for families in the developmental disabilities service system has been a role claimed by social workers (e.g., Hanley & Parkinson, 1994; Levy, 1995). However, in a study of case managers in New York State by MacEachron, Pensky, and Hawes (1986), the necessity of social work training for case managers in developmental disabilities was challenged. The sample for this study included 157 case managers from state agencies and 85 case managers from nonprofit agencies across New York State. The study was not designed to assess the effectiveness of case manager services; however, the authors found that a full array of services was provided, regardless of the type of certification or training of the case manager. MacEachron et al. concluded that their study did not support the restriction of case management in developmental disabilities to a particular profession such as social work. A review of the social work literature during the past 5 years identified one article describing social workers as case managers for persons with developmental disabilities (Fiene & Taylor, 1991). This article presented an innovative case management program in a rural community and included one case study. Other outcome data were not reported, however. Case managers can provide a beneficial service for individuals with mental retardation (Lozano, 1993), and their families (Dunst, Trivette, Gordon, & Pletcher, 1989); however, there are currently no data supporting the superiority of one profession over another as case managers. If social workers are to be given preference as primary case managers in developmental disabilities and mental retardation service systems, more empirically based research is needed to justify this preference.

Another innovative approach to providing family support has been assisting families in developing their own informal social support network. Dunst et al. (1989) developed a program to assist families in locating informal sources of community support. Following an assessment of family strengths and needs, a case manager assisted the family in identifying informal sources of support in the local community. The program included families with young children and infants who had a variety of disabilities in a rural community in North Carolina. A number of outcome measures was used. Assessments conducted 2 and 12 months after the initial intervention indicated that the majority of the families had developed informal supports that were helpful in caring for their child. This approach has potential benefits for families of children with mental retardation. Dunst et al. (1989) provided an excellent foundation for empirical research by developing valid and reliable assessment instruments for this type of intervention.

Parents with mental retardation have been the focus of a number of interventions over the past 10 to 15 years since they are at greater risk for being neglectful of their children, often because of deficient parenting skills (Feldman, Case, Rincover, Towns, & Betel, 1989). Feldman et al. designed a training package for mothers with mental retardation focused on increasing physical affection and on praise and imitation of the children's vocalizations. The 3 mothers in the study all had young children or infants with developmental delays. Using verbal instructions, systematic feedback, and modeling of appropriate behaviors, the researchers were able to increase affection, praise, and imitation to levels similar to those of nonhandicapped parents in a comparison group. These gains were maintained at 3- and 18-month follow-up, with generalization to other child care activities, such as diaper changing and feeding. Two of the young children in the study also made gains in their language skills. In a later study, Feldman, Case, Garrick, MacIntyre-Grand, Carnwell, and Sparks (1992) provided services to 11 mothers with developmental disabilities who had been referred to Child Protective Services for failure to properly care for their infants and young children. Basic child care skills, such as diapering, cleaning baby bottles, and treating diaper rash, were targeted in this intervention. Training techniques included verbal instructions, the use of picture manuals, and systematic modeling, feedback, and reinforcement. All of the mothers rapidly acquired the necessary skills, and at follow-up assessment 17 months later, 6 of the mothers maintained their skills. The other 5 mothers in the study could not be located for follow-up.

A number of other programs have also concentrated on the specific needs of parents with mental retardation. Sarber, Halasz, Messmer, Bickett, and Lutzker (1983) used verbal instructions, visual cues (picture cards and color codes), and modeling to teach a mother with mental retardation menu planning and grocery shopping. The mother acquired the skills and maintained them at a 19-week follow-up. Tymchuk, Hamada, Andron, and Anderson (1990) developed a program to assess potential safety hazards in the homes of 4 mothers with mental retardation. Mothers were trained in group sessions to recognize and manage safety hazards, and individual sessions were later conducted in their own homes. The group also reviewed accidents suffered by the children, and mothers were given feedback on correcting the hazards that resulted in injury. The authors found that very specific training and information was needed for each hazard category (for example, poisons or electrical hazards). One of the subjects dropped out of the study; for the remaining 3 mothers, implementation of safety precautions varied widely. Most of the precautions were implemented; however, at 1-month follow-up a number of safety skills had begun to fade. The authors recommended that some parents with mental retardation may require considerable in-home assistance and ongoing monitoring in order to maintain a safe home.

Bakken, Miltenberger, and Schauss (1993) studied 5 parents with mild mental retardation who previously had contact with Child Protective Services (CPS) for suspected child abuse or neglect (none had an open case with CPS during the course of the study). Baseline observations were conducted in the homes before training began. The parents were involved in a discussion group in which they were given information on appropriate child-rearing practices and behavioral skills training in a small group format. Although the parents could verbally describe appropriate practices and skills, observations indicated that these practices were not implemented at home. Only when individual skills training was practiced in the home, were the skills successfully implemented. The authors suggested that informational or training groups for parents with mental retardation may not result in appropriate implementation without assessment and follow-up in the home.

Programs also have been designed for pregnant teenagers with mental retardation. Levy, Perhats, Nash-Johnson, and Welter (1992) studied the 3-year outcomes of a program designed to serve pregnant teenagers with mild to moderate mental retardation. Services included special education, information and support groups, training in problem solving and decision making, individual counseling, and follow-up home visits. Services continued for up to 18 months following the birth of the child. Measures including birth rate, infant mortality, repeat pregnancy, and school attendance indicated superior outcomes for the teenagers in the program as compared with teenagers in the community. One of the authors of this study is a social worker. Based on the findings of the Bakken et al. (1993) study previously discussed, the success of the Levy et al. study may be partly attributable to the home visiting component of the program.

Although many of these family intervention studies report impressive outcomes, there are some serious limitations to this research. With very few exceptions, the interventions previously described involved mothers as the focus of the intervention. Many projects did not include fathers in the studies. This is common in family research and intervention studies in general, although efforts are now being made to include fathers in research and intervention programs (Greenspan & Budd, 1986; Parke, 1986). Another limitation is that most of the studies of families included in the preceding used samples of families with infants or preschool children living at home. Since the parenting burden changes as children get older, programs that are effective in helping parents care for an infant or young child may not be effective interventions for parents of older children. This issue is especially relevant to parents with mental retardation. Although advocates argue that all parents with mental retardation are capable of properly caring for their children with proper support, the research data do not support this generalization (Greenspan & Budd, 1986). The authors recommend appropriate evaluation of parents' potential to care for children with available support. More information on this complex issue can be found in the article by Greene, Norman, Searle, Daniels, and Lubeck (1995). This paper reviews outcomes of two families headed by parents with disabilities who received intensive in-home services. All the parents rapidly acquired the necessary child care skills. In one case the child was successfully returned home, whereas in the second, parental rights were terminated.

CONCLUSIONS

A large number of empirically based interventions are reviewed in this chapter. This literature has many limitations in research design, sample selection, outcome measures, and long-term assessment of effectiveness. Despite these limitations, empirical studies provide the foundation for future research and the development of effective service programs. A number of social workers have made important contributions to the processes of developing interventions for persons with mental retardation and their families and of providing empirical support for the effectiveness of these interventions. The foundation has been laid. The challenge for social workers who work in programs for persons with mental retardation is to master the current empirical literature and to develop a new literature of innovative, responsive, effective, empirically based interventions to serve the needs of children and adults with mental retardation and their families.

REFERENCES

Alberto, P. A., & Troutman, A. C. (1990). *Applied behavior analysis for teachers* (3rd ed.). New York: Macmillan.

Aman, M. G., Burrow, W. H., & Wolford, P. L. (1995). The Aberrant Behavior Checklist-Community: Factor validity and effect of subject variables for adults in group homes. *American Journal on Mental Retardation, 100,* 283–292.

American Psychiatric Association. (1994). *Diagnostic and statistical manual of mental disorders* (4th ed.). Washington, DC: Author.

Baker, B. L. (1989). *Parent training and developmental disabilities* (Monographs of the American Association on Mental Retardation, 13). Washington, DC: American Association on Mental Retardation.

Baker, B. L., & Brightman, A. J. (1989). *Steps to independence: A skills training guide for parents and teachers of children with special needs* (2nd ed.). Baltimore: Brookes.

Baker, B. L., Landen, S. J., & Kashima, K. J. (1991). Effects of parent training on families of children with mental retardation: Increased burden or generalized benefit? *American Journal on Mental Retardation, 96,* 127–136.

Bakken, J., Miltenberger, R. G., & Schauss, S. (1993). Teaching parents with mental retardation: Knowledge versus skills. *American Journal on Mental Retardation, 97,* 405–417.

Braddock, D. (1987). *Federal policy toward mental retardation and developmental disabilities.* Baltimore: Brookes.

Braddock, D., & Hemp, R. (1996). Medicaid spending reductions and developmental disabilities. *TASH Newsletter, 22,*(5), 12–15.

Braddock, D., Hemp, R., Lakin, K. C., & Smith, G. (1994). Continuing expansion of financial resources for MD/DD services. *Mental Retardation, 32,* 446.

Bregman, J. D. (1991). Current developments in the understanding of mental retardation. Part II: Psychopathology. *Journal of the American Academy of Child and Adolescent Psychiatry, 30,* 861–872.

Bregman, J. D. (1995). Psychopharmacologic treatment of neuropsychiatric conditions in mental retardation. *Child and Adolescent Psychiatric Clinics of North America, 4,* 401–433.

Bregman, J. D., & Gerdtz, J. (1995). Psychiatry. In B. A. Thyer & N. P. Kropf (Eds.), *Developmental disabilities. A handbook for interdisciplinary practice* (pp. 160–171). Cambridge, MA: Brookline.

Bregman, J. D., & Harris, J. C. (1995). Mental retardation. In H. I. Kaplan & D. J. Sadock (Eds.), *Comprehensive textbook of psychiatry* (6th ed., pp. 2207–2241). Baltimore: Williams & Wilkins.

Clayton, J. M., Glidden, L. M., & Kiphart, M. J. (1994). The Questionnaires on Resources and Stress: What do they measure? *American Journal on Mental Retardation, 99,* 313–316.

Colond, J. S., & Wieseler, N. A. (1995). Preventing restrictive placements through community support services. *American Journal on Mental Retardation, 100,* 201–206.

Criscione, T., Walsh, K. K., & Kastner, T. A. (1995). An evaluation of care coordination in controlling inpatient hospital utilization of people with developmental disabilities. *Mental Retardation, 33,* 364–373.

Davidson, P. W., Cain, N. N., Sloane-Reeves, J. E., Giesoe, V. E., Quijano, L. E., Van Heyningen, J., & Shoham, I. (1995). Crisis intervention for community-based individuals with developmental disabilities and behavioral and psychiatric disorders. *Mental Retardation, 33,* 21–30.

DePoy, E., & Miller, M. (1996). Preparation of social workers for serving individuals with developmental disabilities: A brief report. *Mental Retardation, 34,* 54–57.

Dunst, C., Trivette, C., & Deal, A. (1988). *Enabling and empowering families. Principles and guidelines for practice.* Cambridge, MA: Brookline.

Dunst, C. J., Trivette, C. M., Gordon, N. J., & Pletcher, L. L. (1989). Building and mobilizing informal family support networks. In G. H. S. Singer & L. K. Irvine (Eds.), *Support for care giving families. Enabling positive adaptation to disability* (pp. 121–141). Baltimore: Brookes.

Dyson, L. L. (1993). Response to the presence of a child with disabilities: Parental stress and family functioning over time. *American Journal on Mental Retardation, 98,* 207–218.

Faw, G. D., Davis, P. K., & Peck, C. (1996). Increasing self-determination: Teaching people with mental retardation to evaluate residential options. *Journal of Applied Behavior Analysis, 29,* 173–188.

Feldman, M. A., Case, L., Garrick, M., MacIntyre-Grande, W., Carnwell, J., & Sparks, B. (1992). Teaching child-care skills to mothers with developmental disabilities. *Journal of Applied Behavior Analysis, 25,* 205–215.

Feldman, M. A., Case, L., Rincover, A., Towns, F., & Betel, J. (1989). Parent Education Project III: Increasing affection and responsivity in developmentally handicapped mothers: Component analysis, generalization, and affects on child language. *Journal of Applied Behavior Analysis, 22,* 211–222.

Fiene, J. I., & Taylor, P. A. (1991). Serving rural families of developmentally disabled children: A case management model. *Social Work, 36,* 323–327.

Figueroa, R. G., Thyer, B. A., & Thyer, K. B. (1992). Extinction and DRO in the treatment of aggression in a boy with severe mental retardation. *Journal of Behaviour Therapy and Experimental Psychiatry, 23,* 133–140.

Foxx, R. M., & Faw, G. D. (1992). An eight-year follow-up of three social skills training studies. *Mental Retardation, 30,* 63–66.

Foxx, R. M., Faw, G. D., Taylor, S., Davis, P. K., Fulia, R. (1993). "Would I be able to . . ."? Teaching clients to assess the availability of their community living life style preferences. *American Journal on Mental Retardation, 98,* 235–243.

Gaylord-Ross, R., Park, H-S, Johnston, S., Lee, M., & Goetz, L. (1995). Individual social skills training and co-worker training for supported employees with dual sensory impairment: Two case examples. *Behavior Modification, 19,* 78–94.

Goetz, L., Anderson, J., & Laten, S. (1989). Facilitation of family support through public school programs. In G. H. S. Singer & L. K. Irvin (Eds.), *Support for care giving families. Enabling positive adaptation to disability* (pp. 239–251). Baltimore: Brookes.

Green, G. (1990). Least restrictive use of reductive procedures: Guidelines and competencies. In A. C. Repp & N. N. Singh (Eds.), *Perspectives on the use of nonaversive and aversive interventions for persons with developmental disabilities* (pp. 479–493). Sycamore, IL: Sycamore Publishers.

Greene, B. F., Norman, K. R., Searle, M. S., Daniels, M., & Lubeck, R. C. (1995). Child abuse and neglect by parents with disabilities: A tale of two families. *Journal of Applied Behavior Analysis, 28,* 417–434.

Greenspan, S., & Budd, K. S. (1986). Research on mentally retarded parents. In J. J. Gallagher & P. M. Vietze (Eds.), *Families of handicapped persons. Research, programs, and policy issues* (pp. 115–127). Baltimore: Brookes.

Gross, E. R. (1994). Nonaversive olfactory conditioning to control aggressive behaviors of a blind, hearing impaired, and noncommunicating child. *Journal of Developmental and Physical Disabilities, 6,* 1–6.

Gumpel, T. (1994). Social competence and social skills training for persons with mental retardation: An expansion of a behavioral paradigm. *Education and Training in Mental Retardation and Developmental Disabilities, 29,* 194–201.

Hanley, B., & Parkinson, C. B. (1994). Position paper on social work values: Practice with individuals who have developmental disabilities. *Mental Retardation, 32,* 426–431.

Harry, B. (1992). Restructuring the participation of African-American parents in special education. *Exceptional Children, 59,* 123–131.

Heller, T., Markwardt, R., Rowitz, L., & Farber, B. (1994). Adaptation of Hispanic families to a member with mental retardation. *American Journal on Mental Retardation, 99,* 289–300.

Herzog, D., & Money, J. (1993). Sexology and social work in a case of Klinefelter (47,XXY) syndrome. *Mental Retardation, 31,* 161–162.

Hester, P. P., Kaiser, A. P., Alpert, C. L., & Whiteman, B. (1996). The generalized effects of training trainers to teach parents to implement milieu teaching. *Journal of Early Intervention, 20,* 30–51.

Horejsi, C. R. (1979). Developmental disabilities: Opportunities for social workers. *Social Work, 24,* 40–43.

Horner, R. H., Thompson, L. S., & Storey, K. (1990). Effects of case manager feedback on the quality of Individual Habilitation Plan objectives. *Mental Retardation, 28,* 227–231.

Irvin, L. K. (1989). Evaluating family support programs. In G. H. S. Singer & L. K. Irvin (Eds.), *Support for care giving families. Enabling positive adaptation to disability* (pp. 329–341). Baltimore: P. H. Brookes.

Irvine, A. B., Singer, G. H. S., Erickson, A. M., & Stahlberg, D. (1992). A coordinated program to transfer self-management skills from school to home. *Education and Training in Mental Retardation, 27,* 241–254.

Iwata, B. A., Vollmer, T. R., & Zarcone, J. R. (1990). The experimental (functional) analysis of behavior disorders: Methodology, applications, and limitations. In A. C. Repp & N. N. Singh (Eds.), *Perspectives on the use of nonaversive and aversive interventions for persons with developmental disabilities* (pp. 301–330). Sycamore, IL: Sycamore Publishing.

Jackson, T. L., & Altman, R. (1996). Self-management of aggression in an adult male with mental retardation and severe behavior disorders. *Education and Training in Mental Retardation and Developmental Disabilities, 31,* 55–65.

Jauss, J. M., Wacker, D. P., Berg, W. K., Flynn, T. H., & Hurd, R. (1994). An evaluation of long-term maintenance in supported employment placements using a hypothesis testing approach. *Journal of Rehabilitation, 60*(1), 52–58.

Kashima, K. J., Baker, B. L., & Landen, S. J. (1988). Media-based versus professionally led training for parents of mentally retarded children. *American Journal on Mental Retardation, 93,* 209–217.

Kirkham, M. A. (1993). Two-year follow-up of skills training with mothers of children with disabilities. *American Journal on Mental Retardation, 97,* 509–520.

Kohr, M. A., Parrish, J. M., Neef, N. A., Driessen, J. R., & Hallinan, P. C. (1988). Communication skills training for parents: Experimental and social validation. *Journal of Applied Behavior Analysis, 21,* 21–30.

Konarski, Jr., E. A., Favell, J. E., & Favell, J. E. (Eds.). (1992). *Manual for the assessment and treatment of the behavior disorders of people with mental retardation.* Morganton, NC: Western Carolina Center Foundation.

Langone, J., Clees, T. J., Oxford, M., Malone, M., & Ross, R. (1995). Acquisition and generalization of social skills by high school students with mild mental retardation. *Mental Retardation, 33,* 186–196.

Levy, J. M. (1995). Social work. In B. A. Thyer & N. P. Kropf (Eds.), *Developmental disabilities: A handbook for interdisciplinary practice* (pp. 188–201). Cambridge, MA: Brookline.

Levy, S. R., Perhats, C., Nash-Johnson, M., & Welter, J. F. (1992). Reducing the risk in pregnant teens who are very young and those with mild mental retardation. *Mental Retardation, 30,* 195–203.

Lindsay, W. R., Baty, F. J., Michie, A. M., & Richardson, I. (1989). A comparison of anxiety treatments with adults who have moderate and severe mental retardation. *Research in Developmental Disabilities, 10,* 129–140.

Lindsay, W. R., Fee, M., Michie, A., & Heap, I. (1994). The effects of cue control relaxation on adults with severe mental retardation. *Research in Developmental Disabilities, 15,* 425–437.

Lindsey, P. (1994). Assessing the ability of adults with mental retardation to give direct consent for residential placements: A follow-up study for the Consent Screening Interview. *Education and Training in Mental Retardation and Developmental Disabilities, 29,* 155–164.

Lozano, B. (1993). Independent living: Relation among training, skills, and success. *American Journal on Mental Retardation, 98,* 249–262.

Luckasson, R., Coulter, D. L., Polloway, E. A., Reiss, S., Schalock, R. L., Snell, M. E., Spitalnik, D. M., & Stark, J. A. (1992). *Mental retardation: Definition, classification, and systems of supports* (9th ed.). Washington, DC: American Association on Mental Retardation.

Luckasson, R., Schalock, R. L., Snell, M. E., & Spitalnick, D. M. (1996). The 1992 AAMR Definition and preschool children: Response from the Committee on Terminology and Classification. *Mental Retardation, 34,* 247–253.

Lutzker, J. R., Campbell, R. V., Newman, M. R., & Harrold, M. (1989). Ecobehavioral interventions for abusive, neglectful, and high-risk families. In G. H. S. Singer & L. K. Irvin (Eds.), *Support for care giving families. Enabling positive adaptation to disability* (pp. 313–326). Baltimore: P. H. Brookes.

MacEachron, A. E., Pensky, D., & Hawes, B. (1986). Case management for families of developmentally disabled clients: An empirical policy analysis of a statewide system. In J. J. Gallagher & P. M. Vietze (Eds.), *Families of handicapped persons. Research, programs and policy issues* (pp. 273–287). Baltimore: Brookes.

Maeser, N. C., & Thyer, B. A. (1990). Teaching boys with severe mental retardation to serve themselves during family-style meals. *Behavioral Residential Treatment, 5,* 239–246.

Meyer, L. H., & Evans, I. M. (1989). *Nonaversive intervention for behavior problems. A manual for home and community.* Baltimore: Brookes.

Mirenda, P. (1986). Respondent conditioning procedures. In G. W. LaVigna & A. M. Donnellan (Eds.), *Alternatives to punishment: Solving behavior problems with non-aversive strategies* (pp. 141–156). New York: Irvington.

Mueser, K. T., Valenti-Hein, D., & Yarnold, P. R., (1987). Dating skills groups for the developmentally disabled: Social skills and problem-solving versus relaxation training. *Behavior Modification, 11,* 200–228.

Munk, D. D., & Repp, A. C. (1994). The relationship between instructional variables and problem behavior: A review. *Exceptional Children, 60,* 390–401.

Nihira, K., Weisner, T. S., & Bernheimer, L. P. (1994). Ecocultural assessment in families of children with developmental delays: Construct and concurrent validities. *American Journal on Mental Retardation, 98,* 551–566.

Nixon, C. D., & Singer, G. H. S. (1993). Group cognitive-behavioral treatment for excessive parental self-blame and guilt. *American Journal on Mental Retardation, 97,* 665–672.

O'Neill, R. E., Horner, R. H., Albin, R. W., Storey, K., & Sprague, J. R. (1990). *Functional analysis of problem behavior: A practical assessment guide.* Sycamore, IL: Sycamore Publishing.

O'Reilly, M. F., & Glynn, D. (1995). Using a process social skills training approach with adolescents with mild intellectual disabilities in a high school setting. *Education and Training in Mental Retardation and Developmental Disabilities, 30,* 187–198.

Parke, R. D. (1986). Fathers, families, and support systems: Their role in the development of at-risk and retarded infants and children. In J. J. Gallagher & P. M. Vietze (Eds.), *Families of handicapped persons. Research, programs and policy issues* (pp. 101–113). Baltimore: Brookes.

Peterson, F. M., & Martens, B. K. (1995). A comparison of behavioral interventions reported in treatment studies and programs for adults with developmental disabilities. *Research in Developmental Disabilities, 16,* 27–41.

Reichertz, D., & Frankel, H. (1993). Integrating family assessment into social work practice. *Research on Social Work Practice, 3,* 243–257.

Repp, A. C., & Karsh, K. G. (1990). A taxonomic approach to the nonaversive treatment of maladaptive behavior of persons with developmental disabilities. In A. C. Repp & N. N. Singh (Eds.), *Perspectives on the use of nonaversive and aversive interventions for persons with developmental disabilities* (pp. 331–347). Sycamore, IL: Sycamore Publishing.

Rockland, L. H. (1993). A review of supportive psychotherapy, 1986–1992. *Hospital and Community Psychiatry, 44,* 1053–1060.

Ryan, R. (1993). Response to "Psychiatric care of adults with developmental disabilities and mental illness in the community." *Community Mental Health Journal, 29,* 477–481.

Sarber, R. E., Halasz, M. M., Messmer, M. C., Bickett, A. D., & Lutzker, J. R. (1983). Teaching menu planning and grocery shopping skills to a mentally retarded mother. *Mental Retardation, 21,* 101–106.

Schalock, R. L., & Genung, L. T. (1993). Placement from a community-based mental retardation program: A 15-year follow-up. *American Journal on Mental Retardation, 98,* 400–407.

Scheerenberger, R. C. (1983). *A history of mental retardation.* Baltimore: Brookes.

Scotti, J. R., Evans, I. M., Meyer, L. H., & Walker, P. (1991). A meta-analysis of intervention research with problem behavior: Treatment validity and standards of practice. *American Journal on Mental Retardation, 96,* 233–256.

Scotti, J. R., Masia, C. L., Boggess, J. T., Speaks, L. V., & Drabman, R. S. (1996). The educational effects of providing AIDS-risk information to persons with developmental disabilities: an exploratory study. *Education and Training in Mental Retardation and Developmental Disabilities, 31,* 115–122.

Sievert, A. L., Cuvo, A. J., & Davis, P. K. (1988). Training self-advocacy skills to adults with mild handicaps. *Journal of Applied Behavior Analysis, 21,* 299–309.

Singer, G. H. S., Irvin, L. K., & Hawkins, N. (1988). Stress management training for parents of children with severe handicaps. *Mental Retardation, 26,* 269–277.

Singer, G. H. S., Irvine, A. B., & Irvin, L. K. (1989). Expanding the focus of behavioral parent training: a contextual approach. In G. H. S. Singer & L. K. Irvin (Eds.), *Support for care giving families. Enabling positive adaptation to disability* (pp. 85–102). Baltimore: Brookes.

Smith, C., Algozzine, B., Schmid, R., & Hennly, T. (1990). Prison adjustment of youthful prison inmates with mental retardation. *Mental Retardation, 28,* 177–181.

Smith, G. C., Majeski, R. A., & McClenny, B. (1996). Psychoeducational support groups for aging parents: development and preliminary outcomes. *Mental Retardation, 34,* 172–181.

Soto, G., Toro-Zambrana, W., & Belfiore, P. J. (1994). Comparison of two instructional strategies on social skills acquisition and generalization among individuals with moderate and severe mental retardation working in a vocational setting: a meta-analytical review. *Education and Training in Mental Retardation and Developmental Disabilities, 29,* 307–320.

Steiner, J. (1984). Group counseling with retarded offenders. *Social Work, 29,* 181–185.

Stoneman, Z., & Malone, M. (1995). The changing nature of interdisciplinary practice. In B. A. Thyer & N. P. Kropf (Eds.), *Developmental disabilities: A handbook for interdisciplinary practice* (pp. 234–247). Cambridge, MA: Brookline.

Sturmey, P., & Bertman, L. J. (1994). Validity of the Reiss Screen for Maladaptive Behavior. *American Journal on Mental Retardation, 99,* 201–206.

Sundel, S. S. (1994). Videotaped training of job-related social skills using peer-modeling: An evaluation of social validity. *Research on Social Work Practice, 4,* 40–52.

Swanson, C. K., & Garwick, G. B. (1990). Treatment for low-functioning sex offenders: Group therapy and interagency coordination. *Mental Retardation, 28,* 155–161.

Swenson-Pierce, A., Kohl, F. L., & Egel, A. L. (1987). Siblings as home trainers: A strategy for teaching domestic skills to children. *The Journal of the Association for Persons with Severe Handicaps, 12,* 53–60.

Torrey, W. C. (1993). Psychiatric care of adults with developmental disabilities and mental illness in the community. *Community Mental Health Journal, 29,* 461–476.

Touchette, P. E., MacDonald, R. F., & Langer, S. N. (1985). A scatter plot for identifying stimulus control of problem behavior. *Journal of Applied Behavior Analysis, 18,* 343–351.

Tymchuk, A. J., Hamada, D., Andron, L., & Anderson, S. (1990). Home safety training with mothers who are mentally retarded. *Education and Training in Mental Retardation, 25,* 142–149.

Umbreit, J. (1996). Functional analysis of disruptive behavior in an inclusive classroom. *Journal of Early Intervention, 20,* 18–29.

Underwood, L. A., Figueroa, R. G., Thyer, B. A., & Nzeocha, A. (1989). Interruption and DRI in the treatment of self-injurious behavior among mentally retarded and autistic self-restrainers. *Behavior Modification, 13,* 471–481.

Valenti-Hein, D., & Mueser, K. (1990). *The dating skills program: Teaching social-sexual skills to adults with mental retardation.* Orland Park, IL: International Diagnostic Systems.

Valenti-Hein, D. C., Yarnold, P. R., & Mueser, K. T. (1994). Evaluation of the dating skills program for improving heterosocial interactions in people with mental retardation. *Behavior Modification, 18,* 32–46.

Wacker, D., Steege, M., Northup, J., Reimers, T., Berg, W., & Sasso, G. (1990). Use of functional analysis and acceptability measures to assess and treat severe behavior problems: an outpatient clinic model. In A. C. Repp & N. N. Singh (Eds.), *Perspectives on the use of nonaversive and aversive interventions for persons with developmental disabilities* (pp. 349–359). Sycamore, IL: Sycamore.

Walker, B. (1989). Strategies for improving parent-professional cooperation. In G. H. S. Singer & L. K. Irvin (Eds.), *Support for care giving families. Enabling positive adaptation to disability* (pp. 103–119). Baltimore: Brookes.

Westling, D. L. (1996). What do parents of children with moderate and severe disabilities want? *Education and Training in Mental Retardation and Developmental Disabilities, 31,* 86–114.

Chapter 3

ATTENTION DEFICIT HYPERACTIVITY DISORDER

Martha J. Markward

OVERVIEW

Operational Definitions

The *Diagnostic and Statistical Manual of Mental Disorders,* fourth edition (*DSM-IV;* American Psychiatric Association [APA], 1994) notes that the individual with Attention Deficit Hyperactivity Disorder (ADHD) presents with a persistent pattern of inattention, hyperactivity-impulsivity, or both that is more frequent and severe than is typically observed in individuals at comparable levels of development. Individuals with attentional problems are frequently unable to focus on details, make careless mistakes, have difficulty sustaining attention on tasks, cannot listen to or follow instructions, are disorganized, and have difficulty engaging in tasks that require sustained mental effort, especially schoolwork. They also lose necessary items, are easily distracted by extraneous stimuli, or are forgetful in daily activities (APA, 1994, p. 84).

In contrast to individuals with attentional problems, hyperactive individuals often fidget or squirm or move around inappropriately (in adolescents or adults, this may be limited to subjective feelings of restlessness); they often are unable to play or engage in leisure activities quietly, or act on the go or driven. By comparison, impulsive individuals respond inappropriately, are unable to wait their turn, and often interrupt or intrude on others (see APA, 1994, p. 84). Clinicians must also consider whether the impairment was present before age 7, the symptoms are present in at least two social environments, the impairment is present in two settings, and the symptoms are not a result of or explained by another disorder (see APA, 1994, p. 84).

In using the *DSM-IV* criteria, ADHD may be subtyped as either "combined, predominantly inattentive" or "predominantly hyperactive-impulsive," contingent on the symptom pattern apparent in the past 6 months (see APA, 1994, pp. 83–85).

Individuals who have had one type at an earlier stage of development may go on to develop the combined type, or vice versa. When the criteria for this disorder cannot be met, and it is unclear whether they have ever been met, the diagnosis is "ADHD not otherwise specified." Relative to these *DSM-IV* diagnostic criteria, it is not surprising that ADHD children, adolescents, and adults have features that distinguish them from others.

Prevalence and Features

Estimates indicate that the prevalence rate of attention deficit hyperactivity disorder (ADHD) is 3% to 5% among children and adolescents; McFarland, Kolstad, and Briggs (1995) noted that the disorder affects 3% to 10% of school-age children. On one hand, Biederman, Faraone, Mick, and Spencer (1995) noted that the disorder persists into adulthood in 10% to 60% of the childhood-onset cases; on the other hand, Shaffer (1994) contended that the prevalence rate for the disorder among adults is somewhat lower than the rates for other important adult psychiatric disorders. Silverthorn, Frick, Kuper, and Ott (1996) noted that ADHD is more predominant among males than among females, especially school-age children.

Depending on age and development, individuals with ADHD exhibit behaviors that others do not. ADHD children typically present with low frustration tolerance, temper outbursts, bossiness, stubbornness, excessive and frequent demands, mood lability, and demoralization. In contrast, Wender (1995, p. 192) indicated that ADHD adolescents are likely to present with immature behaviors that include laughing excessively and inappropriately, becoming overly excited, fooling around without regard for the feelings of others, and overreacting to teasing or other peer interactions (see also Hechtman, 1989; Barkley, Fischer, Edelbrock, & Smallish, 1990). Those ADHD adolescents with Oppositional Defiant Disorder (ADHD-ODD) or Conduct Disorder (ADHD-CD) present with disobedience and talking back, frequent fighting, or both.

Weinstein (1994) indicated that ADHD adults are likely to make careless mistakes, have difficulty sustaining attention, listen marginally, and lose items they need for leisure or work activities. Adults can also be distracted either internally by their own thoughts or externally by the activities of others. Moreover, they may be unable to participate meaningfully or appropriately even in leisure-time activities due to impulsivity, or they may fail to analyze the consequences of their behaviors and, as a result, do stupid things.

The most common manifestations of behaviors that typify ADHD children, adolescents, and adults are impaired academic achievement and social relationships. ADHD adolescents with ODD and CD are likely to encounter problems with the law and substance abuse or both (see Gittelman, Mannuzza, Shenker, & Bonagura, 1985). ADHD adults experience problems in the workplace; for example, they may not meet deadlines due to organizational problems. Some evidence suggests that

ADHD adults have more auto accidents, lower college grades, more marital problems, and more job changes than others (Barkley, Guevremont, Anastopoulos, DuPaul, & Shelton, 1993).

Individuals with ADHD generally function at a lower intellectual level than others; a substantial number also have either ODD or CD. Tannock, Purvis, and Schachar (1993) noted that 10% to 50% of ADHD children have a learning disability. In this context, Tannock et al. found that ADHD children exhibit deficits in executive processes or in organizing and monitoring output of information rather than deficits in extracting and comprehending main ideas. In addition, there may be a higher prevalence of mood, anxiety, learning, and communication disorders among ADHD children than among other children which, in turn, impact negatively on school outcomes. Interestingly, Hoza, Pelham, Milich, Pillow, and McBride (1993) found that, although ADHD children see themselves as similar to nonreferred children in terms of self-perceived competence and global self-worth, they deny responsibility for negative social events.

Social and Financial Costs

The major social cost of ADHD to society is that a significant number of its children, adolescents, and adults exhibit behaviors that cause serious interactional and relational problems in both the private and public spheres of functioning (see Andersen, Hinshaw, & Simmel, 1994; Anastopoulos, Guevremont, Shelton, & DuPaul, 1992; Barkley, Anastopoulos, Guevremont, & Fletcher, 1992; Cousins & Weiss, 1993; Nathan, 1992). Given the prevalence of ADHD across the life span and the possibility that many more individuals suffer from the disorder than are diagnosed, the financial costs of the disorder are incalculable. However, it is plausible that problems associated with the ADHD syndrome impact on education, health, labor, and rehabilitation costs in both the public and private sectors of the economy.

Relevance to Social Work Practice

The ADHD syndrome is especially relevant to those who work in human services—particularly social workers, who are more likely than other practitioners to work with ADHD sufferers of all ages in a variety of settings. For some time, social workers have been called upon to work in the schools with ADHD students who are labeled *behavior disordered*. Currently, social workers are challenged to work in a variety of settings with individuals whose problems, such as substance abuse, may very well be associated with the ADHD syndrome. In accepting this new challenge, social workers have a moral and ethical responsibility to implement the most effective practices available in treating individuals with ADHD.

ASSESSMENT METHODS

There are currently no laboratory tests available for diagnosing ADHD, although it is likely that one will eventually be developed in light of support for the biological basis of the disorder. Hendrick (1995) highlighted the finding that blood flow in the areas of the brain that process information is slower than normal in ADHD patients. Researchers suspect that this problem could explain why ADHD sufferers have more trouble than others understanding and following verbal instructions, as well as why they must first visualize verbal instructions before understanding and responding to tasks. In the absence of a laboratory test, Kronenberger and Meyer (1996) noted that clinicians rely on cognitive, behavioral, syndrome-specific, psychological, and global assessment measures to diagnose ADHD.

Cognitive Assessment

Cognitive assessment focuses on intelligence, achievement, and adaptive behavior. Social workers can rely on the results of the Wechsler intelligence scales (Wechsler Adult Intelligence Scale—Revised [WAIS-R], Wechsler, 1981; Wechsler Preschool and Primary Scale of Intelligence—Revised [WPPSI-R], Wechsler, 1989; Wechsler Intelligence Scale for Children—Third Edition [WISC-III], Wechsler, 1991) to measure an individual's learning potential, as well as learning strengths and weaknesses. Relative to performance potential, social workers can rely on the results of the Woodcock-Johnson Tests of Educational Achievement—Revised (WJ-R; Woodcock & Johnson, 1989) and the Wechsler Individual Achievement Test (WIAT; Psychological Corporation, 1992) to measure actual performance or achievement. To explain any discrepancy between achievement and learning potential, as well as to better understand an individual's capacity to function appropriately on a day-to-day basis in a variety of settings, social workers might also administer a measure of adaptive behavior, such as the Vineland Adaptive Behavior Scales (VABS; Sparrow, Balla, & Cicchetti, 1984).

Behavioral Assessment

Parent and teacher reports of children's behaviors are especially important. To obtain those reports, social workers might administer the Child Behavior Checklist (CBCL; Achenbach, 1991), as well as the CBCL teacher and youth self-report forms and the Conners Parent Rating Scales (CPRS; Conners, 1990). Considering that most adolescents typically spend little time in the company of parents or a single teacher, Wender contended that the ADD/H Adolescent Self-Report Scale (ADD/HSRS; Conners & Wells, 1985) may actually elicit better information about the here-and-now behaviors of a referred adolescent than do other assessment techniques. Shaffer (1994) cautioned that adults may remember being more or less hyperactive as children than they actually were.

DuPaul and Barkley (1993) noted the importance of using direct observations and teachers' ratings of behavior in the assessment process to measure individual differences in children's responses to medication that vary as a function of (a) the dose, (b) the behavior targeted for change, (c) the uniqueness of individuals, and (d) the amount or strength of the behavioral intervention. One means of measuring the degree to which medication results in behavioral changes is to calculate the reliable change index (RCI; see Christensen & Mendoza, 1986; Jacobsen, Follette, & Revenstorf, 1984). For each measure of treatment response, the RCI statistic is calculated by taking the change score (that is, the child's mean score at medication dosage minus the child's placebo score) and dividing by the standard error of difference between the two scores (see DuPaul & Barkley, pp. 53–55).

Syndrome-Specific Tests

In diagnosing ADHD, social workers can use specific tests to assess individuals' attentional, impulsivity, and distractibility problems. For example, they may administer a continuous performance test, such as the Gordon Diagnostic System (GDS; Gordon, 1983), to measure attention and impulsivity. At the same time, social workers may find it necessary to administer the Matching Familiar Figures Test (MFFT; Cairns & Cammock, 1978) as a means of assessing distractibility.

Psychological Assessment

Social workers may want to assess the psychological functioning of individuals with ADHD, especially adolescents and adults. Cotugno (1995) concluded that the Rorschach Inkblot Test (Exner, 1993) has utility in measuring an ADHD child's ability to manage the chronic distress and discomfort that is related to his or her disorder. By administering the Revised Children's Manifest Anxiety Scale (RCMAS; Reynolds & Richmond, 1978), Locus of Control Scale for Children (N-SLOC; Nowicki & Strickland, 1973), and Persistence Scale for Children (PSC; Lufi & Cohen, 1987), Lufi and Parish-Plass (1995) found that ADHD children tend to manifest a higher level of worry due to out-of-control situations, an external locus of control, and a lower level of persistence.

Global Assessment

Kronenberger and Meyer (1996) stressed the point that no assessment measure is more important in the assessment process than a clinical interview. In the case of an ADHD diagnosis, most clinicians use an interview to obtain a comprehensive history of an individual's behavior and development since early childhood. With respect to children, clinicians rely on information they obtain from parents and teachers; in particular, teachers are able to observe a referred child's academic and nonacademic behaviors in the school setting. As do clinicians in psychiatric settings, social workers can use both structured and semistructured interviews.

EFFECTIVE INTERVENTIONS

A review of the literature indicates that effective psychosocial treatment of ADHD focuses primarily on behavioral treatment that involves an emphasis on the selection of reinforcement and rewards and on the amount of treatment used. Although behavior treatment is usually the most effective short-term intervention with children with ADHD, cognitive treatment is often more effective with adolescents and adults. Specifically, cognitive-behavioral treatment is a relatively effective intervention with groups of ADHD children and adolescents, as well as with their parents. In the classroom group, teacher factors—such as how teachers view parents' treatment of a child's ADHD—may be salient in the teacher's treatment of that child in the classroom. Multiple-modality treatment may ultimately prove to be the most effective intervention with ADHD sufferers of all ages when the methodological problems involved in measuring outcomes are overcome.

Individual Treatment

In working with ADHD children, social workers can generally rely on a behavioral approach that involves the use of certain rules and boundaries to govern actions and a system of both positive and negative reinforcement developed to change targeted inappropriate behaviors. In this system, parents and teachers are usually taught to follow specific plans or strategies in a stepwise fashion. Studies validate the salience of focusing on reinforcement and behavioral dosage in the treatment of ADHD children (Abramowitz, Eckstrand, O'Leary, & Dulcan, 1992; Ajibola & Clement, 1995; Gittelman et al., 1980; Guevremont, Tishelman, & Hull, 1985; Hoza, Pelham, Sams, & Carlson, 1992; Pelham, Vodde-Hamilton, Murphy, Greenstein, & Vallano, 1991; Schweitzer & Sulzer-Azaroff, 1995).

Behavioral Approach.   Gittelman et al. (1980) found that when parents and teachers used contingent reinforcers the behavior of latency-age ADHD children who were also on medication improved and was similar to that of classmates without ADHD. Guevremont et al. (1985) found that two latency-age boys improved in the percentage of classroom work that they completed when they participated in a self-instructional training program and their mothers were trained to use contingency management. Moreover, others also perceived the two boys to be less disruptive and to have more self-control.

Ajibola and Clement (1995) found that ADHD children need to self-reinforce with a reward that provides them with maximum incentive to change targeted negative behaviors. Those researchers employed a modified Latin square design in which each of six boys ages 9 to 12 were offered a job that would last 65 school days. The boys were paid $1 for each day that they attended a special 30-minute tutoring class at 7:30 A.M. and carried out duties specified in weekly employment contracts (see Ajibola & Clement, 1995, p. 215 for a detailed description of the intervention).

The subjects began with a 5-day baseline phase followed by six 10-day treatment phases in which each child received one of six treatment combinations. Those combinations included drug placebo plus noncontingent reinforcers, low-dosage medication plus noncontingent reinforcers, high-dosage medication plus noncontingent reinforcers, low-dosage medication plus self-reinforcement, high-dosage medication plus self-reinforcement, and drug placebo plus self-reinforcement. The major finding in the study was that boys who received a low dosage of medication and were taught to reinforce themselves gained more in terms of academic performance than did boys in other groups (see also Chase & Clement, 1985; Fantuzzo & Polite, 1990).

In an earlier study, Hoza et al. (1992) examined the dosage effects of behavior therapy and medication on the classroom performance of two ADHD boys. The results of this examination showed that the extent of the behavioral intervention, such as the extent to which an ADHD child's environment at home and school is structured, can significantly impact a child's response to therapy. Thus, a social worker can be instrumental in helping a child identify a reinforcer or reward that provides him or her with the most incentive to behave appropriately. In light of Schweitzer and Sulzer-Azaroff's (1995) finding that ADHD children can comprehend the choices they make regarding contingencies, social workers can be instrumental in reinforcing an ADHD child's understanding of the importance of following rules, waiting for more advantageous consequences, and making the best choice given the particular set of circumstances.

Pelham et al. (1991) compared the effects of Ritalin on adolescents with ADHD in a day treatment program in which a multifaceted behavioral intervention was used. The researchers found that psychosocial and educational interventions, such as the use of a point system, addressed a variety of negative behaviors and interactions with others in adolescents with ADHD. Although this finding is consistent with some studies on the treatment of adolescents with ADHD, it is inconsistent with others.

Similarly, Abramowitz et al. (1992) also examined the response of ADHD children in a summer day treatment program to stimulant medication and two intensities or dosages of a behavioral intervention. Based on the results of this examination, the researchers drew three conclusions. First, a simple behavioral intervention, such as structure in the environment, can be as effective as medication when implemented in its most intense form. Second, even though a particular dosage of medication may be needed to achieve positive results, an inappropriate dosage of medication may obviate the need for the most intense form of behavioral intervention. For example, a medication dosage that is too high might conceal the need for a more highly structured environment in order to address a child's problems with impulsivity. Third, individual differences in the responses of children appear to be normative rather than nonnormative.

Cognitive Approach.   Cognitive therapy helps individuals assess situations, plan what to do, solve problems, and be self-reflective. Although several studies show that a cognitive approach is relatively ineffective in the treatment of ADHD children (see Abikoff & Gittelman, 1985; Brown, Borden, Wynne, Schleser, & Clingerman, 1986; Brown, Wynne, & Medenis, 1985), Faigel, Sznajderman, Tishby, Turel, and Uri (1995) noted that cognitive therapy may be more appropriate in the treatment of adolescents with ADHD, primarily because adolescents often lose interest in rewards quickly (see Liu, Robin, Brenner, & Eastman, 1991), view behavior management as a control that threatens their autonomy (Schneider, 1992), or both. Adolescents with ADHD who learn to be compulsive in completing tasks are more successful than those who do not (Faigel et al., 1985).

Similarly, Weinstein (1994) noted that cognitive remediation strategies are especially effective in the treatment of adults with ADHD (see also Guevremont, 1992; Sohlberg & Mateer, 1989). Cognitive remediation strategies take on importance in helping adults with ADHD manage the anger and stress often associated with the disorder. Based on the results of various clinical case studies, adult ADHD patients have reported being able to function more effectively as a result of using cognitive remediation strategies to address attentional, memory, and problem-solving difficulties (see also Sohlberg & Mateer, 1989; Guevremont, 1992; Weinstein, 1994).

Group Treatment

A cognitive-behavioral approach can be effective in working with groups of ADHD children and their parents. In light of findings that indicate that the most lasting deficit of the ADHD syndrome is the lack of social competence (see Hechtman, 1989), clinicians can facilitate parent training and child social skills groups in combination to enhance the social competence of ADHD children. In school settings, some evidence suggests that teacher factors may also be particularly important in the treatment of ADHD students.

Ialongo et al. (1993) found that behavioral group training with parents in combination with medication treatment of the child and child self-control instruction resulted only in parents having a more positive orientation toward their child's disorder. After group training, parents rated the cardinal features of their child's disorder, as well as the child's externalizing behaviors, more positively. Although researchers reasoned that group work with parents might also result in improved family relations, they concluded that parents might need videotaped modeling to change their behavior in such a way as to positively impact their interactions with an ADHD child.

For example, Webster-Stratton, Kolpacoff, and Hollinsworth (1989) demonstrated that a therapist-led, group-based, videotaped modeling approach to working with parents was as effective as an individual-based, time-limited approach in treating conduct problems among preschoolers. Even though the researchers conceded that the effectiveness of the group approach may have been a function of early intervention, they concluded that it may have been a function of the emphasis in the approach on intensive teacher, parent, and therapist training in social learning theory. Regardless, Ialongo et al. (1993) posited that modifications in the curriculum of group intervention benefit teachers in teaching children with ADHD to compensate for their deficits.

Preliminary findings in another study suggest that parents can be involved to a great extent in the generalization and maintenance of socially competent behavior in their ADHD children. Cousins and Weiss (1993) combined a parent training and a child social skills training program to address the social competence deficits of school-age ADHD children in one clinical setting. In planning the intervention, the researchers adapted Barkley's (1987) parent training program and designed a social skills training program for the children.

Thus, social workers can emphasize a combination of cognitive and behavioral training in implementing parent groups. In the 12 to 16 weekly sessions, they could cover the following topics: (a) orientation and review of ADHD; (b) understanding causes of children's misbehavior; (c) improving parents' skills at attending, issuing effective commands, and reinforcing positive behavior; (d) establishing a home points system; (e) reviewing the points system and introducing response cost; using time-out reinforcement; (f) extending time-out to other misbehavior; (g) managing behavior problems in public places; and (h) handling future behavior problems. Each hourly session consists of homework take-up, didactic presentation of material, modeling, group discussion, feedback, and a new homework assignment.

In implementing the child's social skills training group, social workers can emphasize skills that children ages 6 to 10 need in their interactions with others. Those skill areas include: (a) basic interactions skills, such as introducing oneself; (b) getting along with others; (c) contacts with adults at home and at school; (d) conversational skills; and (e) problem situations. A session might involve a review of homework, general greeting, presentation of the week's skill, reading the component steps of the skill aloud, modeling of the skill by the leader, children giving feedback about positive and negative aspects of the modeling, and children ultimately role-playing the skill.

In light of the constraints that managed care can impose on intervention, the results of one study suggest that brief cognitive-behavioral treatment might decrease impulsivity in ADHD children. Cocciarella, Wood, and Low (1995) administered brief behavioral therapy to 7 latency-age children with ADHD, 4 of whom took psychostimulant medication for the condition. The intervention included reinforcing appropriate behaviors and punishing negative behaviors, skills training, and parent education. Children were assigned to one of two groups ($n = 3$; $n = 4$) that met once a week for seven sessions of the three treatments.

The 90-minute group meetings consisted of skills training, a planned activity, and free play. Children were reinforced for prosocial behavior using a star system in which they lost stars when they interrupted, behaved impulsively, or could not control their activity. In addition to meeting four to six times to learn more about ADHD, parents in the program engaged in token economies at home, monitored behavior, and established reward systems. Cocciarella et al. found significant decreases in children's impulsivity at home and at school after treatment.

Greene (1995) contended that teacher factors, including teacher-treatment and teacher-student compatibility, have been largely ignored as they relate to the treatment of ADHD. Several studies indicate that some teachers are more effective than others in working with difficult students (see Cannon, Idol, & West, 1992). For example, grouping students as a means of achieving on-task behavior may be in the best academic and psychological interests of ADHD students only if teachers' facilitation of the groups is based on sound principles of group dynamics. Power, Hess, and Bennett (1993) noted that teachers' treatment of ADHD students may be contingent on perceptions about the extent to which parents are also willing to work with ADHD children. Clearly, teacher interactions with and expectations of students with ADHD are important (see Good & Brophy, 1991).

Family Treatment

Vinson (1994) noted that, although they may be appealing, family therapies appear to have weak effects and little empirical validation in the psychosocial treatment of ADHD. Nonetheless, evidence suggests that a critical measure of successful family therapy in the treatment of individuals with ADHD is the degree to which it prepares parents to understand, cope with, and raise children who suffer from the ADHD syndrome. In light of the finding that hyperactivity can be a precursor to a wide variety of patterns, such as criminality, Meyer and Deitsch (1996) suggested that family therapy should be directed toward helping parents and siblings reduce the stress, guilt, and wear and tear that ADHD children generate in their families. Wender (1995) noted that family therapy is especially salient in working with ADHD adolescents.

Barkley, Guevremont, Anastopoulos, and Fletcher (1992) examined the effects of three family therapy programs on conflict in the families of 61 ADHD adolescents ages 12 to 18. In the absence of a no-treatment group, the adolescents were randomized to either behavior management ($n = 20$), problem-solving and communication training ($n = 21$), or structural family therapy ($n = 20$). Although pre- and posttest measures showed that all treatments resulted in the reduction of negative communication, conflicts, and anger during conflicts, as well as in improved ratings of school adjustment, reduced internalizing and externalizing symptoms, and decreased maternal depressive symptoms, only 5% to 30% of subjects improved within groups and only 5% to 20% improved after treatment.

Anastopoulos, Shelton, DuPaul, and Guevremont (1993) examined changes in parents' functioning resulting from participation in a behavioral parent training (PT) program specifically designed for parents of school-age children with ADHD. Relative to waiting-list controls, subjects who completed the nine-session program showed significant posttreatment gains in both child and parent functioning, which were maintained 2 months after treatment. Specifically, there were reductions in parenting stress and increases in parenting self-esteem, which accompanied parent-reported improvements in the overall severity of the child's ADHD symptoms.

Similarly, Long, Rickert, and Ashcraft (1993) investigated the effectiveness of bibliotherapy with parents as an adjunct to stimulant medication in the treatment of children with ADHD. Researchers randomly assigned parents of ADHD children to either an experimental group or a control group. Parents in the experimental group received a written protocol or bibliotherapy outlining behavioral techniques for managing oppositional child behaviors. Posttreatment results showed significant differences favoring the experimental group on standardized measures of the intensity of behavior problems in the home, parental knowledge of behavioral principles, and teacher ratings of behavior. This approach appears to offer an inexpensive adjunct to stimulant medication in the treatment of ADHD when individual or group behavior management is not feasible.

Hallowell and Ratey (1994) contend that the distractibility, impulsivity, and excessive energy associated with ADHD often impact negatively on the intimate relationships of adults with ADHD. Thus, psychoeducation for the family of the ADHD sufferer can be quite helpful in changing communication patterns in the family system and the ability of members to understand the patient's functioning within that system. For example, an ADHD adult may need to ask family members to repeat verbal instructions; in turn, family members must learn to do this. In some instances, adults with ADHD tend to jump to the next task at hand in an attempt to avoid experiencing emotion; they must learn how to be in touch with their emotions, and other family members can help them to do this.

Multiple-Modality Treatment

Nathan (1992) proposed that the use of multiple-modality treatment of ADHD produces a contribution to outcomes greater than the sum of each modality's contribution. With this in mind, Nathan contended that psychodynamic understanding is key in determining how to combine various therapies and make them mutually effective. Contingent on the developmental age of both parents and child, multiple-modality treatment may be necessary to address the manifestations of problems at different times; hence, as a child grows older, the character of the therapeutic work changes. Given the methodological concerns about multiple-modality treatment, several researchers have focused on the efficacy of this type of treatment.

Kolko (1992) evaluated the short-term outcomes for 65 children ages 6 to 13 who were followed for 2, 4, or 6 months after psychiatric hospitalization for a number of conditions. During hospitalization, multidisciplinary teams were responsible for small groups of patients. Each team consisted of child psychologist, senior clinician or child resident, social worker, special educator, primary nurse, and several members of the nursing or clinical staff. Based on a unitwide point system, the team individualized plans for the patients that exposed each of them to some combination of contingencies, social-cognitive skills training, socialization practice, individual therapy, family counseling, or parent training.

Kolko (1992) found that this approach resulted in poor short-term outcomes for those children in the study with ADHD and for the older children in the study, as well as for those with depressive symptoms, neurological dysfunction, limited aftercare, a history of physical abuse, and higher intelligence. Despite those outcomes, Kolko recommended continued developments in assessing therapeutic outcomes. Specifically, those developments might focus on the effects of sources of difficulty (parents versus children), time (e.g., pretreatment versus follow-up), and diagnosis (e.g., externalizing versus internalizing behaviors) on standardized measures of dysfunction (e.g., childhood disorders) and adaptation (e.g., competence; p. 276).

Grizenko, Papineau, and Sayegh (1993) evaluated the efficacy of multimodal day treatment in addressing the academic, social, and self-esteem deficits of 30 children with disruptive disorders, 8 of whom were diagnosed with ADHD. The children were assigned to either the day treatment program or to a waiting list and were then compared on measures of behavior, self-perception, academics, peer relations, and family functioning. The preadolescent day treatment program provided multiple-modality therapy with a psychodynamic orientation; activities included a daily 150-minute block of special education and a 180-minute block of psychotherapy that might involve a variety of individual and group therapies.

Interestingly, the treatment group improved significantly over the control group on outcome measures of behavior and self-perception. Moreover, the follow-up findings indicated that treated children improved over time on all outcomes measures except academic performance. Within the context that only one fourth of the patients in this study were children with ADHD, the researchers concluded that multiple-modality treatment is needed to deal effectively with the problems of disruptive children.

There is considerable support for multiple-modality treatment of ADHD. Weinstein, Seidman, Feldman, and Ratey (1991) suggested that a critical issue in working with an ADHD individual is to avoid an either/or approach; instead, they argued for making use of all relevant psychological, biological, and social information in treatment. Lipowski (1989) pointed out that identifying strategies to help individuals function more effectively is less of a problem than is helping individuals perceive their self-worth as deserving it (in Weinstein, 1994, p. 51). Clinical experience suggests that social workers should use an integrated approach focused on both the cognitive and affective domains of functioning in helping ADHD adults manage negative behaviors associated with the disorder that they have.

Medication

Evidence suggests that medication treatment, primarily in the form of methylphenidate (Ritalin), has a positive, short-term effect on the behavioral and social interactions of ADHD children (Abikoff & Gittelman, 1985). In fact, Gomez and Cole (1991) noted that approximately 70% to 80% of children diagnosed with ADHD respond favorably to stimulant medication. Several other studies validate the use of either stimulant or antidepressant medication in the treatment of ADHD.

The results in two studies show that medication can improve academic achievement (Douglas, Barr, O'Neill, & Britton, 1986; Pelham, Bender, Caddell, Booth, & Moorer, 1985). Specifically, research indicates that children on medication perform much better in the areas of auditory processing and reading (Forness, Swanson, Cantwell, Youpa, & Hanna, 1992; Pelham et al., 1993). ADHD patients treated with Ritalin showed more normal blood flow in the visual association cortex region of the brain; they performed better on tests than those not treated with Ritalin (see Hendrick, 1995).

Antidepressants, such as imipramine and desipramine, can be used as alternatives to stimulant medications in the treatment of ADHD. Biederman, Baldessarini, Wright, Knee, and Hermatz (1989) found that children and youths ages 6 to 17 who had previously responded poorly to stimulant medications responded favorably to desipramine. Of 62 ADHD children, 68% of those treated with desipramine improved, compared to only 10% of those receiving a placebo. Some advantages to using antidepressants rather than stimulants include the longer lasting effects of those drugs, flexibility in dosage, and lower risks of abuse or dependency; for example, one dose of antidepressants per day is usually adequate, whereas stimulant drugs require multiple doses.

Ialongo, Lopez, Horn, Pascoe, and Greenberg (1994) assessed the effects of Ritalin on self-perceptions of competence, control, and dysphoria (anxiety) in 48 children with ADHD who were ages 7 to 11. The researchers randomly assigned the children to either a medication placebo, low-dose stimulant, or high-dose stimulant group and then dispensed medication in a double-blind fashion. In so doing, they found little evidence that the use of stimulant medication undermines ADHD children's self-perceptions of competence and self-control or that it engenders dysphoria in children.

Despite the clearly positive short-term effects of medication treatment, medication is usually inadequate as the sole treatment for ADHD. In fact, many professionals and laypersons have expressed concerns about the negative side effects of stimulant medication, as well as about parents' and teachers' high expectations that medication will solve the problem (see Divoky, 1989). Relative to those concerns, many experts agree that additional factors, such as a structured environment, also contribute to the effective treatment of ADHD.

CONCLUSIONS

Based on the evidence, the most plausible conclusion that can be drawn is that effective psychosocial treatment of ADHD is related to the development of individuals with the disorder. First, short-term behavioral treatment appears to be effective with children who lack insight into deficits and who are unmotivated to change in the absence of that insight. Second, long-term cognitive treatment appears to be effective with adolescents and adults who do have insight into their deficits and can learn to compensate for them. Third, multiple-modality treatment, such as the combination of behavioral treatment for the individual, some type of therapy for the individual's family, and skills training for the individual's parents or spouse, may be effective. In this way, the individual's functioning in the cognitive, affective, and behavioral domains can be addressed.

Moving away from single-modality treatment toward multiple-modality treatment of ADHD has particular policy, practice, and research implications for social work. Curricular policy at the graduate level that requires students to attain a high level of competence in assessing and treating individuals with ADHD seems to be warranted. In turn, social work practice with ADHD sufferers that is based on and validated in empirical evidence about what works with ADHD children, adolescents, and adults, respectively, seems to be critically needed. Last, investigations that focus on determining which aspects of either single- or multiple-modality treatment impact on a range of outcomes for individuals with ADHD, both in the short and long term, seem to be needed.

REFERENCES

Abikoff, H., & Gittelman, R. (1985). Hyperactive children treated with stimulants: Is cognitive training a useful adjunct? *Archives of General Psychiatry, 42,* 953–961.

Abramowitz, A., Eckstrand, D., O'Leary, S., & Dulcan, M. (1992). ADHD children's responses to stimulant medication and two intensities of a behavioral intervention [Special issue: Treatment of children with attention-deficit hyperactivity disorder (ADHD)]. *Behavior Modification, 16,* 193–203.

Achenbach, T. (1991). *Manual for the child behavior checklist/4-18 and 1991 profile.* Burlington, VT: University of Vermont Department of Psychiatry.

Ajibola, O., & Clement, P. (1995). Differential effects of methylphenidate and self-reinforcement on attention-deficit hyperactivity disorder. *Behavior Modification, 19,* 211–233.

American Psychiatric Association. (1994). *Diagnostic and statistical manual of mental disorders* (4th ed.). Washington, DC: Author.

Anastopoulos, A., Guevremont, D., Shelton, T., & DuPaul, G. (1992). Parenting stress among families of children with attention deficit hyperactivity disorder. *Journal of Abnormal Child Psychology, 20,* 503–520.

Anastopoulos, A., Shelton, T., DuPaul, G., & Guevremont, D. (1993). Parent training for attention-deficit hyperactivity disorder: Its impact on parent functioning. *Journal of Abnormal Child Psychology, 2,* 581–596.

Anderson, C., Hinshaw, S., & Simmel, C. (1994). Mother-child interactions in ADHD and comparison boys: Relationships with overt and covert externalizing behavior. *Journal of Abnormal Child Psychology, 22,* 247–265.

Barkley, R. (1987). *Defiant children: A clinician's guide to parent training.* New York: Guilford Press.

Barkley, R., Anastopoulos, A., Guevremont, D., & Fletcher, K. (1992). Adolescents with attention deficit hyperactivity disorder: Mother-adolescent interactions, family beliefs and conflicts, and maternal psychopathology. *Journal of Abnormal Child Psychology, 20,* 263–288.

Barkley, R., Fischer, M., Edelbrock, C., & Smallish, L. (1990). The adolescent outcome of hyperactive children diagnosed by research criteria I: An 8-year prospective follow-up study. *Journal of the American Academy of Child and Adolescent Psychiatry, 29,* 546–557.

Barkley, R., Guevremont, D., Anastopoulos, A., DuPaul, G., & Shelton, T. (1993). Driving-related risks and outcomes of attention deficit hyperactivity disorder in adolescents and young adults: A 3- to 5-year follow-up survey. *Pediatrics, 92,* 212–220.

Barkley, R., Guevremont, D., Anastopoulos, A., & Fletcher, K. (1992). A comparison of three family therapy programs for treating family conflicts in adolescents with attention-deficit hyperactivity disorder. *Journal of Consulting & Clinical Psychology, 60,* 450–462.

Biederman, J., Baldessarini, R., Wright, V., Knee, D., & Hermatz, J. (1989). A double-blind placebo controlled study of desipramine in the treatment of ADD: Efficacy. *Journal of the American Academy of Child & Adolescent Psychiatry, 28,* 777–784.

Biederman, J., Faraone, S., Mick, E., & Spencer, T. (1995). High risk for attention deficit hyperactivity disorder among children of parents with childhood onset of the disorder: A pilot study. *American Journal of Psychiatry, 152,* 431–435.

Brown, R., Borden, R., Wynne, M., Schleser, R., & Clingerman, S. (1986). Methylphenidate and cognitive therapy with ADD children: A methodological reconsideration. *Journal of Abnormal Child Psychology, 14,* 481–497.

Brown, R., Wynne, M., & Medenis, R. (1985). Methylphenidate and cognitive therapy: A comparison of treatment approaches with hyperactive boys. *Journal of Abnormal Child Psychology, 13,* 69–87.

Cairns, E., & Cammock, T. (1978). Development of a more reliable version of the Matching Familiar Figures Test. *Developmental Psychology, 11,* 244–248.

Cannon, G., Idol, L., & West, J. (1992). Educating students with mild handicaps in general classrooms: Essential teaching practices for general and special educators. *Journal of Learning Disabilities, 25,* 300–317.

Chase, S., & Clement, P. (1985). Effects of self-reinforcement and stimulants on academic performance in children with attention deficit disorder. *Journal of Clinical Child Psychology, 14,* 323–333.

Christensen, L., & Mendoza, J. (1986). A method of assessing change in a single subject: An alteration of the RC index. *Behavior Therapy, 17,* 305–308.

Cocciarella, A., Wood, R., & Low, K. (1995). Brief behavioral treatment for attention-deficit hyperactivity disorder. *Perceptual and Motor Skills, 81,* 225–226.

Conners, C. (1990). *Conners' rating scales manual.* North Tonawanda, NY: MHS.

Conners, C., & Wells, K. (1985). Adolescent self report scale. *Psychopharmacology Bulletin, 21,* 921–922.

Cotugno, A. (1995). Personality attributes of attention deficit hyperactivity disorder (ADHD) using the Rorschach Inkblot Test. *Journal of Clinical Psychology, 51,* 554–562.

Cousins, L., & Weiss, G. (1993). Parent training and social skills training for children with attention-deficit hyperactivity disorder: How can they be combined for greater effectiveness. *Canadian Journal of Psychiatry, 38,* 449–457.

Divoky, D. (1989). Ritalin: Education's fix-it drug. *Phi Delta Kappan, 70,* 599–605.

Douglas, V., Barr, R., O'Neill, M., & Britton, B. (1986). Short term effects of methylphenidate on the cognitive learning and academic performance of children with attention deficit disorder in the laboratory and the classroom. *Journal of Child Psychiatry, 27,* 191–211.

DuPaul, G., & Barkley, R. (1993). Behavioral contributions to pharmacotherapy: The utility of behavioral methodology in medication treatment of children with attention deficit hyperactivity disorder. *Behavior Therapy, 24,* 47–65.

Exner, J. (1993). *A Rorschach workbook for the comprehensive system* (3rd ed.). Ashville, NC: Rorschach Workshops.

Faigel, H., Sznajderman, S., Tishby, O., Turel, M., & Uri, P. (1995). Attention deficit disorder during adolescence: A review. *Journal of Adolescent Mental Health, 16,* 174–184.

Fantuzzo, J., & Polite, K. (1990). School-based, behavioral self-management: A review and analysis. *School Psychology Quarterly, 5,* 180–198.

Forness, S., Swanson, J., Cantwell, D., Youpa, D., & Hanna, G. (1992). Stimulant medication and reading performance: Follow-up on sustained dose in ADHD boys with and without conduct disorders. *Journal of Learning Disabilities, 2,* 115–123.

Gittelman, R., Abikoff, H., Pollack, E., Klein, D., Katz, S., & Mattes, J. (1980). A controlled trial of behavior modification and methylphenidate in hyperactive children. In C. Whalen & B. Henker (Eds.), *Hyperactive children: The social ecology of identification and treatment* (pp. 221–243). New York: Academic Press.

Gittelman, R., Mannuzza, S., Shenker, R., & Bonagura, N. (1985). Hyperactive boys almost grown up: I. Psychiatric status. *Archives of General Psychiatry, 42,* 937–947.

Gomez, K., & Cole, C. (1991). Attention deficit hyperactivity disorder: A review of treatment alternatives. *Elementary School Guidance & Counseling, 26,* 106–114.

Good, T., & Brophy, J. (1991). *Looking in classrooms* (5th ed.). New York: HarperCollins.

Gordon, M. (1983). *The Gordon diagnostic system.* Boulder, CO: Gordon Systems.

Greene, R. (1995). Students with ADHD in school classrooms: Teacher factors related to compatibility, assessment, and intervention. *School Psychology Review, 24,* 81–93.

Grizenko, N., Papineau, D., & Sayegh, L. (1993). Effectiveness of a multimodal day treatment program for children with disruptive behavior problems. *Journal of the American Academy of Child & Adolescent Psychiatry, 32,* 127–134.

Guevremont, D. (1992). Social skills and peer relationship training in attention deficit hyperactivity disorder. In R. Barkley (Ed.), *A Handbook for diagnosis and treatment* (pp. 540–572). New York: Guilford Press.

Guevremont, D., Tishelman, A., & Hull, D. (1985). Teaching generalized self-control to attention deficit boys with mothers as adjunct therapists. *Child & Family Behavior Therapy, 7,* 23–37.

Hallowell, E., & Ratey, J. (1994). *Driven to distraction.* New York: Guilford Press.

Hechtman, L. (1989). Attention-deficit hyperactivity disorder in adolescence and adulthood: An updated follow-up. *Psychiatric Annals, 19,* 597–603.

Hendrick, B. (1995, November 16). Study suggests attention deficit disorder is biological, not psychiatric. *The Atlanta Journal/Constitution,* p. B1.

Hoza, B., Pelham, W., Milich, R., Pillow, D., & McBride, K. (1993). The self-perceptions and attributions of attention deficit hyperactivity disordered and nonreferred boys. *Journal of Abnormal Child Psychology, 21,* 271–286.

Hoza, B., Pelham, W., Sams, S., & Carlson, C. (1992). An examination of the "dosage" effects of both behavior therapy and methylphenidate on the classroom performance of two ADHD children. *Behavior Modification, 16,* 164–192.

Ialongo, N., Horn, W., Pascoe, J., Greenberg, G., Packard, T., Lopez, M., Wagner, A., & Puttler, M. (1993). The effects of a multimodal intervention with attention-deficit hyperactivity disorder children: A 9-month follow-up. *Journal of the American Academy of Child & Adolescent Psychiatry, 32,* 182–189.

Ialongo, N., Lopez, M., Horn, W., Pascoe, J., & Greenberg, G. (1994). Effects of psychostimulant medication on self-perceptions of competence, control, and mood in children with attention deficit hyperactivity disorder. *Journal of Clinical Child Psychology, 23,* 161–173.

Jacobsen, N., Follette, W., & Revenstorf, D. (1984). Psychotherapy outcome research: Methods for reporting variability and evaluating clinical significance. *Behavior Therapy, 15,* 336–352.

Kolko, D. (1992). Short-term follow-up of child psychiatric hospitalization: Clinical description, predictors, and correlates. *Journal of the American Academy of Child & Adolescent Psychiatry, 31*(4), 719–727.

Kronenberger, W., & Meyer, R. (1996). *The child clinician's handbook.* Boston: Allyn & Bacon.

Lipowski, Z. (1989). Psychiatry: Mindless or brainless, both or neither. *Canadian Journal of Psychiatry, 34,* 249–254.

Liu, C., Robin, A., Brenner, S., & Eastman, J. (1991). Social acceptability of methylphenidate and behavior modification for treating attention deficit hyperactivity disorder. *Pediatrics, 88,* 560–565.

Long, N., Rickert, V., & Ashcraft, E. (1993). Bibliotherapy as an adjunct to stimulant medication in the treatment of attention-deficit hyperactivity disorder. *Journal of Pediatric Health Care, 7,* 82–88.

Lufi, D., & Cohen, A. (1987). A scale for measuring persistence in children. *Journal of Personality Assessment, 51,* 178–185.

Lufi, D., & Parish-Plass, J. (1995). Personality assessment of children with attention deficit hyperactivity disorder. *Journal of Clinical Psychology, 51*, 94–99.

McFarland, D., Kolstad, R., & Briggs, L. (1995). Educating attention deficit hyperactivity disorder children. *Education, 115*, 597–603.

Meyer, R., & Deitsch, S. (1996). *The clinician's handbook: Integrated diagnostics, assessment, and intervention in adult and adolescent psychopathology* (4th ed.). Needham Heights, MA: Simon & Schuster.

Nathan, W. (1992). Integrated multimodal therapy of children with attention-deficit hyperactivity disorder. *Bulletin of the Menninger Clinic, 56*, 283–312.

Nowicki, S., & Strickland, B. (1973). A locus of control scale for children. *Journal of Consulting and Clinical Psychology, 40*, 138–154.

Pelham, W., Bender, M., Caddell, J., Booth, S., & Moorer, S. (1985). Methylphenidate and children with attention deficit disorder: Dose effects on classroom academic and social behavior. *Archives of General Psychiatry, 42*, 948–952.

Pelham, W., Carlson, C., Sams, S., Vallano, G., Dixon, M., & Hoza, B. (1993). Separate and combined effects of methylphenidate and behavior modification on boys with attention deficit-hyperactivity disorder in the classroom. *Journal of Consulting and Clinical Psychology, 61*, 506–515.

Pelham, W., Vodde-Hamilton, M., Murphy, D., Greenstein, J., & Vallano, G. (1991). The effects of methylphenidate on ADHD adolescents in recreational, peer group, and classroom settings. *Journal of Clinical Child Psychology, 20*, 293–300.

Power, T., Hess, L., & Bennett, D. (1993, August). *The accountability of interventions for ADHD among elementary and middle school teachers.* Paper presented at the annual convention of the American Psychological Association, Toronto, Canada.

Psychological Corporation. (1992). Wechsler Individual Achievement Test. San Antonio, TX: Author.

Reynolds, C., & Richmond, B. (1978). What I think and feel: A revised measure of children's manifest anxiety. *Journal of Abnormal Child Psychology, 2*, 271–280.

Schneider, S. (1992). Separation and individuation issues in psychosocial rehabilitation. *Adolescence, 27*, 137–144.

Schweitzer, J., & Sulzer-Azaroff, B. (1995). Self-control in boys with attention deficit hyperactivity disorder: Effects of added stimulation and time. *Journal of Child Psychology and Psychiatry, 36*, 671–686.

Shaffer, D. (1994). Attention deficit hyperactivity disorder in adults. *American Journal of Psychiatry, 151*, 633–638.

Silverthorn, P., Frick, P., Kuper, K., & Ott, J. (1996). Attention deficit hyperactivity disorder and sex: A test of two etiological models to explain the male predominance. *Journal of Clinical Child Psychology, 25*, 52–59.

Sohlberg, M., & Mateer, C. (1989). *Introduction to cognitive rehabilitation.* New York: Guilford.

Sparrow, S., Balla, D., & Cicchetti, D. (1984). Vineland Adaptive Behavior Scales. Circle Pines, MN: American Guidance Service.

Tannock, R., Purvis, K., & Schachar, R. (1993). Narrative abilities in children with attention deficit hyperactivity disorder and normal peers. *Journal of Abnormal Child Psychology, 21*, 103–117.

Vinson, D. (1994). Therapy for attention-deficit hyperactivity disorder. *Archives of Family Medicine, 3*, 445–451.

Webster-Stratton, C., Kolpacoff, M., & Hollinsworth, T. (1989). The long-term effectiveness and clinical significance of three cost-effective training programs. *Journal of Consulting Clinical Psychology, 57,* 550–553.

Wechsler, D. (1981). *Manual for the Wechsler Adult Intelligence Scale.* San Antonio, TX: Psychological Corporation.

Wechsler, D. (1989). *Manual for the Wechsler preschool and primary scale of intelligence.* San Antonio, TX: Psychological Corporation.

Wechsler, D. (1991). *Manual for the Wechsler intelligence scale for children—third edition.* San Antonio, TX: Psychological Corporation.

Weinstein, C. (1994). Cognitive remediation strategies: An adjunct to the psychotherapy of adults with attention-deficit hyperactivity disorder, *Journal of Psychotherapy Practice & Research, 3,* 44–57.

Weinstein, C., Seidman, L., Feldman, J., & Ratey, J. (1991). Neurocognitive disorders in psychiatry: A case example of diagnostic and treatment dilemmas. *Psychiatry, 54,* 65–75.

Wender, E. (1995). Attention-deficit hyperactivity disorders in adolescence. *Journal of Developmental & Behavioral Pediatrics, 16,* 192–195.

Woodcock, R., & Johnson, M. (1989). *Woodcock-Johnson psycho-educational battery—revised, tests of achievement.* Allen, TX: DLM Teaching Resources.

Chapter 4

CONDUCT DISORDER

Lisa A. Rapp
John S. Wodarski

OVERVIEW

The diagnosis of Conduct Disorder (CD) in children and adolescents refers to a diverse range of behaviors that violate societal norms or the basic rights of others. Firesetting, defiance, truancy, stealing, lying, criminal activity, and aggressiveness are the most common behaviors evinced by youths with CD. The *Diagnostic and Statistical Manual of Mental Disorders, Fourth Edition, (DSM-IV;* American Psychiatric Association [APA], 1994) has now grouped these behaviors into four main categories: (a) aggressive conduct that results in physical harm to others, (b) nonaggressive conduct that results in property damage, (c) deceitfulness or theft, and (d) serious violations of rules. The prevalence of youths with this disorder has been found to be between 4% and 10% of the population (Institute of Medicine, 1989). Webster-Stratton (1991) indicated that one third to one half of all child and adolescent clinic referrals were estimated to be youths with CD.

Males are diagnosed with CD 3 to 4 times more often than females (Kaplan, Sadock, & Grebb, 1994; Zoccolillo, 1993). Males with CD exhibit more aggressive behavior than females. Fighting, vandalism, and discipline problems are more common for males, while females are more apt to engage in lying, truancy, and running-away behaviors (APA, 1994). Robins and Rutter (1990) found that females usually develop symptoms of CD later than males, who more often exhibit symptoms in early childhood. Males with a history of CD are more likely to continue antisocial behavior into adulthood, whereas females with CD are more likely to shift into disorders of depression or anxiety (Robins & Rutter, 1990).

Although all children and adolescents exhibit occasional antisocial behaviors throughout their development, youths with CD consistently display antisocial behaviors that impair their functioning in the home, school, and community. Youths with CD often evince different problem behaviors in different settings. For instance, a youth may be defiant in the home, steal in the community, and lie at school. When observed together, these behaviors form a pattern of problem behaviors. This pattern delineates the youth with CD from other adolescents. A pattern of problem behaviors that are stable over the course of development presents a poor prognostic picture for the adolescent.

Risk Factors

Risk factors are events or characteristics that increase the likelihood or severity of CD. One risk factor does not necessarily imply the later development of CD; rather, risk factors should be viewed as components that, when combined, magnify the chances of children later developing conduct problems. Numerous risk factors have been hypothesized to lead to CD in youths. Several empirically based factors are discussed in this chapter.

Child Factors

Child temperament—such as moods, emotional responsiveness, activity level, and adaptability—has been found to be related to later behavioral problems. For instance, "difficult" children who are characterized by negative, irritable moods, high intensity reactions to new stimuli, and poor adaptability to change are likely to show behavioral problems later in life (Rutter, Birch, Thomas, & Chess, 1964). These children often begin coercive interaction with others early in life and continue this pattern into adolescence and adulthood (Patterson, 1982).

Likewise, early disruptive behaviors have been found to presage later delinquent behaviors in adolescence and adulthood. White, Moffitt, Earls, Robins, & Silva (1990) reported from longitudinal studies that parent- and teacher-reported problems at age 3, such as "externalizing behavior" and "difficult to manage," are highly indicative of later behavioral findings. Behavioral problems in preschool are the best predictors of antisocial behavior at age 11 (White et al., 1990). These findings match the reports that have found early problem behavior to be stable over time and more severe in nature.

Cognitive Deficits

Cognitive deficits include the domains of cognitive processes, intelligence, and language and speech development. Moffitt (1993) found that cognitive deficits early in life place youth at risk for subsequent conduct problems, as well as delinquency. Dodge (1993) found that children with CD tend to demonstrate deficient and biased encoding of the environment. For example, children with CD usually fail to interpret positive cues from others and presume hostile and negative intentions in their peers. These youth selectively attend to hostile acts directed toward them. Consequently, they consistently attribute hostile intentions in others and have difficulty in accurately labeling emotions (Dodge, 1993).

In addition to these deficits, lower verbal IQ scores have been found to be predictive of later CD (Schonfeld, Shaffer, O'Connor, & Portnoy, 1988). Verbal learning, verbal fluency, memory, abstract reasoning and attention control have also been factors that predict subsequent conduct problems (Kazdin, 1995; Robins, 1991). These difficulties suggest that there may be neurological factors affecting problem behaviors, which indicates that a different approach to intervention may be necessary.

Academic Failure

Academic deficits have been found to be significantly correlated with CD and violent behavior in adolescents. Specific deficits include verbal intelligence, reading achievement, and homework completion (Bramblett, Wodarski, & Thyer, 1991; Kazdin, 1993).

Academic failure often produces rejection by adults, reduction in prosocial attachments and values, and a reduction in commitment to conventional norms. This alienation from prosocial relationships further exacerbates school functioning and, consequently, affects behavior. Evidence has shown that youths who do poorly in school are more likely to terminate their formal education earlier and, therefore, acquire fewer skills and more socioeconomic disadvantages (White et al., 1994). This places these youths at risk for later failure in the workplace and the community.

Parent-Child Interaction (Parenting)

One of the most well known risk factors for CD is poor parental discipline. Parents of children with CD are often either too harsh or too lax in their parenting styles (Kazdin, 1995; Patterson, 1982; Robins, 1991). Widom (1989) reported that youths with CD are more likely to be victims of child abuse and to be in homes where spouse abuse is present. Patterson, Reid, & Dishion (1992) suggested that parental punishment may be a response to child conduct problems rather than an antecedent to it. In other words, harsh parental discipline and child conduct problems may reinforce each other in a vicious cycle. Consequently, both parental and child behaviors become more extreme (Patterson et al., 1992).

Besides extremely harsh parental discipline, neglectful, erratic, and overly lax discipline practices are a risk factor for later CD. This type of parenting fails to provide structure or boundaries for the child. Chaotic or inconsistent parenting fails to teach consequences of behaviors and does not reinforce prosocial behaviors.

Poor parent-child interactions and family relationships can also serve as risk factors. Numerous studies have clearly demonstrated that families of children with CD often have problematic interactions (Kazdin, 1995; Miller & Prinz, 1990; Patterson, 1982). Henggeler (1989) found that parents of children with CD tend to show less affection, emotional support, and overall warmth for their children than other parents. These parents were found to be more coercive in their interactions with their children.

Family Dysfunction

Family violence, criminal behavior, and parental alcoholism have all been found to be critical risk factors for CD (Quinton, Rutter, & Gulliver, 1990; Robins, 1991). Should the mother of a child be involved with criminal behavior, alcoholism, or violence, the risks of CD for that child are even more potent than if the father is involved with these activities.

Social learning theory asserts that imitation, modeling, and observational learning are influential in the acquisition of behaviors, and that children are highly influenced by significant others' behaviors (Burman & Allen-Meares, 1994). The chronicity associated with family violence, parental alcoholism, and parental criminal activity provides an opportunity for children to imitate dysfunctional, antisocial behaviors. It also provides ample opportunity for children to learn poor coping skills, poor social skills, and poor impulse control. Any one of these family problems alone does not significantly increase a youth's risk for CD; however, a combination of these family dysfunctions most notably places a juvenile at risk for later antisocial behavior. A genetic contribution from the parents to the child with CD has yet to be determined.

Environmental Influences

Poverty has been found to be one of the greatest predictors of CD and violence in youth (Sampson, 1993). Poverty defined as simply a lack of resources is not predictive of CD. Rather, the definition of poverty that includes the lack of sufficient resources to meet the basic necessities of a family, compounded by the inability to access more resources because of either neighborhood deterioration or racism, is what portends conduct problems. Sampson (1993) found that the factors of poverty and community problems (rapid population turnover, limited access to socially approved means to improve economic resources, and high crime rate) interact to increase the risk for families and children. McLoyd (1990) reported that poverty also influences children through its effect on the parents' behavior toward their children. She found that the psychological distress caused by poverty diminished the parents' capacity for supportive and consistent parenting and increased their use of coercive parenting techniques. These combined risk factors were especially damaging for African American families.

Minority Status

Ethnic minority research regarding conduct disorder is sparse and has limited usefulness (Hill, Soriano, Chen, & La Fromboise, 1994). That is because the limited research done on CD has dealt with minorities in a homogenous fashion, disregarding variations in socioeconomic factors, culture, values, and traditions within each ethnic group. What is known is that ethnic minority youths have a disproportionately high rate of experience with crime and violence, both as victims and perpetrators, when compared to white youths (Hill et al., 1994).

The environmental risk factors previously identified (such as poverty, poor neighborhoods, unemployment, and public assistance) are overrepresented among members of minority groups (Sampson, 1993). This places ethnic minority youths in even more peril for developing conduct problems than white youths. Limited structural opportunities, such as poorer schools and fewer opportunities for prosocial economic success, greatly increase the risks for minority youths. In addition, institutionalized inequities, including dominant group control over minority access to jobs, job ceilings, and unequal pay scales, limit employment and economic opportunities and actually reinforce antisocial means for obtaining economic success. The media's view of crime and violence as normative responses to thwarted desires and frustrations further augments youths' understanding of appropriate methods to achieve needs (Hill, 1994).

The structural and economic barriers generated by racism tend to reinforce antisocial behaviors in minority youths. Although some of these barriers may be present for poor white youths, they do not have to confront the perpetual racism and discrimination that minority youths do. Consequently, minority status in itself may be considered a risk factor for CD.

Protective Factors

Not all youths who are at risk for conduct problems develop the disorder. There may be positive influences, or protective factors, that affect the onset of CD. These protective factors may cancel or weaken already present risk factors, or they may bolster the youth's resistance to future risk factors. Although these factors are critical, insufficient research has been done. Like risk factors, protective factors may combine and interact differently for individuals depending on age, sex, and ethnic group (Kazdin, 1995). More information regarding these factors is needed to clarify their effect on youths. Intervention and prevention programs could then incorporate these factors for more effective outcomes.

Kazdin (1995) found several factors that reduce the rate of conduct problems. These include being born first, high self-esteem, strong internal locus of control, and above-average intelligence. Rae-Grant, Thomas, & Offord (1989) also found that having good social skills and friends helped protect youths from the risks of CD. Academic success also helps insulate youths from risk factors by promoting positive self-esteem and a hopeful future.

Ethnic culture can also serve as a protective mechanism for children. Ethnic groups can assist in uniting and binding individuals to protect them from damaging risk factors (Nobles, 1991). Cultures can provide a sense of identity, positive self-esteem, and purpose for individuals. Ethnic cultures can also provide values and norms that help families socialize their children and handle racism and discrimination in their environment (Hill et al., 1994).

One of the strongest protective factors noted is a positive relationship, or bonding, between the child and an adult. This bonding can occur with the parent or with another significant adult in the child's life. Bonding has been found to aid in the healthy development of the child and to promote appropriate socialization and resilience from the stressors that may induce conduct problems (McCord, 1991).

Many protective factors appear to be the inverse of previously identified risk factors. Like the risk factors, these protective factors should be thought of as dynamic and interacting. Increasing the number of protective factors should reduce the risk of CD; however, there is no specific formula to be applied. Rather, these factors should be conceived as buffers in protecting children from environmental and familial risks.

Diagnostic Considerations

DSM-IV requires the presence of only three symptoms to make the diagnosis of CD (APA, 1994). Because the severity, chronicity, and combination of symptoms varies greatly within this diagnosis, there is a large diversity among youths diagnosed with CD. The heterogenous nature of this population presents problems for the practitioner with regard to accurate assessment and effective treatment. Because of the large diversity of problem behaviors within the diagnosis of CD, there have been attempts to discriminate categories or subtypes. The differentiation of subtypes is especially important in order for treatment to be matched to the specific needs of the child and family. Thus far, two subtypes have been deciphered: (a) *overt behaviors* (fighting and property destruction) versus *covert behaviors* (lying and stealing); and (b) *childhood onset* versus *adolescent onset* of symptomatology.

Overt behaviors consist of confrontive antisocial behaviors, such as arguing, aggression, destruction of property, and temper tantrums. Covert behaviors consist of sneaky, secretive behaviors. These behaviors include lying, truancy, stealing, firesetting, and substance abuse. Studies have shown that youths with CD are likely to have behaviors clustered in one of these two categories. Social workers should assess youth with these categories in mind. If a youth presents with one or two symptoms in a category, chances are that further symptoms within that category will emerge later.

Other studies have found that youths have different individual and family characteristics depending on the subtype of conduct disorder that they present. For instance, youths with more overt conduct disorder symptoms are usually more resentful, negative, irritable, and hostile. They also tend to come from families with more conflict (Kazdin, 1995). Youths with covert conduct disorder symptoms tend to be suspicious, anxious, and less social. They have been found to come from homes with less social cohesion (Kazdin, 1995).

Not all youths with CD fall neatly into one of these two categories. There are youths who evince behaviors from both categories, indicating mixed behaviors. These youths tend to have more complex, chronic symptoms with a poorer prognosis (Kazdin, 1995). These youths also have more severe family dysfunction (Loeber et al., 1993).

Childhood versus adolescent onset of CD has been identified as another subtype of conduct disorder. Childhood onset distinguishes children who develop conduct disorder symptoms prior to age 10. Although this type of conduct disorder is less prevalent than adolescent onset, it has been noted to be more serious, in that these children are often more aggressive, come from more dysfunctional homes, are more chronic with regard to duration, and have poorer prognostic pictures. These youths exhibit behaviors that are more persistent, inflexible, and refractory to change than are those of youths who begin acting out in adolescence (Moffitt, 1993). Males are most often diagnosed with childhood onset CD (Kazdin, 1995). Conduct problems in childhood usually presage later problems in adulthood, including criminal behavior, alcoholism, depression, poor employment record, marital discord, aggression, and continued antisocial behavior (Kazdin, 1995; Robins, 1991). These serious long-term effects of CD result in necessary long-term mental health treatment, substance abuse treatment, unemployment benefits, and incarceration. These consequences of CD greatly affect other people (such as relatives and victims of crime) and also pose an extremely costly burden for society. Children diagnosed with early onset CD usually are identified as having Oppositional Defiant Disorder (ODD) or Attention Deficit Hyperactivity Disorder (ADHD) prior to CD and often continue to have symptoms of these disorders in addition to conduct disorder symptoms (Kazdin, 1995; Moffitt, 1993).

Adolescent onset of CD is much more common in youth. This subtype is more transient and less severe. Youths with this type of conduct disorder have been found to be less chronic, to be more amenable to treatment, and to evince less severe covert category problem behaviors. These youths exhibit more lying and stealing behaviors and are apt to engage in delinquent behavior when that behavior is profitable to them, but they are able to abandon it when prosocial behaviors are more rewarding (Kazdin, 1995; Moffitt, 1993). Females are classified with this type of conduct disorder more often than males. These two categories of CD should be conceptualized together, in that overt CD tends to be found more often in youths who begin their problem behaviors in childhood, while covert CD tends to be identified more often in youths who begin their problem behaviors in adolescence.

One other diagnostic difficulty that needs to be addressed is the occurrence of separate diagnostic conditions in addition to CD (comorbidity). A comorbid diagnosis is defined as two distinct diagnoses being present in an individual at the same time. CD has been found to often cooccur with several other diagnoses. These include ODD, ADHD, Depression, and Anxiety (Angold & Costello, 1993; Loeber & Keenan, 1994; Zoccolillo, 1991). These compound diagnoses are quite complex and suggest that a separate diagnostic category may be necessary to delineate and understand these disorders.

The hypothesized subtypes of conduct disorder are not only relevant for diagnostic and assessment purposes; they are also critically important for intervention and prevention. These categories of conduct disorder suggest that separate and specific treatments may be necessary to intervene effectively with affected youth (Rapp & Wodarski, 1997).

ASSESSMENT METHODS

Standardized assessment instruments should be used whenever possible to assist the social worker with diagnosis and evaluation of the youth and his or her family. A complete assessment should include the evaluation of the youth's behavior at home, in the school, and in the community. Multiple sources should be used to compile a complete profile of the youth's functioning. For instance, parents, siblings, relatives, teachers, and community contacts (such as coach, church leader, or probation officer), as well as the youth, should be interviewed and given assessment measurements to complete.

The youth should not only be evaluated for conduct disorder, but also should be evaluated for other disorders and difficulties that are usually correlated with antisocial behaviors. These include mood and anxiety disorders, ADHD, substance abuse, learning difficulties and cognitive deficits, peer rejection, and poor social and coping skills.

As previously referenced, only three symptoms out of a wide range of features are required to make the diagnosis of CD. This leaves a very heterogeneous group that can be distinguished as conduct disordered and makes diagnosis and accurate assessment an arduous task. Currently, there is no one standardized instrument consistently used for assessment of CD. However, several have been identified as useful (see Table 4.1). Social workers should use more than one assessment instrument to get a comprehensive evaluation of the youth and the family. More research is still needed to further our knowledge about the reliability and validity of these scales.

EFFECTIVE INTERVENTIONS

The problems encountered with assessment and the consequent heterogeneous characteristics of youths with CD continue to pose difficulties for the practitioner when it comes time to intervene. No one intervention can be used for every youth with CD because these youths are so diverse. This factor has made intervention research quite complex, but just that much more critical. Currently, there are only

**Table 4.1   Selected Rapid Assessment Instruments Useful
in the Social Work Evaluation of Conduct Disorder**

Adolescent Antisocial Self-Report Behavior Checklist
    (Kulik, Stein, & Sarbin, 1968)
Anger Inventory
    (Novaco, 1979)
Behavior Rating Index for Children
    (Stiffman, Orme, Evans, Feldman, & Keeney, 1984)
Children's Action Tendency Scale
    (Deluty, 1979)
Children's Hostility Inventory
    (Kazdin, Rodgers, Colbus, & Siegel, 1987)
Conflict Behavior Questionnaire
    (Prinz, Foster, Kent, & O'Leary, 1979)
Conflict Tactics Scale
    (Straus & Gelles, 1990)
Eyberg Child Behavior Inventory
    (Eyberg & Robinson, 1983)
Impulsivity Scale
    (Hirschfield, Sutton-Smith, & Rosenberg, 1965)
Interview for Aggression
    (Kazdin & Esveldt-Dawson, 1986)
Jesness Inventory
    (Kelly & Baer, 1969)
Self-Control Rating Scale
    (Kendall & Wilcox, 1979)
Self-Report Delinquency Scale
    (Elliott, Dunford, & Huizinga, 1987)

a few empirically based interventions that have been shown to be moderately effective with youths with CD; these are described in the following.

Cognitive-Behavior Therapy

Youths who engage in conduct disordered behaviors have been shown to have distortions and deficiencies in various cognitive processes, including hostile attributions, the inability to generate alternative solutions to problems, and the inability to identify consequences to behaviors (Dodge, 1993; Kazdin, 1995; Kendall, 1993). The goal of cognitive or problem-solving skills training is to reduce negative behaviors while developing interpersonal skills to handle problems effectively (Kazdin, 1993). The focus of this type of treatment is on how the child approaches a situation or problem. The problem-solving skills training (PSST) developed by Kazdin, Esveldt-Dawson, French, and Unis (1987) teaches youth to engage in a step-by-step procedure to solve problems. Tasks, games, and activities are applied to real-life situations to practice effective problem solving. Modeling, role-playing and reinforcement schedules are important additional components. Kazdin et al. (1987) have also added a parent training module to their intervention. As expected, this combined intervention is more efficacious than the PSST program alone.

Research has also supported the use of anger-control training for youths with CD (Kazdin, 1994; Kendall, 1993; Kendall & Panichelli-Mindel, 1995; Lochman, Burch, Curry, & Lampron, 1984). Treatment is based on the view that anger arousal is mediated by a person's expectations and appraisals of external events (Kazdin, 1994; McMahon, 1994). This intervention uses the same techniques as for problem-solving skills, but focuses on controlling anger in a socially appropriate manner. Youths learn to identify triggers or cues that make them angry and then identify alternative behaviors to handle their anger. They also learn to use specific relaxation techniques to control impulses and anger.

Lochman et al. (1984) demonstrated a decrease in disruptive behaviors and an increase in self-esteem in youths using this approach. Long-term maintenance was also indicated. Further and more specific research needs to be completed to indicate whether these interventions would be appropriate for covert antisocial behaviors or females with CD.

Family Therapy

Functional family therapy (FFT) is an integrative approach to treatment which utilizes systems, behavioral and cognitive views on dysfunction (Kazdin, 1995). The feature of this mode of treatment is to help the family understand how the clinical problem serves a function within the family. The goals are to improve communication, use negotiation constructively, increase positive reinforcement, and increase problem solving (Kazdin, 1994; Kazdin, 1995). An individualized reinforcement system is developed for the family to increase positive interactions and communication between family members. Researchers have found positive effects for seriously disordered male and female adolescents. A treatment manual is also available for the clinician's convenience. Although few outcome studies on FFT have been completed, this therapy has been found to be effective for youths with CD. However, replication is sorely needed to solidify reliability.

Pharmacotherapy

Pharmacotherapy for adolescent CD has been suggested for those youths who do not benefit from other psychosocial treatments first. Pharmacotherapy has been found to be useful for adolescents with CD who exhibit mixed forms of the disorder, including aggressiveness, stealing, firesetting, truancy, and temper tantrums (Campbell, Gonzalez, and Silvan, 1992; Sylvester and Kruesi, 1994). Neuroleptics are the most commonly used medications in the treatment of youths with CD, particularly those who are aggressive (Campbell et al., 1992). Haldol has specifically been shown to be superior to a placebo and to be equally as effective as lithium with most children with CD (Campbell et al., 1992; Campbell, Small, & Green, 1984; Sylvester & Kruesi, 1994). A concern about long-term use of neuroleptics in youth poses a dilemma for the clinician due to the risk of side effects, particularly tardive dyskinesia (Campbell et al., 1984; Werry & Aman, 1975). Lithium, on the other hand, has been shown to be equally as effective as Haldol without the side effects (Campbell et al., 1984; Sylvester & Kruesi, 1994). Controlled studies with double-blind placebo conditions repeatedly found fewer side effects of lithium in children (Bennet, Korein, & Kalmijn, 1983; Campbell et al., 1984; Campbell et al., 1992).

Research on medications for youths with CD are somewhat limited. Two of the most effective medications for this disorder to date are Haldol and lithium. These medications have been prescribed most often to reduce aggression and severe acting-out behaviors; however, not all youths with CD exhibit these behaviors. Future research studies should focus on the possible effectiveness of medications with nonaggressive youths, as well as the effectiveness of medications in conjunction with other empirically based treatments.

Parent Management Training (PMT)

Studies on parent management training (PMT) interventions with youths with CD not only constitute the largest and most sophisticated body of treatment research in this area, they have also evinced the most promising results (Kazdin, 1993; McMahon, 1994; Webster-Stratton, 1991). Studies have shown immediate improvement in the child's behavior, improvements in parental perceptions of the child, and generalization of the effects to the home (McMahon, 1994).

The impact of PMT can be broad and useful for a variety of disruptive behaviors, which often makes it applicable in the case of youths with CD. PMT has also been shown to reduce sibling dysfunctional behavior, even when these youths are not the direct focus of treatment (Kazdin, 1995; Webster-Stratton, 1991).

The most influential PMT program was developed by Patterson at the Oregon Social Learning Center (Patterson, 1982). This program focuses on developing effective parenting techniques. Parents are seen by the practitioner to learn how to identify problem behaviors, code these behaviors and intervene effectively. Parents are taught such social learning skills as reinforcement, planned ignoring, mild punishment, negotiation, and contingency contracting. Parents are then asked to practice these techniques at home.

PMT research is the most comprehensive and promising treatment to date for youths with CD (Kazdin, 1995; Miller & Prinz, 1990; Webster-Stratton, 1991). PMT needs to further explore its effectiveness with parents of youths with CD. Although it may not be able to prevent severe CD in this group, it may be able to reduce escalation. An increase in specific intervention manuals would also be beneficial.

CONCLUSIONS

The diagnosis of Conduct Disorder includes a very broad and all-encompassing pattern of behaviors. Youths who have been diagnosed with this disorder tend to be better described within such categories as overt versus covert (or mixed) behaviors, or childhood versus adolescent onset. The necessity of more specific categories within this diagnosis leads to the necessity of more specific interventions for these youths. In other words, interventions that target covert versus overt (or mixed) behaviors and interventions that target the specific problems of childhood versus adolescent onset are now required. Furthermore, social work interventions need to be specialized to intervene with youths who have an additional condition to CD. These youths are especially at risk for long-term mental health problems and generally have a poorer prognosis than do singly diagnosed youths.

Treatment for minority youths has been especially misdirected and lacking. These youths are usually included in the same intervention groups as majority youths. These programs rarely target the risk factors associated with minority status and are, therefore, less successful with these youths.

Research has identified clear risk factors and protective factors for CD. Preventive and interventive programs should utilize this knowledge to reduce risks and enhance protective mechanisms.

The interventions that have been used with youths with CD have been fairly effective in reducing antisocial behaviors. However, more precise interventions need to be developed to assist those youths who do not evince typical, short-term CD. Females, minority youths, and overtly aggressive youths require specialized interventive techniques. The current techniques have been found to be inadequate for these groups.

Despite the need for further research, there is still plenty that practitioners can do to intervene with youths with CD. A complete social work assessment should be done, utilizing standardized assessment instruments, evaluating multiple problem areas, and gathering information from multiple sources. This assessment should also include the specific risk and protective factors that affect the youth and family. The social work interventive program should be as individualized as possible, should intervene with respect to the onset and type of behaviors evinced, and should incorporate the specific risk and protective factors pertinent to that youth.

Within the past several years, great advances in the areas of assessment and treatment of youths with CD and their families have been made. Despite these improvements, much more work is needed to further our knowledge and our ability to assist with one of the most severe and debilitating disorders of youth and, subsequently, adulthood.

REFERENCES

American Psychiatric Association. (1994). *Diagnostic and statistical manual of mental disorders* (4th ed.). Washington, DC: Author.

Angold, A., & Costello, E. (1993). Depressive comorbidity in children and adolescents: Empirical, theoretical, and methodological issues. *American Journal of Psychiatry, 150,* 1779–1791.

Bennett, W., Korein, J., & Kalmijn, M. (1983). Electroencephalogram and treatment of hospitalized aggressive children with haloperidol or lithium. *Biological Psychiatry, 18,* 1427–1440.

Bramblett, R., Wodarski, J., & Thyer, B. (1991). Social work practice with antisocial children: A review of current issues. *Journal of Applied Social Sciences, 15,* 169–182.

Burman, S., & Allen-Meares, P. (1994). Neglected victims of murder: Children's witness to parental homicide. *Journal of the National Association of Social Workers, 39,* 28–34.

Campbell, M., Gonzalez, N., & Silvan, R. (1992). The pharmacologic treatment of conduct disorders and rage outbursts. In D. Shaffer (Ed.), *The Psychiatric clinics of North America* (pp. 69–86). Philadelphia: Saunders.

Campbell, M., Small, A., & Green, W. (1984). Behavioral efficacy of haloperidol and lithium carbonate: A comparison of hospitalized aggressive children with conduct disorder. *Archives of General Psychiatry, 41,* 650–656.

Deluty, R., (1979). Children's Action Tendency Scale: A self-report measure of aggressiveness, assertiveness, and submissiveness in children. *Journal of Consulting and Clinical Psychology, 47,* 1061–1071.

Dodge, K. (1993). Social-cognitive mechanisms in the development of conduct disorder and depression. *Annual Reviews Psychology, 44,* 559–584.

Elliott, D., Dunford, F., & Huizinga, D. (1987). The identification and prediction of career offenders utilizing self-reported and official data. In J. D. Burchard & S. N. Burchard (Eds.), *Preventing delinquent behavior* (pp. 90–121). Newbury Park, CA: Sage.

Eyberg, S., & Robinson, E. (1983). Conduct problem behavior: Standardization of a behavioral rating scale with adolescents. *Journal of Clinical Child Psychology, 12,* 347–354.

Henggeler, S. (1989). *Delinquency in adolescence.* Newbury Park, CA: Sage.

Hill, H. (1994). *The role of developmental mandates of adolescents in understanding youth violence: Instant being versus the agony of becoming.* Paper presented at the Leadership Washington Conference on Violence, Washington, DC.

Hill, H., Soriano, F., Chen, A., & LaFromboise, T. (1994). Sociocultural factors in the etiology and prevention of violence among minority youth. In L. Eron, J. Gentry, & P. Schlegel (Eds.), *Reason to hope: A psychosocial perspective on violence and youth.* (pp. 59–97). Washington, DC: American Psychological Association.

Hirshfield, P., Sutton-Smith, B., & Rosenberg, B. (1965). Response set in impulsive children. *Journal of Genetic Psychology, 107,* 117–126.

Institute of Medicine. (1989). *Research on children and adolescents with mental, behavioral, and developmental disorders.* Washington, DC: National Academy Press.

Kaplan, H., Sadock, B., & Grebb, J. (1994). *Kaplan & Sadock's synopsis of psychiatry* (7th ed.). Baltimore: Williams & Wilkins.

Kazdin, A. (1993). Treatment of conduct disorder: Progress and directions in psychotherapy research. *Development and Psychopathology, 5,* 277–310.

Kazdin, A. (1994). Psychotherapy for children and adolescents. In A. Bergin & S. Garfield (Eds.), *Handbook of psychotherapy and behavior change* (pp. 543–594). New York: Wiley.

Kazdin, A. (1995). *Conduct disorders in childhood and adolescence* (2nd ed.). Thousand Oaks, CA: Sage.

Kazdin, A., & Esveldt-Dawson, K. (1986). The interview for antisocial behavior: Psychometric characteristics and concurrent validity with child psychiatric inpatients. *Journal of Psychopathology and Behavioral Assessment, 8,* 289–303.

Kazdin, A., Esveldt-Dawson, K., French, N., & Unis, A. (1987). Problem-solving skills training and relationship therapy in the treatment of antisocial child behavior. *Journal of Consulting and Clinical Psychology, 55,* 76–85.

Kazdin, A., Rodgers, A., Colbus, D., & Siegel, T. (1987). Children's Hostility Inventory: Measurement of aggression and hostility in psychiatric inpatient children. *Journal of Clinical Child Psychology, 16,* 320–328.

Kelly, F., & Baer, D. (1969). Jesness Inventory and self concept measures for delinquents before and after participating in Outward Bound. *Psychological Reports, 25,* 719–724.

Kendall, P. (1993). Cognitive-behavioral therapies with youth: Guiding theory, current status, and emerging developments. *Journal of Consulting and Clinical Psychology, 61,* 235–247.

Kendall, P., & Panichelli-Mindel, S. (1995). Cognitive-behavioral treatments. *Journal of Abnormal Child Psychiatry, 23,* 107–124.

Kendall, P., & Wilcox, L. (1979). Self-control in children: Development of a rating scale. *Journal of Consulting and Clinical Psychology, 47,* 1020–1029.

Kulik, J., Stein, K., & Sarbin, T. (1968). Dimensions and patterns of adolescent antisocial behavior. *Journal of Consulting and Clinical Psychology, 32,* 375–382.

Lochman, J., Burch, P., Curry, J., & Lampron, L. (1984). Treatment and generalization effects of cognitive-behavioral and goal-setting interventions with aggressive boys. *Journal of Consulting and Clinical Psychology, 52,* 915–916.

Loeber, R., & Keenan, K. (1994). Interaction between conduct disorder and its comorbid conditions: Effects of age and gender. *Clinical Psychology Review, 14,* 497–523.

Loeber, R., Wung, P., Giroux, B., Stouthamer-Loeber, M., Van Kammen, W., & Maughan, B. (1993). Developmental pathways in disruptive child behavior. *Development and Psychopathology, 5,* 103–133.

McCord, J. (1991). Family relationships, juvenile delinquency, and adult criminality. *Criminality, 29,* 397–412.

McLoyd, V. (1990). The impact of economic hardship on black families and children: Psychological distress, parenting, and socioemotional development. *Child Development, 61,* 311–346.

McMahon, R. (1994). Diagnosis, assessment, treatment of externalizing problems in children: The role of longitudinal data. *Journal of Consulting and Clinical Psychology, 62,* 901–917.

Miller, G., & Prinz, R. (1990). Enhancement of social learning family interventions for childhood conduct disorder. *Psychological Bulletin, 108,* 291–307.

Moffitt, T. (1993). Adolescence-limited and life-course-persistent antisocial behavior: A developmental taxonomy. *Psychological Review, 100*(4), 674–701.

Nobles, W. (1991). W. African philosophy: Foundations for black psychology. In R. Jones (Ed.), *Black psychology* (3rd ed., pp. 47–63). Berkeley, CA: Cobb & Henry.

Novaco, R. (1979). *Anger control.* Lexington, MA: Lexington Books.

Patterson, G. (1982). *Coercive family process.* Eugene, OR: Castalia.

Patterson, G., Reid, J., & Dishion, T. (1992). *Antisocial boys.* Eugene, OR: Castalia.

Prinz, R., Foster, S., Kent, R., & O'Leary, K. (1979). Multivariate assessment of conflict in distressed and non-distressed mother-adolescent dyads. *Journal of Applied Behavior Analysis, 12,* 691–700.

Quinton, D., Rutter, M., & Gulliver, L. (1990). Continuities in psychiatric disorders from childhood to adulthood in the children of psychiatric patients. In L. N. Robins & M. Rutter (Eds.), *Straight and devious pathways from childhood to adulthood* (pp. 259–278). Cambridge: Cambridge University Press.

Rae-Grant, N., Thomas, B., & Offord, D. (1989). Risk, protective factors, and the prevalence of behavioral and emotional disorders in children and adolescents. *Journal of the American Academy of Child and Adolescent Psychiatry, 28,* 262–268.

Rapp, L. & Wodarski, J. (1997). The comorbidity of conduct disorder and depression in adolescents: A comprehensive interpersonal treatment technology. *Family Therapy, 24*(2), 81–100.

Robins, L. (1991). Conduct disorder. *Journal of Child Psychology and Psychiatry, 32*(1), 193–212.

Robins, L., & Rutter, M. (Eds.). (1990). *Straight and devious pathways from childhood to adulthood.* Cambridge: Cambridge University Press.

Rutter, M., Birch, H., Thomas, A., & Chess, S. (1964). Temperamental characteristics in infancy and the later development of behavioral disorders. *British Journal of Psychiatry, 110,* 651–661.

Sampson, R. (1993). The community context of violent victimization and offending. In W. J. Wilson (Ed.), *Sociology and the public agency* (pp. 259–286). Newbury Park, CA: Sage.

Schonfeld, I., Shaffer, D., O'Connor, P., & Portnoy, S. (1988). Conduct disorder and cognitive functioning: Testing three causal hypotheses. *Child Development, 59,* 993–1007.

Stiffman, A., Orme, J., Evans, D., Feldman, R., & Keeney, P. (1984). A brief measure of children's behavior problems: The Behavior Rating Index for Children. *Measurement and Evaluation in Counseling and Development, 16,* 83–90.

Straus, M., & Gelles, R. (1990). *Physical violence in American families: Risk factors and adaptations to violence in 8,145 families.* New Brunswick, NJ: Transaction.

Sylvester, C., & Kruesi, M. (1994). Child and adolescent psychopharmacotherapy: Progress and pitfalls. *Psychiatric Annals, 24,* 83–90.

Webster-Stratton, C. (1991). Annotation: Strategies for helping families with conduct disordered children. *Journal of Child Psychology and Psychiatry, 32*(7), 1047–1062.

Werry, J., & Aman, M. (1975). Methylphenidate and haloperidol in children: Effects on attention, memory and activity. *Archives of General Psychiatry, 32,* 790–795.

White, J., Moffitt, T., Caspi, A., Bartusch, D., Needles, D., & Stouthamer-Loeber, M. (1994). Measuring impulsivity and examining its relationship to delinquency. *Journal of Abnormal Psychology, 103,* 192–205.

White, J., Moffitt, T., Earls, F., Robins, L., & Silva, P. (1990). How early can we tell? Predictors of childhood conduct disorder and adolescent delinquency. *Criminology, 28,* 507–533.

Widom, C. (1989). Does violence beget violence? A critical examination of the literature. *Psychological Bulletin, 106,* 3–28.

Zoccolillo, M. (1991). Co-occurrence of conduct disorder and its adult outcomes with depressive and anxiety disorders: A review. *Journal of the American Academy of Adolescent Psychiatry, 31*(3), 547–556.

Zoccolillo, M. (1993). Gender and the development of conduct disorder. *Development and Psychopathology, 5,* 65–78.

Chapter 5

OPPOSITIONAL DEFIANT DISORDER

Peter Lehmann
Richard F. Dangel

OVERVIEW

One of the most common reasons that schools, the courts, and parents refer children to social workers and other mental health professionals is disruptive behavior (Kazdin, 1987, 1991). Noncompliance, attention seeking, delinquency, lying, physical aggression, impulsivity, short attention span, academic underachievement, and social skill deficiencies may all prompt a referral. Each of these behaviors is represented to some degree in the list of characteristics found in the fourth edition of the *Diagnostic and Statistical Manual of Mental Disorders* (*DSM-IV;* American Psychiatric Association [APA], 1994) criteria for Conduct Disorders, Antisocial Disorders, Attention Deficit Hyperactivity Disorder, or Oppositional Defiant Disorder. Because most children display some or all of these behaviors during typical child development, social workers must determine the extent to which the behaviors warrant specialized intervention.

The purpose of this chapter is to present an overview of one diagnostic category, Oppositional Defiant Disorder (ODD). Oppositional Defiant Disorder has been viewed as a collection of behavior problems that both persist and exceed the intensity or severity of similar behaviors in same-age children (Christophersen & Finney, 1993). This chapter is divided into three main sections. First, an overview of the main features of ODD is presented. The second section summarizes commonly used assessment methods. The final section reviews alternative interventions. The conclusions present a best practices approach for assessment and intervention purposes.

Description of Oppositional Defiant Disorder (ODD)

The term *Oppositional Defiant Disorder* refers to a pattern of behaviors displayed by children that includes disobedience, negativism, argumentativeness, and stubbornness. Levy (1955) first drew attention to this group of behaviors, which he named *oppositional behavior.* The Group for the Advancement of Psychiatry (1966) changed the name to *Oppositional Personality Disorder* to describe children who express aggressiveness through oppositional behavior. In 1980, the third edition of the American Psychiatric Association's *Diagnostic and Statistical Manual of Mental Disorders* (*DSM-III;* APA, 1980) introduced Oppositional Disorder in the category Disorders Usually First Evident in Infancy, Childhood, or Adolescence to classify children who show a form of persistent negative, provocative, and disobedient opposition to authority figures. Seven years later, *DSM-III-R* (APA, 1987) changed the name to Oppositional Disorder and placed it with Conduct Disorder and Attention Deficit Hyperactivity Disorder, under the heading of Disruptive Disorders.

Table 5.1 outlines the specific behavioral features of ODD adopted by the fourth edition of the *Diagnostic and Statistical Manual of Mental Disorders* (APA, 1994). To meet the diagnosis of ODD, a number of criteria must be met. First, the behaviors must have lasted at least 6 months. Second, the behaviors must cause impairment in academic and social functioning and must not occur during a psychotic episode or mood disorder. Finally, *DSM-IV* acknowledges that many of the features are also evident in other behavior disorders, such as Conduct Disorder (CD). When symptoms meet both the CD and ODD criteria, *DSM-IV* specifies that a diagnosis of Conduct Disorder is given. Likewise, when characteristics of ODD and Attention Deficit Hyperactive Disorder (ADHD) are present, a dual diagnosis is given.

Researchers believe two existing pathways contribute to a progression of symptoms. The first has been called the *aggressive/versatile onset* path (Loeber, 1991). Children who follow this course often develop disruptive and aggressive behaviors as early as preschool and demonstrate serious behavior problems prior to the onset of adolescence. These children have usually been diagnosed with CD and ODD (Frick et al., 1993; Lahey, Loeber, Quay, Frick, & Grimm, 1992; Loeber, Lahey, & Thomas, 1991). The second or *late onset* pathway typically consists of behaviors that emerge during early adolescence; for example, shoplifting or school truancy. Typically, these adolescents do not demonstrate behaviors typical of ODD during childhood (Hinshaw, Lahey, & Hart, 1993).

Table 5.1 Behavioral Features for Oppositional Defiant Disorder

1. Often loses temper
2. Often argues with adults
3. Often actively defies or refuses to comply with adults' requests or rules
4. Often deliberately annoys people
5. Often blames others for his or her mistakes or misbehavior
6. Often is touchy or easily annoyed by others
7. Often is angry and resentful
8. Often is spiteful or vindictive

Although many children who exhibit ODD do not develop more serious behavior problems, such as those that make up conduct disorders, three known risk factors may contribute to the development and maintenance of negative behavior. These include: (a) child risk variables, such as a difficult temperament, impulsivity, inattention, and aggression (Lilienfeld & Waldman, 1990; Webster-Stratton, 1993); (b) parenting variables, such as providing inconsistent consequences to the child's behavior, ineffective monitoring of the child's behavior, and failing to present a positive affect or provide reinforcement to the child (Patterson & Stouthamer-Loeber, 1984; Webster-Stratton, 1993); and (c) family variables apart from the parent-child relationship. Specific family variables include: parental conflict (Kazdin, 1987; McMahon & Forehand, 1988; O'Leary & Emery, 1982; Webster-Stratton, 1985, 1990, 1994; Webster-Stratton & Herbert, 1994); family violence (Jouriles, Murphy, & O'Leary, 1989); substance abuse and parental psychopathology (Frick et al., 1992); and life stressors, such as poverty, unemployment, crowded living conditions, and illness (Rutter & Giller, 1983).

Prevalence of Oppositional Defiant Disorder

As many as 50% of all referrals of children for mental health services are due to disruptive behaviors (Kazdin, 1987; Robins, 1981). Current reviews of epidemiologic studies of preschool and early school-age children have found that 7% to 25% of the surveyed population display characteristics of ODD or CD (Campbell & Ewing, 1990; Crowther, Bond, & Rolf, 1981). Theorists have argued that young children who develop disruptive behaviors in the early school years are at high risk for continuing on a trajectory toward future conduct problems, including delinquency, school dropout, and interpersonal violence (Loeber, 1991; White, Moffit, Earls, & Robins, 1990).

Empirical findings on gender differences have been mixed. Although most studies have suggested that boys are diagnosed with this disorder more often than girls (Robins & Price, 1991) one study found that a larger percentage of adolescents diagnosed with ODD are female (McGee, Feehan, Williams, & Anderson, 1992). Likewise, Webster-Stratton (1996) concluded that preadolescent girls diagnosed with ODD and CD exhibit the same levels of externalizing behaviors as boys and are just as noncompliant to parents.

Despite prevalence rates, the exact estimate of ODD is unknown. Two reasons may exist for this gap. First, rates of comorbidity or cooccurrence usually exist between the disruptive behavior typologies (Conduct Disorder, Oppositional Defiant Disorder and Attention Deficit Disorder) (Nottelmann & Jensen, 1995). Consequently, when dual diagnoses overlap, such as in the case of ODD and CD, it is unlikely that the true prevalence rates will ever be known. Second, in recent years the diagnostic criteria for ODD (APA, 1987, 1994) have changed. Therefore, as symptom categories have changed, the rates of diagnoses have also changed.

ASSESSMENT METHODS

No single method has been accepted as the standard for assessing Oppositional Defiant Disorder. However, sound assessment strategies share several characteristics. First, they aim to consider what intraorganismic factors, such as genetics, temperament, physiology, and neurology, contribute to early childhood behavior (Costello & Angold, 1993). Second, assessment strategies recognize the developmental pathways that lead to the onset of ODD; and, last, they consider how relational and environmental factors, such as parenting practices, parental psychopathology, socioeconomic disadvantage, and substance abuse, mediate the progression or cessation of ODD (Alexander & Pugh, 1996).

Social workers gather information about ODD in a variety of ways. These include face-to-face interviews with the child, parent, and teacher; direct observation in the environment; and paper-and-pencil tests. Each of these sources provides information for social workers when planning treatment interventions for children with ODD.

Direct Interviews

Most social workers can begin their initial assessments by interviewing parents, children, or both. Hanf (1970) developed a behavioral interview format in which parents are asked about a number of specific situations that may lead to conflict with children (for example, when asked to do chores). Parents describe whether the situation is a problem, how they respond, and how the child typically responds. Barkley and Edelbrock (1987) have devised a short-version questionnaire of Hanf's interview process called the Home and School Questionnaire (HSQ). The HSQ looks at how behavior problems may vary across a range of common situations. The answers identify which situations are most problematic.

An additional version of Hanf's work was developed by Forehand and McMahon (1981) for children ages 3 to 8. Both parents are asked a series of questions about problematic situations (for example, mealtimes, bedtimes, and following rules). If a behavior is reported as problematic, questions are asked about events immediately preceding and following negative child behavior. Answers provide the interviewer with a behavioral analysis of the interactions between parents and child. La Greca and Santogrossi (1980) ask similar questions about adolescent problem behaviors, in addition to questions about peers, school, interests, future plans, feelings, sexual behavior, and alcohol and other drug use.

Patterson and his colleagues (e.g., Patterson, 1975, 1976, 1982; Patterson, Reid, Jones, & Conger, 1975; Patterson & Forgatch, 1987a, 1987b) have structured their assessment somewhat differently. Instead of focusing on situations, parents fill out a symptom checklist containing 31 specific child behavior problems, such as arguing, bed-wetting, complaining, crying, defiance, and talking back. Parents then detail the setting in which each behavior occurs, how they have tried to handle these behaviors, and what they think caused the problem. Parents are asked a series of questions that assess child-rearing practices, including their own style of communicating, discipline, rejection, problem solving, and positive reinforcement. Similar models of interviewing have been devised by Kazdin (1985) and more recently by Loeber, Green, Keenan, and Lahey (1995).

Currently, researchers in the family therapy field have written very little on the assessment of ODD in children. For example, Webster-Stratton and Herbert (1994) use a behavioral family therapy approach. In this assessment approach, less emphasis is placed on specifying specific target behaviors; more emphasis is placed on what function the child's behavior serves in terms of family dynamics and what solutions the child's actions provide. Essentially, the child's behavior is seen in terms of its function within the family system. Other family therapists have included brief therapy methods for assessing and treating ODD (Phelps, 1993). Here, the intent is to go beyond a behavioral approach, with an eye toward developing hypotheses about the child's behavior. Three levels of hypotheses include the *behavioral* (what people do), the *emotional* (what people feel), and the *ideational* (what people think). Exploring each level is helpful in understanding the context of the behavior and in determining where previously attempted solutions have failed.

Although much of the preceding section focuses on parent interviewing, there are a number of child interview guides currently available to assess ODD. One of the most widely used interview formats is the NIMH Diagnostic Interview Schedule for Children (DISC), Parents (DISC-P), and Teachers (DISC-T; Costello, Edlebrock, & Costello, 1985). In approximately 1 hour, informants are asked highly structured questions that provide scores in 27 symptom areas, leading to a determination of a *DSM-III* and *DSM-III-R* diagnosis of children (APA, 1980, 1987). Newer versions of the DISC have been developed to accommodate changes in *DSM-IV* (Schwab-Stone, Shaffer, Dalcan, & Jensen, 1996; Shaffer, Schwab-Stone, Fisher, & Cohen, 1993). A similar interview format is the Diagnostic Interview for Children and Adolescents (DICA; Herjanic & Reich, 1982). The DICA also has a parent version (DICA-P). Both versions make use of *DSM* diagnoses.

Interviewing a child's subjective views of the situation has also been noted in the literature. For example, Cautela, Cautela, and Esonis (1983) ask children about their understanding of family, school, and peer relationships. Likewise, Patterson and Bank (1986) have developed a structured interview with children from the fourth through tenth grades that gauges the child's perceptions of parental discipline, family relations, chores, positive reinforcement, and future expectations. Other practitioners (Valla, Bergeron, Berube, & Gaudet, 1994) use drawings as part of their interview to make a diagnosis of ODD. Children respond to 99 drawings representing situations that correspond to *DSM-III-R*-based behavior disorders.

In summary, face-to-face interviews may be seen as an indispensable tool for social workers in that a large amount of information can be collected quickly and efficiently. Such interviews may also yield data that would not be made available using alternative assessment strategies. Finally, the training backgrounds of most social workers would suggest that the structured interview format can be quickly learned and used.

Direct Observation

McMahon and Forehand (1984) have suggested that direct observation may be a helpful assessment procedure for obtaining an objective estimate of behavior disorders in children. Since characteristics of CD and ODD often overlap, direct observation provides another method of distinguishing between the two disorders. Direct observations can be made in the clinic and in such natural environments as school, home, and playground.

Two widely used observation instruments include one developed by Forehand and associates (Forehand & McMahon, 1981; Forehand et al., 1978) and the Dyadic Parent-Child Interaction Coding System (DPICS; Eyberg & Robinson, 1983; Robinson & Eyberg, 1981). Both instruments can be used in the home or in the clinic. In the Forehand observation system, parents are instructed to engage children in a child's game and a parent's game. In the child's game, the child makes up the rules; in the parent's game, the parents make up the rules. In each situation, parent and child behavior is coded according to praise, commands, and compliance. The Eyberg observation involves parent-child dyads in three standard situations: (a) child-directed, (b) parent-directed, and (c) cleanup. Twelve parent and seven child behaviors, such as praise, attending, commanding, and noncompliance are coded.

Chamberlain and Reid (1987) and Patterson et al. (1975) developed a parent observation checklist for children ages 4 to 10. The Parent Daily Report (PDR) is a parent observation measure that can be administered during brief (5 to 10 minute) telephone interviews. The PDR records a total of 31 child behaviors, such as noncompliance, aggression, tantrums, and lying. Parents sum up all behaviors targeted as problematic during a 24-hour period and note whether the behaviors occurred at school, at home, in the community, or elsewhere. Parents are also asked if they spanked their child during this time period.

Specific home-based observation assessment instruments are also available for social workers. The Family Interaction Coding System (FICS; Patterson et al., 1969; Reid, 1978) and the Standardized Observation Codes (SOC; Wahler, House, & Stambaugh, 1976) are used to describe child-family interactions. Both sets of instruments have been designed for in-home observations of no more than 60 minutes. In both formats a variety of categories of behavior (for example, command, laugh, touch, ignore, instruction adult-nonaversive, attention child-aversive, nonaversive) are coded, recorded, and used to calculate percentages of occurrence.

Two additional coding systems have been developed from the FICS: the Family Process Code (FPC; Dishion et al., 1984) and the Observer Impressions Inventory (OII; Weinrott, Reid, Bauske, & Brummett, 1981). Although these instruments were designed specifically for children with CD, many of the target behaviors are characteristic of ODD. Further, both instruments have been developed to provide more current and long-term rigorous assessments of interactions between parents and children.

Oppositional behaviors also occur in the classroom, and teachers may provide valuable assessment data for the social worker. Several classroom observation formats are currently in use for teachers. Harris (1979, 1980) and Harris and Reid (1981) have adapted the work of Patterson and Forehand for use in the classroom. In his assessment format, 22 categories of behaviors estimate prosocial and aggressive responses. Cobb and Hops (1972) have also designed a coding system for the acting-out child in the classroom. Teachers code 37 behaviors under eight categories. Typical categories include commands, disruption and inappropriate responses, and approval and positive behaviors. Similarly, Reed and Edelbrock (1983) developed the Direct Observation Form (DOF). Observations of behavior problems and on-task behavior are noted at different times of the day.

Trad (1992) has suggested that teachers use diagnostic peer groups in the school to evaluate ODD. The underlying premise of this approach is that children will exhibit characteristic behaviors when interacting with peer groups at school that otherwise might not be evident. The diagnostic peer group allows the social worker to observe the child's prosocial behaviors and attachment relationships. For example, Trad summarized factors to observe that may be indicative of the strengths or weaknesses in the child's relationship network. Some of these factors include the effects of peers on the child's activities; the child's coping abilities; the child's tendency to socialize, reciprocate, or withdraw; and the child's ability to separate from caretakers.

While direct observation may generate reliable information, the use of coding instruments does not appear to be routinely used in clinical practice and may be impractical in some social work agencies and school settings. Many of the instruments require lengthy training before being used. The recording of individual observations can be complex, and small errors can skew results. Finally, the instruments generally call for a great deal of flexibility on the part of families, children, and administrators due to the extensive time period needed for assessment. In many cases time constraints, large caseloads, family crises, or incompatible observation environments may prevent their use.

Pencil-and-Paper Checklists

There are literally hundreds of paper-and-pencil checklists available that include behaviors characteristic of ODD and CD. Several standardized checklists commonly used to assess ODD in children are summarized in the following. Measures of parent and family functioning are considered, as well.

The Child Behavior Checklist (CBCL; Achenbach & Edelbrock, 1983) is designed for use with children ages 2 to 16. The main objective of the CBCL is to provide a complete assessment inventory of behavior problems in children. Parallel forms of the CBCL have been made for parents, teachers, and youths.

The parent form has two different checklists, one for children ages 2 to 3 and one for children ages 4 to 16. The CBCL can be completed in 10 to 20 minutes and provides a profile of three types of behavioral syndromes: (a) internalizing (sad and psychosomatic), (b) externalizing (aggressive, delinquent, and cruel), and (c) social competence (items related to school activities, social relationships, and success in school). A total behavior problem score is available. Separate profiles are provided for boys and girls.

The CBCL-Teacher's Report Form (Edelbrock & Achenbach, 1984) has been adapted from the parent version of the CBCL, with some items replaced by others more appropriate to classroom settings. The teacher version of the CBCL has nine behavior problem scales, derived from the internalizing, externalizing, and social competency syndromes. A total behavior problem score is available. Most of the questionnaire relates to academic and adaptive functioning in the school setting, with separate profiles for boys and girls.

Three additional checklists also use parallel parent and school versions. The Revised Behavior Problem Checklist (Quay & Peterson, 1983) consists of 89 items that cover six main behavioral areas, including aggression, attention problems, immaturity, withdrawal, psychotic behavior, and motor excess. The instrument can be completed in approximately 10 minutes and is intended for children and adolescents ages 5 to 17. The Connors Rating Scales (Goyette, Conners, & Ulrich, 1978) have short and long rating forms for parents and teachers for children ages 3 to 17. The scales range from 28 through 93 items, depending on the specific forms used, and can be completed in less than 30 minutes. The behavior problems covered include conduct disorders, learning problems, anxiety, and hyperactive-immature, anxious-passive, restless-disorganized, psychosomatic, obsessional, and antisocial behavior.

The third checklist is called the Home and School Situations Questionnaire (HSQ; Barkley & Edelbrock, 1987) and is completed by parents and teachers. This measure provides a format for learning about various behavior problems across situations. The HSQ lists 16 different situations in which parents commonly manage children's behaviors. Parents indicate yes or no to the situation along with a rating of 1 (mild) through 9 (severe). The School Situations Questionnaire (SSQ) is the teacher counterpart and consists of 12 situations with a yes or no problem and a severity score. Both instruments are intended to be completed within 15 minutes.

The Eyberg Child Behavior Inventory (ECBI; Eyberg, 1980), developed to measure conduct problems, is commonly used in ODD assessments. The ECBI is completed by parents for children ages 2 to 16 and can be administered in less than 15 minutes. The instrument includes 36 items that describe overt behavior problems, such as "argues with parents about rules" and "destroys toys or other objects." Other items refer to attentional (has short attention span) and developmental (wets bed) problems. Parents indicate whether it is a problem and how frequently it occurs.

Parent and Family Functioning Measures

Since any number of risk factors may contribute to the development and maintenance of ODD, parent and family functioning measures may play an important role in the social worker's assessment. A number of these measures are presented.

Parent-child interactions are important in determining overall family functioning, and a number of instruments are used as evaluation tools. The Dyadic Parent-Child Interaction Coding System—Revised (DPICS-R; Robinson & Eyberg, 1981) codes parent-child interactions according to target variables. Parent-child dyads are observed on two separate visits in order to measure mother-father interactions with the child. Child variables include physical and verbal deviance, noncompliance, and physical warmth; parent variables include praise, affect, nonintrusive statements, critical statements, and physical negative behaviors. A second coding instrument, the Family Problem-Solving Behavior Coding System (FPSBCS; Nickerson, Light, Blechman, & Gandelman, 1976) describes family interaction during a problem-solving discussion. Trained raters view problem-solving discussions among family members and code positive solution, negative solution, and off-task behavior scores.

Another measure of parent-child interactions is the parent Daily Discipline Interview (DDI; Webster-Stratton & Spitzer, 1991). Parents respond to 66 different parenting strategies summarized into five categories. These include physical negative force, limit setting, empathy, spanking, and inappropriate disciplinary strategy. The DDI can be administered at different phases of treatment. In a similar vein, Patterson (1983) devised the Oregon Social Learning Center's Family Crisis List. Parents rate the intensity of 101 items using a 7-point scale. The items include stressful events in the family, transportation problems, and economic, health, school, social, and legal concerns. Parents complete the measure on three separate days and note any crises that have occurred within the past 24 hours.

A popular measure of parental stress is the Parenting Stress Index (PSI; Abidin, 1983). The PSI is a 101-item scale that assesses sources of stress to the parent. The PSI takes approximately 25 minutes to complete and is divided into two major domains, child and parent. The parent domain measures certain parental risk factors, including depression, attachment, role performance and sense of competence, relationship with spouse, and parental health. The child domain measures adaptability, acceptability, demandingness, moodiness, hyperactivity, and parental reinforcement. In addition, the Beck Depression Inventory (BDI; Beck, Rush, Shaw, & Emery, 1980) has been used extensively for measuring parental depression. The

BDI consists of 21 items, each of which is scored on a 4-point scale, with higher scores indicating elevated depression.

Two instruments that measure parental psychopathology include the Structured Clinical Interview for *DSM-III-R* (SCID; Spitzer, Williams, & Gibbon, 1987) and the Schedule for Affective Disorder and Schizophrenia (SADS; Spitzer & Endicott, 1978). Using these instruments, social workers may assess a number of parental risk factors, including depression, mania, dysthymia, Antisocial Personality Disorder, and alcohol or drug abuse.

Finally, a number of measures have been used to evaluate interpersonal relationships and the organizational structure of the family. The Family Environment Scale (FES; Moos, Insel, & Humphrey, 1974) includes 90 true-false items on ten scales loading on three broad dimensions: (a) relationships, (b) personal growth, and (c) system maintenance. A total relationship score is also available. The Beavers-Timberlawn Family Evaluation Scale (BTFES; Lewis, Beavers, Gossett, & Phillips, 1976) was developed to assess the interactional patterns of families. The measure consists of 13 single-item scales subsumed under five theoretical domains: (a) structure, (b) autonomy, (c) affect, (d) perception of reality, and (e) task efficiency. The Life Experience Survey (LES; Sarason, Johnson, & Siegel, 1978) is a 57-item measure that assesses positive and negative life experiences over the past years. Two scales have been used to measure couple hostility and violence. The O'Leary-Porter Scale (Porter & O'Leary, 1980) is a nine-item instrument designed to assess the frequency of overt hostility including quarrels, sarcasm, and physical abuse. Likewise, the Conflict Tactics Scale (CTS; Straus, 1979) indicates how many times in a given time period (for example, the last 6 months) a couple used reasoning and argument, verbal and symbolic aggression, or physical aggression during conflicts. Respondents report their own and their partner's behavior on a scale ranging from 0 (never) to 6 (over 20 times).

EFFECTIVE INTERVENTIONS

A significant number of children display behaviors characteristic of ODD and if left untreated there is an increased risk for developing more serious life-altering behavior disorders and mental health disturbances (Lilienfeld & Waldman, 1990). This section highlights a number of treatment interventions that social workers may find useful in their work with children.

Parent Training

Teaching parents improved management techniques appears to be one of the most frequently used approaches for treating ODD in children. A number of parent training programs are commercially available. Many of the programs place an emphasis on the use of prosocial behaviors, administering tangible reinforcers, using nonviolent punishment procedures, and communicating at a level of development consistent with the child.

One of the most influential parent training programs was developed by Patterson, Reid, and colleagues at the Oregon Social Learning Center (OSLC; Patterson, 1975; Patterson, Reid, Jones, & Conger, 1975; Patterson, 1982; Reid, 1978). This program was originally developed for children ages 3 to 12, with limited application for the older adolescent. In summary, parents first learn the language and concepts of social learning theory, such as positive and negative reinforcement, antecedent behavior, and consequences. They are also taught how to pinpoint, define, and observe behavior and to use time-out, extinction, and praise for good behavior. Once parents have become proficient in the concepts, they define, track, monitor, and record two negative and two prosocial behaviors that their child exhibits. With this information, parents develop their own intervention program to modify the child's behaviors.

Patterson's program has also been adapted for use with adolescents (Marlowe, Reid, Patterson, Weinrott, & Bank, 1988; Reid, 1987). Changes include targeting behaviors that could put the adolescent at risk for future delinquency, such as drug use, curfew violations, and choosing negative peer relations. There is an emphasis on parental monitoring and supervision, using behavioral contracts, and implementing punishment, such as work details or restriction of free time. Training usually involves one-to-one contact between parents and therapist. More intensive training is used with parents who are living with chronically delinquent adolescents.

A number of parent training programs have been developed for young children. Parent-Child Interaction Therapy (PCIT; Eyberg & Robinson, 1982; Eyberg & Boggs, 1989; Eyberg, 1992; Eyberg, Boggs, & Algina, 1995; Maddux, Eyberg, & Funderburk, 1989) assumes that children's behaviors are likely to improve when there is some freedom in their play and when they have their parent's undivided attention. Further, PCIT assumes that in a positive environment caretaking is less likely to be negative. A two-phase approach is used. First, parents are taught a number of communication skills to be used with their children. Here, parents are encouraged to let their child lead a play situation while they imitate, describe, and praise the child's appropriate behavior. Parents are also encouraged to avoid criticizing the child and using commands that prevent the child from leading the play. A major goal of the second phase is to increase positive behavior while decreasing negative or disruptive behavior. Parents are taught how to direct their child's activity with clear, direct, and positively stated commands (for example, "Please put those toys back in the play box," or "Put on your shoes") and to use praise for appropriate behaviors. Negative behavior and noncompliance are addressed with verbal warnings and time out.

Forehand and McMahon (1981) and McMahon and Forehand (1984) have developed a parent training program for use with oppositional children ages 3 to 8. This program also has two phases and is used individually with parents, rather than with groups. In phase 1, parents learn a basic set of skills for improving their child's prosocial behavior. They increase their use of social rewards for appropriate behavior and reduce their commands, questions, and criticisms. The trainers use modeling, behavioral rehearsal, and feedback to help the parents learn the skills. Phase 2 teaches parents how to decrease noncompliant child behavior. Parents learn skills including the use of clear, direct warnings, age-appropriate commands, and implementing time-outs for noncompliance.

Webster-Stratton (1993, 1994, 1996) and Webster-Stratton and Herbert (1994) have one of the most comprehensively researched parenting programs for ODD and CD in young children. The heart of their model focuses around the concept of parent-therapist collaboration. Collaboration is an ongoing process with parents that includes respect for their ideas, values, perceptions, feelings, and contributions. Therapists build on collaboration by acknowledging cultural differences, developing a sense of trust, and fostering open communication. Therapists avoid giving advice or lecturing about what the parents are doing wrong or what the "right" approach is.

There are two parts to a collaboration model of parent training (Webster-Stratton & Herbert, 1994). First, parents participate in a general discussion of child behavior disorders, looking at characteristics, causal factors, and the course of negative behaviors. During this discussion, the therapist works to understand the parents' and child's perspectives. Part two uses a cognitive behavioral model of treatment involving the use of training videotapes. Many of the principles are behavioral and are intended to promote prosocial behavior, enhance individual and social skills, and promote a better quality of family life. Webster-Stratton and Herbert's collaborative model is particularly sensitive to what parents experience as a result of living with a child who exhibits behavior problems. For example, their model considers a number of transitions that parents go through from the beginning (feeling shamed and stigmatized) to the end of treatment (accepting the hard work of parenting)

In addition to changing parental interactions, a recent shift in parent training has focused on modifying beliefs or cognitions about parenting (Hanish, Tolan, & Guerra, 1996). Because the family provides the context for the child's social and cognitive development, parental beliefs and cognitions may play a role in maintaining a child's defiance and oppositional behavior. The initial goals of treatment are to assess the child's presenting problem, self-control, and response to limits, followed by assessing each parent's attributions and behavior-management style. Tolan (1989, 1991) argues that parents may use inconsistent discipline techniques because of fears and anxieties with regard to imposing limits or because of negative childhood experiences. Parent training involves learning what beliefs may exist that interfere with parenting skills, followed by changing some strategies as a way of challenging erroneous cognitions.

One final approach to parent training encompasses a broader family-based training model. This model assumes that parental stressors such as marital conflict, maternal depression, or life stresses are associated with fewer positive changes in child behavior. Consequently, the focus of treatment involves helping parents reduce their stressors and learn problem-solving skills to deal with stressors that interfere with parenting (Dadds, Schwartz, & Sanders, 1987; Griest & Forehand, 1982). For example, when Webster-Stratton (1994) added a treatment component to deal specifically with parental distress, improvement in parent communication, problem solving, and satisfaction with the training program was found in addition to children's increased knowledge of prosocial solutions.

Videotaped Parent Training

Several training programs rely extensively on videotape demonstration to communicate complex interactional skills. Videotaped parent training permits standardization and exportability. Dangel and Polster (1984, 1988) developed WINNING!, the first training program to use professionally developed videotapes and systematic, replicable training procedures. The program is based on three assumptions: (a) all behavior is learned, (b) parents can take control of environmental circumstances that contribute to the behavior of the child, and (c) there are any number of causes of child problem behaviors.

Skills training is divided into three main categories. The first category includes skills to increase appropriate child behavior, such as using praise and developing rewards and privileges. The second category includes skills to decrease inappropriate behaviors, such as ignoring the behavior, removing rewards and privileges, imposing time-out, and spanking. The third category includes skills that are taught to manage specific child problem behaviors, such as arguing, temper tantrums, and refusal to do homework. A main intervention approach is parent group training, and the authors describe in detail how such parent training may be set up, led, and evaluated.

WINNING! (Dangel & Polster, 1984; 1988) consists of 22 videotaped lessons for educational or therapeutic use with children ages 3 to 12. Each videotape is 14 to 25 minutes long and uses 35 to 50 brief scenes of parent-child interactions. The first eight videotapes consist of lessons on praise, rewards, ignoring, time-out, removal, punishment, and compliance. The lessons follow one another, and parents must proceed through each one before advancing. Techniques also address specific child-management problems, showing how to apply the skills covered in the earlier lessons. The systematic training procedures used in the program include quantitative and qualitative feedback, cumulative mastery of skills by difficulty, and opportunities for practice in group and at home.

Burke and Herron (1996) developed a similar program, Common Sense Parenting (CSP), that uses written materials and instructional videotapes. CSP was adapted for use with children and adolescents in group home settings through Father Flanagan's Boys Home. In group settings, all parents are taught the same skills, including the use of clear communication, positive reinforcement and consequences, preventive and corrective teaching, self-control, and problem solving. Videotaped vignettes are used to help parents understand the application of each skill. Examples and role-playing situations are varied to demonstrate applications of the skills with children at different ages.

The Parent and Child Video Series (BASIC) (Webster-Stratton 1981a, 1981b; 1982, 1992; 1994) was designed for parents of children ages 3 to 8. The program has generally been used with groups of parents but may be used individually over a series of 12 or 13 weekly two hour sessions. The ten videotapes show parents and children of different sexes, ages, cultures, socioeconomic backgrounds, and temperaments interacting at play and at mealtimes, when getting children dressed, during toilet training, and when dealing with disobedience. Scenes depict parents handling situations correctly and incorrectly.

Webster-Stratton (1994) has modified her earlier work and developed ADVANCE, a parent training program using videotapes and therapist-led discussions. The goal of ADVANCE is to improve family communication, problem solving, and coping skills. Therapists follow a comprehensive 400-page manual that includes the rationale for each group therapy session, questions to use, homework assignments, and parent handouts. Six videotape programs cover personal self-control (coping with anger, depression, and stress), communication (destructive and effective communication styles and giving and getting support), teaching children how to solve problems, and strengthening social support and self-care.

Follow-up studies of treatment effectiveness with videotaped parent training appear to be positive. Dangel and Polster (1984) evaluated 62 families in four separate studies. Families were observed in their homes and data was collected on parent and child behaviors covered in the training program. Comparisons of baseline and follow-up data indicated that overall improvement occurred in child and family responses to positive and negative consequences, attention to inappropriate behavior, and general positive family interaction. Webster-Stratton and colleagues (Webster-Stratton, 1984; Webster-Stratton, Kolpacoff, & Hollinsworth, 1989) found that therapist-led groups based on videotaped modeling were superior to therapist-led group discussion without videotapes. Likewise, Webster-Stratton (1994) compared the differences between a parent skills training group using videotaped discussion modeling (GVDM) and ADVANCE videotape use, including additional parental problem-solving groups, with parents. While both methods improved child and parent responses in the short term, ADVANCE produced significant additional changes in parental and child functioning. Finally, a review of archival data on mothers who attended CSP programs revealed that parent training was less effective with adolescents. Reasons cited included the long-standing nature of the problems, their severity, and the increased time spent with peers away from home (Ruma, Burke, & Thompson, 1996).

Child Training

Child training refers to programs in which children are instructed, coached, or taught prosocial skills. The instruction may occur either individually or in small groups. Typically, the programs are school- or clinic-based and are time limited, lasting between 4 and 12 weeks. Methods used to produce change include verbal instruction, role-playing or behavioral rehearsal, corrective feedback, and praise.

Because oppositional children demonstrate poor peer relationships and inadequate social skills, remediation programs emphasize social behaviors. Such programs coach children in positive social skills including play, friendship development, and the development of appropriate conversation skills (Bierman & Furman, 1984; Gresham & Nagle, 1980; Mize & Ladd, 1990). For example, in one group program, La Greca and Santogrossi (1980) focused specifically on eight target behaviors, including smiling, greeting, joining, inviting, conversing, sharing, cooperating, and complimenting. The authors found that social skills training led to increased skills and knowledge of how to interact with peers.

An additional treatment approach aims to influence children's thinking processes about problem solving, self-control, or self-statements (Kazdin, 1987; Kendall & Braswell, 1985; Lochman, Burch, Curry, & Lampron, 1984; Spivak, Platt, & Shure, 1976). Most of the preceding programs are school-based and do not involve parents in the training. For example, Feindler (1987) developed an anger control training program for oppositional adolescents that teaches arousal-management skills and cognitive strategies to promote self-control. This model is based on the belief that adolescents lose control of their anger because of behavioral and cognitive skill deficits. The anger control training sessions focus on self-monitoring, learning new cognitive skills, and behavioral rehearsal. The training includes: (a) self-monitoring of anger provocations, (b) relaxation training, (c) coping self-statements, (d) self-reinforcement strategies, (e) self-control contingencies, (f) assertiveness, and (g) problem-solving skills training. Many of the anger control skills are presented using videotapes (Feindler, Ecton, Kingsley, & Dubey, 1986) and a session-by-session training manual (Feindler & Ecton, 1986). Dangel, Deschner, and Rasp (1989) provided anger control training for 12 adolescents in a residential treatment center. Six weeks of training consisted of thought stopping, relaxation training, and changing problem-solving self-talk patterns. Results showed that rates of aggression decreased for 9 of the adolescents. Although child training continues to be a valuable part of treatment, in her review of the social skill and cognitive intervention research, Webster-Stratton (1993) found the results only mildly encouraging. Some evidence suggests that the younger, immature, and more aggressive child may be unaffected by social skills training. Furthermore, studies of child training programs fail to show that skills improvement in the clinic or school setting generalizes to home, that long-term effects were maintained, or what contributes to success or failure in child training. Consequently, child training should be considered only one small part of a treatment regimen provided for children with ODD.

Family Therapy

Although family therapy is a popular approach to treating children and their families, little has been written about using family therapy as a treatment strategy for ODD. In one report, Wells and Egan (1988) compared social learning-based parent training with a structural family therapy approach. Using a sample of 24 families, the authors found that the social learning approach was more effective in reducing oppositional behavior. Another family therapy approach treating ODD used a model of intervention based on hypotheses that looked at the function of symptoms. In this case, Phelps (1993) focused interventions on three levels: (a) behavioral, (b) emotional, and (c) ideational. Although each level presents a different focus, an understanding of all three was necessary in order to focus on the context of behavior and on how previously attempted solutions had gotten stuck. Last, Webster-Stratton and Herbert (1994) discussed some strategies of behavioral family therapy in their work with ODD and CD children. The authors emphasized broad principles of child management that include setting limits or boundaries, increasing the interpersonal communication among family members, supporting the parents as caregivers, and working with the marital relationship.

From the preceding literature, it is clear that there is an absence of empirical studies focusing on family therapy and ODD. Yet the family therapy literature is filled with practical intervention approaches with children and adolescents who exhibit common ODD symptoms yet are not diagnosed as such (e.g., Selekman, 1993, 1995; Durrant, 1995; Metcalf, 1995, 1997). Given the popularity of current family therapy modalities, there is a need for the field to evaluate these approaches and determine their effectiveness with children who exhibit oppositional behaviors.

School and Community Intervention

Webster-Stratton (1993) suggests that once children enter school with ODD, a variety of new risk factors such as peer rejection and academic failure operate independently from family variables. Social workers in school settings may face the task of assessing a new set of circumstances that exacerbate oppositional behaviors. Thus, one role may be to assist teachers and community workers in preventing school-related difficulties.

The Houston Parent-Child Development Center (H-PCDC) program was designed to prevent behavior problems in young Hispanic families. The philosophy of the program is that parent-child education programs can be optimally effective if they are designed to meet the specific needs of the participating families (Johnson, 1988). Consequently, the program is intended to be ethnically sensitive, keeping in mind various needs of its group members. H-PCDC consists of a two-stage program, beginning at age 1 and ending at age 3. The program is designed so that intervention can move from the home in the first year to a local day center in the second year. Bilingual communication is encouraged with the use of materials that are culturally sensitive. Although the model is designed to include the entire family, one major focus is on mother-child interactions. Discussions progress from learning about early infant development and physical growth and change to a specific curriculum that deals with such problem behaviors as temper tantrums and separation anxiety. Teaching techniques centered around parenting include the use of videotapes of mothers interacting with children.

The I Can Problem Solve program (ICPS; Shure & Spivak, 1988; Shure, 1992, 1993) is applicable for young children who may be at risk for behavioral dysfunction and interpersonal maladjustment. There are two programs; one starting in nursery school, followed by a second program in kindergarten. Teachers work with small groups of children for about 20 minutes per day. ICPS assumes that young children who cannot think through ways to solve interpersonal problem or who do not consider the consequences of behavior may be susceptible to impulsive mistakes, frustrations, and aggressive behaviors. Over a period of 4 months, children are helped to learn about the meaning and importance of words, that particular solutions may succeed with some people but not with others, about how other people feel, and how feelings can influence behaviors.

In the Boys Town model, preventive teaching (Boys Town Press, 1989) is used to teach aggressive youth prosocial skills both in group home settings and in the classroom. Adolescents are taught a number of skills to help them prepare for circumstances that they might later encounter. For example, dealing with conflict and with being told no and being assertive are taught in eight separate steps. Some of the preventive teaching steps include initial praise, explanation of the skill, demonstration of the skill, practice, and feedback.

Finally, Webster-Stratton (1993) has underlined the importance of *bonding* (p. 442), a positive relationship process between school, parents, and child in preventing further occurrences of such negative behaviors as ODD and CD. The author has convincingly argued that a teacher's negative reaction to a child's disruptive behavior coupled with a parent's helplessness and demoralization is likely to lead to a lack of coordination and support between home and school. A lack of connection will erode the child's academic learning, beginning a negative slide into additional risk factors: peer rejection, negative peer group membership, and academic underachievement.

Pharmacotherapy

Cantwell (1989) has stated that the use of medications should not be the sole treatment for children or adolescents with ODD. However, a substantial body of literature does support medical intervention for the treatment of disorders that may be related to ODD, such as dysthymia and ADHD (Abikoff & Klein, 1992; Shelton & Barkley, 1995; Anastopoulos, Barkley, & Shelton, 1996).

Best Practices

No definitive protocols exist for the treatment of children with Oppositional Defiant Disorder, and its etiology remains elusive. The literature does, however, illustrate several important points. First, the disorder is prevalent, and if children with the diagnosis do not receive effective treatment they may develop more serious disorders, such as Conduct Disorder or Antisocial Personality Disorder. A careful assessment should gather information about the specific behaviors exhibited by the child, the frequency and intensity of the behaviors, and the settings and circumstances under which they occur. The assessment should also identify parent characteristics, such as maternal depression or fears and anxieties about parenting; family stressors, such as poverty or marital discord; parenting knowledge and skill deficiencies; and family resources and strengths. The most effective intervention will include individual work with parents to address issues that interfere with their ability to parent; parent training that uses videotape modeling to teach specific skills; child training to teach the child self-control methods and social skills; and structured activities in the home and at school to enhance the generalization and maintenance of new child and parent behaviors. Finally, for children with companion disorders such as ADHD or dysthymia, medication may be useful.

CONCLUSIONS

Social workers who treat children are likely to see many symptoms of Oppositional Defiant Disorder (ODD). Depending on the stage of development, these children will exhibit a host of symptoms, ranging from being annoying, spiteful, and disobedient to temper problems and persistent arguments with adults. The intent of this chapter is to provide an overview of the symptoms and prevalence of the disorder along with some assessment and treatment intervention strategies.

ODD appears to be a widespread problem, and each year many children referred for mental health concerns exhibit many of the symptoms. The role of identifying the behaviors is important, and social workers have access to a number of instruments and treatment approaches that may be helpful. Given the state of the field, social work has a dual role for the future. First, the profession needs to develop more collaborative models of intervening effectively with ODD. Such an approach may include integrating theoretical models as well as incorporating treatment regimens from professions such as psychology and marriage and family therapy. Finally, this chapter reveals an absence of grounded research from the profession. Empirical studies reflecting a social work perspective are needed. Evaluation of treatment programs and studies that focus on gender and minority differences are some of the issues deserving the attention of the social work researcher. Although our knowledge of children who exhibit ODD is not complete, social work has a great deal to contribute in making advances toward more and better assessment and intervention approaches.

REFERENCES

Abidin, R. R. (1983). *Parenting Stress Index: Manual.* Charlottesville, VA: Pediatric Psychology Press.

Abikoff, H., & Klein, R. G. (1992). Attention deficit hyperactivity and conduct disorder: Comorbidity and implications for treatment. *Journal of Consulting and Clinical Psychology, 60,* 881–892.

Achenbach, T. M., & Edelbrock, C. S. (1983). *Manual for the child behavior checklist and revised child behavior profile.* Burlington: University of Vermont, Department of Psychiatry.

Alexander, J. F., & Pugh, C. A. (1996). Oppositional behavior and conduct disorder of children and youth. In F. Kaslow (Ed.), *Handbook of relational diagnosis and dysfunctional family patterns* (pp. 210–224). New York: Wiley.

American Psychiatric Association. (1980). *Diagnostic and statistical manual of mental disorders* (3rd ed.). Washington, DC: Author.

American Psychiatric Association. (1987). *Diagnostic and statistical manual of mental disorders* (3rd ed., rev.). Washington, DC: Author.

American Psychiatric Association. (1994). *Diagnostic and statistical manual of mental disorders* (4th ed.). Washington, DC: Author.

Anastopoulos, A. D., Barkley, R. A., & Shelton, T. L. (1996). Family based treatment: Psychosocial intervention for children and adolescents with attention deficit hyperactivity disorder. In E. D. Hibbs & P. S. Jenson (Eds.), *Psychosocial treatments for child and adolescent disorders: Empirically based strategies for clinical practice* (pp. 267–284). Washington, DC: American Psychiatric Association.

Barkley, R. A., & Edelbrock, C. S. (1987). Assessing situational variation in children's behavior problems: The home and school situation questionnaires. In R. Prinz (Ed.), *Advances in behavioral assessment of children and families* (Vol. 3, pp. 157–176). Greenwich, CT: JAI Press.

Beck, A. T., Rush, A. J., Shaw, B. F., & Emery, G. (1980). *Cognitive therapy of depression.* New York: Guilford Press.

Bierman, K. L., & Furman, W. (1984). The effect of social skills training and peer involvement on the social adjustment of preadolescents. *Child Development, 55,* 151–162.

Boys Town Press. (1989). *Working with aggressive youth.* Boys Town, NE: Author.

Burke, R., & Herron, R. (1996). *Common sense parenting.* Boys Town NE: Boys Town Press.

Campbell, S. B., & Ewing, L. J. (1990). Follow-up of hard-to-manage preschoolers: Adjustment at age 9 and predictors of continuing symptoms. *Journal of Child Psychology and Psychiatry, 31,* 871–889.

Cantwell, D. P. (1989). Oppositional defiant disorder. In H. I. Kaplan & B. J. Shaddock (Eds.), *Comprehensive textbook of psychiatry* (3rd ed., pp. 1842–1845). Baltimore: Williams & Wilkins.

Cautela, J. R., Cautela, J., & Esonis, S. S. (1983). *Forms for behavior analysis with children.* Champaign, IL: Research Press.

Chamberlain, P., & Reid, J. B. (1987). Parent observation and report of child symptoms. *Behavioral Assessment, 5,* 349–362.

Christophersen, D. R., & Finney, J. W. (1993). Oppositional defiant disorder. In R. T. Ammerman, C. G. Last, & M. Hersen (Eds.), *Handbook of prescriptive treatments for children and adolescents* (pp. 102–114). Boston: Allyn & Bacon.

Cobb, J. A., & Hops, H. (1972). *Coding manual for continuous observation of interactions by single subjects in an academic setting* (Report No. 9). Eugene: University of Oregon, Center at Oregon for Research in the Behavioral Education of the Handicapped.

Costello, E. J., & Angold, A. (1993). Toward a developmental epidemiology of the disruptive behavior disorders. *Development and Psychopathology, 5,* 91–101.

Costello, E. J., Edelbrock, C. S., & Costello, A. J. (1985). Validity of the NIMH Diagnostic Interview Schedule for Children: A comparison between psychiatric and pediatric referrals. *Journal of Abnormal Child Psychology, 13,* 579–595.

Crowther, J. K., Bond, L. A., & Rolf, J. E. (1981). The incidence, prevalence, and severity of behavior disorders among preschool-aged children in day care. *Journal of Abnormal Child Psychology, 21,* 5–18.

Dadds, M. R., Schwartz, M. R., & Sanders, M. R. (1987). Marital discord and treatment outcome in behavioral treatment of child conduct disorders. *Journal of Consulting and Clinical Psychology, 16,* 192–203.

Dangel, R. F., Deschner, J. P., & Rasp, R. (1989). Anger control training for adolescents in residential treatment. *Behavior Modification, 13,* 447–458.

Dangel, R. F., & Polster, R. A. (Eds.). (1984). *Parent training: Foundations of research and practice.* New York: Guilford Press.

Dangel, R. F., & Polster, R. A. (1988). *Teaching child management skills.* New York: Pergamon Press.

Dishion, T., Gardner, K., Patterson, G., Reid, J., Spyrou, S., & Thibodeaux, S. (1984). The Family Process Code: A multidimensional system for observing family interactions. Unpublished document. Oregon Social Learning Center, Eugene.

Durrant, M. (1995). *Creative strategies for school problems.* New York: W. W. Norton.

Edelbrock, C. S., & Achenbach, T. M. (1984). The teacher version of the child behavior profile: I. Boys aged 6–11. *Journal of Consulting and Clinical Psychology, 52,* 207–217.

Eyberg, S. M. (1980). Eyberg child behavior inventory. *Journal of Clinical Child Psychology, 9,* 29.

Eyberg, S. M. (1992). Assessing therapy outcome with preschool children: Progress and problems. *Journal of Clinical Child Psychology, 21,* 306–311.

Eyberg, S. M., & Boggs, S. R. (1989). Parent training for oppositional defiant preschoolers. In C. E. Schaefer & J. M. Briesmeister (Eds.) *Handbook of parent training: Parents as cotherapists for children's behavior problems* (pp. 105–132.). New York: Wiley.

Eyberg, S. M., Boggs, S. R., & Algina, J. (1995). Parent-child interaction therapy: A psycho-social model for the treatment of young children with conduct problem behaviors and their families. *Psychopharmacology Bulletin, 31,* 83–91.

Eyberg, S. M. & Robinson, E. A. (1982). Parent-child interaction training: Effects on family functioning. *Journal of Clinical Child Psychology, 37,* 130–137.

Eyberg, S. M., & Robinson, E. A. (1983). Dyadic Parent-Child Interaction Coding System: A manual. *Psychological Documents, 13* (Ms. No. 2582).

Feindler, E. L. (1987). Clinical issues and recommendations in adolescent anger control train-ing. *Journal of Child and Adolescent Psychotherapy, 4,* 267–274.

Feindler, E. L., & Ecton, R. B. (1986). *Adolescent anger control: Cognitive-behavioral tech-niques.* Elmsford, NY: Pergamon.

Feindler, E. L., Ecton, R. B., Kingsley, D., Dubey, D. (1986). Group anger control training for institutionalized psychiatric male adolescents. *Behavior Therapy, 17,* 109–123.

Forehand, R. L., & McMahon, R. J. (1981). *Helping the non-compliant child: A clinician's guide to parent training.* New York: Guilford Press.

Forehand, R. L., Peed, S., Roberts, M., McMahon, R., Griest, D., & Humphreys, L. (1978). Coding manual for scoring mother-child interaction (3rd ed.). Unpublished manuscript, Uni-versity of Georgia.

Frick, P. J., Lahey, B. B., Loeber R., Stouthamer-Loeber, M., Christ, M. G., & Hanson, K. (1992). Familial risk factors to oppositional defiant disorder and conduct disorder: Parental psychopathology and maternal parenting. *Journal of Consulting and Clinical Psychology, 60,* 49–55.

Frick, P. J., Lahey, B. B., Loeber, R., Tannenbaum, L., Van Horn, Y., Christ, M. A. G., Hart, E. A., & Hanson, K. (1993). Oppositional defiant disorder and conduct disorder: A meta-analytic review of factor analyses and cross-validation in a clinic sample. *Clinical Psychology Review, 13,* 319–340.

Goyette, C. H., Conners, C. K., & Ulrich, R. F. (1978). Normative data on revised conners par-ent and teacher rating scales. *Journal of Abnormal Child Psychology, 6,* 221–236.

Gresham, F. M., & Nagle, R. J. (1980). Social skills training with children: Responsiveness to modeling and coaching as a function of peer orientation. *Journal of Consulting and Clinical Psychology, 48,* 718–729.

Griest, D. L., & Forehand, R. (1982). How can I get any parent training done with all these other problems: The role of family variables in child behavior training. *Child and Family Behav-ior Therapy, 4,* 73–80.

Group for the Advancement of Psychiatry. (1966). *Psychopathologicald disorders in childhood: Theoretical considerations and a proposed classification* (Report 62). New York: Author.

Hanf, C. (1970). Shaping mothers to shape their children's behavior. Unpublished manuscript, University of Oregon Medical School.

Hanish, L. D., Tolan, P. H., & Guerra, N. G. (1996). Treatment of oppositional defiant disorder. In M. A. Reineke, F. M. Dattilio, & A. Freeman (Eds.), *Cognitive therapy with adolescents and children* (pp. 62–77). New York: Guilford Press.

Harris, A. (1979). An empirical test of the situation specificity/consistency of aggressive behav-ior. *Child Behavior Therapy, 1,* 257–270.

Harris, A. (1980). Response class: A Guttman scale analysis. *Journal of Abnormal Child Psy-chology, 9,* 219–227.

Harris, A., & Reid, J. B. (1981). The consistency of a class of coercive child behaviors across school settings for individual subjects. *Journal of Abnormal Child Psychology, 9,* 219–227.

Herjanic, B., & Reich, W. (1982). Development of a structured psychiatric interview for children: Agreement between child and parent on individual symptoms. *Journal of Abnormal Child Psychology, 10,* 307–324.

Hinshaw, S. P., Lahey, B. B., Hart, E. L. (1993). Issues of taxonomy and comorbidity in the development of conduct disorder. *Development and Psychopathology, 5,* 31–49.

Johnson, P. (1988). The Houston Parent–Child Development Center. In R. H. Price, E. L. Cowen, R. P. Lorion, & J. Ramos-McKay (Eds.), *Fourteen ounces of prevention: A casebook for practitioners* (pp. 83–97). Washington, DC: American Psychological Association.

Jouriles, E., Murphy, C., & O'Leary, K. (1989). Interspousal aggression, marital discord, and child problems. *Journal of Consulting and Clinical Psychology, 57,* 453–455.

Kazdin, A. E. (1985). *Treatment of antisocial behavior in children and adolescents.* Homewood, IL: Dorsey.

Kazdin, A. E. (1987). Treatment of antisocial behavior in children: Current status and future directions. *Psychological Bulletin, 102,* 187–203.

Kazdin, A. E. (1991). Effectiveness of psychotherapy with children and adolescents. *Journal of Consulting and Clinical Psychology, 60,* 785–798.

Kendall, P. C., & Braswell, L. (1985). *Cognitive-behavioral therapy for impulsive children.* New York: Guilford Press.

La Greca, A. M., & Santogrossi, D. A. (1980). Social skills training with elementary school students: A behavioral group approach. *Journal of Consulting and Clinical Psychology, 48,* 220–227.

Lahey, B. B., Loeber, R., Quay, H. C., Frick, P. J., & Grimm, J. (1992). Oppositional defiant and conduct disorders: Issues to be resolved for DSM-IV. *Journal of the American Academy of Child and Adolescent Psychiatry, 31,* 539–546.

Lewis, J. M., Beavers, W. R., Gossett, J. T., & Phillips, V. A. (1976). *No single thread: Psychological health in family systems.* New York: Brunner/Mazel.

Levy, D. M. (1955). Oppositional Syndromes and Oppositional behavior. In P. Hoch & J. Zubin (Eds.), *Psychopathology in Childhood.* New York: Grune & Stratton.

Lilienfeld, S. O., & Waldman, I. D. (1990). The relation between childhood attention-deficit hyperactivity disorders and adult antisocial behavior reexamined; The problem of heterogeneity. *Clinical Psychology Review, 10,* 669–725.

Lochman, J. E., Burch, P. R., Curry, J. F. & Lampron. (1984). Treatment and generalization effects of cognitive-behavioral and goal-setting interventions with aggressive boys. *Journal of Consulting and Clinical Psychology, 52,* 915–916.

Loeber, R. (1991). Antisocial behavior: More enduring than changeable? *Journal of the American Academy of Child and Adolescent Psychiatry, 30,* 393–397.

Loeber, R., Green, S. M., Keenan, K., & Lahey, B. B. (1995). Which boys will fare worse? Early predictors of the onset of conduct disorders in a 6 year longitudinal study. *Journal of the American Academy of Child and Adolescent Psychiatry, 34,* 499–509.

Loeber, R., Lahey, B. B., & Thomas, C. (1991). The diagnostic conundrum of oppositional defiant disorder and conduct disorder. *Journal of Abnormal Psychology, 100,* 379–390.

Maddux, J. E., Eyberg, S. M., & Funderburk, B. W. (1989). Parent-child interaction therapy: Issues in case management of early conduct child problems. In M. C. Roberts & C. E. Walker (Eds.), *Casebook of child and pediatric psychology* (pp. 161–175). New York: Guilford Press.

Marlowe, H., Reid, J. B., Patterson, G. R., Weinrott, M. R., & Bank, L. (1988). A comparison evaluation of parent training for families of chronic delinquents. Unpublished manuscript. Oregon Social Learning Center, Eugene.

McGee, R., Feehan, M., Williams, S., & Anderson, J. (1992). DSM-III disorders in a large sample of adolescents. *Journal of the American Academy of Child and Adolescent Psychiatry, 29,* 611–619.

McMahon, R. J., & Forehand, R. L. (1984). Parent training for the noncompliant child: Treatment outcome, generalization and adjunctive therapy procedures. In R. F. Dangel & R. A. Polster (Eds.), *Parent training: Foundations of research and practice* (pp. 298–328). New York: Guilford Press.

McMahon, R. J. & Forehand, R. L. (1988). Conduct disorders. In E. J. Mash & L. G. Terdal (Eds.), *Behavioral assessment of childhood disorders* (pp. 105–156). New York: Guilford Press.

Metcalf, L. (1995). *Counseling toward solutions: A practical solution-focused program for working with students, teachers, and parents.* New York: Center for Applied Research in Education.

Metcalf, L. (1997). *Parenting toward solutions: How parents can use skills they already have to raise responsible, loving kids.* Englewood Cliffs, NJ: Prentice Hall.

Mize, J. & Ladd, G. W. (1990). A cognitive social-learning approach to social skill training with low status pre-school children. *Developmental Psychology, 26,* 388–297.

Moos, R. H., Insel, P., & Humphrey, B. (1974). *Family, work, and group environment scales.* Palo Alto, CA: Consulting Psychologists Press.

Nickerson, M., Light, R., Blechman, E., & Gandelman, B. (1976). Three measures of problem-solving behavior: A procedural manual. *JSAS Catalog of Selected Documents in Psychology, Winter Issue* (Ms1190).

Nottelmann, E. D., & Jensen, P. S. (1995). Comorbidity of disorders in children and adolescents. *Advances in Clinical Child Psychology, 17,* 109–155.

O'Leary, K. D., & Emery, R. E. (1982). Marital discord and child behavior problems. In M. D. Levine & P. Satz (Eds.), *Middle childhood: Developmental variation and dysfunction* (pp. 345–364). New York: Academic Press.

Patterson, G. R. (1975). *Families: Applications of social learning to family life.* Champaign, IL: Research Press.

Patterson, G. R. (1976). *Living with children: New methods for parents and teachers.* Champaign, IL: Research Press.

Patterson, G. R. (1982). *Coercive Family Processes.* Eugene, OR: Castalia.

Patterson, G. R. (1983). Stress: A change agent for family process. In N. Garmezy & M. Rutter (Eds.), *Stress, coping and development in children* (pp. 235–262). New York: McGraw-Hill.

Patterson, G. R., & Bank, L. (1986). Bootstrapping your way in the nomological thicket. *Behavioral Assessment, 8,* 49–73.

Patterson, G. R., & Forgatch, M. S. (1987a). *Parents and adolescents living together. Part 1: the basics.* Eugene, OR: Castalia.

Patterson, G. R., & Forgatch, M. S. (1987b). *Parents and adolescents living together. Part 2: Family problem solving.* Eugene, OR: Castalia.

Patterson, G. R., Ray, R. S., Shaw, D. A., Cobb, J. A. (1969). *Manual for coding of family interactions* (rev. ed.). New York: Microfiche Publications.

Patterson, G. R., Reid, J. B., Jones, R. R., & Conger, R. E. (1975). *A social learning approach to family intervention: Vol. 1. Families with aggressive children.* Eugene, OR: Castalia.

Patterson, G. R., & Stouthamer-Loeber, M. (1984). The correlation of family management practices and delinquency. *Child Development, 55,* 1299–1307.

Phelps, P. A. (1993). The case of oppositional cooperation. In R. A. Wells & V. J. Gianetti (Eds.), *The casebook of brief psychotherapies* (pp. 287–302). New York: Plenum Press.

Porter, B., & O'Leary, K. D. (1980). Types of marital discord and child behavior problems. *Journal of Abnormal Child Psychology, 8,* 287–295.

Quay, H. C., & Peterson, D. R. (1983). Interim manual for the revised behavior problem checklist. Unpublished manuscript. University of Miami.

Reed, M. L., & Edelbrock, C. (1983). Reliability and validity of the direct observation form of the child behavior checklist. *Journal of Abnormal Child Psychology, 11,* 521–530.

Reid, J. B. (1978). *A social learning approach to family intervention: Vol. II. Observation in home settings.* Eugene, OR: Castalia.

Reid, J. B. (1987). Therapeutic interventions in the families of aggressive children and adolescents. Paper presented at the meeting of the Oreganizzato dalle Catterde di Psicologia Clinicae delle Teorie di Personalita dell Universita di Roma, Rome.

Robins, L. N. (1981). Epidemiological approaches to natural history research: Antisocial disorders in children. *Journal of the American Academy of Child Psychiatry, 20,* 566–580.

Robins, L. N., & Price, R. K. (1991). Adult disorders predicted by childhood conduct problems: Results from the NIMH epidemiological catchment area project. *Psychiatry, 54,* 116–132.

Robinson, E. A., & Eyberg, S. M. (1981). The Dyadic Parent-Child Interaction Coding System: Standardization and validation. *Journal of Consulting and Clinical Psychology, 49,* 245–250.

Ruma, R. R., Burke, R. V., & Thompson, R. W. (1996) Group parent training: Is it effective for children of all ages? *Behavior Therapy, 27,* 159–169.

Rutter, M., & Giller, H. (1983). *Juvenile delinquency: Trends and perspectives.* Harmondsworth, Middlesex: Penguin.

Sarason, I. G., Johnson, G. H., & Seigel, J. M. (1978). Assessing the impact of life changes: Development of the life experiences survey. *Journal of Consulting and Clinical Psychology, 46,* 932–946.

Schwab-Stone, M. E., Shaffer, D., Dalcan, M. K., & Jensen, P. S. (1996). Criterion validity of the NIMH Diagnostic Interview Schedule for Children version 2.3 (DISC-2.3). *Journal of the American Academy of Child and Adolescent Psychiatry, 35,* 878–888.

Selekman, M. D. (1993). *Pathways to change: Brief therapy solutions with difficult adolescents.* New York: Guilford Press.

Selekman, M. D. (1995). Rap music with wisdom. In S. Friedman (Ed.), *The reflecting team in action: Collaborative practice in family therapy* (pp. 205–219). New York: Guilford Press.

Shaffer, D., Schwab-Stone, M., Fisher, P. W., & Cohen, P. (1993). The Diagnostic Interview Schedule for Children—DISC-R: Preparation, field testing, interrater reliability, & acceptability. *Journal of the American Academy of Child and Adolescent Psychiatry, 32,* 643–650.

Shelton, T. L., & Barkley, R. A. (1995). The assessment and treatment of attention-deficit/hyperactivity disorder in children. In M. C. Roberts (Ed.), *Handbook of pediatric psychology* (2nd Ed.), (pp. 633–654). New York: Guilford Press.

Shure, M. B. (1992). *I can problem solve. An interpersonal cognitive problem-solving approach for kindergarten and primary grades.* Champaign, IL: Research Press.

Shure, M. B. (1993). I can problem solve: Interpersonal problem solving for young children. Special issue: Enhancing young children's lives. *Early Child Development and Care, 96,* 49–64.

Shure, M. B., & Spivak, G. (1988). Interpersonal cognitive problem solving. In R. H. Price, E. L. Cowen, R. P. Lorion, & J. Ramos-McKay (Eds.), *Fourteen ounces of prevention: A casebook for practitioners* (pp. 69–82). Washington, DC: American Psychological Association.

Spitzer, R. L., & Endicott, J. (1978). *Schedule for affective disorders and schizophrenia.* New York: New York State Psychiatric Institute.

Spitzer, R. L., Williams, J. B. W., & Gibbon, M. (1987). *Structured clinical interview for DSM-III-R non-patient version.* New York: New York State Psychiatric Institute.

Spivak, G., Platt, J. J. & Shure, M. G. (1976). *The problem-solving approach to adjustment.* San Francisco: Jossey-Bass.

Straus, M. A. (1979). Measuring family conflict and violence: The conflict tactics scale. *Journal of Marriage and the Family, 41,* 75–88.

Tolan, P. H. (1989). Guidelines and pitfalls: Applying structural-strategic approaches in a multiple level perspective. *Journal of Psychotherapy and the Family, 6,* 151–156.

Tolan, P. H. (1991). The impact of therapist outcome conception on child and adolescent family therapy. *Journal of Family Psychotherapy, 1,* 61–78.

Trad, P. V. (1992). Evaluating the mental status of preschoolers through the use of diagnostic peer groups. *Journal of Child and Adolescent Group Therapy, 2,* 113–139.

Valla, J. P., Bergeron, L., Berube, H., & Gaudet, N. (1994). A structured pictorial questionnaire to assess DSM III-R based diagnoses in children (6–11 years): Development, validity, and reliability. *Journal of Abnormal Child Psychology, 22,* 403–423.

Wahler, R., G., House, A. E., Stambaugh, E. E. (1976). *Ecological assessment of child problem behavior: A clinical package for home, school, and institutional settings.* New York: Pergamon Press.

Webster-Stratton, C. (1981a). Modification of mothers' behaviors and attitudes through a videotape modeling group discussion program. *Behavior Therapy, 12,* 634–642.

Webster-Stratton, C. (1981b). Videotape modeling: A method of parent education. *Journal of Clinical Child Psychology, 10,* 93–98.

Webster-Stratton, C. (1982). Teaching mothers through videotape modeling to change their children's behavior. *Journal of Pediatric Psychology, 7,* 279–294.

Webster-Stratton, C. (1984). Randomized trial of two parent training programs for families with conduct-disordered children. *Journal of Consulting and Clinical Psychology, 52,* 666–678.

Webster-Stratton, C. (1985). Comparisons of behavior transactions between conduct disordered children and their mothers in the clinic and at home. *Journal of Abnormal Child Psychology, 13,* 169–184.

Webster-Stratton, C. (1990). Stress: A potential disrupter of parental perceptions and family interactions. *Journal of Clinical Child Psychology, 19,* 302–312.

Webster-Stratton, C. (1992). Individually administered videotape parent training: Who benefits. *Cognitive Therapy and Research, 6,* 31–52.

Webster-Stratton, C. (1993). What really happens in parent training? *Behavior Modification, 17,* 407–456.

Webster-Stratton, C. (1994). Advancing videotape parent training: A comparison training. *Journal of Consulting and Clinical Psychology, 62,* 583–593.

Webster-Stratton, C. (1996). Early-onset conduct problems: Does gender make a difference? *Journal of Consulting and Clinical Psychology, 64,* 540–551

Webster-Stratton, C., & Herbert, M. (1994). *Troubled families, troubled children.* Chichester, England: Wiley.

Webster-Stratton, C., Kolpacoff, M., & Hollinsworth, T. (1989). The long-term effectiveness and clinical significance of three cost-effective training programs for families with conduct-problem children. *Journal of Consulting and Clinical Psychology, 57,* 550–553.

Webster-Stratton, C., & Spitzer, A. (1991). Development, reliability and validity of the daily telephone discipline interview: DDI. *Behavioral Assessment, 13,* 221–239.

Weinrott, M. R., Reid, J. B., Bauske, R. W., & Brummett, B. (1981). Supplementing naturalistic observations with observer impressions. *Behavioral Assessment, 3,* 151–159.

Wells, K. C., & Egan, J. (1988). Social learning and systems family therapy for childhood oppositional disorder: Comparative treatment outcome. *Comprehensive Psychiatry, 29,* 138–146.

White, J. H., Moffit, T., Earls, F. & Robins, L. (1990). Preschool predictors of persistent conduct disorders and delinquency. *Criminology, 28,* 443–454.

Chapter 6 ─────────────────────────────

FEEDING DISORDERS OF INFANCY AND EARLY CHILDHOOD

MaryLouise E. Kerwin
Nancy Hale Sills

OVERVIEW

Nutrition is critical for brain growth and development, especially before age 2. (Ashem & Jones, 1978). Adequate nutrition is assured by a variety of factors, ranging from physiological to family systems. The diagnoses of feeding disorders require assessment of these myriad variables for effective intervention. The fourth edition of the *Diagnostic and Statistical Manual of Mental Disorders* (*DSM-IV;* American Psychiatric Association [APA], 1994) categorizes feeding disorders of infancy and early childhood into three diagnoses: Pica, Rumination Disorder, and Feeding Disorder of Infancy or Early Childhood. All three diagnoses are prevalent in young children and individuals with developmental delays and mental retardation. Each of these feeding problems can affect the individual's nutrition and health as well as cognitive development, emotional development, and social relationships. In addition to the consequences for the individual, the parents of children with feeding abnormalities may feel helpless and distraught when faced with these problems. This chapter reviews the diagnostic criteria, assessment, and treatment of each diagnosis separately. Social workers will benefit from familiarity with these feeding disorders to facilitate appropriate referrals for evaluation and treatment, and to provide supportive counseling to parents.

PICA

According to the diagnostic criteria delineated in *DSM-IV* (APA, 1994), pica refers to (a) the ingestion of nonnutritive substances for at least 1 month, when (b) the ingestion is inappropriate to the developmental level, and (c) the ingestion is not part of a culturally sanctioned practice. Other definitions have included unusual, compulsive cravings for food and nonfood items (Abu-Hamden, Sondheimer, & Mahajan, 1985) and the excessive eating of food and food-related substances (Crosby, 1971). This chapter will utilize the *DSM-IV* criteria of nonfood items as the definition of pica. Common inedible objects consumed in pica are cigarette butts, feces, paper, paint chips, hair, and cloth.

Pica is most prevalent in young children, individuals with mental retardation, and pregnant women (Feldman, 1986). Young children (under the age of 3) often mouth objects and are, therefore, at risk for pica. One serious outcome of mouthing objects or engaging in pica is lead poisoning. Children most at risk for the ingestion of lead are children living in older homes, not children of lower income levels (Lacey, 1993). For individuals with mental retardation living in institutions, prevalence estimates of pica vary from 15.5% to 21%, with an inverse relationship between intelligence test scores and frequency of pica (Danford & Huber, 1982). In some cultures, dirt and clay are eaten by pregnant women for their proported medicinal value in treating nausea, vomiting, and diarrhea or for personal and symbolic connotations (Reid, 1992). Even though a substance is used in a cultural context, it does not mean that the ingestion of that substance is harmless.

Pica can be associated with serious health problems including, but not limited to, intestinal obstruction, poisoning, nicotine toxicity, lead poisoning, and parasitism (Lacey, 1993). Pica resulting in the ingestion of even low levels of lead can have serious side effects, including delayed cognitive development, reduced IQ, impaired hearing, kidney problems, impaired regulation of vitamin D, and decreased synthesis of heme in red blood cells (Agency for Toxic Substances and Disease Registry, 1988).

Assessment

Individuals most at risk for pica are not likely to self-report pica due to limited speech. Therefore, the assessment of pica is typically accomplished through direct observation not only of the pica, but also the events that precede the pica (antecedents) and the events that come after the pica (consequences). For research purposes, pica has been operationalized as the placing of a nonfood item on or past the lips (Finney, Russo, & Cataldo, 1982). A potential disadvantage of direct observation is that of interrupting the pica response by removing the inedible object from the individual before it is consumed. The attention generated by removing the object is now another potential consequence of the pica, thereby contaminating the observation. By baiting the environment with edible items resembling nonfood items (for example, using flour and water to make "paint chips"), pica can be observed safely under naturally occurring conditions without interrupting the pica (Fisher et al., 1994).

According to Mace, Lalli, and Lalli (1991), pica and other aberrant behaviors may be maintained by the positive attention received, the sensory or perceptual consequences of the behavior, the avoidance of a difficult task, and the events that precede the behavior. Bauer, Shea, and Gaines (1988) describe a comprehensive, multistage methodology for conducting a functional analysis of pica.

Treatment

There are two major theories describing the etiology of pica: *nutritional* and *environmental*. The first theory suggests that individuals engage in pica as a result of mineral or nutritional deficiencies in the diet, specifically of zinc (Chisholm & Martin, 1981) and iron (Arbiter & Black, 1991). For those individuals with documented nutritional or mineral deficiencies, dietary changes and mineral supplements have resulted in decreases in pica (Arbiter & Black, 1991; Lofts, Schroeder, & Maier, 1990).

Although nutritional alterations and supplementation have decreased pica for some individuals, the explanation for this effect is unclear. Specifically, does the nutritional deficit cause pica or do the dietary changes resulting from pica produce nutritional deficits? The process may be circular. For example, the underlying state of malnutrition produces dietary iron deficiency in individuals who consume clay in third world countries; however, increased ingestion of clay also inhibits iron absorption. The effect of nutrition on pica is a promising area for future research, especially in light of animal studies demonstrating that pica can be induced in rats through mineral deprivation (Snowdon, 1977) and through the repeated injection of small doses of an intestinal hormone that purportedly produces gastric distress (McCutcheon, Ballard, & McCaffrey, 1992).

A second theory proposes that pica results from persistent hand-mouth behavior, which becomes a learned behavior (Robischon, 1971). As a result, the majority of interventions utilized for pica manipulate the consequences for pica and nonpica behavior. In their review of the literature, Bell and Stein (1992) classified behavioral interventions into broad categories: (a) application of either a jacket or mask to prevent hand-mouth behavior; (b) overcorrection (repetitive sequence of spitting out the nonfood item, toothbrushing, personal hygiene, picking up trash, and emptying the trash can); (c) holding the arms for 10 seconds after each occurrence of pica; and (d) application of an aversive substance such as ammonia, lemon juice, or facial screen after each occurrence of pica.

Self-protection devices (for example, the mask) decreased pica, but also decreased social interaction between the individual and other people (Rojahn, Schroeder, & Mulick, 1980). Of the remaining techniques, overcorrection appears to be the least effective. In general, pica returns once overcorrection is stopped; the effects of overcorrection do not generalize to other settings; and overcorrection does not eliminate the precursors to pica (for example, searching and picking). In contrast, the contingent application of physical restraint or any other stimuli (for example, the facial screen) decrease pica; the effects generalize to other settings; and the effects are maintained without using these procedures for as long as 2 years.

Positive behavioral interventions for pica have included attempts to train discrimination of food and nonfood items and the differential reinforcement of an acceptable behavior (for example, work behavior or gum chewing). Discrimination training alone was ineffective in decreasing the pica of 3 toddlers with lead poisoning; however, the addition of differential reinforcement resulted in a rapid decrease in pica (Madden, Russo, & Cataldo, 1980a). Unfortunately, these results have not been replicated and punishment procedures were needed to decrease pica (Finney et al., 1982; Fisher et al., 1994).

Other theories suggest that pica results from stress (Bithoney, Snyder, Michalek, & Newberger, 1985) or a lack of stimulation in the environment (Madden, Russo, & Cataldo, 1980b). Agarwala and Bhandari (1994) taught progressive relaxation in combination with self-management to 4 women who craved chalk and mud. Pica was eliminated and did not return for 6 months. Similarly, when individuals with profound mental retardation and pica were placed in an enriched environment and toy-holding was reinforced, pica was reduced and replaced with chewing on toys (Favell, McGimsey, & Schell, 1982). Mace and Knight (1986) analyzed pica as a function of staff interaction and protective equipment in individuals with mental retardation who were living in an institution. Pica was lowest when increased interaction with the staff was combined with no protective equipment. Staff initiated more interactions when the client was not wearing a helmet. In conclusion, these results indicate that enriching the environment with social interaction and alternative activities may decrease pica in individuals with mental retardation who are in institutions. The generalizability of these effects to young children has not yet been investigated.

In summary, pica appears to be associated with or caused by a variety of factors, including diet and nutrition, developmental functioning, environment, and pregnancy. Assessment should begin with a screening to explore possible nutritional deficits. The assessment should then include a thorough functional analysis of the pica, attending to those aspects of the environment that may be contributing to the pica (level of enrichment, amount of social interaction, and use of protective equipment). Intervention should manipulate these environmental variables before attempting to target the pica directly with behavioral interventions. Less restrictive interventions should be attempted before more aversive alternatives; therefore, differential reinforcement of nonpica behavior should be attempted before a punishment procedure. If needed, punishment procedures should be implemented in conjunction with reinforcement of appropriate, nonpica behavior.

RUMINATION DISORDER

According to *DSM-IV,* Rumination Disorder is defined as "repeated regurgitation and rechewing of food for a period of at least one month following a period of normal functioning, not due to an associated gastrointestinal or other medical condition" (APA, 1994, p. 98). Rumination Disorder should not be diagnosed when the rumination occurs exclusively during periods of anorexia nervosa or bulimia nervosa. In individuals with mental retardation or pervasive developmental disorder, Rumination Disorder should be diagnosed when the rumination is severe enough to warrant independent clinical attention.

Two populations are more likely to experience rumination disorder: (a) typically developing infants, for whom rumination emerges between 3 and 12 months of age; and (b) individuals with mental retardation, for whom rumination disorder is recognized at a mean of 5.7 years (Mayes, 1992). Boys outnumber girls by 3.7:1 among infants and 3:1 among individuals with mental retardation. Among infants, the prevalence of rumination has not been estimated. For individuals with mental retardation who are living in institutions, prevalence estimates of rumination are 8% (Johnston, 1993). Although not common, rumination has been observed in adults (Tamburrino, Campbell, Franco, & Evans, 1995).

Historically, rumination has been associated with weight loss, growth retardation, malnutrition, dehydration, aspiration, tooth decay and erosion, anemia, electrolyte imbalance, and even death (Johnston, 1993). As a function of medical advances, mortality rates appear to be declining among infants while the number of individuals for whom nutrition and growth problems are not as critical is increasing (Mayes, 1992). In addition to the physical effects, rumination may also have social consequences. Rumination detracts from the individual's appearance and can be a barrier to social interaction with parents and peers.

Three major causes of rumination have been hypothesized: (a) organic, (b) emotional deprivation, and (c) environmental (Johnston, 1993). Rumination may be a function of a physiologic cause, such as hiatal hernia, intestinal obstruction, pyloric stenosis, or gastroesophageal reflux (Herbst, Friedland, & Zboralske, 1971). In contrast, rumination is also believed to result from a disturbance in the parent-child relationship for infants, and from a lack of environmental stimulation for individuals with mental retardation (Mayes, 1992). Although *DSM-IV* criteria specify the exclusion of organic causes, differential diagnosis may be complicated. Recent research suggests that the physiological basis for rumination may be underestimated in individuals with mental retardation (Rogers, Stratton, Victor, Kennedy, & Andres, 1992). Of individuals diagnosed with both rumination disorder and mental retardation, 91% had undiagnosed gastrointestinal problems, and 83% had oropharyngeal dysfunctions (that is, pharyngeal and esophageal dysmotility) documented via radiographic techniques.

Assessment

Medical evaluation should be a first step in the assessment of rumination. Typical medical tests include an upper gastrointestinal series, milk scan, pH probe, and endoscopy. When the medical tests are not definitive, clinical observation and a detailed history must inform the differential diagnosis. Rumination must also be discriminated from operant vomiting. Although both Rumination Disorder and operant vomiting are learned responses, in operant vomiting the vomitus is expelled from the mouth, while in rumination the rumitus is played with in the mouth and reswallowed (Johnston, 1993).

As with pica, the most reliable method of assessment is direct observation. The ruminative cycle may begin with the manual stimulation of the gag reflex, pitching forward, specific movements of the head and neck, or no noticeable movements. Regardless of the facilitating movements that begin the cycle, observers should detect enlarged or bulging cheeks, chewing or reswallowing in the absence of food intake, or rumitus in the mouth (Johnston, 1993). Rumination tends to be highest immediately following a meal and decreases with time elapsed since eating (Mayes, 1992), although some individuals may continue to ruminate at low rates until the next meal.

Humphrey, Mayes, Bixler, and Good (1989) investigated the relationship between the frequency of rumination and a variety of environmental, interpersonal, and temporal variables in a boy with profound retardation. Low levels of rumination were associated with participation in school, receiving individual attention, and time spent with caregivers who liked interacting with the child. Rumination was less frequent as time elapsed after a meal, but increased across the day (more frequent at night than in the morning).

Treatment

Interventions for rumination can be classified as medical, dietary, behavioral, and psychosocial.

Medical.   When the ruminative behavior is unambiguously attributed to a physiological or anatomical cause, medical interventions are more likely to be employed. Examples of some medical interventions are positioning, medication, and surgery (Fleisher, 1994). Medical interventions range on a continuum from least to most conservative and are matched to each individual's needs. A review of the efficacy of these procedures is not in the purview of this chapter; however, many of these interventions can be effective for some individuals. The results documenting a relationship between physiological problems and Rumination Disorder suggest that medical interventions may be useful when combined with other treatment approaches (Rogers et al., 1992).

Dietary.   The most effective dietary manipulation for rumination is satiation. With satiation, the individual continues to eat from a full plate until three consecutive refusals of food despite persistent encouragement to eat and physical guidance back to the meal (Rast, Johnston, Drum, & Conrin, 1981). Most satiation procedures utilize large portions of carbohydrates.

The mechanism underlying the satiation procedure is not known; however, texture and caloric density influence the effectiveness of this procedure. Pureed foods increase rumination when compared to the same food of normal consistency (Johnston et al., 1990). Increasing calories without increasing the volume of food consumed corresponds to modest decreases in rumination (Rast, Johnston, Ellinger-Allen, & Drum, 1985). Similarly, Greene et al. (1991) found an inverse relationship between the rate of rumination and the amount of peanut butter consumed; however, this effect appears to be due to the increased number of calories, not to the consistency of the peanut butter.

In general, dietary manipulations reduce rumination, but the effects vary across individuals. In addition, rumination is likely to return when the procedure is discontinued. Inaccurate implementation of these procedures may also exacerbate the rumination. Eating larger quantities of food without achieving satiation may increase rumination (Rast, Ellinger-Allen, & Johnston, 1985). Finally, excessive weight gain is a possible consequence of satiation. Although low-calorie foods can be used (Johnston, Greene, Rawal, Vazin, & Winston, 1991), low-calorie diets are not associated with as large reductions in rumination as high-calorie diets.

Behavioral.   Starin and Fuqua (1987) reviewed behavioral interventions for rumination in individuals with mental retardation. The majority of behavioral interventions reviewed are punishment procedures, including squirting aversive-tasting substances into the individual's mouth during or immediately after rumination; oral hygiene; exercising after each occurrence of rumination; removal of a preferred event after rumination; and remaining in the setting to complete all required tasks despite rumination (extinction). The final type of behavioral intervention, differential reinforcement, is not punishment. With differential reinforcement of another response, rumination is ignored and the individual is given access to preferred events based on a more appropriate response (McKeegan, Estill, & Campbell, 1987; Mulick, Schroeder, & Rojahn, 1980). Although differential reinforcement decreased rumination in these studies, the use of edible reinforcers may have substituted an external food source for the internal food source ruminated. In addition, these studies often added extinction or controlled eating to the treatment package, making it difficult to evaluate the independent contribution of differential reinforcement.

Unfortunately, because of the complex variables maintaining rumination, the effects of behavioral interventions vary across individuals. Although these interventions may be effective, they require expert design, implementation, and monitoring, long-term application, and constant supervision of the individual.

Psychosocial. These interventions emanate from the theory that rumination in infants results from inadequate parenting (for review see Fleisher, 1994). Rumination is the infant's attempt to receive attention from parents who are not responding appropriately to the infant. As a result, treatment consists of techniques to facilitate attention and love. One typical technique is holding the infant, especially around mealtime (Whitehead & Schuster, 1981). Unfortunately, the effectiveness of these interventions cannot be evaluated because of the lack of experimental design. Although the published case studies do suggest some efficacy of these procedures, there is a variable confounding the interpretation of these results: holding the infant in an upright position. Positioning is a medical treatment used to decrease the symptoms of gastroesophageal reflux (Herbst et al., 1971). Shepherd, Wren, Evans, Lander, and Ong (1987) reported that 99% of infants experiencing gastroesophageal reflux (the backing up of stomach contents into the esophagus) could be diagnosed with rumination disorder. A review of the reported case studies of holding therapy reveals that most of the infants had some gastrointestinal abnormality documented by radiographic or other medical tests (Sauvage, Leddet, Hameury, & Barthelemy, 1985); however, these results were ignored due to observations of poor parenting.

In summary, dietary manipulation and satiation appear to be the most promising interventions because they are effective, easily administered, and minimally intrusive. However, recent research indicates that rumination disorder may have more of a physiological basis than was previously recognized. As a result, a thorough medical evaluation is dictated in addition to a functional analysis (Bauer et al., 1988).

FEEDING DISORDER OF INFANCY OR EARLY CHILDHOOD (FAILURE TO THRIVE [FTT])

Feeding Disorder of Infancy or Early Childhood culminates decades of research in failure to thrive (FTT). FTT is defined as a pattern of weight gain either below the 5th or 3rd percentile for chronological age or crossing two standard deviations (e.g., 50% to the 10%) on the National Center for Health Statistics growth charts (Hamill et al., 1979). FTT has traditionally been categorized as organic or nonorganic (Freud, 1946). *Organic FTT* refers to insufficient growth due to an underlying medical diagnosis, such as cystic fibrosis or metabolic disorder. *Nonorganic FTT* refers to poor growth caused by psychosocial factors, such as inadequate parenting, poverty, significant family stress, substance abuse, or parental psychopathology (Benoit, 1993).

DSM-IV criteria for Feeding Disorder of Infancy or Early Childhood (APA, 1994) reflect the distinction between organic and nonorganic FTT. The diagnostic criteria are: (a) failure to eat adequately with either significant failure to gain weight or weight loss over a minimum of one month; when (b) it is not due to a medical condition, an associated mental disorder or lack of food; and (c) onset occurs before age 6. For ease of presentation, FTT will be used here to represent the Feeding Disorder of Infancy or Early Childhood.

FTT typically begins before age 1 and affects boys and girls equally. Many infants with FTT are developmentally delayed and exhibit unusual behaviors and affect, such as depression and anger. FTT has historically been attributed to poor quality of the mother-child relationship (Freud, 1946). Although clinical observations of mothers of infants with FTT suggest a variety of psychological problems and interactional dysfunctions; controlled studies produce more conflicting results (Ramsay, Gisel, & Boutry, 1987).

Social workers are critical for identifying, assessing, and treating children with FTT and their families. Because social workers often work with families of children at risk, they are in a unique position to identify children who may be failing to thrive and who are not receiving regular medical supervision as well as those patterns of parent-child interactions that may place a child at risk for FTT. Social workers can provide assessment through interview and direct observation, especially in natural settings, such as the home. In addition, they design and implement effective interventions and provide guidance and support to parents to ensure the maintenance and generalization of these gains.

Assessment

Assessing inadequate growth is a simple process involving the measurement of a child's height and weight over at least a 1-month period. Determining the reason for or cause of poor growth is potentially more complex. Assessment should begin with medical tests to rule out metabolic or absorption problems that cause the body to not efficiently use sufficient calories. After medical explanations for FTT have been excluded, the social worker should assess the quality and quantity of food available to the child, the resources available to provide for the nutritional needs of the child (financial, physical space), the parent's level of concern about weight and feeding, and the possibility of neglect or abuse. These problems should be addressed before investigating more complex causes for FTT. If the feeding history includes early signs of discomfort and irritability related to feedings or dysfunctional feeding behavior, then a more focused assessment is needed.

The evaluation process should include a thorough medical and feeding history, medical and developmental testing, oral-motor evaluation, and clinical observation of feeding and nonfeeding situations (Stevenson & Allaire, 1991). Ideally, the assessment team should be comprised of the parents, a physician knowledgeable in medical variables impacting on feeding and development, a nutritionist, a developmental and oral-motor specialist (for example, a speech pathologist or occupational therapist), a social worker, and a psychologist (Chatoor et al., 1992).

Table 6.1 lists the components of the interview and assessment procedures. The literature on children with FTT emphasizes the mother-child interaction as the pri-

Table 6.1   Assessment of Feeding Disorders of Infancy or Early Childhood

Interview
- Parental concerns and interventions attempted
- Medical history (special emphasis on respiratory, gastrointestinal, elimination pattern, neurological, motoric, and allergic factors)
- Growth patterns (height, weight, and head circumference)
- Developmental milestones
- Eating (environment, meal behavior, and diet history)
- General behavior of child (attention, following rules or requests, aggression, independence, and communication)
- Parenting styles (discipline, limit setting, attention, consistency, and routines; include all caretakers and both parents)
- Psychosocial factors (family stressors or events, relationships, and supports)

Assessment
- Observation of feeding (utensils, food type and texture, meal routine, and interaction)
- Oral-motor skills and patterns
- Child's positioning and motoric functioning during eating
- Medical testing (pH probe, upper GI series, barium swallow, milk scan, and allergy testing)
- Observation of parent-child interaction across many situations

NOTE: It is crucial to involve all family members to gather information on family beliefs, experiences, and interactions involving the child.

mary focal point for assessment (Benoit, 1993). However, all caregivers may impact—either directly through interaction with the child, or indirectly through interaction with the mother—on the child's eating patterns, behavior, and emotional functioning (Drotar & Sturm, 1987). Excluding a primary caregiver, such as a father, may provide a skewed and potentially false impression of family relationships and interactions. In addition to parental report, direct observation of feeding provides a wealth of information, especially when a parent has limited abilities to report objectively what is happening at home. For the feeding observation, the parent is asked to bring food to the appointment, and to feed the child as he or she would feed the child at home. If possible, observer effects on the child should be minimized by watching the feeding interaction through a one-way mirror.

Treatment

Treatment for FTT focuses on the child, the parent, the parent-child dyad, and the family system or home environment.

Child.   Historically, hospitalization has been used to document the child's ability to gain weight out of the home environment (Berwick, Levy, & Kleinerman, 1982). However, this intervention has not guaranteed weight gain for all children (Powell, 1988), and the effects have not generalized to the home without additional interventions. In contrast, behavioral interventions have successfully improved eating of children with FTT (e.g., Koepke & Thyer, 1985). Behavioral techniques are typically paired with parent training, education, and supportive counseling to facilitate maintenance of gains (Benoit, 1993).

Parent.   Intervention for the parent of the child with FTT may include psychotherapy aimed at increasing the mother's emotional availability, decreasing stress by improving the quality of social support, increasing sense of competence as a parent, modifying the distorted perception of the child, and treating any affective disorders (Benoit, 1993). These interventions require parental introspection and motivation for change. Unfortunately, parents of children with FTT may not be willing to participate fully in this process (Benoit, Zeanah, & Barton, 1989).

Parent-Child.   Based on the theory that a disordered parent-child relationship creates and perpetuates FTT in the child, interventions addressing the parent-child relationship are psychodynamic or interactional (Chatoor et al., 1984). By improving parental responsiveness to the child's signals, it is thought that the child will have more success with eating. Chatoor et al. (1984) hypothesize that feeding disturbance and FTT result from problems in three developmental stages of feeding (attachment, individuation, and homeostasis); therefore, specific techniques of intervention are matched to the tasks of the failed stage. Although parent-child relationships are believed to cause FTT, the reliance on case studies and poorly controlled research designs limits the objective evaluation of the effectiveness of these procedures.

Family and Home.   Interventions that impact on the family system or home environment are multimodal. They include any of the previously mentioned approaches, as well as marital therapy, family therapy, problem solving about basic issues (such as financial resources, transportation, and housing), and substance abuse services (Bithoney et al., 1989). Unfortunately, the effect of these interventions on the child's FTT have not been documented in controlled studies (Black, Dubowitz, Hutcheson, Bernson-Howard, & Starr, 1995).

In summary, the only seemingly effective intervention for FTT involves behavioral intervention combined with parent training (Koepke & Thyer, 1985). The lack of documented effectiveness for other interventions may reflect the heterogeneity within this diagnosis. Many researchers have questioned FTT as a diagnostic label, stating that it is merely a set of symptoms caused by a variety of medical, developmental, psychosocial or environmental conditions (cf. Woolston, 1985; Boddy & Skuse, 1994). The analogy is that "high fever" is not a diagnosis on its own, but merely a symptom of an illness or disease. Unfortunately, the criteria for Feeding Disorder of Infancy or Early Childhood continue to reflect this false dichotomy between organic and nonorganic causes of FTT.

Recent literature suggests that some organic causes of FTT may be more subtle than was previously realized or acknowledged (Heffer & Kelley, 1994; Ramsay et al., 1993; Boddy & Skuse, 1994). Children diagnosed with FTT are more likely to have exhibited feeding difficulties during infancy than children growing adequately (Pollit & Eichler, 1976). In the literature describing psychosocial interventions for FTT, signs of possible organic abnormality are minimized in favor of problems in the parent-child relationship (cf., Chatoor et al., 1992; Drotar & Sturm, 1987). Although dysfunctional parent-child interactions are exhibited, they may not be the cause of the feeding difficulty or FTT. It is equally plausible that an organic feeding problem present at birth influenced the way parents interact with their child. Perhaps attention should be switched from FTT to the assessment and treatment of the underlying feeding problem.

FEEDING PROBLEMS

Linscheid (1983) estimates that 25% to 35% of all children exhibit a feeding problem at one time or another. These feeding problems may or may not result in failure to thrive. Luiselli (1989) proposes the following categorization of feeding problems in individuals with developmental disabilities: (a) food refusal, (b) food selectivity (eats only a few foods as entire diet), (c) limited food intake, (d) self-feeding deficits, (e) improper pacing (rapid or extremely slow), and (f) mealtime behavior problems (throwing food, temper tantrums, and aggression). In addition, the literature suggests specific neurologic or motoric feeding problems, including dysphagia (swallowing dysfunction) and oral-pharyngeal dysfunction (forming the food bolus and propelling it towards the back of the mouth to initiate the swallowing process) (Morris & Klein, 1987).

The final feeding problem mentioned by Luiselli (1989) is vomiting. With *psychogenic* vomiting, the vomiting is an attempt to control or manipulate the environment. For example, a child who vomits when her parent leaves may be vomiting to get her parent to return and pay attention to her. In contrast, *involuntary* vomiting has a physiological cause, such as gastroesophageal reflux. Thorough medical testing can rule out gastroesophageal reflux as the cause of vomiting.

Feeding problems are not mutually exclusive. Consider the hypothetical example of a 5-year-old girl. Carrie presents with improper pacing, which results in limited food intake, culminating eventually in failure to thrive. If the pace of the meal is faster, Carrie usually vomits. This example indicates the complex interdependence of both the feeding problems and the causes of the feeding problems. Suppose Carrie experiences gastroesophageal reflux, which is associated with heartburn. Because she only vomits when an adult controls the pace of the meal, her pediatrician has determined that the vomiting is psychogenic. An alternative hypothesis suggests that Carrie may be controlling the pace of the meal in an attempt to control her symptoms of gastroesophageal reflux. Therefore, increasing the pace of the meal may result in vomiting not because Carrie is responding to the control of the adult, but because the increased rate of food consumption results in increased frequency of gastroesophageal reflux episodes. Hyman (1994) hypothesizes that gastroesophageal reflux may cause more feeding problems than has been recognized previously.

Assessment

Feeding problems are assessed in the same manner as Feeding Disorder of Infancy or Early Childhood (see Table 6.1), with only a few exceptions. The child and parent responses during the feeding observation are recorded and quantified to identify the most problematic behaviors. The most common child responses recorded are bites of food consumed, number of bites refused for children being fed by an adult, number of bites expelled, number of bites swallowed, meal duration, and other negative responses (such as gagging, throwing utensils, and hitting) (Iwata, Riordan, Wohl, & Finney, 1982). Parent behaviors include verbal prompts to eat, rate of food presentation, and verbal and physical rewards and reprimands (Iwata et al., 1982). Munk and Repp (1994) extended this assessment paradigm by evaluating the child's feeding responses as a function of foods of different texture and type.

Treatment

Interventions for feeding problems target either the feeding skills of the child or the parent's reaction to the child's response. *Feeding skills of the child* refers to the ability to self-feed or accept the food into the mouth, to prepare the food bolus, and to swallow the food bolus. Behavioral interventions have been quite successful in improving self-feeding skills (Luiselli, 1991), in increasing food acceptance (Riordan, Iwata, Finney, Wohl, & Stanley, 1984), and even in increasing the number of times the child swallows food (Babbitt et al., 1994). These interventions are successful because the mealtime becomes a structured environment in which each bite is a trial and each eating response (acceptance, expelling food, and swallowing food) has clear consequences. Babbitt et al. (1994) and Luiselli (1989) provide comprehensive reviews of this literature.

Behavioral interventions are only effective if they address the child's oral-pharyngeal skills. These skills are sensitive to the position of the child, muscle tone abnormalities, texture or consistency of food or liquid, and the method of delivering the food or liquid (such as type of utensil or nipple). Wolf and Glass (1992) describe various interventions traditionally used to improve feeding; however, research investigating their effectiveness has not eliminated potential confounds in the experimental designs.

In most studies, the behavioral interventions are initially implemented by trained staff. Parents are introduced after acceptance increases. Using instruction, discussion, handouts, role-playing, behavioral rehearsal, verbal feedback, and periodic review of videotapes of themselves interacting with their children, parents have been trained to implement the procedures from the beginning of the intervention (Stark et al., 1993; Werle, Murphy, & Budd, 1993). However, parents were more effective in increasing acceptance and calories consumed after sequential instruction in differential attention, access to privileges dependent upon mealtime behaviors, setting realistic expectations of behavior at mealtime, and systematically introducing nonpreferred foods (Stark, Powers, Jelalian, Rape, & Miller, 1994).

These results highlight the importance of parental reactions and responses for the success of any intervention. Satter (1990) recommends a division of responsibility—the child is responsible for what to eat and parents are responsible for how much the child eats. "If a child must have food intake increased above the amount taken willingly, it is better to consider supplemental tube feeding or parenteral feeding than to increase the pressure of feeding and distort the feeding relationship." (Satter, 1990, p. S187). This quote highlights an area of controversy within feeding. Behavioral interventions have been documented to be effective across children and feeding problems (Babbitt et al., 1994); however, they are perceived to be artificially forcing a structure onto the parent-child relationship (Satter, 1990). In contrast, other interventions do not have reliable evidence of effectiveness. As a result, there is increased risk of the placement of a feeding tube. Threading a tube through the child's nose or surgically placing a gastric tube into the stomach is physically invasive to the child. Controlled research of both the effectiveness of interventions and of parental perceptions of interventions will assist in the resolution of this controversy.

Providing adequate nutrition is the most basic of tasks for parents. Not only is feeding a time to receive nutrition, it is also the primary source of social interaction and emotional development (Satter, 1990). Difficulties in this process can attack the parent's sense of ability and competence and the parent's perception of the child. This gradual, insidious undermining of the image of an effective parent may generalize to the parent's affect and emotional functioning and to the relationship with the child. Parenting skills, interaction patterns, emotional health, and marital relationships should be assessed and considered for intervention, while being careful not to assign blame. A promising line of research is one that encompasses the dynamic interplay of organic, developmental, behavioral, and interactional characteristics of the child and the parent. Heffer and Kelley (1994) offer a biopsychosocial model of feeding disturbance and FTT that takes into account child-specific variables (biological, emotional, and behavioral), family and environment variables (stress, financial resources, educational level, and supports), and parent-child interaction variables (reciprocity and response to cues) that interact to impact feeding and growth.

CONCLUSIONS

This review of the treatments for feeding disorders indicates similar hypotheses about the etiology of the three diagnoses within *DSM-IV:* Pica, Rumination Disorder, and Feeding Disorder of Infancy or Early Childhood. Specifically, each of these problems is caused by dysfunctional parent-child relationships. However, evidence increasingly suggests that organic factors may contribute more to these problems than has been recognized previously. Therefore, the assessment of each feeding problem should include a thorough medical and nutritional evaluation (cf. Fleisher, 1994). Social workers must utilize appropriate specialized professionals to observe and assess the child before diagnosing psychosocial causes. However, even if organic factors affect the feeding problem, the complexity of these problems warrants detailed evaluation of the child's skills, each parent's skills, and other psychosocial and environmental correlates. Behavioral interventions have been effective in improving the child's responses for each of these feeding problems. Parent training has been effective in maintaining these skills. Supportive counseling and interventions were needed to facilitate long-term maintenance and generalization of gains. Whether social workers participate actively in *developing* psychosocial and behavioral interventions for pica, rumination disorders, and feeding problems, they are crucial to the overall success of implementing treatments for each of these conditions.

REFERENCES

Abu-Hamden, D. K., Sondheimer, J. H., & Mahajan, S. K. (1985). Cautopyreiophagia. Cause of life-threatening hyperkalemia in a patient undergoing hemodialysis. *The American Journal of Medicine, 79,* 517–519.

Agarwala, S., & Bhandari, A. (1994). Modification of pica by progressive relaxation and self-management. Special section: Relaxation techniques and psychological management. *Journal of Personality and Clinical Studies, 10,* 37–43.

Agency for Toxic Substances and Disease Registry. (1988). *The nature and extent of lead poisoning in children in the United States: A report to Congress.* Washington, DC: U.S. Department of Health and Human Services.

American Psychiatric Association. (1994). *Diagnostic and statistical manual of mental disorders* (4th ed.). Washington, DC: Author.

Arbiter, E. A., & Black, D. (1991). Pica and iron-deficiency anaemia. *Child: Care, Health & Development, 17,* 231–234.

Ashem, B., & Jones, M. (1978). Deleterious effects of chronic undernutrition on cognitive abilities. *Journal of Child Psychology and Psychiatry, 19,* 23–31.

Babbitt, R. L., Hoch, T. A., Coe, D. A., Cataldo, M. E., Kelly, K. J., Stackhouse, C., & Perman, J. A. (1994). Behavioral assessment and treatment of pediatric feeding disorders. *Journal of Developmental and Behavioral Pediatrics, 15,* 278–291.

Bauer, A. M., Shea, T. M., & Gaines, H. (1988). Primer on self-injury. *Education and Treatment of Children, 11,* 157–165.

Bell, K. E., & Stein, D. M. (1992). Behavioral treatments for pica: A review of empirical studies. *International Journal of Eating Disorders, 11,* 377–389.

Benoit, D. (1993). Phenomenology and treatment of failure to thrive. *Child and Adolescent Psychiatric Clinics of North America, 2,* 61–73.

Benoit, D., Zeanah, C. H., & Barton, D. L. (1989). Maternal attachment disturbances in failure to thrive. *Infant Mental Health Journal, 10,* 185–202.

Berwick, D., Levy, J., & Kleinerman, R. (1982). Failure to thrive: Diagnostic yield of hospitalization. *Archives of Disease in Children, 57,* 347–351.

Bithoney, W., McJunkin, J., Michalek, J., Egan, H., Snyder, J., & Munier, A. (1989). Prospective evaluation of weight gain in both non-organic and organic failure to thrive children: An outpatient trial of a multi-disciplinary team intervention strategy. *Journal of Development and Behavioral Pediatrics, 10,* 27–31.

Bithoney, W. G., Snyder, J., Michalek, J., & Newberger, E. H. (1985). Childhood ingestion as symptoms of family distress. *American Journal of Diseases in Children, 139,* 456–459.

Black, M. M., Dubowitz, H., Hutcheson, J., Bernson-Howard, K., & Starr, R. J. (1995). A randomized clinical trial of home intervention for children with failure to thrive. *Pediatrics, 95,* 807–614.

Boddy, J. M., & Skuse, D. H. (1994). The process of parenting in failure to thrive. *Journal of Child Psychology & Psychiatry & Allied Disciplines, 35,* 401–424.

Chatoor, I., Dickson, L., Schaefer, S., Egan, J., Connors, C., & Long, N. (1984). Pediatric assessment of nonorganic failure to thrive. *Pediatric Annals, 13,* 844–851.

Chatoor, I., Kerzner, B., Zorc, L., Persinger, M., Simenson, R., & Mrazek, D. (1992). Two-year-old twins refuse to eat: A multidisciplinary approach to diagnosis and treatment. *Infant Mental Health Journal, 13,* 252–268.

Chisholm, J. C., & Martin, H. I. (1981). Hypozincemia, ageusia, dysosmia, and toilet tissue pica. *Journal of the National Medical Association, 73,* 163–164.

Crosby, W. H. (1971). Food pica and iron deficiency. *Archives of Internal Medicine, 127,* 960–961.

Danford, D. E., & Huber, A. M. (1982). Pica among mentally retarded adults. *American Journal of Mental Deficiency, 87,* 141–146.

Drotar, D., & Sturm, L. (1987). Paternal influences in nonorganic failure to thrive: Implications for management. *Infant Mental Health Journal, 8,* 37–50.

Favell, J. E., McGimsey, J. F., & Schell, R. M. (1982). Treatment of self-injury by providing alternate sensory activities. *Analysis and Intervention in Developmental Disabilities, 2,* 83–104.

Feldman, M. D. (1986). Pica: Current perspectives. *Psychosomatics, 27,* 519–523.

Finney, J. W., Russo, D. C., & Cataldo, M. F. (1982). Reduction of pica in young children with lead poisoning. *Journal of Pediatric Psychology, 7,* 197–207.

Fisher, W. W., Piazza, C. C., Bowman, L. G., Kurtz, P. F., Sherer, M. R., & Lachman, S. R. (1994). A preliminary evaluation of empirically derived consequences for the treatment of pica. *Journal of Applied Behavior Analysis, 27,* 447–457.

Fleisher, D. R. (1994). Functional vomiting disorders in infancy: Innocent vomiting, nervous vomiting, and infant rumination syndrome. *The Journal of Pediatrics, 125,* S84–S94.

Freud, A. (1946). The psychoanalytic study of infantile feeding disturbances. *Psychoanalytic Study of the Child, 2,* 119–132.

Greene, K. S., Johnston, J. M., Rossi, M., Rawal, A., Winston, M., & Barron, S. (1991). Effects of peanut butter on ruminating. *American Journal of Mental Retardation, 95,* 631–645.

Hamill, P., Drizd, T., Johnson, C., Reed, R., Roche, A., & Moore, W. (1979). Physical growth: National Center for Health Statistics percentiles. *American Journal of Clinical Nutrition, 32,* 607–629.

Heffer, R. W., & Kelley, M. L. (1994). Non-organic failure to thrive: Developmental outcomes and psychosocial assessment and intervention issues. *Research in Developmental Disabilities, 15,* 247–268.

Herbst, J., Friedland, G. W., & Zboralske, F. F. (1971). Hiatal hernia and "rumination" in infants and children. *The Journal of Pediatrics, 78,* 261–265.

Humphrey, F. J., Mayes, S. D., Bixler, E. O., & Good, C. (1989). Variables associated with frequency of rumination in a boy with profound mental retardation. *Journal of Autism and Developmental Disorders, 19,* 435–447.

Hyman, P. E. (1994). Gastroesophageal reflux: One reason why baby won't eat. *The Journal of Pediatrics, 125,* S103–S109.

Iwata, B. A., Riordan, M. M., Wohl, M. K., & Finney, J. W. (1982). Pediatric feeding disorders: Behavioral analysis and treatment. In P. J. Accardo (Ed.), *Failure to thrive in infancy and early childhood: A multidisciplinary approach* (pp. 297–329). Baltimore: University Park Press.

Johnston, J. M. (1993). Phenomenology and treatment of rumination. *Child and Adolescent Psychiatric Clinics of North America, 2,* 93–107.

Johnston, J. M., Greene, K., Rawal, A., Vazin, T., & Winston, M. (1991). Effects of caloric level on ruminating. *Journal of Applied Behavior Analysis, 24,* 597–603.

Johnston, J. M., Greene, K., Vazin, T., Winston, M., Rawal, A., & Chuang, S. (1990). Effects of food consistency on ruminating. *Psychological Reports, 40,* 609–618.

Koepke, J., & Thyer, B. (1985). Behavioral treatment of failure-to-thrive in a two year old. *Child Welfare, 64,* 511–516.

Lacey, E. P. (1993). Phenomenology of pica. *Child and Adolescent Psychiatric Clinics of North America, 2,* 75–91.

Linscheid, T. R. (1983). Eating problems in children. In C. E. Walker & M. C. Roberts (Eds.), *Handbook of clinical child psychology* (pp. 616–639). New York: Wiley.

Lofts, R. H., Schroeder, S. R., & Maier, R. H. (1990). Effects of serum zinc supplementation on pica behavior of persons with mental retardation. *American Journal of Mental Retardation, 95,* 103–109.

Luiselli, J. K. (1989). Behavioral assessment and treatment of pediatric feeding disorders in developmental disabilities. In M. Hersen, R. M. Eisler, & P. M. Miller (Eds.), *Progress in behavior modification* (Vol. 24, pp. 91–131). Newbury Park, CA: Sage.

Luiselli, J. K. (1991). Acquisition of self-feeding in a child with Lowe's Syndrome. *Journal of Developmental and Physical Disabilities, 3,* 181–189.

Mace, C. F., & Knight, D. (1986). Functional analysis and treatment of severe pica. *Journal of Applied Behavior Analysis, 19,* 411–416.

Mace, C. F., Lalli, J. S., & Lalli, E. P. (1991). Functional analysis and treatment of aberrant behavior. *Research in Developmental Disabilities, 12,* 155–180.

Madden, N. A., Russo, D. C., & Cataldo, M. F. (1980a). Behavioral treatment of pica in children with lead poisoning. *Child Behavior Therapy, 2,* 67–81.

Madden, N. A., Russo, D. C., & Cataldo, M. F. (1980b). Environmental influences on mouthing in children with lead intoxication. *Journal of Pediatric Psychology, 5,* 207–216.

Mayes, S. D. (1992). Rumination disorder: Diagnosis, complications, mediating variables, and treatment. In B. B. Lahey & A. E. Kazdin (Eds.), *Advances in clinical child psychology* (Vol. 14, pp. 223–261). New York: Plenum Press.

McCutcheon, B., Ballard, M., & McCaffrey, R. J. (1992). Intraperitoneally injected cholecystokinin-octapeptide activates pica in rats. *Physiology & Behavior, 51,* 543–547.

McKeegan, G. F., Estill, K., & Campbell, B. (1987). Elimination of rumination by controlled eating and differential reinforcement. *Journal of Behavior Therapy and Experimental Psychiatry, 18,* 143–148.

Morris, S. E. & Klein, M. D. (1987). *Pre-feeding skills.* Tucson, AZ: Therapy Skill Builders.

Mulick, J. A., Schroeder, S. R., & Rojahn, J. (1980). Chronic ruminative vomiting: A comparison of four treatment procedures. *Journal of Autism and Developmental Disorders, 10,* 203–213.

Munk, D. D., & Repp, A. C. (1994). Behavioral assessment of feeding problems of individuals with severe disabilities. *Journal of Applied Behavior Analysis, 27,* 241–250.

Pollit, E., & Eichler, A. W. (1976). Behavioral disturbances among failure to thrive children. *American Journal of Disabled Children, 130,* 24–29.

Powell, G. F. (1988). Nonorganic failure to thrive in infancy: An update of nutrition, behavior, and growth. *Journal of the American College of Nutrition, 7,* 345–353.

Ramsay, M., Gisel, G., & Boutry, M. (1993). Non-organic failure to thrive: Growth failure secondary to feeding skills disorder. *Developmental Medicine & Child Neurology, 35,* 285–297.

Rast, J., Ellinger-Allen, J. A., & Johnston, J. M. (1985). Dietary management of rumination: Four case studies. *American Journal of Clinical Nutrition, 42,* 95–101.

Rast, J., Johnston, J. M., Drum, C., & Conrin, J. (1981). The relation of food quantity to rumination behavior. *Journal of Applied Behavior Analysis, 14,* 121–130.

Rast, J., Johnston, J. M., Ellinger-Allen, J., & Drum, C. (1985). Effects of nutritional and mechanical properties of food on ruminative behavior. *Journal of Experimental Analysis of Behavior, 44,* 195–206.

Reid, R. (1992) Cultural and medical perspectives on geophagia. *Medical Anthropology, 13,* 337–351.

Riordan, M. M., Iwata, B. A., Finney, J. W., Wohl, M. K., & Stanley, A. E. (1984). Behavioral assessment and treatment of chronic food refusal in handicapped children. *Journal of Applied Behavior Analysis, 17,* 327–341.

Robischon, P. (1971). Pica practice and other hand-mouth behavior and children's developmental level. *Nursing Research, 20,* 4–16.

Rogers, B., Stratton, P., Victor, J., Kennedy, B., & Andres, M. (1992). Chronic regurgitation among persons with mental retardation: A need for combined medical and interdisciplinary strategies. *American Journal of Mental Retardation, 96,* 522–527.

Rojahn, J. Schroeder, S. R., & Mulick, J. A. (1980). Ecological assessment of self-protective devices in three profoundly retarded adults. *Journal of Autism and Developmental Disorders, 10,* 59–66.

Satter, E. (1990). The feeding relationship: Problems and interventions. *Journal of Pediatrics, 117,* S181–S189.

Sauvage, D., Leddet, I., Hameury, L., & Barthelemy, C. (1985). Infantile rumination: Diagnosis and follow-up study of twenty cases. *Journal of the American Academy of Child Psychiatry, 24*, 197–203.

Shepard, R. W., Wren, J., Evans, S., Lander, M., & Ong, T. H. (1987). Gastroesophageal reflux in children: Clinical profile, course, and outcome with active therapy in 126 cases. *Clinical Pediatrics, 26*, 55–60.

Snowdon, C. T. (1977). A nutritional basis for lead pica. *Physiology & Behavior, 18*, 885–893.

Starin, S. P., & Fuqua, R. W. (1987). Rumination and vomiting in the developmentally disabled: A critical review of the behavioral, medical, and psychiatric treatment research. *Research in Developmental Disabilities, 8*, 575–605.

Stark, L. J., Knapp, L. G., Bowen, A. M., Powers, S. W., Jelalian, E., Evans, S., Passero, M. A., Mulvihill, M. M., & Hovell, M. (1993). Increasing caloric consumption in children with cystic fibrosis: Replication with 2-year follow-up. *Journal of Applied Behavior Analysis, 26*, 435–450.

Stark, L. J., Powers, S. W., Jelalian, E., Rape, R. N., & Miller, D. L. (1994). Modifying problematic mealtime interactions of children with cystic fibrosis and their parents via behavioral parent training. *Journal of Pediatric Psychology, 19*, 751–768.

Stevenson, R. D., & Allaire, J. H. (1991). The development of normal feeding and swallowing. *Pediatric Clinics of North America, 38*, 1439–1453.

Tamburrino, M. B., Campbell, N. B., Franco, K. N., & Evans, C. L. (1995). Rumination in adults: Two case histories. *International Journal of Eating Disorders, 17*, 101–104.

Werle, M. A., Murphy, T. B., & Budd, K. S. (1993). Treating chronic food refusal in young children: Home-based parent training. *Journal of Applied Behavior Analysis, 26*, 421–433.

Whitehead, W. E., & Schuster, M. M. (1981). Behavioral approaches to treatment of gastrointestinal motility disorders. *Medical Clinics of North America, 65*, 1397–1411.

Wolf, L. S., & Glass, R. P. (1992). *Feeding and swallowing disorders in infancy.* Tuscon, AZ: Therapy Skill Builders.

Woolston, J. (1985). Diagnostic classification: The current challenge in failure to thrive syndrome research. In D. Drotar (Ed.), *New directions in failure to thrive: Implications for research and practice* (pp. 225–235). New York: Plenum Press.

Chapter 7

ENURESIS AND ENCOPRESIS

John F. Butler
Rick L. Campise

OVERVIEW

The elimination disorders of enuresis and encopresis are common childhood problems and often are frequent presenting complaints for clinical social workers, primary care physicians and other mental health care professionals. Both disorders
are truly family problems and therefore involve not only the child, but also his or
her adult caretakers. Social work actually has a long track record of involvement in
treating children with these disorders. For example, in the field of enuresis the
social work articles by Sluckin (1989), Young and Morgan (1973), Morgan and
Young (1972), Butler (1976a, 1976b), Jehu, Morgan, Turner, and Jones (1977), and
Ronen and Wozner (1995) are representative. With encopresis, those of Sluckin
(1975), Buchanan (1992) and Butler (1977) are representative.

This chapter presents an overview on the assessment and effective psychosocial
and pharmacological treatments for the elimination disorders of nocturnal enuresis
and encopresis. The focus is atheoretical and is primarily on clinical practice. Clinical assessment strategies for these disorders and the controlled research evidence
regarding effective treatments, demonstrated by experiments with randomized subject assignment, are highlighted. Thus, information on the human physiology of
these problems and the current theories relating to treatment will not be addressed.
The overall objective of the chapter is to offer contemporary practice guidelines for
social work clinicians based on the current empirical research evidence.

ENURESIS

The treatment of enuresis has a long and, at times, colorful history. Even prior to
Mowrer and Mowrer's (1938) demonstration that certain conditioning principles

could be utilized to treat nocturnal enuresis, other clinicians had similar ideas. In 1936, Svorlousk, a Russian scientist, published a report on a light device that would flash when a child wet (Forsythe & Butler, 1989). A German pediatrician, Pfaundler, developed equipment in 1902 that signaled when an infant was wet and applied this to cases of enuretic children (Forsythe & Butler, 1989). In ancient times, as early as 1500 B.C., childhood incontinence was mentioned in the Ebers papyrus (Norgaard & Djurhuus, 1993). Last, in the 18th century, drug therapies such as camphor, opium, ergot, and belladonna were routinely given to children to increase bladder muscle tone (Norgaard & Djurhuus, 1993).

According to the fourth edition of the *Diagnostic and Statistical Manual of Mental Disorders* (*DSM-IV,* American Psychiatric Association [APA], 1994), several criteria must be met for the diagnosis of Enuresis. The child must urinate either involuntarily or intentionally into clothing or bedding twice a week for at least 3 months, must have reached age 5 chronologically and developmentally, and the incontinence cannot be due to medication or a general medication condition.

While estimates vary, *DSM-IV* estimates that at age 5 about 7% of males and 3% of females have some type of enuresis. At age 10, the incidence decreases to about 3% for males and 2% for females, and at age 18 about 1% of males have enuresis (APA, 1994). In addition, *DSM-IV* recognizes two types of enuresis: *primary,* where the child has never been continent; and *secondary,* where enuresis develops after a period of continence. Last, after age 5, about 5% to 10% of children will have a spontaneous remission from enuresis.

Several authors have noted the social stigma associated with enuresis that often impacts social functioning and family life (Mellon & Houts, 1995; Houts, Berman, & Abramson, 1994). Studies have also found that children treated for enuresis demonstrate better adjustment on certain measures of self-control and peer relationships (Houts et al., 1994).

Assessment Methods

Although any assessment can have a variety of components, three areas have been suggested (Ciminero & Doleys, 1976; Doleys, 1978). These are a *medical evaluation,* the *clinical interview,* and some type of *baseline recording.*

In today's environment, any child presenting with the symptom of enuresis should be referred to a physician for a medical evaluation. Even though only about 3% to 5% of children may have a medical condition that will explain the enuresis, a medical screening is essential to rule out any pathology (Scott, Barclay, & Houts, 1992). Such conditions as urinary tract infections, nephritis, and diabetes can cause children to display poor bladder control (Mellon & Houts, 1995). As with other areas of practice, receiving medical clearance of the child prior to any intervention is the standard of care. In addition, either a pediatrician or a primary care physician who is knowledgeable about enuresis and encopresis is an essential consultant when practicing in this area. In exchange, establishing such a professional relationship may result in referrals for behavioral treatments from these physicians.

The clinical interview should include the family, the parents, and the child. It is certainly appropriate to structure the initial interview with the entire family and the parents and child alone.

In addition to the required medical evaluation, there are many potential areas of inquiry possible in a clinical interview, and a review of the literature indicates six important areas. First, the history of the problem, including previous attempts at treatment, should be obtained (Doleys, 1978). The onset and frequency of wetting behavior will aid in determining the type of enuresis (Scott et al., 1992). Specific questions concerning what interventions have been used and their results are often instructive, since possible misuses of urine alarms may be revealed (Mellon & Houts, 1995.)

The second area concerns family history, illnesses, and medical history. Children with enuresis may have a parent or sibling who is also enuretic (Scott et al., 1992). In fact, *DSM-IV* estimates that about 75% of enuretic children will have a first-degree biological parent who had enuresis. One study noted an association between a positive family history and attrition from treatment (Young & Morgan, 1973). Questions concerning medical history may indicate the coexistence of an illness that can produce bladder problems (Fielding & Doleys, 1988).

A third area concerns parental attitudes. The clinical interview should clarify the parents' reactions to enuresis and their current feelings regarding this behavior (Fielding & Doleys, 1988). Some parents may believe that the child should be able to control the wetting behavior and, thus, may be punishing the child (Mellon & Houts, 1995). In fact, Hague et al. (1981) surveyed parents and found that about one third punished their child for bed-wetting.

Another area is that of behavior problems. Scott et al. (1992) noted that children having conduct problems might be likely to relapse following treatment (Dishe, Yule, Corbett, & Hand, 1983; Sacks, DeLeon, & Blackman, 1974). Thus, a careful assessment of this area is important. If noncompliance is an issue, then this must be given attention prior to any treatment for enuresis.

Specific attention to family circumstances is also needed. An assessment of the current family stresses, marital problems, and the home enviroment in general is extremely important (Mellon & Houts, 1995). Increased family stress has also been found to predict relapse (Scott et al., 1992). If the urine alarm is used as the treatment of choice, the participation of parents is critical to successful treatment.

The last are of inquiry highlighted by many authors focuses on obtaining a baseline of wetting behavior prior to treatment. Several authors have recommended that a 2- to 3-week baseline be obtained prior to treatment (Barclay & Houts, 1995; Fielding & Doleys, 1988; Doleys 1978; Mellon & Houts, 1995). Such baseline recording is important for several reasons. First, the baseline will serve as a standard to evaluate the success of treatment. Second, this recording may reveal if the child is a multiple wetter. Typically, a child who wets more than once a night may take longer to achieve being dry (Scott et al., 1992). A comprehensive handout for both clinicians and parents is available from chapter coauthor Campise that includes history, an overview of current functioning, recording charts, praise and reward handouts, a glossary, treatment resources, and references.

The overall goal in the clinical interview is to obtain medical clearance of the child and to adequately assess if the parents can, in fact, carry out the treatment regimen. Especially in the case of the urine alarm, which often involves 10 or more weeks of treatment, the essential question is whether the parents can follow through on the selected treatment. If there are any circumstances that might preclude this, then these issues must be addressed before beginning the treatment of enuresis.

Effective Interventions

As stated in the overview, the focus of this section is to highlight the psychosocial, behavioral, and somatic treatments for nocturnal enuresis that can be supported by controlled research. Specifically, only those treatments studied with randomized assignment to treatment conditions and the presence of a control group are considered.

Houts et al. (1994) have provided a comprehensive review of 112 treatment groups and 53 placebo or control groups from 78 published controlled research reports on the effectiveness of psychological and pharmacological treatments for nocturnal enuresis. They compared several types of treatment, including psychological treatments (that is, the urine alarm) and several types of medication at posttreatment and follow-up. In addition, the efficacy of the interventions was studied after adjusting for the allegiance of the particular investigator. This is important, since past reviews have indicated that researcher preference does influence outcome (Houts et al., 1994). This article is the most comprehensive review to date of the empirical research on both the psychological and somatic treatments of nocturnal enuresis. Table 7.1 presents the mean percentages of children who stopped bed-wetting with different types of treatment.

Houts et al. (1994) concluded that at posttreatment and follow-up, children receiving psychological treatment (the bell and pad) were more likely to stop bed-wetting than those receiving no treatment or placebos. The adjusted percentage was also higher for various pharmacological treatments compared to controls, but there was no significant difference when compared to those children given a placebo (Houts et al., 1994). Both psychological and pharmacological treatments were more effective compared to controls, but psychological treatments were found to be more effective at posttreatment and follow-up than pharmacological treatments.

Substantiating the prior findings of researcher adherence to certain treatments affecting outcome, Houts et al. (1994) also found bias in favor of the particular treatment orientation of the researcher.

**Table 7.1   Percentage of Children Who Ceased Bed-Wetting
for Different Categories of Treatment**

Type of treatment	Number of groups	Ceased bed-wetting, %	
		M (SD)	Adjusted M
Posttreatment			
Psychological			
With urine alarm	46	66(25)	60
Without urine alarm	16	31(26)	34
Tricyclics	28	40(14)	39
Desmopressin	4	46(12)	46
Other medications	9	23(25)	25
Follow-Up			
Psychological			
With urine alarm	30	51(21)	44
Without urine alarm	11	21(26)	26
Tricyclics	12	17(18)	18
Desmopressin	3	22(17)	21
Other medications	5	13(10)	17

SOURCE: Houts, A. C., Berman, J. S. & Abramson, H. (1994). Effectiveness of psychiatric treatments for nocturnal enuresis. *Journal of Clinical & Consulting Psychology, 62,* 737–745. Used by permission.

As can be seen in Table 7.1, the greatest percentage of children who had stopped bed-wetting at posttreatment were those receiving the urine alarm alone or the medication desmopressin (60% versus 46%). Concerning follow-up, the best overall outcome was the urine alarm. Actually, the urine alarm resulted in the greatest percentage of children who ceased bed-wetting both at posttreatment and at follow-up.

Additionally, Houts et al. (1994) concluded that there was no significant difference between the subcategories of either psychological or pharmacological treatments. Specifically, at posttreatment or follow-up there was no difference between imipramine versus other tricyclic medications or between the urine alarm alone versus a package approach (using the urine alarm plus other components). The authors also concluded that the longer children received treatment, opposite findings held for treatment by medication. Here, the longer the treatment, the lower the rates of cessation of bed-wetting.

The results of Houts et al. (1994) offer no support for so-called *treatment packages* that include the basic urine alarm plus other behavioral procedures. However, given the rather high relapse rates for the urine alarm, the authors express caution in dismissing procedures to reduce relapse rates outright. Two such packages have been evaluated: *Dry Bed Training* (DBT) and *Full Spectrum Home Training* (FSHT).

Initially presented by Azrin, Sneed, and Foxx (1974) and Azrin and Foxx (1974), Dry Bed Training (DBT) involves four components (Barclay & Houts, 1995). In addition to the urine alarm, there is a nightly hourly waking schedule; overcorrection in the form of positive practice after accidents and prior to bedtime; and clean-liness training, where the child changes his or her wet clothing and linens. Scott et al. (1992) summarized the results of several controlled outcome studies of Dry Bed Training (DBT). DBT has been found to add to the effectiveness of the basic urine alarm. The waking schedule assists children to reach the treatment criteria more rapidly than those not using the schedule (Scott et al., 1992).

Full Spectrum Home Training (FSHT) is the second treatment package to be evaluated. Developed by Houts, Peterson, and Whelan, (1986), this treatment package has four components. Similarly to DBT, the basic urine alarm and clean-liness training are utilized. Also employed are retention control training, which rewards the child for postponing urination in a gradual fashion up to 45 minutes, and overlearning. Overlearning has the child consume about 16 ounces of water 1 hour before bedtime (Houts, 1995).

Recent work has employed a modification of overlearning where the amount of water consumed is gradually increased (Mellon & Houts, 1995). Outcome studies of FSHT have reported a significant reduction in relapse rates, 10% to 15% ver-sus about 40% with the urine alarm alone (Mellon & Houts, 1995; Barclay & Houts, 1995).

Practice Guidelines

1. Obtaining medical clearance of the child prior to treatment is the standard of care.

2. On the basis of strong research evidence, health care providers can suggest with confidence that parents or caretakers obtain treatment for their enuretic child rather than letting them outgrow the problem. Unfortunately, most children do not outgrow nocturnal enuresis (Houts et al., 1994).

3. The urine alarm has been successfully utilized as a treatment for nocturnal enuresis for over 50 years. The treatment outcome review by Houts et al. (1994) provides additional confirmation that the treatment of choice is a version of the urine alarm. This robust finding was true at posttreatment and follow-up.

4. The average length of treatment using the urine alarm is about 10 to 12 weeks; thus, it demands persistent parental involvement. A careful screen-ing of the adult caretakers is crucial to a successful outcome. Parental sup-port and coaching is also important. If it is determined that there are other significant problems that may prevent parents from focusing on the alarm, these should be addressed before treatment begins.

5. In spite of demonstrated effectiveness, relapse rates for the urine alarm remain a problem. Houts (1991) estimates this rate at about 35% to 41%. A meta-analysis of 15 studies ($N = 1,049$ children) found that the mean relapse

percentage was 33%; relapse ranged from 12% to 69% (Van Londen, Van Londen-Barentsen, Van Son & Mulder, 1995). The use of a package of procedures, such as DBT and FSHT, should thus be carefully considered. Some clinicians find it useful to start treatment with the urine alarm; after the criterion of dry nights is reached, other procedures such as overcorrection and positive practice can be suggested.

6. Arousibility appears to be a factor in the successful treatment of nocturnal enuresis (Barclay & Houts, 1995). Thus, it is important that the child wake up and turn off the alarm him- or herself.

7. Research and clinical practice indicate that children who are multiple wetters may take longer to respond to the urine alarm (Houts, 1991). Informing parents about this in advance is helpful.

8. In spite of the success of the urine alarm compared to other treatment, pharmacological treatment is often used first. In fact, insurance estimates are that about 38% of enuretic children and their parents will first seek out a physician and that about one third of these will initially receive medication (Houts, 1991). Thus, if persuasion or lobbying for the urine alarm is needed with physician or managed care colleagues, provide a reprint of the paper by Houts et al. (1994).

9. Regarding the criteria for success, most psychological approaches have used the criteria of stopping bed-wetting, with the results usually given as the percentage of children under study who reach a given criterion, such as 14 continuous dry nights (Butler, 1991). However, the research on somatic treatments has generally reported results on reductions of the frequency of wetting behavior (Houts et al., 1994).

10. Several commercial alarms are available that vary by cost. Inexpensive models (about $45) can be obtained from the JCPenney or Sears catalog. The product from JCPenney is called the Elexis® Wet Alert Bed Wetting Alarm (item number ZP 864-4486; $39.99). The Sears Health Care Catalog offers three devices, called the Palco Wet-Stop (item number 1313; $59.99), the Wee-Alert (item 1302; $89.99), and the Lite-Alert® (item number 1303; $114.99). The toll-free number for the Sears Health Care Catalog is 1-800-326-1750. Additional products can be obtained from Palco (1-800-346-4488), which produces a wearable alarm device called the Wetstop, with a buzzer by the child's ear ($65 plus tax and shipping).

11. In summary, psychotherapy for nocturnal enuresis continues to be dominated by behavioral treatment procedures, where the treatment of choice is a version of the urine alarm. While certainly successful, it is not a magical device that can be blindly applied without careful thought and assessment. Particularly critical are the motivation and compliance of the adult caretakers. Marital, family, or child behavior problems can significantly inter-

fere with the use of the urine alarm. If so, these must be addressed first. Relapse is often a problem and should be anticipated, and the use of a relapse prevention package such as DBT or FSHT should certainly be considered. Carefully applied, the urine alarm and relapse prevention procedures will prove very useful for many children and their families.

ENCOPRESIS

The term *encopresis* was first used in 1925 by Pototosky, but it was Weissenberg, in 1926, who recommended that *encopresis* serve as the fecal equivalent of *enuresis* (Walker, Kenning, & Faust-Campanile, 1989). Today, *DSM-IV* provides the standard for the diagnosis of Encopresis. *DSM-IV* requires the voluntary or involuntary passage of feces into inappropriate places at least once a month for a minimum of 3 months by an individual who has reached age 4 chronologically and developmentally. In addition, the fecal activity cannot be exclusively due to a medical problem (other than constipation) or be a response to medication (APA, 1994).

Encopresis is divided into two types by *DSM-IV*. The first type, *Encopresis with Constipation and Overflow Incontinence,* is characterized by the presence of constipation by history or during the physical examination, poorly formed feces, continuous leakage, the passage of small amounts of feces when toileting, and resolution of the incontinence after treatment of the constipation. The second type, *Encopresis without Constipation and Overflow Incontinence,* includes an absence of constipation by history or during the examination, feces of normal form and consistency, intermittent soiling, and, at times, the depositing of the feces in a prominent location.

With each type of encopresis, a further delineation is made that speaks to the history of the problem. The term *primary encopresis* is used if the person has never been successfully toilet trained, whereas *secondary encopresis* describes the return of fecal accidents after successful toilet training.

DSM-IV suggests that the prevalence rate for encopresis is 1% for 5-year-olds and decreases with age (APA, 1994). Researchers agree that encopresis is more common in boys, but some studies find the boy-to-girl ratio to be as low as 2 to 1 (Young, Brennen, Baker, & Baker, 1995) and as high as 6 to 1 (Levine, 1982).

Encopresis is a treatment issue for social workers and other mental health professionals. Young et al. (1995) suggests that encopresis can have a detrimental effect on parent-child relationships and the self-concept of children. Many parents delay seeking treatment for their child, ascribing the child's problem to laziness, inattention, poor hygiene, or stress rather than to a medical need (Benninga, Buller, Heymans, Tytgat, & Taminiau, 1994). The child's denial, hiding of soiled underwear, and resistance to clothing changes creates an emotionally charged atmosphere (Sprague-McRae, Lamb, & Homer, 1993). Parents of children with encopresis often vacillate between punitive responses, coaxing, bribing, coercing, and ignoring the child (Dawson, Griffith, & Boeke, 1990). It is not unusual for parents to occasionally lose control, use corporal punishment, or yell in response to an act of soiling (Fireman & Koplewicz, 1992). Parents and other family members resent the embarrassment and interruption of family activities caused by the fecal accidents (Becker, 1994). Self-esteem is impacted, and the child can be saddled with a legacy of shame (Owens-Stively, 1987).

Assessment Methods

Before considering the psychosocial assessment of a child for encopresis, a thorough medical exam must be performed to rule out disease, anatomical abnormalities, and constipation. For present purposes, the physiological etiology of encopresis will not be pursued and medical clearance is assumed.

Structured Clinical Interviews.   One of the best sources of information for the evaluation and treatment of encopresis is the clinical interview. Structured and semistructured interviews for assessing encopresis are typically developed by the therapists themselves. See Sprague-McRae (1990), and Campise (1993) for examples of such interviews.

Encopresis interviews typically cover a wide variety of areas related to toileting and the child's general well-being. These areas include previous medical and mental health evaluations or treatment for encopresis; current or recently discontinued medication; family toileting history; the child's ability to remove clothing, past and current urinary and fecal patterns, perception of the urge to defecate, and physical discomfort; response of the child and the family to accidents; past management attempts; motivation of the parents and the child; the child's compliance with commands; any history of unwanted sexual acts; and family relationships.

Rather than a specific interview geared to assess encopresis, some therapists use generic structured or semistructured diagnostic interviews, such as the Diagnostic Interview Schedule for Children (DISC; Costello, Edelbrock, & Costello, 1985), Interview Schedule for Children (ISC; Kovacs, 1985) or Child Assessment Schedule (CAS; Hodges, 1987). These generic interviews can then be supplemented with questionnaires specifically addressing encopresis, such as the History of Encopresis (HE) by Stark, Spirito, Lewis, and Hart (1990) or Levine and Barr's (1980) Encopresis Evaluation System (EES).

Rating Scales.   Most rating scales for fecal activity are generated by the therapists themselves and given to the parents and child to complete. Such scales typically include columns for the date and time of sittings, accidents, accident-free days, and medication. Examples of these rating scales can be found in Wright (1980), Campise, (1993), or Nolan and Oberklaid (1993).

Though not designed to produce information specifically about encopresis, many therapists also use a variety of assessment devices to obtain additional information about the child or the family. Information regarding the child is often obtained by having the parents complete the Child Behavior Checklist (CBCL; Achenbach, 1991a) or by requesting that a teacher complete the Teacher's Report Form (TRF; Achenbach, 1991b). Since family conflict and cohesion do, at times, contribute to treatment failures, therapists often use family assessment devices, such as the Family Adaptability and Cohesion Evaluation Scale II (FACES-II; Olson & Portner, 1983) or Family Environment Scale (FES; Moos & Moos, 1984). For the same reason, many therapists use assessment devices for marital satisfaction, such as the Marital Satisfaction Scale (MSS; Burnett, 1987) or Dyadic Adjustment Scale (DAS; Spanier, 1976).

Physiological Measures.   Biofeedback equipment is useful in detecting difficulties associated with encopresis. Loening-Baucke (1995) reported that 25% to 50% of children experiencing chronic constipation with or without encopresis display abnormal contraction of the external anal sphincter muscle during defecation. Benninga et al. (1994) found that a high percentage of children exhibit contraction rather than relaxation of the anal sphincter during defecation attempts. Loening-Baucke, Cruikshank, and Savage (1987) found a positive correlation between treatment outcome and the ability to relax the external sphincter muscle.

Effective Interventions

Over the years there have been a variety of treatments for encopresis, including behavioral programs, biofeedback, hypnosis, medication, dietary alterations, psychotherapy, play therapy, dream analysis, and hospitalization (Walker et al., 1989). Unfortunately, research on these treatments for the past 10 years has suffered from such methodological limitations as small sample sizes and an absence of comparison groups. Only rarely have randomized group treatment-outcome studies been performed.

Young et al. (1995) reported that early work in the assessment and treatment of encopresis was approached quite differently by the medical and mental health fields. Medical practitioners and researchers initially tended to see encopresis as a physiological problem and discounted the contributions of psychological factors (Stern, Prince, & Stroh, 1988). In contrast, mental health professionals focused upon the emotional, behavioral, and family factors contributing to the problem, or they saw encopresis as a disorder ripe for the judicious application of positive and negative reinforcers. Fortunately, most current assessment and treatment approaches take into account contributions from both the medical and mental health fields.

Behavioral Programs.   Behavioral programs for encopresis primarily focus upon the use of rewards to increase appropriate fecal behavior and negative consequences to decrease inappropriate fecal behavior. Many current behaviorally based encopresis programs are based upon Azrin and Foxx's (1974) procedures. Components of a behaviorally based program for encopresis may include pants checks, token systems, positive reinforcement, punishment, overcorrection or positive practice (sitting on the toilet for increasing amounts of time, or requiring the child to rapidly practice going to the bathroom 10 times after a soiling accident), stimulus control (prompted toilet sitting), stress management, self-monitoring, and charting.

Behavioral approaches to encopresis have shown positive results, with a success rate of 70% or better (Smith & Smith, 1993), but most studies are single case reports or consist of small samples with no control groups and are mostly anecdotal (Thapar, Davies, Jones, & Rivett, 1992). A pure behavioral study is difficult to find, because most current research takes into account the need for a combined medical and behavioral treatment. One primarily behaviorally based study possessing a large sample but no comparison group by Fireman and Koplewicz (1992) found that 85% of the 52 children who started their treatment program reached the criterion of being accident-free for 2 weeks by 28 days and found that 93% (14 of 15) of subjects chosen at random for a 1-year follow-up were still accident-free. For information on additional behavioral treatment regimens, see O'Brien, Ross, and Christophersen (1986) or Nolan, Debelle, Oberklaid, and Coffey (1991).

Combined Medical and Behavioral Treatment.   The use of both medical and behavioral components in treatments is now typical, with success rates for these programs of 63% to 93%. An excellent example of a combined medical and behavioral approach is Young et al.'s 1995 study, in which 38 children in an encopresis experimental group were compared with a nonclinical matched comparison group. Medical treatment began with an initial evacuation procedure, followed by an increase in dietary fiber and the daily use of a stool softener and a bulking agent. The psychological intervention consisted of four phases: (a) education and demystification (removing negative attributions for soiling and creating a consistent, positive, and supportive parental attitude), (b) behavior modification within the context of a structural family therapy paradigm (with scheduled toilet sittings; clean pants checks; small rewards for unsoiled clothing, appropriate toileting behaviors, and the size of bowel movements; overcorrection for soiling—changing own pants and cleaning mess made in bathroom; and charts for monitoring progress), (c) phasing out of rewards (making criteria for rewards increasingly more stringent), and (d) termination (emphasizing relapse prevention). Six months after treatment termination, 37% of children were accident-free; an additional 42% had one or fewer accidents per week; and 92% had experienced improvement.

In a randomly controlled study of 169 children assigned to either a behavior modification or a multimodal treatment (behavior modification plus laxatives), Nolan et al. (1991) found that the multimodal group (83 children) improved sooner, showed greater elimination of the problem at the 3-month follow-up (39% versus 12%) and the 12-month follow-up (51% versus 36%), and showed greater improvement (soiled no more than once per week) at the 3-month follow-up (47% versus 31%) and the 12-month follow-up (63% versus 43%).

There are a number of other useful studies that highlight the effectiveness of a combined treatment approach that bear mentioning despite their methodological weaknesses. Gleghorn, Heyman, and Rudolph (1991) performed a retrospective review of 45 patients and found that education, an initial evacuation, daily dosages of mineral oil, an increase in fluid intake, a high-fiber diet, habit training, and a reward system resulted in 93% of the children being without encopresis or constipation at the 6-month follow-up.

Stark, Owens-Stively, Spirito, Lewis, and Guevremont (1990) conducted a combined behavioral and medical management approach (education, enema clean-out, dietary fiber increase, toileting techniques, and behavioral child-management skills) with 18 children over 6 sessions, and at the 6-month follow-up only 2 of the 18 children continued to soil.

Biofeedback.   Children treated with biofeedback typically experience a recovery rate of 50% to 79% that is maintained at the 1-year follow-up. Such treatment typically consists of exercising the external sphincter muscle, training in discrimination of rectal sensations, and synchronizing the internal and external sphincter responses.

Loening-Baucke (1995) found that at the 4-year follow-up, 50% of successful biofeedback patients who had received two to six treatment sessions had recovered versus 62% of conventionally treated patients, which she attributed to the greater impairment in anorectal functioning in the biofeedback sample. Iwata, Iwai, Nagashima, and Fukata (1995) found their biofeedback treatment program to be effective in 12 of 13 patients (93%). Twice a day for 1 week, children watched a colored ellipse on a computer that represented the sphincter pressure they generated by squeezing their anal sphincter muscles. Cox, Sutphen, Borowitz, Dickens, and Singles (1994) found that 79% of the 13 standard medical care (SMC) children who also received one to six biofeedback sessions completely eliminated soiling, versus 49% for the 13 SMC-only children, at the 16-month follow-up. Loening-Baucke (1990) found, in a randomly assigned study with 19 children receiving 6 months of conventional treatment (laxatives, education, dietary changes, scheduled toileting, and charting) versus 22 children receiving conventional treatment and six sessions of biofeedback, that at the 1-year follow-up 50% of the biofeedback-treated patients were successful, versus 16% of the conventionally treated patients (successful being defined as less than two soiling episodes per month). Wald, Chandra, Gabel, and

Chiponis (1987) reported that in a study with 18 subjects, 67% of the children treated with biofeedback markedly improved or recovered after 1 year, compared with a 33% improvement rate in children who received conventional treatment (mineral oil) alone.

Though biofeedback has been proven to be effective, it has a few significant limitations. It depends upon sophisticated equipment and specialized personnel, and is intrusive in the sense that the training includes the insertion of a sensor into the anal canal or the attachment of electrodes around the anal canal opening. Loening-Baucke (1995) suggested that biofeedback therapy is more effective in patients who do not have anorectal malformations or congenital functional problems with the external sphincter.

Family Therapy.   In the early 1980s some individuals began to emphasize the family and family problems as a contributor to encopresis, and these issues became a focus of treatment. Walker et al. (1989) found much of the family therapy for encopresis to be ineffective; unfortunately, research during the past 10 years has focused on specific case studies and has lacked group comparisons. An example of a single-subject case is Roesler, Savin, and Grosz's (1993) use of family and play therapy to assist a 4-year-old with soiling who had been sexually abused. An unusual example of brief family therapy in which the family is not required for treatment is illustrated by Shapiro and Henderson (1992), who successfully treated 2 children in two sessions by treating the father, who was the person most distressed and motivated to change. Wells and Hinkle (1990) used a family systems approach (strategic and structural) to eliminate encopresis in 2 boys in ten sessions.

Other Treatments.   There are a number of other treatment approaches for encopresis, such as hypnosis, play therapy, and cognitive-behavioral therapy. Unfortunately, the treatment research in these areas consists of case reports or small samples lacking comparison groups. For examples of such encopresis studies, please consult Tilton (1980) for hypnosis; Feldman, Villanueva, Lanne, and Devoroede (1993) for play therapy; and Knell and Moore (1990) for cognitive-behavioral therapy.

Practice Guidelines

1. Prior to the psychosocial treatment of encopresis, it is essential that a physician rule out disease, anatomical abnormalities, and constipation. See Hyman and Fleisher (1994) for a listing of medical causes of encopresis.

2. Be sensitive to the issue of constipation, because it can sabotage the best psychosocial treatment plans. Stool frequency for 95% of children ranges from every other day to three times per day (Hatch, 1988). See Walker et al. (1989) for a description of the mechanics and signs of constipation.

3. A thorough clinical interview should be conducted using an interview of your own construction, an interview specifically designed to elicit information about encopresis (Sprague-McRae, 1990; Campise, 1993), or a generic child interview (CAS, DISC, or ISC) supplemented with an encopresis questionnaire (HE or EES). You may also wish to consider administering an assortment of other assessment devices if you desire more information about the child (CBCL or TRF), the family (FACES-II or FES), or the marriage (MSS or DAS).

4. Explain to the parents and the child that there are three phases to treatment with a different emphasis in each phase. During phase 1, establish a sitting schedule where the child sits on the toilet for 5 minutes after breakfast, lunch, and dinner. The breakfast sitting is very important, because the gastrocolonic reflex is most prominent just after this meal (Becker, 1994).

5. The parents and the child should be given a thorough explanation of the treatment and its effectiveness. Steege and Harper (1989) suggest that with chronic encopresis, parental and child noncompliance can often be directly related to both the parents' and the child's lack of understanding of a recommended intervention or to their judgments about the effectiveness of the intervention.

6. Give the parents and the child a picture and an explanation of how the digestive process works, with the aim of neutralizing the guilt and anger both the parents and the child may feel by discussing the accidents as a function of physiology and habits (Sprague-McRae, 1990).

7. Have the parents and the child construct a daily chart on which they record the date and time of sittings, accidents, accident-free days, and medication.

8. Encourage the parents to develop a reward system for sitting behavior. The emphasis is not on bowel movements or on being accident-free. If sitting requires great effort, buy two toys that the child is allowed to play with only when sitting on the toilet. If the child continues to resist sitting, the toys lack the appropriate attraction value and should be replaced. Wright's (1980) excellent article on compliance reports that by adhering to the compliance guidelines, only 1 of the 500 patients studied failed to overcome encopresis.

9. Train the parents in the use of praise for each act of compliance and success by the child. Too often, commands, factual statements, and "yes, but"s are mistakenly given as praise.

10. The child should assume responsibility for changing him- or herself and for washing out the soiled clothing in an environment free from parental anger. An accident should be followed by time spent sitting in the bath to clean up.

11. Phase 2 begins after the child has been consistently sitting for a week. In phase 2, rewards are earned only for producing a movement when sitting on the toilet.

12. Phase 3 begins 1 week after the child consistently earns rewards for experiencing bowel movements on the toilet. In phase 3, the reward system is changed so that reinforcers are earned only for accident-free days.

13. Once the child has been accident-free for 2 weeks, begin to phase out the program by increasing the number of accident-free days required for rewards.

14. If constipation returns at any time during treatment, refer the child back to the physician and continue the program.

15. Children vary in the time they take to pass through the various treatment phases, but if there is an absence of progress in 2 months consider several alternatives. Biofeedback is not usually the first choice of therapists since it requires special training and equipment, but if the child fails conventional therapy biofeedback offers a positive rate of success. Another alternative is to examine the level of behavioral difficulties presented by the child and to address them, as well as to refer the parents to a parent training course to gain additional skills for dealing with the child's behavioral problems.

REFERENCES

Achenbach, T. M. (1991a). *Manual for the Child Behavior Checklist 4-18 and 1991 profile.* Burlington: University of Vermont, Psychiatry Department.

Achenbach, T. M. (1991b). *Manual for the Teacher's Report Form and 1991 profile.* Burlington: University of Vermont, Psychiatry Department.

American Psychiatric Association (1994). *Diagnostic and statistical manual of mental disorders* (4th ed.). Washington, DC: American Psychiatric Association.

Azrin, N., & Foxx, R. (1974). *Toilet training in less than a day.* New York: Simon & Schuster.

Azrin, N. H., Sneed, T. J., & Foxx, R. M. (1974). Dry bed training: Rapid elimination of childhood enuresis. *Behaviour Research and Therapy, 12,* 147–156.

Barclay, D. R., & Houts, A. C. (1995). Childhood enuresis. In C. E. Schaefer (Ed.), *Clinical handbook of sleep disorders in children* (pp. 223–252). Northvale, NJ: Jason Aranson.

Becker, J. (1994). An approach to the treatment of encopresis. *Surgery Annual, 26,* 49–66.

Benninga, M., Buller, H., Heymans, H., Tytgat, G., & Taminiau, J. (1994). Is encopresis always the result of constipation? *Archives of Disease in Childhood, 71,* 186–193.

Buchanan, A. (1992). *Children who soil: Assessment and treatment.* New York: Wiley.

Burnett, P. (1987). Assessing marital adjustment and satisfaction: A review. *Measurement and Evaluation in Counseling and Development, 20,* 113–121.

Butler, J. (1976a). Toilet training a child with spina bifida. *Journal of Behavior Therapy and Experimental Psychiatry, 7,* 63–65.

Butler, J. (1976b). The toilet training success of parents after reading "Toilet training in less than a day." *Behavior Therapy, 7,* 185–191.

---

* The views expressed in this chapter are those of the authors and do not necessarily represent the view of the Department of Defense or its components.

Butler, J. (1977). Treatment of encopresis by overcorrection. *Psychological Reports, 40,* 639–646.

Butler, R. J. (1991). Establishment of working definitions in nocturnal enuresis. *Archives of Disease in Childhood, 66,* 267–271.

Campise, R. L. (1993). *Encopresis assessment and treatment package for psychology interns.* Unpublished manuscript. Andrews Air Force Base, MD.

Ciminero, A. R. & Doleys, D. M. (1976). Childhood enuresis. *Journal of Pediatric Psychology, 1,* 17–20.

Costello, E. J., Edelbrock, C. S., & Costello, A. J. (1985). Validity of the NIMH Diagnostic Interview Schedule for Children: A comparison between psychiatric and pediatric referrals. *Journal of Abnormal Child Psychology, 13,* 579–595.

Cox, D. J., Sutphen, J., Borowitz, S., Dickens, M. N., Singles, J. (1994). Simple electromyographic biofeedback treatment for chronic pediatric constipation/encopresis: Preliminary report. *Biofeedback and Self-Regulation, 19,* 41–50.

Dawson, P., Griffith, K., & Boeke, K. (1990). Combined medical and psychological treatment of hospitalized children with encopresis. *Child Psychiatry and Human Development, 20,* 181–190.

Dische, S., Yule, W., Corbett, J., & Hand, D. (1983). Childhood nocturnal enuresis: Factors associated with outcome of treatment with an enuresis alarm. *Developmental Medicine and Neurology 25,* 67–80.

Doleys, D. M. (1978). Assessment and treatment of enuresis and encopresis in children. In M. Hersen, R. Eisler, & P. Miller (Eds.), *Progress in behavior modification* (pp. 85–123). New York: Academic Press.

Feldman, P. C., Villanueva, S., Lanne, V., & Devoroede, G. (1993). Use of play with clay to treat children with intractable encopresis. *Journal of Pediatrics, 122,* 483–488.

Fielding, D. M. & Doleys, D. M. (1988). Elimination problems: Enuresis and encopresis. In E. J. Mash & L. G. Terdal (Eds.), *Behavioral assessment of childhood disorders* (pp. 586–623). New York: Guilford Press.

Fireman, G., & Koplewicz, H. (1992). Short-term treatment of children with encopresis. *Psychotherapy: Practice and Research, 1,* 64–71.

Forsythe, W. I., & Butler, R. J. (1981). Fifty years of enuretic alarms. *Archives of Disease in Childhood, 64,* 879–885.

Gleghorn, E., Heyman, M., & Rudolph, C. (1991). No-enema therapy for idiopathic constipation and encopresis. *Clinical Pediatrics, 30,* 669–672.

Hague, J. M., Ellerstein, N. S., Gundy, J. H., Shelov, S. P., Weiss, J. C., McIntire, M. S., Olness, K. N., Jones, D. J., Heagarty, M. C., & Starfield, B. H. (1981). Parental perceptions of enuresis: A collaborative study. *American Journal of Diseases of Childhood, 135,* 809–811.

Hatch, T. (1988). Encopresis and constipation in children. *Pediatric Clinics of North America, 35,* 257–280.

Hodges, V. K. (1987). Assessing children with a clinical research interview: The child assessment schedule. In R. J. Priz (Ed.), *Advances in behavioral assessment of children and families* (pp. 203–233). Greenwich, CT: JAI Press.

Houts, A. C. (1991). Nocturnal enuresis as a biobehavioral problem. *Behavior Therapy, 22,* 133–151.

Houts, A. C. (1995). Behavioral treatment for enuresis. *Scandinavian Journal of Urology & Nephrology, 173,* 83–87.

Houts, A. C., Berman, J. S., & Abramson, H. (1994). Effectiveness of psychological and pharmacological treatments for nocturnal enuresis. *Journal of Consulting and Clinical Psychology, 62,* 737–745.

Houts, A. C., Peterson, J. K., & Whelan, J. P. (1986). Prevention of relapse in full-spectrum home training for primary enuresis: A component analysis. *Behavior Therapy, 17,* 462–469.

Hyman, P. E., & Fleisher, D. R. (1994). A classification of disorders of defecation in infants and children. *Seminars in Gastrointestinal Disease, 5,* 20–23.

Iwata, G., Iwai, N., Nagashima, M., & Fukata, R. (1995). *European Journal of Pediatric Surgery, 5,* 231–234.

Jehu, D., Morgan, R. T., Turner, R. K., & Jones, A. (1977). A controlled trial of the treatment of nocturnal enuresis in residential homes for children. *Behaviour Research and Therapy, 15,* 1–16.

Knell, S. M., & Moore, D. J. (1990). Cognitive-behavioral play therapy in the treatment of encopresis. *Journal of Clinical Child Psychology, 19,* 55–60.

Kovacs, M. (1985). The Interview Schedule for Children (ISC). *Psychopharmacology Bulletin, 21,* 991–994.

Levine, M. (1982). Encopresis: Its potentiation, evaluation, and alleviation. *Pediatric Clinics of North America, 29,* 315–330.

Levine, M. D. & Barr, R. (1980). *Evaluation system.* Boston: Children's Hospital Medical Center, Division of Ambulatory Pediatrics.

Loening-Baucke, V. (1990). Modulation of abnormal defecation dynamics by biofeedback treatment in chronically constipated children with encopresis. *Journal of Pediatrics, 116,* 214–222.

Loening-Baucke, V. (1995). Biofeedback treatment for chronic constipation and encopresis in childhood: Long-term outcome. *Pediatrics, 96,* 105–110.

Loening-Baucke, V., Cruikshank, B., & Savage, C. (1987). Defecation dynamics and behavior profiles in encopretic children. *Pediatrics, 80,* 672–679.

Mellon, M. W., & Houts, A. C. (1995). Elimination disorders. In R. T. Ammerman & M. Hersen (Eds.), *Handbook of child behavior therapy in the psychiatric setting* (pp. 341–366). New York: Wiley.

Moos, R. H., & Moos, B. S. (1984). *Family Environment Scale manual.* Palo Alto, CA: Consulting Psychologists Press.

Morgan, R. T., & Young, G. C. (1972). The conditioning treatment of childhood enuresis. *British Social Work Journal, 2,* 503–509.

Mowrer, O. H., & Mowrer, W. M. (1938). Enuresis: A method for its study and treatment. *American Journal of Orthopsychiatry, 8,* 436–459.

Nolan, T., Debelle, G., Oberklaid, F., & Coffey, C. (1991). Randomized trial of laxatives in treatment of childhood encopresis. *Lancet, 338,* 523–527.

Nolan, T., & Oberklaid, F. (1993). New concepts in the management of encopresis. *Pediatrics in Review, 14,* 447–451.

Norgaard, J. P., & Djurhuus, J. C. (1993). The pathophysiology of enuresis in children and young adults. *Clinical Pediatrics, July,* 5–9.

O'Brien, S., Ross, L. V., & Christophersen, E. R. (1986). Primary encopresis: Evaluation and treatment. *Journal of Applied Behavior Analysis, 19,* 137–145.

Olson, D., & Portner, J. (1983). Family adaptability and cohesion evaluation scales. In E. E. Filsinger (Ed.), *Marriage and family assessment: A sourcebook for family therapy* (pp. 299–315). Beverly Hills, CA: Sage.

Owens-Stively, J. (1987). Self-esteem and compliance in encopretic children. *Child Psychiatry and Human Development, 18,* 13–21.

Roesler, T. A., Savin, D., & Grosz, C. (1993). Family therapy of extra familial sexual abuse. *Journal of the American Academy of Child and Adolescent Psychiatry, 32,* 967–970.

Ronen, T., & Wozner, Y. (1995). A self-control intervention package for the treatment of primary nocturnal enuresis. *Child and Family Behavior Therapy, 17,* 1–20.

Sacks, S., DeLeon, G., & Blackman, S. (1974) Psychological changes associated with conditioning functional enuresis. *Journal of Clinical Psychology, 29,* 271–276.

Scott, M. A., Barclay, D. R., & Houts, A. C. (1992). Childhood enuresis: Etiology, assessment, and current behavioral treatment. In M. Hersen, R. M. Eisler, & P. M. Miller (Eds.), *Progress in behavior modification* (pp. 84–117). Beverly Hills, CA: Sage.

Shapiro, L. E., & Henderson, J. G. (1992). Brief therapy for encopresis. *Journal of Family Psychotherapy, 3,* 1–12.

Sluckin, A. (1975). Encopresis: A behavioural approach described. *Social Work Today, 5*(21), 643–646.

Sluckin, A. (1989). Behavioral social work treatment of childhood nocturnal enuresis. *Behavior Modification, 13,* 482–497.

Smith, L., & Smith, P. (1993). Psychological aspects of fecal incontinence in the elderly. In J. A. Barrett (Ed.), *Fecal incontinence in the older adult.* Sevenoaks, NY: Edward Arnold.

Spanier, G. (1976). Measuring dyadic adjustment: New scales for assessing the quality of marriage and similar dyads. *Journal of Marriage and the Family, 38,* 15–28.

Sprague-McRae, J. (1990). Encopresis: Developmental, behavioral, and physiological considerations for treatment. *Nurse Practitioner, 15,* 8–24.

Sprague-McRae, J., Lamb, W., & Homer, D. (1993). Encopresis: A study of treatment alternatives and historical and behavioral characteristics. *Nurse Practitioner, 18,* 52–63.

Stark, L. J., Owens-Stively, J., Spirito, A., Lewis, A., & Guevremont, D. (1990). Group behavioral treatment of retentive encopresis. *Journal of Pediatric Psychology, 15,* 659–671.

Stark, L. J., Spirito, A., Lewis, A. V., & Hart, K. J. (1990). Encopresis: Behavioral parameters associated with children who fail medical management. *Child Psychiatry and Human Development, 20,* 169–179.

Steege, M., & Harper, D. (1989). Enhancing the management of secondary encopresis by assessing acceptability of treatment: A case study. *Journal of Behavior Therapy and Experimental Psychiatry, 20,* 333–341.

Stern, H., Prince, M., & Stroh, S. (1988). Encopresis responsive to non-psychiatric interventions. *Clinical Pediatrics, 27,* 400–402.

Thapar, A., Davies, G., Jones, T., & Rivett, M. (1992). Treatment of childhood encopresis: A review. *Child-Care, Health, and Development, 18,* 343–353.

Tilton, P. (1980). Hypnotic treatment of a child with thumbsucking, enuresis, and encopresis. *American Journal of Clinical Hypnosis, 22,* 238–240.

Van Londen, A. A., Van Londen-Barentsen, M. W., Van Son, M. J., and Mulder, G. A. (1995). Relapse rate and subsequent parental reaction after successful treatment of children suffering from nocturnal enuresis: A 2½ year follow-up of bibliotherapy. *Behaviour Research & Therapy, 33,* 309–311.

Wald, A., Chandra, R., Gabel, S., & Chiponis, D. (1987). Evaluation of biofeedback in childhood encopresis. *Journal of Pediatric Gastroenterological Nutrition, 6,* 554–558.

Walker, E. C., Kenning, M., & Faust-Campanile, J. (1989). Enuresis and encopresis. In E. J. Mash & R. A. Barkley (Eds.), *Treatment of childhood disorders* (pp. 423–448). New York: Guilford Press

Wells, M. E., & Hinkle, J. S. (1990). Elimination of childhood encopresis: A family systems approach. *Journal of Mental Health Counseling, 12,* 520–526.

Wright, L. (1980). The standardization of compliance procedures, or the mass production of ugly ducklings. *American Psychologist, 35,* 119–122.

Young, G. C., & Morgan, R. T. (1973). Rapidity of response to the treatment of enuresis. *Developmental Medicine and Child Neurology, 15,* 488–496.

Young, M., Brennen, L., Baker, R., & Baker, S. (1995). Functional encopresis: Symptom reduction and behavioral improvement. *Developmental and Behavioral Pediatrics, 16,* 226–232.

Chapter 8

SEPARATION ANXIETY DISORDER

Karen P. Sowers-Hoag
Toni M. DiDona

OVERVIEW

Operational Definitions

The fundamental feature of Separation Anxiety Disorder (SAD) is excessive anxiety about separation from an attachment figure—typically, although not exclusively, a parent—or from home. When separated, children and youth with this disorder typically become socially withdrawn and display apathy, sadness, or difficulty in concentration and attention to work or play.

Although some anxiety regarding separation from a parent is developmentally normal, this disorder is present when the anxiety is extreme. Thyer and Sowers-Hoag (1988) note that most diagnostic features of SAD are different in quantity, not quality, from behaviors exhibited in all children, and that the phenomena is considered part of normal development in infants. They make an interesting note that normal separation anxiety generally coincides with the time when infants become more mobile. Thyer (1991) notes that an essential difference in children with SAD is that although independent activities are severely restricted, such as spending the night away from home, going to camp or school, or going on errands, these activities are often greatly enjoyed if the caregiver accompanies the child.

The fourth edition of the *Diagnostic and Statistical Manual of Mental Disorders* (*DSM-IV;* American Psychiatric Association [APA], 1994) states that the criteria for SAD are met when the excessive anxiety appears before age 18, has a duration of over 4 weeks, and is the cause of significant distress or impairment in functioning.

By definition, this disorder must be present before age 18; however, SAD has been documented in adults as well (cf. Butcher, 1983). SAD is often associated with school refusal. In fact, there is evidence to suggest that SAD may be present in as many as 80% of all cases of school phobia (Gittleman-Klein & Klein, 1984; Popper, 1993).

exist. Children with SAD are more likely to be female, white, and come from a household where the head is from a poor socioeconomic class (Last, Francis, Hersen, Kazdin, & Strauss, 1987; Last, Strauss, & Francis, 1987; Velez, Johnson, & Cohen, 1989). They are also more likely than children with school refusal to meet diagnostic criteria for additional disorders (Last, Francis et al., 1987).

Accurate diagnosis is crucial in selecting the most efficacious treatment approach. However, even some experts have difficulty accurately differentiating between school phobia and SAD. Clinicians must take special care applying in the diagnostic criteria appropriately to the client situation. The term *school phobia* was introduced in the clinical literature in 1941 (Johnson, Falstein, & Szurek, 1941). The term was used to denote a syndrome of childhood characterized by marked anxiety about attending school and by absenteeism. The syndrome was thought to be precipitated by fear of leaving the mother or home rather than by fear of school. Estes, Hayless, & Johnson (1956) substituted the term *separation anxiety* to better communicate the focus of the pathology. Some investigators (Berg, Nichols, & Pritchard, 1969) favor a fear-of-school hypothesis in which the child is viewed as having a phobic reaction to some aspect of the school environment. Most clinicians and researchers, however, assert that anxiety about attending school can stem from separation problems or from excessive fear about some aspect of school itself (Ollendick & Mayer, 1985). This diagnostic confusion has been compounded by the inclusion of *Separation Anxiety Disorder* in *DSM-III* (APA, 1980), *DSM-III-R* (APA, 1987), and *DSM-IV* (APA, 1994). The diagnostic criteria for this disorder include nine symptoms, only three of which must be met to receive the diagnosis. Although reluctance or refusal to go to school is included as one of the nine symptoms characteristic of SAD, a child need not exhibit this particular behavior to meet criteria for the disorder. Unfortunately, over the years and into the present, the label *school phobia* has been applied to both types of children (that is, those who evidence separation anxiety and those who show a phobic reaction toward school). However, it is clear that not all children with school phobia show separation anxiety problems, nor do all children with SAD exhibit school refusal.

Many authors have suggested that SAD may be a precursor or risk factor for the later development of adult anxiety disorders. Although this may appear to make theoretical sense, the evidence is not quite clear and there have been numerous contradictory findings. Despite the lack of clear empirical confirmation, the theory that SAD is fundamentally related to the later development of adult anxiety disorders is so popular that it is referred to by some authors as the separation anxiety hypothesis (SAH).

Thyer (1993) discusses the SAH and states that although early separation anxiety may appear to be related to the development of panic attacks and agoraphobia in adulthood theoretically, there is no sound empirical support for this relationship. Other reviews of the literature have discussed numerous studies that either support the SAH or discredit it. Research that supports this hypothesis seems to be flawed, primarily in the methodology and the external validity of the conclusions. A careful review of the evidence suggests that in fact childhood SAD is not a precursor to the later development of adult panic disorder or agoraphobia (Thyer et al., 1993).

There do appear to be several risk factors for the development of SAD itself, however. Children and adolescents with chronic illnesses may be at higher risk for SAD. Specifically, those with end-stage renal disease have been found to have a significantly higher incidence than matched healthy controls (Fukunishi, Honda, Kamiyama, & Ito, 1993).

Ethnicity is another important factor to consider. In Japan, school refusal is the most common diagnosis in child and adolescent psychiatry and is divided into two categories, separation anxiety in younger children and self-discipline problems associated with adolescence (Honjo, Kasahara, & Ohtaka, 1992). Bird, Gould, Yager, Staghezza, and Canino (1989) evaluated the risk factors for maladjustment in children in Puerto Rico. They found that SAD is most common in the middle age group (ages 6 to 11) and that there are no significant demographic variables, such as gender, social class, or family characteristics associated with the disorder.

The evidence about family structure and characteristics is contradictory. Brar and Brar (1990) found that children who are less intelligent and whose mothers have marital conflicts and poor child-rearing attitudes in fostering dependency, encouraging verbalization, excluding outside influences, approving of activities, and accelerating development have more separation anxiety.

Relevance of Social Work's Involvement

Social work's particular emphasis among the helping professions is to assist people in relating to their social environment. That places the social worker in the position of being the person most likely to facilitate linkages between the client and appropriate referral resources. Social workers in a variety of settings are poised to be the first professionals to have contact with families that have a child with SAD. School social workers are often a direct referral source for children who have been identified as consistently truant. Similarly, child protective service workers investigate alleged child neglect cases that are reported due to children's frequent absence from school or apparent isolation in the home. Clinical social workers in family service agencies, private practice, and mental health facilities receive referrals from other agency-based social workers for treatment of children with SAD. Because of the profession's commitment to a holistic perspective (physical, environmental, social, and psychological), social workers are uniquely well suited to provide appropriate assessment and treatment. For example, because somatic complaints are common among children with SAD who are separated from their attachment figures, non–social work professionals may assess the situation only from a physical perspective and submit children to physical examinations, treatments, and medical procedures that are unnecessary and perhaps harmful. To provide appropriate referrals and treatment, it is critical that the social worker have sufficient knowledge and skills to assess the situation accurately. The social worker is uniquely trained to employ a person-in-environment assessment that includes the cultural, environmental, psychological, physical, and socially interactive elements of the client system. Given this unique perspective among the helping professions and our profession's commitment to basing clinical decisions on a conceptual knowledge base and empirical findings, social workers are perhaps best suited to address the problems associated with SAD. Social workers have made a number of contributions to studies on the descriptive psychopathology and treatment of SAD (e.g., Leader, 1978; Thyer, 1993; Thyer & Sowers-Hoag, 1986, 1988; Thyer et al., 1993).

ASSESSMENT METHODS

The diagnosis of any disorder using the current *DSM-IV* (APA, 1994) criteria can be difficult. Clinicians often complain that the criteria are like a Chinese menu and are not necessarily helpful in the choice of interventive strategies or the development of treatment plans. Further, many *DSM-IV* diagnoses—especially those of childhood—are not stable over time. Cantwell and Baker (1989) found in a semi-blind study that the *DSM-III* (APA, 1980) diagnosis of separation anxiety lacks predictive validity. Other researchers, however, have found that the criteria for SAD are, in fact, stable. King, Gullone and Tonge (1991) found that the classification criteria in *DSM-III* and *DSM-III-R* (APA, 1987) are reliable for SAD but not for the other anxiety-related diagnosis in children.

The diagnosis of SAD is probably less difficult than that of other disorders. Thyer et al., (1993) point out that all of the criteria for SAD are not defining of the diagnosis in and of themselves. They reason that these features must be clearly related to the primary feature of the condition—specifically, excessive anxiety about separation.

There are a wide variety of empirically supported methods for ascertaining the diagnosis of SAD. They can be broken down into types of assessment strategies including but not limited to structured clinical interviews, self-report scales, and observational methods.

Structured Clinical Interviews

There are a number of structured clinical interviews that can be used to diagnose SAD. The Diagnostic Interview for Children and Adolescents (DICA; Wellner, Reich, Herjanic, Jung, & Amado, 1987) and the Child Assessment Schedule (CAS; Hodges, Kline, Stern, Cytryn, & McKnew, 1982) are two such interviews that can assess for the symptoms of SAD and lead to an accurate diagnosis. These interviews, however, are not specifically designed for the assessment of anxiety disorders. Therefore, there are a number of questions related to other potential problems that can be extraneous if the clinician already suspects an anxiety disorder. Since clients typically present with a problem that is at least related to an overall class of disorders, such as anxiety or depression, a structured interview of a broad base of all potential problems may not be the most efficient use of the clinician's time. When the object is to evaluate a wide variety of potential problems, or it is important to have a large set of normative data, such as is necessary in large epidemiological studies, these measures are an appropriate choice. However, in today's managed care environment, when the time for assessment and diagnosis is often limited to 1 therapeutic hour, there are better and more efficient uses of the clinician's time.

The Anxiety Disorders Interview Schedule for Children (ADIS-C; Silverman & Nelles, 1988) is specific to the assessment of anxiety disorders and therefore does not have superfluous questions. It also has both parent and child versions and has relatively high interrater agreement. It does take a rather long time to administer, however, and there are other equally accurate and much more cost effective means of diagnosing SAD. Again, it may be more time-efficient to focus on other exacerbating factors or psychosocial considerations for intervention than to use a measure that is so time-consuming.

Self-Report Methods

There are several multidimensional scales that include a measure or subscale of separation anxiety. These include the revised Ontario Child Health Study (OCHS; Boyle, Offord, Racine, & Flemming, 1993), the Kiddie-Infant Descriptive Instrument for Emotional States (KIDIES) (Stern, MacKain, Raduns, & Hopper, 1992); and the Visual Analog Scale for Anxiety (VASA) (Bernstein & Garfinkel, 1992).

Boyle et al. (1993) developed and evaluated the revised Ontario Child Health Study (OCHS) scales to measure a number of disorders of childhood, including SAD, according to *DSM-III-R* (APA, 1987) criteria. They evaluated their scale with a large sample drawn from the general population ($N = 1751$), as well as a sample from mental health clinics ($N = 1027$), and found that the OCHS is a valid and reliable means of diagnosis for a wide variety of disorders, including SAD. Test-retest reliability for SAD was higher (.65) when assessed by parents of younger children (ages 6 to 11) than older children (.55 for ages 12 to 16) or when assessed by the children themselves. The authors report that the convergent and discriminant validity is not as strong for measures of internalizing disorders, such as SAD, as it is for externalizing disorders, such as Conduct Disorder. They also admit that the scale is probably best suited for studies of large populations where a *DSM-III-R* diagnosis is sought.

The Interpersonal Sensitivity Measure (IPSM) (Boyce & Parker, 1989) is a self-report measure that generates subscale scores for separation anxiety, interpersonal awareness, need for approval, timidity, and fragile inner self. It is reported to have high internal consistency and stability over time. It was normed on 265 non-psychiatric clients of a general practice, 81 nursing and social work students, 30 medical students and, 122 depressive in- and outpatients. Again, this measure is not the most direct means to assess SAD.

The Fear Survey Schedule for Children (FSSC) (Scherer & Nakamura, 1968) is a pencil-and-paper self-test with 80 questions scored in a Likert fashion. Benefits of this method are that it is inexpensive and easy to administer, and both total and subscale scores are available. Drawbacks include the lack of a subscale specific to SAD and being rather long and time-consuming both to administer and to score.

The Separation Anxiety Test (SAT) (Wright, Binney, & Smith, 1995) has good interrater reliability but poor test-retest reliability. In addition, the internal consistency of the self-reliance subscale is low. As a result, this measure is not a suitable choice for diagnosis or ongoing measurement. Also not recommended for clinical use at present are the Children's Manifest Anxiety Scale (Mattison, Bagnato, & Brubaker, 1988) or the Hansberg (1980) Separation Anxiety Test, because of poor or unknown psychometric properties.

The Child Assessment Schedule was found to be a reliable measure with good reliability for both diagnosis and treatment. It has symptom summary scores for separation anxiety, conduct disorder, major depressive episodes, and dysthymia (Hodges, Cools, & McKnew, 1989). The assessment of this scale was conducted with 32 psychiatric inpatients whose mean age was 9 years. However, like several of the structured clinical interviews, it has questions that would seem superfluous if the presenting problem is known to be anxiety-related.

Kim, Hahn, Kish, Rosenberg, and Harris (1991) reported the development, reliability, and validity of the Children's Separation Rating Scale (CSRS) with psychiatrically hospitalized children ($n = 22$). This is a 5-item scale utilizing a 4-point rating for each item. A specific example of each rating is provided for each item. Interrater reliability was high (.92) as was test-retest reliability. The CSRS was found to have good internal consistency (coefficient alpha .77) and adequate concurrent validity. The measure was administered with the Children's Behavior Checklist, and, although correlation coefficients decreased over time, they were statistically significant. This measure has several advantages. First and foremost, it is short, easy to administer and score, and has adequate reliability (albeit demonstrated with a small population). Unfortunately, the authors' support for discriminant validity was quite weak. They state that separation reaction should and did decrease over the course of hospitalization. It would be more clinically relevant if the authors had employed another method to evaluate discriminant validity. It would be far more beneficial to demonstrate that the CRSS can discriminate between known groups—for example, between those with SAD and those with school phobia.

Thyer et al. (1993) suggest that these types of measures are best used on an ongoing basis in the context of treatment for the evaluation of change, rather than exclusively as diagnostic tools. They point out that even in measures that have normative data, it is not logical to assume that a measure that is capable of distinguishing between groups based on diagnostic criteria is necessarily capable of determining a diagnosis for any *individual* child. Given the relative lack of confusion and ease of diagnosis of SAD compared to other disorders of childhood, it would seem that Thyer et al. (1993) are correct in suggesting that these types of measures be used to evaluate progress instead of as a means of diagnosis. Clearly, these measures are useful in research as a means to provide standardized assessment and comparison, but for the clinician in direct practice, these measures are better left for the documentation of successful treatment.

Observational Methods

Trad (1992) recommends the use of diagnostic peer groups that involve a small number of children of equal age and development. He reports that this small group allows the practitioner to observe separation and reunion behaviors, peer interactions, social skills, and overall developmental status, which may be useful in diagnosis in that it provides a reference group for the clinician. No other observational methods were found after an extensive review of the literature.

EFFECTIVE INTERVENTIONS

Social work intervention with SAD can occur in several different modalities by use of multiple models of intervention. SAD is traditionally treated in an individual format, although there are some examples in the literature of group and family therapy. As with other anxiety-related disorders, there are medications that are used in the treatment of SAD. However, the literature clearly presents strong evidence that chemical management of this disorder is typically not necessary. An extensive review of the literature produced several interesting findings. Although the empirically based literature on the treatment of SAD is not extensive, there is quite a bit known about this disorder. Compared to other disorders first evident in childhood, the literature base is actually substantial. What follows is a review of the treatment-based literature. The focus is predominately on treatments that have been documented to be effective. However, a few modalities and models that are not well documented are also included. This is primarily due to the fact that they represent all that is published with regard to the modality and SAD. They are included to offer support by means of their contrast with well established findings of the treatment of choice. Often, clinicians are reluctant to use an intervention— even if it has the clearest empirical support—if they do not see the contrast with the model they are most comfortable using. For this reason, psychodynamic and play therapy models are included in the discussion so that clinicians can compare the models they may be using to models that have far greater empirical support.

Individual Therapies

Psychodynamic Models.   Since the early days of social work intervention, psychodynamic models of intervention have been utilized in the treatment of almost every disorder. Although proponents of this model speak eloquently about the insights, defense mechanisms, and neuroses that are intensely evaluated and resolved via therapy, there has been little empirical support for this methodology. The review of the SAD treatment literature is not substantially different from other disorders in this respect. One case study was found that recommends the use of this intervention with SAD. Kaufman (1990) reports the use of fantasy transformation in a psychodynamically based intervention with a 5-year-old girl who was diagnosed with separation disorder in a borderline personality organization. Although she reports a successful outcome, this intervention can not be recommended due a number of inherent problems. First, the therapy took 5 years to complete. Although this is typical in many psychodynamically oriented models, it is blatantly not cost-efficient in time, money, or—more important—in immediately assuaging the distress of the client. Other problems include a lack of specificity about the actual intervention, reification of the problem, and a lack of reliable or valid measures to document progress.

Other documentation of the success of psychodynamically based intervention can only be gathered unobtrusively. The literature has several examples of children who completed a course of traditional psychotherapy that failed, resulting in their referral to another therapist and successful treatment with a behaviorally based model (cf. Butcher, 1983; Garvey & Hegrenes, 1966).

Thyer and Sowers-Hoag (1986) summarize the literature for school phobia and note that separation anxiety may be a factor. Interestingly, they conclude that although the psychodynamic literature provides numerous potential explanations for the etiology of school phobia, effective corresponding treatment techniques do not exist. They conclude that the behavioral literature, due to its documentation of treatment success, demonstrates that school phobia—and SAD, as one of the possible explanations for school phobia—can be treated successfully without an investigation of psychodynamic causes.

Play Therapy Models.   Play therapy has been utilized with children since the early days of Anna Freud. It has progressed significantly in the past two decades. It is often considered the best method of intervention with children whose verbal skills have not yet developed the complexity necessary for other models. Since SAD is a disorder of childhood, and since it occurs in younger children more frequently than in adolescents, it would seem that play therapy should be considered as a possible treatment. Unfortunately, research in this area has demonstrated that play therapy is not effective in reducing the anxiety symptoms associated with SAD (see Milos & Reiss, 1982).

Virtually all of the other literature on the treatment of SAD recommends an intervention that is behavioral in nature. Effective interventions range from prolonged exposure to anxiety-evoking situations, to contingency management procedures and several combinations of techniques. These findings are similar to what is known about the effective psychosocial treatment of all anxiety disorders, both with adults and with children. Of course, there are a few necessary variations that must be considered when working with children, but many of the basic procedures are analogous.

In a review of the literature on the treatment of anxiety disorders in childhood and adolescents, Thyer (1991) found that exposure-based treatments are the treatment of choice when the anxiety-evoking stimulus can be clearly identified. This conclusion is based on a number of single-subject studies. He warns that pharmacological therapy should not be used as a first treatment in any anxiety-related disorder without concurrent behavioral interventions, due to the lack of clear empirical evidence for such a course of treatment. More specifically, Thyer (1993) reports that children with SAD respond well to behavior-based therapies. These interventions, such as gradual real-life exposure therapy, are effective in the treatment of other phobia-based disorders.

Cognitive-Behavioral Treatments. The evidence supporting cognitive-behavioral treatments for SAD is sparse and mixed. Cognitive-behavioral psychotherapy was used with success to treat both a 10-year-old boy and a 12-year-old girl by Mansdorf and Lukens (1987). Their intervention included a six-step process: (a) cognitive analysis of the child, (b) cognitive analysis of the parents, (c) environmental analysis, (d) cognitive restructuring of the child, (e) cognitive restructuring of the parents, and (f) restructuring of the environment. They reported success by week 4 for the boy and week 2 for the girl. Details about the intervention are not clearly operationalized, however; therefore, the intervention and corresponding success might be difficult to replicate.

Ollendick, Hagopian, and Huntzinger (1991) also used a cognitive-behavioral model to resolve the separation anxiety of two girls, ages 10 and 8, who had initially presented with night fears. They chose a multiple baseline design across subjects to evaluate the effectiveness of their intervention. The intervention specifically consisted of instruction in the nature of anxiety, deep breathing relaxation, use of positive self-talk, problem solving, self-reinforcement, and praise. They found that self-control training was not effective without the addition of reinforcement. The symptoms of SAD had not returned at follow-up at 1 and 2 years, respectively.

The other successful interventions in the treatment of SAD are all behaviorally based. All of these interventions can be categorized into groups, including systematic desensitization, flooding, contingency management, or some combination thereof. Although school phobia is fundamentally different from SAD, some of the literature on the treatment of school phobia is included, because the description of symptoms mirrors SAD rather than school phobia, and there has been a great deal of confusion in the differentiation between these disorders in some of the literature.

Exposure-Based Procedures.   There are six basic variations of exposure therapy: (a) group systematic desensitization in imagination, (b) real-life systematic desensitization, (c) automated systematic desensitization in imagination, (d) self-directed desensitization and emotive imagery, (e) contact desensitization, and (f) self-control desensitization (Morris & Kratochwill, 1985). Desensitization with emotive imagery, self-control desensitization, and in vivo desensitization have all been documented to be effective in the treatment of SAD. Of these, no one variation appears to have the best empirical support.

Lazarus, Davidson, and Polefka (1965) treated a 9-year-old boy with real-life desensitization. The description of the boy's symptoms are in keeping with SAD, even though he is reported to have school phobia. Their case study is somewhat confounded by the use of a tranquilizer for anticipatory anxiety, even though they report that the anxiety was diminished even when the medication was forgotten. They conclude that a placebo would have been just as effective. Furthermore, they combine classical and operant conditioning techniques but are not clear about when which model should be employed (Lazarus et al., 1965).

Houlihan and Jones (1989) used real-life systematic desensitization to treat a 13-year-old boy reported to be diagnosed with school phobia, although the authors note that the child also had overanxious disorder of childhood. The child may have actually had SAD. Their real-life procedure reduced symptoms rapidly and resulted in the child being able to return to school regularly.

Desensitization was also effectively used in the treatment of a 10-year-old boy by Garvey and Hegrenes (1966) after 6 months of traditional psychotherapy had failed. Although they report that the boy had school phobia, their description of his symptoms clearly represents SAD. They completed the desensitization procedure with the use of a fear hierarchy in 20 consecutive sessions of 20 to 40 minutes each.

Martin and Korte (1978) utilized a behavioral program to desensitize a 7-year-old with SAD and school refusal, which resulted in a rapid reduction of symptoms and a return to school within 1 week.

Montenegro (1968) reports the successful treatment of two preschool-age children, a 6-year-old Caucasian boy and a 3½-year-old African American girl. He used a modification of Wolpe's desensitization procedure, reciprocal inhibition. He employed food as a reinforcer along with the desensitization procedure. In order to enhance the effectiveness of the reinforcer, he instructed the parents of the children not to feed them dinner the night before or breakfast the day of the morning session. He then had the parents bring in favorite treats, such as cookies, cake, and ice cream. The food reinforcers were gradually decreased.

Lazarus and Abramovitz (1962) report that emotive imagery was successful in the treatment of 7 out of 9 phobic children. The primary diagnosis was not SAD in all nine of the cases, and it is not clear how many of the subjects had SAD exclusively. Their technique basically involves Wolpe's systematic desensitization, using a superhero or alter ego as the focus for the guided imagery into stress-inducing situations.

Bornstein and Knapp (1981) used a multiple baseline design to evaluate the effectiveness of self-control desensitization in a 12-year-old boy who presented with multiple phobias, including SAD. After the initial 2-week baseline for anxiety regarding separation, 1 month of treatment resulted in significant improvement. The entire intervention, across travel- and illness-related fears as well as separation, was completed in 6 weeks, and the boy continued to be symptom free at 1-year follow-up.

Miller (1972) reports a successful intervention with a 10-year-old-boy with multiple phobias, including SAD, using visual imagery and relaxation for counterconditioning. He based his choice on Wolpe's systematic desensitization technique. His use of an A-B single-system design for the evaluation is further supported by follow-up at 3 and 18 months with no evidence of recurrence or of new problem behaviors.

Hamilton (1994) used a combination of behavior modification techniques to alleviate a 4-year-old girl's SAD, which developed shortly after beginning kindergarten. Specific techniques used were instruction, modeling, relaxation, and real-life exposure. Treatment was completed in 5 weeks, and success was supported by the child riding the school bus with no problems. Contingency management procedures, such as positive reinforcement, shaping, stimulus fading, and extinction have also been successfully utilized in the treatment of SAD.

Contingency Management Procedures.   Contingency management has been reported to be effective in the treatment of SAD. Patterson (1965) reports success in the treatment of a 7-year-old boy in 23 sessions of 20 minutes each. Total time of intervention was only 4 hours and 40 minutes. His intervention is based on learning theory and operant conditioning, with the ubiquitous chocolate-covered candies used to reinforce adaptive separation behavior. He further reports utilizing the same intervention with a second child, with dramatic success in less than 6 clinical hours.

Neisworth, Madle, and Goeke (1975) developed an intervention based on stimulus fading with a 4-year-old girl, who primarily displayed separation anxiety at preschool. Traditional techniques used prior to the intervention, such as rechanneling interest, cuddling, and ignoring behavior, had failed. They used differential reinforcement for nonanxious behaviors, with an increasing criterion for reinforcement by the mother's appearance. A kitchen timer was used to indicate to the child that her mother was about to reappear and to increase the time in between her appearances. A baseline was conducted for 10 preschool sessions, and intervention occurred for 17 hours beginning with delay intervals of a few seconds, which were gradually increased over several days. The child was reinforced for progressively longer periods of nonanxious behavior. The length of time the mother remained with the child for reinforcement was also gradually decreased. In addition, the child was also reinforced for participating in the program. The timer was removed on the 17th day, which resulted in an immediate increase in anxious behavior. The timer was then also gradually faded, by being moved farther and farther away from the child. Monthly follow-up data indicated no recurrence of anxious behavior (Neisworth et al., 1975). There were several advantages to this study. First, high interrater agreement (over 90%) on observations of duration of anxious behavior was found, and very little distress for the child occurred during an intervention that was very short in duration. Although the authors didn't test for autocorrelation of baseline data or generalization to other situations where the child was separated from the mother, this study supports the use of stimulus fading in the treatment of SAD (Neisworth et al., 1975).

Hagopian and Slifer (1993) utilized a treatment that consisted of graduated exposure with reinforcement for appropriate behavior for a 6½-year-old girl with SAD. The primary target was school attendance, but they also worked on having the girl sleep in her own bed at night. A changing criterion design, which resulted in the shaping of appropriate behavior, was used; the amount of time that the child was required to stay in class without her mother was gradually increased, and inter-action with and proximity to her mother were concurrently faded. During the base-line period separation was not attempted; rather, the child's avoidant behavior and anxious episodes were recorded.

Specifically, the treatment involved several steps. The subject's mother initially left her in class four times an hour for 30 seconds each time. The criterion was increased based on meeting requirements two times successfully and the comfort of both the child and her mother in moving on. Reinforcement was initiated on the 4th day of treatment. She received a sticker for each day she remained in her seat while her mother was gone. No punitive component for failure was used. Stickers could be exchanged for prizes at the end of each week, and verbal praise was provided during treatment. Concurrent to this graduated exposure, questions about parental safety were extinguished by providing minimal attention and ignoring crying. Once school attendance was regular, a reinforcement schedule was initiated to increase the inci-dence of the child sleeping in her own bed. The treatment resulted in regular school attendance, sleeping through the night in her own bed, and, at the child's request, attendance without her mother at Brownie meetings (Hagopian & Slifer, 1993). Follow-up at both 2- and 6-month intervals showed no return of symptoms. Strengths of this single-subject design include extensive evaluation before diagnosis, multiple measures, 2- and 9-month follow-up, and demonstrated generalizability to other conditions, such as sleeping in her own bed and attending Brownie meetings.

Behavioral methods have also been documented to be successful in the treat-ment of an adult with a long history of SAD (Butcher, 1983). Traditional methods of psychoanalysis had not been successful during his adolescence after 2 years of treatment.

Real-Life Exposure Techniques.   If one were to evaluate the number of documented cases where one type of intervention was successful in the treatment of SAD, real-life exposure to separation clearly has the most support. This is due in large part to a single report published by Kennedy (1965) where the outcomes of a large number of cases are reported. He reports the success of treatment of 50 different cases with flooding and operant conditioning. The children all presented for treatment due to school phobia, and it is unclear how many of them had simple school phobia and how many had SAD. However, the author demonstrates success over an 8-year period with both boys and girls ranging from nursery school to tenth grade. He details six essential components to the intervention: (a) good public relations, (b) avoidance of emphasis on somatic complaints, (c) forced school attendance, (d) structured interview with the parents, (e) brief interview with the child, and (f) follow-up. The technique basically involves placing the child in school, positive reinforcement of adaptive behavior, and ignoring (that is, extinguishing) any and all negative complaints or symptoms (Kennedy, 1965). The major weakness of this report is that the follow-up involved only a call to parents for a self-report of recurrence of symptoms. However, his success with 50 cases across gender, age, and race provides strong support for the use of this intervention. In fact, this report provides the single largest study to date, even though the report is over two decades old. Although any individual case cannot by its very nature provide external validity, the aggregation of 50 similar cases, similarly treated and with similar positive results, can be argued to approach the generalizability of a classical experiment.

In a comparative study, Blagg and Yule (1984) evaluated the effectiveness of four different treatment conditions for school refusal. Although they did not randomly assign the subjects to groups, this study is the only one to comparatively look at behavioral treatment ($n = 30$), hospitalization ($n = 16$), psychotherapy, and home schooling ($n = 20$). They found that the behavioral treatment was significantly more effective ($p < .001$) than either hospitalization or traditional psychotherapy with home-based education in terms of school attendance after treatment. They also found significantly less separation anxiety in the group that received the behavioral treatment than with either of the other intervention strategies. They further documented that the behavioral treatment is by far the more economic use of the therapist's time, with an average length of treatment for this condition being only 2.53 weeks, as compared to 45.3 weeks for the hospitalization and 72.1 weeks for home schooling plus traditional psychotherapy. Their behavioral intervention consisted of in vivo flooding, contingency management for maintenance, and follow-up.

Given that there appear to be no published reports of true, experimental outcome studies in the area of SAD, the existing research supports the contention that behavioral interventions are the best supported and can be considered the first-choice treatment approach. Typically, a combination of different behavioral methods is most efficient and successful. Graduated exposure in real life to experiencing separation from caregivers appears to be a key feature of successful therapy. Increased success also appears to be related to positive reinforcement for appropriate behaviors and by the planful failure to attend (by parents, teachers, and therapists) to anxious behaviors. This conclusion is also consistent with what is known about the treatment of other anxiety disorders (cf. Morris & Kratochwill, 1985).

Group Therapies

A thorough review of the literature uncovered only one empirically based article on the use of a group modality in the treatment of separation anxiety. That study evaluated variations of group therapy and correspondence to alleviate the separation anxiety of students in a boarding school. The subjects were not diagnosed with SAD but were, rather, having separation issues after leaving home to attend a boarding school.

Group therapy was used to alleviate separation anxiety and was found to increase adjustment and reduce dropout rate in a study of 12-year-olds of lower socioeconomic status who were enrolled in boarding school (Itskowitz, Orbach, & Yablon, 1990). This study compared four groups: (a) group therapy only, (b) structured correspondence with family, (c) group therapy and structured correspondence, and (d) no intervention (control). The specific model of group therapy was not delineated. Structured correspondence had a similar effect on adjustment but did not affect dropout rate. With an *n* of 110 students, this study demonstrates that group therapy may be a modality to consider in future research.

Marital and Family Therapies

Only one article in support of family therapy could be found in the literature (Leader, 1978). That article offers no empirical support, but, rather, a clinical opinion after consideration of the nature of separation anxiety and the relationship between the child and the primary caregiver.

Drug Therapies

No discussion about an anxiety disorder would be complete without a review of what is known and recommended regarding pharmacological treatments. Although social workers, psychologists, and other mental health professionals may not legally prescribe medication, they are in a position to refer to a physician when necessary for evaluation with regard to the appropriateness of medication.

After thorough reviews of the literature, Popper (1993), Kanner, Klein, Rubinstein, and Mascia (1989), and Reiter, Kutcher, and Gardner (1992) recommended the use of several medications, mostly evaluated through open, nonblind clinical trials, although some stronger studies do exist. For example, the antidepressant imipramine has been reported to be helpful by Rabiner and Klein (1969), Gittelman-Klein and Klein (1971, 1973, 1980), Gittelman-Klein (1975), Klien, Koplewicz, and Kanner (1992), Ballenger, Carek, Steele, and Cornish-McTighe (1989), and Deltito and Hahn (1993).

Several different forms of tranquilizers may also be beneficial (see Balon, 1994; Reiter, Kutcher, & Gardner, 1992), as may be some other compounds (Birmaher, Waterman, Ryan, & Cully, 1994). Long-term efficacy, relapse, and side-effect profiles have not been, for the most part, investigated systematically. Often, in these drug trials, medication was provided concurrently with supportive counseling and implicit or explicit behavioral strategies, rendering the relative role of medication alone difficult to evaluate. Given the efficacy of psychosocial therapies, it can be argued that the use of medications to treat SAD should be limited to those children who fail to respond to less intrusive, nonpharmacological interventions; or, perhaps, to use as aids to facilitate exposure work. Medication use is usually not necessary.

REFERENCES

American Psychiatric Association. (1980). *Diagnostic and statistical manual of mental disorders* (3rd ed.). Washington, DC: Author.

American Psychiatric Association. (1987). *Diagnostic and statistical manual of mental disorders* (3rd ed. rev.). Washington, DC: Author.

American Psychiatric Association. (1994). *Diagnostic and statistical manual of mental disorders* (4th ed.). Washington, DC: Author.

Ballenger, J. C., Carek, D. J., Steele, J. J., & Cornish-McTighe, D. (1989). Three cases of panic disorder with agoraphobia in children. *American Journal of Psychiatry, 146,* 922–924.

Balon, R. (1994). Buspirone in the treatment of separation anxiety in an adolescent boy. *Canadian Journal of Psychiatry, 39,* 581–582.

Berg, J., Nichols, K., & Pritchard, C. (1969). School phobia: Its classification and relationship to dependency. *Journal of Child Psychology and Psychiatry 10,* 123–141.

Bernstein, G. A., & Garfinkel, B. D. (1992). The Visual Analogue Scale for Anxiety—Revised: Psychometric properties. *Journal of Anxiety Disorders, 6,* 223–239.

Bird, H. R., Gould, M. S., Yager, T., Staghezza, B., & Canino G. (1989). Risk factors for maladjustment in Puerto Rican children. *Journal of the American Academy of Child and Adolescent Psychiatry, 28,* 847–850.

Birmaher, B., Waterman, G. S., Ryan, N., & Cully, M. (1994). Fluoxetine for childhood anxiety disorders. *Journal of the American Academy of Child and Adolescent Psychiatry, 33,* 993–999.

Blagg, N. R., & Yule, Y. (1984). The behavioral treatment of school refusal: A comparative study. *Behaviour Research and Therapy, 22,* 119–127.

Bornstein, P. H., & Knapp, M. (1981). Self-control desensitization with a multi-phobic boy: A multiple-baseline design. *Journal of Experimental Psychiatry and Behavior Therapy, 12,* 281–285.

Bowen, R. C., Offord, D. R., & Boyle, M. H. (1990). The prevalence of overanxious disorder and separation anxiety disorder: Results from the Ontario Child Health Study. *Journal of the American Academy of Child and Adolescent Psychiatry, 29,* 753–758.

Boyce, P., & Parker, G. (1989). Development of a scale to measure interpersonal sensitivity. *Australian and New Zealand Journal of Psychiatry, 23,* 341–351.

Boyle, M. H., Offord, D. R., Racine, Y. A., Fleming, J. E. (1993). Evaluation of the revised Ontario Child Health Study scales. *Journal of Child Psychology and Psychiatry and Allied Disciplines, 34,* 189–213.

Brar, S., & Brar, S. S. (1990). Separation anxiety in preschool children. *Journal of Personality and Clinical Studies, 6,* 13–17.

Butcher, P. (1983). The treatment of childhood-rooted separation anxiety in an adult. *Journal of Behavior Therapy and Experimental Psychiatry, 14,* 61–65.

Cantwell, D. P., & Baker, L. (1989). Stability and natural history of DSM-III childhood diagnoses. *Journal of the American Academy of Child and Adolescent Psychiatry, 28,* 691–700.

Cohen, P., Cohen, J., Kasen, S. Velez, C. N., Hartmark, C., Johnson, J., Rojas, M., Brook, J., & Streuning, E. L. (1993). An epidemiological study of disorders in late childhood and adolescence: Age and gender specific prevalence. *Journal of Child Psychology and Psychiatry and Allied Disciplines, 34,* 851–867.

Deltito, J. A., & Hahn, R. (1993). A three-generational presentation of separation anxiety in childhood with agoraphobia in adulthood. *Psychopharmacology Bulletin, 29,* 189–193.

Estes, H. R., Hayless, C. H., & Johnson, A. M. (1956). Separation anxiety. *American Journal of Orthopsychiatry, 10,* 682–695.

Francis, G., Last, C. G., & Strauss, C. C. (1987). Expression of separation anxiety disorder: The roles of age and gender. *Child Psychiatry and Human Development, 18,* 82–89.

Fukunishi, I., Honda, M., Kamiyama, Y., & Ito, H. (1993). Anxiety disorders and pediatric continuous ambulatory peritoneal dialysis. *Child Psychiatry and Human Development, 24,* 1, 59–64.

Garrison, C. Z., Valleni, B., Laura, A., Jackson, K. L., & Waller, J. L. (1995). Frequency of obsessive-compulsive disorder in a community sample of young adolescents. *Journal of the American Academy of Child and Adolescent Psychiatry, 34,* 128–129.

Garvey, W., & Hegrenes, J. (1966). Desensitization techniques in the treatment of school phobia. *American Journal of Orthopsychiatry, 36,* 147–152.

Gittelman-Klein, R. (1975). Pharmacotherapy and management of pathological separation anxiety. *International Journal of Mental Health, 4,* 255–271.

Gittelman-Klein, R., & Klein, D. F. (1971). Controlled imipramine treatment of school phobia. *Archives of General Psychiatry, 25,* 204–207.

Gittelman-Klein, R., & Klein, D. F. (1973). School phobia: Diagnostic considerations in the light of imipramine effects. *Journal of Nervous Mental Disorders, 156,* 199–215.

Gittelman-Klein, R., & Klein, D. F. (1980). Separation anxiety in school refusal and its treatment with drugs. In L. Hersov & B. Berg (Eds.), *Out of School* (pp. 321–341). New York: Wiley.

Gittelman-Klein, R., & Klien, D. F. (1984). Relationship between separation anxiety and panic and agoraphobia disorders. *Psychopathology, 17,* 56–65.

Hagopian, L. P., & Slifer, K. J. (1993). Treatment of separation anxiety disorder with graduated exposure and reinforcement targeting school attendance: A controlled case study. *Journal of Anxiety Disorders, 7,* 271–280.

Hamilton, B. (1994). A systematic approach to a family and school problem: A case study in separation anxiety disorder. *Family Therapy, 21,* 149–152.

Hansburg, H. G. (1980). *Adolescent separation anxiety: A method for the study of adolescent separation problems.* Huntington, NY: Krieger.

Hodges, K., Cools, J., & McKnew, D. (1989). Test-retest reliability of a clinical research interview for children: The child assessment schedule. *Psychological Assessment, 1,* 317–322.

Hodges, K., Kline, J., Stein, L., Cytryn, L., & McKnew, D. (1982). The development of a child assessment schedule for research and clinical use. *Journal of Abnormal Child Psychology, 10*(2), 173–189.

Honjo, S., Kasahara, Y., & Ohtaka, K. (1992). School refusal in Japan. *Acta Paedopsychiatrica—International Journal of Child and Adolescent Psychiatry, 55,* 29–32.

Houlihan, D. D., & Jones, R. N. (1989). Treatment of a boy's school phobia with in vivo systematic desensitization. *Professional School Psychology, 4,* 285–293.

Itskowitz, R., Orbach, I., & Yablon, Y. (1990). The effect of group therapy and correspondence with family on students' adjustment to boarding school. *School Psychology International, 11,* 243–252.

Johnson, A. M., Falstein, E. I., & Szurek, S. A. (1941). School phobia. *American Journal of Orthopsychiatry, 11,* 702–711.

Kanner, A. M., Klein, R. G., Rubinstein, B., & Mascia, A. (1989). Use of imipramine in children with intractable asthma and psychiatric disorders: A warning. *Psychotherapy Psychosomatic, 51,* 203–209.

Kaufman, A. M. (1990). The role of fantasy in the treatment of a severely disturbed child. *Psychoanalytic Study of the Child, 45,* 235–256.

Kennedy, W. A. (1965). School phobia: Rapid treatment of fifty cases. *Journal of Abnormal Psychology, 70,* 285–289. 53–67.

Kim, W. J., Hahn, S. U., Kish, J., Rosenberg, L., & Harris, J. (1991). Separation reaction of psychiatrically hospitalized children. *Child Psychiatry and Human Development, 22,* 53–67.

King, N. J., Gullone, E., & Tonge, B. J. (1991). Childhood fears and anxiety disorders. Special issue: Research in anxiety and fear. *Behavior Change, 8,* 124–135.

Klien, R. G., Koplewicz, H. S., & Kanner, A. (1992). Imipramine treatment of children with separation anxiety disorder. *Journal of the American Academy of Child and Adolescent Psychiatry, 31,* 21–28.

Last, C. G. (1991). Somatic complaints in anxiety disordered children. Special issue: Assessment of childhood anxiety disorders. *Journal of Anxiety Disorders, 5,* 125–138.

Last, C. G., Francis, G., & Strauss, C. C. (1989). Assessing fears in anxiety-disordered children with the Revised Fear Survey Schedule for Children (FSSC-R). *Journal of Clinical Child Psychology, 18,* 137–141.

Last, C. G., Francis, G., Hersen, M., Kazdin, A. E., & Strauss, C. C. (1987). Separation anxiety and school phobia: A comparison using DSM-III criteria. *American Journal of Psychiatry, 144,* 653–657.

Last, C. G., Strauss, C. C., & Francis, G. (1987). Comorbidity among childhood anxiety disorders. *Journal of Nervous and Mental Disease, 175,* 726–730.

Lazarus, A. A., & Abramovitz, A. (1962). The use of "emotive imagery" in treatment of children's phobias. *Journal of Mental Science, 108,* 191–195.

Lazarus, A. A., Davidson, G., & Polefka, D. (1965). Classical and operant factors in the treatment of a school phobic. *Journal of Abnormal Psychology, 70,* 225–229.

Leader, A. L. (1978). Intergenerational separation anxiety in family therapy. *Social Casework, 59,* 138–144.

Mansdorf, I. J., & Lukens, E. (1987). Cognitive-behavioral psychotherapy for separation anxious children exhibiting school phobia. *Journal of the American Academy of Child and Adolescent Psychiatry, 26,* 19–36.

Martin, C. A., & Korte, A. O. (1978). An application of social learning principles to a case of school phobia. *School Social Work Journal, 2,* 77–82.

Mattison, R. E., Bagnato, S. J., & Brubaker, B. H. (1988). Diagnostic utility of the Revised Children's Manifest Anxiety Scale in children with DSM-III anxiety disorders. *Journal of Anxiety Disorders, 2,* 147–155.

Miller, P. M. (1972). The use of visual imagery and muscle relaxation in the counterconditioning of a phobic child: A case study. *Journal of Nervous and Mental Disease, 151,* 457–460.

Milos, M. E., & Reiss, S. (1982). Effects of three play conditions on separation anxiety in young children. *Journal of Consulting and Clinical Psychology, 50,* 389–395.

Montenegro, H. (1968). Severe separation anxiety in two preschool children successfully treated by reciprocal inhibition. *Journal of Child Psychology and Psychiatry, 9,* 93–103.

Morris, R. J., & Kratochwill, T. R. (1985). Behavioral treatment of children's fears and phobias: A review. *School Psychology Review, 14,* 84–93.

Neisworth, J. T., Madle, R. A., & Goeke, K. E. (1975). "Errorless" elimination of separation anxiety: A case study. *Journal of Behavior Therapy and Experimental Psychiatry, 6,* 79–82.

Ollendick, T. H., & Francis, G. (1988). Behavioral assessment and treatment of childhood phobias. *Behavior Modification, 12,* 165–204.

Ollendick, T. H., Hagopian, L. P., & Huntzinger, R. M. (1991). Cognitive behavior therapy with nighttime fearful children. *Journal of Behavior Therapy and Experimental Psychiatry, 22,* 113–121.

Ollendick, T. H., & Mayer, J. R. (1985). School phobia. In S. Turner (Ed.), *Behavioral treatment of anxiety disorders.* New York: Plenum Press.

Patterson, G. R. (1965). A learning theory approach to the treatment of a school phobic child. In L. Ullmann & L. Krasner (Eds.), *Case studies in behavior modification* (pp. 279–285) New York: Holt, Rinehart & Winston.

Popper, C. W. (1993). Psychopharmacologic treatment of anxiety disorders in adolescents and children. *Journal of Clinical Psychiatry, 54*(5 suppl.), 52–63.

Rabiner, C. J., & Klien, D. F. (1969). Imipramine treatment of school phobia. *Comprehensive Psychiatry, 10,* 387–390.

Reiter, S., Kutcher, S., & Gardner, D. (1992). Anxiety disorders in children and adolescents: Clinical and related issues in pharmacological treatment. *Canadian Journal of Psychiatry, 37,* 432–438.

Scherer, M. W., & Nakamura, C. Y. (1968). A fear survey schedule for children (FSS-FC): A factor analytic comparison with manifest anxiety (CMAS) *Behaviour Research and Therapy, 6,* 173–182.

Silverman, W. K., & Nelles, W. B. (1988). The anxiety disorders interview schedule for children. *Journal of the American Academy of Child and Adolescent Psychiatry, 27,* 772–778.

Stern, D. N., MacKain, K., Raduns, K., Hopper, P. (1992). The Kiddie-Infant Descriptive Instrument for Emotional States (KIDIES): An instrument for the measurement of affective state in infancy and early childhood. *Infant Mental Health Journal, 13,* 107–118.

Thyer, B. A. (1991). Diagnosis and treatment of child and adolescent anxiety disorders. Special issue: Current perspective in the diagnosis, assessment, and treatment of child and adolescent disorders. *Behavior Modification, 15,* 310–325.

Thyer, B. A. (1993). Childhood separation anxiety disorder and adult-onset agoraphobia: Review of evidence. In C. G. Last (Ed.), *Anxiety across the lifespan: A development perspective* (pp. 128–147). New York: Springer.

Thyer, B. A., Himle, J., & Fischer, D. J. (1993). Separation anxiety disorder. In R. T. Ammerman, C. G. Last, & M. Hersen (Eds.), *Handbook of prescriptive treatments for children and adolescents* (pp. 144–158). Boston: Allyn & Bacon.

Thyer, B. A., & Sowers-Hoag, K. M. (1986). The etiology of school phobia: A behavioral approach. *School Social Work Journal, 10,* 86–98.

Thyer, B. A., & Sowers-Hoag, K. M. (1988). Behavior therapy for separation anxiety disorder. *Behavior Modification, 12,* 205–233.

Trad, P. V. (1992). Diagnostic peer group assessments in preschoolers with anxiety disorder. *Journal of Child and Adolescent Group Therapy, 2,* 175–196.

Velez, C. N., Johnson, J., & Cohen, P. (1989). A longitudinal analysis of selected risk factors for childhood psychopathology. *Journal of the American Academy of Child and Adolescent Psychiatry, 28,* 861–864.

Wellner, Z., Reich, W., Herjanic, B., Jung, K. G., & Amado, H. (1987). Reliability, validity, and parent child agreement studies of the Diagnostic Interview for Children and Adolescents (DICA). *Journal of the American Academy of Child and Adolescent Psychiatry, 26,* 649–653.

Wright, J. C., Binney, V., & Smith, P. K. (1995). Security of attachment in 8–12 year-olds: A revised version of the Separation Anxiety Test, its psychometric properties and clinical interpretation. *Journal of Child Psychology and Psychiatry and Allied Disciplines, 36,* 757–774.

PART II

Substance-Related Disorders

Chapter 9

ALCOHOL ABUSE

Nancy J. Smyth

OVERVIEW

Operational Definitions

Alcohol problems can take many forms and can be defined in many ways. Most often they are defined by diagnosis; however, in recent years there has been increased focus on the health risks of heavy drinking, irrespective of whether or not an individual qualifies for an alcohol-related diagnosis (Heather, 1993).

Moderate and Heavy Drinking. Moderate drinking has been defined by the U.S. Department of Agriculture and the U.S. Department of Health and Human Services as no more than two drinks a day for most men, and one drink a day for most women (National Institute on Alcohol Abuse and Alcoholism [NIAAA], April 1992). Definitions of heavy drinking vary, but recent surveys from the federal government define it as drinking five or more drinks per day on each of five or more days in the past month (Rouse, 1995).

Alcohol-Related Disorders. Alcohol-related disorders are divided into two major categories by the *Diagnostic and Statistical Manual of Mental Disorders, Fourth Edition* (*DSM-IV;* American Psychiatric Association [APA], 1994): *alcohol use disorders* and *alcohol-induced disorders.* The latter includes such diagnoses as Alcohol-Withdrawal Delirium and Alcohol-Induced Anxiety Disorder; the former includes two diagnoses, Alcohol Abuse and Alcohol Dependence, the second of which is considered to be more severe. This chapter focuses primarily on alcohol use disorders, not alcohol-induced disorders, because they are more commonly of concern in social work practice.

In order to qualify for a diagnosis of *Alcohol Abuse,* individuals must, within a 1-year time period, demonstrate a "maladaptive pattern of . . . [alcohol] use" (APA, 1994, p. 182) that results in significant "impairment or distress" (APA, 1994, p. 182) in one of four ways: (a) failure, as a consequence of drinking, to adequately complete one's responsibilities in some significant life role or setting (for example, work, school, and family); (b) alcohol use in physically dangerous situations (for example, drinking heavily and then driving or operating heavy machinery); (c) continuing to drink despite having social or interpersonal problems that result from, or are worsened by, drinking; and (d) experiencing repeated difficulties with the law as a result of drinking. Qualifying for a diagnosis of Alcohol Dependence is an exclusion criteria for the diagnosis of Alcohol Abuse.

A *DSM-IV* (APA, 1994) diagnosis of *Alcohol Dependence* is assigned if an individual experiences three or more of the following seven symptoms within a 1-year period: (a) withdrawal symptoms; (b) tolerance, that is, needing more alcohol to achieve the same effect or finding that the same amount of alcohol has a markedly reduced effect; (c) drinking more than planned, or for a longer period of time than was planned; (d) failed attempts to reduce or control drinking or a persistent wish to do so; (e) spending a lot of time acquiring alcohol, drinking, or recovering from drinking; (f) decreasing or giving up "important social, occupational or recreational activities" (p. 181) due to drinking; and (g) continuing to drink in spite of the awareness that drinking causes or exacerbates an ongoing or recurring physical or psychological problem.

The term *alcohol problems* is often used to refer to any negative consequence that results from alcohol use or abuse. While this clearly includes the diagnoses of Alcohol Abuse and Alcohol Dependence, it also includes those situations that do not qualify for either diagnosis, such as someone with one or two Alcohol Dependence symptoms.

People with Alcohol Problems.   A wide range of terms is used to refer to people who have problems with alcohol, specifically, alcohol abusers, alcoholics, and problem drinkers. The distinctions between these terms can be confusing and different people may use them differently. *Alcohol abuser* is usually a label applied to people who meet the diagnostic criteria for alcohol abuse, although it is sometimes used more generically to refer to anyone with an alcohol problem. *Alcoholic* is a label applied to people with more chronic alcohol problems. Some authors and researchers use the term for anyone who meets *DSM-IV* Alcohol Dependence criteria, while others apply it only to people who meet those criteria and who also meet criteria for physical dependence on alcohol (withdrawal or tolerance). *Problem drinker* is often used to refer to people with Alcohol Abuse or Alcohol Dependence, particularly dependence without significant withdrawal symptoms or without significant physical deterioration due to alcohol use, although it also may incorporate people who have experienced an alcohol problem and who do not quite fit *DSM-IV* criteria. In light of the variable use of these terms in the literature, the phrases *people with alcohol problems, alcoholics, alcohol abusers,* and *problem drinkers* are used interchangeably in this chapter.

Prevalence, Incidence, and Social and Financial Costs

Almost 19% of the U.S. adult (age >18) population report never drinking alcohol, 18.5% identify themselves as former drinkers, and 11.3% as lifetime infrequent drinkers, leaving slightly more than half (51.6%) of adults who identify themselves as current drinkers (Grant, 1994). In the U.S. general population, 4.72% qualify for a current (within the past year) diagnosis of Alcohol Abuse, 3.84% qualify for Alcohol Dependence, and 8.56% qualify for either Alcohol Dependence or Alcohol Abuse (Grant, 1994). In examining rates for current alcohol abuse or dependence among subpopulations, White males have the highest rate (13.93%), followed by non-White males (9.12%), White females (4.62%), and non-White females (2.53%; Grant, 1994). The age group with the highest rates of alcohol abuse or dependence is 18 to 29 (16.78%; Grant, 1994).

A 1993 U.S. survey found that 5.3% of Americans age 12 and up reported heavy alcohol drinking in the past month (Substance Abuse and Mental Health Services Administration [SAMHSA], 1995). On average, men in this survey reported a much higher rate of heavy drinking than women (9.5% vs. 1.5%). The age group with the highest rate of heavy drinking was 18 to 25; their overall rate was 10.4%, with men at 16.8% and women at 4.0%. Whites had the highest rates of heavy drinking (5.7%), followed by Hispanics (5.2%) and Blacks (4.3%; SAMHSA, 1995).

While all heavy drinkers may not be experiencing current alcohol-related problems, they are at risk of developing future problems (NIAAA, April 1992). Among all people who reported some alcohol use, 17.7% reported experiencing at least one alcohol-related problem in the past year (SAMHSA, 1995). Among heavy drinkers, this rate was reported at 70.3% (SAMHSA, 1995).

Alcohol use and abuse play a significant role in many problems, including a wide range of medical diseases, accidental deaths and injuries, suicides and attempted suicides, homicides, family violence, criminal behavior, birth defects, and job productivity losses (NIAAA, 1994). For example, 49.5% of all fatal crashes in 1990 were alcohol-related (NIAAA, 1994). While this is an alarmingly high rate, it reflects a 12.9% decrease since 1982 (NIAAA, 1994). Alcohol involvement among emergency room patients ranges from 15% to 25% (NIAAA, 1994). The incidence of Fetal Alcohol Syndrome, a cluster of birth defects attributable to maternal alcohol use during pregnancy, is estimated at 0.33 to 1.9 cases per 1,000 births in the United States, although the rate for some special populations can be much higher. To illustrate, some Native American populations in the United States have rates of 10 per 1,000 births, while rates as high as 120 per 1,000 have been reported among Native Americans in Canada (NIAAA, 1994). Taken together, the direct and indirect economic costs of alcohol problems in the United States were estimated at $98.7 billion for 1990 (Rouse, 1995).

Relevance of Social Work's Involvement

Social workers can be involved in the assessment of and intervention with alcohol problems in one of two ways: in alcohol and other drug practice settings, or through contact with alcohol-involved clients in other practice settings (Smyth, 1995). Since alcohol abuse may affect people in any number of ways, people with alcohol problems (and their family members) often seek services for a wide range of presenting problems, including family conflict, depression, anxiety, financial difficulties, legal problems, declining performance in school or at work, and physical disorders (Smyth, 1995). Therefore, social workers employed in child welfare, family service, health, mental health, criminal justice, employee assistance, school, and private practice settings will frequently encounter clients who are experiencing alcohol-related problems, either as a result of the client's own use of alcohol, or because of alcohol abuse by someone the client knows.

In many cases, clients do not connect their use of alcohol with the cause of their difficulties, so they may not volunteer information about their alcohol and other drug use. For these reasons, it is essential for social workers in all practice settings to be familiar with how alcohol abuse can affect individuals and families. Alcohol and other drug use information should also, therefore, be routinely gathered.

Recent years have seen an increase in interest among social workers in working with people with alcohol problems and their families. For example, the National Association of Social Workers recently formed a special section for members interested in this field of practice ("Substance section," 1995). While the percentage of social workers providing service in substance abuse agencies is still relatively small, it has been slowly increasing; in 1991, social workers constituted 8.5% of the direct care staff in alcohol and drug treatment agencies (National Institute on Drug Abuse/NIAAA, 1993), a slight increase from the 1982 figure of 6.9% (NIAAA, 1983).

ASSESSMENT METHODS

As with all good social work practice, the assessment of alcohol problems provides the foundation for case conceptualization and treatment planning. Alcohol assessment should take place within the context of a comprehensive biopsychosocial assessment of clients and their environments. Factors such as social support, family environment, psychopathology, use of drugs other than alcohol, and employment all affect the client's probability of success in addressing an alcohol problem (Moos, Finney, & Cronkite, 1990). As a general rule, the more aspects of the client's life that are impaired, whether due to alcohol use or other problems, the more involved and comprehensive treatment will need to be.

In addition to conducting clinical interviews, there are many different types of assessment strategies that can be employed to facilitate the assessment process, including structured interviews, computerized assessment tools, self-report methods, observation, and biological methods. An excellent source book on assessment, assessment methods, and assessment scales and interviews is available from the NIAAA (Allen & Columbus, 1995). Unless indicated otherwise, all of the assessment instruments discussed here have demonstrated good psychometric characteristics; that is, they have demonstrated reliability and validity.

Structured Clinical Interviews

There are several structured clinical interviews that can be used in alcohol assessment and treatment. The alcohol section of the Diagnostic Interview Schedule (DIS; Robins, Helzer, Croughan, & Ratcliff, 1981) is often used to establish a reliable and valid diagnosis of Alcohol Abuse or Alcohol Dependence. A structured interview that often is used for treatment planning or measurement of treatment outcome is the Addiction Severity Index (ASI; McLellan et al., 1992). The ASI yields composite and severity scores in seven areas of client functioning: (a) alcohol use, (b) drug use, (c) medical, (d) employment, (e) legal, (f) family/social, and (g) psychiatric (McLellan et al., 1992). The Comprehensive Problem Drinker Profile (Miller & Marlatt, 1984) is another structured interview that provides useful information for treatment planning.

Computerized Assessment Methods

Computerized versions of many of the assessment scales discussed in this chapter are available. Among the structured interviews, there is a computerized version of the Diagnostic Interview Schedule (Robins et al., 1981). The computerized version of the Time Line Follow Back (Sobell & Sobell, 1995c), an alcohol consumption assessment tool, greatly facilitates the collection and scoring of this information. Many of the self-report assessment instruments, such as the Inventory of Drinking Situations (IDS; Annis, Graham, & Davis, 1987), also have computerized versions. In general, there is a trend to computerize more assessment instruments, so it is advisable to contact the source of the original version to determine if one is available. Practitioners should also be aware that computerized assessment instruments should be evaluated for psychometric characteristics separately from their non-computerized counterparts (Finnegan, Ivanoff, & Smyth, 1991).

Self-Report Methods

Many self-report methods are used in the assessment and treatment of Alcohol Abuse and Alcohol Dependence, although they can be conceptualized in three major categories: (a) measures of alcohol consumption, (b) screening and diagnostic measures, and (c) measures of characteristics of drinking that are helpful in the treatment planning process (Allen & Columbus, 1995). Accurate self-reports are more likely to be ensured when interviews are conducted under the following conditions: (a) clients are alcohol-free, (b) confidentiality is ensured, and (c) interviews are conducted in clinical or research settings, rather than legal settings (Sobell & Sobell, 1995a).

Alcohol Consumption Measures.   Common measures of alcohol consumption include the Time Line Follow Back method (TLFB; Sobell & Sobell, 1995b), a range of Quantity-Frequency (QF) measures (Room, 1990), and the use of diaries or self-monitoring logs (Miller, Westerberg, & Waldron, 1995). All measures of alcohol consumption evaluate drinking in terms of the number of standard drinks. One standard drink is equivalent to 0.5 oz of ethyl alcohol. Alcoholic beverages vary in the amount of alcohol contained in each; According to Miller (1992, p. 77), the following beverages are equal to one standard drink:

Beverage	Usual % alcohol	×	Ounces	=	Alcohol content (oz)
Beer	0.05	×	10.0	=	0.5
Table wine	0.12	×	4.0	=	0.5
80 Proof Spirits	0.40	×	1.25	=	0.5

Diaries and drinking self-monitoring logs are useful for collecting current or prospective levels of drinking, since clients can fill them out on a day-by-day basis. Log entries usually include information about the situation in which alcohol is consumed, the client's mood or thoughts at the time, and the amount and type of alcoholic beverage consumed (Allen & Columbus, 1995). In addition to providing information about levels of consumption, this assessment method can provide useful clinical information about drinking antecedents, which, in turn, can facilitate treatment planning.

QF measures usually retrospectively assess an average pattern of alcohol use, based upon the average number of drinks per drinking occasion and the average frequency of drinking occasions, although the frequency of the maximum quantity of drinking also may be measured. While QF measures provide information about total alcohol consumption and the number of drinking days, they assume that drinking is constant, and, therefore, do not provide information about the variation in drinking over time (Sobell & Sobell, 1995a).

The TLFB method utilizes a calendar to collect detailed information about an individual's past daily drinking over a designated time period, anywhere from 30 days to 12 months prior to the interview (Sobell & Sobell, 1995b). Several memory aids are used to enhance accurate recall, and it can be administered by a trained interviewer or be self-administered by clients in either paper-and-pencil or computerized formats (Sobell & Sobell, 1995b, 1995c).

Screening and Diagnostic Measures.   Screening and diagnostic measures aid in the determination of the existence and severity of an alcohol problem. Screening measures are designed to detect people with alcohol problems who have not yet been identified as having an alcohol problem; for example, people seeking primary health care. For this reason, they are usually brief (Connors, 1995). Diagnostic measures are used to assess the severity of an alcohol problem among clinical populations. There are some instruments, such as the Michigan Alcoholism Screening Test (MAST; Selzer, 1971), that are sometimes used for both screening and diagnosis.

Two common brief screening tools are the MAST (Selzer, 1971), and the CAGE (Mayfield, McLeod, & Hall, 1974). There are several brief versions of the MAST, including a 10-item, a 13-item, and a 24-item version (Allen & Columbus, 1995). CAGE is the simplest of the screening tools; it involves asking the following four questions about alcohol use (two positive responses are clinically significant):

C   Have you ever felt you should **C**ut-down on your drinking?

A   Have people **A**nnoyed you by criticizing your drinking?

G   Have you ever felt bad or **G**uilty about your drinking?

E   Have you ever had a drink first thing in the morning to steady your nerves or to get rid of a hangover (**E**ye-opener)? (Mayfield et al., 1974, p. 1121)

Both the CAGE and the MAST inquire about lifetime alcohol problems, so they are best used to identify individuals who need further assessment and not to determine a current drinking problem. In contrast, the Alcohol Use Disorders Identification Test (AUDIT; Saunders, Aasland, Babor, de la Fuente, & Grant, 1993) is a 10-item screening instrument developed by the World Health Organization that assesses recent drinking, with questions on quantity and frequency, alcohol problems, and alcohol dependence.

Finally, some screening instruments have been designed for the detection of alcohol problems in special populations. Among these are the TWEAK (Russell, Czarnecki, Cowan, McPherson, & Mudar, 1991), for women, and the Rutgers Alcohol Problem Index (White & Labouvie, 1989), for adolescents.

Diagnostic measures are used to assess the severity of an alcohol problem; they are more often employed in situations where an alcohol problem is already suspected, as in the case of evaluation interviews conducted in an alcohol treatment clinic. Common diagnostic measures are the Alcohol Dependence Scale (ADS; Skinner & Horn, 1984), an instrument that assesses severity of alcohol dependence; the Impaired Control Scale (Heather, Tebbot, Mattick, & Zamir, 1993), a measure of actual and perceived control over drinking, and the DrInc (Miller, Tonigan, & Longabaugh, 1995), a scale that measures the consequences of alcohol use. Information from these measures can be useful in making some clinical decisions.

For example, the ADS can be used to determine if a moderate drinking (versus abstinence) treatment goal is likely to be successful for a particular client (Skinner & Horn, 1984).

Treatment Planning Tools.   There are a plethora of assessment instruments that provide useful information in designing treatment plans (Donovan, 1995). These tools provide information about clients' motivation to change, alcohol-related beliefs, drinking relapse risk, and self-efficacy, as well as other aspects of clients' alcohol-related behavior (Donovan, 1995).

One key factor that should be assessed is client motivation and readiness to change. The Readiness to Change Questionnaire (RTCQ; Heather, Gold, & Rollnick, 1991) and Stages of Change Readiness and Treatment Eagerness Scale (SOCRATES; Miller & Tonigan, 1994) are two instruments that assess clients according to the stages-of-change model developed by Prochaska and associates (Prochaska & DiClemente, 1984; Prochaska, DiClemente, & Norcross, 1992). They have identified five stages of change that people go through in changing addictive behaviors: (a) pre-contemplation, (b) contemplation, (c) preparation or determination, (d) action, and (e) maintenance. This model was derived from psychotherapy research (Prochaska & DiClemente, 1984), and subsequent studies have confirmed that clients with the best outcomes are those who are in the preparation or action stages during intervention (Prochaska, DiClemente, & Norcross, 1992; Prochaska, Norcross, Fowler, Follick, & Abrams, 1992). Clients in the earlier stages of precontemplation and contemplation should receive interventions designed to move them from one stage to the next (Prochaska, Norcross, et al., 1992; Miller & Rollnick, 1991).

Clients' beliefs or expectancies about alcohol use also are important to consider in assessment; research indicates that people with alcohol problems hold different alcohol expectancies than people without these problems (Donovan, 1995). When expectancies maintain problematic drinking, they should be specifically targeted for change through cognitive intervention. Among the many scales used to assess alcohol expectancies are the Alcohol Effects Questionnaire (AEFQ; Rohsenow, 1983) and the Alcohol Beliefs Scale (Connors & Maisto, 1988).

The assessment of relapse risk is often done through examination of two aspects of clients' behavior: situational patterns of heavy drinking and self-efficacy; that is, beliefs about their ability to successfully maintain changes in their drinking (Dimeff & Marlatt, 1995). Two assessment instruments that are frequently used for these respective purposes are the Inventory of Drinking Situations (IDS; Annis, Graham, & Davis, 1987) and the Situational Confidence Questionnaire (SCQ; Annis & Graham, 1988). Both scales are based upon the relapse research conducted by Marlatt and colleagues that identifies the following common situations for relapse risk: unpleasant emotions, physical discomfort, pleasant emotions, testing personal control, urges or temptations to use, conflict with others, social pressure to use, and pleasant times with others (Marlatt, 1985).

Observational Methods. Observational methods are not used as frequently in the assessment and treatment of alcohol abuse as they are in clinical research, where observation in simulations, such as a simulated bar, may be used. The most common observational method relevant to practice is that of observing clients in role-playing scenarios. While practitioners can develop client-specific scenarios, there are several role-play tests that have been developed for this purpose. One such instrument is the Alcohol-Specific Role-Play Test (ASRPT; Monti et al., 1993), a ten-situation role-play that is used to assess relapse risk in intrapersonal and interpersonal situations.

Physiological Measures. While many physiological measures of acute and chronic alcohol use exist, most involve testing blood or urine for specific biological markers (Anton, Litten, & Allen, 1995). One exception to this rule is the alcohol breath test, or breathalyzer, a test that measures the amount of alcohol on the breath. This test is often used in clinical as well as legal settings to determine if an individual is under the influence of alcohol; results are normally reported as a blood alcohol count (BAC) or blood alcohol level (BAL). While there are no biological tests that test for alcoholism, there are some liver function tests that detect chronic alcohol intake, the most sensitive of which is the gamma glutamyltransferase (GGT) test (Anton et al., 1995). Unlike the breathalyzer, which is often utilized by social workers and other nonmedical personnel, the GGT test is more exclusively utilized by medical personnel or researchers.

EFFECTIVE INTERVENTIONS

There are many empirically validated approaches available for intervening with alcohol problems. However, it has often been the case that alcohol treatment agencies do not use treatment approaches that are supported by research; instead, many agencies have relied on approaches that either have not been effectively tested or have been shown to be less effective than other methods (Miller & Hester, 1986; Miller et al., 1995). With one or two exceptions (which are clearly noted), treatment approaches that have not been demonstrated to be effective are not discussed in this chapter.

While most alcohol treatment agencies identify abstinence as the goal of treatment, research indicates that moderate drinking is a realistic goal for problem drinkers (Connors, 1993). Generally, research indicates that stable positive moderate drinking outcomes are more likely for low to moderate severity problem drinkers than for severely dependent alcoholics (Connors, 1993).

Among the most important trends in alcohol treatment research has been an emphasis on matching clients to alcohol treatments; that is, recognizing that no one treatment approach works for everyone (Institute of Medicine, 1990; Allen & Kadden, 1995). The range of characteristics that have been found to predict differential treatment outcome includes psychosocial, demographic, and alcohol-related characteristics (Allen & Kadden, 1995). Examples of relevant psychosocial characteristics are sociopathy, autonomy, locus of control, and social stability; important demographic variables include gender and age; and relevant alcohol-related characteristics are the client's view of alcoholism, motivation to change drinking, and urge to drink (Allen & Kadden, 1995).

Individual Therapies

Most alcohol treatment settings provide some type of individual counseling, although many place a greater emphasis on group and self-help approaches (Straussner, 1993). There is a wide range of empirically validated individual treatment methods, the majority of which come from a cognitive-behavioral perspective (Miller et al., 1995).

Brief intervention for alcohol problems is receiving increasing attention in the treatment literature, particularly for clients with low or moderate alcohol dependence; for this population it seems to be more effective than no treatment and as effective as more extensive treatment (Heather, 1995). Brief treatment most often involves some assessment of the client's drinking followed by the provision of personalized feedback; this can include advice from a physician to cut down on drinking as well as a clear message about the nature of sensible and problematic drinking (Babor, Ritson, & Hodgson, 1986). There is more research evidence supporting brief intervention than there is for any other type of alcohol treatment (Miller et al., 1995).

Motivational interventions are a specialized type of brief intervention designed to enhance people's commitment to changing their drinking. The most well known of these approaches, motivational interviewing (MI; Miller & Rollnick, 1991), synthesizes elements of several effective motivational strategies. The goal of motivational interviewing is to assist clients in recognizing that they have problems with alcohol, and to help them decide to change and to move toward making desired changes in their lives. Miller and Rollnick (1991) identify five basic principles of motivational interviewing: (a) express empathy, (b) develop discrepancy between individuals' perceptions of where they are and where they want to be, (c) avoid argumentation, (d) roll with resistance, and (e) support clients' sense of self-efficacy. Motivational interviewing utilizes many of the principles of empathic and nondirective communication in a systematic effort to facilitate change. Client resistance is managed through empathy, reflection, and paraphrasing instead of by challenging it directly. The practitioner attempts to engage the client in a collaborative, mutual exploration of his or her drinking, using active listening skills to reinforce any information related to a drinking problem. Labels (such as *alcoholic, problem drinker,* or *having an alcohol problem*) are deemphasized and are not envisioned as necessary for change to occur.

Outcome research on motivational interventions indicates that they are quite effective; Miller et al. (1995) ranked these strategies third (out of 30 different categories of alcohol treatment) in cumulative evidence of effectiveness. Recent results from Project MATCH, a nine-site national study funded by the NIAAA, indicate that 4 sessions of Motivational Enhancement Therapy (MET; Miller, Zweban, DiClemente, & Rychtarik, 1992) are as effective as 12 sessions of the comparative treatments, coping skills training and 12-step facilitation (Project MATCH Research Group, 1997). In addition, preliminary research indicates that even one motivational counseling session at the beginning of an inpatient stay significantly improves treatment outcome (Brown & Miller, 1993).

Behavioral Self-Control Training (BSCT) is a treatment method that can be used for drinking goals of either abstinence or moderation and can be delivered in individual or group treatment formats (Hester, 1995b). The most recent innovation in BSCT is an interactive computer software program that teaches clients BSCT skills with minimal therapist involvement (Hester, 1995a). BSCT involves setting limits on drinking, self-monitoring of drinking, utilizing moderation strategies such as drink refusal and drinking rate control skills, designing reward systems for goal achievement, analysis of the antecedents for overdrinking, and development of alternative coping skills to manage overdrinking trigger situations (Hester, 1995b). Overall, BSCT has good empirical support, having been evaluated in over 30 outcome studies (Hester, 1995b; Miller et al., 1995); it has not performed well only when compared to brief intervention (Miller et al., 1995). These findings suggest that BSCT should be provided after efforts with brief intervention have failed (Hester, 1995b; Miller et al., 1995); in addition, research indicates that moderation goals may be appropriate for problem drinkers but are not recommended for severely dependent alcoholics (Hester, 1995b).

Relapse prevention is a treatment approach that has been offered in individual, family, and group treatment formats, although it has been most consistently evaluated as part of group treatment (Dimeff & Marlatt, 1995). Therefore, it is discussed in the section on group therapies.

Pharmacological treatment is the primary intervention for alcohol withdrawal (detoxification), generally with benzodiazepines such as diazepam and chlorodiazepoxide (Anton, 1994). Beyond their use with detoxification, medications alone are rarely used to treat alcohol problems; however, they can be important supplements to other treatment (Anton, 1994). The most well known drug used in alcoholism treatment is disulfiram (Antabuse), a medication that causes nausea if alcohol is ingested (Fuller, 1995). The extensive research on disulfiram suggests that when used in combination with other alcoholism treatment approaches it enhances treatment outcome (Fuller, 1995). In addition to disulfiram, recent research on naltrexone suggests that when used as an adjunct to treatment it can prevent alcoholism relapse (O'Malley et al., 1992; Volpicelli, Alterman, Hayashida, & O'Brien, 1992). Finally, research on two other medications, buspirone and acamprosate, suggests that they also hold promise for enhancing treatment outcome (Schuckit, 1996).

Aversion therapy is another form of effective treatment for alcohol problems (Miller et al., 1995; Rimmele, Howard, & Hilfrink, 1995). Historically, aversion therapy involved the use of electrical shock; this form of aversion therapy is not effective (Miller et al., 1995). However, aversion therapy utilizing either nausea-inducing drugs or covert sensitization both have empirical support (Miller et al., 1995; Rimmele et al., 1995). The most applicable form of this treatment for out-patient settings is covert sensitization, a procedure that involves pairing, through imagery, drinking scenes with an unpleasant scene, such as feeling nauseous. In addition, drinking scenes are paired with scenes where the client utilizes coping strategies to avoid drinking (Rimmele et al., 1995).

There is a range of other treatment strategies with empirical support for treating alcohol problems. Most of these treatment methods are types of cognitive-behavioral treatment, including behavior contracting, cognitive therapy, and the use of self-help manuals, which usually teach BSCT (Miller et al., 1995). In addition, client-centered therapy has empirical support (Miller et al., 1995). It should be noted that some of these treatment approaches are incorporated into other interventions discussed in this chapter. For example, MI incorporates many strategies from client-centered therapy, and both BSCT and the community reinforcement approach (discussed later) incorporate behavioral contracting. In addition, there are a few treatment strategies that have demonstrated promise for the treatment of alcohol problems, but that need to be subjected to further investigation and replication (Miller et al., 1995). Among these methods are acupuncture (Bullock, Uman, Culliton, & Olander, 1987), sensory deprivation (Cooper, Adams, & Scott, 1988), and developmental counseling (Alden, 1988).

Group Therapies

Although practitioners consider group therapy to be the treatment of choice for people with alcohol problems (Galanter, Castaneda, & Franco, 1991), the comparative effectiveness of group versus other treatment modalities has not been systematically examined (Cartwright, 1987). One study of problem drinkers found no difference between the two treatment modalities, although group therapy clients achieved their gains earlier in treatment than those in individual therapy (Duckert, Amundsen, & Johnsen, 1992). Another study compared individual and group guided self-change treatment, a motivationally based four-session BSCT intervention, and found no difference in alcohol treatment outcome, retention in treatment, or client satisfaction between the two modalities (Sobell, Sobell, Brown, Cleland, & Buchan, November 1995).

As noted earlier, relapse prevention (RP) is often provided as a type of group treatment. Its components include self-monitoring of drinking or drinking urges, identifying high-risk situations, assessment of the client's current coping skills or resources and self-efficacy, developing coping strategies and a plan to manage high-risk situations, and developing or strengthening more lifestyle balance with regard to shoulds and wants (Dimeff & Marlatt, 1995). Research generally supports the effectiveness of RP (Dimeff & Marlatt, 1995; Miller et al., 1995). Some research suggests that RP is most likely to benefit people with moderate to severe alcohol dependence (Dimeff & Marlatt, 1995) and alcoholics with differentiated rather than undifferentiated drinking profiles; that is, drinking that varies over different types of situations (Annis & Davis, 1989).

Coping and social skills training (CSST; Monti, Rohsenow, Colby, & Abrams, 1995) for treating alcohol problems has been most often delivered and investigated as a group intervention, although it has been adapted for individual treatment, as well (Monti, Abrams, Kadden, & Cooney, 1989; Monti et al., 1995). These approaches usually include interpersonal and mood-management skills, particularly as they relate to alcohol use (Monti et al., 1989, 1995). Topics might include coping with alcohol cravings and drinking-related thoughts, problem solving, managing anger, assertiveness, giving and receiving criticism, planning for emergencies, coping with a lapse, and managing negative thinking. CSST has strong empirical support for its effectiveness (Miller et al., 1995; Monti et al., 1989). In addition, research suggests that it may be particularly effective for more severe alcoholics and for alcoholics with concurrent psychopathology (Monti et al., 1995).

Another group treatment is interactional group therapy for alcohol problems, developed by Getter (1984) and based on work by Yalom and colleagues (Brown & Yalom, 1977; Yalom, 1974); interactional group therapy has demonstrated important matching effects for specific types of alcoholics when compared to coping skills group treatment (Allen & Kadden, 1995). Alcoholics rated higher in either psychopathology or sociopathy are less likely to relapse in coping skills than in interactional group therapy, whereas alcoholics rated lower in these two characteristics, or who have high levels of cognitive impairment, are less likely to relapse in interactional group therapy (Cooney, Kadden, Litt, & Getter, 1991).

No discussion of group treatment would be complete without mention of self-help groups. The largest and most widely known self-help group is Alcoholics Anonymous (AA), but there are others, including Rational Recovery (RR), Secular Organizations for Sobriety/Save Our Selves (SOS), Women for Sobriety (WFS) and Self-Management and Recovery Training (SMART) (McCrady & Delaney, 1995; Horvath, July 1996). There is some research on the type of individuals likely to affiliate with AA and RR. Specifically, AA affiliators are likely to have severe drinking histories, have experienced loss of control over their drinking, and have anxiety about their drinking (Emrick, Tonigan, Montgomery, & Little, 1993). RR affiliators often place a high value on rationality and low value on spirituality (Galanter, Egelko, & Edwards, 1993).

While most alcohol treatment settings and treatment professionals refer clients to AA, there is no empirical evidence supporting the effectiveness of AA as an intervention by itself (McCrady & Delaney, 1995). A review of studies examining AA's effectiveness as an adjunct to treatment did indicate that AA attendance is associated with modest improvements in outcome (Emrick et al., 1993). No published studies have been conducted on the effectiveness of the other self-help groups mentioned in this chapter (McCrady & Delaney, 1995).

Marital and Family Therapies

Marital and family treatment (MFT) of alcohol problems, particularly behavioral MFT, has relatively strong empirical support for its effectiveness (Miller et al., 1995; O'Farrell, 1995). However, by and large, most of these studies have been conducted with white male alcoholics (O'Farrell, 1995).

While there are no data on the types of people who have the best response to MFT, clients who accept and complete MFT are most likely to have the following characteristics (O'Farrell, 1995): (a) have full-time employment; (b) have a minimum of a high school education; (c) have serious alcohol problems of relatively long duration; (d) have a spouse or other family members who are not alcoholic; (e) come into treatment after a crisis, usually one that threatens the marriage; (f) alcoholic, spouse and other members of the family have no concurrent drug abuse or serious psychopathology; (g) have no history of serious family violence (that is, violence that is life-threatening or that has resulted in serious injury); and (h) live with the spouse, or will move back in with the spouse for the course of treatment. One study found that alcoholics who are rated high in autonomy have better post-treatment family functioning when treated with social learning (SL) MFT than when treated with individual SL treatment, whereas alcoholics who are rated low in autonomy have better family functioning when treated with individual SL treatment (McKay, Longabaugh, Beattie, Maisto, & Noel, 1993).

MFT can be divided into two major categories: interventions designed to work with spouses of treatment-resistant alcoholics and interventions used when the alcoholic is in treatment. The former category includes several interventions that have some empirical support, although all require further replication, while the latter has more outcome research to support treatment effectiveness (O'Farrell, 1995).

MFT Interventions for Treatment-Resistant Alcoholics.   One intervention targeting spouses of treatment-resistant alcoholics is unilateral family therapy (UFT), an approach that works with spouses of alcoholics to enhance their family functioning and coping skills, as well as teach them how to encourage problem drinkers' sobriety (Thomas, 1994). Preliminary trials evaluating UFT have supported its effectiveness in decreasing spouses' distress, increasing marital satisfaction, and facilitating alcoholics' entry into treatment (O'Farrell, 1995; Thomas, Santa, Bronson, & Oyserman, 1987).

Another unilateral approach to working with spouses of alcoholics, Reinforcement Training (RT), focuses on teaching the partner how to avoid physical abuse and how to facilitate sobriety and the alcoholic's entry into treatment (Sisson & Azrin, 1986). A pilot study comparing RT to supportive counseling and disease concept education plus referral to Alanon (a self-help group) found that RT was more successful in getting alcoholics both to enter treatment and to reduce their drinking prior to entering treatment (Sisson & Azrin, 1986).

Both UFT and RT are interventions that can involve several months of treatment. In an effort to develop a brief unilateral intervention, Barber and Crisp (1995) developed the Pressures to Change (PC) approach, a five- or six-session treatment method that teaches the spouse or partner behavioral strategies to encourage the alcohol abuser to either reduce drinking or seek treatment. When compared to both a control group and to Alanon, partners receiving the PC approach were more likely to have spouses who reduced drinking and entered treatment (Barber & Gilbertson, 1996). In addition, partners who received PC through individual counseling, as opposed to group work, had higher marital consensus scores than both the Alanon and control conditions (Barber & Gilbertson, 1996).

The Johnson Institute Intervention model (JII; Johnson, 1973), an approach that involves educating and preparing family members to confront the alcohol abuser, was evaluated in one study and found to be successful in facilitating alcoholics' entry into treatment (Liepman, Nirenberg, & Begin, 1989). However, the JII condition had a very high dropout rate. A retrospective study comparing the JII with four other types of referrals found that JII referrals had higher rates of entering treatment than did coerced and voluntary referrals, as well as referrals from unsupervised interventions (USI) and unrehearsed interventions (URI; interventions that deviated from JII model; Loneck, Garrett, & Banks, 1996a). Although the JII clients were more likely to relapse than the clients from the other four referral types, they were equally as likely to complete treatment as coerced, USI, and URI clients and were more likely to complete than voluntary clients (Loneck, Garrett, & Banks, 1996b).

The final intervention approach with some promise of empirical support is disease-concept oriented group therapy for spouses of alcoholics. One study found that wives in this group treatment had less enabling and anxiety, and greater self-concept, than wives in a waiting list control condition (Dittrich & Trapold, 1984).

Self-help groups for family members of alcoholics also exist, specifically Alanon (for adult family members), Alateen and Alatot (for children), and Alanon-Adult Children of Alcoholics (ACOA), for adults who grew up in an alcoholic family (McCrady & Delaney, 1995). Of these groups, only Alanon has received any study, and that has been minimal (O'Farrell, 1995). In the one small controlled study comparing Alanon to the PC unilateral approach (Barber & Gilbertson, 1996), Alanon participants had fewer personal problems than control participants and PC group work participants, but not PC individual counseling participants. However, as previously noted, Alanon was not effective in helping spouses facilitate their partners' entry into treatment. There also have been several uncontrolled, correlational studies that reported positive outcomes for wives who participated in Alanon (O'Farrell, 1995).

MFT Interventions When the Alcoholic Is in Treatment.

Most alcohol treatment agencies treat couples by enrolling the spouse and the alcoholic in separate, concurrent treatment; however, there are no controlled studies evaluating the effectiveness of this treatment approach (O'Farrell, 1995). In contrast, there is quite a bit of research on the effectiveness of conjoint MFT when the alcoholic is enrolled in treatment (O'Farrell, 1995). As previously noted, most of the effective MFT interventions are behavioral approaches. However, there also is some empirical support for nonbehavioral couples group treatment compared to treating only the alcoholic (Cadogan, 1973; Corder, Corder, & Laidlaw, 1972; McCrady, Paolino, Longabaugh, & Rossi, 1979). The only study of family systems conjoint treatment of alcohol abuse indicated that participants receiving one conjoint session of advice counseling did as well as participants receiving eight sessions of couples treatment based on a family systems approach (Zweben, Pearlman, & Li, 1988).

Behavioral MFT (BMFT) can be conducted with one couple or with a group of couples; it generally includes communication skills and problem-solving training, teaching constructive strategies for changing a spouse's behavior, and as a focus on drinking and alcohol-related interaction (O'Farrell, 1995). A review of treatment outcome studies on BMFT indicated that it is more effective in treating alcoholics than treatment methods that do not include conjoint or family treatment, and that adding relapse prevention sessions can minimize deterioration of treatment gains (O'Farrell, 1995).

Community Interventions

Community interventions can range from interventions that utilize environmental components in the treatment of individuals to interventions that target population subgroups or whole communities.

The Community Reinforcement Approach (CRA; Meyers & Smith, 1995; Smith & Meyers, 1995) is a broad-spectrum behavioral treatment method that utilizes environmental reinforcers (social, recreational, vocational, and familial) to intervene in alcohol and other drug problems. Treatment strategies are chosen from a wide array of options, including coping skills training, job training, social clubs, marital therapy, relapse prevention, disulfiram, and social or recreational counseling, depending upon the assessment of the antecedents and consequences of the individual's drinking. In a comprehensive review of alcohol treatment research, CRA was rated as fourth (among 30 different modalities) in the amount of cumulative evidence that supports its effectiveness (Miller et al., 1995).

A very different type of community intervention can be found in the application of brief interventions to such community settings as hospitals and primary health care settings. These interventions may be conducted as part of health screening programs, regular physical exams, or in the context of a medical hospitalization (Heather, 1995). As with brief intervention in general, these community-based brief treatment approaches have excellent empirical support (Heather, 1995).

Intervention with driving under the influence (DUI) offenders is another area for community intervention. A meta-analysis of DUI remediation programs concluded that such programs are generally successful in preventing recidivism (Wells-Parker, Bangert-Drowns, McMillen, & Williams, 1995). The best combination of interventions was identified as education, psychotherapy, and probation contact (Wells-Parker et al., 1995). A new approach to intervening with multiple DUI offenders, the Probation Alcohol Treatment (PAT) approach, integrates alcoholism treatment and probation into a single intervention; research on the PAT program found that it reduces recidivism among repeat drinking and driving offenders ("Combination of alcohol treatment . . .", 1995).

Many of the communitywide interventions for alcohol problems focus on preventing the development of alcohol problems—primary prevention—as opposed to intervention with people with early stage or more serious alcohol problems (NIAAA, 1994). A discussion of prevention strategies follows.

Prevention

Prevention interventions can target multiple system levels, from individuals to an entire nation (NIAAA, 1994). Efforts to prevent alcohol problems can be divided into several categories, including policies targeting the availability (physical, economic, and social) of alcohol, social controls, and primary prevention programs (Moskowitz, 1989).

Availability-reduction approaches can encompass limiting the type or number of outlets where alcohol is sold, raising the price of alcoholic beverages, limiting advertising of alcohol, and limiting the sale and consumption of alcohol. While there are data indicating that limiting the availability of alcohol is correlated with a reduction in alcohol consumption and in alcohol problems (NIAAA, 1994), methodological limitations in many of these studies do not allow for the identification of clear cause-and-effect relationships (Moskowitz, 1989). In a review of alcohol problem prevention research, Moskowitz (1989) identified that the research offers strong support for maintaining a higher, rather than lower (that is, age 21 versus 18), minimum drinking age. Policies that increase taxation on alcoholic beverages also appear to reduce alcohol problems.

Social control approaches to reducing alcohol problems have focused on public intoxication laws and, more recently, drinking-and-driving laws. To date, there is good empirical support for increased enforcement of drinking-and-driving laws as a policy to reduce alcohol-related fatalities (Moskowitz, 1989; NIAAA, 1994).

The research on primary prevention approaches provides little guidance for prevention intervention. There is little research to support mass media and education programs as an intervention strategy, and there is some research to indicate that these programs can sometimes result in increased drinking (Moskowitz, 1989). At best, mass media and education programs appear to influence knowledge, but rarely behavior (Moskowitz, 1989; Schinke, Botvin, & Orlandi, 1991); in other cases, as with the introduction of warning labels on alcoholic beverages, mass education campaigns appear to have had no impact even on knowledge and awareness of the hazards of alcohol consumption (NIAAA, 1994).

The few effective primary prevention interventions have been cognitive-behavioral approaches, primarily skills training, particularly for the prevention of adolescent alcohol use and abuse (Botvin, Baker, Dusenbury, Botvin, & Diaz, 1995; NIAAA, 1994; Schinke et al., 1991; Wodarski & Feit, 1993) and, more recently, reduction of alcohol use among blue-collar workers (Cook, Back, & Trudeau, 1996). In addition, the data supporting the effectiveness of alcohol server training interventions (that is, for bartenders) on the prevention of alcohol impairment also is promising (Moskowitz, 1989).

CONCLUSIONS

In conclusion, social workers have at their disposal a range of empirically validated interventions for intervention with alcohol problems. Miller and colleagues (Miller et al., 1995) have noted that in the United States there continues to be a sizable gap between the alcohol treatment interventions supported by clinical research and those offered in clinical practice. As a profession, social work is well positioned to provide leadership to ensure that clients have access to interventions with demonstrated effectiveness.

REFERENCES

Alden, L. E. (1988). Behavioral self-management controlled-drinking strategies in a context of secondary prevention. *Journal of Consulting and Clinical Psychology, 56,* 280–286.

Allen, J. P., & Columbus, M. (Eds.). (1995). *Assessing alcohol problems: A guide for clinicians and researchers* (NIAAA Treatment Handbook, Series 4, NIH Publication No. 95-3745). Bethesda, MD: U.S. Department of Health and Human Services.

Allen, J. P. & Kadden, R. M. (1995). Matching clients to alcohol treatments. In R. K. Hester & W. R. Miller (Eds.), *Handbook of alcoholism treatment approaches* (2nd ed., pp. 170–182). Boston: Allyn & Bacon.

American Psychiatric Association (1994). *Diagnostic and Statistical Manual of Mental Disorders* (4th ed.). Washington, DC: Author.

Annis, H. M., & Davis, C. S. (1989). Relapse prevention. In R. K. Hester & W. R. Miller (Eds.), *Handbook of alcoholism treatment approaches* (2nd. ed., pp. 278–291). New York: Pergamon Press.

Annis, H. M., & Graham, J. M. (1988). *Situational Confidence Questionnaire (SCQ-39) Users Guide.* Toronto: Addiction Research Foundation.

Annis, H. M., Graham, J. M., & Davis, C. S. (1987). *Inventory of Drinking Situations (IDS) user's guide.* Toronto: Addiction Research Foundation.

Anton, R. F. (1994). Medications for treating alcoholism. *Alcohol Health and Research World, 18,* 265–271.

Anton, R. F., Litten, R. Z., & Allen, J. P. (1995). Biological assessment of alcohol consumption. In J. P. Allen & M. Columbus (Eds.), *Assessing alcohol problems: A guide for clinicians and researchers* (NIAAA Treatment Handbook, Series 4, NIH Publication No. 95-3745, pp. 31–39). Bethesda, MD: U.S. Department of Health and Human Services.

Babor, T. F., Ritson, E. B., & Hodgson, R. J. (1986). Alcohol-related problems in the primary health care setting: A review of early intervention strategies. *British Journal of Addiction, 81,* 23–46.

Barber, J. G., & Crisp, B. R. (1995). The pressures to change approach to working with the partners of heavy drinkers. *Addiction, 90,* 269–276.

Barber, J. G., & Gilbertson, R. (1996). An experimental study of brief unilateral intervention for the partners of heavy drinkers. *Research on Social Work Practice, 6,* 325–336.

Botvin, G. J., Baker, E., Dusenbury, L., Botvin, E. M., & Diaz, T. (1995). Long-term follow-up results of a randomized drug abuse prevention trial in a white middle-class population. *Journal of the American Medical Association, 273,* 1106–1112.

Brown, J. M., & Miller, W. R. (1993). Impact of motivational interviewing on participation and outcome in residential alcoholism treatment. *Psychology of Addictive Behaviors, 7,* 211–218.

Brown, S., & Yalom, I. D. (1977). Interactional group therapy with alcoholics. *Journal of Studies on Alcohol, 38,* 426–456.

Bullock, M. L., Umen, A. J., Culliton, P. D., & Olander, R. T. (1987). Acupuncture treatment of alcoholic recidivism: A pilot study. *Alcoholism: Clinical and Experimental Research, 11,* 292–295.

Cadogan, D. A. (1973). Marital group therapy in the treatment of alcoholism. *Quarterly Journal of Studies on Alcohol, 34,* 1187–1194.

Cartwright, A. (1987). Group work with substance abusers: Basic issues and future research. *British Journal of Addiction, 82,* 951–953.

Combination of alcohol treatment and probation shown to reduce criminal behavior by repeat DWI offenders. (1995). *Drinking, Drugs & Driving,* Research Note 95-3. Buffalo, NY: Research Institute on Addictions.

Connors, G. J. (1993). Drinking moderation training as a contemporary therapeutic approach. In G. J. Connors (Ed.), *Innovations in alcoholism treatment* (pp. 117–134). Binghamton, NY: Haworth.

Connors, G. J. (1995). Screening for alcohol problems. In J. P. Allen & M. Columbus (Eds.), *Assessing alcohol problems: A guide for clinicians and researchers* (NIAAA Treatment Handbook, Series 4, NIH Publication No. 95-3745, pp. 17–29). Bethesda, MD: U.S. Department of Health and Human Services.

Connors, G. J., & Maisto, S. A. (1988). The Alcohol Beliefs Scale. In M. Hersen & A. S. Bellack (Eds.), *Dictionary of behavioral assessment techniques* (pp. 24–26). New York: Pergamon Press.

Cook, R. F., Back, A. S., & Trudeau, J. (1996). Preventing alcohol use problems among blue-collar workers: A field test of the *working people* program. *Substance Use & Misuse, 31*, 255–275.

Cooney, N. L., Kadden, R. M., Litt, M. D., & Getter, H. (1991). Matching alcoholics to coping skills or interactional therapies: Two-year follow-up results. *Journal of Consulting & Clinical Psychology, 59*, 598–601.

Cooper, G. O., Adams, H. B., & Scott, J. C. (1988). Studies in REST: I. Reduced environmental stimulation therapy and reduced alcohol consumption. *Journal of Substance Abuse Treatment, 5*, 61–68.

Corder, B. F., Corder, R. F., & Laidlaw, N. D. (1972). An intensive treatment program for alcoholics and their wives. *Quarterly Journal of Studies on Alcohol, 33*, 1144–1146.

Dimeff, L. A., & Marlatt, G. A. (1995) Relapse prevention. In R. K. Hester & W. R. Miller (Eds.), *Handbook of alcoholism treatment approaches* (2nd. ed., pp. 176–194). Boston: Allyn & Bacon.

Dittrich, J. E., & Trapold, M. A. (1984). Wives of alcoholics: A treatment program and outcome study. *Bulletin of the Society of Psychologist in Addictive Behaviors, 3*, 91–102.

Donovan, D. (1995). Assessments to aid in the treatment planning process. In J. P. Allen & M. Columbus (Eds.), *Assessing alcohol problems: A guide for clinicians and researchers* (NIAAA Treatment Handbook, Series 4, NIH Publication No. 95-3745, pp. 75–122). Bethesda, MD: U.S. Department of Health and Human Services.

Duckert, E., Amundsen, A., & Johnsen, J. (1992). What happens to drinking after therapeutic intervention? *British Journal of Addiction, 87*, 1457–1467.

Emrick, C. D., Tonigan, S., Montgomery, H., & Little, L. (1993). Alcoholics Anonymous: What is currently known? In B. S. McCrady & W. R. Miller (Eds.), *Research on alcoholics anonymous: Opportunities and alternatives* (pp. 41–79). New Brunswick, NJ: Alcohol Research Documentation, Inc., Rutgers University.

Finnegan, D. J., Ivanoff, A. M., & Smyth, N. J. (1991). A computer applications explosion: What practitioners and managers need to know. *Computers in Human Services, 8*, 1–19.

Fuller, R. K. (1995). Antidipsotropic medications. In R. K. Hester & W. R. Miller (Eds.), *Handbook of alcoholism treatment approaches* (2nd. ed., pp. 123–133). Boston: Allyn & Bacon.

Galanter, M., Castaneda, R., & Franco, H. (1991). Group therapy and self-help groups. In R. J. Frances & S. I. Miller (Eds.), *Clinical textbook of addictive disorders* (pp. 431–451). New York: Guilford Press.

Galanter, M., Egelko S., & Edwards H. (1993). Rational Recovery: Alternative to AA for addiction. *American Journal of Drug and Alcohol Abuse, 19*, 499–510.

Getter, H. (1984). *Aftercare for alcoholism: Short term interactional group therapy manual.* Unpublished manuscript. Storrs: University of Connecticut, Department of Psychology.

Grant, B. F. (1994). Alcohol consumption, alcohol abuse and alcohol dependence. The United States as an example. *Addiction, 89*, 1357–1365.

Heather, N. (1993). Application of harm-reduction principles to the treatment of alcohol problems. In N. Heather, A. Wodak, E. Nadelmann, & P. O'Hare (Eds.), *Psychoactive drugs & harm reduction: From faith to science* (pp. 168–183). London: Whurr Publishers.

Heather, N. (1995). Brief intervention strategies. In R. K. Hester & W. R. Miller (Eds.), *Handbook of alcoholism treatment approaches* (2nd. ed., pp. 105–122). Boston: Allyn & Bacon.

Heather, N., Gold, R. & Rollnick, S. (1991). *Readiness to Change Questionnaire: User's manual* (Technical Report 15). Kensington, Australia: University of New South Wales, National Drug and Alcohol Research Center.

Heather, N., Tebbott, J. S., Mattick, R. P., & Zamir, R. (1993). Development of a scale for measuring impaired control over alcohol consumption: A preliminary report. *Journal of Studies on Alcohol, 54,* 700–709.

Hester, R. (1995a). *Behavioral self-control program for Windows, version 3.0.* Albuquerque, NM: Alcohol Self-Control Program, 4300 San Mateo NE, Ste. B-285, 87110.

Hester, R. K. (1995b). Behavioral self-control training. In R. K. Hester & W. R. Miller (Eds.), *Handbook of alcoholism treatment approaches* (2nd. ed., pp. 148–159). Boston: Allyn & Bacon.

Horvath, A. T. (1996, July). Is SMART as effective as AA? *SMART recovery: News and views,* 1–2. Beachwood, OH: SMART Recovery, 24000 Mercantile Rd., Ste. 11, 44122.

Institute of Medicine (1990). *Broadening the base of treatment for alcohol problems.* Washington, DC: National Academy Press.

Johnson, V. A. (1973). *I'll quit tomorrow.* New York: Harper & Row.

Liepman, M. R., Nirenberg, T. D., & Begin, A. M. (1989). Evaluation of a program designed to help family and significant others to motivate resistant alcoholics into recovery. *American Journal of Drug and Alcohol Abuse, 15,* 209–221.

Loneck, B., Garrett, J. A., & Banks, S. M. (1996a). A comparison of the Johnson intervention with four other methods of referral to outpatient treatment. *American Journal of Drug and Alcohol Abuse, 22,* 233–246.

Loneck, B., Garrett, J. A., & Banks, S. M. (1996b). The Johnson intervention and relapse during outpatient treatment. *American Journal of Drug and Alcohol Abuse, 22,* 363–375.

Marlatt, G. A. (1985). Situational determinants of relapse and skill-training interventions. In G. A. Marlatt & J. R. Gordon (Eds.), *Relapse prevention: Maintenance strategies in the treatment of addictive behaviors* (pp. 71–127). New York: Guilford Press.

Mayfield, D., McLeod, G., & Hall, P. (1974). The CAGE questionnaire: Validation of a new alcoholism screening instrument. *American Journal of Psychiatry 131,* 1121–1123.

McCrady, B. S., & Delaney, S. I. (1995). Self-help groups. In R. K. Hester & W. R. Miller (Eds.), *Handbook of alcoholism treatment approaches* (2nd. ed., pp. 160–175). Boston: Allyn & Bacon.

McCrady, B. S., Paolino, T. J., Jr., Longabaugh, R., & Rossi, J. (1979). Effects of joint hospital admission and couples treatment for hospitalized alcoholics: A pilot study. *Addictive Behaviors, 4,* 155–165.

McKay, J. R., Longabaugh, R., Beattie, M. C., Maisto, S. A., & Noel, N. E. (1993). Changes in family functioning during treatment and drinking outcomes for high and low autonomy alcoholics. *Addictive Behaviors 18,* 355–363.

McLellan, A. T., Kushner, H., Metzger, D., Peters, R., Smith, I., Grissom, G., Pettinati, H., & Argeriou, M. (1992). The fifth edition of the addiction severity index: Historical critique and normative data. *Journal of Substance Abuse 9,* 199–213.

Meyers, R. J., & Smith, J. E. (1995). *Clinical guide to alcohol treatment: The community reinforcement approach.* New York: Guilford Press.

Miller, W. R. (1992). Appendix A: Assessment feedback procedures. In W. R. Miller, A. Zweben, C. C. DiClemente, & R. G. Rychatarik (Eds.), *Motivational enhancement therapy manual: A clinical research guide for therapists treating individuals with alcohol abuse and dependence* (NIAAA Project MATCH Monograph Series, Vol. 2, DHHS Publication No. ADM 92-1894, pp. 67–86). Washington, DC: U.S. Government Printing Office.

Miller, W. R., Brown, J. M., Simpson, T. L., Handmaker, N. S., Bien, T. H., Luckie, L. F., Montgomery, H. A., Hester, R. K., & Tonigan, J. S. (1995). What works? A methodological analysis of the alcohol treatment outcome literature. In R. K. Hester & W. R. Miller (Eds.), *Handbook of alcoholism treatment approaches* (2nd. ed., pp. 12–44). Boston: Allyn & Bacon.

Miller, W. R., & Hester, R. K. (1986). The effectiveness of alcoholism treatment: What research reveals. In W. R. Miller & N. Heather (Eds.), *Treating addictive behaviors: Processes of change* (pp. 121–174). New York: Plenum Press.

Miller, W. R. & Marlatt, G. A. (1984). *Manual for the comprehensive drinker profile.* Odessa, FL: Psychological Assessment Resources.

Miller, W. R., & Rollnick, S. (1991). *Motivational interviewing.* New York: Guilford Press.

Miller, W. R., & Tonigan, J. S. (1994). Assessing drinker's motivation for change: The Stages of Change Readiness and Treatment Eagerness Scale (SOCRATES). Unpublished manuscript, University of New Mexico, Albuquerque, Center on Alcoholism, Substance Abuse, and Addictions.

Miller, W. R., Tonigan, J. S., & Longabaugh, R. (1995). *The Drinker Inventory of Consequences (DrInC): An instrument for assessing adverse consequences of alcohol abuse. Test manual* (NIAAA Project MATCH Monograph Series, Vol. 4, NIH Publication No. 95-3911). Washington, DC: U.S. Government Printing Office.

Miller, W. R., Westerberg, V. S., & Waldron, H. B. (1995). Evaluating alcohol problems in adults and adolescents. In R. K. Hester & W. R. Miller (Eds.), *Handbook of alcoholism treatment approaches* (2nd. Ed., pp. 61–88). Boston: Allyn and Bacon.

Miller, W. R., Zweben, A., DiClemente, C. C., & Rychtarik, R. G. (Eds.). (1992). *Motivational enhancement therapy manual: A clinical research guide for therapists treating individuals with alcohol abuse and dependence* (NIAAA Project MATCH Monograph Series, Vol. 2, DHHS Publication No. ADM 92-1894). Washington, DC: U.S. Government Printing Office.

Monti, P. M., Abrams, D. A., Kadden, R. M., & Cooney, N. L. (1989). *Treating alcohol dependence: A coping skills guide.* New York: Guilford Press.

Monti, P. M., Rohsenow, D. J., Abrams, D. B., Zwick, W. R., Binkoff, J. A., Munroe, S. M., Fingeret, A. L., Nirenberg, T. D., Liepman, M. R., Pedraza, M, & Kadden, R. M. (1993). Development of a behavior analytically derived alcohol-specific role-play assessment instrument. *Journal of Studies on Alcohol, 54,* 710–721.

Monti, P. M., Rohsenow, D. J., Colby, S. M., & Abrams, D. B. (1995). Coping and social skills training. In R. K. Hester & W. R. Miller (Eds.), *Handbook of alcoholism treatment approaches* (2nd. ed., pp. 221–241). Boston: Allyn & Bacon.

Moos, R. H., Finney, J. W., & Cronkite, R. C. (1990). *Alcoholism treatment context, process and outcome.* New York: Oxford University Press.

Moskowitz, J. M. (1989). The primary prevention of alcohol problems: A critical review of the research literature. *Journal of Studies on Alcohol, 50,* 54–88.

National Institute on Alcohol Abuse and Alcoholism (1983). *National drug and alcoholism treatment utilization survey: September 1983 comprehensive report.* Rockville, MD: Alcohol, Drug Abuse, and Mental Health Administration.

National Institute on Alcohol Abuse and Alcoholism (1992, April). Moderate Drinking. *Alcohol Alert* (DHHS Publication No. 16). Rockville, MD: Alcohol, Drug Abuse, and Mental Health Administration.

National Institute on Alcohol Abuse and Alcoholism (1994). *Eighth special report to the U.S. Congress on alcohol and health.* (NIH Publication No. 94-3699). Alexandria, VA: U.S. Department of Health and Human Services.

National Institute on Drug Abuse and National Institute on Alcohol Abuse and Alcoholism (1993). *National drug and alcoholism treatment unit survey: 1991 main findings report* (DHHS Publication No. ADM 93-2007). Washington, DC: U.S. Government Printing Office.

O'Farrell, T. J. (1995). Marital and family therapy. In R. K. Hester & W. R. Miller (Eds.), *Handbook of alcoholism treatment approaches* (2nd. ed., pp. 195–220). Boston: Allyn & Bacon.

O'Malley, S. S., Jaffe, A. J., Chang, G., Schottenfeld, R. S., Meyer, R. E., & Rounsaville, B. (1992). Naltrexone and coping skills therapy for alcohol dependence. *Archives of General Psychiatry, 49,* 881–887.

Prochaska, J. O., & DiClemente, C. C. (1984). *The transtheoretical approach.* Homewood, IL: Dorsey Press.

Prochaska, J. O., DiClemente, C. C., & Norcross, J. C. (1992). In search of how people change: Applications to addictive behaviors. *American Psychologist, 47,* 1102–1114.

Prochaska, J. O., Norcross, J. C., Fowler, J. L., Follick, M. J., & Abrams, D. B. (1992). Attendance and outcome in a work site weight control program: Processes and stages of change as process and predictor variables. *Addictive Behaviors, 17,* 35–42.

Project MATCH Research Group. (1997). Matching alcoholism treatments to client heterogeneity: Project MATCH posttreatment drinking outcomes. *Journal of Studies on Alcohol, 58,* 7–29.

Rimmele, C. T., Howard, M. O., & Hilfrink, M. L. (1995). Aversion therapies. In R. K. Hester & W. R. Miller (Eds.), *Handbook of alcoholism treatment approaches* (2nd. ed., pp. 134–147). Boston: Allyn & Bacon..

Robins, L. N., Helzer, J. E., Croughan, J., & Ratcliff, K. S. (1981). National Institute of Mental Health Diagnostic Interview Schedule. *Archives of General Psychiatry, 38,* 381–389.

Rohsenow, D. J. (1983). Drinking habits and expectancies about alcohol's effects for self versus others. *Journal of Consulting & Clinical Psychiatry, 55,* 411–417.

Room, R. (1990). Measuring alcohol consumption in the United States: Methods and rationales. In L. T. Kozlowski, H. M. Annis, H. D. Cappell, F. B. Glaser, M. S. Goodstadt, Y. Israel, H. Kalant, E. M. Sellers, & E. R. Vingilis (Eds.), *Research advances in alcohol and drug problems* (Vol. 10, pp. 39–80). New York: Plenum Press.

Rouse, B. A. (Ed.). (1995). *Substance abuse and mental health: Statistics sourcebook.* (DHHS Publication No. SMA 95-3064). Rockville, MD: U.S. Department of Health and Human Services.

Russell, M., Czarnecki, D. M., Cowan, R., McPherson, E., & Mudar, P. (1991). Measures of maternal alcohol use as predictors of development in early childhood. *Alcoholism: Clinical & Experimental Research, 15,* 991–1000.

Saunders, J. B., Aasland, O. G., Babor, T. F., de la Fuente, J. R., & Grant, M. (1993). Development of the Alcohol Use Disorders Screening Test (AUDIT). WHO collaborative project on early detection of persons with harmful alcohol consumption. II. *Addiction, 88,* 791–804.

Schinke, S. P., Botvin, G. J., & Orlandi, M. A. (1991). *Substance abuse in children and adolescents evaluation and intervention.* Newbury Park, CA: Sage.

Schuckit, M. A. (1996). Recent developments in the pharmacotherapy of alcohol dependence. *Journal of Consulting and Clinical Psychology, 64,* 669–676.

Selzer, M. L. (1971). The Michigan Alcoholism Screening Test: The quest for a new diagnostic instrument. *American Journal of Psychiatry, 127,* 1653–1658.

Sisson, R. W., & Azrin, H. H. (1986). Family-member involvement to initiate and promote treatment of problem drinking. *Journal of Behavior Therapy and Experimental Psychiatry, 17,* 115–121.

Skinner, H. A., & Horn, J. L. (1984). *Alcohol Dependence Scale: Users guide.* Toronto: Addiction Research Foundation.

Smith, J. E., & Meyers, R. J. (1995). The community reinforcement approach. In R. K. Hester & W. R. Miller (Eds.), *Handbook of alcoholism treatment approaches* (2nd. ed., pp. 251–266). Boston: Allyn & Bacon.

Smyth, N. J. (1995). Substance abuse: Direct practice. In R. L. Edwards et al. (Eds.), *Encyclopedia of Social Work* (19th ed., pp. 2328–2337). Washington, DC: National Association of Social Workers.

Sobell, L. C., & Sobell, M. B. (1995a). Alcohol consumption measures. In J. P. Allen & M. Columbus (Eds.), *Assessing alcohol problems: A guide for clinicians and researchers* (NIAAA Treatment Handbook, Series 4, NIH Publication No. 95-3745, pp. 55–73). Bethesda, MD: U.S. Department of Health and Human Services.

Sobell, L. C., & Sobell, M. B. (1995b). *Alcohol Timeline Followback (TLFB) users manual.* Toronto: Addiction Research Foundation.

Sobell, L. C., & Sobell, M. B. (1995c). *Timeline followback computer software.* Toronto: Addiction Research Foundation.

Sobell, L. C., Sobell, M. B., Brown, J. C., Cleland, P. A., & Buchan, G. (1995, November). *A randomized trial comparing group versus individual guided self-change treatment for alcohol and drug abusers.* Poster presented at the 29th Annual Meeting of the Association for Advancement of Behavior Therapy, Washington, DC.

Straussner, S. L. (1993). Assessment and treatment of clients with alcohol and other drug problems: An overview. In S. L. Straussner (Ed.), *Clinical work with substance-abusing clients* (pp. 3–30). New York: Guilford Press.

Substance Abuse and Mental Health Services Administration (1995). *National household survey on drug abuse: Main findings 1993.* Rockville, MD: U.S. Department of Health and Human Services.

Substance section wins full status. (1995, October). *NASW News,* pp. 1, 10.

Thomas, E. J. (1994). Appendix B. The unilateral treatment program for alcohol abuse—background, selected procedures, and case applications. In J. Rothman & E. J. Thomas (Eds.), *Intervention research, design and development for human service* (pp. 427–447). New York: Haworth Press.

Thomas, E. J., Santa, C. A., Bronson, D. & Oyserman, D. (1987). Unilateral family therapy with spouses of alcoholics. *Journal of Social Service Research, 10,* 145–162.

Volpicelli, J. R., Alterman, A. I., Hayashida, M., & O'Brien, C. P. (1992). Naltrexone in the treatment of alcohol dependence. *Archives of General Psychiatry, 49,* 876–880.

Wells-Parker, E., Bangert-Drowns, R., McMillen, R., & Williams, M. (1995). Final results from a meta-analysis of remedial interventions with drink/drive offenders. *Addiction, 90,* 907–926.

White, H. R., & Labouvie, E. W. (1989). Toward a multisource approach. In C. E. Stout, J. L. Levitt, & D. H. Ruben, (Eds.), *Handbook for assessing and treating addictive disorders* (pp. 83–96). New York: Greenwood.

Wodarski, J. S., & Feit, M. D. (1993). *Adolescent substance abuse.* Binghamton, NY: Haworth.

Yalom, I. D. (1974). Group therapy and alcoholism. *Annals New York Academy of Sciences, 233,* 85–103.

Zweben, A., Pearlman, S., & Li, S. (1988). A comparison of brief advice and conjoint therapy in the treatment of alcohol abuse: The results of the marital systems study. *British Journal of Addiction, 83,* 899–916.

Chapter 10 ——————————————————————

COCAINE ABUSE

Patrick S. Bordnick
Joy Schmitz
Judith R. Bordnick

OVERVIEW

Over the past 100 years there have been several cycles of stimulant abuse, including cocaine use. The prevalence of Cocaine Abuse in the United States has gradually increased since the 1970s (Manschreck, 1993), reaching its peak with the introduction of crack cocaine in the mid-1980s (National Institute on Drug Abuse [NIDA], 1993). In the following years, several National Institute on Drug Abuse (NIDA) surveys indicated a decrease in use from the mid-1980s to 1992, with a stabilization in 1993 among high school students (Johnston, O'Malley, & Bachman, 1994a), college students, and young adults (ages 19 to 29) (Johnston, O'Malley, & Bachman, 1994b). Current estimates of the number of people who have tried cocaine are 20 to 30 million (Manschreck, 1993; U.S. Department of Health and Human Services [DHHS], 1993). In 1992, it was estimated that 805,000 persons age 12 or older had used crack cocaine and 4.9 million had used cocaine during the past year (U.S. DHHS, 1992a). In 1993, 4.5 million reportedly used cocaine and 996,000 used crack (U.S. DHHS, 1993). It is estimated that, among adults, approximately 25% of those ages 25 to 34 have used cocaine (Manshreck, 1993) and, by age 28, 33% have tried cocaine (Johnston, O'Malley, & Bachman, 1994b). Even with the downward trend, millions of Americans are abusing cocaine and may require varying degrees of intervention.

The cocaine-related costs to society are high. Crime and health care issues represent the greatest costs to society. According to the Drug Abuse Warning Network (DAWN) survey of admissions at approximately 700 emergency rooms in 21 metropolitan areas, the number of cocaine-related emergency room admissions from 1988 to 1991 was 80,335 to 110,113 (U.S. DHHS, 1992b). During this time period, the total number of cocaine-related fatalities quadrupled. By 1991, cocaine was the primary drug mentioned in reports of drug-related deaths (U.S. DHHS, 1992b).

Cocaine-related criminal activity is a major concern to society. The U.S. Department of Justice reported that, in 1991, criminals who used either marijuana or cocaine were more likely to commit crimes than nonusers (U.S. Department of Justice, 1994b). In 1991, approximately 1 in 4 of convicted state prison inmates had used cocaine or crack in the month prior to their arrest (U.S. Department of Justice, 1994a), and 14% reported to have committed their offense under the influence of either cocaine or crack (U.S. Department of Justice, 1993). The data collected in these surveys are subject to various confounds and do not represent a causal link with drug use.

Roles of Social Workers

Social workers have been involved in various roles with regard to cocaine abuse. Large numbers of clinicians treating cocaine-abusing patients are licensed social workers and social work students. For this reason, social workers need to keep abreast of the current state-of-the-science treatments for cocaine-abusing patients in order to provide the most efficacious interventions available. Research in cocaine abuse has not been a strong role for social workers. This is evident in the sparse number of research outcome studies published in the literature by social workers. However, social workers are beginning to realize the vital role that research plays in providing effective practice, and this could lead to more participation in empirically based treatment outcome research on cocaine and other drugs of abuse.

ASSESSMENT METHODS

Several categories in the fourth edition of the *Diagnostic and Statistical Manual of Mental Disorders* (*DSM-IV;* American Psychiatric Association [APA], 1994) pertain to cocaine use. Substance use and substance-induced disorders are the two major groups listed for cocaine-related disorders. *Substance use disorders* are divided into two classes: Cocaine Dependence (304.20) and Cocaine Abuse (305.69). The major difference between these diagnostic categories is that Cocaine Dependence involves repeated administration that leads to tolerance, withdrawal, or compulsive drug-use behavior. Also, cocaine use is less frequent and less intense in individuals who meet the criteria for Cocaine Abuse. *Cocaine-induced disorders* encompass problems that are associated with cocaine use, such as withdrawal, intoxication, or physiological or psychological problems that manifest during use episodes (APA, 1994).

Currently, a variety of physiological and psychological assessment methods are being used to assess and evaluate treatment outcome in cocaine abusers. The standard in evaluating outcome is urine analysis. Urine samples are collected from patients and analyzed to detect the level of cocaine metabolites. The metabolite levels are compared with a cutoff value and are deemed either positive or negative. Urine drug screens are the most effective means of evaluating treatment outcome. Several self-report instruments are also valuable in evaluating cocaine-dependent patients, if they are used in conjunction with the urine screens.

Self-Report Instruments

The Addiction Severity Index (ASI; McLellan, Lubrosky, Woody, & O'Brien, 1980) is an instrument that assesses substance use and the severity of difficulties in the following areas: medical, employment, drug and alcohol, legal, family and social, and psychiatric problems; both the past 30 days and the lifetime history are assessed. The ASI has high reliability and validity, but does require training to administer. The ASI can provide the clinician with a vast amount of information regarding substance-use history and the impact of that use on several areas of the patient's life (McLellan et al., 1980).

The Cocaine Relapse Inventory (CRI) is a structured clinical interview that purports to measure several factors (onset, course, and termination) of cocaine relapse episodes (McKay, Rutherford, Alterman, Cacciola, & Kaplan, 1994). The CRI must be administered by trained personnel; it takes approximately 30 minutes to complete all six sections of the CRI interview. The initial psychometric properties of the CRI appear to be acceptable (McKay et al., 1994). The CRI provides detailed accounts of the relapse episode, how the patient handled the relapse, and what happened after the relapse. Clinicians can use this information to assess the patient's potential reasons for returning to use, and what skills, if any, the patient utilized to terminate use.

The University of Minnesota Cocaine Craving Scale (CCS) is a rapid assessment instrument designed to measure the intensity, frequency, and duration of a craving (Halikas, Kuhn, Crosby, Carlson, & Crea, 1991). The CCS can be administered daily, weekly, or at other set intervals. Intense levels of craving have been purportedly shown to be related to future levels of cocaine use (Bordnick & Schmitz, in press). Clinicians who encounter patients with higher levels of craving can adjust their treatment to potentially decrease future relapse episodes. However, caution should be used when utilizing this or other craving instruments due to the lack of reliability and validity of the data regarding craving measures.

EFFECTIVE INTERVENTIONS

An extensive review of the treatment literature was undertaken to determine current state-of-the-science interventions for Cocaine Dependence and Cocaine Abuse. This review focused on empirically supported interventions that have been shown to offer effective strategies for treating cocaine-dependent individuals. Currently, interventions to treat Cocaine Abuse cover a wide range of inpatient and outpatient therapies, including—but not limited to—psychotherapy, behavior therapy, pharmacotherapy, and various combinations of these therapeutic approaches. While some progress has been made in finding effective pharmacological and psychosocial interventions, more work needs to be done (Leukefeld & Tims, 1993). Currently, there appears to be no consensus with regard to the treatment of Cocaine Dependence (Higgins, Budney, Bickel, Foerg, et al., 1994). The following subsections review psychosocial and psychopharmacological approaches to the treatment of Cocaine Dependence, with the empirical status of each. Studies selected for review represent current state-of-the-science outcome evaluations in Cocaine Abuse and Cocaine Dependence treatment.

Psychotherapy

Currently, an arsenal of psychotherapies is applied to cocaine dependence, ranging from 12-step model approaches (that is, Cocaine Anonymous) to peer-led counseling programs, used on both an inpatient and outpatient basis. The efficacy of these psychotherapeutic approaches is currently unknown, since most psychotherapeutic treatments for Cocaine Abuse have not been subjected to controlled trials (Carroll, Rounsaville, & Gawin, 1991). The treatment literature contains only one randomized clinical trial evaluating purely psychotherapeutic approaches for Cocaine Abuse (Carroll, 1993).

Outpatient Therapy. In an uncontrolled study, Washton, Gold, & Pottash (1986) reported data on 63 outpatients who were treated with a combination of intervention strategies. They reported that 51 patients were presently abstinent at 7- to 19-month follow-up, but that half of those patients had used cocaine without returning to compulsive use.

In an evaluation of supportive expressive individual therapy, structural family therapy, and peer-led group therapy on a sample of 148 cocaine abusers, Kleinman et al. (1991) determined from data analysis that the three therapies offered were insufficient to produce remission in a large majority of those patients.

Carroll et al. (1991) compared interpersonal psychotherapy to cognitive-behavioral relapse prevention treatments on 42 patients in outpatient therapy. Overall, 23 of the 42 subjects failed to achieve abstinence, defined in this study as not using cocaine for 3 weeks while in treatment. Abstinence rates between the two treatments were not statistically significant. The investigators found that patients who were rated *high severity* at pretreatment were more likely to become abstinent if they were given the relapse prevention intervention. These results indicate that drug severity may be an important treatment-matching variable. Unfortunately, no conclusions regarding the overall relative efficacy of interpersonal psychotherapy versus relapse prevention can be offered on the basis of these findings. However, aside from having a small sample size, this study has fewer methodological shortcomings than previously reviewed studies. In particular, the researchers used random assignment to treatment condition, manual-driven therapy, and biological verification of drug use.

In a study to determine the efficacy of psychotherapy, family therapy, and group therapy, 168 patients were treated, and follow-up data were collected at 6 to 12 months posttreatment (Kang et al., 1991). Findings revealed that only 23 patients became abstinent. The abstinence criteria were defined as having a negative urine test and reporting abstinence for the prior three months. The investigators concluded that the interventions tested do not appear to be effective on a weekly visit basis for cocaine use disorders.

A manual-driven treatment referred to as a *neurobehavioral model,* utilizing a combination of psychotherapeutic and behavioral methods according to presumed stages in cocaine recovery, has been practiced by the Matrix Center since 1985 (Rawson, Obert, McCann, & Ling, 1993). In an open trial of this treatment model involving 486 patients at two locations in California (Rancho Cucamonga and Beverly Hills, California), self-report and urinalysis revealed abstinence rates of 40% and 44%, respectively, for the two sites (Rawson et al., 1993). A controlled trial on 100 cocaine abusers compared the Matrix treatment to community-based inpatient and outpatient treatments (Rawson et al., 1995). Results revealed that subjects in both treatment conditions significantly reduced their cocaine use. No differences were found between the two treatment conditions. Subjects in the Matrix treatment had higher rates of treatment retention and participation, which were positively related to improvements on several psychosocial measures and urine results (Rawson et al., 1995). Although promising, this multicomponent treatment approach has not been shown to be superior to other treatment approaches. Research continues on the utility of this model as an outpatient treatment.

Wells, Peterson, Gainey, Hawkins, & Catalano (1994) compared cognitive-behavioral relapse prevention and the 12-step approach in a sample of 110 cocaine-abusing outpatients. The results failed to demonstrate differences in outcome between the two treatments. One interesting finding was a significant decrease in alcohol use in the relapse prevention group. The investigators also found that the length of time spent in treatment had an effect on use. Again, the results are clouded with various methodological problems. The authors noted that the treatments were not manual-based and may have been inadvertently similar in the two groups. Also, the confound of concurrent history as a probable cause for improvements and the provision of a control group comparison would indeed improve, if not clarify, these results.

Inpatient Therapy.   The drug abuse treatment community appears to be turning away from inpatient services for substance abusers, perhaps because studies have found virtually no differences in outcome that favor inpatient treatment. However, it has been suggested that patients with significant physical or psychiatric problems, or those prone to drop out, might particularly benefit from inpatient stays (Alterman, O'Brien, & Droba, 1993; Alterman et al., 1994). Miller (1993) indicates that the literature of the past 20 years reveals that inpatient and residential settings have consumed the bulk of treatment dollars, even though studies have concluded that inpatient settings offer no overall benefit above outpatient settings (U.S. Congress, 1983; Annis, 1985).

Empirical research with regard to the efficacy of inpatient cocaine treatment is virtually nonexistent, and mostly consists of uncontrolled studies. Miller, Millman, and Keskinen (1990) studied 1,627 inpatients admitted for polysubstance abuse (alcohol, alcohol and other drugs, and cocaine and other drugs) and found that a sample of patients who responded to a survey of treatment reported abstinence rates of 76% at 6 months and 62% at 12 months.

Another treatment setting is the day hospital program. Galanter, Egelko, De Leon, and Rohrs (1993) evaluated a day hospital program having both peer-led and professional treatment components; they found that 59 patients, out of 150 who had completed treatment or were still involved in the program, had acceptable outcomes. An acceptable outcome was defined as three consecutive negative urine samples immediately before termination.

A comparison of the costs of inpatient and day hospital treatment on 111 patients found that 50% of the patients in the sample were abstinent from cocaine 7 months after admission (confirmed with urine samples) and that the two treatments were equally effective (Alterman et al., 1994). The results of this study provide important information with regard to the cost-effectiveness of inpatient versus outpatient treatment. The cost of inpatient treatment in this study was 1.5 to 3.0 times greater than outpatient care, leading to the suggestion that only patients with significant physical or psychological problems should be admitted for inpatient treatment (Alterman et al., 1994).

Research on inpatient treatment for Cocaine Abuse provides little support for the hospitalization of patients for drug abuse treatment in the absence of acute hospitalization for related medical problems. Results from the preceding review indicate that inpatient treatment programs do not offer an advantage over outpatient programs. The costs of inpatient treatment programs are approximately double the costs of outpatient programs, and the additional costs are not justified. Inpatient programs should be utilized for only the most severe cases, or when patients suffer from significant physical or psychological problems (Alterman et al., 1994).

Self-Help Group Therapy.   Another mechanism discussed in cocaine treatment is the use of self-help groups, such as Drugs Anonymous (DA), Narcotics Anonymous (NA), and Cocaine Anonymous (CA). These groups closely parallel the Alcoholics Anonymous (AA) format. Spitz and Rosecan (1987) state that these groups provide emotional support to members and serve a vital therapeutic function. Washton and Stone-Washton (1991) claim that thousands of addicts around the world have benefited from these groups, and they encourage all patients to get involved. However, this approach suffers from a lack of empirical study, so information regarding the efficacy of the strategy is sparse. However, the view that self-help groups are opposed to research on their efficacy is changing (Miller, 1993). Information claiming the beneficial nature of these groups is rampant in the research and self-help literatures, but it is based primarily on anecdotal case reports and patient testimonials.

Behavior Analysis and Therapy

Treatment strategies in the behavioral arena have deep conceptual roots in the processes of classical conditioning (Pavlov, 1927) and operant conditioning (Skinner, 1953) in both humans and animals. The role of conditioned responses to drug-related stimuli was originally proposed by Wikler (1948) and continues to form the basis for various behavior therapy approaches, such as cue exposure (Childress, Ehrman, McLellan, & O'Brien, 1988), coping skills training (Marlatt, 1988), and aversion procedures (Smith, 1982; Smith & Frawley, 1990). This subsection reviews the empirical findings from studies testing these behaviorally based treatments.

Operant Conditioning.   Operant-based treatment approaches focus on eliminating cocaine use by decreasing its reinforcing effects (for example, aversion methods) or increasing the positive consequences of alternative abstinence-oriented behaviors (for example, the community reinforcement approach [CRA]). The operant conditioning paradigm or model views drug use as behavior that operates on the environment and is at least partially maintained by the pharmacological and psychosocial consequences associated with drug use (Grabowski, Higgins, & Kirby, 1993). Drugs themselves can serve as powerful reinforcers for abusers (Grabowski et al., 1993), and interventions usually involve implementing changes in the patient's environment, changes in the consequences associated with drug use, or both. Researchers have continued to use operant principles in developing new interventions. These strategies, as described in the literature, are reviewed and evaluated.

Contingency Management.   In the contingency management approach, the drug-abusing patient agrees to the implementation of certain positive or negative consequences, contingent upon abstinence or drug use. Contingency management procedures are used to ultimately reinforce abstinence (Higgins & Budney, 1993). Bigelow, Stitzer, Griffiths, and Liebson (1981) have discussed the role of reinforced operant behaviors and believe that drug self-administration behaviors can be positively changed with the contingency management approach. Several studies utilizing the contingency management approach have offered findings of possible efficacy for cocaine abusers.

Anker and Crowley (1982) and Crowley (1984) used a contingency management approach coupled with psychotherapy or pharmacotherapy if needed. The contingency program consisted of a contract with the patient that if a urine test was positive for cocaine, letters would be mailed to specific individuals or agencies, which could result in various negative legal and other consequences. Results on a sample of 67 patients indicated that of the 32 patients who used contingency contracts, 31 remained abstinent in treatment, whereas the 35 patients who did not participate continued to use cocaine (Anker & Crowley, 1982).

Budney, Higgins, Delaney, Kent, and Bickel (1991) utilized a contingency management approach in a trial with two patients who were abusing marijuana and cocaine. Patients could earn vouchers contingent upon cocaine and marijuana abstinence. Abstinence was measured by urine samples, which were collected on a fixed schedule 2 to 4 times per week and analyzed immediately. The patient and therapist jointly selected items or activities, which were bought with the earned vouchers (Budney et al., 1991). During the first phase of treatment, vouchers were contingent upon negative urine sample tests for cocaine. Both patients were abstinent from cocaine use but continued to use marijuana during this phase. In the next phase of treatment, vouchers were contingent upon the urine samples testing negative for both cocaine and marijuana. During this phase, the two patients' samples were 96% and 100% negative, respectively, for cocaine and marijuana (Budney et al., 1991). Urine testing at 1- and 5-month posttreatment follow-up revealed continued cocaine abstinence in both patients, but resumption of marijuana use (Budney et al, 1991). The results of these early uncontrolled trials appear promising, but extensive follow-up research is required.

Community Reinforcement Approach.   Several outcome studies utilizing the community reinforcement approach (CRA; Sisson & Azrin, 1989) have yielded successful and provocative findings. The CRA behavioral program consists of the following components. First, patients receive points for negative urine tests, which can be exchanged for various reinforcers—favorable consequences, tangible items, or activities. Second, drug use (a positive urine test) results in the loss of positive reinforcement (that is, points). Third, by agreement with the patient, significant others in the patient's life who have agreed to participate in pleasurable activities with the patient contingent upon negative urine tests are notified of the urine test results. Fourth, patients are instructed on how to identify antecedents and consequences of their drug use. Fifth, adjunctive pharmacotherapies may be used. For example, disulfiram therapy may be used if alcohol is causing problems in achieving cocaine abstinence. The main goal of the community reinforcement approach is to increase the number of natural sources of reinforcement for non-drug-using prosocial behavior and abstinence (Higgins, Budney, Bickel, & Badger, 1994).

A controlled trial comparing the effectiveness of behavioral treatment based on the community reinforcement approach with a 12-step program demonstrated that 3 of 13 patients in the behavioral group achieved 12 consecutive weeks of abstinence, compared to 0 of 12 patients in the 12-step program group (Higgins et al., 1991). More patients in the behavioral group remained in treatment and had longer periods of statistically significant continuous abstinence (Higgins et al., 1991). These positive, yet preliminary, results were later replicated in a larger study involving 38 patients. A second study with 38 patients (Higgins et al., 1993) that compared the CRA with 12-step counseling found that significantly more patients in the CRA group remained in treatment. At 16 weeks in treatment, significantly more patients were abstinent in the CRA group (42%) than in the 12-step group (5%), and the use of other drugs did not differ significantly between groups.

In a further assessment of the CRA, Higgins, Budney, Bickel, Foerg, et al. (1994) compared a community reinforcement approach with incentives to a community reinforcement approach without incentives, using a sample of 40 patients. The incentives included, but were not limited to, sporting equipment, gift certificates for restaurants, fishing licenses, and educational materials. The incentive group showed greater abstinence rates according to urine test data at 5-, 10-, and 20-week intervals compared to the nonincentive group, thus demonstrating that the community reinforcement approach with incentives is helpful in achieving significant periods of abstinence during treatment (Higgins, Budney, Bickel, Foerg, et al., 1994). The authors discuss two limitations of the study: the incentive group was in treatment longer, and the cost of utilizing this approach may not be practical (Higgins, Budney, Bickel, Foerg, et al., 1994). Thus, long-term outcome data from two clinical trials of the CRA (Higgins, Budney, Bickel, Foerg, et al., 1994; Higgins et al., 1993) have been reported. One-year follow-up data in both trials revealed that the CRA combined with incentives was more efficacious than controls (Higgins, et al., 1995).

Respondent Conditioning

Cue Exposure.   The principles of respondent (Pavlovian) conditioning have been used in studies directed toward eliminating conditioned responses that are elicited by conditioned stimuli. Ehrman, Robbins, Childress, McLellan, and O'Brien (1991) demonstrated that cues relevant to a specific drug user play a role in maintaining abuse and appear to be conditioned. In studies comparing nonusers to cocaine abusers, several investigators have found marked physiological responses (changes in skin temperature, galvanic skin response, and heart rate) to cocaine-related cues (video tapes of cocaine use and handling of paraphernalia) in abusers, whereas nonusers did not display these responses (Childress et al., 1988; Ehrman, Robbins, Childress, & O'Brien, 1992; Negrete & Emil, 1992).

Passive cue exposure (extinction) treatment involves repeatedly exposing the patient to cocaine-related stimuli without allowing the exposure to be followed by drug use (Childress, Hole, et al., 1993). During this treatment, patients receive individual sessions involving the presentation of cocaine-related stimuli (for example, pipes, razor blades, white powder, mirrors, and syringes), while discussing their feelings and thoughts during this exposure. Craving ratings are taken periodically. These sessions are repeated until conditioned cravings diminish. Cue exposure may be combined with other behavioral treatments or traditional psychotherapeutic treatments.

Extinction of cocaine-related cues was studied in 60 detoxified cocaine patients to determine if adding passive cue exposure to drug counseling or psychotherapy would be beneficial (Childress, Ehrman, et al., 1988; Childress, McLellan, & O'Brien, 1988). Results indicated that patients who received passive exposure had better retention in treatment and more negative urine tests for cocaine use (Childress, Ehrman, MacRae, McLellan, & O'Brien, submitted). Results also indicated that repeated cue exposure produced a nearly complete reduction in self-reported craving (Childress et al., submitted).

Similar preliminary results were reported comparing extinction programs combined with either psychotherapy or standard drug counseling to psychotherapy or standard drug counseling without extinction (O'Brien, Childress, McLellan, & Ehrman, 1990). The results indicated that subjects in therapies combined with extinction had more negative urine screens for cocaine, compared to the non-extinction programs, and had better retention in treatment (O'Brien et al., 1990).

In an ongoing study of 16 cocaine-abusing outpatients, Childress (1991) found preliminary results indicating that craving for cocaine may be reduced with a treatment program combining passive cue exposure, relaxation, and imagery techniques. The results of the extinction studies should be interpreted with caution because most of the patients resumed or never stopped using, despite reporting reduced craving on exposure to specific stimuli after treatment (Childress, McLellan, & O'Brien, 1988). It can be argued from previous research that cues may be an important element for some patients but not for others. Based on past trials, results of the extinction programs are varied, so definitive conclusions regarding their efficacy cannot yet be made.

Aversion Therapy.   The respondent model has led to the testing of aversion treatments to eliminate craving, induce an aversion to drugs, and potentially increase abstinence rates in cocaine abusers. Aversion treatments have been utilized in the study of alcohol abuse, and are currently being investigated for their efficacy on cocaine abuse. Aversion therapy involves the repeated pairing of the abused drug and associated paraphernalia with an aversive stimulus (such as shock or nausea), in order to eliminate pleasant associations (McLellan & Childress, 1985; Smith, 1982). By pairing the aversive experience with cocaine use and associated stimuli, the addict should develop an aversion to the sight, smell, taste, thoughts, and other cues associated with the use of the drug. The three forms of aversion therapy presently utilized in substance abuse treatment include chemical aversion, electrical aversion (faradic), and verbal aversion (covert sensitization).

Chemical (Emetic) Aversion Treatment.   Chemical aversion involves the pairing of emetically induced nausea or vomiting with the taste, sight, and smell of the abused substance (Elkins, 1991; Smith, 1982). Studies on the efficacy of chemical aversion therapy for cocaine abuse are becoming more common in the literature. Frawley and Smith (1990), in a study of 21 cocaine-only and cocaine and alcohol abusers treated with chemical aversion therapy, found on self-report measures that 38% of cocaine-only patients and 50% of the cocaine and alcohol patients were abstinent at 18-month posttreatment follow-up.

Faradic Aversion Treatment.   Faradic therapy involves the pairing of an aversive electrical shock stimulus with the sight, smell, and taste of the abused substance. Faradic therapy has been in use since the 1970s to treat substance abusers at the Schick Shadel Hospital (Jackson & Smith, 1978). In a large study on 600 chemically dependent patients who were treated with either chemical or faradic aversion therapy, investigators interviewed a random sample of treated patients by phone and determined relapse rates. These interviews revealed that of the 49 patients contacted who had been treated for cocaine abuse, 83.7% were reported to be abstinent at 12-month posttreatment follow-up (Smith & Frawley, 1993). The results of this study are plagued with methodological problems, including lack of controlling for concurrent history and multiple treatment effects, lack of randomization, and the questionable validity of self-report information obtained in phone interviews.

Covert Sensitization.   Covert sensitization (CS) involves the pairing of verbally induced nausea with imagined use, taste, and ingestion of the abused substance (Elkins, 1980). The goal of CS is to have the patients develop conditioned nausea (Elkins, 1980). Conditioned nausea is a response that occurs by the pairing of the abused substance with imagery-induced nausea (Elkins, 1980). Currently, CS treatment studies on cocaine-dependent subjects are being conducted. However, completed research with alcoholics indicates that covert sensitization is helpful to some patients in achieving abstinence (Ashem & Donner, 1968; Fleiger & Zingle, 1973), and similar results regarding abstinence might be expected in cocaine dependent subjects.

   Bordnick, Elkins, Orr, Walters, & Thyer (1996) evaluated the effects of three aversion therapies (chemical, faradic, and covert sensitization) on cocaine craving in a sample of 70 crack cocaine abusers. These investigators found that craving ratings were reduced in all of the treatment groups. At the end of treatment, fully

100% of the patients who had received chemical aversion treatment reported a complete absence of craving for cocaine, whereas 78% of the patients in the faradic and covert sensitization groups had completely eliminated cocaine craving. In addition, the chemical aversion therapy produced the most rapid reduction in craving (approximately 1 session) compared to the other two aversion treatments. These results are promising, but must be interpreted with caution due to their preliminary nature. Currently, no definitive empirical evidence suggests which, if any, aversion therapy is more effective at reducing or eliminating craving or drug use.

Pharmacological Treatments

The development of medications for cocaine abusers has been on the rise and trials are continuing. The research on medications to combat cocaine abuse focuses on the neurobiological aspects of cocaine use. In 1988, $2.7 billion was allocated by legislators for the war on drugs, of which $10 million was used for medication research; that budget item has increased over time (Johnson & Vocci, 1993). Several drugs are being studied that are presumed to affect different brain systems (for example, dopamine and serotonergic) or aspects of behavior and are being used to treat addiction, withdrawal, and craving and to maintain abstinence.

Although there have been a number of studies, no pharmacological agent has been approved for management of Cocaine Dependence (Johnson & Vocci, 1993). Currently, a variety of medication trials are demonstrating potentially promising results, but the data supporting these results are limited and not uniform (Kosten, 1992). A number of review articles provide a more detailed analysis of medication treatments for cocaine abuse (Tutton & Crayton, 1993; Mendelson & Mello, 1996).

Current Research.   L-type calcium channel blockers have been shown in ongoing research to attenuate cocaine's toxic effects in the brain and reduce some of its subjective effects (Muntaner, Kumor, Nagoshi, & Jaffe, 1991; Johnson et al., 1997). These results suggest that L-type calcium channel blockers may be useful in treating the behavioral and toxic effects of cocaine (Johnson et al., 1997).

The opiate antagonist naltrexone, an agent that has been shown to reduce alcohol use and craving (Volpicelli, Alterman, Hayashida, & O'Brien, 1992), is currently being investigated for its effect on Cocaine Dependence in a double-blind placebo-controlled study comparing relapse prevention versus direct counseling therapies by Dr. Joy Schmitz and her research team at the University of Texas Medical School, Houston.

As stated at the beginning of this subsection, no medication has been proven to be efficacious in the treatment of Cocaine Abuse. The results of present and ongoing research appear promising, but more replications with larger samples and strict experimental controls are needed before definitive conclusions can be reached.

CONCLUSIONS

Clearly, a universally effective intervention has not been developed from the previously described psychotherapeutic, biological, and behavioral approaches. That is not to say that some patients have not been successfully treated, but those who have been represent a small minority of cocaine abusers. Interpreting the results is difficult when faced with the methodological problems that plague most of the investigations. Generalizing results from patient studies to various populations is problematic, due to the fact that the vast majority of studies use sample groups that are all white males.

Investigators are still unsure of exactly what to address when providing interventions. Some have concentrated on withdrawal symptoms, others have targeted abstinence behaviors, and still others have treated both. Combining therapies to create a more extensive approach (that is, combining both biological and behavioral treatments) may increase the efficacy rates in future treatment research trials. There is a consensus among researchers that treatment development needs to take into account different types of patient characteristics. The matching of patient to treatment may be crucial to achieving positive outcomes (Pearsall & Rosen, 1992). Clinicians working with patients who abuse crack need to change strategies or develop new ones for assessing and assigning patients to treatment (Marlatt, 1988).

Currently, the recommendation is to use those interventions that have been shown to be the most efficacious in empirically based outcome evaluations. Indeed, it can be argued that to apply treatments for which there are no efficacy or effectiveness data is unethical, or borders on it. In this period of search and research, each clinic is obligated to keep current on knowledge and the application rationale for particular techniques and should closely monitor programs under clearly defined regimens. Behavioral treatment approaches that include contingent reinforcement, skills training, and situational analysis of behavior appear to provide the most effective interventions. Relapse prevention and community reinforcement approaches that utilize these behavioral strategies have been shown to be the most effective in achieving abstinence in cocaine-dependent subjects. Withers, Pulvirenti, Koob, and Gillin (1995) propose that treatments that combine medications and behavior or cognitive therapies based on current research may offer the most efficacious intervention approaches. However, further trials are needed to determine the efficacy of these combined approaches before definitive conclusions can be reached.

Much more information with regard to the treatment of Cocaine Abuse needs to be learned if an effective treatment for Cocaine Dependence is to be discovered. Controlled treatment outcome evaluation research is needed so that more definitive conclusions can be reached regarding the efficacy of interventions, due to the fact that no specific intervention strategy has been shown to be effective. Combining multiple strategies appears to be warranted based on the current research. Future research on cocaine dependence also needs to focus on treatment development in order to provide more effective interventions for this complex problem.

REFERENCES

Alterman, A. I., O'Brien, C. P., & Droba, M. (1993). Day hospital vs. inpatient rehabilitation of cocaine abusers: An interim report. In F. M. Tims & C. G. Leukefeld (Eds.), *Cocaine treatment: Research and clinical perspectives* (National Institute on Drug Abuse Research Monograph 135, pp. 150–162). Washington, DC: National Institute of Health.

Alterman, A. I., O'Brien, C. P., McLellan, A. T., August, D. S., Snider, E. C., Droba, M., Cornish, J. W., Hall, C. P., Raphaelson, A. H., & Schrade, F. X. (1994). Effectiveness and costs of inpatient versus day hospital cocaine rehabilitation. *Journal of Nervous and Mental Disease, 182,* 157–163.

American Psychiatric Association (1994). *Diagnostic and statistical manual of mental disorders* (4th ed.). Washington, DC: Author.

Anker, A., & Crowley, T. J. (1982). Use of contingency contracts in specialty clinics for cocaine abusers. In L. S. Harris (Ed.), *Problems of drug dependence 1981: Proceedings of the 43rd annual scientific meeting, the Committee on Problems of Drug Dependence, Inc.* (National Institute on Drug Abuse Research Monograph 41, pp. 452–459). Washington, DC: National Institute of Health.

Annis, H. M. (1985). Is inpatient rehabilitation of the alcoholic cost effective? Con position. *Advances in Alcohol and Substance Abuse, 5,* 175–190.

Ashem, B., & Donner, L. (1968). Covert sensitization with alcoholics: A controlled replication. *Behaviour Research and Therapy, 6,* 7–12.

Bigelow, G. E., Stitzer, M. L., Griffiths, R. R., & Liebson, I. A. (1981). Contingency management approaches to drug self-administration and drug abuse: Efficacy and limitations. *Addictive Behaviors, 6,* 241–252.

Bordnick, P. S., Elkins, R. L., Orr, T. E., Walters, P., & Thyer, B. A. (1996). *Evaluating the relative efficacy of three aversion therapies designed to reduce craving among male cocaine abusers.* Manuscript submitted for publication.

Bordnick, P. S., & Schmitz, J. M. (in press). Cocaine craving: An evaluation across treatment phases. *Journal of Substance Abuse.*

Budney, A. J., Higgins, S. T., Delaney, D. D., Kent, L., & Bickel, W. K. (1991). Contingent reinforcement of abstinence with individuals abusing cocaine and marijuana. *Journal of Applied Behavior Analysis, 24,* 657–665.

Carroll, K. M. (1993). Psychotherapeutic treatment of cocaine abuse: Models for its evaluation alone and in combination with pharmacotherapy. In F. M. Tims & C. G. Leukefeld (Eds.), *Cocaine treatment: Research and clinical perspectives* (National Institute on Drug Abuse Research Monograph 135, pp. 116–131). Washington, DC: National Institute of Health.

Carroll, K. M., Rounsaville, B. J., & Gawin, F. H. (1991). A comparative trial of psychotherapies for ambulatory cocaine abusers: Relapse prevention and interpersonal psychotherapy. *American Journal Drug Alcohol Abuse, 17,* 229–247.

Childress, A. R. (1991, January). *Integrating cue exposure techniques with standard psychosocial treatments for cocaine dependence.* Paper presented at National Institute on Drug Abuse Symposium, Research and Treatment: "Alliance for the 21st Century", Washington, DC.

Childress, A. R., Ehrman, R., MacRae, J., McLellan, A. T., & O'Brien, C. P. (1993). *Cue reactivity and a cue exposure intervention in cocaine dependence.* Manuscript submitted for publication.

Childress, A. R., Ehrman, R., McLellan, A. T., & O'Brien, C. P. (1988). Conditioned craving and arousal in cocaine addiction: A preliminary report. In L. S. Harris (Ed.), *Problems of drug dependence 1987. Proceeding of the 49th annual scientific meeting, the Commission on Problems of Drug Dependence, Inc.* (National Institute on Drug Abuse Research Monograph 81, pp. 74–80). Washington, DC: National Institute of Health.

Childress, A. R., Hole, A. V., Ehrman, R. N., Robbins, S. J., McLellan, A. T., & O'Brien, C. P. (1993). Cue reactivity and cue reactivity interventions in drug dependence. In L. S. Onken, J. D. Blaine, & J. J. Boren (Eds.), *Behavioral treatment for drug abuse and dependence.* (National Institute on Drug Abuse Research Monograph 137, pp. 73–95). Washington, DC: National Institute of Health.

Childress, A. R., McLellan, A. T., & O'Brien, C. P. (1988). Classically conditioned responses in cocaine and opioid dependence: A role in relapse? In B. A. Ray (Ed.), *Learning factors in substance abuse* (National Institute on Drug Abuse Research Monograph 84, pp. 25–43). Washington, DC: National Institute of Health.

Crowley, T. J. (1984). Contingency contracting treatment of drug-abusing physicians, nurses, and dentists. In J. Grabowski, M. Stitzer, & J. Henningfield (Eds.), *Behavioral intervention techniques in drug abuse treatment* National Institute on Drug Abuse Research Monograph 46, pp. 68–83). Washington, DC: National Institute of Health.

Ehrman, R. N., Robbins, S. J., Childress, A. R., McLellan, A. T., & O'Brien, C. P. (1991). Responding to drug-related stimuli in humans as a function of drug use history. In R. A. Glennon, T. Jarbe, & J. Frankenhein (Eds.), *Drug discrimination: Applications to drug abuse research* (National Institute on Drug Abuse Research Monograph 116, pp. 231–244). Washington, DC: National Institute of Health.

Ehrman, R. N., Robbins, S. J., Childress, A. R., & O'Brien, C. P. (1992). Conditioned responses to cocaine-related stimuli in cocaine abuse patients. *Psychopharmacology, 107,* 523–529.

Elkins, R. L. (1980). Covert sensitization treatment of alcoholism: Contributions of successful conditioning to subsequent abstinence maintenance. *Addictive Behaviors, 5,* 67–89.

Elkins, R. L. (1991). An appraisal of chemical aversion (emetic therapy) approaches to alcoholism treatment. *Behaviour Research and Therapy, 29,* 387–413.

Fleiger, D. L., & Zingle, H. W. (1973). Covert sensitization treatment with alcoholics. *Canadian Counsellor, 7,* 269–277.

Frawley, P. J., & Smith, J. W. (1990). Chemical aversion therapy in the treatment of cocaine dependence as part of a multimodal treatment program: Treatment outcome. *Journal of Substance Abuse Treatment, 7,* 21–29.

Galanter, M., Egelko, S., De Leon, G., & Rohrs, C. (1993). A general hospital day program combining peer-led and professional treatment of cocaine abusers. *Hospital and Community Psychiatry, 44,* 644–649.

Grabowski, J., Higgins, S. T., & Kirby, K. C. (1993). Behavioral treatments of cocaine dependence. In F. M. Tims & C. G. Leukefeld (Eds.), *Cocaine treatment: Research and clinical perspectives* (National Institute on Drug Abuse Research Monograph 135, pp. 133–149). Washington, DC: National Institute of Health.

Halikas, J. A., Kuhn, K. L., Crosby, R., Carlson, G., & Crea, F. (1991). The measurement of craving in cocaine patients using the Minnesota Cocaine Craving Scale. *Comprehensive Psychiatry, 32,* 22–27.

Higgins, S. T., & Budney, A. J. (1993). Treatment of cocaine dependence through the principles of behavior analysis and behavioral pharmacology. In L. S. Onken, J. D. Blaine, & J. J.

Boren (Eds.), *Behavioral treatments for drug abuse and dependence* (National Institute on Drug Abuse Research Monograph 137, pp. 97–122). Washington, DC: National Institute of Health.

Higgins, S. T., Budney, A. J., Bickel, W. K., & Badger, G. J. (1994). Participation of significant others in outpatient behavioral treatment predicts greater cocaine abstinence. *American Journal of Drug and Alcohol Abuse, 20,* 47–56.

Higgins, S. T., Budney, A. J., Bickel, W. K., Badger, G. J., Foerg, F. E., & Ogden, D. (1995). Outpatient behavioral treatment for cocaine dependence: One-year outcome. *Experimental and Clinical Psychopharmacology, 3,* 205–212.

Higgins, S. T., Budney, A. J., Bickel, W. K., Hughes, J. R., Foerg, F., & Badger, G. (1993). Achieving cocaine abstinence with a behavioral approach. *American Journal of Psychiatry, 150,* 763–769.

Higgins, S. T., Budney, A. J., Bickel, W. K., Foerg, F. E., Donham, R., & Badger, G. J. (1994). Incentives improve outcome in outpatient behavioral treatment of cocaine dependence. *Archives of General Psychiatry, 51,* 568–576.

Higgins, S. T., Delaney, D. D., Budney, A. J., Bickel, W. K., Hughes, J. R., Foerg, F., & Fenwick, J. W. (1991). A behavioral approach to achieving initial cocaine abstinence. *American Journal of Psychiatry, 148,* 1218–1224.

Jackson, T. R., & Smith, J. W. (1978). A comparison of two aversion treatment methods for alcoholism. *Journal of Studies on Alcohol, 39,* 187–191.

Johnson, B. A., Lamki, L., Simms, D., Chen, R., Fang, B., Barron, B., Wells, L. Abramson, D., Dhother, S., Meisch, R., & Oderinde, V. (1997, June). *Reversal of cocaine-induced changes in brain blood flow by isradipine.* Paper presented at the 59th annual scientific meeting of the College on Problems of Drug Dependence, Nashville, TN.

Johnson, D. N., & Vocci, F. J. (1993). Medications development at the National Institute on Drug Abuse: Focus on cocaine. In F. R. Tims & C. G. Leukefeld (Eds.), *Cocaine treatment: Research and clinical perspectives* (National Institute on Drug Abuse Research Monograph 135, pp. 57–70). Washington, DC: National Institute of Health.

Johnston, L. D., O'Malley, P. M., & Bachman, J. G. (1994a). *National survey results on drug use from the monitoring the future study, 1975–1993: Vol. 1. Secondary school students.* Washington, DC: National Institute on Drug Abuse.

Johnston, L. D., O'Malley, P. M., & Bachman, J. G. (1994b). *National survey results on drug use from the monitoring the future study, 1975–1993: Vol. 2. College students and young adults.* Washington, DC: National Institute on Drug Abuse.

Kang, S., Kleinman, P. H., Woody, G. E., Millman, R. B., Todd, T. C., Kemp, J., & Lipton, D. S. (1991). Outcomes for cocaine abusers after once-a-week psychosocial therapy. *American Journal of Psychiatry, 148,* 630–636.

Kleinman, P. H., Woody, G. E., Todd, T. C., Millman, R. B., Kang, S., Kemp, J., & Lipton, D. S. (1991). Crack and cocaine abusers in outpatient psychotherapy. In L. S. Onken & J. D. Blaine (Eds.), *National Institute on Drug Abuse Research Monograph 104* (pp. 24–35). Washington, DC: National Institute of Health.

Kosten, R. T. (1992). Pharmacotherapies. In T. R. Kosten & H. D. Kleber (Eds.), *Clinician's guide to cocaine addiction* (pp. 273–289). New York: Guilford Press.

Leukefeld, C. G., & Tims, F. M. (1993). Treatment of cocaine abuse and dependence: Directions and recommendations. In F. M. Tims & C. G. Leukefeld (Eds.), *Cocaine treatment: Research and clinical perspectives* (National Institute on Drug Abuse Research Monograph 135, pp. 260–266). Washington, DC: National Institute of Health.

Manschreck, T. C. (1993). The treatment of cocaine abuse. *Psychiatric Quarterly, 64,* 183–197.

Marlatt, G. A. (1988). Matching client to treatment: Treatment models and stages of change. In D. M. Donovan & G. A. Marlatt (Eds.), *Assessment of Addictive Behaviors* (pp. 474–483). New York: Guilford Press.

McKay, J. R., Rutherford, M. J., Alterman, A. I., Cacciola, J. S., & Kaplan, M. R. (1995). An examination of the cocaine relapse process. *Drug and Alcohol Dependence, 38,* 35–43.

McLellan, A. T., & Childress, A. R. (1985). Aversive therapies for substance abuse: Do they work? *Journal of Substance Abuse Treatment, 2,* 187–191.

McLellan, T. A., Luborsky, L., Woody, G. E., & O'Brien, C. P. (1980). An improved diagnostic evaluation instrument for substance abuse patients: The Addiction Severity Index. *Journal of Nervous and Mental Disease, 168,* 26–33.

Mendelson, J. H., & Mello, N. K. (1996). Drug therapy: Management of cocaine abuse and dependence. *The New England Journal of Medicine, 334,* 965–972.

Miller, N. S., Millman, R. B., & Keskinen, S. (1990). Outcome at six and twelve months post inpatient treatment for cocaine and alcohol dependence. *Advances in Alcohol & Substance Abuse, 9,* 101–120.

Miller, W. R. (1993). Behavioral treatments for drug problems: Where do we go from here? In L. S. Onken, J. D. Blaine, & J. J. Boren (Eds.), *Behavioral treatments for drug abuse and dependence* (National Institute on Drug Abuse Research Monograph 137, pp. 303–321). Washington, DC: National Institute of Health.

Muntaner, C., Kumor, K. M., Nagoshi, C., & Jaffe, J. H. (1991). Effects of nifedipine pretreatment on subjective and cardiovascular responses to intravenous cocaine in humans. *Psychopharmacology, 105,* 37–41.

National Institute on Drug Abuse. (1993). *Capsules cocaine abuse* (pp. 1–5). Washington, DC: National Institute of Health.

Negrete, J. C., & Emil, S. (1992). Cue-evoked arousal in cocaine users: A study of variance and predictive values. *Drug and Alcohol Dependence, 30,* 187–192.

O'Brien, C. P., Childress, A. R., McLellan, T., & Ehrman, R. (1990). Integrating systematic cue exposure with standard treatment in recovering drug dependent patients. *Addictive Behaviors, 15,* 355–365.

Pavlov, I. P. (1927). *Conditioned reflexes.* London: Oxford University Press.

Pearsall, H. R., & Rosen, M. I. (1992). Inpatient treatment of cocaine addiction. In T. R. Kosten & H. D. Kleber (Eds.), *Clinician's guide to cocaine addiction* (pp. 314–334). New York: Guilford Press.

Rawson, R. A., Obert, J. L., McCann, M. J., & Ling, W. (1993). Neurobehavioral treatment for cocaine dependence: A preliminary evaluation. In F. R. Tims & C. G. Leukefeld (Eds.), *Cocaine treatment: Research and clinical perspectives* (National Institute on Drug Abuse Research Monograph 135, pp. 92–115). Washington, DC: National Institute of Health.

Rawson, R. A., Shoptaw, S. J., Obert, J. L., McCann, M. J., Hasson, A. L., Marinelli-Casey, P. J., Brethen, P. R., & Ling, W. (1995). An intensive outpatient approach for cocaine abuse treatment: *The MATRIX model. Journal of Substance Abuse Treatment, 12,* 117–127.

Sisson, R. W., & Azrin, N. H. (1989). The community reinforcement approach. In R. K. Hester & W. R. Miller (Eds.), *Handbook of alcoholism treatment approaches: Effective alternatives* (pp. 242–258). New York: Pergamon Press.

Skinner, B. F. (1953). *Science and human behavior.* New York: Macmillan.

Smith, J. W. (1982). Treatment of alcoholism in aversion conditioning hospitals. In E. M. Pattison & E. Kaufman (Eds.), *Encyclopedic handbook of alcoholism* (pp. 874–884). New York: Gardener Press.

Smith, J. W., & Frawley, P. J. (1990). Long-term abstinence from alcohol in patients receiving aversion therapy as part of a multimodal inpatient program. *Journal of Substance Abuse, 7,* 77–82.

Smith, J. W., & Frawley, P. J. (1993). Treatment outcome of 600 chemically dependent patients treated in a multimodal inpatient program including aversion therapy and pentothal interviews. *Journal of Substance Abuse Treatment, 10,* 359–369.

Spitz, H. I., & Rosecan, J. S. (1987). *Cocaine abuse new directions in treatment and research.* New York: Brunner/Mazel.

Tutton, C. S., & Crayton, J. W. (1993). Current Pharmacotherapies for cocaine abuse: A review. *Journal of Addictive Diseases, 12,* 109–127.

U.S. Congress, Office of Technology Assessment. (1983). *The effectiveness and costs of alcoholism treatment.* Washington, DC: U.S. Government Printing Office.

U.S. Department of Health and Human Services. (1992a). *National household survey on drug abuse: Population estimates 1992* (DHHS Publication No. 93-2053). Rockville, MD: Author.

U.S. Department of Health and Human Services. (1992b). *Annual emergency room data. Data from the drug abuse network (DAWN;* DHHS Publication No. 94-2080). Rockville, MD: Author.

U.S. Department of Health and Human Services, (1993). *National household survey on drug abuse: Population estimates 1993* (DHHS Publication No. 94-3017). Rockville, MD: Author.

U.S. Department of Justice. (1993, March). *Survey of state prison inmates, 1991,* (p. 21). Rockville, MD: Author.

U.S. Department of Justice. (1994a, January). *Drugs & crime data. Fact sheet: Drug use trends,* (p. 3). Rockville, MD: Author.

U.S. Department of Justice. (1994b, September). *Drugs & crime data. Fact sheet: Drugs and related crime,* (USDJ Publication No. NCJ-149286, p. 1). Rockville, MD: Author.

Volpicelli, J. R., Alterman, A. I., Hayashida, M., & O'Brien, C. P. (1992). Naltrexone in the treatment of alcohol dependence. *Archives of General Psychiatry, 49,* 876–880.

Washton, A. M., Gold, M. S., & Pottash, A. C. (1986). Treatment outcome in cocaine abusers. In L. S. Harris (Ed.), *Problems of drug dependence, 1985: Proceedings of the 47th annual scientific meeting, the Committee on Problems of Drug Dependence, Inc.* (National Institute on Drug Abuse Research Monograph 67). Washington, DC: National Institute of Health.

Washton, A. M., & Stone-Washton, N. (1991). Outpatient treatment of cocaine addiction: Suggestions to increase its effectiveness. *The International Journal of the Addictions, 25,* 1421–1429.

Wells, E. A., Peterson, P. L., Gainey, R. R., Hawkins, J. D., & Catalano, R. F. (1994). Outpatient treatment for cocaine abuse: A controlled comparison of relapse prevention and twelve-step approaches. *American Journal Drug and Alcohol Abuse, 20,* 1–17.

Wikler, A. (1948). Recent progress in research on the neurophysiological basis of morphine addiction. *American Journal of Psychiatry, 105,* 328–338.

Withers, N. W., Pulvirenti, L., Koob, G. F., & Gillin, J. C. (1995). Cocaine abuse and dependence. *Journal of Clinical Psychopharmacology, 15,* 63–78.

Chapter 11

OPIATE ABUSE

Cheryl Davenport Dozier
J. Aaron Johnson

OVERVIEW

The use of opiates as psychoactive drugs has occurred for hundreds of years, because they are naturally occurring substances. Even heroin, a semisynthetic opiate compound, was synthesized nearly a century ago. Ironically, while most members of the general public could probably identify the term *opiate* as referring to an illicit substance, probably relatively few could provide more than a cursory definition. For this reason, it is necessary to clarify a few key terms.

Opiates may occur naturally, such as *morphine, codeine,* and *opium;* as semisynthetic compounds, such as *heroin* or *dilaudid;* or as synthetic compounds, such as *methadone.* All of these substances have the potential for abuse, but the opiate most frequently associated with abuse and addiction is heroin. Also of interest is methadone, which can be used as an effective treatment for heroin addiction but may itself be abused.

Opiates are highly addictive drugs that produce drowsiness, slurred speech, mood changes, and analgesia. Frequently the opioid-intoxicated individual will appear to be unaware of the surrounding environment. Smaller doses of some opiates are used effectively by physicians as pain killers and cough suppressants, while higher doses of these drugs may lead to depression of the central nervous system.

Operational Definitions

Addiction, as a concept, is difficult to define. Professionals in various fields have difficulty agreeing upon a universal definition. Official definitions may range from the heavily theoretical to the more practical. Some groups (such as the American Psychiatric Association [APA], 1994) avoid the use of the term *addiction* altogether, relying instead on terms such as *abuse* and *dependence.* On the other hand, some researchers and clinicians use the term *addiction* in referring to many abuses not necessarily marked by physical dependence. Many self-help groups (such as Alcoholics Anonymous and Narcotics Anonymous) define addiction as a disease of the body, mind, and spirit (Raskin & Daley, 1991); the individual is said to be "powerless" over alcohol or drugs. Others argue that addiction refers to the dependence of normal functions (such as working, eating, and sleeping) on alcohol or drugs regardless of the quantity or effects of the drugs on behavior (Raskin & Daley, 1991). The Substance Abuse and Mental Health Services Administration (SAMHSA) officially defines addiction as "a progressive, chronic, primary, relapsing disorder that generally involves the compulsion, loss of control, and continued use of alcohol or drugs, despite adverse consequences" (Landry, 1995, p. 9). SAMHSA's official position is that addiction need not involve the development of physical dependence, tolerance, and withdrawal.

Because of this confusion over the term *addiction,* and the fact that the overwhelming majority of treatment facilities now treat both alcohol and drugs, the term *chemical dependency* is now commonly used to refer to the harmful use of either alcohol or illicit psychoactive substances. This lack of clarity as to the definition of addiction, combined with the inconsistency of terminology in the treatment arena, highlights the necessity for valid, reliable assessment methods, some of which are discussed later in this chapter.

Withdrawal is one of the symptoms commonly associated with opiate dependence. *Withdrawal* can also be an ambiguous concept, and the term therefore requires clarification. The characteristics of withdrawal differ from substance to substance, but in the case of opiates, they include dysphoric mood, nausea or vomiting, dilation of the pupils, diarrhea, fever, weeping, muscle aches, and insomnia.

After discussing the prevalence and social costs of opiate use and abuse, this chapter elaborates on some of the most common methods used in the assessment of Opiate Abuse. The primary focus of the chapter, effective social work interventions in the treatment of opiate addiction, follows the section on assessment methods.

Prevalence and Social Costs of Opiate Use and Abuse

Opiate use—specifically, heroin use—is somewhat of an anomaly in terms of drug-use trends. Whereas the use of most substances (such as marijuana and cocaine) peaked during the early 1980s and then showed a marked decrease throughout the remainder of the decade, reported lifetime use of heroin has generally remained at around 2 million persons since 1979 (Gfroerer, 1996). The numbers of past-year and past-month users show wide variability from year to year, but the figures are too small for the variability to be statistically significant. Estimates from the 1995 National Household Survey on Drug Abuse (NHSDA) show the numbers of past-year and past-month users of heroin to be 428,000 and 196,000, respectively (Gfroerer, 1996). SAMHSA cautions that these estimates of heroin use should be considered very conservative, because the heroin-using population is probably undersampled in the NHSDA. For instance, efforts were made by the National Institute on Drug Abuse in 1991 and 1992 to estimate the prevalence of drug abuse among all population subgroups in the Washington, DC area. The survey found that for some categories of drug users—notably, heroin users—the nonhousehold population included a substantial proportion of users. Approximately 20 percent of past-year heroin users were found in the nonhousehold population (Gfroerer, 1996). Similar sampling problems could also explain much of the wide variability from year to year among past-year and past-month users.

The relative inaccessibility of opiate users further results in widely varying estimates of the number of opiate addicts. Estimates of the number of chronic opiate addicts range from 50,000 to more than 1,000,000 (Vocci, Jaffe, & Jain, 1992; Straussner, 1993; Kreek, 1990). Estimates of the number of abusers are likewise difficult to obtain. However, one means of determining the trends in opiate abuse is to look at the number of heroin-related emergency department episodes, using data from the Drug Abuse Warning Network (DAWN). The number of heroin-related episodes rose by about 400 percent from 1978 to 1994 (11,700 to 64,000) and increased another 19 percent from 1994 to 1995 (64,000 to 76,000; McCaig, 1996).

Furthermore, the proportion of drug-related emergency department episodes involving heroin increased steadily from 4 percent in 1978 to almost 13 percent in 1994 (McCaig, 1996). According to DAWN's estimates, while injection continues to be the most popular route of administration in terms of heroin-related episodes, an increasing percentage of episodes are occurring in which the route of administration is by snorting or is unknown. Overdose, seeking detoxification, and chronic effects are the most frequently cited reasons given for an emergency department visit. When asked their motive for heroin use, approximately 80% of the individuals involved in heroin-related episodes cite dependence (McCaig, 1996).

As a result of the longevity and persistence of opiate use and abuse, drug abuse treatment has largely focused on opiate addiction—principally heroin addiction—since the 1950s (Hubbard et al., 1989). However, there are signs that this may be changing. The number of annual admissions to drug abuse treatment for heroin addiction doubled between 1981 and 1993 (90,000 to 180,000; Rouse, 1995). Despite this increase, heroin addiction actually comprises a smaller percentage of overall admissions to drug abuse treatment, having been superseded by admissions for cocaine addiction.

While the numbers of users and abusers of opiates are not as prevalent in the population as those of some of the more common illicit substances, such as cocaine or marijuana, one can only speculate as to the severity of Opiate Abuse in terms of social and financial costs to society. When estimating the costs of abuse of illicit substances as opposed to the costs of Alcohol Abuse, two distinctions are clear. Whereas the primary costs associated with Alcohol Abuse are related to the loss of productivity due to premature death and the loss of productivity due to illness, these costs are nominal for the drug abuser (Rouse, 1995). On the other hand, the costs associated with crime, criminal justice, or property loss (affecting 69% of users) and AIDS (affecting 9.5% of users) are cause for major concern in the area of drug abuse (Rouse, 1995).

While the social and financial costs of Opiate Abuse are difficult to separate from the costs of substance abuse in general, one may assume that Opiate Abuse represents a substantial proportion of the combined costs for two reasons. First, intravenous administration remains the most popular means of use among opiate abusers. With a shortage of needle exchange programs through which used needles can be traded for clean needles, many abusers share needles, which contributes to the spread of HIV. Kreek (1990) found that approximately 60% of all heroin addicts were infected with the HIV virus. This can be attributed largely to the sharing of needles with HIV-infected persons. Second, because persons with opiate addictions are often unable to function normally without the drug, many are unable to maintain employment. The addicted user, though unemployed, still needs money to secure the drug. In an effort to avoid withdrawal, the addicted user is likely to resort to illegal means, including theft and violence, to obtain the drugs. Unemployment and criminal behavior are more commonly associated with opiate abusers than with the abusers of other illicit substances.

Another social cost common among opiate abusers but frequently overlooked is depression. Researchers (Steer, 1990; Milby et al., 1996) estimate that 25% to 60% of opiate addicts suffer from some form of psychiatric comorbidity. Milby et al. (1996) found the most common disorders to be Major Depressive Disorder (31.4%) and Post-Traumatic Stress Disorder (31.4%). In the case of depression, it is often difficult to determine if the depressive symptoms are a result of the individual's opiate addiction, or if the addiction arose as a result of efforts to relieve the depression. Beeder and Millman (1995) note that "self-medication with opiates commonly occurs in a variety of psychiatric conditions" (p. 94). These findings have important implications for the social worker involved in the treatment of Opiate Abuse. Treatment cannot be effective unless comorbid symptoms are detected in assessment and are systematically addressed.

Physiologically, Opiate Abuse is much more costly for women than for men. Hormone secretion is altered and the menstrual cycle is disrupted. Amenorrhea, dysmenorrhea, and venereal disease are common among the female opiate-abusing population, as is sexual dysfunction and lack of sexual desire (Pape, 1993). Continuous drug use often causes premature aging, and women may suffer more physical deterioration than men. Opiates also pose significant health risks to the fetus, and, hence, to infants born to addicted women. Many women with addictions to opiates do not use birth control methods because they believe they are incapable of getting pregnant (Rosenbaum & Murphy, 1990). Unanticipated children are often neglected and may be raised by relatives or end up in foster care.

Relevance of Opiate Treatment to Social Work Practice

A large yet poorly integrated service delivery system for persons experiencing problems related to substance abuse has emerged (Hanson, 1991). "As clinicians struggle with the dilemmas that accompany addictions," Hanson points out, "they discover few clear explanations for the problems and few effective intervention strategies" (Hanson, 1991, p. 66). Social workers and other clinicians continue to search for the most effective and least expensive treatments for opiate addiction. Social work practitioners should attempt to utilize the least intrusive methods of treatment, including self-help programs, outpatient drug-free programs, detoxification, and inpatient treatment (Dozier, 1997).

Recognizing the impact that managed care is having on substance abuse treatment, many providers are raising concerns regarding the cost-effectiveness of various treatment interventions. Given the fiscal constraints on substance abuse treatment, social workers must support interventions that are empirically based, clinically justifiable, and cost-efficient (Patterson, 1997). Social workers should utilize client-treatment matching to improve the impact of initial intervention and decrease the expense and frustration of repeated treatment attempts (Miller, 1992). Treatment matching also lends itself to the more empowering model of viewing a failed treatment as possibly being the result of a wrong approach, rather than the failure of an individual client. Social workers can then seek an alternative treatment approach that may be more beneficial for that particular client.

Social workers' role in the treatment of Opiate Abuse need not be confined to the treatment center. While they are less prevalent than employees who abuse alcohol and cocaine, there are opiate abusers who are able to maintain employment. To effectively manage such populations, Barabander (1993) believes that industrial social workers must assume three roles. First, they must act as trainers, educating managers to be aware of performance deficiencies as an indicator of drug abuse. Second, they must work closely with management in devising and implementing substance abuse policies and procedures. Finally, they must serve as clinicians, making accurate assessments of addictive disorders and appropriate referrals for treatment.

ASSESSMENT METHODS

Currently, admission for treatment at most treatment centers requires a diagnosis of Opiate Dependence (304.00) or Opiate Abuse (305.50) as defined by the *Diagnostic and Statistical Manual of Mental Disorders,* Fourth Edition (*DSM-IV;*

American Psychiatric Association [APA], 1994, pp. 175–194). An individual must have experienced three of more of the following seven symptoms in the past 12 months in order to be diagnosed as substance dependent: (a) tolerance to a particular drug; (b) feelings of withdrawal when not taking the substance; (c) taking larger amounts of a substance over a longer period than was intended; (d) persistent desire or unsuccessful efforts to control or reduce substance use; (e) spending a great deal of time in an effort to obtain the substance; (f) giving up or reducing important social, occupational, or recreational activities because of substance use; and (g) continuing substance use despite knowledge of having a persistent or recurrent physical or psychological problem that is likely to have been caused or exacerbated by the substance.

To be diagnosed with a substance abuse disorder, the individual need only exhibit one or more of the following substance abuse symptoms (APA, 1994): (a) recurrent substance use that results in a failure to fulfill major role obligations at work, school, or home; (b) recurrent substance use in situations in which it is physically hazardous; (c) recurrent substance-related legal problems; and (d) continued substance use despite having persistent or recurrent social or interpersonal problems that are caused or exacerbated by the effects of the substance.

The primary difference between Opiate Dependence and Opiate Abuse is that the dependence diagnosis is marked by tolerance of the opiate and withdrawal when the opioid substance is discontinued (APA, 1994). Opiate abusers typically use the substance less frequently and do not develop tolerance or experience withdrawal. *DSM-IV* also provides the means for diagnosing a number of opioid-related disorders, including Withdrawal, Intoxication, Delirium, Psychosis, Sexual Dysfunction, and Sleep Disorders (APA, 1994).

Straussner (1993, p. 14) identifies five tasks or goals that must be completed during the assessment process: (a) determine a formal diagnosis, (b) ascertain the severity and impact of substance abuse on the patient and those around him or her, (c) establish a baseline of the patient's status for future comparison, (d) provide a guide to treatment planning and the patient's progress, and (e) evaluate the impact of environmental influences and appropriate preventative efforts. Urine drug screens are effective in detecting the presence of opiates in the body, and the medical exam can accurately assess the opiate abuser's physical condition, but both these methods are incapable of determining many of the other problems associated with the abuse of an illicit substance (such as family, legal, and psychological problems). For these reasons, it is necessary to use a self-report instrument capable of making a reliable assessment of even the most complex cases of Opiate Abuse and Opiate Dependence. While there is some question as to whether the self-reports of opiate users are reliable and valid, Foy, Cline, and Laasi (1987) found self-reports among this population to be quite accurate. However, factors such as assessment setting, interviewer characteristics, and subject characteristics may serve to limit the reliability and validity of these self-reports (Foy et al., 1987).

Self-Report Instruments

Perhaps the most widely used instrument in the field, both for client assessment purposes and for research, is the Addiction Severity Index (ASI; Friedman and Granick, 1994). The fifth edition of the ASI (McLellan et al., 1992) is a 161-item structured interview that identifies personal and family background characteristics and assesses the patient's relative status in the following six treatment-related life problem areas: (a) drug and alcohol use, (b) medical problems, (c) psychological or psychiatric problems, (d) legal or criminal justice involvement, (e) family and social relations, and (f) employment and financial support. The instrument is administered to the client by a trained clinician and has a high level of validity and reliability.

The Drug Abuse Treatment for AIDS Risk Reduction (DATAR) is another comprehensive assessment instrument that is particularly valuable for the opiate-abusing population. As previously mentioned, extensive needle sharing puts opiate abusers at high risk for HIV. DATAR is advantageous in that it collects data on high-risk sexual behavior and needle use (Friedman & Granick, 1994). DATAR consists of two parts: an intake form that, like the ASI, is administered by the clinician, and a self-rating form that is self-administered by the client. DATAR has also been shown to have a high level of validity and reliability.

One notable weakness of the ASI and DATAR—as well as of nearly all other self-report assessment instruments—is that they do not collect adequate information on the special problems and issues of female clients (Friedman & Granick, 1994). As mentioned earlier, women face health issues that may require special attention in treatment, yet most assessment instruments are not designed to detect these issues.

Social worker Walter Hudson has recently prepared a rapid-assessment instrument called the Index of Drug Involvement (IDA), a 25-item survey designed to assess a client's self-reported degree or severity of drug abuse. A strength of the IDA is that it may be easily administered on a repeated basis to assess the effectiveness of social work treatment as it occurs, consistent with the expectations of empirically based practice. Low-cost copies of the IDA, along with information on its reliability and validity, and scoring instructions, are available from the author of the scale (Hudson, 1996).

Self-Rating versus Observation of Opiate Withdrawal

While most instruments assess generic drug and alcohol abuse, specifically for the assessment of opiate withdrawal instruments are available. The Subjective Opiate Withdrawal Scale (SOWS) is a 16-item scale that asks the client to rate on a 5-point scale the intensity of each symptom currently being experienced (National Institute on Drug Abuse [NIDA], 1993). The Objective Opiate Withdrawal Scale (OOWS) is completed by an observer who rates the presence of 13 physically observable signs over a 10-minute observation period (NIDA, 1993). Both these scales have demonstrated reliability and validity in assessing opiate withdrawal syndrome. When the SOWS and the OOWS were compared with each other in an ultrashort detoxification, both measures demonstrated a steady reduction of withdrawal distress (Loimer, Linzmayer, & Grunberger (1991). However, Loimer et al. (1991) found that the clinical assessment (OOWS) significantly underestimated the psychological distress experienced by the patients. For this reason, the clinician should consider using both scales, as subjective withdrawal may persist even when few objective signs of distress remain. The measurement of subjective distress may be important in preventing discontinuation of treatment and early relapse (Loimer et al., 1991).

EFFECTIVE INTERVENTIONS

Research on the effectiveness of drug treatment varies rather widely in the quality of the designs and methodologies (Berg, 1992). This section presents the findings of an extensive literature review and assesses the empirical evidence regarding effective treatment interventions for Opiate Abuse and Opiate Dependence. It is worth noting that there are two primary types of treatment interventions for opiate addiction, one that leaves the opiate-addicted person completely drug-free, and one that successfully maintains and monitors the opiate-addicted person on drug medication. This section primarily focuses on the psychosocial treatment approaches that are drug-free.

This section primarily addresses intervention and treatment approaches related to heroin abuse and addiction, as it is the prevalent opiate of choice. It is important to note that inpatient and outpatient substance abuse treatment programs admit persons whose opiates of choice include morphine, codeine, oxycodone (Percodan), meperidine (Demerol), dilaudid, Darvon, and other prescribed and illicit drugs. Opiate abusers working in the health-related fields (that is, physicians and nurses) are often abusers of these prescribed opiates. Heroin addicts sometimes abuse these prescribed opiates in combination with illicit drugs. Many of these prescribed drugs are legally obtained from emergency rooms, private physicians, and health and mental clinics as pain relievers for real or fictitious ailments. Social workers need to be especially cognizant of this licit opiate use. The literature regarding effective treatment interventions with these opiates is limited.

The following subsections present both psychosocial and pharmacological treatments that represent the most current empirically based interventions for opiate abuse and addiction.

Detoxification

Detoxification is a clinical process aimed at the relief of symptoms associated with the opioid abstinence syndrome while eliminating physical dependence. Acute detoxification of opioid dependence usually takes 5 to 7 days and currently may be allowed less time due to managed care restrictions. Methadone is commonly chosen as the detoxification agent. The detoxification process usually requires large doses of methadone to prevent withdrawal symptoms during the stabilization stage, followed by daily reductions of the drug. There is controversy around the use of detoxification as the sole treatment modality. After detoxification, patients should be referred to an appropriate inpatient or outpatient treatment modality. Detoxification usually occurs in a medical setting but may take place in a therapeutically supervised outpatient setting for persons with less severe dependence.

Inpatient Rehabilitation

Historically, substance abuse treatment for heroin addiction included some form of inpatient treatment. Treatment for opiate addictions (primarily heroin addiction) began to include hospitalization in the 1920s and by the 1960s the long-term residential therapeutic communities (TCs) were developed (Dozier, 1997)

Therapeutic Communities

The residential therapeutic community (TC) was primarily developed for the treatment of hard-core heroin addicts with long-term dependence and, usually, criminal histories. Prior to the 1980s the TC population was made up largely of heroin-addicted clients, but since the 1980s cocaine-dependent clients have emerged as the largest population group in most TCs (Gerstein & Harwood, 1990). It is important for the social worker to note that not all residential drug treatment programs follow a therapeutic community model.

In TCs, opiate addicts are involved in intensive social therapy that lasts for about 9 to 18 months (the length of stay is constantly being reduced, primarily due to financial constraints). This group-centered approach encompasses the following methods, grounded in an interdependent social environment: (a) firm behavioral norms; (b) reality-oriented group and individual psychotherapy, which extends to lengthy encounter sessions; (c) a system of clearly specified rewards and punishments; (d) a series of hierarchical responsibilities, privileges, and esteem achieved by working up a ladder of tasks; and (e) some degree of potential mobility from client to staff status (Gerstein & Harwood, 1990, p. 155). Interventions in TCs often include more forceful confrontative and encounter approaches (Hanson, 1991) than most social workers are comfortable with or are trained to perform. The staffers have traditionally been recovering addicts trained by the TC but currently include an increasing number of masters-level professionals, including social workers.

Numerous outcome studies have evaluated the effectiveness of TCs (Jainchill & DeLeon, 1992; Tims, Jainchill, & DeLeon, 1994; Gerstein & Harwood, 1990; Goldapple & Montgomery, 1993). However, conclusions about the effectiveness of TCs are limited by the difficulties of applying standard clinical trial methodologies to this treatment milieu and by a population often not willing to participate in such research. Some of the strongest conclusions on the effectiveness of TCs are based on nonrandomized but rigorously conducted studies of clients seeking admission to TCs (Gerstein & Harwood, 1990).

Research on client outcomes has usually included one of the three types of studies: (a) single TCs, such as the Phoenix House study (DeLeon and others in Condelli & Hubbard, 1994); (b) multiple TCs, such as the Drug Abuse Reporting Program (DARP; Bales et al. and Sells & Simpson in Gerstein & Harwood, 1990); and (c) multiple long-term residential programs that included TCs such as the Treatment Outcome Prospective Study (TOPS; Hubbard et al., 1989). The results of these different types of studies have been very similar and their findings are widely reported in the literature. The major finding is that clients who stay in treatment programs for long periods of time have lower rates of drug use and criminal behavior, and higher rates of employment and school attendance, than clients who stay in programs for short periods of time (Condelli & Hubbard, 1994; Gerstein & Harwood, 1990).

One TC outcome study was completed by social workers Gary Goldapple and Dianne Montgomery (1993). Sixty-six clients admitted to a Miami TC were randomly assigned to receive a cognitive-behavioral intervention designed to reduce drop out from the TC, or to receive no special treatment (that is, the standard TC program). Clients receiving the retention-promotion intervention had a 100% rate of retention in TC-treatment; those receiving the standard TC program had a 63% dropout rate. It seems clear that some form of retention promotion can be a useful adjunct to TC programs.

Psychotherapy Treatment

Psychodynamic psychotherapy in inpatient or outpatient psychiatric settings was the usual form of treatment available for persons with opiate addictions before the widespread use of methadone maintenance. There is one known published study, by Nyswander and colleagues in 1958, that attempted to evaluate the effects of psychotherapy for persons with opiate addictions before 1970 (Rounsaville & Kleber, 1985, Rawson, 1995). This study indicated that psychotherapy could not be an important intervention for the great majority of addicts.

Addiction typically affects four major areas of functioning: (a) physical and medical, (b) psychological or emotional, (c) social or family, and (d) spiritual (Kingery-McCabe & Campbell, 1991). For opiate addiction treatment to be effective, all major problem areas must be addressed. For instance, methadone maintenance treatment may eliminate the client's physical or medical complications, but it in no way improves his or her psychological well-being or social and spiritual difficulties. By comparing a methadone-maintenance-only control group with a group receiving counseling, on-site medical and psychiatric care, family therapy, and employment counseling, McLellan, Arndt, Metzger, Woody, & O'Brien (1993) found that the group receiving enhanced services showed significantly improved outcomes when compared to the methadone-only group.

Another study of opiate users found that persons who stopped drug use changed their social network interaction patterns so that they had fewer contacts with opiate users and more links with positive, non-drug-using role models (Hawkins & Fraser, 1983). This study illustrated that effective social network intervention requires not only that pro-drug-use patterns be disrupted, but also that anti-drug-use (or non-drug-use) contacts be established (Hanson, 1991, p. 86). The social workers' skills and understanding of emotional illness separate from drug abuse are particularly beneficial in helping the addicted client confront any existing social and family problems.

A controlled study (often referred to as the Philadelphia Study) was done in the methadone treatment unit of the Philadelphia Veterans Administration Medical Center to test whether professional psychotherapy can provide additional benefits when combined with standard drug counseling services in a methadone maintenance program (Woody et al., 1983). This study included 110 subjects who were offered random assignment to three types of treatment modalities: drug counseling alone, or counseling plus 6 months of either supportive-expressive (SE) psychotherapy or cognitive-behavioral (CB) psychotherapy. Patients who completed the study's intake procedure had to keep three appointments with a counselor and, if they were assigned to SE or CB, three appointments with a therapist. The major findings of this study were that all patients in all three groups showed improvement in many outcome measures, including lessened drug use, crime days, and illegal income, and improved psychological function. The study also indicated that patients who receive psychotherapy in addition to drug counseling make more and larger gains than those who receive drug counseling alone (Woody et al., 1983).

Another study presented data about the potential role of psychotherapy for psychiatrically impaired clients on methadone maintenance for opiate addictions (Woody, McLellan, Luborsky, & O'Brien, 1994). The findings indicated that professional psychotherapy is a helpful supplement to ongoing drug counseling services for these patients. However, there was no evidence that psychotherapy cures addiction or that it could be used successfully without integrating it into other ongoing clinical services, such as methadone treatment and drug counseling. These authors further identified differences between therapist and programs (structure, staffing, dosing procedures, physical plant, and leadership) that may play a significant role in the feasibility and success of attempts to use psychotherapy in drug treatment programs.

The issue of systemic differences between therapists in psychotherapy outcome studies in the area of drug-dependence treatment was studied by Christoph, BeeBe, & Connolly (1994). One of the implications of their research is that knowledge of therapist effects—particularly studies of effective versus noneffective therapists—

may be useful for understanding how psychotherapy works and how therapists can be better trained to be successful.

Outpatient Drug-Free Treatment

Outpatient drug-free treatment (OPDF) is usually described as a nonresidential form of therapy that does not use methadone or any narcotic antagonists. Outpatient, nonmethadone treatment for opiate addictions varies in duration from one-time assessments and referrals to long-term intensive outpatient treatment with daily psychotherapy and counseling (Gerstein and Harwood, 1990). This type of treatment is usually for the client who is in the early stages of opiate dependence, is without a criminal history, and usually is still employed and connected to some support systems. Historically, a primary approach of psychotherapy in an outpatient drug-free setting was viewed to be of little value in treating opiate addictions (Rounsaville & Kleber, 1985).

However, there are some outpatient studies that do suggest treatment efficacy. In the DARP study previously mentioned, the outcomes were generally quite favorable for the drug-free treatment modality. The large-scale TOPS study evaluated the treatment course and outcome for more than 11,000 substance abusers between 1979 and 1981. It compared four types of treatment modalities: (a) methadone maintenance, (b) residential drug-free treatment, (c) outpatient drug-free treatment, and outpatient detoxification. The findings indicated significant improvements in rates of illicit drug use and criminal activity and decreases in psychological symptoms for those who stayed in treatment for at least 3 months. The patterns of improvement were similar except in the area of weekly opiate use, which was 23.6% for OPDF compared to 78.3% for the methadone maintenance group (Rounsaville & Kleber, 1985).

Methadone Maintenance Treatment

Methadone maintenance continues to be the most commonly used pharmacotherapy for heroin addiction. At the same time it has been the most controversial, because methadone is a narcotic that addicted persons continue to use to control addiction to a more harmful opiate, heroin. Methadone maintenance is a treatment that is designed primarily for persons with serious addictions to heroin. According to the Institute of Medicine, one of the major conclusions of the extensive evaluation literature on methadone maintenance is that there is strong evidence from clinical trials and similar study designs that heroin-dependent individuals have better outcomes, on average, when they are maintained on methadone (Gerstein & Harwood, 1990). One of the other major arguments is that many persons with opiate addictions who are on methadone maintenance continue to use alcohol and illicit street drugs, such as cocaine or crack and benzodiazepines. In controlled studies measuring heroin in urine, criminal activity, and engagement in socially productive activities, clients in methadone maintenance programs have consistently done better than those not taking methadone (Gerstein & Harwood, 1990).

There has been ongoing controversy as to whether methadone should be used as a long-term pharmacological treatment for heroin addiction or as a short-term medical intervention. Moolchan and Hoffman (1994) developed a clinical model for methadone treatment that incorporates both the psychosocial and the medical aspects of treatment. This phases-of-treatment model is based on the understanding of opiate addiction as a biopsychosocial process. This clinical model provides a means of meeting the individual treatment needs of all patients (Moolchan & Hoffman, 1994).

One problem with methadone maintenance programs is the client's continued or newly developed abuse of other, nonopiate, drugs. The use of low-cost urine-testing procedures affords one way to empirically evaluate the client's abuse of these drugs. Various contingency-management programs involving positive reinforcers for maintaining clean urine samples and mildly punitive consequences for samples showing drug use have been shown to be of great value in reducing the methadone maintenance client's abuse of nonopiate drugs (see Kidorf & Stitzer, 1996; Stitzer, Bigelow, Liebson, & Hawthorne, 1982; McCaul, Stitzer, Bigelow, & Liebson, 1984).

Naltrexone Treatment

Naltrexone was once thought to be the antagonist agent that would become the primary treatment for opiate addiction. Clinical trials began in the 1970s; it was introduced to the market in 1986. Still, naltrexone treatment is virtually unknown outside the academic and research settings where most of the studies were conducted. Naltrexone has had a limited impact in the treatment community, and research on naltrexone for opiate addiction has been at a standstill for the past decade. Naltrexone's greatest advantages are that it is nonaddicting and is less costly than methadone (Rousaville, 1995).

Polyaddiction Treatment

A number of clinical research reports address the combined treatment of drug addiction and alcoholism in the same treatment setting. It is becoming more infrequent to treat a pure drug abuser, one who abuses only a single drug (including alcohol). Often, clients will identify one drug as their drug of choice but after further exploration will disclose a number of other drugs that they use either in combination with the drug of choice or when they are unable to obtain that drug. One study at the Eagleville Hospital and Rehabilitation Center, a residential abstinence-based therapeutic community, reported empirical findings based on two decades of experience with combined treatment. Their findings have been favorable, supporting the thesis that alcoholics and opiate addicts can achieve desirable abstinence (Craig, 1987).

In methadone maintenance treatment programs, large numbers of the patients are also addicted to alcohol, crack or cocaine, or other substances. Treatment providers are either referring these patients to outpatient drug-free treatment and alcoholism treatment programs or are developing therapeutic groups in their own settings to address polyaddiction.

Dual-Diagnosis Treatment

Both substance abuse and psychiatric patient populations demonstrate significant comorbid psychopathology. The terms *dual diagnosis* and *mentally ill chemical abuser* (MICA) were developed to identify those patients with psychopathology who are primarily treated in substance abuse programs. The etiology of a dual-diagnosis condition may vary, but it is usually either a patient with a primary mental illness and subsequent substance abuse or a patient with a primary substance dependence with a concurrent psychopathology. Self-medication with opiates is a common occurrence with a variety of psychiatric conditions (Beeder & Millman, 1995).

Natural Recovery

A number of researchers are readdressing the need for more research on *natural recovery* in drug addiction. They refer to earlier studies by Charles Winick regarding his *maturing out* hypothesis, and Lee Robins's study of Vietnam veterans who were addicted to opiates (see Biernacki, 1990; Mariezcurrena, 1994).

Rousaville and Kleber's (1985) study consisted of a group of subjects with opiate addictions who received treatment compared to an untreated group. Both groups had the same criteria, which included a minimum of 2 years of opiate use at least three times weekly, withdrawal symptoms on drug cessation, and a recent use of opiates during the past 2 months. A further requirement for the untreated group was no history of treatment interventions for the previous 3 years except brief involuntary hospitalization for detoxification. Findings indicated that the nontreated subjects had more adequate social functioning, lower rates of depressive disorders, and fewer drug-related legal problems. The treated subjects received equivalent or higher ratings on all of the ratings of drug-use severity. There was no difference in functioning in marital, nuclear family, and work roles.

Graeven and Graeven's study (as cited in Mariezcurrena, 1994) discussed treated and untreated adolescents with heroin addictions, focusing on factors associated with participation in treatment and cessation of heroin use. In this study the treated and untreated populations were separated, which possibly contributed to a more reliable analysis of natural recovery and an analysis of the difference between groups. The results indicated that the untreated adolescents were less likely to be in trouble at high school, less likely to be incarcerated or unemployed, and more likely to go to college. They also had higher self-esteem than the treated adolescents and more cohesive families that exercised more control over their behavior. The untreated adolescents were more likely to have stopped using heroin than treated ones. The researchers suggested that treating people who have supportive families and do not want treatment may be less effective than no treatment at all. Clearly, there is a need for further research of this approach by social workers.

Self-Help Groups

There is limited empirical support but much clinical evidence for the benefit of participation in self-help groups. Self-help groups in substance abuse treatment are primarily the traditional 12-step programs, such as Alcoholics Anonymous and Narcotics Anonymous, and may include such nontraditional groups as Women for Sobriety. These programs can provide the opiate-addicted person with a positive clean and sober support system (Morgan, 1996). Most outpatient drug-free treatment programs depend heavily on 12-step groups, and attendance at their meetings is often built into the treatment regimen. There is still controversy regarding the use of 12-step self-help groups by methadone maintenance patients in the treatment community.

CONCLUSIONS

Having established the current state of opiate abuse and treatment, several implications may be drawn from the preceding discussion. First, better methods need to be devised for gaining access to those persons affected by Opiate Abuse and Opiate Dependence. Because much of this population is inaccessible to conventional survey methods, estimates of the numbers of users and abusers vary tremendously from year to year. Without an accurate estimate of the numbers and characteristics of abusers, implementing an efficient and effective strategy for treatment is virtually impossible.

Efficient treatment would include the placement of treatment centers in areas with a high concentration of opiate abusers. Strategic placement and easy accessibility of centers may make the abuser more willing to receive treatment. While data from the Drug Abuse Warning Network (DAWN) is obviously limited, it may offer the best solution to this problem. By coordinating the placement of treatment facilities with DAWN's findings, treatment efforts could be concentrated in those areas whose hospitals report the greatest numbers of heroin-related episodes. The recent increase in the potency of street-level heroin has led to significant increases in the number of heroin-related emergency department episodes. If substance abuse treatment professionals were to coordinate their efforts using data from DAWN, perhaps a number of these episodes—and a substantial number of deaths—could be prevented.

Second, few professionals understand the complexity of chemical dependency better than social workers. Surprisingly, the principal creators of assessment instruments remain psychiatrists and clinical psychologists. Rather than relying on these clinicians to devise such instruments, social workers need to take a more active role in developing assessment tools. Social workers' knowledge of the potential societal difficulties faced by persons with addictions seems to make them a vital resource for collaboration on the development of these instruments. Of particular importance is the development of an instrument specifically designed to assess female opiate abusers. As previously mentioned, opiates are physically more detrimental to females than to males. Unwanted pregnancies are an additional concern, as are the effects of opiate abuse on newborns, and the effects of the abuser's lifestyle on the well-being of children. Again, this is an area where the social worker's knowledge is advantageous and should prove invaluable in the development of a female-oriented assessment instrument.

Finally, there is evidence that many substance abuse treatment programs and clinicians have relied upon modalities that have never been proven to be effective. However, many more treatment outcome studies have been conducted over the past couple of decades that address treatment efficacy (Miller, 1992). According to the Institute of Medicine's report on treatment effectiveness, treatment providers are not utilizing the results of research to develop the most effective treatment interventions. This is an area where great improvement is needed—the integration of empirically based research with clinical practice.

There is not a clear consensus, based on the empirical evidence of treatment of Opiate Abuse and Opiate Dependence, regarding a single universally accepted approach. In the area of Opiate Dependence, methadone maintenance has been the subject of the most extensive studies using all of the main techniques of evaluation research. Therapeutic communities have been the subject of the next most extensive research, followed by outpatient drug-free treatments. As McLellan et al. (1993) have shown, a patient should never be maintained on methadone without the aid of counseling. Because of the continued controversy over methadone maintenance, the gradual removal of the patient from this narcotic is both socially desirable and expedient. Given the complexity of chemical dependency—and, particularly, opiate abuse—the social worker may again be an invaluable resource in these removal efforts. The therapeutic community is perhaps one of the most ideal drug-free treatment settings, particularly for younger patients. There is clear evidence of the effectiveness of therapeutic communities with younger populations. For this reason, TCs should be increasingly utilized, and social workers should play an integral role in these communities.

There are a number of factors that contribute to treatment effectiveness or that may be limitations for research. For example, attention needs to be paid to the effects that the therapist or counselor's style, the staff's credentials, and the patient's race, ethnicity, gender, sexual orientation, age, and socioeconomic status have on treatment outcomes. There are many hidden populations of opiate users that need particular consideration, such as women, racial and ethnic groups, prescription drug abusers, adolescents, inner-city residents, and the elderly. Social workers must incorporate the use of the strengths perspective and recognition of diversity issues when addressing treatment of these special populations.

Social workers' use of psychotherapy as a clinical intervention still needs further research, especially in non-substance-abuse settings. However, there is substantial research that does indicate a positive relationship between psychotherapy intervention and opiate addiction treatment outcomes. Social workers must continue to be involved in the provision of and evaluation of opiate abuse treatment in both substance abuse and non-substance-abuse settings. Collaboration with other substance abuse professionals at all levels is essential.

REFERENCES

American Psychiatric Association. (1994). *Diagnostic and statistical manual of mental disorders* (4th ed.). Washington, DC: Author.

Barabander, C. S. (1993). Alcohol and drugs in the workplace. In S. L. A. Straussner (Ed.), *Clinical work with substance-abusing clients* (pp. 69–87). New York: Guilford Press.

Beeder, A. B., & Millman, R. B. (1995). Treatment strategies for co-morbid disorders: Psychopathology and substance abuse. In A. Washton (Ed.), *Psychotherapy and substance abuse: A practitioners handbook* (pp. 76–102). New York: Guilford Press.

Berg, W. E. (1992). Evaluation of community-based drug abuse treatment programs: A review of the literature. In E. Freeman (Ed.), *The addiction process* (pp. 81–95). New York: Longman.

Biernacki, P. (1990). Recovery from opiate treatment: A summary. In E. Y. Lambert, *The collection and interpretation of data from hidden populations* (NIDA Research Monograph 98, pp. 113–119). Washington, DC: U.S. Department of Health and Human Services.

Christoph, P. C., BeeBe, K., & Connolly, M. B. (1994). Therapist effects in the treatment of drug dependence: Implications for conducting comparative treatment studies. In *Psychotherapy and counseling in treatment of drug abuse* (NIDA Research Monograph 104, pp. 39–49). Washington, DC: U.S. Department of Health and Human Services.

Condelli, W. S., & Hubbard, R. L. (1994). Client outcomes from therapeutic communities. In F. Tims, G. DeLeon & N. Jainchill (Eds.), *Therapeutic community: Advances in research and application* (NIDA Research Monograph 144, pp. 80–98). Washington, DC: U.S. Department of Health and Human Services.

Craig, R. J. (1987). *Clinical management of substance abuse programs.* Springfield, IL: Charles C. Thomas.

Dozier, C. D. (1997). Should social workers support the inpatient treatment of substance abusers who do not require detoxification? Yes! In B. A. Thyer (Ed.), *Controversial issues in social work practice* (pp. 81–87). Boston, MA: Allyn & Bacon.

Foy, D. W., Cline, K. A., & Laasi, N. (1987). Assessment of alcohol and drug abuse. In T. D. Nirenberg & S. A. Maisto (Eds.), *Developments in the assessment and treatment of addictive behaviors* (pp. 89–114). Norwood, NJ: Ablex.

Friedman, A. S., & Granick, S. (1994). *Assessing drug abuse among adolescents and adults: Standardized instruments* (NIH Publication No. 94-3757). Washington, DC: U.S. Government Printing Office.

Gerstein, D. R., & H. J. Harwood (Eds.). (1990). *Treating drug problems* (Vol. 1). Washington, DC: National Academy Press.

Gfroerer, J. (1996). *Preliminary estimates from the 1995 National Household Survey on Drug Abuse* (DHHS Advance Report No. 18). Washington, DC: U.S. Government Printing Office.

Goldapple, G., & Montgomery, D. (1993). Evaluating a behaviorally-based intervention to improve client retention in therapeutic community treatment for drug dependency. *Research on Social Work Practice, 3,* 21–39.

Hanson, M. (1991). Alcoholism and other drugs. In A. Gitterman (Ed.), *Handbook of social work practice with vulnerable populations* (pp. 65–100). New York: Columbia University Press.

Hawkins, J. D., & Fraser, M. (1983). Social support networks in treating drug abuse. In J. K. Whittaker & James Garbarino (Eds.), *Social support networks: Informal helping in the human services* (pp. 355–380). Hawthorne, NY: Aldine.

Hubbard, R. L., Marsden, M. E., Rachal, J. V., Harwood, H. J., Cavanaugh, E. R., & Ginzburg, H. M. (1989). *Drug abuse treatment: A national study of effectiveness.* Chapel Hill, NC: University of North Carolina Press.

Hudson, W. W. (1996). *The Index of Drug Involvement.* Tempe, AZ: Walmyr.

Jainchill, N., & G. DeLeon. (1992). Therapeutic community research: Recent studies of psychopathology and retention. In G. Buhringer & J. Platt (Eds.), *Drug addiction treatment research: German and American Perspectives* (pp. 367–388). Malabar, FL: Krieger.

Kidorf, M., & Stitzer, M. L. (1996). Contingent use of take-homes and split-dosing to reduce illicit drug use of methadone patients. *Behavior Therapy, 27,* 41–51.

Kingery-McCabe, L. G., & Campbell, F. A. (1991). Effects of addiction on the addict. In D. C. Daley & M. S. Raskin (Eds.), *Treating the chemically dependent and their families* (pp. 57–78). Newbury Park, CA: Sage.

Kreek, M. J. (1990). Methadone maintenance treatment for heroin addiction. In J. J. Platt, C. D. Kaplan, & P. J. McKim (Eds.), *The effectiveness of drug abuse treatment* (pp. 275–293). Malabar, FL: Krieger.

Landry, M. J. (1995). *Overview of addiction treatment effectiveness.* (DHHS Publication No. SMA 96-3081). Washington, DC: U.S. Government Printing Office.

Loimer, N., Linzmayer, L., & Grunberger, J. (1991). Comparison between observer assessment and self rating of withdrawal distress during opiate detoxification. *Drug and Alcohol Dependence, 28,* 265–268.

Mariezcurrena, R. (1994). Recovery from addictions without treatment: Literature review. *Scandinavian Journal of Behavior Therapy, 23,* 131–154.

McCaig, L. (1996). *Historical estimates from the Drug Abuse Warning Network* (DHHS Advance Report No. 16). Washington, DC: U.S. Government Printing Office.

McCaul, M. E., Stitzer, M. L., Bigelow, G. E., & Liebson, I. A. (1984). Contingency management interventions: Effects on treatment outcome during methadone detoxification. *Journal of Applied Behavior Analysis, 17,* 35–43.

McLellan, A. T., Arndt, I. O., Metzger, D. S., Woody, G. E., & O'Brien, C. P. (1993). The effects of psychosocial services in substance abuse treatment. *Journal of the American Medical Association, 269,* 1953–1959.

McLellan, A. T., Kushner, H., Metzger, D., Peters, R., Smith, I., Grissom, G., Pettinati, H., & Argeriou, M. (1992) The fifth edition of the Addiction Severity Index. *Journal of Substance Abuse Treatment, 9,* 199–214.

Milby, J. B., Sims, M. K., Khuder, S., Schumacher, J. E., Huggins, N., McLellan, A. T., Woody, G. E., & Haas, N. (1996). Psychiatric comorbidity: Prevalence in methadone maintenance treatment. *American Journal of Drug and Alcohol Abuse, 22,* 95–107.

Miller, W. R. (1992). The effectiveness of treatment for substance abuse: Reasons for optimism. *Journal of Substance Abuse Treatment, 9,* 93–102.

Moolchan, E. T., Hoffman, J. A. (1994). Phases of treatment: A practical approach to methadone maintenance treatment. *International Journal of the Addictions, 29,* 135–160.

Morgan, T. (1996). Behavioral treatment techniques for psychoactive substance use disorders. In F. Rotgers, D. S. Keller, & J. Morgenstern (Eds.), *Treating substance abuse: Theory and technique* (pp. 202–240). New York: Guilford Press.

National Institute on Drug Abuse. (1993). *Diagnostic source book on drug abuse research and treatment* (NIH Publication No. 93-3508). Washington, DC: U.S. Government Printing Office.

Pape, P. A. (1993). Issues in assessment and intervention with alcohol- and drug-abusing women. In S. L. A. Straussner (Ed.), *Clinical work with substance-abusing clients* (pp. 251–269). New York: Guilford Press.

Patterson, D. (1997). Should social workers support inpatient treatment of substance abusers, No! In B. A. Thyer, (Ed.), *Controversial issues in social work practice* (pp. 88–94). Needham Heights, MA: Allyn & Bacon.

Raskin, M. S., & Daley, D. C. (1991). Introduction and overview of addiction. In D. C. Daley & M. S. Raskin (Eds.), *Treating the chemically dependent and their families* (pp. 1–21). Newbury Park, CA: Sage.

Rawson, R. A. (1995). Is psychotherapy effective for Substance Abusers? In A. Washton (Ed.), *Psychotherapy and substance abuse: A practitioners' handbook* (pp. 55–75). New York: Guilford Press.

Rosenbaum, M., & Murphy, S. (1990). Women and addiction: Process, treatment, and outcome. In E. Y. Lambert (Ed.), *The collection and interpretation of data from hidden populations* (NIDA Research Monograph 98, pp. 120–127). Washington, DC: U.S. Department of Health and Human Services.

Rounsaville, B. J. (1995). Can psychotherapy rescue naltrexone treatment of opioid addiction? In L. S. Onken, J. D. Blaine, & J. J. Boren (Eds.), *Integrating behavioral therapies with medications in the treatment of drug dependence* (NIDA Research Monograph 150, pp. 37–51). Washington, DC: U.S. Department of Health and Human Services.

Rounsaville, B. J., & Kleber, H. D. (1985). Psychotherapy/counseling for opiate addicts: Strategies for use in different treatment settings. *International Journal of the Addictions, 20,* 869–896.

Rouse, B. A. (Ed.). (1995). *Substance abuse and mental health statistics sourcebook* (DHHS Publication No. SMA 95-3064). Washington, DC: U.S. Government Printing Office.

Steer, R. A. (1990). Psychopathology and depression in heroin addicts. In J. J. Platt, C. D. Kaplan, & P. J. McKim (Eds.), *The effectiveness of drug abuse treatment* (pp. 161–167). Malabar, FL: Krieger.

Stitzer, M. L., Bigelow, G. E., Liebson, I. A., & Hawthorne, J. W. (1982). Contingent reinforcement for benzodiazepine-free urines: Evaluation of a drug abuse treatment intervention. *Journal of Applied Behavior Analysis, 15,* 493–503.

Straussner, S. L. A. (1993). Assessment and treatment of clients with alcohol and other drug abuse problems: An overview. In S. L. A. Straussner (Ed.), *Clinical work with substance-abusing clients* (pp. 3–30). New York: Guilford Press.

Tims, F., Jainchill, N., & DeLeon, G. (1994). Therapeutic communities and treatment research. In F. Tims, G. DeLeon, & N. Jainchill (Eds.), *Therapeutic community: Advances in research and application* (NIDA Research Monograph 144, pp. 1–15). Washington, DC: U.S. Department of Health and Human Services.

Woody, G. E., McLellan, A. T., Luborsky, L., & O'Brien, C. P. (1994). Psychotherapy and counseling for methadone-maintained opiate addicts: Results of research studies. In *Psychotherapy and counseling in treatment of drug abuse* (NIDA Research Monograph 104, pp. 9–23). Washington, DC: U.S. Department of Health and Human Services.

Woody, G. E., Luborsky, L., McLellan, A. T., O'Brien, C. P., Beck, A. T., Blaine, J., Herman, I., & Hole, A. (1983). Psychotherapy for opiate addicts: Does it help? *Archives of General Psychiatry, 40,* 639–645.

Vocci, F. J., Jaffe, J. H., & Jain, R. B. (1992). Drug dependence (addiction) and its treatment. In R. B. Jain (Ed.), *Statistical issues in clinical trials for treatment of opiate dependence* (NIDA Research Monograph 128, pp. 6–13). Washington, DC: National Institute of Health.

PART III

Schizophrenia and Other Psychotic Disorders

Chapter 12

SCHIZOPHRENIA

Rosemary L. Farmer
Joseph Walsh
Kia J. Bentley

OVERVIEW

Schizophrenia is described as "one of today's best known and most common forms of madness" (Gottesman, 1991, p. 1). It is specifically a disorder of thought, and is considered, along with such others as Bipolar Disorder and unipolar depression, to be one of the major mental disorders. The term *major* implies a high degree of severity and a pervasive negative impact on the everyday lives of those who struggle with the symptoms of these disorders, particularly those whose illness runs a chronic long-term course.

Definition and Description

The diagnosis of Schizophrenia is made on the basis of the existence of an array of symptoms in an individual over time. In general, there are thought to be two defining groups of symptoms in schizophrenia. The first is psychosis, characterized by hallucinations (false perceptions), delusions (false beliefs), unusual (bizarre or inappropriate) behavior, and disturbed thinking and speech (tangential and illogical, with loose associations). In recent years these symptoms have come to be known as *positive* symptoms because they reflect *excesses* or *distortions* of typical human functioning. Second, schizophrenia is also characterized by so-called deficit or *negative* symptoms which reflect a *loss* of typical functioning, such as social withdrawal, avolition, and a flattening or restricting of affect. For the diagnosis to be applied, the current *Diagnostic and Statistical Manual of Mental Disorders,* fourth edition (*DSM-IV*) criteria require symptoms to be present for 6 months, with 1 month in an active phase (American Psychiatric Association [APA], 1994). A person whose disorder is characterized more by positive symptoms is said to be *Type 1* and those characterized more by negative symptoms are *Type 2*. The distinctions of *positive* and *negative* have proved especially meaningful in distinguishing medication effects, although there is great hope that further research into this typology will aid in our understanding of the causes and course of schizophrenia, as well.

In addition, *DSM-IV* provides a separate and slightly older list of subtypes of Schizophrenia, also based on the predominant features in a presenting individual. These are *paranoid* (characterized by persecutory delusions), *disorganized* (characterized by inappropriate affect), *catatonic* (characterized by bizarre body movements, posturing or lack of responsiveness to the environment), *undifferentiated* (not meeting the criteria of other subtypes) and *residual* (has had a previous episode, but currently has no prominent positive symptoms). The manual warns of the difficulty in diagnosing Schizophrenia in the context of other cultures and the need to be sensitive to differences in an individual's presentation and communication style. Schizophrenia is also considered a *diagnosis of exclusion,* meaning that all other potential diagnoses (for example, organic disorders, substance abuse, and affective disorders) must be ruled out before this one may be applicable.

Prevalence, Incidence, and Social and Economic Costs

Data from the National Institute of Mental Health (NIMH)-sponsored Epidemiologic Catchment Area (ECA) research showed the lifetime prevalence of schizophrenia (total number who have or will have the disorder) to be 1.3% of the population in the United States. The incidence (in 1 year) was estimated at 0.025% to 0.05% of the population. Gottesman (1991) notes that by the year 2000 there will be 2.06 million people in America who have or will have had schizophrenia.

Males tend to have their first episode of schizophrenia in their late teens and early 20s, while this happens a bit later, the late 20s, for females. In general, however, there are equal prevalence rates for males and females and an even geographical distribution in the United States and in the world. In addition, people with schizophrenia tend to be born in winter or early spring. These statistics seem to hold across time (the past 200 years), and space (pastoral villages to industrial societies) with only modest variations by culture. Sadly, given the many effective medications and psychosocial interventions available (see following), it is estimated that only about half of all people with schizophrenia receive treatment.

Complete and total remission in schizophrenia is thought to be relatively uncommon. While not considered a necessarily progressive illness, in that it does not automatically get worse over a lifetime (indeed, the opposite is true), its course is typically described as *variable.* This is usually reflected in either a chronic course, with symptoms becoming less or more florid but never really disappearing, or one in which periods of substantial symptomatology are interspersed with periods of remission. As with many physical and mental disorders, while a typical course can be described, reliable and accurate prediction of any individual's course is still impossible. Some of the risk factors for a poorer prognosis are poor premorbid functioning, gradual onset, earlier age at onset, being male, having a long active phase, existence of structural brain abnormalities, having abnormal neurological functioning, having a history of schizophrenia in the family, being unmarried, and social isolation. This information can tell us only so much, however, because studies show that risk factors can only account for 38% of the variance in outcome (Black, Yates, & Andreasen, 1988). We *don't* know so much more than we *do* know with respect to the outcome and course of schizophrenia.

Black et al. (1988) summarize 80 years of research on the devastating personal and social costs of the illness. Many people with schizophrenia live under extreme social and economic limits. For example, two thirds of people with schizophrenia never marry, and only 34% live in their own home or in a relative's home. The *social drift hypothesis* explains the higher concentrations of people with schizophrenia in poverty by noting the impairments in vocational functioning and the impact of stigma. Perhaps most startling (and underreported) is that 50% of people with schizophrenia attempt suicide. Ten percent succeed, contributing to the lower life expectancy of people with schizophrenia. These statistics approach those of persons with affective disorders. In fact, suicide is the number-one cause of premature death in schizophrenia (Fenton, McGlashan, Victor, & Blyler, 1997).

It is estimated that 25% of all hospital beds are filled with someone diagnosed with schizophrenia. Total societal costs are put at 2% of our gross national product (GNP). In today's dollars that is close to $100 *billion.* This includes direct costs, such as treatment and public assistance, as well as indirect costs, such as the loss of employment productivity by persons with schizophrenia (Black et al., 1988). Emotional costs and family costs are not included.

Relevance of Social Work Involvement

In spite of the grim picture painted thus far of the symptoms and costs of this disorder, many would say we are in a time of great optimism with respect to schizophrenia. Our expanding knowledge base relates to new brain-imaging techniques; related discoveries in neurotransmission, brain anatomy, brain function and genetics; the introduction of a new breed of antipsychotic medications; and a new appreciation of psychosocial influences on onset, course, and treatment. As this chapter will show, the newer diagnostic and assessment techniques and effectiveness research in schizophrenia are also causes for tremendous hope for all people with schizophrenia, for their families, and for all providers in mental health fields. Social workers, the largest professional group of providers in public and nonprofit mental health agencies, have been participating in these developments since Edith Horton, a graduate of what is now the Columbia University School of Social Work, was sent out as an aftercare agent for two mental hospitals in 1904—a social work role that has continued to the present (Hudson, 1978). Developments in the first 50 years of this century—such as the rise of social psychiatry, the aftercare and mental hygiene movements, and two world wars—set the stage for expanded social work roles in mental health and mental illness. Today, social workers provide services to people with schizophrenia in state and private hospitals, other psychiatric units, community mental health centers, private clinics, residential treatment centers, group homes, rehabilitation centers, psychosocial clubhouses, and drop-in centers. They function as therapists, discharge planners, case managers, counselors, brokers, advocates, educators, group leaders, community organizers, researchers, program planners and evaluators, and, most important, as *partners* with people diagnosed with schizophrenia, their families, and other providers who are trying to help improve the quality of human life.

ASSESSMENT METHODS

Described in the following are a range of scales that may be used by social workers to assess symptoms, symptom changes, quality of life, and levels of social functioning for persons with schizophrenia. While several of the diagnostic measures are out of date with regard to *DSM-IV* criteria, they remain in wide use. In general, these scales tend to demonstrate moderate and sometimes high levels of validity and reliability, but the reader is referred to the original articles for those details. As a rule, more structured scales demonstrate higher reliability.

Structured Clinical Interviews

The first three instruments included here are lengthy diagnostic tools, generally used in research studies. They are not always practical for use in single case assessments and thus are not described in detail.

The *Diagnostic Interview Schedule* (DIS) is a highly structured interview designed for making *DSM* diagnoses of schizophrenia and other disorders (Robins, Helzer, Croughan, & Ratcliff, 1981). It bases diagnoses on well-defined frequency, duration, and age of onset criteria and does not require that the social worker seek additional information from external sources. All questions and rules for probes are specified. The DIS is scored by computer and requires 45 to 75 minutes to complete.

The *Structured Clinical Interview* (SCID) guides the social worker in making Axis I *DSM-III-R* diagnoses and symptom change ratings (Spitzer, Williams, Gibbon, & First, 1992). Among the 33 diagnoses included are Schizophrenia, Schizophreniform Disorder, and Schizoaffective Disorder. There are two editions of the SCID available, one of which includes psychotic symptoms as a major area of focus. The instrument is formatted to include questions, diagnostic criteria, and a 4-point rating scale for each symptom. The output of the SCID is a record of the presence or absence of a disorder for both current and lifetime occurrence. The social worker is encouraged to formulate his or her own questions and to use all available sources of information about a client in completing the form, including past records and family observations.

The *Schedule for Affective Disorders and Schizophrenia* (SADS), consisting of 120 scaled items, is designed to facilitate the diagnosis of clients based on DSM criteria (Endicott & Spitzer, 1978). The SADS provides for descriptions of a disorder when it was most severe and the severity of symptoms during the preceding week (which can be used as a measure of change). The SADS, which requires 1 to 2 hours for completion, is available in three versions. The standard version is the most general assessment tool. A lifetime version (SADS-L) focuses on the presence of a disorder over a lifetime, and a change version (SADS-C) focuses on symptom severity during the previous week. The eight summary scales include measures of delusions or hallucinations and thought disorder. The social worker is encouraged to make use of all available information about a client in rating symptoms.

The *Present State Examination* (PSE) is a tool for determining the mental status of clients with schizophrenia and other psychoses (Manchanda & Hirsch, 1986; Wing, Cooper, & Sartorius, 1974). Its 140 items assess symptoms and monitor changes. The instrument, which can be computer scored, provides scores on 38 syndromes that can be summarized into subscales, two of which are specific to psychotic behavior (delusions/hallucinations and behavior/speech). Ratings are based on client reports and social worker observations during the interview, utilizing 2- and 3-point scales. Normally, symptoms observed during the previous month are rated. Suggestions for some interview questions and probes are provided. Most symptoms are rated on the basis of frequency of occurrence and severity, and all items are defined in a glossary. Statistical output provides symptom profiles, subscores, a total score, and symptom classification into diagnostic categories. The interview usually takes 1 hour to complete. Reported limitations of the instrument include its failure to address organic symptoms, a bias toward reported versus observed behavior, a lack of utility in assessing noncommunicative clients, and an insensitivity to mild symptoms. The PSE has been amended to function with greater sensitivity as a change-rating scale, with symptom ratings expanded to a 7-point range (Tress, Bellenis, Brownlow, Livingston, & Leff, 1987).

Rating Scales

The following six scales have great utility for social workers as measures of symptom change. All are short, easy to administer, and rely heavily on clinical judgment.

The *Brief Psychiatric Rating Scale* (BPRS) measures symptom changes in persons with schizophrenia (Overall & Gorman, 1962). It is not a diagnostic tool, but provides a clinical profile at a single point in time. There are several versions of this instrument, but the most well-known includes 18 items, each rated on a 7-point scale. The BPRS includes 12 items specific to schizophrenia and 6 for depression.

The scale is constructed for measuring symptoms of schizophrenia, but along with the depression items may also be considered a schizoaffective scale. It includes recommended cutoff scores for evaluating the severity of symptoms. Scores for the four domains of thinking disturbance, withdrawal and retardation, hostility and suspicion, and anxiety and depression may be obtained by summing item subsets. The social worker is instructed to assess most client symptoms at the specific time of the interview, but guidelines suggest rating six items on the basis of conditions during the prior 3 days. There is no standardized interview protocol included with this instrument, although it is recommended that the task not exceed 30 minutes. When the BPRS is applied in repeated ratings, each assessment should be uninfluenced by prior reviews. Interrater reliability of the BPRS, when jointly conducted by social workers with nurses or psychiatrists is quite high (see Ligon, 1997).

The *Psychiatric Symptom Assessment Scale* (Bigelow & Berthot, 1989) is a revised version of the BPRS. The 23-item scale uses concrete, behavioral anchor points as guides for the social worker's decision making about ratings. The instrument includes the 18 BPRS items (although 5 are renamed) with 4 items added to expand the range of ratings for depression, mania, and schizophrenia. A global *loss of functioning* item has also been added. The items, all of which include guidelines and examples, are rated on a 7-point scale. The order of items is arranged to reflect the sequence in which information is usually gathered in a clinical interview, and the social worker is instructed to rate the quality of a given behavior rather than its duration.

The *Manchester Scale* (Krawiecka, Goldberg, & Vaughan, 1977) is a short, easy-to-administer instrument, sensitive to symptom change, for assessing persons with schizophrenia. It consists of eight items with 5-point rating scales that cover the three domains of positive symptoms, negative symptoms, and affect (anxiety and depression). The first four ratings are based on client responses to questions (no interview guidelines are provided), and the other four on observations made during the interview. A manual offers probe questions and guidelines for rating. The scale is not intended to be used blindly; familiarity with the client's history is desirable, and the scale is most useful with clients whom the social worker knows well. Software is available for data management in longitudinal studies.

As noted earlier, specifying clients whose symptoms tend to be predominantly positive or negative can have implications for intervention. The *Scale for the Assessment of Negative Symptoms* (SANS) and *Scale for the Assessment of Positive Symptoms* (SAPS) are used to quantify these client characteristics (Andreasen, 1982; Andreasen & Olsen, 1982). The SANS is a 25-item instrument, rated along a 6-point scale with five subscales (affect, poverty of speech, apathy, anhedonia, and impairment of attention). The SAPS is a 35-item instrument with four subscales (hallucinations, delusions, bizarreness, and positive thought disorder), and one global assessment of affect. Subscales for both instruments contain a global rating index. Symptom ratings are to be considered within a time frame of 1 month, although this may be adjusted. The SANS and SAPS are designed to be used in conjunction with client interviews, clinical observations, family member observations, reports from professionals, and self-reports by clients. All scores for each instrument are hand-calculated.

The *Positive and Negative Syndrome Scale for Schizophrenia* (PANSS) is an instrument that measures positive and negative symptoms, the relative predominance of one type to the other, and is also a measure of global psychopathology (Kay, Fiszbein, & Opler, 1987). The PANSS includes 18 items adapted from the BPRS and 12 items derived from another source. Seven items represent each of the positive and negative symptom scales, and 16 represent general psychopathology. Each item includes a definition and anchoring criteria for the 7-point ratings. PANSS ratings are based on information specific to a time period, usually the previous week. The social worker derives information primarily from the clinical interview but may also utilize input from other professionals and family members. The 30- to 40-minute semiformal interview consists of four prescribed phases, including rapport development; probes of themes of pathology; questions about mood, anxiety, orientation, and reasoning; and a probing of areas where the client seems ambivalent.

Quality of Life Scales

The development of instruments to measure the quality of life and social functioning of persons with schizophrenia acknowledges the current emphasis on comprehensive community-based services for these clients. With the shift from custodial to community care has come an awareness of the need for new methods to evaluate client characteristics that go beyond symptom assessment.

The *Quality of Life Interview* (QOLI), the best-known scale, is a structured, 45-minute instrument for use with persons who have serious mental illnesses, including schizophrenia (Lehman, 1988). The QOLI can provide quality-of-life measures at a single point in time or measures of change in any of nine domains, including living situation, family relations, social relations, leisure, work, finances, legal and safety concerns, physical health, and mental health. It is organized by first asking the client for demographic information and a rating of general life satisfaction, and then proceeding through the life domains, asking first about objective life conditions and then about satisfaction with those conditions. It concludes with another question about life satisfaction and some open-ended probes. Clients receive scaled or dichotomous scores in all domains. The QOLI, which includes directions and scoring instructions, is highly structured to minimize interviewer effects. Still, interviewing skills are important in setting limits on a respondent's tendency to digress and in judging whether a respondent is too disturbed to tolerate the interview or to provide valid responses.

The *Quality of Life Scale* (QLS) is a 21-item instrument utilizing a semistructured interview to assess and monitor changes in deficit symptoms specific to schizophrenia (Heinrichs, Hanlon, & Carpenter, 1984). It is scored on a 7-point scale and requires approximately 45 minutes to administer. The conceptual framework of the QLS asserts that symptom fluctuations occur in the areas of intrapsychic, interpersonal, and instrumental functioning. These domains are supported by factor analysis, along with a fourth domain reflecting the client's participation in routine activity patterns. The QLS elicits information on symptoms and functioning during the preceding 4 weeks. The process is organized similarly to that of a clinical interview, and the social worker is instructed to use his or her own probes in making judgments about ratings. Scoring is based on client self-report only.

The *Quality of Life* questionnaire (QOL) measures a client's general happiness or satisfaction of needs, and performance or actualization of abilities (Bigelow, Gareau, & Young, 1990). It is a semistructured interview including 146 items, rated either dichotomously or on a 4-point scale. Domains covered by the interview include housing, self and home maintenance, finances, employment, psychological distress, psychological well-being, and interpersonal functioning. Satisfaction of need and performance are assessed within domains. Human service items pertaining to domains are included to facilitate the instrument's use in program evaluation. The primary source of data is the client, but additional information may be gathered from clinical observations and from the client's significant others. The QOL interview may have limited utility in that it is lengthy, but it is a well-known measure that has been used in psychosocial rehabilitation program evaluation projects.

Social Functioning Scales

The *Social Adjustment Scale for Schizophrenics* (SAS-II) was developed in 1980 as an adaptation of an earlier SAS scale that assessed the social adjustment of depressed women (Schooler, Hogarty, & Weismann, 1979). The SAS-II consists of 52 items measuring interpersonal and instrumental performance in the five areas of work, relationships with household members, relationships with other relatives, performance of leisure and recreational activities, and personal well-being. In addition, there are four global ratings of the domain areas. Each item is rated on a 5-point scale based on information obtained during a 45- to 90-minute semistructured interview with the client or a significant other. Scores can be combined to yield an average performance per role, and any items that do not apply can be eliminated. Additionally, ten factors have been statistically derived for the SAS-II from a large sample of persons with schizophrenia, including personal anguish, intimate relations, parental role, primary relationship, social relationships, work affect, sexual practices, major role performance, self-care, and economic independence.

The next two scales provide potentially useful and varied types of information about social functioning, but are quite lengthy and thus impractical for use in some clinical settings. The *Katz Adjustment Scale* (KAS) is a self-report inventory that exists in two forms: one for use by the client and the other for use by a close relative (Katz & Lyerly, 1963; Platt, 1986). The relative's scale consists of 205 items in five sections that rate symptoms and social behavior, performance of socially expected activities, extent of free-time activities, and the relative's satisfaction with the client's functioning. The client's scales are identical, except that they include a different symptoms-distress checklist (55 items rated on a 4-point global scale). The instrument measures behaviors occurring during the previous few weeks. The difference between the two ratings provides an index of significant others' dissatisfaction with the client's current role performances. Advantages of the KAS are its assessment of psychopathology and inclusion of significant others' perspectives.

The *Social Behavior and Adjustment Scale* (SBAS) assesses a client's performance of major life roles and the effects of that performance on members of the client's household (Platt, 1986; Platt, Weyman, Hirsch, & Hewett, 1980). Information is obtained during a 60- to 90-minute interview with a significant other about the client's behavior during the previous month. It includes 329 items, but not all of these must be used when assessing aspects of social functioning. Scores from each of six sections yield measures of the client's demographics, performance of socially expected behaviors, the objective burden experienced by the family, the subjective distress experienced by the household related to the client's behavior, changes in the family's performance of socially expected activities, and the family's needs for assistance from external sources. The SBAS includes a rating manual and training guide. A strength of the SBAS is its provision of data about the support offered to, and the demands imposed upon, the client by the immediate household environment. A limitation of the instrument is the expectation that the significant other understands the client's functioning thoroughly.

Clearly, the social worker providing services for persons meeting the criteria for a diagnosis of Schizophrenia has many assessment options available. Apart from their value in corroborating the diagnosis, some of them, if used repeatedly, can serve as useful outcome measures to ascertain the client's responses to medication or psychosocial interventions.

EFFECTIVE INTERVENTIONS

While the treatment of persons with schizophrenia remains a daunting task, the advances of the past 30 years demonstrate that numerous effective psychosocial interventions exist. This section presents an up-to-date summary of these interventions. Five subsections serve to organize the material being presented, including individual therapies, group therapies, family therapies, community interventions, and prevention. To be sure, the informed use of contemporary antipsychotic agents remains a mainstay of treatment for persons meeting the criteria for a diagnosis of Schizophrenia, but a review of this vast literature falls outside the scope of this chapter. Social workers do, of course, need to be thoroughly familiar with such medications, their indications and contraindications, dosage regimens, and potential side effects (Bentley & Walsh, 1996).

Individual Therapies

This category includes those interventions defined as psychodynamic therapy, supportive therapy, psychosocial skills training (SST), behavioral and cognitive-behavioral interventions, and cognitive adaptation training, as conducted between a social worker and an individual client. While individual psychoanalytic treatment of persons with schizophrenia has a long history—and includes such respected names as Sullivan, Fromm-Reichmann, Sechehaye, and Searles—many of these treatments were presented as case reports that have limited empirical support. Since the 1960s there have been few controlled studies of individual psychotherapy of any type, and those that do exist have serious methodological problems. In a review of these studies, Gomes-Schwartz (1984) finds that, for the most part, individual psychodynamically oriented treatment is not effective on the criteria of symptom reduction, reduced number of hospitalizations, and improved community adjustment. One example of successful analytic therapy with regard to these same measures involves 36 clients with schizophrenia who were treated over a period of 20 months with Rosen's direct analysis, which interprets psychotic communications as expressions of the client's infantile impulses (Karon & VandenBos, 1972). Still, it is believed that therapist characteristics not directly related to analytic technique (for example, having more experience, being sensitive and tolerant, and having a strong desire to work with persons who have schizophrenia) may play an important role in these endeavors. In another review of psychotherapy studies, Mueser and Berenbaum (1990) conclude that supportive, reality-oriented approaches appear to be superior to dynamic, insight-oriented therapies on three of four outcome criteria (rehospitalization, vocational adjustment, and social adjustment), but the two modalities demonstrate no differences related to symptoms.

Supportive Therapy.   In recent years, disappointment with the potential of psychodynamic approaches to produce symptom alleviation has led to a greater interest in supportive psychotherapies. The definition of *supportive* is generally understood to include strengthening the therapeutic alliance; providing environmental interventions; offering education, advice, and suggestion; offering encouragement and praise; setting limits and prohibitions; strengthening adaptive defenses while undermining maladaptive defenses; and emphasizing client strengths and talents (Rockland, 1993). Supportive psychotherapies are demonstrated to be more effective in helping persons with schizophrenia make positive adjustments in their desired lifestyles (Gunderson et al., 1984). Social worker Gerald Hogarty's personal therapy (PT) is a cognitive intervention featuring a modified level of cognitive restructuring to accommodate the neuropsychological vulnerability found in schizo-phrenia. It is currently being studied in a controlled trial comparing PT with sup-portive therapy, family psychoeducation and management, and a combination of both. The study is also comparing PT with supportive therapy only. Early results show a significant positive effect of the PT on those subjects who are living with their families (Hogarty et al., 1995).

Social Skills Training.   Social skills training (SST) attempts to address the deficits in interpersonal relating that are frequently found among persons with schizophrenia by directing training at specific skills needed for successful every-day living. SST is a very popular mode of behavioral intervention. Its research base includes large numbers of both noncontrolled and controlled studies that frequently use single-subject and multiple baseline designs. Some studies have concluded that after 1 year of SST interventions, rehospitalization rates have decreased. However, while Hogarty et al. (1991) found significant improvements in symptomatology 1 year after treatment with SST, gains were no longer evident after 2 years. Other studies report improvement in anxiety and social adjustment but no improvement in depression or hallucinations. In a meta-analysis of 27 stud-ies, Benton and Schroeder (1990) concluded that SST leads to major improve-ments in social behavior when the outcome measures are specific and behaviorally defined. In a comparison group study where inpatients received either intensive SST for ten hours per week or milieu treatment, researchers found that the SST group demonstrated more improvement in negativism and overall psychopathol-ogy, and experienced only one half the rehospitalization rate (Liberman, Mueser, & Wallace, 1986). Liberman, Kopelowicz, and Young (1994) have found that biobehavioral therapy, which employs behavioral assessment, social learning prin-ciples, and skills training, improves the course and outcome of schizophrenia as measured by symptom reduction, social functioning, and quality of life.

One of the more controversial issues related to SST is whether or not treatment gains can be generalized from the treatment situation to the everyday world. Scott and Dixon (1995), in their review of the SST literature, note that some simple behaviors (for example, improving interpersonal eye contact) demonstrate gener-alizability to novel situations, but it is unclear whether or not more complex behav-iors are transferred. Dobson (1996), using two meta-analytic studies, asserts that more recent data support the contention that generalization does occur. In sum-mary, the positive results of SST appear to be promising but results may be time-limited. Longitudinal research and strategies for generalization are especially needed.

Cognitive-Behavioral Interventions.   Cognitive and behavioral interventions are increasingly being used in the treatment of schizophrenia, and while some are considered to be part of SST, others are categorized differently. Cognitive-behavioral interventions focus on reducing the symptoms of the illness and their meaning to the individual. They are based on the premise that affect and behavior are largely mediated by a person's beliefs, rather than being caused by earlier life events. Such interventions include psychoeducation, modifying dysfunctional assumptions, improving coping responses, and relabeling psychotic experiences. Initial results of an ongoing study of cognitive-behavioral treatment of the affective symptoms of schizophrenia have demonstrated significant clinical improvement in the experimental group (Kuipers, Garety, & Fowler, 1996). Other studies indicate that cognitive interventions can influence hallucinations and delusions by decreasing their frequency and the subjective distress associated with them, and by increasing the person's belief that the voices are really thoughts. These studies have made effective use of such cognitive interventions as Socratic questioning, modifying distressing cognitions that interfere with functioning, correcting maladaptive assumptions about the experience of psychosis, and teaching new coping strategies. Many of these interventions place a strong emphasis on the importance of developing a solid relationship between social worker and client to engage the client actively in his or her own treatment. These practices are very familiar to social workers and tap into their strengths as practitioners. These positive results notwithstanding, it should be noted that some researchers are more pessimistic about influencing the information-processing deficits of persons with schizophrenia by cognitive rehabilitation, since it is difficult to precisely identify the cognitive functions that are deficient in schizophrenia (Bellack, 1992). Related to this, Hogarty and Flesher (1992) have found that persons with schizophrenia appear "unable to develop a coherent and integrated cognitive schema" (p. 54) and that what seems most important is that individual cognitive styles be identified as needing corrective action.

Cognitive Adaptation Training.   Cognitive adaptation training is also being used to treat persons with schizophrenia, who frequently have deficits in adaptive functioning and role performance as a result of cognitive impairments. Based on neuropsychological, behavioral, and occupational therapy principles, cognitive adaptation training uses an individualized approach to environmental manipulation. In a study that compares standard psychosocial treatment (defined as inpatient supportive group therapy, medication education, occupational therapy, and socialization) with cognitive adaptation training, preliminary results demonstrate greater improvement in adaptation among patients who were assigned to a specialized cognitive adaptation group, as opposed to those who received the standard treatment procedures (Velligan, Mahurin, True, Lefton, & Flores, 1996).

Behavioral interventions have also been shown to be extremely useful in helping clients to alleviate both positive and negative symptoms of schizophrenia. The work of social worker Stephen Wong is particularly notable in this regard (e.g., Wong, 1996; Wong & Liberman, 1996; Wong et al., 1993; Wong, Massel, Mosk, &

Liberman, 1986; Wong & Woolsey, 1989; Wong, Woolsey, & Gallegos, 1987). Such interventions can be conducted in both inpatient and outpatient contexts. Highly structured behavioral inpatient units can be quite effective in reducing psychotic behavior and restoring effective functioning, with positive treatment effects lasting well after discharge to the community (see Paul & Menditto, 1992, for a review), but the intensive training and supervision required to effectively administer such programs has, sadly, retarded their widespread use and adoption.

Group Therapies

Group therapies include psychodynamic or insight-oriented, supportive, and behaviorally oriented types of group intervention, which may be used in inpatient or outpatient settings. In general, there are few controlled studies of group therapy, and those that do exist have methodological limitations that may limit utility and generalizability (Scott & Dixon, 1995). Though group interventions are widely used in inpatient settings, there is little evidence for their effectiveness in helping persons who are recently admitted and, usually, highly psychotic (Schooler & Keith, 1993). The positive results that have been achieved are with group interventions that are clear about the behaviors targeted for change and the nature of the intervention. In his review of the effectiveness of inpatient and outpatient groups, Kanas (1993) found that interaction-oriented groups are preferable to insight-oriented groups for persons with schizophrenia.

For outpatient groups, there is a lack of evidence that group therapy results in a reduction in rehospitalization rates or psychopathology (Mosher & Keith, 1980). However, for persons with poor social skills, there is evidence for the positive benefit of participating in a group experience. Group therapy can reduce the client's social isolation, increase the client's sense of cohesiveness, and improve the client's reality testing. Group modalities are often used in conjunction with other interventions, such as medication and social skills training. In one such combined treatment approach, Malm (1982) found that though relapse rates were not affected, the addition of group therapy to medication and SST resulted in increases in emotional communication, free-time activities, and social interactions, and a decrease in anhedonia, or the pervasive absence of pleasure. In an art therapy group, used as part of a comprehensive social work treatment for clients with chronic schizophrenia, group goals included expression of feelings and thoughts, interaction among group members, and increased self-esteem via creativity. The group process was found to assist clients with self-disclosure, awareness, interaction with others, self-esteem, and enhanced social functioning outside the group (Potocky, 1993). While this study did not provide a controlled research design, it does demonstrate some possible strengths of group interventions.

In the area of psychoeducation, group methods are often used effectively, and multifamily groups provide such an example. A 4-year study was conducted comparing psychoeducational multifamily groups, psychoeducation in a single-family format, and multifamily groups without psychoeducation. The outcome criterion was symptomatic relapse, and it was found that the psychoeducational multifamily groups are significantly more effective in extending the time until relapse than are the single-family formats (McFarlane, Link, Dushay, & Marchal, 1995). The results of this study demonstrate the importance of multifamily group treatment, in conjunction with maintenance antipsychotic medication and family psychoeducation.

Family Therapies

Psychoeducational family interventions are of primary interest in schizophrenia research, since social workers see the family members as important allies in coping with and managing the illness, rather than as persons to be treated. Since the majority of persons with a severe mental illness reside with or near their families, and families provide a natural support system, it is important that social workers understand what has been demonstrated to be effective in working with family members.

As reviewed by Dixon and Lehman (1995), there is substantial evidence that psychoeducational family interventions reduce the rate of relapse among persons with schizophrenia. Out of 15 studies reported, 8 demonstrated significantly fewer relapses in the families exposed to family interventions. Effective interventions included crisis-oriented weekly sessions (for 6 months), behavioral family therapy including problem-solving and communication skills training in the family's home (for 9 months), education, discussion, communication, and problem-solving training (for 2 years), and psychoeducational multifamily groups (for 4 years). In addition to lower relapse rates, several of these modalities also demonstrated improvement in client functioning, reduced family burden, an increase in the family's well-being, reduced psychiatric symptomatology, and reduced cost in the treatment group, although the evidence in these areas is not conclusive. These 15 studies are methodologically rigorous, but 7 of them required that the identified clients be from families rated high in levels of negative emotional expression; thus, the results cannot be generalized to all families.

During the past 20 years psychosocial interventions for families of persons with schizophrenia have expanded tremendously, and their effective components can now be demonstrated. The most frequently used models are psychoeducation, behavioral problem solving, family support, and crisis management. It should be noted that psychodynamic approaches to family intervention have been found to be ineffective. When types of family intervention are compared, such as behavioral family management and supportive family management, there are significant improvements in the person with schizophrenia. However, there are no differences in family member functioning based on which type of intervention the family received. It cannot be concluded at the present time that any specific type of family intervention is consistently superior to any other. However, the key elements that are found in any effective intervention include taking a positive approach, establishing a collaborative working relationship, providing structure and stability, focusing on the here and now, using family systems concepts, working on cognitive restructuring with all members, taking a behavioral approach, and improving family communication (Lam, 1991). In addition, several characteristics that appear to be related to less of a treatment effect include time-limited interventions that are not focused on a specific type of client (for example, 10 weeks or less), interventions conducted in the hospital, those restricted to family members who are not ill, and those that are less oriented toward education and support (Kottgen, Sonnichsen, Mollenhauser, & Jurth, 1984; Vaughan et al., 1992).

As some models of family intervention were developed, services were provided in the homes of families of a person with schizophrenia, since it was believed that this would increase the participation of all members. There is no evidence that in-home services are preferable to those in clinical settings (Randolph et al., 1994). Based on several studies that either included the client or treated the client separately from the family, it is suggested that the client's participation in at least some aspect of the family intervention is important.

In recent years more use has been made of the multifamily group, and this has been compared to interventions using a single-family group. As noted previously in this section, psychoeducation delivered within a multifamily group was compared to psychoeducation in a single-family group and in a multifamily group without psychoeducation. This study found that the 2- and 4-year relapse rates were significantly higher in the psychoeducational single-family group than in the multifamily group. In fact, the multifamily group that received no psychoeducation demonstrated such a high relapse rate that it was discontinued (McFarlane, 1994). Replicated in a randomized trial in six New York State public hospitals, this study design again revealed that the multifamily group intervention resulted in many fewer relapses than did the single-family intervention (McFarlane et al., 1995). This study also found differences based on race and negative expressed emotion (EE) status. Within the more effective multifamily groups, Caucasian families and high-EE families had lower relapse rates than those receiving single-family intervention. These differences were not seen among minority and low-EE families. These results provide a beginning understanding of the types of family interventions that may be beneficial for specific client populations. As Bentley and Harrison (1989) note in their review of models of family-based management of schizophrenia, it is often difficult to generalize research interventions to populations that did not participate in the study. More research is needed so that effective interventions can be demonstrated for specific racial, gender, and ethnic groups, as well as for those persons with schizophrenia who have no access to their families.

Community Interventions

Since the time of deinstitutionalization, which began in the 1950s but was more aggressively realized in the 1970s, the primary site for the treatment of serious mental illnesses like schizophrenia has become the community. As such, many new interventions have been developed to help persons with schizophrenia manage the illness with minimal reliance on inpatient stays. This subsection considers those interventions that have demonstrated effectiveness, including assertive community treatment, case management, and vocational rehabilitation. While there is frequent overlap among these categories of services, they are distinguished here for descriptive purposes.

Assertive Community Treatment.   Assertive community treatment (ACT) was initially developed as the Training in Community Living (TCL) program by Stein and Test (1980) in Madison, Wisconsin. It has since been replicated in Australia, in England, and at several other sites in the United States. The core characteristics of the ACT model of service delivery are assertive engagement, in vivo delivery of services, a multidisciplinary team approach, staff continuity over time, low staff-to-client ratios, and frequent client contacts. At referral, clients are contacted by team members who use telephone calls and in-person visits to actively solicit client participation. Services are provided in the client's home, at shopping malls or places of work, or wherever the person may focus on everyday needs. Frequency of contact may be once per week to as often as several times daily, depending on need. Staff-to-client ratios are usually approximately 1 to 10, and the staff may include a support worker who has experienced a serious mental illness. Other kinds of intensive case-management programs share some, but not all, characteristics of the ACT model; these are included in the summary results reported here. A review of 22 studies of the ACT model (and other case-management models that include the key elements of ACT) conducted between 1973 and 1991 found that these programs reduce the rate and duration of psychiatric hospitalizations. Nine of the studies reported a reduction of about 50% in inpatient days (Bond, McGrew, & Fekete, 1995). In programs where hospitalization rates were similar for experimental and control patients, the length of stay was about 80% shorter. It should be noted that as the ACT treatment is discontinued, and as the model is modified, the lowered hospitalization rates tend to diminish. It appears to be crucial that the original components of the ACT model be maintained (Scott & Dixon, 1995).

The issue of cost is becoming increasingly important in community intervention, and it is reasonable to conclude that the most cost-effective programs are most likely to survive, regardless of research results. It is thus heartening to find that the studies to date demonstrate that ACT programs may be less costly than standard outpatient treatment, at least in the short term, and the cost-benefit ratio may be preferable in most cases. In the original TCL program in Madison, average treatment costs per client were higher, but these increased costs were offset by increased benefits, which included a doubling of work productivity by clients. Australian researchers have found a substantial decrease in treatment costs for experimental subjects and a difference in where the costs are incurred. For clients participating in the TCL program, 81% of costs were spent in the community; for the control group, 79% of the cost was due to inpatient treatment (Hoult & Reynolds, 1984). In a replication study in London, the TCL model resulted in significantly less costly treatment than the standard hospital and outpatient care (Knapp et al., 1994). In other cost-effectiveness studies conducted in the United States, results have been less consistent. Two studies of the Thresholds program in Chicago showed costs to be significantly reduced for the experimental subjects, but later studies in Indiana found one program in which costs were higher than standard community mental health center care, one program where costs were equivalent, and a third instance where costs were lower. These contrasting results may be a function of the type of TCL program being studied, and how faithful it is to the original model (Bond, Miller, Krumwied, & Ward, 1988).

In addition to reducing the rate and duration of hospitalizations, ACT programs have also been found to reduce symptomatology, improve social functioning, and promote residential stability and independent living. The clients who receive these services find the programs agreeable, which increases treatment compliance. Further, family involvement has been found to be crucial in assertive community treatment. In a recently completed 24-month follow-up study, McFarlane et al. (1995) found that ongoing family involvement (via multifamily groups or crisis family intervention) in assertive community treatment enhances the rehabilitation of clients and improves family-related outcomes. While ongoing maintenance treatment with medication is now seen as necessary, not all social workers have reached this same understanding with psychosocial interventions, and this oversight is costly. When participation in an ACT program is discontinued, the earlier treatment gains are lost.

Case Management.   Many case-management models exist, and researchers are not always careful in defining the specific components of the model being studied. Poorly defined case management, not enough studies that use the same program model, and methodological limitations make it difficult to compare different case-management interventions and demonstrate degrees of effectiveness (Draine, 1997). Intensive case management and generalist or rehabilitation case management are two of the models frequently reported. Though there is much variation in models (based on their specific focus and the availability of community resources), there are five core functions that traditionally comprise case management—client assessment, planning for needed services, linkage, advocacy, and monitoring the match between client needs and services received.

Studies of intensive case management show mixed results in regard to use of inpatient care. Several studies report that the average rehospitalization rate is significantly reduced and the number of days of hospital use (when this is necessary) are diminished. Other studies demonstrate no statistically significant differences in admission rates or in the number of days of hospital use. It should be noted that these studies often involve clients with several types of serious mental illness, which tends to confound the results. Evaluations of other models of case management also demonstrate mixed results. For example, a study of the generalist model, where case managers have large caseloads and function primarily as brokers of services from other providers, showed a significant increase in inpatient care among clients exposed to case management (Franklin, Solovitz, Mason, Clemons, & Miller, 1987). The rehabilitation model, where caseloads are generally smaller in size and case managers provide some services directly, does not always significantly reduce rehospitalization rates (Goering, Wasylenki, Farkas, Lancee, & Ballantyne, 1988).

On another outcome measure—use of other mental health services—the results are less equivocal. Six of seven reported studies found that clients exposed to intensive case management make greater use of other mental health services. However, future research will need to focus more on the quality of these other services and what they might be providing, and less on the quantity of services (Scott & Dixon, 1995). Intensive case-management models have also been found to be less costly than other interventions, but in some situations costs are shifted. For example, Borland, McRae, and Lycan (1989) found that hospitalization costs were significantly reduced during a 5-year period, while the costs of residential care were significantly increased. In a 2-year follow-up to this study, it was found that treatment costs decreased by 12% after the case-management services were discontinued. These researchers suggest that there may be long-lasting effects from 5 years of continuous and intensive case management, and that these effects continue after intervention is terminated (McRae, Higgins, Lycan, & Sherman, 1990).

Several case-management models are being used in interventions with persons who have a severe mental illness and are homeless. In the NIMH McKinney Project, 894 homeless mentally ill adults in four cities were exposed to rehabilitation, assertive community treatment, or intensive case-management services, depending on which model was offered in each city. Though the specific intervention models differed, all of them utilized teams of case managers and assertive outreach methods. The project report notes a 47.5% increase in individuals living in community housing among those who were exposed to the treatment conditions. In addition, 78% of participants were considered to be housed in permanent sites (Shern et al., 1997). While the focus of this study is on housing outcomes for those who were homeless, the multisite project did use a randomized experimental design and structured interviews, and the researchers concluded that the services provided were effective. As in other studies of case management, residential stability, independence, and instrumental role functioning in daily life activities seemed to improve with the provision of case-management activities. However, case-management outcomes are less impressive in the areas of reduced psychiatric symptomatology and medication compliance (Chamberlain & Rapp, 1991).

Vocational Rehabilitation. *Vocational rehabilitation* is defined as work-related activity that provides financial remuneration and a normalizing experience of participation in society. Vocational rehabilitation includes sheltered work, psychosocial rehabilitation, prevocational training, transitional employment, volunteer placements, and supported employment. The goals of vocational programs may be full-time competitive employment; any paid or volunteer job; or the development of job-related skills, job satisfaction, and job performance. There are several limitations to the effectiveness of research in this area. The number of controlled trials, especially of single models, is small, and their quality is limited. Many of the studies include heterogeneous client groups, so it is difficult to determine the relationship between a specific client group (for example, persons with schizophrenia) and a vocational outcome (Lehman, 1995).

Many studies have found that vocational rehabilitation programs have a positive influence on such work-related activities as paid employment, job starts, duration of employment, and earnings. Yet, these outcomes are achieved within the confines of a rehabilitation program (that is, sheltered or transitional employment) and it can be concluded that independent competitive employment is less positively influenced (Bond, 1992). Two recent studies suggest more positive results. In a quasi-experimental study conducted in New Hampshire, a traditional partial hospitalization program was compared with a supportive employment program that was closely aligned with a clinical service team. At follow-up, clients in the supportive employment group had a significantly increased rate of competitive employment as compared with those in the partial hospitalization group (Drake et al., 1994). This same partial hospitalization program was converted to a supported employment program the following year, and when clients in the two previous groups were compared on vocational outcomes, all had increased their rate of competitive employment (Drake, Becker, Biesanz, Wyzik, & Torrey, 1996). The authors conclude that this replication study demonstrates the greater effectiveness of assertive supported employment services for clients with serious mental illnesses.

While vocational status is an important consideration in itself, the broad ramifications of employment are also important. In a study of three psychosocial rehabilitation programs in South Carolina, researchers found that getting a job has a positive impact on self-esteem and quality of life (Arms & Linney, 1993). Another consistent result, though not surprising, is that clients who are paid for sheltered work activity are more likely to begin and remain in such a job, work more hours, and earn more money (Bell, Milstein, & Lysaker, 1993). Regarding client characteristics that might predict a favorable response to vocational rehabilitation services, several studies have found a significant negative correlation between severity of symptoms and work performance. Anthony, Rogers, Cohen, and Davies

(1995), who followed 275 clients in a psychosocial rehabilitation setting, reported that current symptoms are negatively correlated with work skills and employability over time. Unfortunately, a diagnosis of Schizophrenia is also negatively related to the attainment of employment and is a negative predictor of response to vocational rehabilitation when compared with other diagnoses. This finding is consistent with research results that relate extensive past employment to a more favorable response to vocational rehabilitation interventions (Lehman, 1995).

Prevention

There are three levels of prevention in the field of mental illness. *Primary prevention* refers to professional activities that result in preventing schizophrenia from developing in at-risk individuals. *Secondary prevention* involves early case finding and intervention with persons having schizophrenia before the disorder becomes severe. *Tertiary prevention* refers to rehabilitation activities that attempt to help clients return to their highest possible level of functioning after the disorder has become severe. Most of the interventions discussed in this chapter address secondary and tertiary prevention efforts. Some exploratory efforts, however, are occurring in the area of primary prevention.

While the neuroscience research of the past two decades has led to a much fuller understanding of the possible etiology of schizophrenia, it is still not known precisely how the illness is caused. Therefore, it is not possible at this time to speak in terms of primary prevention. However, a biological basis to this brain disorder has been established. There is a genetic component to schizophrenia, but its exact mechanism and extent are unknown. Genetic vulnerability may result in a neuro-developmental process that goes awry (either in utero, in the perinatal stage, or during adolescence) and adversely affects brain structure and function. Still, the genetic and biological components are not the whole story, and perhaps account for only about 50% to 60% of the etiology. The other contributors to the development of schizophrenia are environmental, including such factors as stress, transitional life events, cognitive processes, coping skills, and social learning.

According to the vulnerability-stress model of schizophrenia (Zubin & Spring, 1977), when a person with biological vulnerability is exposed to environmental stressors that exceed his or her coping capacity, the threshold of vulnerability is crossed and a psychotic episode is likely to occur. Yank, Bentley, and Hargrove (1993) used vulnerability models to demonstrate how biological and psychosocial approaches to schizophrenia can be integrated for effective interventions that include the mediation of stress in vulnerable individuals. A recent study in Buckingham County, England included an attempt to intervene prior to the onset of illness. Teams of mental health practitioners worked closely with family practitioners to educate them about the prodromal symptoms of schizophrenia (for example, marked peculiar behavior, speech that is difficult to follow, and marked preoccupation with odd ideas). When persons were found to have some of these symptoms (and therefore were considered to possibly be in the prodromal phase of schizophrenia), they were provided with psychoeducation, usually in their own homes. Intervention was ongoing and included home-based stress management, problem-solving strategies, and medication, if indicated. Results of this four-year pilot study demonstrate that the occurrence of the florid psychotic episodes of schizophrenia were noticeably reduced (Falloon, Kydd, Coverdale, & Laidlaw, 1996). However, the authors caution that there is a distinction between avoiding a psychotic episode of schizophrenia and preventing the disorder. This study is an important beginning and needs to be replicated, using a random-controlled design.

Another example of intervention in the prodromal phase of psychosis, with the goal of preventing or minimizing psychosocial disruption, is a study currently in progress in Victoria, Australia (Yung et al., 1996). In 1994 a clinic was established to care for and monitor young people ages 16 to 30 who were thought to be at high risk for psychosis. In order to address issues of stigma, the service was named Personal Assistance and Crisis Evaluation (PACE) and was housed in an adolescent health center. Psychosocial treatment was provided with the goals of reducing stress, enhancing coping and problem solving, and emphasizing individualized case management and support. Preliminary results show that it is possible to identify and follow individuals in the community who may be experiencing a prodromal phase of schizophrenia. Based on this data, the researchers are narrowing the family history criteria for inclusion in their study. While it is too early to reach any conclusions about effective interventions with this population, the study is on the frontier of knowledge concerning the prevention of schizophrenia.

In recent years a major area for research in schizophrenia has been the early course of the illness, or what is referred to as *first episode schizophrenia*. It is thought that by studying persons who are at the very beginning of a psychotic illness, treatment can be provided earlier (and possibly be more effective) and that these first-episode clients may increase insight into the nature of schizophrenia, especially as the clients have had little or no exposure to psychotropic medications. Since these studies do not focus on psychosocial interventions, but rather attempt to enhance knowledge of course and outcome, they are not described here in detail.

CONCLUSIONS

Great strides in knowledge have been made in recent years regarding effective psychosocial interventions for persons diagnosed with Schizophrenia. While psychodynamic approaches have been largely discredited, other approaches have been empirically validated. There is much evidence that family psychoeducation and support, assertive community treatment programs, behavioral interventions, social skills training, and case management can have positive effects on the management of schizophrenia. Researchers are still in the beginning stages of determining what interventions work best for whom under what circumstances. This is complicated by the fact that Schizophrenia is probably not one disorder but a group of brain disorders. Social workers practicing in the field of mental illness must keep informed of, and perhaps participate in, the ongoing research concerning schizophrenia and its treatment, and apply the most effective intervention methods in the context of caring partnerships with clients and their families.

REFERENCES

American Psychiatric Association. (1994). *Diagnostic and statistical manual of mental disorders* (4th ed.). Washington, DC: Author.

Andreasen, N. C. (1982). Negative symptoms of schizophrenia: Definition and reliability. *Archives of General Psychiatry, 39,* 784–788.

Andreasen, N. C., & Olsen, S. (1982). Negative vs. positive schizophrenia: Definition and validation. *Archives of General Psychiatry, 39,* 789–794.

Anthony, W. A., Rogers, E. S., Cohen, M., & Davies, R. R. (1995). Relationships between psychiatric symptomatology, work skills, and future vocational performance. *Psychiatric Services, 46,* 353–358.

Arms, P. G., & Linney, J. A. (1993). Work, self, and life satisfaction for persons with severe and persistent mental disorders. *Psychosocial Rehabilitation Journal, 17,* 63–79.

Bell, M. D., Milstein, R. M., & Lysaker, P. H. (1993). Pay as an incentive in work participation by patients with severe mental illness. *Hospital and Community Psychiatry, 44,* 684–686.

Bellack, A. S. (1992). Cognitive rehabilitation for schizophrenia: Is it possible? Is it necessary? *Schizophrenia Bulletin, 18* (1), 43–50.

Bentley, K. J., & Harrison, D. F. (1989). Behavioral, psychoeducational, and skills training approaches to family management of schizophrenia. In B. Thyer (Ed.), *Behavioral family therapy.* Springfield, IL: Charles C. Thomas.

Bentley, K. J., & Walsh, J. (1996). *The social worker and psychotropic medication.* Pacific Grove, CA: Brooks/Cole.

Benton, M. K. & Schroeder, H. E. (1990). Social skills training with schizophrenics: A meta-analytic evaluation. *Journal of Consulting and Clinical Psychology, 58,* 741–747.

Bigelow, D. A., Gareau, M. J., & Young, D. J. (1990). A quality of life interview. *Psychosocial Rehabilitation Journal, 14,* 94–98.

Bigelow, L. B., & Berthot, B. D. (1989). The psychiatric symptom assessment scale (PSAS). *Psychopharmacology Bulletin, 25,* 168–179.

Black, D. W., Yates, W. R., & Andreasen, N. C. (1988). Schizophrenia, schizophreniform disorder, and delusional (paranoid) disorders. In J. A. Talbott, R. E. Hales, & S. C. Yudofsky (Eds.), *The American Psychiatric Press textbook of psychiatry* (pp. 357–402). Washington, DC: American Psychiatric Press.

Bond, G. R. (1992). Vocational rehabilitation. In R. P. Liberman (Ed.), *Handbook of psychiatric rehabilitation.* New York: Macmillan.

Bond, G. R., McGrew, J. H., & Fekete, D. M. (1995). Assertive outreach for frequent users of psychiatric hospitals: A meta-analysis. *Journal of Mental Health Administration, 22,* 4–16.

Bond, G. R., Miller, L. D., Krumwied, R. D., & Ward, R. S. (1988). Assertive case management in three CMHCs: A controlled study. *Hospital and Community Psychiatry, 39,* 411–418.

Borland, A., McRae, J., & Lycan, C. (1989). Outcome of five years of continuous intensive case management. *Hospital and Community Psychiatry, 40,* 369–376.

Chamberlain, R., & Rapp, C. A. (1991). A decade of case management: A methodological review of outcome research. *Community Mental Health Journal, 27,* 171–188.

Dixon, L. B., & Lehman, A. F. (1995). Family interventions for schizophrenia. *Schizophrenia Bulletin, 21,* 631–643.

Dobson, D. (1996). Long-term support and social skills training for patients with schizophrenia. *Psychiatric Services, 47,* 1195–1199.

Draine, J. (1997). A critical review of randomized field trials of case management for individuals with serious and persistent mental illness. *Research on Social Work Practice, 7,* 32–52.

Drake, R. E., Becker, D. R., Biesanz, J. C., Torrey, W. C., McHugo, G. J., & Wyzik, P. F. (1994). Partial hospitalization vs. supported employment: I. Vocational outcomes. *Community Mental Health Journal, 30,* 519–532.

Drake, R. E., Becker, D. R., Biesanz, J. C., Wyzik, P. F. & Torrey, W. C. (1996). Day treatment versus supported employment for persons with severe mental illness: A replication study. *Psychiatric Services, 47,* 1125–1127.

Endicott, J., & Spitzer, R. L. (1978). A diagnostic interview: The schedule for affective disorders and schizophrenia. *Archives of General Psychiatry, 35,* 837–844.

Falloon, I. R. H., Kydd, R. R., Coverdale, J. H., & Laidlaw, T. M. (1996). Early detection and intervention for initial episodes of schizophrenia. *Schizophrenia Bulletin, 22,* 271–282.

Fenton, W. S., McGlashan, T. H., Victor, B. J., & Blyler, C. R. (1997). Symptoms, subtypes, and suicidality of patients with schizophrenia spectrum disorders. *American Journal of Psychiatry, 154,* 199–204.

Franklin, J., Solovitz, B., Mason, M., Clemons, J., & Miller, G. (1987). An evaluation of case management. *American Journal of Public Health, 77,* 674–678.

Goering, P. N., Wasylenki, D. A., Farkas, M., Lancee, W. J., & Ballantyne, R. (1988). What difference does case management make? *Hospital and Community Psychiatry, 39,* 272–276.

Gomes-Schwartz, B. (1984). Individual psychotherapy of schizophrenia. In A. S. Bellack (Ed.), *Schizophrenia: Treatment, management, and rehabilitation* (pp. 307–335). New York: Grune & Stratton.

Gottesman, I. I. (1991). *Schizophrenia genesis: The origins of madness.* New York: W. H. Freeman.

Gunderson, J. G., Frank, A., Katz, H. M., Vannicelli, M. L., Frosch, J. P., & Knapp, P. H. (1984). Effects of psychotherapy in schizophrenia: II. Comparative outcomes of two forms of treatment. *Schizophrenia Bulletin, 10,* 564–598.

Heinrichs, D. W., Hanlon, T. E., & Carpenter, W. T. (1984). The quality of life scale: An instrument for rating the schizophrenic deficit syndrome. *Schizophrenia Bulletin, 10,* 388–398.

Hogarty, G. E., & Flesher, S. (1992). Cognitive remediation in schizophrenia: Proceed with caution. *Schizophrenia Bulletin, 18,* 51–57.

Hogarty, G. E., Kornblith, S. J., Greenwald, D., DiBarry, A. L., Cooley, S., Flesher, S., Reiss, D., Carter, M., & Ulrich, R. (1995). Personal therapy: A disorder-relevant psychotherapy for schizophrenia. *Schizophrenia Bulletin, 21,* 379–393.

Hogarty, G. E., Anderson, C. M., Reiss, D. J., Kornblith, S. J., Greenwald, D. P., Ulrich, R. F., Carter, M., and the EPICS Research Group (1991). Family psychoeducation, social skills training, and maintenance chemotherapy in the aftercare treatment of schizophrenia: II. Two-year effects of a controlled study on relapse and adjustment. *Archives of General Psychiatry, 48,* 340–347.

Hoult, J., & Reynolds, I. (1984). Schizophrenia: A comparative trial of community-oriented and hospital-oriented psychiatric care. *Acta Psychiatrica Scandinavica, 69,* 359–372.

Hudson, B. (1978). Behavioural social work with schizophrenic patients in the community. *British Journal of Social Work, 8,* 159–170.

Kanas, N. (1993). Group psychotherapy with schizophrenia. In H. I. Kaplan & B. J. Sadock (Eds.), *Comprehensive group psychotherapy,* (pp. 407–417). Baltimore: Williams & Wilkins.

Karon, B., & VandenBos G. R. (1972). The consequences of psychotherapy with schizophrenic patients. *Psychotherapy; Theory, Research and Practice, 9,* 111–119.

Katz, M. M., & Lyerly, S. B. (1963). Methods for measuring adjustment and social behavior in the community: I. Rationale, description, discriminative validity and scale development. *Psychological Reports, 13,* 502–535.

Kay, S. R., Fiszbein, A., & Opler, L. A. (1987). The positive and negative syndrome scale for schizophrenia. *Schizophrenia Bulletin, 13,* 261–275.

Knapp, M., Beecham, J., Koutsogeorgopoulou, V., Hallam, A., Fenyo, A., Marks, I. M., Connolly, J., Audini, B., & Muijen, M. (1994). Service use and costs of home-based versus hospital-based care for people with serious mental illness. *British Journal of Psychiatry, 165,* 195–203.

Kottgen, C., Sonnichsen, I., Mollenhauser, K., & Jurth, R. (1984). Group therapy with families of schizophrenia patients: III. Results of the Hamburg Camberwell family interview study. *International Journal of Family Psychiatry, 5,* 84–94.

Krawiecka, M., Goldberg, D., & Vaughan, M. (1977). A standardized psychiatric assessment scale for rating chronic psychotic patients. *Acta Psychiatrica Scandinavica, 55,* 299–308.

Kuipers, E., Garety, P., & Fowler, D. (1996). An outcome study of cognitive-behavioural treatment for psychosis. In G. Haddock & D. Slade (Eds.), *Cognitive-behavioural interventions with psychotic disorders* (pp. 116–136). London: Routledge.

Lam, D. H. (1991). Psychosocial family intervention in schizophrenia: A review of empirical studies. *Psychological Medicine, 21,* 423–441.

Lehman, A. F. (1995). Vocational rehabilitation in schizophrenia. *Schizophrenia Bulletin, 21,* 645–656.

Lehman, A. F. (1988). A quality of life interview for the chronically mentally ill. *Evaluation and Program Planning, 11,* 51–62.

Liberman, R. P., Kopelowicz, A., & Young, A. (1996). Biobehavioral treatment and rehabilitation of schizophrenia. *Behavior Therapy, 25,* 89–107.

Liberman, R. P., Mueser, K. T., & Wallace, C. J. (1986). Social skills training for schizophrenic individuals at risk for relapse. *American Journal of Psychiatry, 143,* 523–526.

Ligon, J. H. (1997). *Crisis psychiatric and substance abuse services: Evaluation of a community program in an urban setting.* Unpublished doctoral dissertation, University of Georgia, School of Social Work.

Malm, U. (1982). The influence of group therapy on schizophrenia. *Acta Psychiatrica Scandinavica, 65* (Suppl. 297).

Manchanda, R., & Hirsch, S. R. (1986). Rating scales for clinical studies on schizophrenia. In P. B. Bradley & S. R. Hirsch (Eds.), *The psychopharmacology and treatment of schizophrenia* (pp. 234–260). New York: Oxford University Press.

McFarlane, W. R. (1994). Multiple-family groups and psychoeducation in the treatment of schizophrenia. *New Directions in Mental Health Services, 62,* 13–22.

McFarlane, W. R., Link, B., Dushay, R., & Marchal, J. (1995). Psychoeducational multiple family groups: Four-year relapse outcome in schizophrenia. *Family Process, 34,* 127–144.

McRae, J., Higgins, M., Lycan, C., & Sherman, W. (1990). What happens to patients after five years of intensive case management stops? *Hospital and Community Psychiatry, 41,* 175–183.

Mosher, L. R., & Keith, S. J. (1980). Psychosocial treatment: Individual, group, family, and community support approaches. *Schizophrenia Bulletin, 6*(1), 10–41.

Mueser, K. T., & Berenbaum, H. (1990). Psychodynamic treatment of schizophrenia. Is there a future? *Psychological Medicine, 20,* 253–262.

Overall, J. E., & Gorman, D. R. (1962). The brief psychiatric rating scale. *Psychological Reports, 10,* 799–812.

Paul, G. L., & Menditto, A. A. (1992). Effectiveness of inpatient treatment programs for mentally ill adults in public psychiatric facilities. *Applied and Preventive Psychology, 1,* 41–63.

Platt, S. (1986). Evaluating social functioning: A critical review of scales and their underlying concepts. In P. B. Bradley & S. R. Hirsch (Eds.), *The psychopharmacology and treatment of schizophrenia* (pp. 263–284). New York: Oxford University Press.

Platt, S., Weyman, A., Hirsch, S., & Hewett, S. (1980). The Social Behavior Assessment Schedule (SBAS): Rationale, contents, scoring, and reliability of a new interview schedule. *Social Psychiatry, 15,* 43–55.

Potocky, M. (1993). An art therapy group for clients with chronic schizophrenia. *Social Work with Groups, 16*(3), 73–82.

Randolph, E. A., Eth, S., Glynn, S. M., Paz, G. G., Leong, G. B., Shaner, A. L., Strachan, A., Van Vort, W., Escobar, J. I., & Liberman, R. P. (1994). Behavioral family management in schizophrenia: Outcome of a clinic-based intervention. *British Journal of Psychiatry, 164,* 501–506.

Robins, L. N., Helzer, J. E., Croughan, J., & Ratcliff, K. S. (1981). National Institute of Mental Health Diagnostic Interview Schedule: Its history, characteristics, and validity. *Archives of General Psychiatry, 38,* 381–390.

Rockland, L. H. (1993). A review of supportive psychotherapy, 1986–1992. *Hospital and Community Psychiatry, 44,* 1053–1060.

Schooler, N., Hogarty, G. E., & Weismann, M. M. (1979). Social Adjustment Scale II (SAS-II). In W. A. Hargreaves, C. C. Atkinson, & J. E. Sorenson (Eds.), *Resource materials for community mental health program evaluators* (pp. 290–303); DHEW Publication No. 79–328). Washington, DC: U.S. Government Printing Office.

Schooler, N. R., & Keith, S. J. (1993). The clinical research base for the treatment of schizophrenia. *Psychopharmacology Bulletin, 29,* 431–446.

Scott, J. E. & Dixon, L. B. (1995). Psychological interventions for schizophrenia. *Schizophrenia Bulletin, 21,* 621–630.

Shern, D. L., Felton, C. J., Hough, R. L., Lehman, A. F., Goldfinger, S., Valencia, E., Dennis, D., Straw, R., & Wood, P. (1997). Housing outcomes for homeless adults with mental illness: Results from the second-round McKinney program. *Psychiatric Services, 48,* 239–241.

Spitzer, R. L., Williams, J. B., Gibbon, M., & First, M. B. (1992). The structured clinical interview for DSM-III-R (SCID) I: History, rationale, and description. *Archives of General Psychiatry, 49,* 624–629.

Stein, L. I., & Test, M. A. (1980). Alternative mental hospital treatment: I. Conceptual model, treatment program, and clinical evaluation. *Archives of General Psychiatry, 37,* 392–397.

Tress, K. H., Bellenis, C., Brownlow, J. M., Livingston, G., & Leff, J. P. (1987). The Present State Examination Change rating scale. *British Journal of Psychiatry, 150,* 201–207.

Vaughan, K., Doyle, M., McConaghy, N., Blaszczynski, A., Fox, A., & Tarrier, N. (1992). The Sydney intervention trial: A controlled trial of relatives' counseling to reduce schizophrenic relapse. *Social Psychiatry and Psychiatric Epidemiology, 27,* 16–21.

Velligan, D. I., Mahurin, R. K., True, J. E., Lefton, R. S., & Flores, C. V. (1996). Preliminary evaluation of cognitive adaptation training to compensate for cognitive deficits in schizophrenia. *Psychiatric Services, 47,* 415–417.

Wing, J. K., Cooper, J. E., & Sartorius, N. (1974). *The measurement and classification of psychiatric symptoms.* Cambridge: Cambridge University Press.

Wong, S. E. (1996). Psychosis. In M. A. Mattaini & B. A. Thyer (Eds.), *Finding solutions to social problems: Behavioral strategies for change* (pp. 319–343). Washington, DC: American Psychological Association.

Wong, S. E., & Liberman, R. P. (1996). Biobehavioral treatment and rehabilitation of schizophrenia. In V. B. Van Hasselt & M. Hersen (Eds.), *Sourcebook of psychological treatment manuals for adult disorders* (pp. 233–256). New York: Plenum Press.

Wong, S. E., Martinez-Diaz, J. A., Massel, H. K., Edelstein, B. A., Wiegand, W., Bowen, L., & Liberman, R. P. (1993). Conversational skills training with schizophrenic inpatients. *Behavior Therapy, 24,* 285–304.

Wong, S. E., Massel, H. K., Mosk, M. D., & Liberman, R. P. (1986). Behavioral approaches to the treatment of schizophrenia. In G. D. Burrows, T. R. Norman, & G. Rubinstein, (Eds.). *Handbook of studies on schizophrenia* (pp. 79–99). Amsterdam: Elsevier Science Publishers.

Wong, S. E., & Woolsey, J. E. (1989). Re-establishing conversational skills in overtly psychotic chronic schizophrenic patients. *Behavior Modification, 13,* 415–430.

Wong, S. E., Woolsey, J. E., & Gallegos, E. (1987). Behavioral treatment of chronic psychiatric patients. *Journal of Social Service Research, 10,* 7–35.

Yank, G. R., Bentley, K. J., & Hargrove, D. S. (1993). The vulnerability-stress model of schizophrenia: Advances in psychosocial treatment. *American Journal of Orthopsychiatry, 63,* 55–69.

Yung, A. R., McGorry, P. D., McFarlane, C. A., Jackson, H. J., Patton, G. C., & Rakkar, A. (1996). Monitoring and care of young people at incipient risk of psychosis. *Schizophrenia Bulletin, 22,* 283–303.

Zubin, J., & Spring, B. (1977). Vulnerability—a new view of schizophrenia. *Journal of Abnormal Psychology, 86,* 103–126.

PART IV

Mood Disorders

Chapter 13

MAJOR DEPRESSIVE DISORDER AND DYSTHYMIC DISORDER

Catherine N. Dulmus
John S. Wodarski

OVERVIEW

Depression ranks as one of the major health problems of today, being so wide-spread that it is often called *the common cold of psychiatry* (Seligman, 1975). Millions of clients suffering from some form of depression fill social workers' caseloads in both inpatient and outpatient settings and account for a large portion of health care dollar expenditures. Depression may appear as a primary disorder, or it may accompany a wide variety of other psychiatric or medical disorders. Beck (1996) states that depression is a prominent cause of human misery, and its correlate—suicide—is a leading cause of death among certain age groups. This chapter examines two of the mood disorders—Major Depressive Disorder and Dysthymic Disorder as manifested in adults—and reviews the symptomatology, assessment, and empirically based treatments available for these diagnoses.

Major Depressive Disorder and Dysthymic Disorder are common clinical problems and are associated with impairment at all levels of functioning. Major Depressive Disorder may occur either as a single episode or as a recurrent problem. Dysthymic Disorder is a less severe but longer lasting depressive state. According to Kline (1964), more human suffering has resulted from depression than from any other single disease (whether depression can be legitimately labeled a *disease* remains controversial, as witnessed by the *DSM-IV* labeling schema). Depression is second only to schizophrenia as a cause for first and second admissions to mental hospitals in the United States, and it has been estimated that the prevalence of depression outside hospitals is five times greater than that of schizophrenia (Dunlop, 1965). At least 12% of people experience depression severe enough to require treatment at some time in their lives, with depression accounting for an estimated 75% of all psychiatric hospitalizations (Fennell, 1995).

At any given time, 15% to 20% of adults suffer significant levels of depressive symptomatology, with a reported 3% to 5% of all persons meeting the criteria for Dysthymic Disorder. The prevalence rate of depression in women can be as high as 25%. Kaplan, Sadock, and Grebb (1994) report that this is a universal observation, independent of country or culture, and hypothesize that it may be related to hormonal differences, the effects of childbirth, differing psychosocial stressors for women and men, and behavioral models of learned helplessness. Fortunately, depression is time-limited in most cases, and untreated episodes usually resolve themselves within 3 to 6 months. However, relapse is frequent, and some 15% to 20% of people follow a chronic course (Fennell, 1995).

The mean age of initial onset for Major Depressive Disorder is about 40, with 50 percent of all patients having onset between ages 20 and 50. Major Depressive Disorder can also have its onset in childhood or in old age, although this is uncommon. Some recent epidemiological data suggest that the incidence of Major Depressive Disorder may be increasing among persons under age 20, and that this may be related to the increased use of alcohol and other substances in that age group (Kaplan, Sadock, & Grebb, 1994).

Symptomatology

The fourth edition of the *Diagnostic and Statistical Manual of Mental Disorders* (*DSM-IV;* American Psychiatric Association [APA], 1994) lists the contemporary features comprising the diagnosis of Major Depressive Disorder (MDD). These criteria require that within the same 2-week period the client have five or more specific symptoms that present a definite change from usual functioning. Specific symptoms include low or depressed mood, sleep or appetite disturbance, loss of interest or pleasure, low energy level, decreased motivation and concentration, feelings of worthlessness or helplessness, and suicidal ideation.

The *DSM-IV* criteria for Dysthymic Disorder (DD) (1994) require the presence of a depressed mood most of the time for at least a 2-year period. It involves the steady presence of symptoms similar to those of Major Depressive Disorder, but it is a less severe form of depression in terms of magnitude. DD is more common among women, among unmarried and young persons, and among persons with low incomes. It coexists frequently with other mental disorders, especially major depression, anxiety disorders, substance abuse, and Borderline Personality Disorder (Kaplan, Sadock, & Grebb, 1994).

Suicide is a serious concern with those diagnosed with depression—about two thirds of all depressed patients contemplate suicide, and 10% to 15% successfully committ suicide (Kaplan, Sadock, & Grebb, 1994). Looking retrospectively at all cases of suicide, 50% to 70% have been identified as individuals who had symptoms characteristic of depression (Goodwin & Guze, 1989). Obviously, suicidal intentions should routinely be assessed when working with depressed clients.

Risk Factors

Although depression (or melancholia) has been recognized as a clinical syndrome for more than 2,000 years, Beck (1996, p. 3) reports that, as yet, "there are still major unsolved issues regarding its nature, its classification, and its etiology." Although there is strong evidence in support of a genetic component to depression, the exact weight of the genetic and psychosocial factors remains to be determined, and the nature of the genetic transmission in depressive disorders is similarly unclear (Institute of Medicine, 1994).

In considering risk factors, Fennell (1995, p. 169) states:

> It seems likely that no single factor can explain the occurrence of depression, but rather that it results from an interaction between many different factors. Its onset and course have been shown to relate to a variety of biological, historical, environmental, and psychosocial variables. These include disturbances in neurotransmitter functioning, a family history of depression or alcoholism, early parental loss or neglect, recent negative life events, a critical or hostile spouse, lack of a close confiding relationship, lack of adequate social supports, and long-term lack of self-esteem.

Additional risk factors that have been identified include downward social mobility; loss of a job; death of a spouse, child, or parent; divorce; and poverty (Institute of Medicine, 1994), and the presence of severe and traumatic events in an individual's life (Coyne & Downey, 1991).

Relevance to Social Work Practice

The National Association of Social Workers (NASW) reports that in 1989, the dominant setting of its members' employment was in mental health (Chess & Norlin, 1991). Over 30% of NASW's members work in this field, and a large percentage of their clients present with a depressive disorder. This requires social workers to obtain ongoing education and maintain up-to-date knowledge regarding the assessment and effective treatment of depression.

Mental illnesses, including depressive disorders, have a substantial emotional and financial cost to society. The Institute of Medicine (1994) estimates that the economic costs for 1990 were $98 billion for alcohol abuse, $66 billion for drug abuse, and $147 billion for other mental disorders. Certainly, persons with depressive disorders present in each of these categories and contribute to the high economic costs associated with mental illness.

Mental health services are underutilized by minority groups (Institute of Medicine, 1994). Although the prevalence of mood disorders does not appear to differ from race to race, clinicians tend to underdiagnose mood disorders and to overdiagnose schizophrenia in patents who have racial or cultural backgrounds different from their own (Kaplan, Sadock, & Grebb, 1994).

ASSESSMENT METHODS

Social work assessment is an important process that should incorporate both the client's and the social worker's perspectives, should result in a diagnosis, and should indicate potential treatments (Dulmus & Wodarski, 1996). Assessing the presumptively depressed client requires the usual array of interviewing and clinical skills that characterize the social work field. The major tools involved in the appraisal of depression include the clinical interview and standarized assessment methods.

The Clinical Interview

The traditional clinical interview, informed by a foundation of therapeutic skills and based upon a thorough familiarity with the *DSM-IV* criteria—not just those for mood disorders but for other common clinical problems, as well—remains the centerpiece of assessing depressed clients. In addition to the usual unstructured interviewing style, several structured interviewing protocols have been developed that can help the social worker focus on the evaluation of specific depressive signs and symptoms.

Structured Clinical Interview for the *DSM*

The Structured Clinical Interview for the *DSM* (SCID; First, Spitzer, Gibbon, & Williams, 1995) is perhaps the most widely used, reliable, and valid means of determining which *DSM-IV* criteria a particular client meets. The Mood Disorders section can be administered in isolation or in combination with other sections of the SCID; when the protocol is properly completed, the result is a clear and fairly unambiguous determination of whether a client meets the criteria for each of the mood disorders. The present version of the SCID, and its predecessors, were codeveloped by social workers.

Schedule for Affective Disorders and Schizophrenia

The Schedule for Affective Disorders and Schizophrenia (SADS) is an older interview protocol, developed to reduce the variance among interviewers in the type and amount of information available to make a diagnosis. Though it covers multiple psychiatric categories, it can assist the social worker in diagnosing depression. The SADS is a highly structured interview whereby the social worker progresses through a series of specific questions related to various psychiatric conditions. The complete interview takes approximately 2 hours, and it is recommended that it be administered only by highly trained individuals with extensive clinical knowledge (Endicott & Spitzer, 1978). While very good at capturing the phenomenology of depression, because of its age the SADS is *not* useful in formalizing a *DSM-IV* diagnosis. At present, the SCID is preferred over the SADS when a structured interview schedule is desired.

Rapid Assessment Instruments

Many rating scales, checklists, and rapid assessment instruments (RAIs) have been devised to quantify depression and to assist the social worker in diagnosis, assessing progress, and gauging termination of treatment. When used as an adjunct to information obtained from clinical interviews, the quantified information provided by these RAIs can be of great benefit in assessing where the client is at, and, if repeatedly administered during the course of treatment, they provide useful information in determining whether clients are improving, deteriorating, or remaining stable in terms of affective symptomatology. The following describes a few RAIs that can assist the social worker in diagnosing depression.

Multi-Problem Screening Inventory.   The Multi-Problem Screening Inventory (MPSI) is a 334-item inventory developed by social workers to gather a large amount of detailed information on many possible problem areas. It is a self-report questionnaire that is comprised of 27 subscales, including one specific to depression. Each subscale can be scored individually, which allows the social worker to individualize the assessment to the client by choosing to administer either the whole questionnaire or just one or more of the subscales. The inventory is somewhat lengthy, but it provides important, detailed information. It has been shown to have good validity and test-retest reliability (Hudson, 1990; Hudson & McMurtry, 1997). A computer scoring program for this instrument is also available.

Generalized Contentment Scale.   Also developed by a social worker, the Generalized Contentment Scale (GCS) is a self-report scale designed to measure the degree, severity, or magnitude of nonpsychotic depression. This scale produces a range of 0 to 100; the scores are regarded as true ratio scale values (Hudson, 1992). A computer scoring program is available from the publisher, although its brevity indicates that the scoring of individual tests does not require anything except a pencil.

Beck Depression Inventory.   The Beck Depression Inventory (BDI) is the most frequently used self-report inventory. It is comprised of 21 items to assess symptoms and attitudes, and it has demonstrated excellent reliability and validity. It has also been found to be applicable across a variety of cultures (Beck, Ward, Mendelson, Mock, & Erbaugh, 1961).

Hamilton Rating Scale for Depression.   The Hamilton Rating Scale for Depression has historically been one of the most commonly used interview measures. Devised in 1960, it has been revised twice. Its current version is a 24-item scale that is most often used to measure the severity of depression in a client. It has demonstrated both reliability and validity (Hamilton, 1960).

Each of the preceding instruments can be readily administered to depressed clients by social workers. The scales' scores can then be graphed to depict changes over time. This information can be helpful to the clinician and his or her supervisor, and it can sometimes be usefully shared with clients. In the aggregate, RAI scores of this type can also help to evaluate agency services.

EFFECTIVE INTERVENTIONS

Once the assessment has been completed and the diagnosis has been made, it is the social worker's ethical responsibility to select the most effective intervention available to treat the disorder (Dulmus & Wodarski, 1996; Myers & Thyer, 1997). Though there is much research yet to be done, there *is* a strong body of empirically based knowledge regarding the treatment of depression that the social worker can draw upon. This places the responsibility on the social worker to continually remain current on what the literature indicates is effective.

Treatment of clients with mood disorders must be directed toward a number of goals. First, the safety of the client must be paramount. Once safety considerations have been dealt with, a treatment plan should be initiated that addresses not only the immediate symptoms but also the patient's prospective well-being (Kaplan, Sadock, & Grebb, 1994). Affective disorders are heterogeneous with respect to treatment response, so the social worker is confronted with the complex problem of selecting the most effective treatment or combination of treatments available for a particular patient (Beck, Rush, Shaw, & Emery, 1979). This section reviews these specific treatments.

Cognitive Therapy

The goal of cognitive therapy is to break down existing negative thoughts and to replace them with more positive and functionally adaptive ones (Goodwin & Guze, 1989). Cognitive therapy, as formulated by Aaron Beck, focuses on the cognitive distortions postulated to be present in major depression. The goal of cognitive therapy is to alleviate depression and to prevent its recurrence by helping clients identify and test negative cognitions; develop alternative, flexible, and positive ways of thinking; and rehearse new cognitive and behavioral responses.

A variety of inventories has been developed for the assessment of cognition related to depression; these inventories are useful both for assessment purposes and for outcome evaluation. Included among the measures specifically relevant to cognitive therapy are the *Autonomic Thoughts Questionnaire* (Hollon & Kendall,

1980), the *Dysfunctional Attitude Scale* (Weissman & Beck, 1978), and the *Attributional Style Questionnaire* (Peterson et al., 1982).

Cognitive therapy is an active, directive, time-limited, structured approach that is used to treat not only depression but a variety of psychiatric disorders (for example, anxiety, phobias, and pain problems). It is based on an underlying theoretical rationale that an individual's affect and behavior are largely determined by the way in which he or she structures the world. An individual's *cognitions* (verbal or pictorial events in his or her stream of consciousness) are based on attitudes or assumptions (*schemas*), developed from previous experiences. The social worker using cognitive therapy helps the patient to think and act more realistically and adaptively about his or her psychological problems and, thus, to reduce the symptoms (Thyer & Myers, in press).

Some research suggests that the central psychological core in the suicidal patient is *hopelessness.* Positive results from using a direct approach to the hopelessness in depressed patients suggests that cognitive therapy might have longer range antisuicidal effects than the use of chemotherapy (Beck et al., 1979). However, a great deal more clinical research is needed to isolate specific predictors for using cognitive therapy alone or in a combined regimen.

Behavioral Therapy

In behavioral therapy, the patient is helped to function effectively in interpersonal interactions so as to maximize reinforcement obtained from others (Goodwin & Guze, 1989). It is based in part on the hypothesis that maladaptive behavioral patterns result in a person receiving little positive feedback—and, perhaps, outright rejection—from society. This leads, for example, to the type of behavioral therapy called *social skills training.* It emphasizes assertiveness, verbal skills, and practice at making others feel more comfortable (Goodwin & Guze, 1989).

Another aspect of the behavioral perspective is the hypothesis that depression is the by-product of living in a particularly aversive environment, or one in which meaningful reinforcers are absent or have been lost (for example, following the death of a loved one). Treatment therefore focuses on reducing the client's exposure to aversive or punitive situations and on the development of coping skills and stress management techniques (see Lewinsohn, 1974). Structured homework exercises aimed at promoting the likelihood of the client encountering reinforcing experiences (and, for example, becoming more social, as opposed to being self-isolated) are also an important element in behavioral treatment of depression. Etiologically, the causes of depression are sought in *what is felt*—that is, in the environment—rather than in feelings per se. The behavioral view suggests that depression is a *consequence* of punitive or aversive experiences, not a cause. One's environment is seen as causing concurrent dysphoric *affect,* depressive *behaviors,* and dysfunctional *thoughts.* One's thoughts are not seen as causing depressive behavior, for example. Rather, unpleasant experiences in life give rise to both depressive thoughts and behavior. The behavioral social worker thereby focuses more on environmental manipulation—on promoting a more reinforcing life—than on office-based verbal therapy.

Though few studies have been conducted on behavioral therapy for Major Depressive Disorder, the data to date does indicate that behavioral therapy may be an effective treatment modality for MDD (Kaplan, Sadock, & Grebb, 1994). Lewinsohn, Munoz, Youngren and Zeiss (1986) have developed a treatment manual, titled *Control Your Depression,* that social workers can use as a guide in providing behavioral therapy for depressed clients. Such treatment has been shown to be very helpful.

Cognitive-Behavioral Therapy

Beck et al. (1979, p. 3) define cognitive-behavioral therapy as "an active, directive, time-limited, structured approach . . . based on an underlying theoretical rationale that an individual's affect and behavior are largely determined by the way in which he structures the world." When applied to the diagnosis of depression, the goal of the therapy is to assist the client in finding solutions to his or her problems, using specific cognitive-behavioral strategies. The first goal is to reduce the symptoms related to depression, and then to apply these newly acquired techniques to solve life problems. This particular therapy is time-limited, with a goal of assisting the client in developing independent self-help skills (Fennell, 1995).

Several studies have been completed to date that provide empirical evidence for the effectiveness of cognitive-behavioral therapy as a treatment for depression. Studies have indicated that applying the strategies of cognitive-behavioral therapy can reduce the frequency and intensity of depressing thoughts, resulting in an immediate beneficial effect on mood (Blackburn & Bonham, 1980; Fennell & Teasdale, 1984; Fennell & Teasdale, 1987; Teasdale & Fennell, 1982). Other studies have indicated that cognitive-behavioral therapy is at least as effective in reducing depression as are tricyclic antidepressants (Beck, Hollon, Young, Bedrosian, & Budenz, 1985; Blackburn, Biship, Glen, Whalley, & Christie, 1981; Rush, Beck, Kovacs & Hollon, 1977; Teasdale, Fennell, Hibbert, & Aimes, 1984). In addition, it has been indicated that cognitive-behavioral therapy may well be more effective in relapse prevention than antidepressant medications (Blackburn, Eunson, & Biship, 1986; Kovacs, Rush, Beck, & Hollon, 1981; Simons, Murphy, Levine, & Wetzel, 1986).

The empirical evidence clearly indicates that cognitive-behavioral therapy is an approach that social workers should consider in treating the depressed client.

Interpersonal Psychotherapy

Interpersonal psychotherapy (IPT) attempts to improve the quality of the patient's social and interpersonal functioning by enhancing his or her ability to cope with internally and externally induced stresses, by restoring morale, and by helping the patient deal with the personal and social consequences of the disorder (Goodwin & Guze, 1989). Interpersonal therapy, developed by Gerald Klerman, focuses on one or two of the patient's current interpersonal problems. It usually consists of 12 to 16 weekly sessions. The therapy is characterized by an active therapeutic approach (Kaplan, Sadock, & Grebb, 1994). While IPT has been shown to be promising in a few well-controlled studies, proper training programs in the procedure remain rare.

Group Therapy

Cost, efficiency, and treatment effectiveness are good arguments for group work (Randall & Wodarski, 1989). Clinical studies have demonstrated the efficacy of interpersonal psychotherapy in groups (Mufson, Moreau, Weissman, & Klerman, 1993) as well as that of cognitive-behavioral group therapy (Lewinsohn, Clarke, Hops, & Andrews, 1990; Reynolds & Coats, 1986) in treating depression. Group work and group therapy are viable treatment options for the social worker to consider in helping the depressed—provided that specific therapies are used.

Marital and Family Therapies

Marital and family therapies are not generally viewed as primary therapies for the treatment of Major Depressive Disorder, but increasing evidence indicates that helping a patient with a mood disorder learn to reduce stress and to cope with stress can reduce the chance of a relapse. Family therapy is indicated if the disorder jeopardizes the patient's marriage or family functioning, or if the mood disorder seems to be promoted or maintained by the family situation (Kaplan, Sadock, & Grebb, 1994).

The efficacy of marital therapy for depression occurring in the context of marital distress is encouraging. Marital therapy appears to decrease depression. In addition, it may lead to increases in marital satisfaction and decreases in negative marital communication, thereby decreasing the probability of relapse among patients with depression (Hooley & Teasdale, 1989).

Pharmacotherapy

If psychosocial interventions such as cognitive, behavioral, or cognitive-behavioral therapies are not effective, then consideration should be given to the use of medication. Although antidepressant drugs are obviously less expensive than psychotherapy, not all patients respond to this medication. Beck (1973) reviewed numerous controlled studies that examined chemotherapy as a treatment for depression and found that only 60% to 65% of individuals show a definite improvement as a result of treatment with a common tricyclic drug. Hence, methods must be developed to help the 35% to 40% of patients who are not helped in their first trial of an antidepressant drug.

As previously stated, antidepressant medication has been of significant benefit in the treatment of various kinds of depression. For the 60% to 65% of individuals who do respond to chemotherapy, it is expected that the use of specific pharmacotherapy approximately doubles the chance that the patient will recover in 1 month. The tricyclic antidepressants (for example, imipramine, amitriptyline, desipramine, nortriptyline, and protriptyline) and related agents are commonly prescribed for patients with moderate to severe depression. Bupropion and the serotonin-specific reuptake inhibitors, such as fluoxetine, paroxetine, and sertraline, are much safer and are much better tolerated than previous drugs and are equally effective (Kaplan, Sadock, & Grebb, 1994). Nevertheless, many patients who might be drug-responsive either refuse to take medication because of personal objections or develop side effects that cause them to terminate the drugs.

When treating the patient with depression, the social worker may consider integrating pharmacotherapy with psychosocial interventions. Studies indicate that the combination of cognitive therapy and pharmacotherapy can be more efficacious than either therapy alone (Kaplan, Sadock, & Grebb, 1994).

Community Interventions

Although the National Institute of Mental Health has begun a program to increase the awareness of depression in the general population and among physicians, the symptoms of depression are often inappropriately dismissed as understandable reactions to stress, as evidence of a weakness of will, or simply as a conscious attempt to achieve some secondary gain (Kaplan, Sadock, & Grebb, 1994). Educating the community, professionals, individuals, and families about depression will provide accurate information regarding the illness, increase early diagnosis and treatment, and—hopefully—decrease the stigma associated with depression.

Prevention

At the present time the majority of resources available for mental health services in the United States, both human and material, are allocated to the treatment or rehabilitation of those experiencing psychiatric disorders (Blair, 1992). In contrast, the promotion of mental health and the prevention of mental illness have been given relatively few resources and relatively little status (Sommerschild, 1987). In preventative research, a risk-reduction model—whereby risk factors are identified and matched to empirically tested interventions—is promising (Institute of Medicine, 1994). Risk factors are those characteristics, variables, or hazards that make it more likely that an individual will develop a disorder than will someone selected from the general population (Werner & Smith, 1982). Risk groups could be identified on the basis of biological, psychological, or social risk factors that are known to be associated with the onset of depression. Once identified, individuals or subgroups of the population at risk for developing depression could be targeted with selective prevention interventions (Institute of Medicine, 1994). If risk factors can be decreased or in some way altered, or if protective factors can be enhanced, the likelihood of at-risk individuals eventually developing a depressive disorder would be decreased. It must be acknowledged, however, that the risk-reduction model remains more a hope than a fulfilled promise, in terms of actual data (Dulmus & Wodarski, 1997).

CONCLUSIONS

When an individual seeks mental health treatment from a social worker it is essential that the social worker's treatment protocol incorporate state-of-the-art assessment technology and empirically based interventions. This chapter provides an overview of both in relation to Major Depressive Disorder and Dysthymic Disorder. Many advances have been made in the treatment of these mood disorders. It is imperative that social workers utilize this knowledge in treating clients with depressive disorders. Anything less is ethically unacceptable.

REFERENCES

American Psychiatric Association. (1994). *Diagnostic and statistical manual of mental disorders* (4th ed.). Washington, DC: Author.

Beck, A. T. (1973). *The diagnosis and management of depression.* Philadelphia: University of Pennsylvania Press.

Beck, A. T. (1996). *Depression: Causes and treatments.* Philadelphia: University of Pennsylvania Press.

Beck, A. T., Hollon, S. D., Young, J. E., Bedrosian, R. C., & Budenz, D. (1985). Treatment of depression with cognitive therapy and amitriptyline. *Archives of General Psychiatry, 42,* 142–148.

Beck, A. T., Rush, A. J., Shaw, B. F., & Emery, G. (1979). *Cognitive therapy of depression.* New York: Guilford Press.

Beck, A. T., Ward, C. H., Mendelson, M., Mock, J., & Erbaugh, J. (1961). An inventory for measuring depression. *Archives of General Psychiatry, 4,* 561–571.

Blackburn, I. M., Biship, S., Glen, A. I., Whalley, L. J., & Christie, J. E. (1981). The efficacy of cognitive therapy in depression: A treatment trial using cognitive therapy and pharmacotherapy, each alone and in combination. *British Journal of Psychiatry, 139,* 181–189.

Blackburn, I. M., & Bonham, K. G. (1980). Experimental effects of a cognitive therapy technique in depressed patients. *British Journal of Social and Clinical Psychology, 19,* 353–363.

Blackburn, I. M., Eunson, K. M., & Biship, S. (1986). A two-year naturalistic follow-up of depressed patients treated with cognitive therapy, pharmacotherapy and a combination of both. *Journal of Affective Disorders, 10,* 67–75.

Blair, A. (1992). The role of primary prevention in mental health services: A review and critique. *Journal of Community and Applied Social Psychology, 2,* 77–94.

Chess, W. A., & Norlin, J. M. (1991). *Human behavior in the social environment: A social systems method* (2nd ed.). Boston: Allyn & Bacon.

Coyne, J. C., & Downey, G. (1991). Social factors and psychopathology: Stress, social support, and coping processes. *Annual Review of Psychology, 42,* 401–425.

Dulmus, C. N., & Wodarski, J. S. (1996). Assessment and effective treatments of childhood psychopathology: Responsibilities and implications for practice. *Journal of Child and Adolescent Group Therapy, 6*(2), 75–99.

Dulmus, C. N., & Wodarski, J. S. (1997). Prevention of childhood mental disorders: Hope and a vision for the future. *Child and Adolescent Social Work Journal, 14,* 181–198.

Dunlop, E. (1965). Use of antidepressants and stimulants. *Modern Treatment, 3,* 543–568.

Endicott, J., & Spitzer, R. (1978). A diagnostic interview: The Schedule for Affective Disorders and Schizophrenia. *Archives of General Psychiatry, 35,* 837–844.

Fennell, M. J. (1995). Depression. In K. Hawton, P. Salkovskis, J. Kirk, & D. Clark (Eds.), *Cognitive behavior therapy for psychiatric problems: A practical guide* (pp. 169–234). Oxford: Oxford University Press.

Fennell, M. J., & Teasdale, J. D. (1984). Effects of distraction on thinking and affect in depressed patients. *British Journal of Clinical Psychology, 23,* 65–66.

Fennell, M. J., & Teasdale, J. D. (1987). Cognitive therapy for depression: Individual differences and the process of change. *Cognitive Therapy and Research, 11,* 253–271.

First, M. B., Spitzer, R. L., Gibbon, M., & Williams, J. B. (1995). *Structured clinical interview for the DSM-IV: Axis-I.* New York: New York State Psychiatric Institute, Biometrics Research Department.

Goodwin, D. W., & Guze, S. B. (1989). *Psychiatric Diagnosis.* New York: Oxford University Press.

Hamilton, M. (1960). A rating scale for depression. *Journal of Neurology, Neurosurgery and Psychiatry, 12,* 56–62.

Hollon, S. D., & Kendall, P. C. (1980). Cognitive self-statements in depression: Development of an automatic thoughts questionnaire. *Cognitive Therapy and Research, 4,* 109–143.

Hooley, J. M., & Teasdale, J. D. (1989). Predictions of relapse in unipolar depressives: Expressed emotion, marital distress, and perceived criticism. *Journal of Abnormal Psychology, 98,* 229–235.

Hudson, W. (1990). *The Multi-Problem Screening Inventory manual.* Tallahassee, FL: WALMYR.

Hudson, W. (1992). *The WALMYR assessment scales scoring manual.* Tallahassee, FL: WALMYR.

Hudson, W. W., & McMurtry, S. L. (1997). Comprehensive assessment in social work practice: The Multi-Problem Screening Inventory. *Research on Social Work Practice, 7,* 79–98.

Institute of Medicine (1994). *Reducing risks for mental disorders: Frontiers for preventive intervention research.* Washington, DC: National Academy Press.

Kaplan, H. I., Sadock, B. J., & Grebb, J. A. (1994). *Kaplan & Sadock's Synopsis of Psychiatry* (7th ed.). Baltimore: Williams & Wilkins.

Kline, N. (1964). Practical management of depression. *Journal of the American Medical Association, 190,* 732–740.

Kovacs, M., Rush, A. J., Beck, A. T., & Hollon, S. D. (1981). Depressed outpatients treated with cognitive therapy or pharmacotherapy: A one-year follow-up. *Archives of General Psychiatry, 135,* 525–533.

Lewinsohn, P. M. (1974). A behavioral approach to depression. In R. J. Freidman & M. M. Katz (Eds.), *The psychology of depression.* New York: Wiley.

Lewinsohn, P. M., Clarke, G. N., Hops, H., & Andrews, J. (1990). Cognitive-behavioral treatment for depressed adolescents. *Behavior Therapy, 21,* 385–401.

Lewinsohn, P. M., Munoz, R., Youngren, M. A., & Zeiss, A. (1986). *Control your depression.* Englewood Cliffs, NJ: Prentice-Hall.

Mufson, L., Moreau, D., Weissman, M. M., & Klerman, G. L. (1993). *Interpersonal psychotherapy for depressed adolescents.* New York: Guilford Press.

Myers, L. L. & Thyer, B. A. (1997). Do social work clients have the right to effective treatment? *Social Work, 42,* 288–298.

Peterson, C., Semmel, A., von Baeyer, C., Abramson, L. Y., Metalsky, G. I., & Seligman, M. E. P. (1982). The Attributional Style Questionnaire. *Cognitive Therapy and Research, 6,* 287–299.

Randall, E., & Wodarski, J. S. (1989). Theoretical issues in clinical social group work. *Small Group Behavior, 20,* 475–499.

Reynolds, W. M., & Coats, K. I. (1986). A comparison of cognitive-behavioral therapy and relaxation training for the treatment of depression in adolescents. *Journal of Consulting and Clinical Psychology, 44,* 653–660.

Rush, A. J., Beck, A. T., Kovacs, M., & Hollon, S. D. (1977). Comparative efficacy of cognitive therapy and pharmacotherapy in the treatment of depressed outpatients. *Cognitive Therapy and Research, 1,* 17–37.

Seligman, M. E. (1975). *Helplessness.* San Francisco: Freeman.

Simons, A. D., Murphy, G. E., Levine, J. L., & Wetzel, R. D. (1986). Cognitive therapy and pharmacotherapy for depression: sustained improvement over one year. *Archives of General Psychiatry, 43,* 43–49.

Sommerschild, H. (1987). *Prevention of Child Psychiatrica Scandinavia 76,* (Suppl. 337), 59–63.

Teasdale, J. D., & Fennell, M. J. (1982). Immediate effects on depression of cognitive therapy intervention. *Cognitive Therapy and Research, 6,* 343–351.

Teasdale, J. D., Fennell, M. J., Hibbert, G. A., & Aimes, P. L. (1984). Cognitive therapy for major depressive disorder in primary care. *British Journal of Psychiatry, 144,* 400–406.

Thyer, B. A., & Myers, L. L. (in press). Behavioral and cognitive theories for clinical social work. In J. Brandell (Ed.), *Theory and practice in clinical social work* (pp. 18–37). New York: Free Press.

Weissman, A. N., & Beck, A. T. (1978). *Development and validation of the Dysfunctional Attitudes Scale: A preliminary investigation.* Paper presented at the annual meeting of the Association for Advancement of Behavior Therapy, Chicago.

Werner, E. E., & Smith, R. S. (1982). *Vulnerable but invincible: A longitudinal study of resilient children and youth.* New York: McGraw-Hill.

Chapter 14

BIPOLAR DISORDER

Bruce Brotter
John F. Clarkin
Daniel Carpenter

OVERVIEW

Bipolar Disorder is a severe, recurrent, often chronic behavioral disorder that affects approximately 1% of the population. Those afflicted with this disorder suffer an average of 12.3 episodes during what are typically the most productive years of adulthood. The growing research on the pharmacological treatment of this crippling condition is in sharp contrast to the relative absence of research on crucial behaviors associated with seeking treatment and the outcome of treatment, such as medication compliance, monitoring of symptoms, and patient and family management of stress. Although it is estimated that the use of lithium therapy from 1969 to 1989 saved the United States $40 billion through reduction of medical costs and restoration of productivity (Goodwin & Jamison, 1990), epidemiological data and rates of treatment noncompliance as high as 53% suggest a serious underutilization of outpatient psychiatric services by bipolar patients. Left untreated, Bipolar Disorder causes personal distress, leads to family disruption, and results in property damage, in bodily harm to the patient and others, and in the use of costly emergency medical services and legal services.

Operational Definitions

The fourth edition of the *Diagnostic and Statistical Manual of Mental Disorders* (*DSM-IV;* American Psychiatric Association [APA], 1994a) describes Bipolar Disorder in terms of cross-sectional symptoms and the course of the illness across time. The diagnosis is made when a patient's symptoms meet the criteria for a manic episode. Typical manic episode symptoms are elated or irritable mood, racing thoughts, pressured speech, decreased sleep, and feelings of omnipotence. *DSM-IV* should be consulted for a comprehensive operational definition.

Relevance of Social Work's Involvement

Bipolar patients experience severe psychiatric symptoms that can often be successfully minimized or ameliorated through psychopharmacologic intervention. However, various psychosocial factors can trigger symptoms and episodes; conversely, symptoms and episodes generally result in psychosocial consequences. For example, the loss of a job (stressor) might trigger symptoms in a bipolar individual, while symptoms might result in job loss (psychosocial consequence); medication noncompliance might then follow as a further consequence of the episode—or it might, in fact, have played an earlier role as a trigger. Bipolar Disorder is thus a condition that requires a biopsychosocial approach to treatment planning and intervention. Due to the many psychosocial variables that both influence and result from the illness course, Bipolar Disorder presents patients, families, and social workers with a challenge to conduct a truly interdisciplinary treatment.

The social worker often functions in the role of coordinator of a patient's overall treatment plan, particularly in inpatient settings. In this role, the social work clinician provides a psychosocial perspective and encourages interdisciplinary collaboration. In addition, the social worker has expertise in treating the range of psychosocial factors that are associated with major psychiatric illnesses and offers flexibility in the modality of treatment, whether individual, marital, or family treatment or case-management services are indicated. Furthermore, in the role of providing clinical services to families of severely ill patients, the social work clinician is in a position to deliver the primary psychoeducational intervention described in this chapter.

ASSESSMENT METHODS

In general clinical practice, the social worker conducts an assessment by identifying particular areas where more information is needed to formulate a treatment plan and exploring those areas via relevant and tactful questioning. The clinical interview is thus the usual method for conducting an assessment. However, if resources permit, or research interests dictate the assessment strategy, standardized methods may be utilized. This chapter suggests primary areas of assessment to be explored in the clinical interview of a bipolar patient and also recommends standardized methods that the researcher or interested clinician might employ.

Clinical Assessment

The areas of assessment depend upon the foci of intervention (described in the following section). There should be an intimate relationship between assessment and intervention, not only in the view of the social worker but also for patients and their families. The areas of assessment are intimately related to the focused psycho-educational intervention program, and are described in more detail in the context of the phases of treatment and the specific interventions to which they relate.

The primary areas to be assessed in the clinical interview with a bipolar patient are as follows:

1. Does the patient meet *DSM-IV* criteria for the diagnosis of Bipolar Disorder? Does comorbid character pathology or another psychiatric disorder exist?

2. Does the patient accept the diagnosis and the need for treatment?

3. What is the patient's history regarding adherence to medication? What is the family's perception of the need for the patient to take medication, and to what degree does the family support it?

4. What is the patient's level of overall psychosocial functioning? What are the patient's and family's expectations for the patient's role performance?

5. What are the patient's early warning signs, and are the patient and family able to identify them?

6. What are the current stressors, and how do the patient and family manage them?

Standardized Instruments for Assessment

A limited number of assessment strategies are clinically useful in addition to the clinical interview. These include patient (and family members) self-report instruments, semistructured interviews, and observational methods, including rating scales and direct observational methods. Selection of strategies should be determined by the advantages and limitations of each method, as well as the purpose of the assessment. In an era of managed care, efficient patient self-report instruments will probably be emphasized, along with brief ratings by clinicians in the course of doing necessary clinical service. While the clinical interview is often an adequate method to assess the treatment needs of a bipolar patient, the following instruments may be clinically useful in arriving at a more careful and comprehensive assessment—and, hence, at a better informed treatment plan.

Diagnosis.   The Structured Clinical Interview for *DSM-IV* (SCID; First, Spitzer, Gibbon, & Williams, 1995)—which was coauthored by social workers—is an effective tool to diagnose Bipolar Disorder in cases where the diagnosis is difficult to assess through a standard clinical interview. At times, additional information is required to determine whether the client is presenting symptoms of a Bipolar I or II Disorder, or to rule out a Schizoaffective Disorder. The SCID is a structured interview, constructed in conjunction with *DSM-IV,* that can be utilized in such cases.

Axis II Diagnosis.   There is a growing literature on the comorbidity of Axis I Affective Disorders and Axis II Personality Disorders, suggesting that concurrent character pathology may influence the diagnosis (Hirschfeld & Klerman, 1979), treatment process, and absorption of the treatment. Our own work (Carpenter, Clarkin, Glick, & Wilner, 1995) suggests that a minority of bipolar patients have a comorbid Axis II or Personality Disorder diagnosis. For this reason, it is important that the clinician determine whether or not significant Axis II pathology exists. While the clinical interview and *DSM-IV* criteria can be used as guides in this process, the Axis II section of the SCID (noted previously) offers a standardized way to obtain a diagnosis of Axis II Personality Disorder in both patient and spouse.

Patient Psychopathology.   Quantifiable measures of patient psychopathology can be quite useful in determining whether a bipolar patient is experiencing early warning symptoms, hypomania, or a full-blown relapse of mania. The Global Assessment Scale (GAS); Endicott, Spitzer, Fleiss, & Cohen, 1976) is a rating scale that offers a global assessment of the patient's overall symptoms and functioning; it can be used to support or clarify clinical impressions. The SADS-C is a variation of the Schedule for Affective Disorder and Schizophrenia (Endicott & Spitzer, 1978) that enables the clinician to measure changes on various dimensions of symptomatology relevant to depression and mania. Data from the SADS-C can also be used to fill out the Brief Psychiatric Rating Scale (BPRS; Lukoff, Nuechterlein & Ventura, 1986), a 24-item rating scale that assesses symptomatic adjustment and relapse. In our own study, the BPRS became the yardstick to measure changes in the patient's mental status, providing the social worker and the psychiatrist with quantifiable data to discuss and utilize in making appropriate modifications to the treatment plan.

Patient Social Functioning.   Since the bipolar client's social functioning can be so dramatically affected by the symptoms and overall course of Bipolar Disorder, a quantifiable method to assess functioning in the various social roles can be clinically useful to determine targets for intervention, as well as to measure changes over the course of treatment. The Social Adjustment Scale (SAS; Weissman & Sholomskas, 1982) is a 48-item structured interview that can be used toward this end. It measures the patient's level of functioning overall and on six major role scales, including work, social and leisure activities, extended family, marital, parental, and general family functioning, over a period of 2 months prior to the interview.

Marital and Family Functioning.   The Camberwell Family Interview (CFI; Brown, Birley, & Wing, 1972; Vaughn & Leff, 1976) is a semistructured interview for use with a significant other or relative that has become a classic in the field for evaluating hostility and overinvolvement with the identified patient. It is a reliable instrument that has predicted relapse in cases of schizophrenia and major depression. While scoring the interview is not always clinically useful or feasible, the interview elicits rich clinical material regarding the family's dynamics and functioning that can be utilized to identify additional goals or to plan family intervention.

The Social Behavior Assessment Schedule (SBAS; Platt, Weyman, Hirsch, & Hewett, 1978) can be used to measure the burden on the spouse before and after treatment, and to determine to what extent family burden should be a focus of attention in the treatment plan. The SBAS assesses several domains: (a) problematic behaviors of the patient, (b) social role performance, (c) adverse effects on others (impact of the patient's illness on the informant's work, social life, and emotional and physical well-being), and (d) social supports. Both global and domain-specific scores for subjective burden can be derived.

The Marital Satisfaction Inventory (MSI; Snyder, Willis & Keiser, 1979) is an additional measure of marital functioning to augment the material reported in a clinical interview. The MSI is an easily administered 280-item self-report instrument that elicits information regarding areas of conflict in the relationship. In our experience, spouses are generally less satisfied with the relationship than patients, but do not always verbalize this during an interview due to concerns about injuring the patient's feelings. Thus, this instrument can offer clinically useful information that might not be reported otherwise.

EFFECTIVE INTERVENTIONS

Background and Rationale

Important aspects of current research on the treatment of severe psychiatric disorders in general, and Bipolar Disorder specifically, provide additional background for social work intervention with this disorder: (a) the patient's family environment and its potential for surrounding the patient with ambient stress, (b) medication compliance, and (c) the impact of psychoeducational intervention. Empirical research in these areas is presented in the following subsections, followed by a detailed description of psychoeducational intervention strategies.

Ambient Family Stress.   Psychosocial stress may be an important determinant of relapse and recurrence in major affective disorders and therefore needs to be addressed both theoretically and pragmatically in the development and evaluation of treatment models. Research on family factors in the major psychiatric disorders has identified several types of stressors confronted by families attempting to cope with mental illness: (a) the objective and subjective burdens imposed on family life by salient aspects of the illness and the need to provide caregiving; (b) the family members' tendency to respond to the patient with criticism or emotional overinvolvement (so-called high expressed emotion [EE]), which is hypothesized to increase the stress climate for the patient (Vaughn & Leff, 1976); and (c) additional stress associated with psychiatric disorders of the patient's spouse, as a consequence of assortative mating.

Medication Compliance and Effects.   Pharmacological treatments for patients with Bipolar Disorder may help buffer or reduce the impact of the stressors described in the preceding for both patient and spouse. However, retrospective reports show that 47% of patients are noncompliant at some time (Jamison & Akiskal, 1983). A recent review (Goodwin & Jamison, 1990) suggests that medication compliance is associated with patient variables, including increasing age, being married, higher education, higher occupational status, lower chronicity of illness, fewer symptoms, a lesser extent of disability, patient belief in the seriousness of the illness and the effectiveness of treatment, a history of good compliance, and social support. Health system issues—convenience of clinical setting, continuity of care, and extent of supervision by others—have also been implicated. Noncompliance is associated with living alone, having unstable and nonsupportive families, having a more complex treatment regimen, and being prescribed more kinds of medication with higher associated costs. These and other studies (Davenport, Ebert, Adland, & Goodwin, 1977; Fitzgerald, 1972) suggest that psychosocial factors contribute substantially to medication noncompliance and that psychosocial interventions may be effective in dealing with the problem (e.g., Cochran, 1984; Fitzgerald, 1972; Shahir, Volkmar, Bacon, & Pfefferbaum, 1979). Even when taken in adequate doses, however, medication may have limited impact on impaired social functioning (DiMascio et al., 1979; Friedman, 1975; Weissman et al., 1979). Furthermore, even with medication, psychosocial stress may provoke relapse and recurrence (Vaughn & Leff, 1976). Thus, research to date demonstrates the need to specify more precisely the critical psychosocial variables mediating medication compliance and, therefore, medication effectiveness.

Psychoeducation and Stress Reduction.   Recent controlled studies have shown that psychosocial treatment with families can have significant effects on patient outcome (Falloon, Boyd & McGill, 1982; Leff, Kuipers, Berkowitz, Eberlein-Vries, & Sturgeon, 1982; McFarlane et al., 1995). Well-controlled clinical research on unipolar depression has demonstrated that outpatient psychotherapy used in conjunction with pharmacologic treatments can improve patient functioning in the areas of social, family, and work adjustment (DiMascio et al., 1979; Rounsaville, Weissman, Prusoff, & Herceg-Baron, 1979; Weissman et al., 1979; Weissman, Myers & Thompson, 1981). Data from our previous work indicates that a combination of inpatient psychosocial and pharmacological treatments can result in improved work and social functioning in bipolar patients (Clarkin, et al., 1990; Clarkin, Haas & Glick, 1988a, 1988b).

Reviews of these psychoeducational treatment programs (e.g., Goldstein, 1982) have identified common features: (a) they all aim to ameliorate the course of the illness and reduce relapse rate rather than to cure the condition, and (b) they try to attain these goals via clearly defined types of family intervention that are largely educational in nature (Anderson, Hogarty & Reiss, 1981; Goldstein, 1982). Psychoeducational interventions are those aimed at obtaining the family's help in working with the patient, educating the family as to the nature of the illness and what can be expected, and helping the family to modify stressful interaction patterns.

Pharmacotherapy

Before discussing interventions inherent to the psychosocial treatment of Bipolar Disorder, the standard psychopharmacological intervention is described. Although this intervention is administered by the patient's physician (usually a psychiatrist), the social work clinician must be familiar with the psychiatric symptoms and biological treatment of the disorder, and be ready to communicate information useful to the somatic treatment regime. In addition, the social worker must provide appropriate psychoeducation about medication treatment to the client and family, with the goal of strengthening the client's understanding of and cooperation with the treatment plan. Finally, in situations where the social worker functions as a coordinator of the patient's overall treatment, an understanding of the psychiatric symptoms of Bipolar Disorder and standard psychopharmacologic interventions is necessary. The following is a very brief overview. The interested reader is referred to one or more of the recently published guidelines on treating Bipolar Disorder (APA, 1994b; Frances, Docherty & Kahn, 1996).

The primary treatment for the symptoms of Bipolar Disorder is pharmacotherapy. Medication treatment has been shown to reduce manic symptoms, ameliorate depressive symptoms, and reduce the likelihood of a recurrence of the disorder once symptoms have abated. It is important that social workers know that patients with Bipolar Disorder who take appropriately prescribed medications are far less likely to experience a recurrence of the disorder than patients who do not take prophylactic medications. Experts in the pharmacotherapy of Bipolar Disorder suggest lifetime prophylaxis with mood-stabilizing medication after as few as two full manic episodes. This is not to say that taking medications prevents episodes; nor will discontinuing medications always result in a reemergence of symptoms.

Helping patients and families understand both the power and the limitations of medications is one of the primary goals of any psychosocial treatment of Bipolar Disorder. This is, in part, because most people with any serious illness have difficulty accepting the prospect of taking medications for the rest of their lives. Moreover, although medications are the most powerful tool to address acute symptoms and prevent relapse, they are much less effective at relieving chronic depression and improving psychosocial functioning. An absence of acute symptoms may represent a good outcome as compared to severe mania or suicidal depression, but is not the same as feeling like oneself again or facing each day with the vigor experienced years before the onset of the illness. Coping with persistent symptoms that are considered subsyndromal and with the loss of optimal functioning requires far more than medications alone can offer.

The primary class of medications prescribed for patients with Bipolar Disorder is the mood stabilizers. Virtually all patients with the disorder will be prescribed lithium, valproate, or carbamazepine. All have been shown to lessen the severity of manic and depressive symptoms and to reduce the likelihood of a reemergence of symptoms. Although lithium has been used far more widely, valproate and carbamazepine have been increasingly used in the past decade as the limitations of lithium have become apparent. Lithium is generally considered to be the treatment of choice when the patient is manic with the typical features of euphoria, grandiosity, and expansiveness. In many cases of mania with atypical features (mania with dysphoric mood or a mixture of mania and depression) or with rapid cycling (4 or more episodes in a year), valproate and carbamazepine are increasingly used as first-line treatments because lithium is less effective. The point is to understand that lithium is not the only mood stabilizer, and there are some situations where valproate or carbamazepine would probably be more effective. In general, mood stabilizers are usually prescribed one at a time. Combination therapies may be used when the patient has broken through adequate trials of a single mood stabilizer. In such cases, pairs can be prescribed. Physicians are hesitant to prescribe valproate and carbamazepine together because of concerns about overtaxing the hepatic system.

Antipsychotics (or neuroleptics) and antidepressents are also prescribed for patients with Bipolar Disorder. As their name suggests, antipsychotics are usually used when psychotic symptoms are present during acute phases of the illness. They may also be used to treat the agitation and aggressiveness associated with mania and some types of depression. In most cases, the doses of antipsychotics are tapered and eventually discontinued once acute symptoms have abated and patients have moved into the maintenance phase of the illness.

Antidepressants are used to alleviate the symptoms of depression. The primary concern about prescribing antidepressants in patients with Bipolar Disorder is that they can *induce* manic symptoms or increase the likelihood of rapid cycling. For patients with a history of manic episodes, an antidepressent is therefore rarely prescribed without a mood stabilizer. This caution must be extended to depressive patients with a history of hypomania or a family history of manic-depressive illness where the precipitation of a manic episode would indicate a worsening in the course of the illness.

Adjunctive medications are also prescribed for patients with Bipolar Disorder, depending on the situation. Benzodiazepines, such as lorazepam or clonazepam, are sometimes prescribed during periods of acute mania or agitation. Anticholinergic medications, such as benztropine, are often prescribed to counteract some side effects of antipsychotics.

The discussion of pharmacotherapy concludes with some notes about working with physicians on cases of Bipolar Disorder. Physicians show a range of receptivity to collaborating with clinical social workers. Some prefer to treat the patient in psychotherapy as well as pharmacotherapy and may have some discomfort in splitting the treatment. Others are quite happy to prescribe medications and leave the issues of family and marital functioning to someone else. Whatever the case, it is important that there be an explicit contract between the patient, the physician, and the social worker regarding the nature and timing of information sharing. It is optimal that the lines of communication be open between patient, physician, and social worker; however, the most important principle is that all three understand and agree on the circumstances of information sharing and think through the potential problems associated with any restrictions on sharing. Some questions follow as a guide.

1. Whom should the patient call in a crisis? And does that clinician call the other? This is a crucial issue because Bipolar Disorder is an illness often characterized by crises, and all involved—including family members—must plan for them in advance.

2. What happens when the crisis contact is on vacation? Clinician vacations are critical times when patients may be more vulnerable and clinicians less prepared. Be certain that issues of coverage are addressed thoroughly and explicitly.

3. In general, what kinds of information will and will not be shared with the other clinician? Specifically, will the social work clinician report medication noncompliance or substance use or abuse to the physician? The kind of situation to be avoided here is where the physician assumes that the social work clinician is another source of information regarding these issues while the social work clinician assumes that the patient's reports are subject to the rules of confidentiality. Similarly, will the physician report changes in medication strategies to the social worker? It is helpful to know about such changes so that support and psychoeducation can be offered during the transition.

Marital and Family Psychosocial Intervention

There are many reasons to think that psychosocial intervention with the bipolar patient and the family is integral to the progress of the patient, both in terms of symptom improvement and—most important—in terms of social support and integration and overall quality of life. The interventions described in the following address the target symptoms and psychosocial problems associated with Bipolar Disorder as reported in the literature and as observed in our clinical experience.

Following discussion of the tasks of marital and family intervention, two models of individual psychosocial intervention that are currently under investigation are presented, with a discussion of similarities and differences in their goals.

Building the Alliance.   The first task of the social worker conducting a psychoeducational intervention is to build an alliance with the patient and any available family member. General principles of accommodation to the particular family are used toward this end (Minuchin, 1974). This includes obtaining the family member's view of the situation, using his or her preferred vocabulary, and accepting the patient's and family's perceptions for the present while getting further details by neutral questioning.

The general attitude of the social work clinician is one of nonblame and acceptance of the patient and family coping with a recent bipolar episode. Family members are quick to blame themselves for the patient's illness, and are often worried that they in some way caused the disorder. The social work clinician accepts the patient as the one needing treatment, and reassures the family members that they did not *cause* the condition.

Particularly in situations of a first illness episode, family members are often in a state of crisis, overwhelmed by anxiety, uncertain about the right treatment for the patient, angry at the patient, guilty about their interactions with the patient prior to the episode or about their inability to do something sooner about a deteriorating situation. Under these conditions, the social worker may appear singularly or alternately as a welcome source of help, an opportunity to avoid further responsibility for the patient, a symbol of family failure, or a convenient scapegoat for all ensuing problems. Whatever the perception, family feelings are intense and members are ready to react quickly. The family structure may have been temporarily disturbed, making it difficult to deal with the crisis in familiar ways. Such a crisis entails specific risks for each family, but also provides opportunities for the therapist at a time when people are most open for change with professional help.

The process of building an alliance is often different depending upon the number of previous episodes. When there have been multiple previous illness episodes and hospitalizations, families may be less obviously disrupted and in crisis. The social worker's ability to allow these families to ventilate about the chronic burden they have experienced will be crucial in building an alliance. Those experiencing the first episode will need much more education and assistance in recognizing the recent episode as an illness and coming to realize that reoccurrences are likely. Only with such a realization of likely future episodes will the patient and family members take seriously the need for continued treatment.

As in conducting any social work intervention, the clinician must gather salient history while making contact with the patient and building the alliance. This information is utilized to confirm the diagnosis and to begin to develop a conceptual schema of the case.

Discussing the Diagnosis and Overall Treatment Plan.   The social worker has now set the stage to go on to the next clinical task: to affirm that the patient is ill and provide psychoeducational information about the disorder. The diagnosis should be conveyed to the patient and family in the following way:

> Your symptoms (and state them here in much the same words the patient and family used during the initial sessions) are part of a manic (or depressive) episode. These symptoms are common for someone in such a period.

By reviewing the course of the symptomatology and past treatment, and by stating the diagnosis, the social worker affirms the patient's temporary role as being ill. Family members who are either guilt-ridden (for example, thinking they caused the disorder) or denying the gravity of the disorder need to hear that the patient is ill and temporarily incapacitated. The sick role involves valid exemption from certain normal social obligations and responsibilities, recognition of a state that is undesirable and to be overcome with professional help, and acknowledgement of a need for cooperating with treatment and getting well. By defining the patient role, the clinician is helping the patient and family accept a *limited* period of illness, a need for psychiatric help, and a plan for treatment that will include giving up the acute patient role.

Psychoeducational information is then provided regarding the general principles of the treatment plan and is reviewed in the context of symptoms already reported. For instance, if the patient's acute manic symptoms have gone untreated in the past, the benefits of neuroleptic medication during the acute phase of illness would be reviewed, while noting the prophylactic use of lithium even during the symptom-free recovery phase of the illness. While variability in the course of illness is discussed, the social worker communicates to the patient and family that there is evidence for a markedly better prognosis in cases where medication regimes and psychoeducational treatment plans are followed.

The general procedures of the psychoeducational intervention are reviewed at this time, including the following: (a) the patient and family members will be present for all sessions; (b) the focus of the treatment will be on increasing information about and improving coping with the bipolar disorder; (c) sessions will be 1 hour in duration and will take place once a week for the first ten sessions, followed by biweekly sessions.

Identifying Treatment Goals.   Before undertaking the work of resolving the psychosocial problems with which a particular patient and family needs help, these must be clearly identified. After developing an alliance and gaining the patient's and family's understanding of the diagnosis and the rationale for the treatment plan, problems and resistances common to patients with Bipolar Disorder, as well as specific ones stated by the individual patient and family, should be explored.

The patient and family are asked:

> What would you like to gain from this treatment.... What problems have you
> encountered in managing your (your spouse's) bipolar disorder that you would like
> help with?

The patient and family are thus encouraged to articulate problems that will then
be worked on during the midphase of treatment. The authors suggest the following
key areas for exploration in order to identify psychosocial targets for intervention.

The Role of Stress.   Stressors that may have precipitated the most recent episode
or past ones should be identified at this time. The social worker then provides
information regarding the role of stress in triggering symptoms and the role of the
family in helping the patient to minimize and manage stressors. The clinician
guides the exploration of stressors, keeping in mind the two general areas of stress
that have been found to influence treatment course and outcome: (a) the family
members' tendency to respond to the patient with criticism or emotional overinvolvement (high EE) and (b) stressful life events, whether environmental (such
as job change or moving), developmental (such as empty nest) or interpersonal
(such as conflict with spouse or boss).

Early Warning Symptoms.   In reviewing stressors that may have been triggers
for previous episodes, the social worker directs the patient's and family's attention
to the intersection of stress and the identification of early warning symptoms. The
patient and family should be told that the ability to identify early warning signs and
to seek additional help promptly (such as emotional support, problem-solving
assistance, and medication changes) is preventative medicine to ward off a full-
blown episode. The patient and family can be asked,

> In hindsight, what do you notice about any changes or signs of trouble before the last
> episode? . . . Did you (your spouse) seem to need less sleep? Become more energetic
> or active than usual? . . . What happened next?

The patient and family are helped to become conscious of signs and symptoms
that might have previously gone unnoticed. This provides important data to be used
later when problem solving is carried out around prevention of future episodes.

Threats to Treatment Adherence.   A variety of threats to treatment adherence for
both patient and family must be addressed in the early phase of psychoeducational
intervention. This is most commonly expressed as medication noncompliance. The
social work clinician should be aware of common resistances to medication compliance and determine which ones should be targets of intervention in a particular case.
These are as follow:

1. Inadequate information regarding the illness, including symptoms, course, and treatment.
2. Denial of illness, though information and evidence is available.
3. Inadequate social (or family) supports to assist in acceptance and maintenance of the treatment plan.
4. Unpleasurable side effects of lithium.
5. Pleasure of mania.
6. Negative feelings regarding having one's mood controlled by medication.
7. Oppositional or other problematic personality traits.

Depending on the patient's history of medication compliance and willingness to discuss this openly, the clinician may decide to focus further on any of the factors noted in the preceding. For example, if the patient evidences denial of illness or of the impact of the illness on his or her family's life, the social worker might supportively confront the patient's views by reviewing again the history reported by the patient and family in the initial sessions, and by enlisting the family members to share their reactions to those events. If the patient complains of unpleasurable side effects of lithium or does not want to give up the pleasure that some patients experience during a manic episode, the clinician should validate and normalize these feelings and then encourage reality-testing regarding the unpleasurable long-term consequences of mania (such as loss of spouse, loss of job, or other psychosocial results of episodes). If medication side effects are severe enough to result in noncompliance, the patient should be encouraged to discuss them with his or her psychiatrist and explore alternate medication trials. In addition, the client should be helped again to think through possible consequences of acting on the impulse to relieve side effects via stopping medications, and be engaged in problem solving regarding other ways of managing side effects.

At times, comorbid character pathology contributes to noncompliance. In fact, comorbid Axis II pathology is said to occur in approximately 23% of cases of Bipolar Disorder (Carpenter et al., 1995; Charney, Nelson, & Quinlan, 1981). Though character pathology is not resolved by psychoeducational intervention, personality traits that interfere in the patient's treatment can be identified by the social worker. While the treatment of character pathology is beyond the scope of this chapter, the social worker must assess whether comorbid Axis II pathology is operating and attempt to identify any behavioral goals that might be addressed in the next phase of treatment.

An additional complication to case management using a psychoeducational intervention can result from Axis I pathology in the spouse. Documented assortative mating among patients afflicted with affective disorders suggests that it is statistically more likely that the spouses of individuals with affective disorder will themselves have affective disorders, alcohol and substance abuse problems, or other pathologies. The active pathology of the spouse of the bipolar patient thus may have a negative effect on the treatment. If the family member has symptoms that cannot be managed within the psychoeducational intervention, the couple is provided with assistance in seeking appropriate treatment for the spouse.

The initial tasks of family psychoeducational intervention are summarized in Table 14.1. During the midphase of treatment, the social worker trains the patient and family in the use of communication and problem-solving skills, which are then applied to the problem areas identified in the early sessions. While the techniques that follow can be carried out with any patient and family member system, they are presented in terms of the typical case of a patient and spouse dyad.

Communication Skills Training.   The social worker will explain in simple terms the overall ideas and specific steps in marital communication skills. The goal here is to teach the couple the methodology of communication skills so that they can be guided in using them on the problems inherent to coping with Bipolar Disorder. It is hoped that following treatment the couple will spontaneously use these skills by themselves. The communication skills are especially important for couples in which the recognition of affect—especially hypomania or mania and depression—may be deficient in the patient, and the communication of feelings, in general, may be disturbed. For example, patients with hypomanic symptoms often are unaware of their feelings or of how they are being expressed. They may be unaware of their impact on others. Patients who are depressed often elicit anger from others, and reduce self-disclosure and problem-solving behavior with significant others. Spouses of depressed and hypomanic patients may need assistance in communicating their perception of the patient's moods to him or her.

There are four modules that are taught and rehearsed (role-played) with the couple in communication training (see Table 14.2): (a) active listening, (b) expressing positive feelings, (c) expressing negative feelings, and (d) making positive requests. Before teaching the couple the techniques of effective communication (such as eye contact and clarity of statements), the patient and spouse are asked: "How do you feel you do in the area of [active listening, . . .]?" Each partner is asked to comment on how he or she communicates positive feelings, negative feelings, and so forth. Common pitfalls to effective communication are reviewed and the couple's particular strengths and weaknesses are noted. The patient and spouse are commended on their ability to have noticed and reported difficulties in their communication so that they can be worked on.

Table 14.1   Initial Tasks of Family Psychoeducational Intervention

1. Build an alliance via appropriate history gathering, reduction of feelings of blame and guilt, and encouraging ventilation of feelings of burden.
2. Affirm the patient's temporary role as being ill and explain the treatment as dictated by the diagnosis.
3. Identify specific patient and family treatment goals, including: (a) management of stressors that might trigger symptoms; (b) management of early warning symptoms; and (c) management of threats to treatment adherence.

Table 14.2   Communication Skills

Active listening
- Look at the person.
- Attend to what is said.
- Use feedback (nod, uh-huh).
- Ask clarifying questions.
- Check out what you heard.

Expressing negative feelings
- Look at the person.
- Speak firmly.
- Say exactly what they did that upset you.
- Say how it made you feel.
- Suggest how they may prevent this in the future.

Expressing positive feelings
- Look at the person.
- Say exactly what they did that pleased you.
- Say how it made you feel.

Making a positive request
- Look at the person.
- Say exactly what you would like them to do.
- Tell how it would make you feel.

The couple is then given instruction regarding the basic behavioral elements in each of the four areas of communication. Role-playing is carried out in each session. For homework between sessions, the couple is encouraged to practice these skills on specific issues, especially those dealing with Bipolar Disorder, its symptomatology, and its management. The occasions and the manner in which these skills are utilized between sessions should be explored in the next session and, when there are difficulties, these should be used as cues to role-play other approaches.

Introduction of Problem Solving.   After completing communication skills training, the social worker describes the elements in effective problem solving: (a) defining the problem in concrete detail, (b) generating alternative solutions, (c) evaluating alternative solutions, (d) deciding on a most optimal solution, (e) executing that solution, and (f) assessing the outcome. The patient and spouse are told that most couples have areas of strength and weakness with various aspects of the problem-solving process, and are asked to identify areas in which they do well and those in which they have difficulty. For instance, some couples might spontaneously brainstorm possible solutions to a problem, but have marked difficulty in deciding on one solution and implementing it; another couple might be impulsively inclined to implement the first available solution without giving adequate consideration to the range of possibilities and the pros and cons of each. These differences are framed in the context of the individual's personality and problem-solving style. All efforts are praised as attempts to cope, while any negative consequences are noted and utilized as motivations to learn new skills.

The couple is then told to try out the problem-solving method in relation to a relatively minor or simple problem. It can be useful to ask the patient and spouse to assign one of them as a secretary who will write down the problem defined by the couple and record possible solutions. For homework, the couple is told to apply the method again in relation to a relatively easy problem and note the difficulties that arise for review in the next session.

Application of Problem-Solving Skills to Target Areas.   In the following months, the couple will practice problem-solving (and communication) skills in relation to the problems they identified during the early sessions. At this point in the treatment, sessions shift to a biweekly schedule while the couple continues homework assignments between sessions.

Based on review of the literature and personal clinical experience, the authors have formulated the modules for problem solving that are summarized in Table 14.3. They are divided into issues related to coping with the disorder and issues related to daily life. Some of these will have been addressed, in part, in the initial sessions.

In general, the modules relating to coping with the disorder should be covered first, followed by the modules related to daily life. However, the social worker can be flexible and apply the models to fit the individual couple. For example, the social worker may want to deal with the module on coping with suicidal ideation first, if that is an issue for a particular patient. The amount of time that each of these modules will take with a particular couple depends upon the presence or absence of that problem, the coping skills that the couple possesses without treatment, and the general acceptance of the couple of the need to learn and change.

Table 14.3   Modules for Problem Solving

Issues directly related to coping with the disorder
1. Acceptance of the disorder
2. Spouse's support of the patient's compliance with treatment, especially medication
3. Patient's and spouse's recognition of early signs of a recurrence of an episode of illness
4. Ability to distinguish behaviors related to Bipolar Disorder from other undesired behaviors of the patient or spouse
5. Coping with suicidal ideation and behavior
6. Managing relapse

Issues related to daily life
7. Regularity of daily routine
8. Spouse's expectation of patient's current and future role performance
9. Managing stress in the form of daily hassles, life events and role transitions
10. Substance use and abuse
11. Intimacy and sexuality

The relative effort that must be given to the various modules is dictated by the assessment and goals identified at the start of treatment. Some examples of applying the problem-solving skills in relation to these common targets for intervention are presented following.

Differentiating Bipolar Behaviors from Other Behaviors.   While the couple has learned to identify symptoms of mania and depression earlier in the treatment, they also need to learn the typical interactional aspects of the depression and mania, learn to recognize these in their own interactional sequences, and learn to distinguish them from other interactions that may be aversive but are unrelated to the disorder. This recognition of the interactions must precede any problem-solving discussions about how to change or modify such interactional sequences. Typical interactional aspects of depression and mania include the following:

- Oversensitivity and self-preoccupation by the patient
- Lack of responsiveness by the patient or negativity by the patient to spouse support, reassurance, and sympathy
- Inability of the patient to function at normal roles and tasks
- Attempts by the spouse to coax, reassure, become overinvolved, or infantalize the patient
- Critical or hostile behavior by the patient followed by counterattacks by the spouse

Problem-solving can be applied to any of the preceding interactional problems. The social worker should keep in mind the hypothesis that positive symptoms (for example, hallucinations and delusions) may be perceived by the nonpatient spouse as unintentional and involuntary. Thus, the spouse will have little difficulty in attributing the cause of florid positive symptoms to the illness and not to the voluntary control of the patient. In contrast, however, negative symptoms such as social isolation, depression, lack of emotion, and routine or leisure time impairment may be attributed not to the illness, but to an unwillingness of the patient to engage in appropriate behavior. It may be appropriate to again bring out the psychoeducational material on the symptoms of Bipolar Disorder.

Managing Relapse.   Since Bipolar Disorder is a condition that involves multiple episodes, it is quite possible that the patient might experience a symptomatic relapse during the course of the treatment. While it is an important goal of family psychoeducational intervention to reduce the number of relapses, it is quite likely and expectable that in some cases relapse will occur during the treatment, and the therapist (and couple) should face relapse not with total discouragement but with optimal coping. The social worker should not only work with the couple to learn and rehearse coping skills to handle potential relapse well, but should also model an attitude change. Relapse should be expected in a chronic illness. A balance of optimism and realism will lead to optimal coping.

There is a sequence of steps to be taken when relapse (either symptom exacerbation or rehospitalization) occurs. This includes: (a) review of the events leading up to the relapse; (b) positive feedback on the improvement in this process as compared to the marital process described concerning the first episode in the beginning of treatment; (c) reinstatement of patient stabilization through increase in medication, additional support, or hospitalization; and (d) resumption of the sequence of family psychoeducational intervention.

Expectations of the Patient's Current and Future Role Performance.   Helping the spouse verbalize his or her expectations of the patient's current and future social (as a spouse, parent, and social individual in the community) and vocational (at work or as a breadwinner) functioning is critical, as this is often an area that can become a significant stressor. If expectations are unrealistic (either those of the spouse or of the patient), a psychoeducational approach—reviewing with the couple what the patient's diagnosis implies in terms of prognosis—may be sufficient. More frequently, however, the spouse needs to verbalize strong feelings of disappointment, frustration, and sadness, especially in a first-break case.

The patient, too, must mourn prior self-expectations and readjust them realistically. By mutual discussion of feelings interjected with realistic goals, the patient and spouse must come to a mutual image of possible future achievements and adjustments to work and social relations outside the home. Through use of the problem-solving model, the couple is helped to arrive at a reasonable plan.

The tasks of the midphase of family psychoeducational intervention are summarized in Table 14.4. After these tasks have been completed, the clinician will spend one or two sessions reviewing the progress made thus far and clarifying problems for ongoing work by the couple following termination. Discharge plans and the need for aftercare will be discussed.

Individual Psychotherapies

Two individual treatment models currently under investigation deserve mention as alternatives to family intervention and should be considered by the social worker when developing intervention strategies to treat a bipolar patient. Each of these

Table 14.4   Midphase Tasks of Family Psychoeducational Intervention

1. The patient and family are trained in the use of effective communication skills.
2. The patient and family are taught to problem solve effectively.
3. The patient and family are helped to manage the problems related to the disorder, as well as daily life stressors, through use of the communication and problem-solving skills.

psychosocial individual treatments are psychoeducational and behavioral in over-all approach, with similarities and differences in relation to each other and to family psychoeducational intervention, with regard to their foci of attention.

Interpersonal and Social Rhythm Therapy of Bipolar Disorder.

Inter-personal and social rhythm therapy (IP/SRT; Frank et al., 1994) is a psychoeducational treatment for patients with Bipolar Disorder based upon the interpersonal psychotherapy of depression (Klerman, Weissman, Rounsaville, & Chevron, 1984) and the social rhythm stability hypothesis (Ehlers, Kupter, Frank, & Monk, 1993). This hypothesis suggests that the stability of social rhythms (patterns of daily activity and social stimulation) affects the stability of circadian rhythms which, in turn, affects the stability of mood. In other words, disruption of the sleep-wake cycle is viewed as the intervening variable between stress and symptoms. Thus, IP/SRT's primary goal is the regulation of social rhythms and sleep-wake cycles. In addition, interpersonal sources of stress are identified, and the patient is helped to strengthen skills at managing interpersonal stressors, such as conflict and loss (Miklowitz & Frank, in press). Like family psychoeducational intervention, IP/SRT achieves these goals by providing the individual patient with psycho-educational information regarding the role of stress and the disruption of social and circadian rhythms, though it takes this as the primary focus of the treatment. IP/SRT also differs from family intervention in deviating from a behavioral approach by utilizing exploratory techniques to resolve interpersonal problems that leave the patient more vulnerable to disruptions and symptoms.

Cognitive-Behavioral Treatment.

In the tradition of the cognitive-behavioral treatment of depression by Aaron Beck, Basco and Rush (1996) have formulated an individual cognitive-behavioral treatment for patients with Bipolar Disorder. CBT differs from the treatment approaches previously described in its focus on the specific thoughts and behaviors associated with the affective changes inherent to Bipolar Disorder. The patient is educated regarding the *negatively biased* thoughts associated with a depressed mood and *positively biased* ones associated with mania, and is then helped to identify these and apply cognitive restructuring techniques to modify them. Similarly, patients are helped to become aware of the ways in which depressive or manic behaviors are influenced by the cognitive distortions associated with mania or depression. Again, traditional cognitive-behavioral techniques are applied to modify these behaviors.

This treatment approach also addresses the central issues presented in family psychoeducational intervention with similar educational and behavioral treatment strategies, such as providing education about the illness and rationale for specific interventions; providing training in communication and problem-solving skills; facilitating the application of skills to the central problems associated with bipolar disorder; and utilizing homework and in-session behavioral practice to achieve treatment goals.

Scott (1996) has also presented a discussion of the value of *manualized* cognitive-behavioral treatment of clients with Bipolar Disorder, which can be used to promote adjustment to the condition, increase the acceptability of prescribed medications, and reduce symptoms. It is clear that cognitive-behavioral methods afford a promising new psychosocial approach to helping clients with Bipolar Disorder and their families.

REFERENCES

American Psychiatric Association. (1994a). *Diagnostic and statistical manual of mental disorders* (4th ed.). Washington, DC: Author.

American Psychiatric Association. (1994b). Practice guidelines for the treatment of patients with bipolar disorder [December suppl.]. *American Journal of Psychiatry, 141*(12).

Anderson, C. M., Hogarty, G. E., & Reiss, D. S. (1981). The psychoeducational family treatment of schizophrenia. In M. J. Goldstein (Ed.), *New developments in interventions with families of schizophrenics* (pp. 79–94). San Francisco: Jossey-Bass.

Basco, M. R., & Rush, A. J. (1996). *Cognitive-behavioral therapy for bipolar disorder.* New York: Guilford Press.

Brown, G. W., Birley, L. T., & Wing, J. K. (1972). Influence of family life on the course of schizophrenic disorders: A replication. *British Journal of Psychiatry, 121,* 241–258.

Carpenter, D., Clarkin, J. F., Glick, I. D., & Wilner, P. (1995). Personality pathology among married adults with bipolar disorder. *Journal of Affective Disorders, 34,* 269–274.

Charney, D. S., Nelson, J. C., & Quinlan, D. M. (1981). Personality traits and disorder in depression. *American Journal of Psychiatry, 138,* 1601–1604.

Clarkin, J. F., Haas, G. L., & Glick, I. D. (1988a). Inpatient family intervention. In J. F. Clarkin, G. L. Haas, & I. D. Glick (Eds.), *Affective disorders and the family: Assessment and treatment* (pp. 134–152). New York: Guilford Press.

Clarkin, J. F., Haas, G. L., & Glick, I. D. (Eds.). (1988b). *Affective disorders and the family: Assessment and treatment.* New York: Guilford Press.

Clarkin, J. F., Glick, I. D., Haas, G. L., Spencer, J. H., Lewis, A. B., Peyser, J., DeMane, N., Good-Ellis, M., Harris, E., & Lestelle, V. (1990). A randomized clinical trial of inpatient family intervention: V. Results for affective disorders.

Cochran, D. S. (1984). Preventing medical noncompliance in the outpatient treatment of bipolar affective disorders. *Journal of Consulting and Clinical Psychology, 52,* 873–878.

Davenport, Y. B., Ebert, M. H., Adland, M. L., & Goodwin, F. K. (1977). Couples group therapy as an adjunct to lithium maintenance in the manic patients. *American Journal of Orthopsychiatry, 47,* 495–502.

DiMascio, A., Weissman, M. M., Prusoff, B. A., Neu, C., Zwilling, M., & Klerman, G. L. (1979). Differential symptom reduction by drugs and psychotherapy in acute depression. *Archives of General Psychiatry, 36,* 1450–1456.

Ehlers, C. L., Kupfer, D. J., Frank, E., & Monk, T. H. (1993). Biological rhythms and depression: The role of zeitgebers and zeitstorers. *Depression, 1,* 285–293.

Endicott, J., & Spitzer, R. L. (1978). A diagnostic interview: Schedule for Affective Disorders and Schizophrenia. *Archives of General Psychiatry, 35,* 837–844.

Endicott, J., Spitzer, R. L., Fleiss, J., & Cohen, J. (1976). The Global Assessment Scale. *Archives of General Psychiatry, 33,* 766–771.

Falloon, I. R. H., Boyd, J. L., & McGill, C. W. (1982). Family management in the prevention of exacerbations of schizophrenia: A controlled study. *New England Journal of Medicine, 30,* 1438–1440.

First, M. B., Spitzer, R. L., Gibbon, M., & Williams, J. B. W. (1995). *Structured Clinical Interview for DSM-IV Axis I disorders—patient edition (SCID-I/P, Version 2.0).* New York: New York State Psychiatric Institute, Biometrics Research Department.

Fitzgerald, R. G. (1972). Mania as a message: Treatment with family therapy and lithium carbonate. *American Journal of Psychotherapy, 136,* 455–456.

Frances, A., Docherty, J. P., & Kahn, D. A. (1996). The expert consensus guideline series: Treatment of bipolar disorder. *Journal of Clinical Psychiatry, 57* (Suppl. 12A), 1–88.

Frank, E., Kupfer, D. J., Ehlers, C. L., Monk, T. H., Cornes, C., Carter, S., & Frankel, D. (1994). Interpersonal and social rhythm therapy for bipolar disorder: Integrating interpersonal and behavioral approaches. *Behavior Therapist, 17,* 143, 149.

Friedman, A. S. (1975). Interaction of drug therapy with marital therapy in depressed patients. *Archives of General Psychiatry, 32,* 619–637.

Goldstein, M. J. (Ed.) (1982). *New developments in interventions with families of schizophrenics.* San Francisco: Jossey-Bass.

Goodwin, F. K., & Jamison, K. R. (1990). *Manic-depressive illness.* New York: Oxford University Press.

Hirschfeld, R. M. A., & Klerman, G. L. (1979). Personality attributes of affective disorders. *American Journal of Psychiatry, 136,* 67–70.

Jamison, K. R., & Akiskal, H. S. (1983). Medication compliance in patients with bipolar disorder. *Psychiatric Clinics of North America, 6,* 175–192.

Klerman, G. L., Weissman, M. M., Rounsaville, B. J., & Chevron, E. (1984). *Interpersonal psychotherapy of depression.* New York: Basic Books.

Leff, J., Kuipers, L., Berkowitz, R., Eberlein-Vries, R., & Sturgeon, D. (1982). A controlled trial of social intervention in the families of schizophrenic patients. *British Journal of Psychiatry, 141,* 121–134.

Lukoff, D., Nuechterlein, K. H., & Ventura, J. (1986). Manual for expanded Brief Psychiatric Rating Scale (BPRS). *Schizophrenia Bulletin, 12,* 594–602.

McFarlane, W. R., Lukens, E., Link, B., Duushay, R., Deakins, S., Newmark, M., Dunne, E., Horen, B., & Toram, J. (1995). The multiple family group, psychoeducation and maintenance medication in the treatment of schizophrenia. *Archives of General Psychiatry.*

Miklowitz, D., & Frank, E. (in press). New psychotherapies for bipolar disorder. In J. Goldberg & M. Harrow (Eds.), *Bipolar disorder: Clinical course and outcome.* Washington, DC: American Psychiatric Press.

Minuchin, S. (1974) *Families and family therapy.* Cambridge, MA: Harvard University Press.

Platt, S., Weyman, A., Hirsch, S., & Hewett, S. (1978). The Social Behavior Assessment Schedule (SBAS): Rationale, contents, scoring and reliability of a new interview schedule. *Social Psychiatry, 15,* 43–55.

Rounsaville, B. J., Weissman, M. M., Prusoff, B. A., & Herceg-Baron, R. L. (1979). Marital disputes and treatment outcome in depressed women. *Comprehensive Psychiatry, 20,* 483–490.

Scott, J. (1996). The role of cognitive behaviour therapy in bipolar disorder. *Behavioural and Cognitive Psychotherapy, 24,* 195–208.

Shahir, S. A., Volkmar, F. R., Bacon, S., & Pfefferbaum, A. (1979). Group psychotherapy as an adjunct to lithium maintenance. *American Journal of Psychiatry, 136,* 455–456.

Snyder, D. K., Willis, R. M., & Keiser, T. W. (1979). Empirical validation of the Marital Satisfaction Inventory: An acturial approach. *Journal of Consulting and Clinical Psychology, 49,* 262–268.

Vaughn, C. E., & Leff, J. P. (1976). The influences of family and social factors on the course of psychiatric illness. *British Journal of Psychiatry, 129,* 125–137.

Weissman, M. M., Myers, J. K., & Thompson, W. D. (1981). Depression and its treatment in a U.S. urban community, 1975–1976. *Archives of General Psychiatry, 38,* 417–421.

Weissman, M. M., Prusoff, B. A., DiMascio, A., Neu, C., Goklaney, N., & Klerman, G. L. (1979). The efficacy of drugs and psychotherapy in treatment of acute depressive episodes. *American Journal of Psychiatry, 136,* 555–558.

Weissman, M. M., & Sholomskas, D. (1982). The assessment of social adjustment by the clinician, the patient, and the family. In E. I. Burdock, A. Sudilovsky, & A. Gershon (Eds.), *The behavior of psychiatric patients: Quantitative techniques for evaluation* (pp. 177–209). New York: Marcel Dekker.

PART V

Anxiety Disorders

Chapter 15

PANIC DISORDER AND AGORAPHOBIA

Joseph A. Himle
Daniel J. Fischer

OVERVIEW

The *Diagnostic and Statistical Manual of Mental Disorders, Fourth Edition* (*DSM-IV;* American Psychiatric Association [APA], 1994) defines a *panic attack* as a discrete period of intense fear or discomfort, in which 4 of a list of 13 symptoms develop abruptly and reach a peak within 10 minutes of the onset of the episode. Panic attack symptoms include palpitating, pounding, or racing heart; sweating; trembling or shaking; shortness of breath or smothering; feeling of choking; chest pain or discomfort; feeling dizzy, unsteady, lightheaded, or faint; derealization or depersonalization; fear of losing control or going crazy; fear of dying; numbness or tingling sensations; and chills or hot flushes. *DSM-IV* describes *Panic Disorder* as recurrent, unexpected, panic attacks where at least one attack is followed by 1 month (or more) of at least one of the following symptoms: persistent concern about having additional attacks, worry about the implications of the attack or its consequences, or a significant change in behavior related to the attacks. There are two types of Panic Disorder, *Panic Disorder without Agoraphobia* and *Panic Disorder with Agoraphobia.*

Agoraphobia is a condition often related to Panic Disorder and is defined in *DSM-IV* as anxiety about being in places or situations from which escape might be difficult (or embarrassing) or in which help may not be available, in the event of having a panic attack or experiencing paniclike symptoms. Agoraphobic fears may include anxiety about being outside the home alone; being in a crowd or standing in a line; being on a bridge; traveling in a bus, train, or automobile; visiting a mall or grocery store; going to the theater; eating in a restaurant; or visiting other places where panic attacks have previously occurred. Formally, the diagnosis of Agoraphobia is present in two varieties, *Panic Disorder with Agoraphobia* and *Agoraphobia without History of Panic Disorder.*

Panic Disorder and agoraphobia are both relatively common conditions. According to the National Comorbidity Survey, Panic Disorder without Agoraphobia is present in about 2% of the population, whereas Panic Disorder with Agoraphobia is somewhat less common, with 1.5% of the general population meeting diagnostic criteria (all rates are for lifetime prevalence; Eaton, Kessler, Wittchen, & Magee, 1994). Agoraphobia without Panic Disorder is the most common of this group of anxiety disorders (5.2%; Eaton et al., 1994; Magee, Eaton, Wittchen, McGonagle, & Kessler, 1996). As with most psychiatric disorders, a range of impairment is noted among persons meeting criteria for agoraphobia and Panic Disorder. However, it is clear that when Panic Disorder and agoraphobia are both present, impairment is often substantial (Magee et al., 1996).

The average age of onset for Panic Disorder and agoraphobia has consistently ranged from the mid- to late-20s across studies from several treatment centers and in epidemiological surveys (Magee, et al., 1996; Thyer, Himle, Curtis, Cameron, & Nesse, 1985; Ost, 1987a). Females, compared to males, are roughly twice as likely to meet criteria for Panic Disorder (0.4% of males, 1% of females), Panic Disorder with Agoraphobia (0.4% of males, 1% of females), and Agoraphobia without History of Panic Disorder (1% of males, 2.1% of females; prevalence rates based on month prior to interview; Eaton et al., 1994; McGee et al., 1996). Several disorders commonly cooccur with Panic Disorder and agoraphobia. Depression is often present among patients with panic attacks and agoraphobia (McGee et al., 1996; Robins, Locke, & Regier, 1991). Panic Disorder and agoraphobia also often coexist with other anxiety disorders, such as Simple Phobia and Social Phobia (McGee et al., 1996). Finally, Alcohol Abuse and Alcohol Dependence are common among subjects meeting criteria for Panic Disorder with Agoraphobia and Panic Disorder but not among those patients meeting criteria for Agoraphobia without Panic Disorder (Himle & Hill, 1991; Thyer, McNeece & Miller, 1987; Thyer, Parrish, Himle, Cameron, Curtis, & Nesse, 1986).

Two general treatment strategies, medication and cognitive-behavioral therapy, have been shown to be effective in the treatment of Panic Disorder and agoraphobia. Several medications, including tricyclic antidepressants (Mavissakalian, 1990), monoamine oxidase inhibitors (Sheehan, Ballenger, & Jacobsen; 1980); selective serotonin reuptake inhibitors (Den Boer & Westenberg, 1988), and the high-potency benzodiazapine, alprazolam (Ballenger et al., 1988) have been shown to be effective in reducing the frequency and intensity of panic attacks. An extensive amount of research has been conducted that clearly demonstrates the effectiveness of behavioral therapies in reducing agoraphobic avoidance (see Barlow, 1988; Thyer, 1987a). These behavioral treatments involve prolonged and repetitive exposures to agoraphobic situations. More recently, various cognitive and behavioral strategies have been developed that have been shown to significantly reduce the frequency and severity of panic attacks (Barlow, Craske, Cerny, & Klosko, 1989). Other psychosocial interventions have not been empirically tested in the treatment of Panic Disorder and agoraphobia and therefore are not reviewed in this chapter. It is the purpose of this chapter to describe the empirically based psychosocial treatments of Panic Disorder and agoraphobia. Each of the empirical treatments described in this chapter would generally be identified as behavioral or cognitive treatments.

ASSESSMENT METHODS

At the most basic level, the task of the social worker evaluating a person suffering from Panic Disorder or agoraphobia involves developing an understanding of three main areas: (a) the nature of the panic symptoms, (b) the extent of phobic avoidance, and (c) the triggering events and circumstances that elicit panic attacks and avoidance.

Clinical Interviews

Structured clinical interviews developed by social workers and others, such as the Structured Clinical Interview for *DSM-IV* (SCID; First, Spitzer, Gibbon, & Williams, 1995) and the Anxiety Disorders Interview Schedule—Revised (ADIS-R; Di Nardo et al., 1985), provide the social worker with a checklist of panic attack symptoms and questions regarding phobic avoidance that can aid the clinician in establishing the diagnosis of Panic Disorder and agoraphobia. The ADIS-R also provides information to the social worker regarding the onset, course, and degree of interference in the client's functioning of the symptoms, as well as an inventory of thoughts related to panic attacks. Beyond the structured interview, a detailed assessment of phobic avoidance is conducted. In this assessment, the social worker and the client review situations that the client avoids, and an attempt is made to place these situations in a hierarchy progressing from easier to more difficult. It is also important to gather information on other variables that trigger panic and avoidance, including distorted thinking, physiological sensations, interpersonal interactions, and affective states. In addition, it is important that the social worker discuss the impact of the client's panic attacks and avoidant behavior on his or her work life, family functioning, and romantic relationships.

As in the assessment of any condition, the clinical interview should include a detailed review of the onset and course of the presenting complaint, a comprehensive review of other comorbid psychiatric conditions, and a thorough investigation of the patient's medical, family, and social history.

Self-Report Measures

Self-rating inventories have been developed to assess the symptoms present during a panic attack, including some designed to assess fear of panic symptoms, such as the Anxiety Sensitivity Index (Peterson & Reiss, 1987) and the Body Sensations Questionnaire (Chambless, Caputo, Bright, & Gallagher, 1984). In addition, panic attack diaries have been developed to record panic frequency and symptoms present during attacks (Rapee, Craske, & Barlow, 1990). Self-report scales used to measure the extent of phobic avoidance include the Fear Questionnaire (Marks & Mathews, 1979), the Agoraphobia Scale (Ost, 1990), and the Mobility Inventory for Agoraphobia (Chambless, Caputo, Jasin, Gracely, & Williams, 1985).

Behavioral Avoidance Test

An additional method of assessing phobic behavior is the behavioral avoidance test (Barlow, O'Brien, & Last, 1984; Williams & Rappoport, 1983). During the behavioral avoidance test, clients are accompanied by the social worker and are instructed to approach a predetermined series of naturalistic situations of increasing difficulty, such as visiting a mall, going to church, or eating at a restaurant. Prior to the behavioral avoidance test, the situations to be encountered are determined using one of two methods. The first method involves the social worker and the client constructing an individualized hierarchy of feared situations together. The second method involves the use of a predetermined series of challenging situations created by the social worker for use with several agoraphobic patients. During the behavioral avoidance test, the social worker records whether the client refuses the task (avoidance), partially completes the task (escape), or successfully completes the task. In addition, the client also rates the degree of anxiety he or she experiences upon encountering each situation.

EFFECTIVE INTERVENTIONS

Real-Life Exposure to External Cues

Agoraphobic behavior includes the avoidance of a variety of situations and circumstances that serve as triggers to panic and extreme anxiety. Real-life exposure therapy is designed to reduce anxiety and avoidance by systematically asking clients to confront feared situations or circumstances until the fear subsides. Marks (1987a) suggests that in order to ensure optimal effectiveness, exposure should be repeated and prolonged, and the client should be encouraged to focus his or her attention on the phobic stimulus. The initial task in conducting successful exposure treatment is to have the client identify situational triggers that are avoided as well as those triggers that elicit anxiety but are not avoided. Once this is completed, the situations are arranged in a hierarchical fashion from least feared to most feared. Clients are taught to rate and monitor the degree of anxiety they experience using a subjective units of distress scale (SUDS; Wolpe, 1973). A SUDS scale is typically a 100-point scale, with 0 representing calm and 100 representing extreme anxiety. This simple self-report method of quantifying subjective anxiety has been shown to correlate reasonably well with physiological indices of fear, such as heart rate and skin temperature (see Thyer, Papsdorf, Davis, & Vallecorsa, 1984). Each item on the graded hierarchy is rated with this scale by the client. In practice, clients may find it easier to generate their hierarchy of feared situations by listing one item at time and rating its anxiety, without initially attempting to list items hierarchically. Later, the feared situations can be arranged in ascending order.

Once a fear hierarchy has been established, clients are given exposure assignments in which they confront the situations that they fear and avoid. Exposure assignments are determined in a collaborative effort between the client and social worker, with the client ultimately dictating the pace of the exposure tasks. As previously mentioned, the keys to effective exposure are that trials must be frequent and prolonged, with the ideal being daily practice totaling at least 90 minutes per day (Marks, 1987a). The more often clients practice, the more rapidly they will improve. Exposure trials are designed to purposefully increase and sustain the client's level of anxiety, until anxiety decreases naturally. This process, whereby an individual becomes less anxious after prolonged contact with fearful stimuli, is known as *habituation*. Movement from one major item in the hierarchy to the next (for example, bus rides to shopping malls) is typically done after the client has mastered the previous step. During exposure trials, clients are asked to focus their attention on the task at hand, as research has shown that distraction reduces the therapeutic effect of exposure (Sartory, Rachman, & Grey, 1982). It is not uncommon for clients to report that they have attempted their own version of real-life exposure without success. Common reasons for their failure include not fully focusing their attention on the exposure task or terminating exposure prematurely.

A common method of real-life exposure involves exposure trials conducted with the social worker present, supplemented by daily homework assignments that are carried out by the client between sessions. However, recent research suggests that clients can also progress well by conducting all of their exposure sessions without the social worker. This can be achieved by using therapy sessions to develop assignments that the client can carry out alone, or the client can utilize self-help books or computer-generated instruction without direct assistance by a therapist (Ghosh & Marks, 1987). Whichever treatment method is selected, exposure to external cues is of critical importance in reducing agoraphobic fear and avoidance. Additional clinical descriptions of the conduct of exposure therapy can be found in the social work literature (e.g., Thyer, 1983, 1985).

Exposure to Internal Cues

Beyond repetitive exposure to external stimuli that prompt panic attacks, researchers (Barlow et al., 1989) have demonstrated that exposure to internal body sensations associated with panic states is also of therapeutic benefit in the treatment of Panic Disorder. Barlow and Cerny (1988) suggest that after certain internal states (for example, dizziness, increased heart rate, and shortness of breath) have been associated with panic attacks, these sensations themselves can serve as conditioned triggers of panic episodes. Many clients with Panic Disorder closely scrutinize internal bodily sensations and often avoid activities that would elicit feelings associated with panic.

Using methods similar to those of treatment programs aimed at external panic triggers, Barlow and Cerny (1988) were first to develop a treatment program aimed at exposing patients in a gradual and repetitive manner to internal sensations (for example, running in place, whirling about, hyperventilating, confronting hot places, and staring at one's hand or at a spot on a wall). Clients are thought to habituate to these exercises in a manner similar to that seen during therapeutic exposure to external cues. The individual internal cue exposure exercises can be combined (for example, spinning about while hyperventilating and running in place) after clients become comfortable confronting one cue at a time.

Internal cue exposures are often initiated in the social worker's office and then assigned to the client as homework. Initially, it is not uncommon for clients to experience panic attacks when practicing their internal cue exercises. These attacks can be alarming to both the client and the therapist. However, with continued practice, attacks become less frequent and decrease in severity, both in the office and in the natural environment. In the authors' experience, internal cue exposure sessions need to be conducted somewhat differently than exposure sessions aimed at external triggers. Rarely can clients hyperventilate, run in place, and whirl about for hours at a time, as is often expected for sessions at the mall or theater. Instead, clients can be asked to repeatedly practice shorter trials of exposure with accompanying rest periods. In the authors' clinic, patients are typically asked to practice their internal cue exposures three times daily in 15-minute sessions. These exercises are often added to longer external cue exposure sessions in order to meet the general guideline of 1.5 to 2 hours of daily exposure.

In determining which internal cue exercises to select, the general rule of focusing on the *first* and the *worst* applies well here. The authors suggest that patients target those symptoms that they notice first during a panic attack and those that are most frightening. Although each patient presents a symptom profile that is somewhat different, certain exercises appear to be especially valuable. In the authors' experience, voluntary hyperventilation is an especially challenging exercise for many patients and mastery over it often results in substantial improvement. Asking the client to breathe rapidly and deeply through the mouth at a rate of about one breath per second is all that is required. Also of particular interest and importance is the production of the feelings of unreality that are common during panic attacks. Several exercises, such as staring at one's hand or a point on a wall, or staring at a light and attempting to read, can trigger feelings of unreality similar to those experienced during naturally occurring panic attacks. Once this unreality trigger has been identified, repetitive exposure can begin.

It is important to note that although internal cue exposure may elicit anxiety and often proves helpful, not all clients with panic disorders respond to these exercises with feelings of anxiety. In fact, some clients find that physical exertion actually reduces their feelings of panic. It is advised that social workers present the technique of exposure to internal cues to clients as a method that may or may not be used, depending on whether the exercises prompt anxiety.

Cognitive Therapy

A cognitive model of Panic Disorder has been described, in which inappropriate and catastrophic thinking exacerbates the physiological symptoms present during panic attacks (Clark, 1986). Ottaviani & Beck (1987) found that patients often report thoughts that they are about to die, collapse, go crazy, lose control, or have a heart attack during panic attacks. These self-statements are thought to maintain a positive feedback loop where disordered thinking exacerbates physical symptoms, which leads to further catastrophic misinterpretations of bodily sensations, followed by further worsening of physical symptoms. As a result, clients often pay close attention to internal sensations and external situations previously associated with panic attacks and follow these triggers with inaccurate thinking. Cognitive therapy for Panic Disorder involves the social worker and the client in a collaborative relationship to address the accuracy of these thoughts and to replace them with more appropriate interpretations of bodily sensations.

Clearly, one source of information that can be used to assess the accuracy of a client's thinking during a panic attack is the client's own history. By the time most clients seek therapy for panic disorder, they have already experienced several attacks of varying severity. Most clients report catastrophic thinking of one sort or another (heart attack, stroke, death, or going crazy) during these attacks. Almost by definition, the feared consequences have not come to pass. The social worker can gently question patients and help them to recount how often they have had panic attacks, erroneously predicted disaster, yet somehow escaped it. Clients can use this information to counter thoughts about panic attacks causing catastrophe. A second source of information that the social worker can utilize is knowledge about other clients with Panic Disorder. The social worker can educate the client about other panic patients he or she has seen, as well as about clients at other centers, informing the client of the high prevalence of predicted catastrophe and the near absence of truly deleterious consequences. Another source of information that can aid the client in countering irrational thinking is information about the physiology of panic attacks. Clients who worry about fainting can be informed that heart rate and blood pressure are higher during panic attacks, whereas fainting requires low heart rate and blood pressure. Clients who worry about smothering, as well as those who experience dizziness or tingling in the extremities, can be instructed in the physiology of hyperventilation and the symptoms it typically produces. Clients can be instructed in the causes of heart attacks and how their efforts to prevent them during panic attacks (fleeing, having a drink of water, or distraction) would have no effect if a real heart attack were on the way.

A fourth source of information is often referred to as a *behavioral test*. It is sometimes puzzling to clinicians why clients maintain the belief that terrible consequences will come from panic attacks when most clients seem to have had several opportunities to discover that panic attacks are not harmful. In fact, most clients do not allow themselves to learn that panic attacks do *not* lead to catastrophe because they engage in several behaviors (distraction, fleeing, taking a pill, taking a drink of water, or supporting themselves) to protect themselves from disaster. Behavioral tests involve asking clients to experience entire attacks from start to finish without engaging in any such rescuing behaviors. This technique allows the client to discover that the panic attack only *seems* to signal true danger. Repetitive behavioral tests can sometimes involve the addition of deliberate attempts to aggravate panic (for example, running in place during a panic attack) in order to build an even more convincing argument that panic attacks will not lead to catastrophic consequences. The four sources of information previously described can be used by the client and the social worker to argue back against the negative thoughts often present during attacks and, thus, reduce the frequency and severity of the episodes.

Given the high prevalence of Panic Disorder and agoraphobia, the potential exists to have a number of clients in treatment at the same time. This suggests the possible role of therapy and support groups in the provision of treatment. Both the psychoeducational aspects of behavior therapy and the exposure treatment elements lend themselves well to delivery in small groups. The segue into supportive therapy is obvious. Often, clients spontaneously develop phone networks to support each other's homework efforts, and they may pair themselves up to practice difficult exposure tasks together, independent of time spent with the social worker. Thyer (1987b) describes the conduct of such groups for clients with these conditions.

Anxiety Management Techniques

When a person experiences a panic attack, the anxiety experienced involves three response classes: (a) a behavioral response (escape or avoidance), (b) a cognitive response (patterns of catastrophic thinking), and (c) a physiological response (heart palpitations, dizziness, shortness of breath, and muscle tension). As has been discussed, behavioral strategies are helpful in ameliorating escape and avoidance patterns through the use of frequent and prolonged exposure to feared situations or body sensations. Cognitive restructuring is helpful in reducing anxiety by assisting clients in developing more accurate thinking about the physiological symptoms of panic. A third approach is to help clients with panic attacks learn strategies to manage and control the physiological component of their anxiety. *Applied relaxation* and *breathing control training* are two effective methods clients can use to manage the physiological symptoms of panic.

Applied relaxation training is a treatment devised by Ost (1987b) that involves teaching clients a graded method of relaxation using several steps. The initial step (session 1) in applied relaxation is designed to increase the client's awareness of the specific early signs of arousal and panic, which then serve as cues for relaxation. Awareness is increased by having clients keep a daily record of their panic attacks. The panic diary record includes situations where panic attacks occurred, physiological symptoms experienced, and a rating of panic intensity.

The second step (sessions 2 and 3) involves instructing clients in a progressive relaxation technique in which initial muscle tension is produced, followed by muscle relaxation. Muscle groups are tensed and relaxed, beginning with the hands and progressing through the arms, shoulders, face, neck, trunk, back, and down through the legs and feet. By alternating tension with relaxation, clients are taught to distinguish the differences between a state of relaxation and muscle tension. Clients are instructed to rate their level of tension before and after the procedure using a 0 to 100 scale. Tension is typically applied for 5 to 10 seconds, followed by 10 to 15 seconds of relaxation.

The short version of progressive relaxation, release only, is introduced during session 4. The goal of this stage is to further decrease the amount of time it takes to relax by omitting the tension portion of the exercise. The social worker instructs the client to relax each muscle group, using a progression similar to that established during the tension-and-release phase. Muscle tension is used only if the client has difficulty relaxing a particular muscle group.

Cue-controlled or conditioned relaxation, which further reduces the time it takes for the client to achieve a state of relaxation, is introduced in session 5. This stage focuses on establishing a conditioned relationship between the self-instruction *relax* and a state of increased relaxation. The session begins by having the client use release-only relaxation until a satisfactory level of relaxation is achieved. Following the client's breathing pattern, the social worker gives verbal cues to "Inhale," and then, just before the client exhales, the social worker gives the verbal cue, "Relax." Eventually, the client is instructed to continue this breathing pattern on his or her own, replacing the social worker's verbal cues with self-generated statements.

Differential relaxation is introduced in session 6 and continued in session 7. The primary goal of this technique is to teach the client to relax while engaged in everyday activities. Session 6 starts with the client using cue-controlled relaxation while sitting comfortably in a chair or couch. The client is then instructed to move parts of the body while continuing to relax. Once the client has practiced these body movements while sitting in a comfortable chair, these same movements are practiced while sitting at a desk, standing, and, eventually, while walking. By the end of this phase of treatment, it is hoped that clients will be able to relax in 60 to 90 seconds.

Sessions 8 and 9 are used to develop and practice rapid relaxation. Rapid relaxation, which further reduces the amount of time (20 to 30 seconds) it takes for the patient to relax, teaches patients how to relax in stressful but nonpanic situations. In rapid relaxation, the client and social worker identify a series of cues (for example, making a telephone call or looking at a watch) that remind the patient to relax. When relaxing, the client is taught to take one to three deep breaths, then to think *relax* before exhaling, all the while scanning the body for tension and trying to relax as much as possible.

Finally, sessions 10, 11, and 12 are used for application training in natural situations and for maintenance instruction. Application training involves teaching the client to apply the learned relaxation skills in stressful, panic-inducing situations. Practice usually involves frequent but brief (10 to 15 minutes) exposure to a variety of anxiety-producing stimuli and applying relaxation at the first signs of arousal. Clients are encouraged to scan their bodies for tension at least once daily and to practice differential or rapid relaxation regularly in order to maintain these skills. During each phase of applied relaxation training, clients are asked to practice the relaxation techniques at home between sessions.

A second commonly used anxiety-management procedure for Panic Disorder is breathing retraining. Barlow and Cerny (1988) describe a breathing control technique that is useful as a method of managing initial symptoms associated with panic attacks, as well as of controlling symptoms during the attacks themselves. The breathing control program involves instructing clients in slow-paced respirations coupled with a meditational counting technique to time the breathing frequency. Clients are instructed to count during each inhalation and to say the word *relax* to themselves when exhaling. The goal of this technique is to gradually slow the client's respiratory rate to about 3 seconds devoted to inhalation and 3 seconds to exhalation. This practice limits breathing to around 10 breaths per minute, making it difficult to hyperventilate. Often, clients will mistakenly accelerate their breathing and gasp in large amounts of air as they begin to practice the breathing control technique. However, with practice, clients can learn to slow their counting, take in normal-volume breaths, and, thus, appropriately regulate their ventilation.

Cognitive-Behavioral Therapies

To date, dozens of controlled studies have documented the efficacy of repetitive and prolonged exposure to agoraphobic situations (see Barlow, 1988; Marks, 1987a). Most studies involve treatment where the therapist is present during real-life exposure sessions or the social worker guides exposure homework exercises from the office without accompanying the client in the field. In addition, Ghosh and Marks (1987) demonstrated that many agoraphobics can also benefit from self-exposure therapy guided by computer-generated exposure instructions or a self-help exposure therapy book. However, Marks (1987b) notes that some clients require more guidance than others, at times making therapist-assisted exposure sessions necessary, provided that the social worker gradually withdraws, leaving the client to conduct exposure on his or her own. Clearly, it is beyond the scope of this chapter to review in detail the numerous studies documenting the benefits of exposure therapy, but it is important to note that this technique has limitations. Jansson and Ost (1982) reviewed several studies and found the average dropout rate for exposure treatment to be 12%. A second limitation is that approximately 30% to 40% of agoraphobic patients who complete exposure treatment fail to gain benefit (Barlow, 1988, p. 409). Finally, exposure to agoraphobic situations does not apply for those panic disorder patients without agoraphobia.

Beyond studies examining the effectiveness of external cue exposure in the treatment of agoraphobia, a body of recent research has demonstrated the efficacy of other cognitive-behavioral strategies that target panic attacks directly. Barlow and colleagues (Barlow et al., 1989) studied a group of clients with Panic Disorder who were assigned to one of four groups: (a) progressive muscle relaxation, (b) panic control treatment (includes internal cue exposure and cognitive restructuring), (c) panic control treatment and relaxation, and (d) wait list (control group). Each active treatment was superior to the wait-list control group. Treatments that included panic control treatment were superior to relaxation therapy alone. The superiority of the panic control treatment was also demonstrated at up to 2 years post treatment (Craske, Brown, & Barlow, 1991). In another study, Clark and colleagues (Clark et al., 1994) compared the effects of cognitive restructuring, applied relaxation (following Ost, 1987b), imipramine, or wait-list control among a group of clients with Panic Disorder. All three treatment conditions included weekly self-conducted external cue exposure. Cognitive therapy was superior to all other treatment conditions in reducing panic attacks and avoidance at both the end of treatment and at 1-year follow-up. Imipramine and applied relaxation, although less effective than cognitive restructuring, were more helpful than the wait-list control group. In contrast, Ost and associates (Ost, Westling, & Hellstrom, 1993), found similar rates of improvement when comparing applied relaxation, real-life external cue exposure, and cognitive therapy in a group of Panic Disorder patients. Like previous studies, all clients also performed self-conducted external cue exposure exercises, making it impossible to determine how effective these treatments would be without this component. However, in a study of panic disordered patients without agoraphobia where external exposure was not used, Ost and Wesling (1994) also found essentially equal efficacy for cognitive therapy and applied relaxation. Beck, Stanley, Baldwin, Deagle, and Averill (1994) investigated the differential effects of relaxation therapy (a version including progressive muscle relaxation and controlled breathing) and cognitive therapy and found both therapeutic conditions to be helpful. However, the cognitive therapy group exceeded the relaxation group in the percentage of clients classified as treatment responders.

Evaluating the efficacy of the technique of exposure to internal cues is difficult, since most studies of cognitive-behavioral methods used in treating Panic Disorder combine this technique in a package including other methods (Barlow et al., 1989). However, preliminary research attempting to separate the relative effects of various cognitive-behavioral strategies used in treating Panic Disorder suggests that internal cue exposure exercises enhance outcome when combined with other cognitive-behavioral methods (Margraf, Barlow, Clark, & Telch, 1993).

The preceding findings related to the efficacy of various cognitive-behavioral treatments reveal inconsistencies with regard to which treatments are superior in reducing panic attacks. These inconsistencies, coupled with the finding that all active treatments studied appear to be helpful, leads one to question whether the techniques themselves were important in achieving change. It is possible that the positive outcomes achieved were related mainly to nonspecific factors associated with simply participating in a credible treatment. Two studies address this issue. Shear and colleagues (Shear, Pilkonis, Cloitre, & Leon, 1994) found that a *nonprescriptive* treatment involving mainly reflective listening and support was essentially equal in effectiveness to a cognitive-behavioral treatment that included cognitive restructuring, breathing retraining, muscle relaxation, and exposure to internal and external cues. However, Craske, Maidenberg, and Bystrinsky (1995) found an opposite result comparing nondirective supportive therapy (modeled after Shear et al., 1994) and cognitive-behavioral therapy. In this study, those who received cognitive-behavioral therapy worried less about their panic attacks, experienced fewer agoraphobic symptoms, and were twice as likely to report being panic-free, compared to nondirective patients. These contrasting results leave the specificity of cognitive-behavioral therapy for Panic Disorder somewhat in doubt and open for further study.

CONCLUSIONS

To the benefit of the many who suffer from Panic Disorder and agoraphobia, a substantial and growing body of empirical research exists to guide the social worker in selecting treatment approaches. The dilemma that presents itself to the social worker is how to select from the two major treatment approaches, medication and cognitive-behavioral therapy. At times, the decision is simple—the client refuses either medication or cognitive-behavioral treatment, leaving the social worker to begin what was not ruled out by the client. More often, the client leaves it up to the social worker to decide what is best. The research literature does not give the social worker a clear choice between the two major treatments, since studies have not indicated that one treatment is clearly superior to the other (Black, Wesner, Bowers, & Gabel, 1993; Klosko, Barlow, Tassinari, & Cerny, 1990; Mavissakalian, 1989). One guideline for treatment selection that is available to the social worker is the use of antidepressant medications (those with antipanic benefits) when the client suffers from significant comorbid depression. Cognitive-behavioral treatments typically require the client to expend a substantial amount of effort, which is sometimes very difficult for clients with severe depression. Clinical experience suggests that antidepressant medications can be helpful in improving mood and, consequently, increasing the likelihood that clients will be able to complete their cognitive-behavioral assignments.

The standard practice in the authors' clinic is to encourage all patients to participate in either group or individual cognitive-behavioral therapy, even if they wish to use medication. Part of the reasoning behind this practice is that most patients will likely wish to stop their medication at some point, either out of necessity (for example, pregnancy) or preference. In addition, a limited amount of research suggests that clients will have greater success discontinuing medication if they have also participated in cognitive-behavioral therapy (Otto, Pollack, Meltzer-Brody, & Rosenbaum, 1992; Spiegel, Bruce, Gregg, & Nuzzarello, 1994). Another reason for encouraging clients taking medication to also participate in cognitive-behavioral therapy is that combined medication and cognitive-behavioral treatment may be superior to medication alone (Mavissakalian, 1990). The final reason for encouraging participation in cognitive-behavioral therapy is that gains made in treatment are often maintained, whereas relapse is common when medication is used alone (Marks, 1987b). One problem with medication treatments for panic is that the risk of unpleasant side effects is high, and serious side effects are not uncommon. Relapse (the return of panic attacks) upon the discontinuation of antipanic medication is high, so in one sense pharmacotherapy is palliative, not curative. Despite these problems, it remains clear that medication can play a valuable role in the treatment of clients with Panic Disorder and agoraphobia. A thorough familiarity with contemporary developments in the pharmacotherapy of these problems is necessary for clinical social workers to be effective practitioners.

REFERENCES

American Psychiatric Association. (1994). *The diagnostic and statistical manual of mental disorders* (4th ed.). Washington, DC: Author.

Ballenger, J. C., Burrows, G., DuPont, R. L., Lesser, I. M., Noyes, R., Pecknold, J. C., Rifkin, A. & Swinson, R. P. (1988). Alprazolam in panic disorder and agoraphobia: Results from a multicenter trial: 1. Efficacy in short-term treatment. *Archives of General Psychiatry, 45,* 413–422.

Barlow, D. H. (1988). *Anxiety and its disorders.* New York: Guilford Press.

Barlow, D. H., & Cerny, J. A. (1988). *Psychological treatment of panic.* New York: Guilford Press.

Barlow, D. H., Craske, M. G., Cerny, J. A., & Klosko, J. S. (1989). Behavioral treatment of panic disorder. *Behavior Therapy, 20,* 261–282.

Barlow, D. H., O'Brien, G. T., & Last, C. G. (1984). Couples treatment of agoraphobia. *Behavior Therapy, 15,* 41–58.

Beck, J. G., Stanley, M. A., Baldwin, L. E., Deagle, E. A., & Averill, P. M. (1994). A comparison of cognitive therapy and relaxation training for panic disorder. *Journal of Consulting and Clinical Psychology, 62,* 818–826.

Black, D. W., Wesner, R., Bowers, W., & Gabel, J. (1993). A comparison of fluvoxamine, cognitive therapy, and placebo in the treatment of panic disorder. *Archives of General Psychiatry, 50,* 44–50.

Chambless, D. L., Caputo, G. C., Bright, P., & Gallagher, R. (1984). Assessment of fear in agoraphobics: The Body Sensations Questionnaire and the Agoraphobic Cognitions Questionnaire. *Journal of Consulting and Clinical Psychology, 52,* 1090–1097.

Chambless, D. L., Caputo, G. C., Jasin, S. E., Gracely, E. J., & Williams, C. (1985). The Mobility Inventory for Agoraphobia. *Behaviour Research and Therapy, 23,* 33–44.

Clark, D. M. (1986). A cognitive approach to panic. *Behaviour Research and Therapy, 24,* 461–470.

Clark, D. M., Salkovskis, P. M., Hackmann, A., Middleton, H., Anastasiades, P., & Gelder, M. (1994). A comparison of cognitive therapy, applied relaxation, and imipramine in the treatment of panic disorder. *British Journal of Psychiatry, 164,* 759–769.

Craske, M. G., Brown, T. A., & Barlow, D. H. (1991). Behavioral treatment of panic disorder: A two year follow-up. *Behavior Therapy, 22,* 289–304.

Craske, M. G., Maidenberg, E., & Bystrintsky, A. (1995). Brief cognitive behavioral versus nondirective therapy for panic disorder. *Journal of Behavior Therapy and Experimental Psychiatry, 26,* 113–120.

Den Boer, J. A. & Westenberg, H. G. M. (1988). The effect of serotonin and noradrealine uptake inhibitor in panic disorder: A double blind comparative study with fluvoxamine and maprotiline. *International Journal of Clinical Psychopharmacology, 3,* 59–74.

Di Nardo, P. A., Barlow, D. H., Cerny, J., Bermilyea, B. B., Himadi, W., & Waddell, M. (1985). Anxiety disorders interview schedule—revised (AIDS-R). Albany: State University of New York, Phobia and Anxiety Disorders Clinic.

Eaton, W. W., Kessler, R. C., Wittchen, H., & Magee, W. J. (1994). Panic and panic disorder in the United States. *American Journal of Psychiatry, 151,* 413–420.

First, M. B., Spitzer, R. L., Gibbon, M., & Williams, J. B. (1995). *Structured Clinical Interview for DSM-IV Axis-I disorders (SCID).* New York State Psychiatric Institute, Biometrics Research Department.

Ghosh, A. & Marks, I. M. (1987). Self-directed exposure for agoraphobia: A controlled trial. *Behavior Therapy, 18,* 3–16.

Himle, J., & Hill, E. (1991). Alcohol abuse and the anxiety disorders. *Journal of Anxiety Disorders, 5,* 237–245.

Jansson, L., & Ost, L. G. (1982). Behavioral treatments for agoraphobia: An evaluative review. *Clinical Psychology Review, 2,* 311–336.

Klosko, J. S., Barlow, D. H., Tassinari, R., & Cerny, J. A. (1990). A comparison of alprazolam and behavior therapy in the treatment of panic disorder. *Journal of Consulting and Clinical Psychology, 58,* 77–84.

Magee, W. J., Eaton, W. W., Wittchen, H., McGonagle, K. A., & Kessler, R. C. (1996). Agoraphobia, simple phobia, and social phobia in the national comorbidity survey. *Archives of General Psychiatry, 53,* 159–168.

Margraf, J., Barlow, D. H., Clark, D. M., & Telch, M. J. (1993). Psychological treatment of panic: Work in progress on outcome, active ingredients, and follow-up. *Behaviour Research and Therapy, 31,* 1–8.

Marks, I. M. (1987a). *Fears, phobias, and rituals.* New York: Oxford University Press.

Marks, I. M. (1987b). Behavioral aspects of panic disorder. *American Journal of Psychiatry, 144,* 1160–1165.

Marks, I., & Mathews, A. M. (1979). Brief standard self-rating for phobic patients. *Behaviour Research and Therapy, 17,* 263–267.

Mavissakalian, M. (1989). Differential effects of imipramine and behavior therapy on panic disorder with agoraphobia. *Psychopharmacology Bulletin, 25,* 27–29.

Mavissakalian, M. (1990). Sequential combination of imipramine and self-directed exposure in the treatment of panic disorder with agoraphobia. *Journal of Clinical Psychiatry, 51,* 184–188.

Ost, L. G. (1987a). Age of onset of different phobias. *Journal of Abnormal Psychology, 96,* 223–229.

Ost, L. G. (1987b). Applied relaxation: Description of a coping technique and review of controlled studies. *Behaviour Research and Therapy, 25,* 397–410.

Ost, L. G. (1990). The Agoraphobia Scale: An evaluation of its reliability and validity. *Behaviour Research and Therapy, 28,* 323–329.

Ost, L. G., and Westling, B. E. (1994). Applied relaxation versus cognitive behavior therapy in the treatment of panic disorder. *Behaviour Research and Therapy, 33,* 145–158.

Ost, L. G., Westling, B. E., & Hellstrom, K. (1993). Applied relaxation, exposure *in vivo,* and cognitive methods in the treatment of panic disorder with agoraphobia. *Behaviour Research and Therapy, 31,* 383–394.

Ottaviani, R., & Beck, A. T. (1987). Cognitive aspects of panic disorders. *Journal of Anxiety Disorders, 1,* 15–28.

Otto, M. W., Pollack, M. H., Meltzer-Brody, S., & Rosenbaum, J. F. (1992). Cognitive behavioral therapy for benzodiazepene discontinuation in panic disorder patients. *Psychopharmacology Bulletin, 28,* 123–130.

Peterson, R. A., & Reiss, S. (1987). *Anxiety Sensitivity Index manual.* Worthington, OH: IDS Publishing.

Rapee, R. M., Craske, M. G., & Barlow, D. H. (1990). Subject described features of panic attacks using a new self-monitoring form. *Journal of Anxiety Disorders, 4,* 171–181.

Robins, L. N., Locke, B. Z., & Regier, D. A. (1991). An overview of psychiatric disorders in America. In L. N. Robins & D. A. Regier (Eds.), *Psychiatric disorders in America: The epidemiologic catchment area study* (pp. 328–366). New York: Free Press.

Sartory, G., Rachman, S., & Grey, S. (1982). Return of fear: The role of rehearsal. *Behaviour Research and Therapy, 20,* 123–133.

Shear, M. K., Pilkonis, P. A., Cloitre, M., & Leon, A. C. (1994). Cognitive behavioral treatment compared with nonprescriptive treatment of panic disorder. *Archives of General Psychiatry, 51,* 395–401.

Sheehan, D. V., Ballenger, J. C., & Jacobsen, G. (1980). Treatment of endogenous anxiety with phobic, hysterical, and hypochondriacal symptoms. *Archives of General Psychiatry, 37,* 51–59.

Spiegel, D. A., Bruce, T. J., Gregg, S. F., & Nuzzarello, A. (1994). Does cognitive behavior therapy assist slow taper alprazolam discontinuation in panic disorder? *American Journal of Psychiatry, 151,* 876–881.

Thyer, B. A. (1983). Treating anxiety disorders with exposure therapy. *Social Casework, 64,* 77–82.

Thyer, B. A. (1985). The treatment of phobias in their natural contexts. *Journal of Applied Social Sciences, 9*(1), 73–83.

Thyer, B. A. (1987a). *Treating anxiety disorders.* Newbury Park, CA: Sage.

Thyer, B. A. (1987b). Community-based self-help groups in the treatment of agoraphobia. *Journal of Sociology and Social Welfare, 14*(3), 135–141.

Thyer, B. A., Himle, J., Curtis, G. C., Cameron, O. G., & Nesse, R. M. (1985). A comparison of panic disorder and agoraphobia with panic attacks. *Comprehensive Psychiatry, 26,* 208–214.

Thyer, B. A., McNeece, A. C., & Miller, M. A. (1987). Alcohol abuse among agoraphobics: A community-based replication. *Alcoholism Treatment Quarterly, 4,* 61–67.

Thyer, B. A., Papsdorf, J. D., Davis, R., & Vallecorsa, S. (1984). Autonomic correlates of the Subjective Anxiety Scale. *Journal of Behavior Therapy and Experimental Psychiatry, 15,* 3–7.

Thyer, B. A., Parrish, R. T., Himle, J., Cameron, O. G., Curtis, G. C., & Nesse, R. M. (1986). Alcohol abuse among clinically anxious patients. *Behaviour Research and Therapy, 24,* 357–359.

Williams, S. L., & Rappoport, J. A. (1983). Cognitive treatment in the natural environment for agoraphobics. *Behavior Therapy, 14,* 299–313.

Wolpe, J. (1973). *The practice of behavior therapy.* New York: Pergamon Press.

Chapter 16

SPECIFIC AND SOCIAL PHOBIAS

Joseph J. Plaud
Keith G. Vavrovsky

OVERVIEW

Specific and Social Phobias belong to the general class of psychiatric classification labeled Anxiety Disorders in the *Diagnostic and Statistical Manual of Mental Disorders, Fourth Edition* (*DSM-IV;* American Psychiatric Association [APA], 1994). *DSM-IV* groups anxiety disorders into 12 categories, which include not only phobias, but also Panic Disorder, Obsessive-Compulsive Disorder, Medically Related and Substance-Induced Anxiety, Post-Traumatic Stress Disorder, and Generalized Anxiety Disorder. As a general guiding principle, anxiety is considered to be a clinical problem if a person is acutely distressed or disabled by the anxiety experience, regardless of its specific etiology. The purpose of this chapter is to define the categories of anxiety disorders known as Specific and Social Phobias, and to provide an overview of psychosocial assessment and treatment techniques relevant to the empirical practice of social work.

Clinical Definitions

The term *phobia* is derived from the name of the Greek god Phobos, who was said to have the ability to frighten his enemies. According to *DSM-IV* (APA, 1994), the essential feature of Specific Phobia is a pronounced as well as persistent fear of clearly discernible, circumscribed objects or situations. *DSM-IV* specifies that encountering the phobic stimulus almost invariably provokes an immediate anxiety response. The authors of *DSM-IV* note that although adolescents and adults with this disorder may understand that their fear is excessive or unreasonable, children do not usually have such understanding. The phobic stimulus is usually avoided, although it is sometimes endured with dread. According to *DSM-IV,* the diagnosis of Specific Phobia is appropriate only if the avoidance, fear, or anxious anticipation of encountering the phobic stimulus interferes significantly with a person's daily schedule, occupational functioning, or social life, or if the person is markedly distressed about having the phobia.

There are several common subtypes of Specific Phobia in *DSM-IV*, which are denoted to indicate the focus of fear or avoidance. Subtypes include Animal Type (if the fear is cued by animals or insects, with childhood onset common); Natural Environment Type (if the fear is elicited by objects in the natural environment, such as storms, heights, or water; also with childhood onset common); Blood-Injection-Injury Type (if the fear is elicited by seeing blood or an injury, receiving an injection or other invasive medical procedure); Situational Type (if the fear is cued by a definable situation, such as public transportation, tunnels, bridges, elevators, flying, driving, or enclosed places—according to *DSM-IV*, this subtype has a bimodal age-at-onset distribution, with one peak in childhood and another peak in the mid-20s); or Other Type.

The essential feature of Social Phobia is a noticeable and persistent fear of social or performance situations in which embarrassment may occur, which provokes an immediate anxiety response that may take the form of a situationally bound or situationally predisposed panic attack. As with Specific Phobia, adults with Social Phobia may recognize that their fear is unreasonable or excessive or unreasonable, though children usually do not make such a discrimination. Also similarly to specific phobias, the feared social situation is usually avoided, and if it is difficult to engage in successful avoidance of the social situation, it will probably be endured with dread.

Barlow (1988) has argued that although anxiety disorders are heterogeneous categories of classification, which may have lead to the low reliability found in many studies attempting to classify anxiety disorders, the advent of *DSM-III* in 1980 (APA, 1980) has lead to greater reliability in classification—a trend that has continued in the subsequent editions of *DSM-III-R* (APA, 1987) and *DSM-IV* (APA, 1994). However, granting the greater diagnostic specificity concerning phobias evident in *DSM-IV*, more studies on the reliability of the anxiety disorders classification system need to be conducted. Even though *DSM-IV* arguably contributes to the scientific efforts to achieve adequate diagnostic reliability, questions still remain over whether *DSM-IV* provides valid diagnoses of the anxiety disorders, and specific and social phobias specifically. Future studies and ongoing research into the classification of behavioral pathology should provide more data to assist in answering this question.

Epidemiology of Phobias

Although the diagnostic criteria in *DSM-IV* have changed somewhat in the classification of Specific Phobias (called Simple Phobias prior to *DSM-IV*) and Social Phobia, several studies during the past 20 years have estimated the prevalence and gender differences in epidemiological studies of the disorders. Schwab, Bell,

Warhelt, and Schwab (1979) found an American prevalence of 10.6% and 10.2% to 30% in men for social and specific phobias, respectively. Costello (1982) found a Canadian 1-point prevalence rate of 5% to 12.5% in females for specific phobias. Myers et al. (1984) estimated 0.9% to 1.7% male and 1.5% to 2.6% female 6-month prevalence rates for social phobia, and 2.3% to 7.3% male and 6% to 15.7% female rates for specific phobias in an urban sample. In another urban setting, Robins et al. (1984) found that 3.8% to 14.5% of men and 8.5% to 25.9% of women met the diagnostic criteria for specific phobias in a lifetime prevalence study. Bourden et al. (1988) estimated a lifetime prevalence rate of 2.3% and 3.2% for males and females respectively for social phobia, and 7.2% and 13.9% for specific phobias, again in an urban setting. A recent study by Fredrikson, Annas, Fischer, and Wik (1996) found that total point prevalence of any specific phobia was 19.9% (26.5% for females and 12.4% for males), with multiple phobias reported by 5.4% of the females and 1.5% of the males. Taken as a whole, then, epidemiological studies consistently show that a significant proportion of the human population is affected by specific and social phobias, with women tending to exhibit more anxiety-related symptomatology.

ASSESSMENT METHODS

Taylor and Agras (1981) described four major techniques of assessment of phobic behavior: (a) *self-report,* including general fear inventories, specific fear inventories, self-report hierarchies, and self-monitoring; (b) *personality measures,* such as the Minnesota Multiphasic Personality Inventory—Second Edition (MMPI-2) and the Eysenck Personality Inventory (EPI); (c) *physiologic and biochemical measures,* such as skin conductance and heart rate; and (d) *overt behavioral analysis,* such as functional analysis and in vitro, in vivo assessment. Each of these areas of clinical assessment is examined in the following.

Self-Report Inventories

There are many questionnaires being utilized in the assessment of fears and phobias. According to Thorpe and Burns (1983), questionnaires have the advantage of eliciting much data in a short period of time. The Anxiety Disorders Interview Schedule—Revised (ADIS-R; Di Nardo & Barlow, 1988) is a structured interview designed to work in conjunction with *DSM* diagnostic criteria. Scales used to identify phobic and panic episodes include the Fear Survey Schedule (Thyer, Tomlin, Curtis, Cameron, & Nesse, 1985; Wolpe & Lang, 1964), the Fear Questionnaire (Marks & Mathews, 1979), the Anxiety Sensitivity Index (Reiss, Peterson, Gursky, & McNally, 1986), and similar scales by Marks & Herst (1970), an agoraphobia questionnaire designed by Burns (1977), the Body Sensations Questionnaire (Chambless, Caputo, Bright, &

Gallagher, 1984), and the *Social Avoidance and Distress Scale* (Watson & Friend, 1969). Scales such as these have been found to be useful as a method of assessment; however, it should be noted that researchers have found it useful to assess anxiety by self-report and other means as well, due to the fact that the different measures do not always correlate well. Many self-monitoring techniques, such as activity checklists and daily diaries, help the therapist to continually assess the effectiveness of intervention. In reference to the reliability of these self-report inventories, the questionnaires mentioned here have all been found to have adequate reliability measures. Thorpe and Burns (1983) report that such scales are relatively short, standardized measures that are quite easy to score. Concerning validity, Hecker and Thorpe (1992) state that phobic rating scales in general tend to correlate well with behavioral observation.

Personality Measures

Personality scales, such as the Eysenck Personality Inventory, (EPI; Eysenck & Eysenck, 1975) and the clinical and content scales of the Minnesota Multiphasic Personality Inventory—Second Edition (MMPI-2; Graham, 1993), are used in assessing how pronounced anxiety responses may be, as well as in assessing the possibility of favorable treatment outcomes. For example, high extraversion on the EPI is correlated with a more efficacious treatment outcome. For differential diagnosis, however, personality measures have been found to have little overall utility (Agras & Jacob, 1980).

Physiological Measures

Heart-rate and skin-conductance levels have been highly correlated with anxiety levels. They provide valid, concrete data in assessing the body activity level of those with phobic response patterns. However, they have not served to differentiate among phobias. Their main utility is in assessing the effectiveness of therapeutic intervention.

Behavioral Analyses

In line with a functional analysis of behavior, Bernstein, Borkovec, and Coles (1986) state that such an analysis does not depart from an assessment of other behavior in any major way. They list a set of crucial questions for the clinician to assess:

1. What is the nature of the stimulus classes that elicit or signal anxiety response components in the presenting problem?
2. What response components are functionally relevant to the presenting problem?

3. Does the client display an anticipatory anxiety reaction and, if so, what is its component structure and spatial and temporal, thematic, and semantic relationship to feared stimuli?

4. Does the client's anxiety response pattern represent an inappropriately conditioned response to an objectively nonthreatening situation, or is it an appropriate reaction to a situation that, for a variety of reasons, is actually harmful, dangerous, or punishing?

5. What are the immediate and long-term consequences of each anxiety response component?

Performance-based assessment measures have also been used, such as the behavioral avoidance test (BAT; Lang & Lazovik, 1963). In such tasks, clients progressively approach feared objects or places. Such real-life assessments directly place the client in a fearful situation. As with physiological measures, activity checklists, and daily diaries, such behavioral tasks allow continual assessment and measures of treatment outcome.

In conducting diagnostic interviews, Barbaree and Marshall (1985) suggest that when dealing with phobic clients, "it will be necessary in a proper analysis of the presenting problem, to identify the magnitude of defects (dependency, passivity, poor relationships, and depression) in each patient in order to define assessment strategies in addition to ascertaining treatment goals and procedures." Supportive data on the nature of functional behavior analytic assessment, and the authors' own clinical experience, suggest using the outline in Table 16.1 to gain the appropriate clinical information on the nature and etiology of specific and social phobias.

EFFECTIVE INTERVENTIONS

Exposure Therapies

The major psychosocial treatment technique shown to be effective in treating clients with specific and social phobias is the procedure known as *real-life exposure*. In exposure therapy, a client is exposed directly to the feared stimulus; through the mechanisms of extinction, fear is reduced and, hopefully, ultimately eliminated over several sessions. Once the anxiety response is extinguished, the operant avoidance response also extinguishes due to the elimination of the negative reinforcement contingency. Therefore, exposure-based procedures are a direct application of one of the major behavioral theories on the acquisition and maintenance of anxiety responses. Hafner and Marks (1976) found that clients do not have to experience extreme levels of anxiety during exposure sessions in order to show clinical improvement. Therefore, low to moderate levels of anxiety may be sufficient for exposure to be effective in the treatment of phobias.

Table 16.1   Functional Behavioral Assessment of Clinically Relevant Behavior

I. Gather specific information on the following:

   1. All problems the client experiences (specific—reasons for wanting therapy).

   2. The antecedents and consequences of these (contingencies and affect).

   3. The onset of each and maintaining factors (reinforcement schedule).

   4. Client's preexisting coping skills and self-control processes.

   5. The developmental history of each problem and organismic variables:

     a. Current medical status.

     b. Reproductive history (females).

     c. Family medical history

     d. Self-care problems.

     e. Past and present drug and alcohol use.

     f. Significant dental problems.

   6. Previous treatment and the nature of such.

   7. Goals of therapy

   8. What client considers "ideal self" to be (performing what behaviors?)

   9. Assets and strengths stated by client:

     a. Academic.

     b. Occupational.

     c. Recreational.

     d. Other interests.

  10. Factors predisposing the development of these problems:

     a. Positive and negative characteristics seen in each parent.

     b. How client is similar and different from parents.

     c. Describe in detail the relationship with parents and significant others.

     d. Describe the rules and regulations in house.

     e. Describe how rules were enforced.

     f. Describe early social behavior (preschool, during school, and nicknames).

  11. Resources for help.

II. Gather collateral information: Reports from others, other information, and test scores.

III. Consider: Cognitive and perceptual features, logic, intelligence, expressions (verbal and otherwise), style, flexibility, and the nature of distortions.

Imaginal exposure techniques have also been used. Rather than exposing the client to the actual feared object or situation in real life, *imaginal exposure,* as its name suggests, has the client attempt to experience situations imaginally over a period of time. Stern and Marks (1973) found that real-life techniques are generally more effective than imaginal approaches, though other studies have shown that both approaches can be clinically efficacious (Thorpe & Olson, 1997). In addition, it has been found that a few long treatment sessions (for example, 2-hour sessions) are more helpful than several short sessions (for example, ½-hour to 1-hour sessions; Stern & Marks, 1973). Further, several studies have also shown that graduated real-life practice (also called *graded practice*) is effective in the treatment of phobias. In this approach, exposure to the feared stimulus is conducted more gradually, and the client is provided with feedback concerning the amount of time that he or she is actually exposed to the stimulus. In addition, clients in several studies were told that they could withdraw from the feared stimulus at any point. A study of patients with specific and social phobias by Al-Kubaisy et al. (1992) showed that 6 hours of self-exposure instruction along with daily homework exercises produced significant reduction in anxiety, and that those gains were not improved upon by 9 additional hours of therapist-directed exposure. In general, exposure techniques have proven to be among the most clinically efficacious treatment approaches to specific and social phobias.

Among the case illustrations further describing the use of real-life exposure therapy by social workers in the treatment of specific and social phobias are Curtis and Thyer (1983), Thyer (1981, 1983, 1985), Thyer and Stocks (1986), and Vonk and Thyer (1995).

Contingency Management and Social Skills Training

Socially-based anxiety responses may be a function, at least in part, of relative deficits in a person's social skills. For example, some clients may lack the skills needed to start conversations, feel comfortable in group situations, and interact with others in social contexts. Social skills training involves using behavioral assessment to identify a client's oral communication abilities, flexibility and resourcefulness in social situations, enthusiasm in group settings, ability to work under pressure, interpersonal sensitivities, and listening skills (Goldstein, 1988). Social skills training usually involves the client and the therapist in role-playing or acting out social situations; the therapist provides appropriate feedback to the client concerning his or her social performance. Research indicates that social skills training can be particularly beneficial in the behavioral treatment of social phobia (Emmelkamp, 1990).

O'Donohue, Plaud, and Hecker (1992) highlighted the importance of positive reinforcement in the maintenance of anxiety-related behavior in a study of whether positive reinforcement contingencies in an agoraphobia patient's home could help maintain avoidance behavior. As in the specific and social phobias, avoidance behavior is a central feature of agoraphobia. The persistence of avoidance behavior can also be mediated by the contingencies of positive reinforcement. Once in the home, a person with agoraphobia does not cease to function. Positive reinforcers exist in the home, and with the help of others who bring needed external reinforcers into the home (such as groceries), the home environment might be considered to be a fairly densely reinforcing environment. O'Donohue et al. hypothesized that if they deprived a homebound agoraphobic client of pleasurable activities in the home (assessed through free operant baseline time frequency), and made such deprived activities available only outside the home, then the amount of activities outside the home would increase relative to baseline: Preferred activities would serve to positively reinforce outside activities, given the changed contingency schedule.

During a 30-day baseline period, O'Donohue et al. gathered data concerning the types and amounts of behavior that the client engaged in within the confines of her home and yard. In addition, reinforcers in the home were identified by survey schedules and interviews. In an attempt to make the home a less positively reinforcing environment, several sources of reinforcement were moved outside the home, and the client agreed to engage in certain reinforcing activities only outside her home (for example, going to a neighbor's house in order to watch television or engage in social activities) during an 18-day intervention period. Postintervention results indicated that for the first time in over 7 years the client began engaging in out-of-home activities, including walking to other parts of the street, visiting several neighbors' homes, and attending parties at neighbors' homes. Moreover, the client evidenced a positive trend in time spent outside the yard during a 60-day follow-up. This finding supports the principle that even anxiety-related behavior can be influenced by positive reinforcement, and that reinforcement contingencies exert a strong control over human behavior (Plaud, 1992).

Rational-Emotive Behavior Therapy (REBT)

Albert Ellis' (1962, 1995) rational-emotive behavior therapy (REBT) is a cognitive-behavioral therapy that proposes that sustained emotional reactions are caused by internal self-statements that people repeat to themselves and that reflect assumptions and beliefs about one's approach to life. According to Ellis, an individual is able to deal with any adversity (such as anxiety-provoking situations) without the necessity of eliciting negative mood states. As a behavior therapy technique, REBT focuses on the client's presentation of a disturbing emotion. This emotional consequence C, according to Ellis, is not in reality caused by the activating event A, but rather the beliefs B that the client has about the relationship between A and C:

$$A \rightarrow B \rightarrow C$$

Ellis hypothesizes that cognitive mechanisms he defines as irrational beliefs iBs account for the negative emotive states surrounding certain classes of imperative words, such as *should, must,* and *terrible.*

The aim of REBT is to identify and eliminate those beliefs that are self-defeating by disputing D the iBs and therefore challenging the veracity of iBs, replacing them with more functional or rational beliefs rBs. For example, a client who presents with fear of negative evaluation by others in particular social situations involving public speaking may complain that he or she feels anxious because he or she is "incapable of speaking adequately while others watch." An REBT therapist would actively investigate whether the client endorsed categorically imperative ways of describing the state of being *incapable* in such situations; for example, "I have to be competent and do a great job when others are watching, otherwise what is the value of living?" In this case, Ellis would probably recommend a course of therapeutic action directed at disputing the necessity of performing in a perfect manner in a social situation, substituting *rB*s such as "It might be preferable to do perfectly and be acknowledged by others in a social situation, but I can live and cope without the constant need of such achievements." Therefore, according to the theoretical mechanism of behavior and emotive change offered by Ellis, negative or maladaptive emotional states are changed by a direct challenge and replacement of *iB*s with *rB*s through verbal disputation (as well as by giving the client homework assignments so that he or she can test out the veracity of the *iB*s in real life).

REBT has been found to be clinically efficacious as a cognitive-behavioral treatment in a variety of clinical populations (e.g., Bernard & DiGiuseppe, 1989; Lipsky, Kassinove, & Miller, 1980; Trexler & Karst, 1972). Thorpe and Olson (1997) have argued, however, that while many behavior therapists are sympathetic to the views put forth by Ellis, there is debate about the scientific status of REBT in terms of its theoretical assumptions. In other words, debate continues on the nature and role of *iB*s and *rB*s in changing emotional consequences. As the preceding discussion of rule-governed behavior suggests, much of what might serve as the active clinical mechanism in REBT is the active changing or restructuring of the rules by which persons operate and changing the verbal context of behavior— in the present case, anxiety-related behavior—in doing so. Therapeutic strategies that systematically alter the emotion-eliciting functions of verbal behavior therefore also function to change reinforcing and directive functions of other verbal-symbolic events in the client's behavioral repertoire. For example, our socially anxious client might be more willing to interact in social situations as a function of changing the rules (that is, the expectations or social contingencies) that go along with public speaking. Reinforcing consequences gained from once again interacting with the social environment could then further decrease or diminish the nature of the original socially phobic response repertoire.

Acceptance and Commitment Therapy (ACT)

Hayes (1994) has elucidated a new clinical application of behavior change that takes into consideration the importance of verbal and rule-governed behavior (and the influence of stimulus equivalence processes). Hayes calls his contextual approach to treatment acceptance and commitment therapy (ACT). ACT is based upon the experimental analysis of human behavior, whether it is overt, covert, or verbal. In other words, contingency-shaped functional behavior relationships are addressed in therapy, so that the contingencies that produce verbal rules and other forms of human action are appropriately addressed in therapy. Verbal communities, according to Hayes, set up three major sets of contingencies that control the contexts in which people operate. First, there is a context of *literality*. In this context, words take on literal meaning. For example, the word *anxiety* has come to mean something to people. Indeed, people are said to possess this word—for example, "I'm anxious;" "I have anxiety."

Second, Hayes defines a context of *reason giving*. This context implies that certain events or internal states control or explain other events. For example, saying "she didn't go to work because she felt anxious about interacting with her boss" is accepted by the verbal community as an explanation of why this person did not end up going to work. However, such a statement just begs the question of why she was anxious in the first place! Furthermore, it is conceivable that a person can go to work and feel anxious at the same time, yet statements such as the preceding one are accepted as a valid explanation of behavior, in this case the behavior of not going to work.

Third, Hayes discusses a context of *control*. Such a context implies that we believe that certain events must follow in order for changes to take place. For example, a person might think that in order to get better he or she must somehow get rid of the anxiety, or control the bad thoughts. According to Hayes, each of these verbal contexts can produce pathological results at times, because each context really refers to sets of *contingencies* established and maintained by the verbal community. A first goal of ACT, therefore, is to create a new verbal community that operates within a different verbal context. Behavior change can be accomplished in several different manners in therapy. One possibility is to teach clients different rules that have more beneficial results (many cognitive techniques, such as cognitive restructuring and REBT [previously discussed], are really variations of attempts to teach clients new rules). However, a problem with this approach is that attempting to modify rule-governed behavior by teaching new rules is just another form of the three verbal contexts previously mentioned, and it is therefore vulnerable to the same aversive consequences. A second approach is to reduce compliance to maladaptive rules so that clients can more directly experience overt contingency-shaped behavior (many behavioral techniques, such as flooding [discussed following], attempt to do this). However, just employing this second approach might not directly address the clinically significant elements of clients' verbal stimulus control of behavior in the form of maladaptive rules and contexts. A third approach (complementary with the second approach) is to reduce the contexts of literality, reason giving, and control in verbal therapy—to challenge the contexts themselves.

Consistent with REBT, Hayes attempts to change the verbal contingencies of reinforcement by exploring the paradoxes of such contexts. One important method used in acceptance and commitment therapy involves the attempt to separate clients' words and actions from the clients—to distinguish people from their behavior. Showing clients that they are not bad, or that they can live with anxiety—in other words, extinguishing the control exerted by the contexts of literality, reason giving, and control—is a major goal of therapy. In essence, ACT attempts to address issues of verbal stimulus control as well as of overt behavioral stimulus control. According to this behavioral approach, one reason why many direct behavioral manipulations do not make adequate changes in clients' lives is because the elements of verbal stimulus control have not been attended to. Acceptance and commitment therapy addresses these elements of verbal behavior. Empirical outcome data on this verbally based approach to behavioral therapy have been encouraging (Hayes, 1994), though at present the approach is just beginning to be regarded as a challenge to REBT as a major behavioral therapy technique.

Systematic Desensitization

Systematic desensitization (SD), developed by Wolpe (1958), represents one of the most clinically efficacious treatments for phobias. In this procedure, clients are first trained in progressive muscle relaxation exercises and are then gradually exposed imaginally or in real life to feared stimuli while simultaneously relaxing using the learned muscle relaxation techniques. Clients construct a fear hierarchy and usually start with the least feared item, then gradually move up the hierarchy to the most feared item. Dyckman and Cowan (1978) have found that real-life exposure to feared objects or situations is superior to imaginal exposure in the treatment of phobias.

SD is based upon a fundamental principle of learning: counterconditioning of fear. Wolpe reasoned that anxious clients could not be simultaneously fearful and relaxed; therefore, learning to respond in a polar opposite fashion to stimuli that originally elicited anxiety would allow the extinction of the anxiety response, a mechanism Wolpe originally labeled *reciprocal inhibition*. This approach to therapy for phobias is based on both Pavlovian and Hullian learning theories, and multiple studies over the past 35 years have supported its clinical efficacy as a main treatment for phobias, especially Specific Phobia (Thorpe & Olson, 1997). Joel Fischer (1978) provides an excellent overview of this approach for social workers in *Effective Casework Practice*.

Individual versus Group Treatment Approaches

Although patients with social phobias may not respond well, at least initially, to group-based behavior therapy approaches, research has demonstrated that group therapy can be beneficial in the management of anxiety. As reviewed by Thorpe and Olson (1997), several researchers have found that the group setting allows for economy of professional time and for the ability of clients to learn how to interact with each other and to become models themselves for other clients. Research has also shown that group therapy—in contrast to individual therapy—can encourage more social contacts among clients and may encourage clients to try harder with exposure regimens. Therefore, group therapy approaches, especially for specific phobias, are a viable and potentially beneficial alternative to the traditional individualized therapy approach.

CONCLUSIONS

Behavior analysis and therapy enjoys a long record of accomplishment in accounting for the etiology of such anxiety disorders as Specific Phobia and Social Phobia, as well as in providing for empirically validated behavioral assessment and in developing effective approaches to mitigating these anxiety-related problems. The assessment and treatment strategies presented in the preceding sections represent the major current empirical approaches in this area, mostly based upon a cognitive-behavioral approach. They represent significant advancements in the assessment of anxiety, as well as validated contingency modification approaches to eliminating anxiety. Very few alternative psychosocial interventions have been shown to be effective in helping clients overcome specific and social phobias.

Empirically oriented social workers emphasize that these assessment and treatment techniques should not be used in isolation, but rather should be viewed in the context of the major etiological paradigms upon which the techniques and procedures are based. In the appropriate assessment and treatment of specific and social phobias, the verbal (cognitive), the visceral (physiological), and the overt behavioral levels of analysis should all be considered for each person, so that treatment can be tailored individually, and clinical results can be empirically verified. The social work practice text *Treating Anxiety Disorders* (Thyer, 1987) provides a more in-depth discussion of psychosocial assessment and treatment procedures for clients with phobias.

REFERENCES

Agras, W. S., & Jacob R. (1980). Phobia: Nature and measurement. In M. Mavissakalian & D. H. Barlow (Eds.), *Phobia: Psychological and pharmacological treatment.* New York: Guilford Press.

Al-Kubaisy, T., Marks, I. M., Logsdail, S., Marks, M. P., Lovell, K., Sungur, M., & Araya, R. (1992). Role of exposure homework in phobia reduction: A controlled study. *Behavior Therapy, 23,* 599–621.

American Psychiatric Association. (1980). *Diagnostic and statistical manual of mental disorders* (3rd ed.). Washington, DC: Author.

American Psychiatric Association. (1987). *Diagnostic and statistical manual of mental disorders* (3rd ed., rev.). Washington, DC: Author.

American Psychiatric Association. (1994). *Diagnostic and statistical manual of mental disorders* (4th ed.). Washington, DC: Author.

Barbaree, H. E., & Marshall, W. L. (1985). Anxiety-based disorders. In M. Hersen & S. M. Turner (Eds.), *Diagnostic interviewing.* New York: Plenum Press.

Barlow, D. H. (1988). *Anxiety and its disorders: The nature and treatment of anxiety and panic.* New York: Guilford Press.

Bernard, M. E., & DiGiuseppe, R. (Eds.). (1989). *Inside rational-emotive therapy: A critical appraisal of the theory and therapy of Albert Ellis.* San Diego, CA: Academic Press.

Bernstein, D. A., Borkovec, T. D. & Coles, M. G. H. (1986). Assessment of anxiety. In A. R. Ciminero, K. S. Calhoun, & H. E. Adams (Eds.), *Handbook of behavioral assessment.* New York: Wiley.

Bourden, K. H., Boyd, J. H., Rae, D. S., Burns, B. J., Thompson, J. W., & Locke, B. Z. (1988). Gender differences in phobias: Results of the ECA community survey. *Journal of Anxiety Disorders, 2,* 227–241.

Burns, L. E. (1977). *An Investigation into the additive effects of behavioral techniques in the treatment of agoraphobia.* Unpublished doctoral dissertation, University of Maine, Fogler Library.

Chambless, D. L., Caputo, G. C., Bright, P., & Gallagher, R. (1984). Assessment of fear in agoraphobics: The Body Sensations Questionnaire and the Agoraphobic Cognitions Questionnaire. *Journal of Consulting and Clinical Psychology, 52,* 1090–1097.

Costello, C. G. (1982). Fears and phobias in women: A community study. *Journal of Abnormal Psychology, 91,* 280–286.

Curtis, G. C., & Thyer, B. A. (1983). Fainting on exposure to phobic stimuli. *American Journal of Psychiatry, 140,* 771–774.

Di Nardo, P. A., & Barlow, D. H. (1988). *Anxiety Disorders Interview Schedule—Revised (ADIS-R).* Albany, NY: Graywind.

Dyckman, J. M., & Cowan, P. A. (1978). Imagining vividness and the outcome of in vivo and imagined scene desensitization. *Journal of Consulting and Clinical Psychology, 48,* 1155–1156.

Ellis, A. (1962). *Reason and emotion in psychotherapy.* New York: Lyle Stuart.

Ellis, A. (1995). Changing rational-emotive therapy (RET) to rational emotive behavior therapy (REBT). *Journal of Rational Emotive and Cognitive Behavior Therapy, 13,* 85–89.

Emmelkamp, P. M. G. (1990). Anxiety and fear. In A. S. Bellack, M. Hersen, & A. E. Kazdin (Eds.), *International handbook of behavior modification and therapy* (2nd ed.), (pp. 283–305). New York: Plenum Press.

Eysenck, H. J., & Eysenck, S. B. (1975). *Manual of the Eysenck Personality Questionnaire.* San Diego: Digits.

Fischer, J. (1978). *Effective casework practice.* New York: McGraw-Hill.

Fredrikson, M., Annas, P., Fischer, H., & Wik, G. (1996). Gender and age differences in the prevalence of specific fears and phobias. *Behaviour Research and Therapy, 34,* 33–39.

Goldstein, A. P. (1988). *The prepare curriculum: Teaching prosocial competencies.* Champaign, IL: Research Press.

Graham, J. R. (1993). *MMPI-2: Assessing personality and psychopathology* (2nd ed.). New York: Oxford University Press.

Hafner, J., & Marks, I. (1976). Exposure in vivo of agoraphobics: Contributions of diazepam, group exposure, and anxiety education. *Psychological Medicine, 6,* 71–88.

Hayes, S. C. (1994). Content, context, and the types of psychological acceptance. In S. C. Hayes, N. S. Jacobson, V. M. Follette, & M. J. Dougher (Eds.), *Acceptance and change: Content and context in psychotherapy* (pp. 13–32). Reno, NV: Context Press.

Hecker, J. E., & Thorpe, G. L. (1992). *Agoraphobia and panic: A guide to psychological treatment.* Boston: Allyn & Bacon.

Lang, P. J., & Lazovik, A. D. (1963). Experimental desensitization of a phobia. *Journal of Abnormal and Social Psychology, 66,* 519–525.

Lipsky, M. M., Kassinove, H., & Miller, N. J. (1980). Effects of rational-emotive therapy, rational role-reversal, and rational-emotive imagery on the emotional adjustment of Community Mental Health Center patients. *Journal of Consulting and Clinical Psychology, 48,* 366–374.

Marks, I. M. & Herst, E. R. (1970). A survey of 1,200 agoraphobics in Britain: Features associated with treatment and ability to work. *Social Psychiatry, 5,* 15–24.

Marks, I. M., & Mathews, A. M. (1979). Brief standard self-rating for phobic patients. *Behaviour Research and Therapy, 17,* 263–267.

Myers, J. K., Weissman, M. M., Tischler, G. L., Holzer, C. E., Leaf, P. J., Orvaschel, H., Anthony, J. C., Boyd, J. H., Burke, J. D., Jr., Kramer, M., & Stoltzman, R. (1984). Six-month prevalence of psychiatric disorders in three communities. *Archives of General Psychiatry, 41,* 959–967.

O'Donohue, W. T., Plaud, J. J., & Hecker, J. E. (1992). The possible function of positive reinforcement in home-bound agoraphobia: A case study. *Journal of Behavior Therapy and Experimental Psychiatry, 23,* 303–312.

Plaud, J. J. (1992). The prediction and control of behavior revisited: A review of the matching law. *Journal of Behavior Therapy and Experimental Psychiatry, 23,* 25–31.

Reiss, S., Peterson, R. A., Gursky, D. M., & McNally, R. J. (1986). Anxiety sensitivity, anxiety frequency, and prediction of fearfulness. *Behaviour Research and Therapy, 24,* 1–8.

Robins, L. N., Helzer, J. E., Weissman, M. M., Orvaschel, H., Gruenberg, E., Burke, J. D., Jr., & Reiger, D. A. (1984). Lifetime prevalence of specific psychiatric disorders in three sites. *Archives of General Psychiatry, 41,* 949–958.

Schwab, J. J., Bell, R. A., Warheit, G. J., & Schwab, R. B. (1979). *Social order and mental health.* New York: Bruner/Mazel.

Stern, R., & Marks, I. M. (1973). Contract therapy in obsessive-compulsive neurosis with marital discord. *British Journal of Psychiatry, 123,* 681–684.

Taylor, C. B., & Agras, S. (1981). Assessment of phobia. In D. H. Barlow (Ed.), *Behavioral assessment of adult disorders.* New York: Guilford Press.

Thorpe, G. L. & Burns, L. E. (1983). *The agoraphobic syndrome.* New York: Wiley.

Thorpe, G. L., & Olson, S. L. (1997). *Behavior therapy: Concepts, procedures, and applications.* Boston: Allyn & Bacon.

Thyer, B. A. (1981). Prolonged in-vivo exposure therapy with a 70-year-old woman. *Journal of Behavior Therapy and Experimental Psychiatry, 12,* 69–71.

Thyer, B. A. (1983). Treating anxiety disorders with exposure therapy. *Social Casework, 64,* 77–82.

Thyer, B. A. (1985). The treatment of phobias in their natural contexts. *Journal of Applied Social Sciences, 9*(1), 73–83.

Thyer, B. A. (1987). *Treating anxiety disorders.* Newberry Park, CA: Sage.

Thyer, B. A., & Stocks, J. T. (1986). Exposure therapy in the treatment of a phobic blind person. *Journal of Visual Impairment and Blindness, 80,* 1001–1003.

Thyer, B. A., Tomlin, P., Curtis, G. C., Cameron, O. G. & Nesse, R. M. (1985). Diagnostic and gender differences in the expressed fears of anxious patients. *Journal of Behavior Therapy and Experimental Psychiatry, 16,* 111–115.

Trexler, L. D., & Karst, T. O. (1972). Rational-emotive therapy, placebo, and no-treatment effects on public-speaking anxiety. *Journal of Abnormal Psychology, 79,* 60–67.

Vonk, M. E., & Thyer, B. A. (1995). Exposure therapy in the treatment of vaginal penetration phobia. *Journal of Behavior Therapy and Experimental Psychiatry, 29,* 359–363.

Watson, D., & Friend, R. (1969). Measurement of social-evaluative anxiety. *Journal of Consulting and Clinical Psychology, 33,* 448–457.

Wolpe, J. (1958). *Psychotherapy by reciprocal inhibition.* Stanford, CA: Stanford University Press.

Wolpe, J., & Lang, P. J. (1964). A fear survey schedule for use in behavior therapy. *Behaviour Research and Therapy, 2,* 27–30.

Chapter 17 ──────────────────────

OBSESSIVE-COMPULSIVE DISORDER

Iris Cohen
Gail Steketee

OVERVIEW

Obsessive-Compulsive Disorder (OCD) is the fourth most common psychiatric disorder in the United States and is one that causes tremendous impact on the lives of patients and family members. The prevalence of the illness strongly suggests that clinical social workers will encounter clients with OCD in many practice settings. It is important that social workers have the knowledge to recognize, assess, and treat OCD, guiding those practices on the substantial existing and developing body of empirical research. This chapter begins with an overview of the characteristic presentation of OCD, followed by a description of the assessment tools currently accepted as most relevant. Finally, common theoretical models for understanding the disorder are presented and the therapeutic interventions derived from them for effective treatment of OCD are specified. Extensive research in the past several decades has permitted important developments in the treatment realm.

Diagnostic and Clinical Characteristics

Accurate assessment of OCD is an important preliminary step toward proper treatment. Over the past several decades, the mental health community has debated the components that differentially define OCD and the models that best describe it. The fourth edition of the *Diagnostic and Statistical Manual of Mental Disorders* (*DSM-IV;* American Psychiatric Association [APA], 1994) outlines the current criteria required for formal diagnosis of OCD. OCD is characterized by the dual presence of distressing obsessions and associated anxiety-reducing compulsions. More specifically, *obsessions* are intrusive thoughts, images, or impulses that cause emotional distress. The most common obsessions, in descending order, are contamination, pathological doubt, somatic fears, need for symmetry, and aggressive and sexual impulses (Rasmussen & Eisen, 1990). *Compulsions* are physical or mental actions undertaken to alleviate the discomfort generated by the obsessions. The most common physical compulsions, in descending order, are checking, washing, counting, needing to ask or confess, ordering, and hoarding (Rasmussen & Eisen, 1990). Also included are repetitive actions and mental compulsions, such as counting, praying, and repeating words or phrases in one's head. Most clients have more than one type of obsession and ritual. Frequently, clients describe obsessions and compulsions to clinicians with little prompting, although embarrassing symptoms may require direct questioning.

The distress associated with obsessions often focuses on catastrophic consequences, such as causing harm to others, forgetting to do important things, or becoming contaminated by illness-causing organisms. Certain behaviors are typically reported in association with specific types of compulsions. For example, checking rituals include repeatedly examining appliances to make sure they are turned off, making sure envelopes are sealed, and excessively seeking reassurance from others. Patients with washing behaviors may take long showers, repeatedly wash their hands, and use disinfectant or excessive amounts of soap. Others may count repeatedly to a "good number" in order to prevent harm. Ordering and arranging rituals tend to reduce general discomfort rather than prevent a negative consequence; symmetrical realigning is an example of this behavior. Hoarding practices revolve around fears of forgetting and fears that ordinary items might be needed in the future. The diagnostic description of OCD now includes a *poor insight* type that applies to patients who do not recognize the unreasonableness of their behavior (APA, 1994).

Determining a precise differential diagnosis of OCD requires close attention to the criteria cited in *DSM-IV* (APA, 1994). Some people may experience obsessive-compulsive behaviors but not have sufficient symptom severity (marked distress; more than an hour per day; and significant interference in daily life) to warrant a diagnosis of OCD. Generalized Anxiety Disorder (GAD) and OCD share some characteristics but are quite distinguishable. GAD is evident in a preoccupation with extreme worries about real-life problems, but the obsessions of OCD tend to be more specific. They are accompanied by a greater awareness of the excessiveness and unreasonableness of the symptoms and a stronger effort to suppress or neutralize the obsessions. Another diagnosis from which OCD should be differentiated is Obsessive-Compulsive Personality Disorder (OCPD), which encapsulates a personality syndrome characterized by orderliness, indecisiveness, perfectionism, and rigidity. Hollander (1993) has suggested that several mental health diagnoses can be considered obsessive-compulsive *spectrum disorders* that lie on a continuum of compulsivity and impulsivity. Examples of compulsive risk-aversive conditions are Anorexia, Bulimia, Hypochondriasis, and Dysmorphobia. These diagnoses and OCD share a pattern of increased anxiety in response to obsessive-like ideas and a reduction of the distress through specific behaviors (Salkovskis & Warwick, 1986; Tynes, White, & Steketee, 1990). Impulse control disorders, such as Trichotillomania, Face Picking, and Gambling, have been likened to OCD but lack functional commonality with it. These conditions lack the unwanted, distressing mental intrusions of OCD and the satisfying, rather than discomfort-reducing, effects of compulsive rituals (see Steketee, 1994). Distinguishing OCD from other diagnoses that appear similar is extremely important for initiation of appropriate treatment of the disorder.

Clients with a variety of other mental health diagnoses also may exhibit obsessions and compulsions. Determination of the primary diagnosis is usually based on the patient's report of his or her main concern and source of functional impairment. Some of the Axis I disorders that may appear in conjunction with OCD are anxiety disorders, depression, substance abuse, eating disorders, hypochondriasis, and schizophrenia. According to Weissman et al. (1994), comorbidity of OCD with other anxiety disorders ranges from 25% to 60%, and family studies have introduced the possibility of genetic relationships linking OCD and other anxiety disorders (Black, Noyes, Pfohl, Goldstein, & Blum, 1993). The highest rates for co-occurrence are with specific phobias (Karno, Golding, Sorenson, & Burnam, 1988) followed by Social Phobia and Panic Disorder in 10% to 50% of samples (Steketee, Henninger, & Pollard, in press). Concurrence of minor or major depression is also high, with rates of 12% to 80% (Steketee et al., in press); Bipolar Disorder is also common, although somewhat less frequent (Kruger, Cooke, Hasey, Jorna, & Persad, 1995). Patient reports indicate that depressive symptoms usually occur following the onset of OCD (Rasmussen & Eisen, 1992) and are often reduced by successful treatment of OCD (e.g., Foa, Steketee, Grayson, Turner, & Latimer, 1984). Among Axis II diagnoses, the personality disorders most often found in OCD patients are OCPD, Avoidant, Dependent, Histrionic, Passive-Aggressive, and Schizotypal Personality Disorder (Steketee et al., in press). Interestingly, the personality disorder long considered most similar to OCD, OCPD, does not co-occur more frequently than other personality disorders (Pfohl & Blum, 1991).

Prevalence and Incidence

Several studies have been conducted on the incidence and prevalence rates of OCD, both in the United States and internationally. A large-scale survey showed a 6-month prevalence of 1.6% and a lifetime prevalence of 2.5% (Karno & Golding, 1991). Other research has shown comparable rates, with 1-year prevalence rates ranging from 0.8% to 2.3% and lifetime prevalence rates from 1.9% to 3.3% (Karno et al., 1988; Robins et al., 1984). It is interesting that despite cultural differences, OCD tends to occur at approximately the same rate in various countries and cultures.

Several demographic characteristics associated with OCD onset have also been investigated. Rapoport (1986) reported that 50% of adults with OCD had developed symptoms by age 15, and less than 15% of patients experienced symptom onset after age 35 (Rasmussen & Tsuang, 1986). Onset of symptoms often begins earlier in boys (ages 14 to 17) and tends to be more severe than in girls, whose symptoms begin around age 19 (Rasmussen & Eisen, 1990). During childhood, boys are diagnosed with OCD twice as often as girls (Flament, 1994; Swedo, Rapoport, Leonard, Lenane, & Cheslow, 1989), but in adulthood the diagnosis occurs nearly equally in men and women (Karno et al., 1988; Rasmussen & Tsuang, 1986). No difference in the racial distribution of OCD has been observed in epidemiological research (Myers et al., 1984). The course of OCD tends to be chronic, with some fluctuation (Eisen & Steketee, 1997). Not surprisingly, the combination of early onset and chronic illness course has produced many people with OCD who have struggled for years with serious functional impairment.

Financial and Social Costs

The role of OCD in clients' lives is often reflected in the tremendous financial and social costs associated with it. The financial cost of the illness is apparent in two important ways: impact on functioning and cost of treatment. A report based on Obsessive Compulsive Foundation members showed that 41% were unable to work due to OCD symptoms, with an average loss of 2 years of wages (Hollander, Rowland, Stein, Broatch, & Himelein, 1995). Examining various anxiety disorders, Turner, Beidel, Spaulding, and Brown (1995) found that OCD required the greatest amount of treatment time (more hours and longer duration, with medians ranging from 6 to 12 months), and the largest associated financial cost. In fact, treatment for OCD cost approximately twice that for GAD and 60% more than treatment for Social Phobia and Panic Disorder. Two studies have examined the national financial costs of mental health treatment for OCD. Hollander et al. (1995) estimated lifetime hospital costs in the $5 billion range and lifetime indirect costs for lost wages at $40 billion. According to a second study, direct expenses, as well as morbidity and mortality costs of OCD, were $8.4 billion; $2.1 billion were spent in 1990 alone on institutional and hospital care, office-based mental health care, medication, and other support costs (Dupont, Rice, Shiraki, & Rowland, 1995). These figures indicate the profound cost of this illness to society.

Although perhaps less quantifiable, OCD involves tremendous social costs to patients and families. The obsessions and compulsions experienced by clients can determine much of their daily behavior and social interaction. Hollander et al. (1995) found that 64% of the OCD sufferers surveyed had lowered their career aspirations, and 62% had difficulty maintaining relationships because of symptoms. Calvocoressi et al. (1995) further confirmed the adverse social impact, noting that 88% of spouses or parents surveyed accommodated to family members' symptoms. Furthermore, family accommodation was associated with poor family functioning, rejecting attitudes toward the patient, and family stress.

Family interactions increasingly are being studied in relation to OCD presentation and treatment.

Social work practitioners have an important role in both the assessment and treatment of OCD. Many sufferers of OCD are not aware that their symptoms represent a formally recognized diagnosis for which treatment exists. When people with OCD pursue medical treatment for symptoms or other associated problems (for example, dermatitis for excessive washing), they may not be recognized by medical professionals as having OCD. As clinical practitioners in a multitude of mental health agencies, medical centers, and private practice settings, social workers are likely to encounter clients or family members of clients with OCD. As noted, OCD impacts relationships within the family and is likely to be a source of stress between family members. Thus, in addition to having OCD clients, social workers may encounter family members who need emotional support and guidance for managing the stress associated with having a family member with OCD. Social workers can have a significant role in providing proper diagnosis, assessment, psychoeducation, and treatment concerning OCD.

ASSESSMENT METHODS

Structured Clinical Interviews

To accurately diagnose OCD and determine the specific types of obsessions and compulsions that are relevant to each client, a number of assessment tools are available. A structured interview tool that measures specific components of OCD is the Anxiety Disorders Interview Schedule—IV (ADIS-IV; DiNardo, Brown, & Barlow, 1994). This interview targets information about frequency, persistence, distress, and resistance associated with specific obsessions and compulsions. In addition, it inquires about insight and gathers information about environmental factors such as stressors regarding family, work, finances, legal matters, and health. The ADIS allows for the diagnosis of other Axis I disorders relevant to OCD, with extensive emphasis on the other anxiety disorders that are most commonly comorbid with OCD, as well as Major Depressive Disorder, Dysthymia, psychotic disorders, and Substance Abuse. The ADIS also contains biographical information and the widely used Hamilton Rating Scale for Depression and Hamilton Anxiety Rating Scale (HRSD, HARS; Hamilton, 1959, 1960), which assess depressed and anxious mood. Finally, the ADIS-IV contains an historical time-line assessment, allowing interviewers to date the onset of all current disorders as an aid to the clinician in determining the possible interrelationship among comorbid disorders and deciding which to treat first. Although the ADIS requires approximately 2 to 3 hours to complete, its value is in its breadth of diagnostic inquiry and its sensitivity to components of OCD.

A highly specific assessment for OCD, and the one that is considered the standard, is the Yale-Brown Obsessive-Compulsive Scale (YBOCS), which can be applied as an adjunct to a structured clinical interview (Goodman et al., 1989a, 1989b). The interviewer administering the scale first explains the definitions of obsessions and compulsions and then asks about the client's current or past experience with 36 obsessions and 23 rituals that constitute the YBOC Checklist. These symptoms are organized according to the following categories: (a) aggressive/harming, (b) contamination, (c) sexual, (d) hoarding and saving, (e) religious, (f) symmetry/exactness, (g) somatic, and (h) miscellaneous. The 10-item YBOC Scale assesses severity on obsessions and compulsions subscales that examine five aspects of OCD pathology: (a) time spent, (b) interference, (c) distress, (d) resistance, and (e) perceived control. The scale has well-established reliability and validity (Woody, Steketee, & Chambless, 1995). One of its significant advantages is that it measures severity of OCD, irrespective of the types of obsessions and compulsions the client exhibits.

The YBOCS was formulated for use by clinicians to determine OCD severity and improvement with treatment, rather than to determine whether a client qualifies for the diagnosis of OCD. YBOCS scores range from 0 to 40, and clients scoring 16 or above are viewed as having sufficient symptom severity to warrant treatment. The YBOCS is an easily implemented, useful guide that enables clinicians to obtain a sense of the specific types and intensity of symptom difficulty an OCD client is experiencing. Application of a broad structured interview combined with the YBOCS should provide basic preliminary information about the clinical profile of a client with OCD.

Observational Measures

One observational measure for assessing OCD outcomes is the Behavioral Avoidance Test (BAT), which measures observable avoidance behavior and self-reported anxiety levels (Steketee, Chambless, Tran, Worden, & Gillis, 1996). The BAT challenges the client to perform one or more multistep tasks (up to 7 steps) that he or she usually associates with significant anxiety or rituals. The client is rated on the percentage of steps completed at least partially, the level of anxiety observed for each step at least partially completed (as measured by subjective units of discomfort [SUDS]), the level of avoidance displayed at each step, and the rituals performed for each step. Complex scoring procedures are used to quantify the preceding four measures, and a composite BAT score that reflects OCD symptom severity is then determined.

Self-Report Measures

Self-report methods have also been developed to measure OCD symptoms and pathology. A modified version of the YBOCS intended as a computerized or self-report method of assessment has been developed and shows promising preliminary reliability and validity (Frost, Steketee, Krause, & Trepanier, 1995). Another measure, the Maudsley Obsessional Compulsive Inventory (MOCI), is a 30-item true/false questionnaire with four subscales: (a) checking, (b) washing, (c) slowness—repetition, and (d) doubting—conscientious (Hodgson & Rachman, 1977); a revised version of the scale (MOCI-R) contains 84 items and is still undergoing preliminary testing for empirical soundness by Rachman and colleagues. The Padua Inventory (PI) is a 60-item instrument that assesses common obsessive-compulsive symptoms (Sanavio, 1988). This measure has also been revised and shortened and has demonstrated good reliability and validity. See Feske and Chambless (in press) for an excellent review of assessment tools for OCD. These authors recommend a multimethod measurement strategy and agree with other researchers and clinicians that the YBOCS remains the instrument of choice and at present enables greater cross-investigational comparison.

EFFECTIVE INTERVENTIONS

Individual Behavioral Treatment

In keeping with a behavioral model of OCD, behavioral treatment attempts both to eliminate the association of emotional distress with obsessive intrusions (deconditioning) and to stop the rituals that reinforce obsessive fears. *Exposure* and *response prevention* (ERP) involves exposing clients to overt and covert cues that provoke obsessions, coupled with blocking of the rituals in order to prevent them from prematurely reducing obsessive fears, thereby interfering with the habituation of the negative emotion generated by the obsession. The technique of ERP was developed by Meyer and colleagues in working with hospital patients who feared contamination and had washing rituals (Meyer, Levy, & Schnurer, 1974). Their intervention employed an intensive program of daily direct contact with contaminants and the complete prevention of rituals. This research inspired a rich continuation of experimentation on the behavioral treatment of OCD.

Many studies have focused on the effects of applying exposure and response prevention techniques in varying formats. Researchers at the Maudsley Hospital in London used a 15-session protocol of exposure and blocking over a 3-week period and found excellent overall effectiveness, even 2 years later; these benefits were considerably more effective than relaxation training (Marks, Hodgson, & Rachman, 1975). Of the 75% of the patients who were responsive to ERP, most showed substantial change. In reviewing findings, Steketee (1993) noted that 85% of clients were at least somewhat improved immediately after treatment and 55% were much or very much improved on the target symptoms. Follow-up reports have shown that an average of 75% were improved, and 50% were considered much or very much improved.

Some research has studied the effects of ERP on specific OCD symptoms and the usefulness of individual treatment components. Foa and Goldstein's (1978) study of 21 patients found that 57% improved substantially on obsessions whereas 86% stopped ritualizing after treatment, implying that the ERP therapy was most effective in addressing the compulsions. Research has not yet determined a precise number of sessions or duration of treatment required for effective ERP, but 15 to 20 sessions applied over 4 to 16 weeks has produced positive results in most clients (Steketee & Shapiro, 1993). Better long-term gains have been associated with longer trials of exposure therapy (O'Sullivan, Noshirvani, Marks, Monteiro, & Lelliott, 1991). Studies examining differences in the frequency of sessions suggest that scheduling exposure sessions more often than weekly does not enhance benefits beyond those produced by weekly sessions (Emmelkamp, van den Heuvell, Ruphan, & Sanderman, 1989; Steketee & Shapiro, 1993). Having the therapist model exposure does not add significantly to benefits of direct exposure without modeling (Boersma, Den Henst, Dekker, & Emmelkamp, 1976; Heyse, 1975). Direct exposure is essential to good outcome (Rabavilas, Boulougouris, & Stefanis, 1976), and imagined exposure may be an especially useful addition for patients who experience obsessions about catastrophic outcomes (Foa, Steketee, & Grayson, 1985). It has been suggested that exposure techniques may be more effective when the therapist guides the client to concentrate on the fears during exposure and avoids distracting conversation that might interfere with the processing of fearful information (Grayson, Steketee, & Foa, 1986). Overall, the extensive outcome research on ERP has produced consistently positive results, and further research may help refine the effective application of ERP techniques for particular patients.

Exposure treatment has several steps. The initial task for the client is to list relevant obsessive situations and then rank each one to create a rated hierarchy of the fears associated with those obsessions. Hierarchy items are rated from 0 to 100, with 0 representing no emotional discomfort and 100 the most discomfort (Steketee & White, 1990). At the outset of treatment, exposure is directed at low items on the hierarchy, gradually increasing up the range of discomfort in subsequent exposure sessions. In planning the approach to exposure treatment, the obsessional fears that are currently distressing to a client are addressed first. However, to obtain complete relief from OCD symptoms, it is important that the most feared situations eventually be treated with exposure, despite some clients' reluctance to do so. Decisions about how long to continue the exposure during a session are determined by ensuring that the client feels noticeably more comfortable at the end of the exposure than at the beginning. The exposure should not be stopped while the client still feels strongly distressed. The goal is to enable the client to experience a decline in the discomfort associated with obsessions without resorting to rituals.

Response prevention can be carried out using a variety of methods. Although complete blocking is highly recommended, some patients require more gradual forms of ritual prevention. At least three gradual methods have been used: (a) response delay, (b) ritual restriction, (c) and selective ritual prevention. *Response delay* challenges the patient to wait a specific period of time after the situational exposure before engaging in compulsive rituals that relieve the distress. This method has rarely been used in research trials; thus, there is little evidence to support its efficacy. *Ritual restriction* involves restricting the amount of time a ritual behavior is actually done; for example, by reducing showers from 30 minutes to 20 minutes or the number of checks from 10 to 2. This strategy may be combined with *selective ritual prevention,* in which rituals related to situations that rate high on the fear hierarchy are permitted (or reduced only somewhat), but those related to situations in which exposure has been practiced are not permitted at all. In other words, rituals are not restricted for those situations not yet included on the list of exposures being targeted, but as exposure items are added to the list, their associated rituals are no longer allowed. Some programs do not allow any ritualizing at all from the commencement of treatment, whereas others encourage patients to stop as completely as possible from the beginning but allow some rituals in the more fearful situations. More complete response prevention methods have shown slightly better gains than gradual methods in research trials (e.g., Foa & Goldstein, 1978), but no direct comparisons of these methods have been studied. Some additional study of this issue would be welcome, since more severe restriction of rituals produces considerable discomfort for some patients during therapy, whereas less restrictive methods might be more tolerable and might lead to less refusal of treatment. With regard to intervention for cognitive rituals, these should be treated with response prevention, *not* exposure. Blocking techniques, such as thought stopping, distraction, or substitution of obsessive thoughts in place of rituals, should be used.

Cognitive Treatment

Two major types of cognitive therapies have been utilized with OCD patients. The first is *Rational-Emotive Therapy* (RET), which focuses on identifying and disputing irrational beliefs and on making rational analyses of obsessional situations. Emmelkamp, Visser, and Hoekstra (1988) studied RET in comparison with self-controlled ERP and found that both treatments produce significant changes in most measures of OCD symptoms; on average, patients improved 78% from their baseline scores. Gains continued at 6-month follow-up, with an average improvement of 94%. Another study by Emmelkamp and Beens (1991) of 21 patients showed that RET is equally effective as exposure, but that combined treatment of RET and ERP does not have an additive effect. It is interesting to note that irrational beliefs declined more after RET and required longer to improve than did obsessive-compulsive symptoms. Rational-emotive cognitive treatment clearly has merit for clinical application and warrants further investigation in more widely distributed centers.

jects making clinically significant improvement. Decreases in depressed and anxious mood and improvement in functioning were also noted. The treatment strategy in this study focused less on exposure and blocking of rituals during sessions than other behavioral methods.

A series of uncontrolled trials by Van Noppen, Steketee, McCorkle, and Pato (1997) of 10- and 12-week ERP programs conducted in groups of 7 to 8 patients led to good outcomes on OCD symptoms, as well as in general functioning. Thirty-one percent showed clinically significant improvement after treatment and 43% did so at 1-year follow-up. Finally, a well-controlled trial of group behavioral treatment for OCD was conducted by Fals-Stewart, Marks, and Schafer (1993). OCD patients were treated in one of three conditions: (a) group exposure (imaginal or in vivo) and response prevention ($N = 30$), (b) comparable individual treatment ($N = 31$), and (c) individual relaxation control treatment ($N = 32$). Therapy took place in 24 sessions over a 12-week period for all patients. Results showed significant improvement for subjects in group exposure and in individual treatment, with individual treatment producing somewhat faster change. The control group changed significantly only on anxiety measures.

To provide a clinical picture of group ERP, procedural highlights from Van Noppen et al.'s (1997) Group Behavior Therapy (GBT) are outlined in the following. The major goals of this therapy are: (a) to establish rapport with the patient; (b) to provide education about OCD; (c) to develop and implement a behavioral treatment plan for the patient; (d) to promote feelings of empowerment, altruism, and empathy and decrease feelings of isolation, stigma, shame, burden, confusion, and impotence through the group process; (e) to encourage self-help skills through homework assignments and behavioral task challenges; and (f) to improve long-term outcome by providing education, a behavioral framework for problem solving, and support to the patient. The treatment course includes two initial individual sessions with each patient to establish treatment goals and develop an initial hierarchy. This is followed by 12 group treatment sessions, which can be co-led by two therapists, and 6 monthly check-in group sessions, for a total treatment plan of 20 sessions. Each group session is formatted to have a Check-In, Go-Round, ERP Therapy, and Homework Go-Round. During the 10-minute Check-In the group reviews what was covered and accomplished the previous week. Go-Round takes 20 minutes; the patients each report on the homework they completed during the week. The ERP Therapy portion of each meeting lasts 60 minutes and focuses on imagined or in vivo exposure and response prevention. During the 30-minute Homework Go-Round, each patient selects a behavioral goal from his or her hierarchy as a homework task. In the last six weekly group treatment sessions, patients are given increasing responsibility for devising the in vivo exposure and response prevention tasks. Finally, monthly check-in group sessions are 90-minute meetings intended to ensure maintenance of treatment gains by reviewing progress and stumbling blocks and reinforcing self-help strategies for OCD symptoms and life stresses. These sessions do not usually include any direct exposure. Group processes are employed to facilitate patient motivation, problem solving skills, peer support, and a rational vantage point for engaging in exposure tasks.

Family Treatment

Although little research has been conducted on family treatment for OCD, some evidence suggests that including family members in patients' treatment may improve their outcome. OCD symptoms have a negative impact on family functioning and often extensively involve the family in the patient's illness (Allsopp & Verduyn, 1990; Marks et al., 1975). Some of the adverse effects on the family include difficulties in managing the patient's reassurance-seeking, confessing, avoidance behaviors, and excessive bathroom and water use; delays due to rituals; and financial costs to replace "contaminated" items. Despite such frustrations, partner relationships among OCD patients are no worse than those of the general population (e.g., Riggs, Hiss, & Foa, 1992). However, Calvocoressi et al. (1995) observed that greater family participation in symptoms is significantly associated with family dysfunction and negative attitudes toward the patient, suggesting that intervention to address these difficulties may be needed. Research in the area of family involvement in OCD therapy has been limited, but some case studies and a few larger projects have provided preliminary information.

Support groups that include family members have been the subject of some reports, but no research has been published to date. Marks et al. (1975) conducted an open-ended monthly group for family members and patients to discuss the effect of OCD on the family, plan coping strategies, and rehearse behavioral exercises. More recent groups have had a psychoeducational focus, with topics intended to improve self-esteem, teach strategies for coping with OCD symptoms, share feelings and experiences, and accept patients' limitations (e.g., Black & Blum, 1992; Tynes, Salins, Skiba, & Winstead, 1992). These time-limited family support groups have also included specific information on the diagnosis, assessment, and theories of OCD, and on behavioral treatment, medication, and relapse prevention. High participant utilization and satisfaction have been reported, but empirical research on the effectiveness of these interventions is needed.

Case studies and a handful of group investigations have examined the impact of including spouses or partners and other family members in OCD treatment. Hafner (1982) reported case studies in which poor marital relationships appeared to adversely affect the outcome of OCD outpatients who returned home after treatment. In addition, two cases showed improvement when spouses participated in the behavioral treatment (Cobb, McDonald, Marks, & Stern, 1980; Hafner, 1988). Benefits were also evident in case studies of parental involvement in the behavioral treatment of children with OCD (Dalton, 1983) and of adolescents and adults (Hafner, Gilchrist, Bowling, & Kalucy, 1981; Hoover & Insel, 1984). Consistent with Hafner, Badenoch, Fisher, and Swift's (1983) suggestions, it appears that including family members in behavioral treatment might lead to better gains than individual treatment alone.

However, larger studies have produced less consistent results concerning the involvement of family members in therapy. Emmelkamp and De Lange (1983) compared the outcome of Dutch clients treated behaviorally with or without the spouse as cotherapist. Patients treated with spouse assistance improved more at posttest but not at follow-up. In a second larger study, spouse assistance made no difference in outcome either after treatment or at follow-up, despite improvement in marital satisfaction (Emmelkamp, de Haan, & Hoogduin, 1990). The researchers themselves noted that spouses were not specifically trained in communication with the patient regarding symptoms and later commented that inclusion of partners and empathic communication may be an important factor in outcome (Emmelkamp, Kloek, & Blaauw, 1992). A study done in India by Mehta (1990) provided quite positive results. Involving family members in ERP for 30 patients led to significantly greater improvement in OCD symptoms, mood state, and social and occupational functioning than did unassisted ERP treatment. Furthermore, family-treated patients showed continued improvement several months later, whereas individually treated patients lost some of the gains they had made. Hafner (1992) proposed that the discrepancy in Emmelkamp's and Mehta's findings may be due to the latter study's less confrontational family role and greater intensity of treatment (24 sessions twice weekly versus 8 sessions in 5 weeks). The discrepant findings could also reflect cultural differences in Indian and Dutch families, particularly in the style of family interaction, as well as differences in the type of participation of marital partners compared to a broader group of family members.

One research group has focused therapy efforts on reducing relatives' involvement in patients' OCD symptoms. In the context of an inpatient treatment program in Great Britain, Thornicroft, Colson, and Marks (1991) taught relatives to assist in a self-treatment ERP program that included training in self-control and social skills. Intervention with family members concentrated on reducing relatives' involvement in rituals by training them to monitor patient behavior and encourage self-exposure in a noncritical manner. Relatives practiced under the supervision of a therapist on the ward. The success of this therapeutic approach was evident in substantial decreases in symptoms of about 45% at discharge and 60% at 6-month follow-up, with improvement in functioning that ranged from 33% for work functioning to 48% for home functioning at follow-up.

A recently studied approach for including families in treatment is multifamily behavioral treatment (MFBT). Two uncontrolled studies tested 8- to 12-week groups of family members and patients together. Groups received education about OCD and ERP, family contracting for behavior change, direct exposure during family group sessions, and communication skills regarding management of OCD symptoms. Modeling by therapists and by other family members appeared to be an important component of therapy. Results in the first study of 13 OCD patients and their families showed a significant decrease in YBOCS scores at posttest, and further reduction at follow-up (Van Noppen, Pato, Rasmussen, & Marsland, 1993). A second study of 19 OCD patients showed similar gains, with 47% at posttest and 58% at follow-up moving out of the clinical range on OCD symptoms (Van Noppen et al., 1997).

To provide a more detailed view of MFBT, highlights of this treatment are outlined in the following. The goals of the treatment are: (a) to establish rapport with the patient and family and provide a supportive therapy context; (b) to provide psychoeducation on OCD; (c) to develop and implement a behavioral treatment plan for the patient to improve his or her level of functioning and decrease the severity of OCD symptoms; (d) to change the family pattern of communication to reduce criticism and overinvolvement and improve problem solving and positive support through family behavioral contracting; (e) to promote feelings of empowerment, altruism, and empathy while decreasing feelings of isolation, stigma, shame, confusion, and impotence through the group process; (f) to teach the patient to utilize self-instruction through exposure and response prevention homework assignments; and (g) to improve long-term outcome by providing the patient with education to enhance insight into OCD and behavioral strategies to manage obsessive compulsive symptoms. In addition, the group modeling offers patients a normative context to rely on when challenging irrational thoughts and unreasonable behaviors after the formal group ends. The format is similar to that of GBT: 20 sessions are divided into 2 information gathering sessions with each patient individually, 12 weekly family group treatment sessions, and 6 monthly follow-up family group sessions. The first three family group treatment sessions focus on psychoeducation, the next session begins an intensive ERP treatment phase, and the remaining sessions focus on the behavioral family treatment phase, during which family members learn behavioral contracting to negotiate specific ERP goals. Exposure planning is gradually shifted from the group leader to the patients. The six check-in family group sessions are meant to reinforce gains made during the treatment period and help patients and families to continue in a self-help mode of therapy.

CONCLUSIONS

It is clear from the preceding review that a considerable amount of information has accumulated regarding the symptoms and psychopathology of OCD, as well as about its treatment. Perhaps the least information is available on determining the etiology of this condition, although most researchers agree that multiple causal factors are undoubtedly responsible. Most certainly these include biological factors, both neurochemical and neuroanatomical. Additional contributors are likely to include specific historical experiences and negative cognitive interpretations regarding common obsessive intrusions. Greater clarity on the specific roles of these causal factors is much needed to enable clinicians to better develop, design, and direct the various effective treatment interventions.

Intensive behavioral treatments that include exposure and ritual prevention have proven highly effective for up to 80% of clients. However, some relapse occurs in up to 25%, and similar refusal rates because of the anxiety provocation associated with this method render it less effective than the initial benefit rates make it appear to be. An additional problem is the difficulty for some clients in rural regions of finding therapists who are well-trained in delivering this therapy. Cognitive treatments appear very promising but are inadequately tested, especially at long-term follow-up. The need for well-trained delivery of cognitive therapy specifically focused on OCD is also likely to be a problem for some time. Like for cognitive therapy, combinations of medication with either ERP or cognitive treatment are also inadequately tested. So far, despite a strong clinical impression of their synergistic action, there is little research evidence to support combined treatment.

Despite these lacks in available research and some of the evident problems in delivering treatment, the overall outlook for clients with OCD is considerably improved over its status 25 years ago. More etiological and treatment research is clearly needed. Also needed are many more social workers who are well trained in delivery of behavioral (ERP) and cognitive therapy. This is a particular need in managed care systems where, despite large numbers of social workers and other clinical providers, few are trained in brief treatment procedures such as ERP that have been demonstrated to be effective for particular disorders. Social workers with proper training are well positioned to provide such effective psychosocial intervention for OCD, especially in group and family contexts.

REFERENCES

Allsopp, M., & Verduyn, C. (1990). Adolescents with obsessive-compulsive disorder: A case note review of consecutive patients referred to a provincial regional adolescent psychiatry unit. *Journal of Adolescence, 13,* 157–169.

American Psychiatric Association. (1994). *Diagnostic and statistical manual of mental disorders* (4th ed.). Washington, DC: Author.

Beck, A., Emery, G., & Greenberg, R. (1985). *Anxiety disorders and phobias: A cognitive perspective.* New York: Basic Books.

Black, D. W., & Blum, N. S. (1992). Obsessive-compulsive disorder support groups: The Iowa model. *Comprehensive Psychiatry, 33,* 65–71.

Black, D., Noyes, R., Pfohl, B., Goldstein, R., & Blum, N. (1993). Personality disorder in obsessive compulsive volunteers, well comparison subjects, and their first degree relatives. *American Journal of Psychiatry, 150,* 1226–1232.

Boersma, K., Den Hengst, S., Dekker, J., & Emmelkamp, P. M. G. (1976). Exposure and response prevention: A comparison with obsessive compulsive patients. *Behaviour Research and Therapy,* 19–24.

Calvocoressi, L., Lewis, B., Harris, M., Trufan, B. S., Goodman, W. K., McDougle, C. J., & Price, L. H. (1995). Family accommodation in obsessive compulsive disorder. *American Journal of Psychiatry, 152,* 441–443.

Cobb, J., McDonald, R., Marks, I. M., & Stern, R. (1980). Marital versus exposure therapy: Psychological treatment of co-existing marital and phobic obsessive problems. *Behavioural Analysis and Modification, 4,* 3–16.

Cottraux, J., Mollard, E., Bouvard, M., Marks, I., Sluys, M., Nury, A. M., Douge, R., & Cialdella, P. (1989). A controlled study of fluvoxamine and exposure in obsessive compulsive disorder. *International Clinical Psychopharmacology, 5,* 1–14.

Dalton, P. (1983). Family treatment of an obsessive-compulsive child: A case report. *Family Process, 22,* 99–108.

DiNardo, P. A., Brown, T. A., & Barlow, D. H. (1994). *Anxiety Disorders Interview Schedule for DSM-IV (ADIS-IV).* Albany, NY: Graywind.

Dupont, R. L., Rice, D. P., Shiraki, S., & Rowland, C. R. (1995). Economic costs of obsessive-compulsive disorder. *Medical Interface,* 102–109.

Eisen, J., & Steketee, G. (1997). Course of illness in obsessive compulsive disorder. In L. J. Dickstein, M. B. Riba, & J. M. Oldham (Eds.), *Review of Psychiatry* (Vol. 16, pp. III73–III95). Washington, DC: American Psychiatric Press.

Emmelkamp, P. M. G., & Beens, H. (1991). Cognitive therapy with obsessive-compulsive disorder: A comparative evaluation. *Behaviour Research and Therapy, 29,* 293–300.

Emmelkamp, P. M. G., de Haan, E., & Hoogduin, C. A. L. (1990). Marital adjustment and obsessive compulsive disorder. *British Journal of Psychiatry, 156,* 55–60.

Emmelkamp, P. M. G., & De Lange, I. (1983). Spouse involvement in the treatment of obsessive-compulsive patients. *Behaviour Research and Therapy, 21,* 341–346.

Emmelkamp, P. M. G., Kloek, J., & Blaauw, E. (1992). Obsessive-compulsive disorders. In P. H. Wilson (Ed.), *Principles and practice of relapse prevention* (pp. 213–234). New York: Guilford Press.

Emmelkamp, P. M. G., van den Heuvell, C. V. L., Ruphan, M., & Sanderman, R. (1989). Home-based treatment of obsessive-compulsive patients: Intersession interval and therapist involvement. *Behaviour Research and Therapy, 27,* 89–93.

Emmelkamp, P. M. G., Visser, S., & Hoekstra, R. J. (1988). Cognitive therapy versus exposure *in vivo* in the treatment of obsessive-compulsives. *Cognitive Therapy and Research, 12,* 103–114.

Enright, S. J. (1991). Group treatment for obsessive-compulsive disorder: An evaluation. *Behavioural Psychotherapy, 19,* 183–192.

Epsie, C. A. (1986). The group treatment of obsessive-compulsive ritualizers: Behavioral management of identified patterns of relapse. *Behavioural Psychotherapy, 14,* 21–33.

Fals-Stewart, W., Marks, A. P., & Schafer, J. (1993). A comparison of behavioral group therapy and individual behavior therapy in treating obsessive-compulsive disorder. *Journal of Nervous and Mental Disease, 181,* 189–193.

Flament, M. F. (1994). Recent findings in childhood onset obsessive compulsive disorder. In E. Hollander, D., Marazziti, & J. Zohar (Eds.), *Current insights in obsessive compulsive disorder* (pp. 23–40). New York: Wiley.

Feske, U., & Chambless, D. L. (in press). A review of assessment measures for obsessive compulsive disorder. In W. K. Goodman, M. Rudorfer, & J. Maser (Eds.), *Treatment challenges in obsessive compulsive disorder.* Rahway, NJ: Erlbaum.

Pfohl, B., & Blum, N. (1991). Obsessive compulsive personality disorder: A review of available data and recommendations for DSM-IV. *Journal of Personality Disorders, 5,* 363–375.

Rabavilas, A., Boulougouris, J., & Stefanis, C. (1976). Duration of flooding sessions in the treatment of obsessive-compulsive patients. *Behaviour Research and Therapy, 14,* 349–355.

Rapoport, J. L. (1986). Childhood obsessive compulsive disorder. *Journal of Child Psychology and Psychiatry, 19,* 134–144.

Rasmussen, S., & Eisen, J. (1990). Epidemiology and clinical features of obsessive-compulsive disorder. In M. A. Jenike, L. Baer, & W. E. Minichiello (Eds.), *Obsessive-compulsive disorders: Theory and management* (pp. 10–27). Chicago: Year Book Medical.

Rasmussen, S., & Eisen, J. (1992). The epidemiology and differential diagnosis of obsessive compulsive disorder. *Journal of Clinical Psychiatry, 53,* 4–10.

Rasmussen, S., Eisen, J., & Pato, M. (1993). Current issues in the pharmacologic management of obsessive compulsive disorder. *Journal of Clinical Psychiatry, 54*(6, Suppl.), 4–9.

Rasmussen, S., & Tsuang, M. (1986). DSM-III obsessive compulsive disorder: Clinical characteristics and family history. *American Journal of Psychiatry, 143,* 317–322.

Riggs, D. S., Hiss, H., & Foa, E. B. (1992). Marital distress and the treatment of obsessive compulsive disorder. *Behavior Therapy, 23,* 585–597.

Robins, L., Helzer, J., Weissman, M., Ovasehel, H., Gruenberg, E., Burke, J., & Reigner, D. (1984). Lifetime prevalence of specific psychiatric disorders in three sites. *Archives of General Psychiatry, 41,* 949–958.

Salkovskis, P. M., & Warwick, H. M. C. (1986). Morbid preoccupations, health anxiety and reassurance: A cognitive behavioural approach to hypochondriasis. *Behaviour Research and Therapy, 24,* 597–602.

Sanavio, E. (1988). Obsessions and compulsions: The Padua Inventory. *Behaviour Research and Therapy, 26,* 169–177.

Stein, D., Spadaccini, E., & Hollander, E. (1995). Meta-analysis of pharmacotherapy trials for obsessive compulsive disorder. *International Clinical Psychopharmacology, 10,* 11–18.

Steketee, G. (1993). Social support and treatment outcomes of obsessive compulsive disorder at 9-month follow up. *Behavioural Psychotherapy, 21,* 81–95.

Steketee, G. (1994). Behavioral assessment and treatment planning with obsessive compulsive disorder: A review emphasizing clinical application. *Behavior Therapy, 25,* 613–633.

Steketee, G., Chambless, D. L., Tran, G. Q., Worden, H., & Gillis, M. M. (1996). Behavioral avoidance test for obsessive compulsive disorder. *Behaviour Research and Therapy, 34,* 73–83.

Steketee, G., Henninger, N., & Pollard, C. A. (in press). Predicting treatment outcome for OCD: Effects of comorbidity. In W. K. Goodman, M. Rudorfer, & J. Maser (Eds.), *Treatment challenges in obsessive compulsive disorder.* Rahway, NJ: Erlbaum.

Steketee, G., & Shapiro, L. J. (1993). Obsessive-compulsive disorder. In A. S. Bellack & M. Hersen (Eds.), *Handbook of behavior therapy in the psychiatric setting* (pp. 199–227). New York: Plenum Press.

Steketee, G., & White, K. (1990). *When once is not enough: Help for obsessive compulsives.* Oakland, CA: New Harbinger.

Swedo, S., Rapoport, J., Leonard, H., Lenane, M. C., & Cheslow, D. L. (1989). Obsessive compulsive disorder in children and adolescents. *Archives of General Psychiatry, 46,* 335–345.

Taylor, C. J., & Sholomskas, D. E. (1993, March). *Group exposure and response prevention for OCD.* Paper presented at the annual meeting of the Anxiety Disorders Association of America, Santa Monica, CA.

Thornicroft, G., Colson, L., & Marks, I. (1991). An in-patient behavioural psychotherapy unit description and audit. *British Journal of Psychiatry, 158,* 362–367.

Turner, S. M., Beidel, D. C., Spaulding, S. A., & Brown, J. M. (1995). The practice of behavior therapy: A national survey of cost and methods. *The Behavior Therapist, 18,* 1–4.

Tynes, L., Salins, C., Skiba, W., & Winstead, D. K. (1992). A psychoeducational and support group for obsessive-compulsive disorder patients and their significant others. *Comprehensive Psychiatry, 33,* 197–201.

Tynes, L. L., White, K., & Steketee, G. (1990). Toward a new nosology of OCD. *Comprehensive Psychiatry, 31,* 465–480.

Van Noppen, B., Pato, M., Rasmussen, S., & Marsland, R. (1993, May). *Family function and family group treatment.* Paper presented at the American Psychiatric Association, San Francisco, CA.

Van Noppen, B., Steketee, G., McCorkle, B. H., & Pato, M. (1997). Group and multi-family behavioral treatment for OCD: A pilot study. *Journal of Anxiety Disorders, 11,* 431–446.

van Oppen, P., deHaan, E., van Balkom, A., Spinhoven, P., Hoogduin, K., & van Dyck, R. (1995). Cognitive therapy and exposure *in vivo* in the treatment of obsessive compulsive disorder. *Research and Therapy, 4,* 379–390.

Weissmann, M., Bland, R., Canino, G., Greenwald, S., Hwo, H., Lee, C., Newman, S., Oakley-Browne, M., Rubio-Stipek, M., Wickramaratne, P., Wittchen, H., & Eng-Kung, Y. (1994). The cross national epidemiology of obsessive compulsive disorder. *Journal of Clinical Psychiatry, 55,* 5–10.

Woody, S. R., Steketee, G., & Chambless, D. L. (1995). Reliability and validity of the Yale-Brown Obsessive Compulsive Scale. *Behaviour Research and Therapy, 33,* 597–605.

Chapter 18

POST-TRAUMATIC STRESS DISORDER

M. Elizabeth Vonk
Bonnie L. Yegidis

OVERVIEW

Although people experienced difficulties related to traumatic events long before the late 20th century, the diagnosis of Post-Traumatic Stress Disorder (PTSD) did not appear in the *Diagnostic and Statistical Manual of Mental Disorders* (*DSM-III*, American Psychiatric Association [APA], 1980) until relatively recently. Since that time, the definition has been revised twice, based on a wealth of clinical and empirical study.

The contemporary definition of PTSD (APA, 1994) includes specifications of the traumatic events, the symptoms, and the duration of symptoms. Criterion A requires that the person must experience or be confronted with a traumatic event that involves the threat of death, serious injury, or loss of physical integrity, to which the person responds with fear, helplessness, or horror. By definition, the event must have occurred prior to the manifestation of symptoms.

Criteria B, C, and D refer to symptomatic requirements of the diagnosis. First, the person must have at least one symptom of persistently reexperiencing the traumatic event, such as intrusive images or thoughts, dreams about the event, a sense that the event is reoccurring, intense distress when confronted with reminders of the event, or physiological reactivity when in the presence of event-related cues. Next, the person must have at least three symptoms of avoidance and numbing, such as avoiding thoughts, feelings, or conversations about the event; avoiding activity, places, or people that are reminders of the event; inability to remember part of the event; decreased participation in important activities; a sense of detachment from others; inability to experience a full range of emotion; or a restricted sense of the future. Third, the person must show at least two symptoms of increased arousal, such as sleep difficulties, increased irritability, difficulty concentrating, exaggerated startle response, or hypervigilance. Finally, Criteria E and F require that the person must have experienced the symptoms for more than 1 month and that the symptoms must cause some type of functional impairment, such as in school, at work, or in relationships.

Post-Traumatic Stress Disorder may be diagnosed at any age, including childhood. The *DSM-IV* (APA, 1994) definition draws a distinction between three types of PTSD. If symptoms are present for less than 3 months, the diagnosis is *Acute.* When symptoms persist for 3 months or longer, PTSD is considered to be *Chronic.* If the symptoms do not occur until at least 6 months following the event, the diagnosis is *with Delayed Onset.* Persons with PTSD may seek treatment for any of the three types.

It is also important to note that many people who have PTSD also have other psychological difficulties, such as substance abuse, depression, and personality disorders (Keane & Wolfe, 1990). They also share many of the same symptoms as those with generalized anxiety disorders, dissociative disorders, or depression (Davidson & Foa, 1991). In one study of Vietnam veterans, it was shown that of the group that demonstrated PTSD symptoms, 66% also met criteria for anxiety or depressive disorder, and 39% met the criteria for Alcohol Abuse or Alcohol Dependence (Centers for Disease Control, 1988). While it is not known whether exposure to trauma or subsequent PTSD results in this variety of pathologies, or if, conversely, the vulnerability to pathology proceeds exposure and subsequent PTSD, the practitioner needs to be aware of potential comorbidity.

The diagnosis of PTSD is unusual in that it requires a *cause* in addition to a particular set of symptoms in its definition. The cause—a traumatic event—may be of a wide variety of types as long as it is perceived by the victim to threaten serious injury or loss of life and is accompanied by fear and helplessness. Traumatic events may be war-related, such as combat exposure or torture of prisoners and refugees; related to natural disasters, such as earthquakes, floods, or hurricanes; crime-related, such as rape, battering, incest, or assault; or accident-related, such as automobile or airplane collisions. When caused by nature or by accident, traumatic events are potent reminders of human vulnerability. When caused deliberately by others, they are reminders of the capability of persons to inflict injury and suffering on one another.

Estimates of exposure to trauma and of PTSD in the general adult population vary. Green (1994) draws several conclusions, based on a review of the epidemiological literature. First, she reports that exposure to at least one traumatic event during one's lifetime is common, citing studies with estimates ranging from approximately 40% to 75% of the general adult population of the United States. She goes on to report that about 25% of those who are exposed go on to develop PTSD. Rates of PTSD for specific types of trauma are also reviewed by Green (1994), as well as by Meichenbaum (1994). For example, the lifetime PTSD rate for Vietnam combat veterans has been found to be 31% for males and 27% for females. High rates of lifetime prevalence of PTSD have been found for women who have been raped (up to 80%) or battered (45% to 84%). Survivors of child sexual abuse are also at high risk for PTSD. Lifetime rates are somewhat lower for those who experience a natural disaster or a traffic accident.

Although the numbers can be somewhat confusing and can seem contradictory at times, the bottom line is that millions of people worldwide are exposed to traumatic events that meet the specifications of Criterion A. The risk of exposure to trauma crosses lines of gender, age, race, class, and nationality. Women are particularly at risk for personal and sexual violence; men for combat, physical assault, and automobile accidents. People who live in developing countries are at higher risk of being greatly affected by natural and technological disasters. All who are exposed are at risk of developing PTSD.

Exposure to trauma alone is insufficient to cause PTSD. From a review of the pertinent literature, Meichenbaum (1994) proposes that there are characteristics of the event, the person, and the environment that may increase a person's vulnerability to developing PTSD. First, predisposing factors related to the traumatic event may include the proximity of the person to a disaster site or to combat, the level of death and destruction that is witnessed, and the intentionality of the acts that cause the trauma. Next, several characteristics have been identified with regard to the person, including a history of prior victimization, a history of prior psychiatric or substance abuse problems, and lower socioeconomic status. There is evidence that the person's perception about the level of threat to his or her life and bodily integrity are of utmost importance. The person's perception of loss of control or self-blame for the traumatic event appear to be equally important. Finally, environmental characteristics include deficient social support, familial or community-wide blaming of victims, or the impossibility of resuming normal routines.

Many of those who develop PTSD show similar symptomatic profiles, regardless of the type of trauma they have experienced. The general pattern that has emerged includes a very high level of distress within the first week that may continue for several weeks. After about 3 months, the acute distress has generally been alleviated, leaving many victims with long-term difficulties in several areas of their lives, including emotional, cognitive, physical or biological, and social or interpersonal problems (Gilmartin, 1994; Meichenbaum, 1994). Emotional responses are generally very intense and include fear, anxiety, depression, anger, grief, numbing, and guilt. It is not unusual for persons to feel overwhelmed by the intensity of their feelings following a trauma. Cognitive difficulties include impaired ability to concentrate, confusion, and intrusive thoughts. The trauma survivor must struggle to make sense of an experience that is shattering to long-held assumptions about the world (Janoff-Bulman, 1985). Assumptions that are disrupted may involve the person's sense of control, beliefs about safety, trust in self and others, beliefs about self-control and power, self-esteem, and beliefs about intimacy (McCann & Pearlman, 1990a). Physical or biological impacts may include sleep disturbance, nightmares, disrupted eating patterns, and psychosomatic complaints. On the interpersonal and social level, trauma victims often experience disruption in intimate relationships, vocational impairment, or general social withdrawal.

The impact of PTSD does not stop with individuals. Families, workplaces, and communities are adversely effected as well. For example, the families of Vietnam veterans with PTSD have more marital problems than do families of veterans without PTSD (Figley, 1995d). Children may also experience more difficulty if a parent suffers from PTSD. Meichenbaum (1994) points out that children are at risk of secondary victimization by a parent with PTSD. For example, children of Holocaust survivors often have adjustment problems, such as low self-esteem and affective impairment. It has already been noted that individuals with PTSD are often unable to perform well at school or at work. PTSD is also thought to be associated with a wide range of community problems, such as homelessness, increased utilization of medical intervention, and substance abuse.

PTSD clearly deserves attention from social work practitioners due to its far-reaching impact. Also, because the risk of exposure to trauma is uniformly high, social workers in a wide variety of settings should be familiar with the assessment and treatment of PTSD.

ASSESSMENT METHODS

Typically, the diagnosis of PTSD is made only after establishing that Criterion A (the stressor) has been experienced and after conducting an in-depth clinical interview. Practitioners often enhance the clinical interview assessment with the use of one or more self-report assessment tools to measure symptoms. It is believed that a multiaxial approach is most effective in making a thorough assessment of the disorder. This section reviews the most well-known assessment measures in the field and presents a brief summary of the usefulness and psychometric properties of each. It should be noted that there is a literature addressing the assessment of physiological symptoms associated with PTSD. These methods are not addressed in this section; however, interested readers are referred to Blanchard, Kolb, Pallmeyer, and Gerardi (1982); Malloy, Fairbank, and Keane (1983); or Lating and Everly (1995) for a thorough discussion of these issues.

Structured Interviews

Structured interviews have been used extensively to assess PTSD. This method allows for the in-depth exploration of the major diagnostic categories of the disorder, including both the experience of a traumatic event and the emotional responses that the person has had to it. Following is a summary of several examples of this kind of assessment:

Structured Clinical Interview for DSM-III (SCID).   The SCID (Spitzer & Williams, 1985) requires the social worker to pose specific questions about the symptoms the client experiences according to *DSM-III* (APA, 1980). The instrument has a PTSD component that has been shown to be a clinically valuable measurement of the disorder (see, for example, McFall, Smith, Mackay, & Tarver, 1990).

Post-Traumatic Stress Disorder Interview (PTSD-I).   The PTSD-I (Watson, Juba, Manifold, Kucala, & Anderson, 1991) is comprised of 20 items related to *DSM III-R* (APA, 1987) criteria. Questions assess whether the respondent has experienced an event that would qualify as *trauma*. The remaining items measure the various symptoms of the disorders. Reliability data show that the instrument is high in internal consistency ($\alpha = .92$). Test-retest estimates are also high (.95). Validity data show that the instrument is useful in cross-validating the assessment of PTSD with other instruments.

Clinician Administered PTSD Scales (CAPS-1).   The CAPS-1 (Blake et al., 1990). is a clinically administered measure of current PTSD status. Data on the CAPS-1 show that it is both a reliable and valid measure of the disorder. The CAPS-2 version is designed to assess symptoms during the previous week and is often used in studies that require repeated measures. Items on the measure assess the 17 symptoms of PTSD described in *DSM-III-R* (APA, 1987) and include eight associated symptoms derived from that source and from the clinical literature on the topic. For example, one item on the CAPS asks respondents if "In the past week, have you had unpleasant dreams about the event(s)?" Responses for the item measure the frequency and the intensity of the distress associated with this symptom. CAPS also assesses the impact of PTSD symptoms on the respondent's social and occupational functioning. CAPS has been used extensively for the assessment of PTSD in combat veterans.

Objective Measures

Numerous self-administered, objective measures have been developed for use in assessing PTSD. In addition, measures of generalized anxiety, such as the State and Trait Anxiety Inventory (Spielberger, Gorsuch, & Lushene, 1970), and depression (Beck, Ward, Mendelson, Mock, & Erbaugh, 1961) have been used extensively in studies of PTSD. This subsection reviews the PTSD measures that appear frequently in the published research on PTSD. It should be noted that in addition to the five instruments presented in the following, other measures of PTSD are mentioned in the literature. However, those that are most often identified in the literature, have evidence of reliability and validity, and have been used successfully in the clinical setting have been selected for discussion. Most of these scales are in the public domain; others must be purchased from the publisher or requested directly from the author; and some are completely reprinted, along with scoring and interpretive instructions, in the valuable compilation of rapid assessment instruments prepared by Fischer and Corcoran (1994).

Impact of Events Scale (IES).   The *IES* (Horowitz, Wilner & Alvarez, 1979) is a 15-item scale designed to measure the frequency of current distress, as shown in symptoms of intrusion and avoidance, relative to a specific traumatic event. Reliability estimates range from .78 to .86 for subscale reliabilities, with a test-retest estimate on total scale scores of .87. The scale has been successfully used to measure changes in stress symptoms following treatment in a study of rape survivors (Resnick, Kilpatrick, Walsh, & Veronen, 1991).

Rape Aftermath Symptom Test (RAST).   The RAST (Kilpatrick, 1988) is a 70-item measure of psychological symptoms and fear-producing stimuli. The scale was derived from items of the Symptom CheckList 90—Revised (SCL-90R; Derogatis, 1977) and the Modified Fear Survey (MFS; Veronen & Kilpatrick, 1980). The RAST has been found to discriminate between matched groups of rape victims and nonvictims at numerous assessment periods postrape (Kilpatrick et al., 1985).

PTSD Symptom Scale (PSS).   The PSS (Foa, Riggs, Dancu, & Rothbaum, 1993) contains 17 items based upon *DSM-III-R* (APA, 1987) criteria for assessing the severity of PTSD symptoms. The scale produces continuous data and yields a severity score for clusters of symptoms that correspond to the diagnostic criteria (reexperiencing, avoidance, and arousal). The reliability estimate of the scale, measured as a coefficient α, has been reported as .85. Subscale reliabilities range from .78 to .82. The validity of the measure was derived by correlating scores on the PSS with two other objective measures of PTSD, the Impact of Events Scale (IES; Horowitz et. al, 1979) and the Rape Aftermath Symptoms Test (RAST; Kilpatrick, 1988). These correlations showed that the PSS correlates highly with the IES (.80) and the RAST (.82), supporting the convergent validity of the scale.

Crime Related PTSD Scale of the Symptom Check List.   This scale (Saunders, Mandoki, & Kilpatrick, 1990) is a 28-item scale derived from the SCL-90R (Derogatis, 1977), designed to measure crime-related PTSD in the community. Study of the instrument has shown that it successfully discriminates between groups of women within the same community who differ with respect to victimization. Reliability estimates of the scale show that it is high in internal consistency ($\alpha = .90$).

Mississippi Scale for Combat Related PTSD (M-PTSD).   The M-PTSD (Keane, Caddell, & Taylor, 1988) is a 35-item instrument that provides a continuous measure of PTSD symptoms as presented in *DSM-III* (APA, 1980). Studies of the instrument show that it successfully discriminates between groups of PTSD veterans as compared to matched groups of successfully adjusted veterans. Reliability estimates of the scale are strong, with a coefficient α of .94.

The development of reliable and valid measures of PTSD in trauma survivors needs further refinement. This is necessary to get a better picture of the incidence and prevalence of the disorder. Also, better measurement provides researchers and clinicians with the opportunity to measure change in symptoms as a function of treatment more accurately.

EFFECTIVE INTERVENTIONS

Several interventions have been found to be at least partially effective for the treatment of Post-Traumatic Stress Disorder. At this time, however, there is no conclusive evidence of the superiority of any one of the effective treatments over the others (Meichenbaum, 1994). In addition, most social workers in clinical practice combine techniques rather than relying exclusively on one type of intervention. For instance, a client may be involved in a form of individual psychotherapy along with taking psychotropic medication. In addition to interventions aimed at individuals, there are group, family, and preventative or community interventions. Freedy and Donkervoet (1995) emphasize that the treatment of PTSD calls for an eclectic or integrative use of treatments based on assessment of the client's individual needs and on what is known about successful treatments. Before reviewing specific interventions, this section provides an overview of the goals and commonalities of many effective interventions. Helpful attitudes and backgrounds for social workers serving people who are traumatized are also briefly reviewed.

Just as trauma may have an effect on a person's emotional, physical, cognitive, and social well-being, so must treatment goals be comprehensive. Several goals can be identified that are compatible with interventions of many types (Kudler & Davidson, 1995; Meichenbaum, 1994; Resick & Schnicke, 1993). These include: (a) a reduction of symptoms, (b) cognitive understanding of the trauma that reduces guilt and does not include self-blame, (c) increased understanding of PTSD, (d) increased coping skills, (e) improvements in the person's social support system, and (f) improved functioning in social roles, such as at work and with family.

Commonalities of successful treatments have also been identified (Freedy & Donkervoet, 1995; Koss, 1993). Effective treatments of PTSD maintain a focus on the trauma and related memories, thoughts, and feelings; avoid blaming or stigmatizing the victim; provide information about responses to trauma; attempt to strengthen the client's internal resources, such as ability to manage anxiety, along with external resources, such as work, family, and social support; and instill hope about the chances for improvement.

Drawing from Resick & Schnicke's (1993) work with those who have been trau-matized by rape, the requirements of social workers can be summarized. First, the practitioner must be knowledgeable about typical reactions to trauma and PTSD. Next, he or she must be familiar with effective treatments. Finally, the social worker must be able to tolerate hearing the details of stories that may be frighten-ing or horrifying at times and be able to tolerate the expression of strong emotion. This is vital so that avoidance is not encouraged.

Several treatments for PTSD that are supported by empirical evidence of effec-tiveness are examined in this section. Presented first are interventions that are designed for individuals or groups, followed by family or systemic interventions, and, finally, preventative or community interventions. When choosing a treatment for PTSD it is important to be mindful of two caveats. One, it is difficult to help someone heal from the effects of trauma when that trauma is continuing to occur. In this case, such as with someone who is in an actively abusive relationship, the first task is to work on issues of safety and protection from further abuse. Two, certain comorbid conditions, such as psychosis, suicidal behaviors, or active substance abuse, require immediate attention and may contraindicate the use of the techniques described in the following. The descriptions that follow are introductions to inter-ventions that are effective in clinical practice. More detailed training resources are referenced and should be studied before putting an intervention to use.

Individual and Group Interventions

Many treatments for PTSD are designed for individual work (i.e., Rothbaum & Foa, 1992), some for group work (i.e., Makler, Sigal, Gelkopf, Kochba, & Horeb, 1990; Perl, Westin, & Peterson, 1985; Rozynko & Dondershine, 1991), and still others can be used either way (i.e., Resick & Schnicke, 1993). While the superior-ity of individual versus group interventions has not been established (although more supportive empirical research has been conducted on individual treatment), some advantages and disadvantages of each have been proposed (Meichenbaum, 1994; Resick & Schnicke, 1993). Group intervention allows members to discover that they are not alone in their experience of trauma. They may also be reassured to find that their reactions to trauma are normal and are acceptable to share with others. Group members may provide support for one another and encourage each other to continue to work on difficult issues. Further, group members can serve as positive models to one another as they see each other learn new coping skills, tol-erate intense affect, and change maladaptive cognitions. Individual treatment, on the other hand, allows the practitioner to give undivided attention to one person and may be the only option for those who are very uncomfortable with self-disclosure in a group setting. Finally, a client may begin individual treatment at any time without having to wait for others to be available to begin a group.

Behavioral Models. The most widely tested group of treatments that have been found effective in reducing symptoms of PTSD are behavioral. These include exposure therapy, cognitive-behavioral therapy, stress inoculation training (SIT), and cognitive processing therapy (CPT).

Exposure therapy has been found to be effective with PTSD following rape and incest (Foa, Rothbaum, Riggs, & Murdock, 1991; Rychtarik, Silverman, Van Landingham, & Prue, 1984; Steketee & Foa, 1987), combat exposure (Keane, Fairbank, Caddell, & Zimering, 1989), and accidents (McCaffrey & Fairbank, 1985; Richards & Rose, 1991). Although most clinical research using this treatment has been conducted with adult clients, there is evidence that the procedures are also effective with children (Saigh, 1987).

Exposure therapy involves activation of the fear and anxiety that is associated with trauma-related memories or external cues. The client is encouraged to fully experience his or her fear in a setting that is actually relatively safe, until the response begins to extinguish. Activation may be accomplished either through imagination or through actual contact with reminders of the trauma, such as the sound of helicopters to a Vietnam veteran. The technique as applied to survivors of rape is described in detail by Rothbaum & Foa (1992), with an illustrative case example. (See Lyons & Keane, 1989 for a description of exposure with combat-related PTSD.) During sessions, the clients are asked to imagine and describe the assault experience, including as much sensory detail as can be remembered. Between sessions, clients are asked to practice exposure through real-life contact with nondangerous situations or objects that have been feared and avoided since the assault. Imaginal and real-life exposure must be long enough that the client's anxiety level begins to decrease, generally about 30 to 45 minutes. The client should not be left in a highly anxious state.

Cognitive-behavioral therapy has been found to be effective for treatment of PTSD following rape (Frank et al., 1988) and is often part of the overall treatment package used with combat veterans (Meichenbaum, 1994). Cognitive-behavioral therapy (Beck, Rush, Shaw, & Emery, 1979) has long been recognized as a successful treatment for anxiety and depression. It involves teaching the client to monitor distressing cognitions and then to challenge and replace them with more adaptive thoughts. For example, a woman who has been raped may think that she is to blame because she did not resist sufficiently. Exploration of this belief should challenge the idea that she is responsible for her own rape. A more adaptive belief might be that she survived the rape by using the best tactics available to her while experiencing extreme duress. Cognitive-behavioral therapy may also be used to explore basic underlying assumptions about the world and self that have been disrupted by trauma. For example, a client of the first author described great distress at the realization that she had briefly aimed—and had intended to discharge—a loaded gun at her rapist during the struggle (Beck, et al., 1979). Prior to this experience, she had believed herself to be nonviolent and incapable of the intensity of rage that she had experienced immediately following the rape. Exploration of this belief resulted in a more adaptive belief for her that included the possibility of taking action against another for the sake of self-preservation.

Stress inoculation training (SIT) is a composite treatment program that has been found to be effective in the treatment of PTSD following rape (Foa et al., 1991). Meichenbaum (1994) describes the treatment and reports that it has been used successfully to treat problems related to PTSD, such as panic disorders and anger control. He describes the treatment in three phases. In the first phase, the client is prepared for treatment through education about traumatic stress and related emotional responses. In the second phase, the client is taught a variety of coping skills for dealing with stress, including relaxation training, cognitive restructuring, anger control, assertive training, and controlled breathing exercises. The client practices these skills both in and out of session. In the third phase, the client learns to apply his or her new coping skills to stress responses aroused through the use of imaginal and in vivo exposure to trauma-related cues.

Cognitive processing therapy (CPT) is also a composite treatment package, combining prolonged exposure with cognitive processing. It was designed by Resick & Schnicke (1992) and has been effective in reducing PTSD and depression following rape. It has yet to be tested with groups of other types of trauma survivors. CPT is based on the idea that trauma disrupts cognitive assumptions and beliefs held by the victim. When these assumptions are disrupted, a person must either alter the new information so that it can be assimilated into existing belief schemas or alter the existing schema so the new information can be accommodated. For example, if a woman who believes that she is invulnerable to rape is raped, either she must distort the information so that the experience is no longer considered a rape, and the information can be assimilated; or the information that she has been raped must be accommodated within a new, altered belief about her vulnerability in the world. The victim will have a more difficult time processing the event when information from the experience is more discrepant from her schematic beliefs. A thorough description of the procedure is available in a treatment manual (Resick & Schnicke, 1993). In the exposure component of treatment, clients are asked to write and then read aloud detailed descriptions of their assault. In the cognitive processing component, clients are taught to identify discrepancies between their prior beliefs and new information based on the traumatic experience. Resolution of those discrepancies often results in modification of the underlying beliefs and symptomatic relief.

Other Treatment Models. While behavioral interventions are the most strongly supported, there are a variety of other interventions for PTSD that have at least some support for their effectiveness. These include pharmacological treatments, Eye Movement Desensitization and Reprocessing (EMDR), psychodynamic therapy, crisis intervention and supportive treatment, and inpatient treatment programs. Each is reviewed briefly, with the acknowledgment that further controlled treatment outcome research is needed.

Pharmacological treatments are sometimes used along with psychosocial interventions to help alleviate particular symptoms related to PTSD. Kudler and Davidson (1995) provide an overview of the use of psychotropic drugs for the treatment of PTSD based on their review of relevant research and clinical practice. Several points are relevant to the nonprescribing practitioner. First, antidepressants have been found to be helpful in alleviating symptoms of chronic PTSD. The choice of a particular antidepressant should be based on the particular symptoms and needs of the client. For example, antidepressants vary in terms of their level of sedating effect, overdose lethality, and affordability. Next, Kudler and Davidson (1995) emphasize that medication should be used in conjunction with other treatment modalities. Finally, the importance of communication between members of the mental health team is stressed. The nonprescribing primary clinician needs to be aware of the benefits and side effects of medications in order to know when to refer for a medical consult and what relevant information to provide to the prescribing physician. Ongoing collaboration between the client, the primary clinician, and the physician is imperative.

Eye movement desensitization and reprocessing (EMDR) is a relatively new and somewhat controversial intervention that combines elements of exposure and cognitive processing with saccadic eye movements. The method is described in a book authored by its founder (Shapiro, 1995) and has been widely promoted to clinicians through workshops. Research evidence in support of the effectiveness of EMDR has been mixed (see Meichenbaum, 1994 for a cautionary review).

Both individual and group forms of *psychodynamic treatments* have been used to treat PTSD. Although descriptions of the methods and case studies are available (Koller, Marmar, & Kanas, 1992; Marmar, 1991), very little support is available from controlled studies. However, Brom, Kleber, and Defares (1989) compared three treatments for PTSD to a waiting-list control group and found all three—trauma desensitization, hypnotherapy, and psychodynamic therapy—to be effective. Again, more research is needed before it can be concluded that psychodynamic treatment is effective for the treatment of PTSD.

Crisis oriented supportive treatment has been successfully used to address the stress-induced symptoms of rape victims. As an example, Perl, Westin and Peterson (1985) used a time-limited, structured group therapy approach in treating four groups of adult female rape survivors. Following 8 weeks of treatment, they found a strong improvement in expressed anxiety, fear, anger, depression, self-esteem, and somatic complaints.

Before leaving the area of individual and group treatments, *inpatient treatment* must be mentioned. Inpatient treatment for PTSD should be considered if the client is acutely self-destructive or is having severe functional difficulties. An excellent description of the advantages, components, and treatment strategies of an inpatient treatment program for combat-related PTSD is provided by Carroll and Foy (1992). The program employs many of the assessment techniques and behavioral interventions that are reviewed in the preceding, with the addition of readily available crisis support and a multidisciplinary team on site.

Dudley, Abueg, Woodward, and Keane (1993) provide an excellent overview of all outcome studies that had been published on the treatment of PTSD, involving a variety of psychosocial interventions. They concluded:

> [I]t is clear that the existing PTSD treatments, particularly behavioral and pharmacological, can significantly reduce PTSD signs and symptoms . . . aside from pharmacotherapy trials, behavioral studies predominate in empirically-based clinical research, and they do so absolutely in single-*n*, group pre-post, and simple controlled studies. Little published data exist demonstrating the efficacy of psychodynamic psychotherapy with PTSD. (Dudley et al., 1993, p. 219)

Family or Systemic Intervention

Family therapy may be an appropriate treatment method to address the needs of those with PTSD, as well as those of their family members. This is important because the traumatized person typically develops chronic symptoms that affect the overall functioning of the family. In addition, PTSD victims may develop relationship problems with family members. Thus, it is critical that clinical social workers consider family treatment as a possible modality of treatment for these individuals and their families. Empirical evidence of the effectiveness of the following models of family intervention is needed to supplement the supporting clinical case materials contained in the descriptive articles that are cited.

Figley (1988) has proposed a systems-oriented approach to working with families in which there is a member with PTSD symptoms. According to this model, the purpose of using family treatment with these families is to facilitate normal family functioning, including maximizing the effectiveness of social support. Treatment includes five general phases: Phase 1 involves developing a relationship with the family and securing a commitment to the goals of treatment. A part of this process includes exploring the sources of family stress, while providing a spirit of hope. Phase II involves framing the problem, including an examination of the traumatic events that have disrupted the balance of the family system. Phase III is a reframing of the problem to help family members view the stress as a challenge to be conquered together. This phase sets the context for Phase IV, which involves the development of a healing theory, providing the family an opportunity to develop alternative ways of coping with future traumatic events. Finally, Phase V is the closure and preparedness phase, in which the successes of treatment are reviewed. A component of this phase is empowering family members to learn from the experience, and therefore become better prepared to deal with future traumatic events (Figley, 1989).

Using a somewhat different approach, Craine, Hanks and Stevens (1992) show that family adaptation theory may be effective in conceptualizing family reactions to PTSD and in formulating clinical treatment. The authors use an approach of mapping how families behave in the face of stressful and traumatic events. They identify three areas of functioning that may provide the basis for understanding family functioning. These areas are the family's regenerativity, resilience, and rhythmicity. Following the assessment of families along these dimensions, treatment is designed to build on the strengths of the family while minimizing the effects of the family's limitations.

Community-Level Interventions

The risk of PTSD is heightened by the occurrence of violence of many types in our society. The reduction of violence has become a great concern in recent years and is often addressed by groups of people who are interested in a particular issue. For example, there is a considerable developing literature addressing community-level interventions for the prevention of sexual assault. Community responses typically include the collaboration of social service agencies, educational institutions, law enforcement, and judicial systems. These collaborations represent the increased awareness of communities with regard to the relative ineffectiveness of more traditional modes of intervention. In hundreds of communities around the nation, violence task forces have been developed to evaluate the effectiveness of various intervention programs and to establish protocols for acceptable treatment methods (Yegidis, 1997). These types of collaborative efforts typically include an ongoing monitoring of police response to victims. In addition, they may include designing and delivering training programs for law enforcement and legal personnel. Training is important to ensure that victims are not revictimized through insensitive legal and criminal processes.

In addition to training relevant personnel, community level interventions often provide for a broad range of services, including victim assistance and support, education concerning normal reactions to traumatic events, medical and legal advocacy, access to 24-hour hot lines and crisis services, referrals to professional counseling, and statewide data analysis. The goal of community programs is to ensure accessible, sensitive, effective, and coordinated service delivery for victims (Koss, 1993).

Social workers have been strong advocates for community intervention. Continuing advocacy is needed to maintain or to increase public funding for prevention, crisis intervention, and treatment programs. This would help to facilitate the use of trained personnel in agencies serving those who are at risk for developing PTSD.

In addition, more funding would permit the ongoing development of resource materials and training manuals for the treatment of PTSD.

SECONDARY TRAUMATIC STRESS SYNDROME

Practitioners who work with people who have Post-Traumatic Stress Disorder have been shown to suffer symptoms similar to those experienced by their clients. This phenomenon has alternatively been termed *vicarious traumatization, compassion fatigue,* or *secondary traumatic stress syndrome* (STS). The concept of vicarious traumatization was first operationalized by McCann and Pearlman (1990b) in providing a framework for understanding the effects of trauma work on therapists. The authors showed that working with survivors of trauma can reactivate therapists' own victimization memories or experiences. Figley has further defined STS as "the stress resulting from helping or wanting to help a traumatized or suffering person" (1995b, p. 7). The primary distinction between PTSD and STS is the nature of the stressor. PTSD victims experience a primary stressor, while victims of STS react to the traumatizing event experienced by another.

The symptoms experienced by victims of STS are similar to those experienced in PTSD. In particular, the STS victim experiences an event as a threat to the traumatized person, including reexperiencing the event through recollections, dreams and intrusive thoughts. STS victims also experience attempts to avoid and numb thoughts, feelings and situations that are stressful along with experiencing irritability, difficulty in falling asleep and exaggerated startle responses (Figley, 1995b). STS has been shown to alter the view one has of self, others, and the world (McCann & Pearlmann, 1990b); as well as to disrupt beliefs about one's own capacities to be helpful to others (Pearlman & Saakvitne, 1995).

STS has been compared to and differentiated from the concept of burnout. Figley (1995b) has indicated that burnout is a kind of exhaustion resulting from long-term work in draining situations. While therapists sometimes experience burnout, burnout does not include the interaction of the therapist with the traumatized individual that is a critical component of the experience of STS. Burnout tends to emerge gradually in therapists and often comes as a result of emotional exhaustion. STS, on the other hand, may emerge suddenly.

STS has been empirically shown to affect a wide range of counselors or therapists who work directly with victims of abuse, including sexual abuse and rape, as well as with victims of other forms of traumatic events (e.g., Cerney, 1995; Schauben & Frazier, 1995). While incidence estimates are not readily available, Schauben and Frazier (1995) showed that counselors who work with a higher percentage of sexual violence survivors report more disrupted beliefs about themselves and others, more PTSD-related symptoms, and more vicarious trauma than counselors who see fewer survivors. In addition, STS has been shown to be present in other mental health and law enforcement professionals (Follette, Polusny, and Milbeck, 1994).

There are numerous strategies and qualities that help to insulate social workers from experiencing STS. Hayes, Gelso, Van Wagoner, and Diemer (1991) have shown that five qualities help therapists manage some of these experiences. These qualities are (a) anxiety management, (b) conceptualization of skills, (c) empathic ability, (d) self-insight, and (e) self-integration. Others have suggested that the coping strategies therapists often teach their clients are the same ones that professional therapists must use to manage their own stress symptoms. These skills include cognitive restructuring, expressing feelings and getting assistance, exercising, and finding new ways to experience life in a joyful or spiritual manner.

It has also been suggested that the formal training of helping professionals should include content on addressing the needs of trauma survivors (Schauben & Frazier, 1995). The inclusion of the methods of assessment and treatment of PTSD in social work curricula, as well as in related clinical disciplines (such as health care) is warranted. If this were to be done, students would have learning opportunities in the classroom and on internship sites to develop their skills and capacities to help these clients. Also, formal education provides a mechanism to get support within the context of clinical supervision, which has been identified as being helpful in preventing STS.

In addition to these methods, social workers must learn to say no to taking on more and more trauma survivors as a part of their caseloads. The belief that one can and should help everyone who requests it contributes to feelings of helplessness. Further, maintaining a sense of perspective about work and balance in life is critical to assuring one's health and competence as a social worker. Thus, it is essential that social workers prepare themselves for work with trauma survivors, both with knowledge of the assessment and effective treatment of PTSD, and with the ability to avoid becoming overwhelmed by the number of clients who will certainly seek them out.

REFERENCES

American Psychiatric Association. (1980). *Diagnostic and statistical manual of mental disorders* (3rd ed.). Washington, DC: Author.

American Psychiatric Association. (1987). *Diagnostic and statistical manual of mental disorders* (3rd ed., rev.). Washington, DC: Author.

American Psychiatric Association. (1994). *Diagnostic and statistical manual of mental disorders* (4th ed.). Washington, DC: Author.

Beck, A. T., Rush, A. J., Shaw, B. F., & Emery, G. (1979). *Cognitive therapy of depression.* New York: Guilford Press.

Beck, A. T., Ward, C. H., Mendelson, M., Mock, J., & Erbaugh, J. (1961). An inventory for measuring depression. *Archives of General Psychiatry, 4,* 561–571.

Blake, D. D., Weathers, F. W., Nagy, L. M., Kaloupek, D. G., Klauminzer, G., Charney, D. S., & Keane, T. M. (1990). A clinical rating scale for assessing current and lifetime PTSD: The CAPS-1. *The Behavior Therapist, 13,* 187–188.

Blanchard, E. B., Kolb, L. C., Pallmeyer, T. P., & Gerardi, R. J. (1982). The development of a psychophysiological assessment procedure for PTSD in Vietnam veterans. *Psychiatric Quarterly, 54,* 220–228.

Brom, D., Kleber, R. J., & Defares, P. B. (1989). Brief psychotherapy for PTSD. *Journal of Consulting and Clinical Psychology, 57,* 607–612.

Carroll, E. M., & Foy, D. W., (1992). Assessment and treatment of combat-related PTSD in a medical center setting. In D. W. Foy (Ed.), *Treating PTSD* (pp. 39–68). New York: Guilford Press.

Centers for Disease Control. (1988). Health status of Vietnam veterans: Psychosocial character-istics. *Journal of the American Medical Association, 259,* 2701–2707.

Cerney, M. (1995). Treating the "heroic treaters". In C. R. Figley (Ed.), *Compassion fatigue* (pp. 131–149). New York: Brunner/Mazel.

Craine, M. H., Hanks, R., & Stevens, H. (1992). Mapping family stress: The application of fam-ily adaptation theory to Post-Traumatic Stress Disorder. *American Journal of Family Ther-apy, 20,* 195–203.

Davidson, J. R. T., & Foa, E. B. (1991). Diagnostic issues in Post-traumatic Stress Disorder: Considerations for the DSM-IV. *Journal of Abnormal Psychology, 100,* 346–355.

Derogatis, L. R. (1977). *SCL-90: Administration, scoring and procedure manual for the R(evised) version.* Baltimore: John Hopkins University, School of Medicine.

Dudley, D., Abueg, F., Woodward, S. & Keane, T. (1993). Treatment efficacy in Post-traumatic Stress Disorder. In T. R. Giles (Ed.), *Handbook of effective psychotherapy* (pp. 195–226). New York: Plenum Press.

Figley, C. R. (1988). A five-phase treatment of post-traumatic stress disorder in families. *Jour-nal of Traumatic Stress, 1,* 127–141.

Figley, C. R. (1989). *Helping traumatized families.* San Francisco: Jossey-Bass.

Figley, C. R. (1995a). Systemic Post-Traumatic Stress Disorder: Family treatment experiences and implications. In G. Everly & J. Lating (Eds.), *Post-traumatic stress* (pp. 3–8). New York: Plenum Press.

Figley, C. R. (Ed.). (1995b). *Compassion fatigue: Coping with STSD in those who treat the trau-matized.* New York: Brunner/Mazel.

Fischer, J., & Corcoran, K. (1994). *Measures for clinical practice* (2nd ed.). New York: Free Press.

Foa, E. B., Riggs, D. S., Dancu, D. V., & Rothbaum, B. O. (1993). Reliability and validity of a brief instrument for assessing Post-traumatic Stress Disorder. *Journal of Traumatic Stress, 6,* 459–473.

Foa, E. B., Rothbaum, B. O., Riggs, D. S., & Murdock, T. B. (1991). Treatment of Post-traumatic Stress Disorder in rape victims: A comparison between cognitive-behavioral pro-cedures and counseling. *Journal of Consulting and Clinical Psychology, 59,* 715–723.

Follette, V. M., Polusney, M. M., & Milbeck, K. (1994). Mental health and law enforcement pro-fessionals: Trauma history, psychological symptoms, and impact of providing services to child sexual abuse survivors. *Professional Psychology: Research and Practice, 25,* 275–282.

Frank, E., Anderson, B., Stewart, B. D., Dancu, C., Hughes, C., & West, D. (1988). Efficacy of cognitive behavior therapy and systematic desensitization in the treatment of rape trauma. *Behavior Therapy, 19,* 403–420.

Freedy, J. R., & Donkervoet, J. C. (1995). Traumatic stress: An overview of the field. In J. Freedy & S. Hobfoll (Eds.), *Traumatic stress from theory to practice* (pp. 3–28). New York: Plenum Press.

Gilmartin, P. (1994). *Rape, incest, and child sexual abuse: Consequences and recovery.* New York: Garland.

Green, B. L. (1994). Psychosocial research in traumatic stress: An update. *Journal of Traumatic Stress, 7,* 341–362.

Hayes, J. A., Gelso, C. J., VanWagoner, S. L, & Diemer, R. A. (1991). Managing countertransference: What the experts think. *Psychological Reports, 69,* 138–148.

Horowitz, M. J., Wilner, N., & Alvarez, W. (1979). Impact of Events Scale: A measure of subjective distress. *Psychosomatic Medicine, 41,* 207–218.

Janoff-Bulman, R. (1985). The aftermath of victimization: Rebuilding shattered assumptions. In C. R. Figley (Ed.), *Trauma and its wake: The study and treatment of Post-Traumatic Stress Disorder* (pp. 15–25). New York: Brunner/Mazel.

Keane, T. M., Caddell, J. M., & Taylor, K. T. (1988). Mississippi Scale for Combat-Related Post-traumatic Stress Disorder: Three studies in reliability and validity. *Journal of Consulting and Clinical Psychology, 56,* 85–90.

Keane, T. M., Fairbank, J. A., Caddell, J. M., & Zimering, R. T. (1989). Implosive (flooding) therapy reduces symptoms of PTSD in Vietnam combat veterans. *Behavior Therapy, 20,* 245–260.

Keane, T. M., & Wolfe, J. (1990). Comorbidity in Post-Traumatic Stress Disorder: An analysis of community and clinical studies. *Journal of Applied Social Psychology, 20,* 1776–1788.

Kilpatrick, D. G. (1988). Rape Aftermath Symptom Test. In M. Hersen & A. S. Bellack (Eds.), *Dictionary of behavioral assessment techniques* (pp. 366–367). New York: Pergamon Press.

Kilpatrick, D. G., Best, C. L., Veronen, L. J., Amick, A., Villeponteaux, L., & Ruff, M. (1985). Mental health correlates of criminal victimization: A random community survey. *Journal of Consulting and Clinical Psychology, 53,* 866–873.

Koller, P., Marmar, C. R., Kanas, N. (1992). Psychodynamic group treatment of PTSD in Vietnam veterans. *International Journal of Group Psychotherapy, 42,* 225–246.

Koss, M. P. (1993). Rape: Scope, impact, interventions, and public policy responses. *American Psychologist, 48,* 1062–1069.

Kudler, H., & Davidson, J. R. T. (1995). General principles of biological intervention following trauma. In J. Freedy and S. Hobfoll (Eds.), *Traumatic stress from theory to practice* (pp. 73–98). New York: Plenum Press.

Lating, J. M., & Everly, G. S. (1995). Psychophysiological assessment of PTSD. In G. Everly & J. Lating (Eds.), *Psychotraumatology* (pp. 129–145). New York: Plenum Press.

Lyons, J. A., & Keane, T. M. (1989). Implosive therapy for the treatment of combat related PTSD. *Journal of Traumatic Stress, 2,* 137–152.

Makler, S., Sigal, M., Gelkopf, M., Kochba, B., & Horeb, E. (1990). Combat-related, Chronic Post-traumatic Stress Disorder: Implications for group therapy intervention. *American Journal of Psychotherapy, 44,* 381–395.

Malloy, P. F., Fairbank, J. A., & Keane, T. M. (1983). Validation of a multimethod assessment of post-traumatic stress disorders in Vietnam veterans. *Journal of Consulting and Clinical Psychology, 51,* 488–494.

Marmar, C. R. (1991). Brief dynamic psychotherapy of PTSD. *Psychiatric Annals, 21,* 405–414.

McCaffrey, R. J., & Fairbank, J. A. (1985). Post-Traumatic Stress Disorder associated with transportation accidents: Two case studies. *Behavior Therapy, 16,* 406–416.

McCann, I. L., & Pearlman, L. A. (1990a). *Psychological trauma and the adult survivor.* New York: Brunner/Mazel.

McCann, I. L., & Pearlman, L. A. (1990b). Vicarious traumatization: A framework for understanding the psychological effects of working with victims. *Journal of Traumatic Stress, 3,* 131–149.

McFall, M. E., Smith, D. E., Mackay, P. W., & Tarver, D. J. (1990). Reliability and validity of the Mississippi Scale for Combat-Related PTSD. *Psychological assessment, 2,* 114–121.

Meichenbaum, D. (1994). *A clinical handbook/practical therapist manual for assessing and treating adults with Post-Traumatic Stress Disorder.* Waterloo, Ontario: Institute Press.

Pearlman, L. A., & Saakvitne, K. W. (1995). Treating therapists with vicarious traumatization and secondary traumatic stress disorders. In C. R. Figley (Ed.), *Compassion fatigue: Coping with secondary traumatic stress disorders in those who treat the traumatized* (pp. 150–177). New York: Brunner/Mazel.

Perl, J., Westin, A. B., & Peterson, L. G. (1985). The female rape survivor: Time limited group therapy with female-male cotherapists. *Journal of Psychosomatic Obstetrics and Gynecology, 4,* 197–205.

Resick, P. A., & Schnicke, M. K. (1992). Cognitive processing therapy for sexual assault victims. *Journal of Consulting and Clinical Psychology, 60,* 748–756.

Resick, P. A., & Schnicke, M. K. (1993). *Cognitive processing therapy for rape victims.* Newbury Park, CA: Sage.

Resnick, H. S., Kilpatrick, D. G., Walsh, C. & Veronen, L. J. (1991). Marital rape. In R. T. Ammerman & M. Hersen (Eds.), *Case studies in family violence,* (pp. 329–355). New York: Plenum Press.

Richards, D. A. & Rose, J. S. (1991). Exposure therapy for Post-Traumatic Stress Disorder: Four case studies. *British Journal of Psychiatry, 158,* 836–840.

Rothbaum, B. O., & Foa, E. B. (1992). Exposure therapy for rape victims with PTSD. *The Behavior Therapist, 15,* 219–222.

Rozynko, V., & Dondershine, H. E. (1991). Trauma focus group therapy for Vietnam veterans with PTSD. *Psychotherapy, 28,* 157–161.

Rychtarik, R. G., Silverman, W. K., Van Landingham, W. P., & Prue, D. M. (1984). Treatment of an incest victim with implosive therapy: A case study. *Behavior Therapy, 15,* 410–420.

Saigh, P. A. (1987). *In vitro* flooding of childhood post-traumatic stress disorders: A systematic replication. *Professional School Psychology, 1,* 135–146.

Saunders, B. E., Mandoki, K. A., & Kilpatrick, D. G. (1990). Development of a crime related Post-traumatic Stress Disorder scale within the Symptom Checklist 90—Revised. *Journal of Traumatic Stress, 3,* 439–448.

Schauben, L. J., & Frazier, P. A. (1995). Vicarious trauma: The effects on female counselors of working with sexual violence survivors. *Psychology Women Quarterly, 19,* 49–64.

Shapiro, F. (1995) *Eye movement desensitization and reprocessing.* New York: Guilford Press.

Spielberger, C. D., Gorsuch, R. L., & Lushene, R. E. (1970). *Manual for the State-Trait Anxiety Inventory (self evaluation questionnaire).* Palo Alto, CA: Consulting Psychologists Press.

Spitzer, R. L., & Williams, J. B. (1985). Structured Clinical Interview for *DSM-III-R,* patient version. New York: New York State Psychiatric Institute, Biometrics Research Department.

Steketee, G., & Foa, E. (1987). Rape victims: Post-traumatic stress responses and their treatment. *Journal of Anxiety Disorders, 1,* 69–86.

Veronen, L. J., & Kilpatrick, D. G. (1980). Self-reported fears of rape victims: A preliminary investigation. *Behavior Modification, 4,* 383–396.

Watson, C. G., Juba, M. P., Manifold, V., Kucala, T., & Anderson, P. E. D. (1991). The PTSD interview: Rationale, description, reliability, and concurrent validity of a *DSM-III* based technique. *Journal of Clinical Psychology, 47,* 179–188.

Yegidis, B. L. (1997). Family violence: Implications for social work practice. In E. Gambrill and M. Reisch (Eds.), *Social work practice in the 21st century* (pp. 127–133). Newbury Park, CA: Sage.

Chapter 19 ————————————————————————————————

GENERALIZED ANXIETY DISORDER

Robert W. McLellarn
Julie Rosenzweig

OVERVIEW

Operational Definitions and Diagnostic Criteria

The criteria for the diagnosis called Generalized Anxiety Disorder (GAD) have evolved considerably in the last two decades. In the second edition of the *Diagnostic and Statistical Manual of Mental Disorders* (*DSM-II;* American Psychiatric Association [APA], 1968), generalized anxiety was embedded in the psychiatric disorder *Anxiety Neurosis,* a vague label used to describe the condition of excessive anxiety experienced over a prolonged period of time without marked phobic avoidance. The diagnosis was applied to individuals who were generally anxious, as well as to those with Panic Disorder (PD).

GAD was first described in *DSM-III* (APA, 1980). Anxiety Neurosis was reformulated as the diagnostic categories of PD and GAD. This reconceptualization identified PD as an independent entity and one of several symptom-specific anxiety disorders, leaving GAD as a residual category. The criteria for GAD required generalized, persistent anxiety manifested by symptoms from three of four categories, including motor tension, autonomic hyperactivity, apprehensive expectation and vigilance, and scanning. The anxious mood could not be due to another mental disorder and must have persisted for 1 month. A diagnosis of GAD was made by default, when the configuration of reported symptoms did not fit any symptom-specific anxiety disorder. This method of diagnosing GAD was ineffective and contributed to low rates of diagnostic reliability for GAD (Barlow & DiNardo, 1991). In addition, the overall lack of conceptual clarity inhibited the development of effective treatments for GAD.

The revised third edition of the diagnostic manual, *DSM-III-R,* included a more clinically useful definition of GAD (APA, 1987). No longer considered a residual category, the symptoms specific to GAD were more clearly identified. GAD's unique feature was defined as excessive and unrealistic worry, referred to as *appre-*

hensive expectation. The minimum duration that persistent anxiety had to be present was extended from 1 month to 6 months, and at least 6 of the 18 associated symptoms needed to have occurred during that time. Previously restricted to individuals 18 years and older, GAD could now be applied to children and adolescents.

In the current and fourth edition, *DSM-IV* (APA, 1994), the revised definition of GAD emphasizes an inability to control the chronic worry. The number of symptoms describing GAD has been reduced to the six that best distinguish GAD from other anxiety disorders—restlessness, fatigue, difficulty concentrating, irritability, muscle tension, and sleep disturbance (Brown, Barlow, & Liebowitz, 1994). Three of these six symptoms must have persisted over a 6-month duration and must be clearly linked to serious distress and impairment in significant life domains.

Epidemiology of GAD

A recent national survey based upon *DSM-III-R* diagnostic criteria found that the lifetime and 12-month prevalence rates of all anxiety disorders combined were 24.9% and 17.2% respectively, while the corresponding GAD rates were 5.1% and 3.1%. For comparison, the lifetime and 12-month prevalence rates for PD were 3.5% and 2.3%, for Agoraphobia were 5.3% and 2.8%, for Social Phobia were 13.3% and 7.9%, and for Simple Phobia were 11.3% and 8.8%. Overall, the anxiety disorders were the most prevalent of all the major groups of disorders (Kessler et al., 1994).

Both community surveys and clinical studies have found significant morbidity associated with anxiety disorders, with the most frequent problem being lost time and productivity at work. GAD in particular has high rates of comorbidity with Simple Phobia and Social Phobia and is associated with high risk for Substance Abuse (Brown & Barlow, 1992; DiNardo & Barlow, 1990; Kushner, Sher, & Beitman, 1990). In clinical settings, 55% to 60% of those diagnosed with GAD are female and in epidemiological studies about two thirds of the adults with GAD are female (APA, 1994). GAD is more common among separated, divorced, or widowed persons than among the married or never married. Finally, GAD may be more common among people of lower socioeconomic status (Blazer, Hughes, George, Swartz, & Boyer, 1991).

Future epidemiological and familial studies will need to explore the role of ethnicity and culture, as well as other sociocultural variables, in the prevalence, development, presentation, and treatment of GAD. Inclusion of a cultural perspective on GAD is illustrated in a review of cross-cultural literature on anxiety by Good and Kleinman (1985) and in a review of anxiety disorders in African Americans by Friedman (1994). The universality of anxiety and anxiety disorders across cultures is not disputed; however, the authors underscore the importance of understanding culture-specific expressions of distress, social reality, and symptomatic resolution.

Continuing Conceptual Concerns

Despite the ongoing research to better understand GAD, several issues continue to hamper progress. First, and perhaps foremost, is the nature of anxiety itself. Anxiety is an intrinsic human response that is universally experienced at times of threat or challenge. Anxiety associated with GAD is not fundamentally different from anxiety associated with daily stress and uneasiness. Assessment and diagnosis of GAD focuses on the magnitude (intensity, pervasiveness, and persistence) of the anxiety reported. Locating the boundary between normal and pathological anxiety is thereby left to the discretion of each clinician (Hoehn-Saric, Borkovec, & Nemiah, 1995; Lipschitz, 1988).

The difference between GAD and high-trait anxiety has also been questioned. For instance, Rapee (1991) identifies three major ways that GAD is similar to high-trait anxiety: (a) the relative stability and early onset of the disorder, (b) the persistent worry without a specific focus, and (c) the parallels in the cognitive similarities between GADs and nonclinical populations compared to the cognitive similarities between high-trait and low-trait anxiety in nonclinical populations. The central, most apparent difference between individuals with GAD and those with high-level trait anxiety is that with GAD the anxiety has a greater impact on daily functioning.

Likewise, anxiety is a common and often indistinguishable component of depression (Riskind et al., 1991). Both are affective responses and share a similar neurobiological reaction to stressful life events (Barlow, 1988). Determining whether GAD or Dysthymic Disorder is the primary diagnosis can be quite challenging for the practitioner. Lipschitz (1988) suggests that in primary depression, severe anxiety occurs only intermittently; whereas, in primary GAD, the depressed mood is a transient expression of defeat and failure to effectively manage the chronic anxiety. Anxiety and depression might also be considered to share different positions on the same continuum. According to Barlow (1991):

> [W]hether one becomes anxious and stays that way, or also becomes depressed, depends on the extent of one's psychological vulnerability, the severity of the current stressor, and the coping mechanism at one's disposal. The greater the vulnerability, the more severe the stressor, and the fewer the coping mechanisms that are available, the more likely the anxiety will be accompanied by depression. (p. 14)

The Role of Social Work

The cost of debilitating anxiety experienced by individuals suffering from GAD is both personal and social. By definition, many spheres of the person's life are affected—managing daily life tasks, employment, and family relationships. Left untreated, the person becomes less able to engage in productive and fulfilling life roles. The effects of GAD are systemic. Not only does the individual suffer; family, friends, and coworkers are affected, as well. GAD is most prevalent in those segments of the population where health care is already compromised. As rising health care costs and managed care continue to shrink the numbers of people eligible to receive health and mental health services, it is likely that the number of individuals with untreated anxiety disorders will grow. The need for intervention will not decrease, but seeking treatment will likely be delayed, resulting in increased chronicity and poor treatment outcomes. Social work contributions to research and practice in this area of mental health are needed. Although some examples of social work research related to the descriptive psychopathology (e.g., Raskin, Rondesvedt, & Johnson, 1972; Williams et al., 1992) and psychosocial treatment of GAD (e.g., Raskin, Johnson, & Rondesvedt, 1973) are available in the literature, these are too few and far between.

The current literature on GAD would greatly benefit from social work's perspective and expertise. For example, very few of the studies reviewed for this chapter offered sample characteristics or analyses based on sociocultural variables of race, gender, age, socioeconomic status, or sexual orientation. Understanding differences in symptoms and treatment responses is essential for accurate diagnosis and provision of the most effective intervention. The current approach to treatment for GAD is individualistic, primarily utilizing cognitive-behavioral therapy and medication. Couple and family-based interventions remain undeveloped. The integration of social work's knowledge about family systems, vulnerable populations, and environmental interventions with the current understanding of anxiety and GAD would enhance assessment and treatment options.

ASSESSMENT METHODS

Structured Clinical Interview

The most clinically useful assessment instrument available specifically for anxiety disorders is a structured interview called the Anxiety Disorders Interview Schedule—IV (ADIS-IV; Brown, DiNardo, & Barlow, 1994a, 1994b). The ADIS has gone through a number of revisions over the years, with the questions being adjusted to reflect the changing diagnostic criteria for the various anxiety disorders in the *DSM* series. The present version, ADIS-IV, thus corresponds to *DSM-IV*. The GAD section begins with several screening questions assessing the degree to which worry is a problem, followed by a series of questions asking specifically about the current episode of worry.

The ADIS-IV has separate sections for each of the anxiety disorders listed in *DSM-IV* and provides suggested questions and various prompts that allow the interviewer to carefully assess the presence of each disorder. In addition, there are separate sections that allow the assessment of accompanying problems, such as Major Depressive Disorder, Dysthymic Disorder, Mania/Cyclothymia, Hypochondriasis, Somatization Disorder, Mixed Anxiety-Depression, Alcohol Abuse, Alcohol Dependence, Substance Abuse, and Substance Dependence. Given the high comorbidity rates between GAD and the other Axis I mood and anxiety disorders (Sanderson &

Wetzler, 1991), as well as with possible alcohol problems (Kushner et al., 1990), these additional sections seem particularly useful and appropriate. Questions inquiring about the client's medical and psychiatric history, as well as family history, are also provided. Finally, the Hamilton Anxiety and Depression scales are provided at the end of the ADIS-IV. The interviewer is free to select from the various sections the ones that seem most relevent to a thorough assessment of the individual case.

Questionnaires

There is not an abundance of self-report questionnaires available for the assessment of GAD. The Hamilton Anxiety and Depression scales previously discussed are potentially useful, as are the Beck Anxiety Inventory (Beck, Brown, Epstein, & Steer, 1988) and the Beck Depression Inventory (Beck, Ward, Mendelson, Mock, & Erbaugh, 1961). These are not specific to GAD, but have frequently been used in outcome studies and are more general measures of anxiety and depression.

One of the few questionnaires that is more specific to GAD is the Penn State Worry Questionnaire (PSWQ). This is a 16-item, easily administered instrument; its results have proven to have favorable psychometric properties in two separate studies. Particularly useful is the finding that the PSWQ successfully distinguishes GAD from the other anxiety disorders (Brown, Anthony, & Barlow, 1992; Meyer, Miller, Metzger, & Borkovec, 1990).

Self-Monitoring

Self-monitoring is a useful and appropriate assessment method for GAD, because the technique can provide a tailor-made assessment of each client's areas of concern or difficulty. David Barlow and colleagues have provided examples of forms that can be used to measure subjective anxiety and depression (Brown, O'Leary, & Barlow, 1993, p. 155), specific episodes of worry (Craske, Barlow, & O'Leary, 1992, p. 2-5) and daily mood (Craske et al., 1992, p. 2-9). Self-monitoring is typically done during the initial baseline period and periodically throughout treatment.

EFFECTIVE INTERVENTIONS

Review of the Literature

A number of excellent reviews of the treatment literature on GAD have recently been published (Borkovec & Whisman, 1996; Butler & Booth, 1991; Butler, 1996; Durham & Allan, 1993; Hoehn-Saric et al., 1995). This section provides a summary of research study results to answer the question, "Based on the extant literature, what do we now know about the best ways to treat GAD?" This section does not cover the medication management of GAD; a recent review by Hoehn-Saric et al. (1995) provides information in that area. This section focuses on adults, as there is very little literature regarding GAD in children or adolescents (Silverman & Ginsburg, 1995).

Outcome studies published since the introduction of *DSM-III* that used a structured interview to assess for GAD were selected for review. These criteria provided some assurance of a relatively homogeneous sample of chronically anxious clients with whom the various treatment approaches could be applied. Twelve separate studies were identified for review (Barlow et al., 1984; Barlow, Rapee, & Brown, 1992; Blowers, Cobb, & Mathews, 1987; Borkovec & Costello, 1993; Borkovec & Mathews, 1988; Borkovec et al., 1987; Butler, Cullington, Hibbert, Klimes, & Gelder, 1987; Butler, Fennell, Robson, & Gelder, 1991; Durham et al., 1994; Power, Jerrom, Simpson, Mitchell, & Swanson, 1989; Power, Simpson, Swanson, & Wallace, 1990; White, Keenan, & Brooks, 1992). Table 19.1 lists these 12 studies and the comparisons made, as well as the primary posttest and follow-up results.

Table 19.1   Summary of Results from GAD Psychosocial Treatment Studies

	Comparisons	Primary posttest results	Primary follow-up results
Barlow et al. (1984)	RX + BF + CBT vs. WL	RX + BF + CBT > WL	Results maintained.
Blowers et al. (1987)	AMT vs. ND vs. WL	AMT > WL	Results maintained.
Butler et al. (1987)	AM vs. WL	AM > WL	Results maintained.
Borkovec et al. (1987)	RX + CT vs. RX + ND	RX + CT > RX + ND	Results not reported.
Borkovec & Mathews (1988)	RX + CT vs. RX + CD vs. RX + ND	RX + CT = RX + CD = RX + ND	Results maintained.
Power et al. (1989)	DZ vs. PL vs. CBT	CBT > PL	Comparisons not reported.
Power et al. (1990)	CBT vs. DZ vs. PL vs. CBT + DZ vs. CBT vs. PL	CBT + DZ & CBT > DZ + PL	CBT groups sought less follow-up treatment.
Butler et al. (1991)	CBT vs. BT vs. WL	CBT > BT > WL	Results maintained.
Barlow et al. (1992)	RX vs. CT vs. RX + CT vs. WL	RX = CT = RX + CT > WL	Results maintained.
White et al. (1992)	CT vs. BT vs. CBT vs. PL vs. WL	CT = BT = CBT = PL > WL	Results maintained.
Borkovec & Costello (1993)	CBT vs. AR vs. ND	CBT & AR > ND	Results maintained.
Durham et al. (1994)	CT vs. AP vs. AMT	CT > AP & AMT	Results maintained.

NOTE: RX = relaxation; BF = biofeedback; CBT = cognitive-behavioral therapy; WL = waiting list; AMT = anxiety management training; ND = nondirective; AM = anxiety management; CT = cognitive therapy; CD = coping desensitization; DZ = diazepam; PL = placebo; BT = behavior therapy; AR = applied relaxation; AP = analytic psychotherapy.

Three of these studies found that treatment is better than no treatment (Barlow et al., 1984; Blowers et al., 1987; Butler et al., 1987), three others found no differences between treatments (Barlow et al., 1992; Borkovec & Mathews, 1988; White et al., 1992), and the final six showed differential efficacy across treatments, favoring packages that involve Cognitive Therapy (CT) combined with other behavioral techniques (Borkovec & Costello, 1993; Borkovec et al., 1987; Butler et al., 1991; Durham et al., 1994; Power et al., 1989; Power et al., 1990).

A number of reviewers have come to the same overall conclusion that the Beck and Emery (1985) version of CT, alone or in combination with other behavioral techniques (for example, relaxation, self-control desensitization, anxiety management training, or biofeedback), is effective in treating GAD (Borkovec & Whisman, 1996; Butler & Booth, 1991; Chambless & Gillis, 1993; Durham & Allan, 1993; Hollon & Beck, 1994). For example, a recent review by Durham and Allan (1993) concluded that psychological treatment will result in a 50% reduction in the severity of somatic symptoms and a 25% reduction in trait anxiety, and that about 50% of clients will achieve normal functioning. These results are likely to be maintained at follow-up. The authors suggest that the best results appear to be obtained by CT, but due to some methodological limitations in the research and some conflicting results, conclusions should not yet be drawn.

Chambless and Gillis (1993) performed a meta-analysis of nine GAD treatment studies that used some form of cognitive-behavioral therapy (CBT) and found that the pretest-posttest effect sizes supported the superior effectiveness of CBT over various control groups, as well as over waiting-list or pill placebo groups. An additional—and, perhaps, more impressive—finding was that, in general, treatment effects were at least maintained or even increased over the follow-up period. Additional findings were that clients treated with CBT were often less likely to seek further treatment than were clients in other treatment conditions; that CBT seemed to produce a relatively low dropout rate of 14%; and that depression-related dropout may also have been reduced, due to CBT's additional impact on clients' depression.

Specific Studies

Two recent, well-designed studies are covered in some detail, because they provide good examples of some of the best treatments currently available for GAD. In fact, a recent report from the American Psychological Association noted that there now exist "Well-Established Treatments" for GAD and cited the Butler et al. (1991) study as support for this conclusion (Chambless et al., 1996).

Results from Butler et al. (1991) provide some of the more impressive results available supporting the efficacy of CBT in the treatment of GAD. Fifty-seven ADIS-diagnosed GAD clients were randomly assigned to one of three groups—behavior therapy (BT), CBT, or waiting-list (WL). The two therapists who treated clients in both conditions were already well-trained behavior therapists, and they visited the Center for Cognitive Therapy in Philadelphia for training to ensure that they were equally well versed in the methods of CBT. Integrity-of-treatment checks done on audiotapes of sessions from the beginning, middle, and end of treatment indicated that the therapists provided appropriate examples of each type of treatment. Clients were treated for 4 to 12 individual 1-hour sessions, plus three booster sessions following treatment at intervals of 2, 4, and 6 weeks. BT consisted of teaching clients progressive muscular relaxation (Bernstein & Borkovec, 1973) and a variety of other behavioral techniques to build confidence. CBT was based upon Beck and Emery (1985) and used activity schedules and dysfunctional thought records to identify, examine, and evaluate thoughts that were believed to maintain the client's anxiety. These thoughts were evaluated primarily via behavioral experiments. Results at posttest were that the CBT group was superior to the WL on all but 1 of the 16 measures used, while BT was superior to WL on only 4 of the 16. Results at 6-month follow-up clearly favored the CBT group. The CBT group was superior to the BT group on three of the six anxiety measures, one of the four depression measures, and five of the six measures of changes in cognition. Additional results supporting the superiority of CBT over BT were that 2 clients had to be withdrawn from the BT condition because they became so depressed, and 3 more dropped out of treatment, while there were no similar losses from the CBT group. Finally, at the last follow-up, conducted between 11 and 24 months following treatment, it was found that 58% of the CBT group versus 21% of the BT group had received no further treatment, while 37% of the BT group versus 11% of the CBT group had received extensive additional treatment.

In Borkovec and Costello (1993), 55 ADIS-diagnosed GAD clients were assigned to nondirective therapy (ND), applied relaxation (AR), or CBT. Treatment was administered over 12 sessions via one of four therapists, two experienced psychologists, and two graduate students who were carefully trained and supervised. Integrity checks done on 20% of the audiotapes of the sessions indicated good adherence to the treatment protocols. AR consisted of careful self-monitoring of anxiety reactions and early intervention in the development of anxiety, primarily via relaxation procedures (Bernstein & Borkovec, 1973). CBT included all that was in AR, except that instead of focusing on the early detection of anxiety cues and the early application of relaxation, Goldfried's (1971) self-control desensitization and brief CT were used. Only 10 to 15 minutes per session were devoted to CT; to the extent possible during this limited time, the authors attempted to identify underlying thoughts and beliefs related to anxiety, engage in logical analysis with probability and evidence searching, and develop alternative thoughts and beliefs followed by behavioral testing of those beliefs. The primary purpose of the CT was to generate coping responses to be used during self-control desensitization. During self-control desensitization, clients imagined anxiety-provoking scenes and used relaxation skills and the coping statements to eliminate the anxiety. At postassessment, AR and CBT were generally equivalent but both were superior to ND. Though AR and CBT were generally equivalent at postassessment, there was some evidence that *differential pathways* (p. 617) led to these results. There was some indication that AR was more effective at reducing daily anxiety (results from a daily diary), while CBT showed superior results on measures of worry and depression. Though follow-up was a bit muddled because some clients received additional therapy between the end of treatment and the follow-up assessments, overall the results were generally maintained; that is, AR and CBT continued to be superior to ND. Moreover, 57.9% of the CBT clients vs. 37.5% of the AR clients met criteria for high endstate functioning, which at least suggests the possibility of some long-term superiority for CBT over AR. As the authors note, these results were obtained with only 10 to 15 minutes per session devoted to CT, and the results would perhaps have been greater if more thorough CT had been provided.

CONCLUSIONS

We can now return to the question posed earlier in this chapter: "Based on the extant literature, what do we now know about the best ways to treat GAD?" This review and the results of other reviews suggest that there is presently no single treatment of choice for GAD and that our current best answer is primarily CT used in conjunction with other behavioral techniques. Virtually all of the authors who used CT cited Beck and Emery (1985) as their source; nonetheless, their application of these procedures appears to have varied considerably. Butler et al. (1991) used the cognitive techniques as their primary intervention method and described their approach as using dysfunctional thought records to identify anxious thoughts, to develop the skills needed to examine these anxious thoughts, and, finally, to formulate alternative thoughts that can then be tested in subsequent behavioral experiments. Borkovec and Costello (1993) also used CT, but it was employed as an adjunct technique to develop additional coping skills for use during imaginal presentation of anxiety-provoking scenes, a segment of their self-control desensitization method. Behavioral techniques used included self-monitoring, relaxation, and exposure.

Much remains to be learned regarding the conceptualization, assessment, and treatment of GAD. Little attention has been devoted so far to the role of sociodemographic variables, such as race, culture, sexual orientation, marital status, gender, and social class, in GAD; so, these areas are especially in need of additional study. Likewise, GAD in children and adolescents remains relatively unexplored territory; this, too, is an area in need of further inquiry. Finally, treatments studied so far have focused upon individual therapy to the exclusion of the more systemically oriented approaches—such as couple or family therapy—that are so familiar to social workers. Social work, with its appreciation of sociodemographic variables and the usefulness of systemic conceptualizations, potentially has much to offer to the future development of more effective treatments for GAD.

REFERENCES

American Psychiatric Association. (1968). *Diagnostic and statistical manual of mental disorders* (2nd ed.). Washington, DC: Author.

American Psychiatric Association. (1980). *Diagnostic and statistical manual of mental disorders* (3rd ed.). Washington, DC: Author.

American Psychiatric Association. (1987). *Diagnostic and statistical manual of mental disorders* (3rd ed., rev.). Washington, DC: Author.

American Psychiatric Association. (1994). *Diagnostic and statistical manual of mental disorders* (4th ed.). Washington, DC: Author.

Barlow, D. H. (1988). *Anxiety and its disorders: The nature and treatment of anxiety and panic.* New York: Guilford Press.

Barlow, D. H. (1991). The nature of anxiety: Anxiety, depression, and emotional disorders. In R. M. Rapee & D. H. Brown (Eds.), *Chronic anxiety: Generalized anxiety disorder and mixed anxiety-depression* (pp. 1–28). New York: Guilford Press.

Barlow, D. H., Cohen, A. S., Waddell, M. T., Vermilyea, B. B., Klosko, J. S., Blanchard, E. B., & DiNardo, P. A. (1984). Panic and generalized anxiety disorders: Nature and treatment. *Behavior Therapy, 15,* 431–449.

Barlow, D. H., & DiNardo, P. A. (1991). The diagnosis of generalized anxiety disorder: Development, current status, and future directions. In R. M. Rapee & D. H. Barlow (Eds.), *Chronic anxiety: Generalized anxiety disorder and mixed anxiety-depression* (pp. 95–118). New York: Guilford Press.

Barlow, D. H., Rapee, R. M., & Brown, T. A. (1992). Behavioral treatment of generalized anxiety disorder. *Behavior Therapy, 23,* 551–570.

Beck, A. T., Brown, G., Epstein, N., & Steer, R. A. (1988). An inventory for measuring clinical anxiety: Psychometric properties. *Journal of Consulting and Clinical Psychology, 56,* 893–897.

Beck, A. T., & Emery, G. (1985). *Anxiety disorders and phobias: A cognitive perspective.* New York: Basic Books.

Beck, A. T., Ward, C. H., Mendelson, M., Mock, J., & Erbaugh, J. (1961). An inventory for measuring depression. *Archives of General Psychiatry, 4,* 561–571.

Bernstein, D. A., & Borkovec, T. D. (1973). *Progressive relaxation training.* Champaign, IL: Research Press.

Blazer, D. G., Hughes, D., George, L. K., Swartz, M., & Boyer, R. (1991). Generalized anxiety disorder. In L. N. Robins & D. A. Regier (Eds.), *Psychiatric disorders in America: The epidemiologic catchment area study* (pp. 180–203). New York: Free Press.

Blowers, C., Cobb, J., & Mathews, A. (1987). Generalized anxiety: A controlled treatment study. *Behaviour Research and Therapy, 25,* 493–502.

Borkovec, T. D., & Costello, E. (1993). Efficacy of applied relaxation and cognitive-behavioral therapy in the treatment of generalized anxiety disorder. *Journal of Consulting and Clinical Psychology, 61,* 611–619.

Borkovec, T. D., & Mathews, A. M. (1988). Treatment of nonphobic anxiety disorders: A comparison of non-directive, cognitive, and coping desensitization therapy. *Journal of Consulting and Clinical Psychology, 56,* 877–884.

Borkovec, T. D., Mathews, A. M., Chambers, A., Ebrahimi, S., Lytle, R., & Nelson, R. (1987). The effects of relaxation with cognitive or non-directive therapy and the role of relaxation-induced anxiety in the treatment of generalized anxiety. *Journal of Consulting and Clinical Psychology, 55,* 883–888.

Borkovec, T. D., & Whisman, M. A. (1996). Psychosocial treatment for generalized anxiety disorder. In M. Mavissakalian & R. Prien (Eds.), *Long-term treatments of anxiety disorders* (pp. 171–199). Washington, DC: American Psychiatric Press.

Brown, T. A., Anthony, M. M., & Barlow, D. H. (1992). Psychometric properties of the Penn State Worry Questionnaire in a clinical anxiety disorders sample. *Behaviour Research and Therapy, 30,* 33–37.

Brown, T. A., & Barlow, D. H. (1992). Comorbidity among anxiety disorders: Implications for treatment and DSM-IV. *Journal of Consulting and Clinical Psychology, 60,* 835–844.

Brown, T. A., Barlow, D. H., & Liebowitz, M. R. (1994). The empirical basis of generalized anxiety disorder. *American Journal of Psychiatry, 151,* 1272–1280.

Brown, T. A., DiNardo, P. A., & Barlow, D. H. (1994a). *Anxiety Disorders Interview Schedule for DSM-IV.* Albany, NY: Graywind.

Brown, T. A., DiNardo, P. A., & Barlow, D. H. (1994b). *Anxiety Disorders Interview Schedule for DSM-IV: Clinicians manual.* Albany, NY: Graywind.

Brown, T. A., O'Leary, T. A., & Barlow, D. H. (1993). Generalized anxiety disorder. In D. H. Barlow (Ed.), *Clinical handbook of psychological disorders: A step-by-step treatment manual* (2nd ed., pp. 137–188). New York: Guilford Press.

Butler, G. (1996). Research and practice in the treatment of complex anxiety disorders: Developing more effective treatments. In W. Dryden (Ed.), *Research in counseling and psychotherapy: Practical applications* (pp. 79–100). New York: Sage.

Butler, G., & Booth, R. G. (1991). Developing psychological treatments for generalized anxiety disorder. In R. M. Rapee & D. H. Barlow (Eds.), *Chronic anxiety: Generalized anxiety disorder and mixed anxiety-depression* (pp. 187–209). New York: Guilford Press.

Butler, G., Cullington, A., Hibbert, G., Klimes, I., & Gelder, M. (1987). Anxiety management for persistent generalized anxiety. *British Journal of Psychiatry, 151,* 535–542.

Butler G., Fennell, M., Robson, P., & Gelder, M. (1991). Comparison of behavior therapy and cognitive behavior therapy in the treatment of generalized anxiety disorder. *Journal of Consulting and Clinical Psychology, 59,* 167–175.

Chambless, D. L., & Gillis, M. M. (1993). Cognitive therapy of anxiety disorders. *Journal of Consulting and Clinical Psychology, 61,* 248–260.

Chambless, D. L., Sanderson, W. C., Shoham, V., Johnson, S. B., Pope, K. S., Crits-Christoph, P., Baker, M., Johnson, B., Woody, S. R., Sue, S., Beutler, L., Williams, D. A., & McCurry, S. (1996). An update on empirically validated therapies. *The Clinical Psychologist, 49,* 5–18.

Craske, M. G., Barlow, D. H., & O'Leary, T. A. (1992). *Mastery of your anxiety and worry.* Albany, NY: Graywind.

DiNardo, P. A., & Barlow, D. H. (1990). Syndrome and symptom co-occurrence in the anxiety disorders. In J. O. Maser & C. R. Cloninger (Eds.), *Comorbidity of mood and anxiety disorders* (pp. 205–230). Washington, DC: American Psychiatric Press.

Durham, R. C., & Allan, T. (1993). Psychological treatment of generalized anxiety disorder: A review of the clinical significance of results in outcome studies since 1980. *British Journal of Psychiatry, 163,* 19–26.

Durham, R. C., Murphy, T., Allan, T., Richard, D., Treliving, L. R., & Fenton, G. W. (1994). Cognitive therapy, analytic psychotherapy and anxiety management training for generalized anxiety disorder. *British Journal of Psychiatry, 165,* 315–323.

Friedman, S. (Ed.). (1994). *Anxiety disorders in African Americans.* New York: Springer.

Goldfried, M. R. (1971). Systematic desensitization as training in self-control. *Journal of Consulting and Clinical Psychology, 37,* 228–234.

Good, B. J., & Kleinman, A. M. (1985). Culture and anxiety: Cross-cultural evidence for the patterning of anxiety disorders. In A. H. Tuma & J. D. Maser (Eds.), *Anxiety and anxiety disorders* (pp. 297–324). Hillsdale, NJ: Erlbaum.

Hoehn-Saric, R., Borkovec, T. D., & Nemiah, J. C. (1995). Generalized anxiety disorder. In G. O. Gabbard (Ed.), *Treatments of psychiatric disorders: The DSM-IV edition* (pp. 1537–1567). Washington, DC: American Psychiatric Association.

Hollon, S. D., & Beck, A. T. (1994). Cognitive therapy and cognitive behavioral therapy. In A. E. Bergin & S. L. Garfield (Eds.), *Handbook of psychotherapy and behavior change* (4th ed., pp. 428–466). New York: Wiley.

Kessler, R. C., McGonagle, K. A., Zhao, S., Nelson, C. B., Hughes, M., Eshleman, S., Wittchen, H. U., & Kendler, K. S. (1994). Lifetime and 12-month prevalence of DSM-III-R psychiatric disorders in the United States. Results from the National Comorbidity Survey. *Archives of General Psychiatry, 51,* 8–19.

Kushner, M. G., Sher, K. J., & Beitman, B. D. (1990). The relation between alcohol problems and the anxiety disorders. *American Journal of Psychiatry, 147,* 685–695.

Lipschitz, A. (1988). Diagnosis and classification of anxiety disorders. In C. G. Last & M. Hersen (Eds.), *Handbook of anxiety disorders,* (pp. 41–65). New York: Pergamon Press.

Meyer, T. J., Miller, M. L., Metzger, R. L., & Borkovec, T. D. (1990). Development and validation of the Penn State Worry Questionnaire. *Behaviour Research and Therapy, 28,* 487–495.

Power, K. G., Jerrom, D. W., Simpson, R. J., Mitchell, M. J., & Swanson, V. (1989). A controlled comparison of cognitive-behavior therapy, diazepam and placebo in the management of generalized anxiety. *Behavioural Psychotherapy, 17,* 1–14.

Power, K. G., Simpson, R. J., Swanson, V., & Wallace, L. A. (1990). A controlled comparison of cognitive-behaviour therapy, diazepam, and placebo, alone and in combination, for the treatment of generalized anxiety disorder. *Journal of Anxiety Disorders, 4,* 267–292.

Rapee, R. M. (1991). Generalized anxiety disorder: A review of clinical features and theoretical concepts. *Clinical Psychology Review, 11,* 419–440.

Raskin, M., Johnson, G., & Rondesvedt, J. W. (1973). Chronic anxiety treated by feedback-induced muscle relaxation. *Archives of General Psychiatry, 28,* 263–267.

Raskin, M., Rondesvedt, J. W., & Johnson, G. (1972). Anxiety in young adults: A prognostic study. *Journal of Nervous and Mental Disease, 154,* 229–237.

Riskind, J. H., Moore, R., Harman, B., Hohmann, A. A., Beck, A. T., & Stewart, B. (1991). The relation of generalized anxiety to depression in general and dysthymic disorder in particular. In R. M. Rapee & D. H. Brown (Eds.), *Chronic anxiety: Generalized anxiety disorder and mixed anxiety-depression,* (pp. 153–171). New York: Guilford Press.

Sanderson, W. C., & Wetzler, S. (1991). Chronic anxiety and generalized anxiety disorder: Issues in comorbidity. In R. M. Rapee & D. H. Barlow (Eds.), *Chronic anxiety: Generalized anxiety disorder and mixed anxiety-depression* (pp. 119–135). New York: Guilford Press.

Silverman, W. K., & Ginsburg, G. (1995). Specific phobias and generalized anxiety disorder. In J. S. March (Ed.), *Anxiety disorders in children and adolescents.* New York: Guilford Press.

White, J., Keenan, M., & Brooks, N. (1992). Stress control: A controlled comparative investigation of large group therapy for generalized anxiety disorder. *Behavioural Psychotherapy, 20,* 97–114.

Williams, J. B. W., Gibbon, M., First, M. B., Spitzer, R. L., Davies, M., Borus, J., Howes, M. J., Kane, J., Pope, H. G., Rounsaville, B., & Wittchen, H. (1992). The Structured Clinical Interview for DSM-III-R (SCID) II. Multisite test-retest reliability. *Archives of General Psychiatry, 49,* 630–636.

PART VI

Sexual Disorders

Chapter 20

SEXUAL DESIRE AND AROUSAL DISORDERS

Sophia F. Dziegielewski
Cheryl Resnick

OVERVIEW

As we progress through the human life cycle, each of us develops into a sexual being with certain needs, desires, and expectations. These expectations can be highly variable, complicating the simple definition of sexual problems.

The fourth edition of the *Diagnostic and Statistical Manual of Mental Disorders* (*DSM-IV;* American Psychiatric Association [APA], 1994) defines *Sexual Dysfunction* as "characterized by disturbance in sexual desire and in the psychophysiological changes that characterize the sexual response cycle and cause marked distress and interpersonal difficulty" (p. 493). *DSM-IV* further delineates *desire* as "fantasies about sexual activity and the desire to have sexual activity" (APA, 1994, p. 493); *excitement* as "a subjective sense of sexual pleasure and the accompanying physiological changes" (p. 494); *orgasm* as "a peaking of sexual pleasure, with release of sexual tension in rhythmic contraction of the perineal muscles and reproductive organs" (p. 394); and *resolution* as "a sense of muscular relaxation and general well-being" (p. 394). Kaplan (1979) delineates a normal cycle of sexual response as beginning with the desire phase, moving next to the excitement or arousal phase, and culminating in the orgasm phase. When disturbances occur at any point in this cycle, a sexual disorder can result.

Once the definition and diagnostic criteria of what constitutes a sexual desire disorder (that is, Hypoactive Sexual Desire Disorder and Sexual Aversion Disorder) or a sexual arousal disorder (that is, Female Sexual Arousal Disorder and Male Erectile Disorder) have been derived, special attention to the application and relevance of this definition for each individual must be explored. Conte (1986) asserts that as many as 50% to 60% of married couples experience sexual difficulties. This statistic, however, can be misleading, because consideration needs to be given to what constitutes a sexual desire or arousal problem. Therefore, the problem of assessing *normal* and *not normal* sexual behavior continues to complicate the definition. According to Knopf and Seiler (1990), the average couple generally have sexual intercourse two to three times a week; however, this number is questioned in appreciation for individual couples' preferences and needs. Simply stated, the number of times a couple have or do not have sexual intercourse is not considered a problem—unless it is deemed so by the participating couple.

The frequency of sexual behavior in a relationship is only one factor to be explored in the determination of a sexual arousal or desire disorder. In the past, the concept of the importance of individual perception in the form of irrational thoughts leading to the inhibition of one's capacity for sexual enjoyment has been questioned. Today, however, many professionals continue to argue just the opposite (Eastman, 1993). It has become clear that an individual's perceptions about sexual desire and arousal can be swayed by a multitude of factors. These factors include personal beliefs, societal attitudes and mores, cultural pressure, parental influence, spiritual and religious teaching, socioeconomic status, and education level (Stuntz, Falk, Hiken, & Carson, 1996). To further complicate understanding, an individual's sexual attitudes and views can—and often do—change throughout the life cycle. This can make certain events problematic that were not considered to be before, and vice-versa.

Sexual Desire Disorders

In *DSM-IV* (APA, 1994), the Sexual Desire Disorders are divided into two diagnostic types: Hypoactive Sexual Desire Disorder and Sexual Aversion Disorder. *Hypoactive Sexual Desire Disorder* occurs at the initial (desire) phase of the sexual response cycle. It is identified when "a deficiency or absence of sexual fantasies and desire for sexual activity" exists (APA, 1994, p. 496). Leif (1977) termed this condition *inhibited sexual desire,* referring to minimal or no interest in sexual activity. Hypoactive sexual desire can be situational (occurring within a specific context) or global (occurring across situations and partners; Fish, Busby, & Killian, 1994). In addition, it can be primary (lifelong) or secondary (occurring after a normal period of sexual functioning).

Sexual Aversion Disorder is defined as "the aversion to and active avoidance of genital sexual contact with a sexual partner" (APA, 1994, p. 499). This antipathy, which may be manifest as anxiety or panic, must be intense enough to cause marked distress or interpersonal dissatisfaction and difficulty and cannot be directly related to another clinical diagnosis. This revulsion can be limited to a particular aspect of sexual conduct, such as vaginal secretions or genital stimulation; or it can be more diverse and include such sexual behaviors as kissing and hugging. An outcome of this disorder is often repeated avoidance of sexual relations.

Sexual Arousal Disorders

In *DSM-IV* (APA, 1994), the Sexual Arousal Disorders are divided into two diagnostic types: Female Sexual Arousal Disorder and Male Erectile Disorder. These disorders of the excitement phase often involve problems with vaginal lubrication or erection. *Female Sexual Arousal Disorder* is described as "a persistent or recurrent inability to attain, or to maintain until completion of the sexual activity, an adequate lubrication-swelling response of sexual excitement" (APA, 1994, p. 500). Individuals with sexual arousal disorders may experience sexual excitation without evidencing physical signs of arousal (for example, erection or vaginal lubrication).

Male Erectile Disorder is delineated as "a persistent or recurrent inability to attain, or to maintain until completion of the sexual activity, an adequate erection"; this difficulty must cause marked distress, and the dysfunction cannot be directly attributed to another major clinical diagnosis or general medical condition (APA, 1994, p. 502). In this disorder the patterns of dysfunction can be diverse, in that some men will have difficulty with penile firmness from the onset of the sexual encounter, while others will develop problems later in the sequence of events. Many males may only be able to experience erections with self-masturbation or at early morning awakening (APA, 1994).

Incidence and Prevalence

In the diagnosis and treatment of sexual dysfunctions, both prevalence and incidence rates should be considered. *Incidence* refers to the number of new cases of sexual dysfunction that occur in a specific population during a discrete period of time, whereas *prevalence* refers to the number of people who actually suffer from the disorder at a given period of time (Spector & Carey, 1990). In regard to the sexual disorders, it is difficult to obtain both prevalence and incidence rates, and the currently reported rates can and do vary.

In the area of the sexual desire disorders, O'Carroll (1991) describes Hypoactive Sexual Desire Disorder as affecting 20% of the total population and 15% of the male population and indicates that this is a major complaint affecting women, with estimates as high as 36% to 49%. In an Oxford study, 17% of the women ages 35 to 59 reported low sexual desire; 42% of the women age 40 reported the same in a Danish study; 35% of the wives in couples studied in the United States described low sexual desire; and 40% to 60% of couples presenting for therapy with a problem that is female-related implicate low sexual desire as the cause (Hawton, Catalan, & Fagg, 1991).

Palace (1995) estimates that 30% of all women exhibit orgasmic disorder and 20% of women exhibit sexual desire disorders. Numerically, that translates to 23.5 and 15 million women, respectively. It is important to differentiate between women who are anorgasmic during masturbation and those who are anorgasmic via coitus (4% and 70%, respectively). Female arousal disorder presents in 62% of women seeking therapy, whereas the rates for vaginismus and dyspareunia are 12% to 17% and 3% to 5%, respectively (Spector & Carey, 1990). Alexander (1993) found the incidence of decreased libido to be 11% to 48%, with help-seeking behavior occurring more often in women. She states that 70% of those who seek assistance for sexual disorders present with decreased libido.

Estimates indicate that nearly 20% of the total population experiences hypoactive sexual desire disorders (Kinzl, Traweger, & Biebl, 1995). Regardless of specific percentages, several studies indicate that inhibited sexual desire disorders are on the rise, climbing to approximately 40% of those seeking sex therapy and 31% of couples seeking treatment (Fish et al., 1994). The Sex Therapy Clinic of the University of New York at Stony Brook found an increase in reported sexual desire disorders from 32% (1974 and 1976) to 46% (1978) and then to 55% (1981 to 1982; Trudel, 1991). Although this disorder appears to be more commonly reported in women, there is a rising incidence of sexual desire disorder among men (Trudel, 1991).

In the area of the sexual arousal disorders, there also appears to be an increasing rate of prevalence. Spector and Carey (1990) estimate the prevalence of inhibited female orgasm to be 5% to 10% of the general population. They also indicate that inhibited female orgasm is the most commonly presented female dysfunction, reported by 18% to 76% of females seeking sex therapy treatment.

In the general population, the prevalence of Male Erectile Disorder is estimated at 4% to 9% of all men, although it is the most common presenting complaint for males. Generally, 36% to 40% of males seeking sex therapy report having this disorder. Fifty percent of these males describe secondary erectile disorder (being able to maintain an erection at some point), whereas only 8% describe primary erectile disorder (never being able to maintain an erection; Spector & Carey, 1990). Current estimates depict premature ejaculation at 36% to 38% and inhibited male orgasm at 4% to 10%, which makes it the least common of the male dysfunctions (Spector & Carey, 1990).

ASSESSMENT METHODS

A skilled, thorough, clinical interview is critical to any social work assessment. Although not included in the scope of this chapter, the authors recommend Fedoroff's (1991) article as an excellent resource for conducting interviews to assess sexual disorders.

Since many sexual desire disorders present concurrently with arousal and orgasm disorders, taking a proper history is essential to the implementation of the best treatment plan. In fact, Segraves and Segraves (1991) report that of the 475 women they studied with a diagnosis of Hypoactive Sexual Desire Disorder, 41% had at least one other sexual disorder and 18% had sexual disorders in all three phases of the sexual response cycle (desire, arousal, and orgasm). Taking an adequate history ensures that the therapist has endeavored to ascertain all the factors that may have caused, may be related to, and may be maintaining the dysfunction.

As the actual etiology of a sexual disorder may be physiological, psychological, environmental, or situational, a physical exam is critical. A physical examination should always be the first line of assessment, since many diseases and physical abnormalities produce or exacerbate sexual dysfunction (age, physical health, depression, stress, and hormone insufficiency; medical illnesses, such as diabetes, renal failure, endocrine disorders, and neurological disorders; and psychiatric illnesses). A multitude of studies have linked sexual arousability to hormonal determinants (Rosen & Leiblum, 1987). Alexander (1993) indicates that estrogen-androgen replacement in postmenopausal women appears to increase sexual desire, arousal, and drive. Research also has suggested that 50% to 60% of men diagnosed with psychogenic impotence may actually suffer from an organic condition (Conte, 1986). Alexander (1993) presents a comprehensive listing of the organic causes of decreased sexual desire. In this review, she delineates both reversible and irreversible organic origins for the pituitary, endocrine, neurological, renal, psychiatric, and pharmacologic determinants.

Some studies have suggested that dysfunctional individuals may experience less of a physiological response during sexual arousal, or are simply less attentive to their own physiological cues than are sexually functional individuals (Barlow, 1986; Palace & Gorzalka, 1992). They may, in turn, also have difficulty labeling physiological genital cues relating to their own sexual arousal. However, the results from studies conducted in this area have been conflicting, and it is suggested that more research is required to establish this as a predictor for understanding sexual responses.

In assessment, it is important to note the use of substances that can affect sexual behavior, including prescription and nonprescription medications, drugs, and alcohol (alcohol may result in difficulty gaining an erection, and certain drugs may interfere with vaginal lubrication). It is important that persons with medical problems recognize the effects of some prescription medications upon sexual response.

In assessment, the psychological aspects that can affect sexual response should be noted. For example, a type of psychological turning off can actively suppress sexual desire (Read, 1995). In such cases the individual actively learns to focus on angry, fearful, or distracting associations that result in the physiological inhibition of desire (Kaplan, 1979). Anxiety, power and control struggles, individual body image, problems with self-esteem, and a history of abuse may also serve to inhibit the sexual response. Postcolostomy and postmastectomy patients have the added complication of the likelihood of body image issues. The fear of intimacy, inability to form commitment, dependency issues, guilt, and conflicts pertaining to sexual preference and identification can also influence the sexual response cycle.

In assessing sexual difficulties, it is always important to take environmental and situational issues into account. This includes examining the nature of the partner relationship and the environmental circumstances. Partner-relationship areas that need to be considered include ways of addressing and relating to intimacy, attraction to the partner, communication problems and means of problem solving, sources of marital conflict and discord, family issues and pressure, the presence of small children, living arrangements, and the sense of security in the relationship. It is frequently useful to gain information regarding both partners' sensitivity to stimulation and responsive body areas (Anderson, 1983). Women displaying inhibited sexual desire are more likely to report greater martial dissatisfaction and refuse sexual invitations from their spouses more often than noninhibited women (Stuart, Hammond, & Pett, 1987). The inhibited women express the view that they experience lower levels of affection and emotional closeness in their marriages. Clearly, the quality and nature of the marital relationship bears relation to most sexual disorders, particularly those of sexual desire.

Parental attitudes and teachings, as well as religious indoctrination, influence lifelong sexuality. Stuart et al. (1987) compared women's perception of parental attitudes toward sex and parental displays of affection, and found significant differences between women exhibiting inhibited sexual desire and noninhibited women. The inhibited women rated both these components much more negatively. Closely tied to the parental environment was the failure of parents to appropriately teach sexual education and knowledge (Stuart et al. 1987).

Another environmental and situational factor that needs to be considered in the social work assessment is life stress. Excessive life stressors frequently result in decreased sexual interest and arousal. It is important to note that environmental and situational factors, although somewhat difficult to isolate and identify clearly, can be extremely amenable to change; therefore, their contribution to intervention success should not be underestimated.

The partners' preferred frequencies of sexual interaction—defined as the frequency of the wish to have sex—should be determined. This is a critical assessment factor, since no criteria for normal sexual desire exist. In fact, when couples are comparable in their levels of desire, disorders may not be identified. Sexual differences are recognized as disorders when one partner's desire differs significantly from the other's. As Stuart et al. (1987) state, "if both partners have a similar level of desire, there is no issue. If their levels of desire diverge, the disparity may create a problem" (p. 93).

The social worker must also be careful to assess the client's *desire* for sexual activity along with the *frequency* of sexual activity, since the two can differ enormously. It is quite conceivable that a person might desire more sexual activity than current circumstances permit (as parents of young children understand all too clearly). In this instance, a low frequency of sexual activity might not reflect a sexual desire disorder. According to Rosen & Leiblum (1987), an individual might experience a strong sexual appetite, manifested through sexual urges, thoughts, and feelings, but fail to initiate or engage in sexual activity because they do not have the opportunity to do so. Perhaps a more useful measurement is *sexual fantasy:* "a conscious mental representation which translates itself in more or less imaginary form with hedonic value and is susceptible to produce sexual activity" (Trudel, 1991, p. 265). Trudel also recommends the cognitive evaluation of irrational beliefs, thoughts, and ideas impacting the cognitive-behavioral dimension of sexuality (also see Thyer & Papsdorf, 1981).

In summary, the social worker's assessment of sexual desire and arousal disorders should always include demographic information; identification of the primary and secondary nature of the problem; global versus situational description of the sexual problem; information about the specificity, intensity, and duration of the presenting problem; the antecedent circumstances at the onset of the problem, as well as concurrent factors; a complete sexual history, including desired as well as actual frequency of sexual activity; and the motivation for seeking treatment. Environmental and situational factors should always be explored. Referral for a physical examination by a well-trained physician is also indicated.

Assessment Scales and Methods

In addition to a thorough clinical interview, other self-report assessment techniques include rapid assessment instruments, questionnaires, and behavioral records. Conte (1986) provides information regarding numerous available questionnaires, including Thorne's 200-item Sex Inventory Scale, the Sexual Orientation Method, the Self-Evaluation of Sexual Behavior and Gratification Questionnaire, the Sexual Interest Questionnaire, the Sexual Interaction Inventory, and the Derogatis Sexual Functioning Inventory. All of these evaluation measures have demonstrated usefulness in the assessment of sexual dysfunctions. Conte (1986) indicates that literature regarding the use of self-report behavioral records is scarce. Weekly checklists or further record keeping in this area could prove extremely useful in the assessment of sexual functioning. Indeed, the systematic client-reported tracking of selected sexual activities is essential for ascertaining whether problems exist and whether clients are benefiting from treatment.

Anderson (1983) delineated a number of assessment tools that are comprehensive and easy to administer. Kinzl et al. (1995) designed a 7-item scale to measure sexual dysfunction for their study of sexual dysfunction in women who had been sexually abused as children. Items on their scale include persistent or recurrent deficiency or absence of sexual fantasy and desire for sexual activity in adulthood; aversion to and avoidance of genital sexual contact with a partner; delay in, or absence of, orgasm following normal sexual excitation; genital pain before, during, or after sexual intercourse; and lack of a subjective sense of sexual excitation.

Hawton et al. (1991) illustrated the type of questions that are essential for assessing the nature of the partners' relationship. These 5-point scales assess level of commitment to the relationship; contentment; tension; communication (both general and sexual); enjoyment of sexual activity; frequency of activity; frequency of sexual thoughts; communication of needs; and each partner's own desired frequency of sexual activity, along with the projected partner's desired frequency. Woody, D'Souza, and Crain (1994) developed the Sexual Interaction System Scale (SISS), an instrument for measuring couples' sexual functioning. It explores the nature of the sexual relationship and interactions, sexual satisfaction, and marital adjustment. Their study found strong correlations between marital adjustment, sexual interaction, and sexual satisfaction.

Kaplan & Harder (1991) developed a 33-item scale for women that measures the subjective discomfort and conflict a woman feels in relation to her sexual arousal and desire. The scale examines the woman's subjective evaluation of her emotional being, as opposed to behavioral factors, such as orgasm. Their study found that women who have been sexually abused display the highest scores. They recommend the development of a similar scale for men to delineate male sexual desire conflicts, which they suggest could produce the recognition of important gender differences.

EFFECTIVE INTERVENTIONS

Social workers across a variety of practice settings are frequently presented with the sex-related problems of clients. Appropriate interventions and referrals for these clients present obstacles for social work professionals. Empirical research studies on clients with sexual desire or arousal disorders have helped social workers to develop and refine treatment options. Knowledge of these current methods is essential for social work professionals, particularly in this era of managed care services, when funding for general mental health treatment is often considered only as a last resort (Dziegielewski, 1996).

Several general techniques have been employed to treat sexual dysfunction. Sex education, communication training, sexual technique training, systematic desensitization, and sensate focus have all been used in treating sexual dysfunction (Harrison, 1987). Many of the practice strategies employed have been administered on an individual, group, marital, family, or combination basis.

Sexual Desire Disorders

Hypoactive Sexual Disorder, or low sexual desire disorder (which includes any type of inhibited sexual desire) is noted as the most common sexual dysfunction. Terms previously used to describe these conditions include *frigidity* and *impo-*

tence. Wincze and Carey (1991) warn against using these labels, since they are imprecise and have often been used to describe other sexual dysfunctions. Diagnosis of the conditions that fall under the umbrella of hypoactive sexual disorders can be difficult, because they are often multifaceted. These disorders appear to have a combination of the following aspects: biological (e.g., neuroendocrine), psychological (e.g., cognitive and affective), social (e.g., relationship oriented), and cultural (e.g., religious upbringing; Wincze & Carey, 1991). This multifaceted composition also makes it difficult to identify specific treatment techniques.

Trudel (1991) indicates that Hyposexual Desire Disorder is highly resistant to treatment, and even when positive results are initially obtained, long-term success rates are low. Results have been particularly poor when this disorder is perceived exclusively as an individual symptom (Fish et al., 1994). Hormonal therapy, sex therapy, treatment for depression, increased recognition and perception of pleasurable body sensations, and couples therapy that attends to the diversification of sensual and sexual activity are all meaningful in the treatment of low sexual desire (Trudel, 1991).

There are two primary methods of reasoning that have often been linked to hyposexuality that influence treatment strategy: conscious motivation and unconscious motivation (Knopf & Seiler, 1990). In *conscious motivation,* individuals are aware of what they are feeling. Here, individuals are believed to make either active or inactive choices as to whether they want to enjoy sex with the chosen partner. In an active choice, individuals may decide not to enjoy sexual acts of expression due to, for example, anger directed at the partner. In an inactive choice, individuals may not be able to identify exactly where the resistance is coming from, only that it exists.

In conscious control, some individuals can pinpoint exactly when their desire was lost; however, many remain unable to actively control desire's on-off mechanism. In *unconscious motivation,* individuals seem unaware of what is happening to them, or why. They often do not understand their situation or recognize how it occurred. Sexual feelings are often repressed or avoided, and it is not uncommon for these urges to be replaced with depression and anxiety (Barlow, 1986).

Hawton et al. (1991) found that the motivation of the male partner plays a significant role in recovery for women presenting with Hypoactive Desire Disorder. The younger the age and the lower the motivation of the male partner, the poorer the outcome. Sexual arousal disorders can occur in both men and women; however, this type of disorder seems to be diagnosed and treated most commonly in males.

In a study that addressed sexual dysfunction in either the male or the female partner, Russell (1990) acknowledged the difficulty that couples have in resolving conflicts in expressing emotional, as well as physical, intimacy. This study attempted to combine some of the well-known strategies for treating sexual difficulties with a new cognitive approach to treatment in couples therapy, where self-disclosure is used in conjunction with sensate focus exercises. Here the individual's past, the couple's past, and family history response patterns are examined. Russell expected the combination of these modes of treatment to increase understanding and intimacy for the couple (1990). In her study of 49 couples, 8 couples communicated concerns regarding one member's low sex desire for the other. In the final results, 15 couples who participated clearly reported an increase in emotional and physical intimacy.

Of the research examined in this area, cognitive-behavioral treatment appears to be one of the most effective therapies in treating Hypoactive Desire Disorder. Attention is given to the anticipation of negative consequences tied to sexual experiences. Initially, exercises to help increase comfort during sexual activity are provided, allowing for the exploration of increasing partner attraction, the creation of fantasies and imagery, and the provision of proper sexual education. Multimodel treatment has been most effective; it focuses on increasing sensuality, achieving of insight on what factors maintain low sexual desire, restructuring the cognitions inhibiting sexual desire, and improving sexual behaviors through the use of traditional sex therapy techniques (Trudel, 1991).

In a study by Fish et al. (1994), the couple was highlighted as the focus of treatment. The researchers supported the contention that a structural form of couples therapy would also be effective in treating inhibited sexual desire when the problem was conceptualized within the context of the "couple". In this study, inhibited sexual desire was examined in such interactive terms as, "sex serves as a function in relationships, and desire depends on that function and the cues each partner has endowed with sexual meaning" (Fish et al., 1994, p. 115).

In summary, working with couples appears to be a viable option for treatment when one or both partners present with Hypoactive Desire Disorder. The prognosis for low sexual desire dysfunctions is poorer than for the excitement and the orgasmic dysfunctions (Friedman & Hogan, 1985). Keeping this in mind, cognitive-behavioral therapy remains a positive treatment modality for dealing with sexual desire disorders. Nevertheless, more research is needed—particularly longitudinal studies—in order to measure the lasting effects of cognitive-behavioral treatment (Russell, 1990). Not only is exploration of new treatment experiences needed—the replication of current treatment results is essential.

The future task of the social work professional in treating clients with sexual desire disorders remains twofold: (a) to measure the effectiveness of new cognitive-behavioral and other treatments, and (b) to establish whether these treatments will prove to be effective over time. There does appear to be a shift in emphasis, with the primary emphasis being focused on the second objective—thus highlighting the need for replication of these treatment studies.

Sexual Arousal Disorders

In general, there are three behavioral treatments that can be helpful in treating clients suffering from erectile dysfunction: (a) communication technique training (to deal with social and relationship issues), (b) sexual technique training (teaching education and the practice of sexual techniques), and (c) a combination treatment that utilizes both. Kilmann et al. (1987) studied 20 couples who were tested to determine the effectiveness of current treatments on secondary erectile dysfunction. In order to participate in the study, the male partner's success/experience ratio during sexual intercourse had to be approximately 20 percent, and erectile dysfunction had to have been a problem over the past 5 years. Five experimental groups were used, and four couples participated in each group. The three treatment groups (consisting of eight 2-hour sessions) were all designed to enhance the male's sexual functioning and included a *communication education group,* which stressed positive communication techniques; a *sexual training group,* which was designed to enhance positive sexual techniques; and a *combination treatment group,* which stressed both communication and sexual training. The fourth group, referred to as the *attention-placebo control group,* implemented controls to limit the degree of treatment received, thus constituting a less powerful treatment procedure than that given the other groups. In this group, highly structured lectures were provided without any planned applicability or practice time being allotted for individual problem solving. The couples in the *no treatment control group* were pretested and waited 5 weeks for treatment to begin. After the posttest, they were provided with the combination treatment. Several pretest measurement inventories and questionnaires were used, and the results were statistically analyzed.

Each of the treatments for secondary erectile dysfunction were found to be statistically significant when compared to no treatment at all. The small number of couples participating (five groups of four couples each) limits the generalizability of the conclusions. Nevertheless, this article clearly supports the importance of including a structured psychological treatment component in the treatment of sexual dysfunction. It also supports the recommendation by Eastman (1993) that the importance of education, communication, and support should not be underestimated, even when a condition is organically generated.

Goldman and Carroll (1990) also highlight the importance of including education when treating secondary erectile dysfunction in older couples. In this study, 20 couples were randomly assigned to two groups; 10 completed a education workshop and 10 were used as controls. The workshop provided a structured educational format that focused on the physiological and psychological changes that occur in the sexual response cycle during aging. Sexual behavior was measured along three dimensions utilizing three standardized scales: (a) the frequency of sexual behavior, (b) sexual satisfaction, and (c) knowledge and attitudes toward sex. Pretest and posttest scores were reviewed and analyzed. Study results suggest that the couples who attended the workshop had a significant increase in knowledge levels after completion of the workshop. A slight increase in sexual behavior was noted for the experimental group, with a slight decline in this behavior for the control group. Overall, the educational workshop was considered a success, with a reported increase in knowledge and positive changes, as well as more realistic attitudes once the etiology related to sexual satisfaction and erectile functioning was explained.

Although the literature has stressed the importance of education in the treatment of erectile difficulty, the addition of *play therapy* has also been considered. Shaw (1990) focused on this option in treating men who had inhibited ejaculation. The central premise of the inclusion of play therapy is the belief that sexuality should be fun and pleasureful, not performance-oriented. However, the reality for many men is that the desire to perform becomes extremely anxiety-provoking. In play therapy, performance anxiety is addressed and males are taught to reduce the focus on performance. The focus of the intervention is on helping clients recognize and increase the spontaneous aspects of their personalities. In Shaw's study (1990), participants were expected to create and act on fantasies, to participate in sensate focus exercises, and to take part in sexual expression board games. Fifteen males (followed over a 3-year period) were able to successfully ejaculate with their own touch, although they were unable to do so with their partners. Of the 12 men who completed the program, all reported relief within 3 to 22 months of the intervention.

In summary, these studies elucidate the need for both biological and social work therapies for sexual arousal disorders. The behavioral and behavioral-cognitive therapies are among the best supported psychosocial treatments in this regard. More research is needed to determine exactly what types of psychosocial treatments work best and if the results remain consistent over time. This makes the social worker's role as a clinical researcher critical in helping clients.

Combination Approaches

Many researchers express interest in combining strategies for treating the sexual desire and arousal disorders and their resulting sexual difficulties. Russell (1990) compared cognitive marital therapy (CMT), a new couples therapy approach, to previously used interventions. In CMT, self-disclosure among couples is strongly encouraged as a means of increasing understanding and intimacy, thus reducing conflict. Self-disclosure is seen as a means to increase both physical and emotional closeness.

With the 49 couples that were assessed in the clinic, the information gathered consisted of a complete psychosocial history, which included both current and past behaviors and trends. The therapist then made an initial decision regarding the type of sexual disorder each couple was suffering from and devised and discussed an appropriate plan with the couple. Most of the couples in this study chose a combination treatment approach. In this approach, specific concern was devoted to correcting the sexual problem and cognitive marital therapy was chosen to address relationship issues. Sensate focus homework assignments were almost always used, along with factual information to dispel myths about what is normal. Of the 24 couples that completed this year-long longitudinal study, 15 reported an increase in physical and emotional intimacy. Based on the results of the study, Russell (1990) strongly believes that sexual dysfunctions cannot be isolated from interpersonal dimensions that ultimately determine the quality of the couple's relationship.

Many current social work and behavioral science researchers concur with the need for the inclusion of a psychosocial component with specific measures to address the marital, social, and personal difficulties an individual may express (Goldman & Carroll, 1990; Kaplan, 1990; Shaw, 1990). Burte and Araoz (1994), in focusing on cognitive processes and their manipulation as a treatment for sexual dysfunction, seek to uncover what they term *negative self-hypnosis.* They define this concept as nonconscious negative statements or defeatist mental images. Cognitive interactions between partners are highlighted, searching for negative imagery and self-talk. Burte and Araoz follow Walen's 8-link model, emphasizing: (a) perception of the sexual stimulus, (b) evaluation of the sexual stimulus, (c) physiological arousal, (d) perception of the arousal, (e) assessment of the arousal, (f) sexual behavior, (g) perception of that behavior, and (h) evaluation of the sexual behavior. Previously discussed studies center on faulty perceptions and self-evaluations of arousal; however, *hypnosex therapy,* as Burte and Araoz designate their approach, focuses on altering the cognitive components of these perceptions and evaluations. Clients awareness of their negative thought patterns is the core of intervention. Some authors have advocated the primary use of traditional hypnotherapy techniques in treatment of the sexual desire disorders (Bakich, 1995); however, more research is needed in this area.

In dealing with disease-related sexual dysfunction, Macaluso & Berkman (1984) implemented the use of three groups. The organic causes of dysfunction included diabetes, hypertension, alcoholic neuropathy, and erectile difficulty following prostate surgery. Groups focused on education, attitude change, the use of adaptive sexual techniques, and improved communications. Using pre- and post-group assessment to measure attitude changes, the group approach was found to be effective in educating couples about sexual dysfunction and offering alternative methods of obtaining sexual gratification (Macaluso & Berkman, 1984).

In investigating 65 couples presenting with sexual dysfunction, LoPiccolo, Heiman, and Hogan (1985) found that single-therapist groups show no significant difference from cotherapy groups. Those assigned to a single male or single female therapist did no better or worse than those assigned to a dual-sex cotherapy team. Sex therapy was effective for either group.

SEXUAL DYSFUNCTION AMONG GAY MEN

Consideration should be given to the particular needs of gay men with sexual dysfunction. Assessment is crucial, and information regarding the use of alcohol and drugs may be pertinent. Fears and concerns relating to HIV and AIDS need to be evaluated, as well as the potential aversion to particular sexual acts (Reece, 1987). Assessment should also include exploration of issues related to homophobia, unresolved childhood conflicts, sexual orientation guilt, sexual trauma, performance pressures, and lack of insight into relationship needs (Reece, 1988).

As with heterosexual couples, Hypoactive Sexual Desire Disorder can be reframed as partner discrepancy in sexual desire. Desire differences may be based in disparity in time, place, style, role, or activities preferences (Reece, 1987). Treatment for sexual dysfunction in the gay community involves evaluation of the couple's level of commitment, general sexual education and information, partner cooperation and compromise, couple awareness and increased communication, as well as combating the boredom and routine of sexual relationships (Reece, 1987).

The most frequently related sexual disorder among gay men is secondary erectile dysfunction, yet retarded ejaculation seems to be reported more frequently among homosexual males than it is in heterosexual males (Reece, 1988). Reece (1988) hypothesizes that inhibited ejaculation may present more often in gay males because they may be more likely to develop rigid patterns in self-stimulation. Such patterns, which include "very rapid stroking of the penis, applied with great pressure and often accompanied by tensed abdominal and leg muscles . . . not only is the body rigid, but the position—usually reclining on the back—seldom varies" may make it difficult for males to orgasm with a partner, under differing circumstances (Reece, 1988).

It is interesting to note that the development of similar rigid patterns of masturbatory behavior may underlie the problem that many women have in experiencing orgasm during coitus. If masturbatory patterns are set to maximize clitoral stimulation, vaginal coitus may not replicate such stimulation with ease. Further research regarding masturbatory patterns and the orgasm phase of the sexual response cycle with partners is indicated for both gay males and women who present as anorgasmic through coitus.

CONCLUSIONS

The importance of the inclusion of cognitive, educational, and behavioral techniques remains a crucial element in the complete treatment of individuals suffering from any type of sexual difficulty, and should not be forgotten or underestimated. In addition to the need for more social work and behavioral science research in the area of sexual dysfunctions, there is the need for more replication of research. There are many different cognitive and behavioral treatments being conducted on either an individual or a group basis; however, the question of whether the results from these studies will remain consistent across individuals over time needs further exploration.

It is recommended that social workers doing empirical practice in this area, whether as part of an interdisciplinary team or independently, clearly denote that they are social work professionals. In this managed care environment, proving what works is no longer just expected—it is required (Dziegielewski, 1996). Social workers have long been involved in the diagnosis, assessment, and treatment of sexual dysfunctions, and it remains essential to emphasize this continuance.

REFERENCES

Alexander, B. (1993). Disorders of sexual desire: Diagnosis and treatment of decreased libido. *American Family Physician, 47,* 832–838; discussion *49, 758.*

American Psychiatric Association. (1994). *Diagnostic and Statistical Manual of Mental Disorders* (4th ed.). Washington, DC: Author.

Anderson, B. L. (1983). Primary orgasmic dysfunction: Diagnostic considerations and review of treatment. *Psychological Bulletin, 93,* 105–136.

Bakich, I. (1995). Hypnosis in the treatment of the sexual desire disorders. *Australian Journal of Clinical and Experimental Hypnosis, 23*(1), 70–77.

Barlow, D. H. (1986). Causes of sexual dysfunction: The role of anxiety and cognitive interference. *Journal of Consulting and Clinical Psychology. 54,* 140–148.

Burte, J. M. & Araoz, D. L. (1994). Cognitive hypnotherapy with sexual disorders. *Journal of Cognitive Psychotherapy, 8,* 299–311.

Conte, H. R. (1986). Multivariate assessment of sexual dysfunction. *Journal of Consulting and Clinical Psychology, 54,* 149–157.

Dziegielewski, S. F. (1996). Managed care principles: The need for social work in the health care environment. *Crisis Intervention and Time Limited Treatment, 3,* 97–111.

Eastman, P. (1993, May/June). Washington report: Treating erectile dysfunction. *Geriatric Consultant,* 10–13.

Fedoroff, J. P. (1991). Interview techniques to assess sexual disorders. *Families in Society, 72,* 140–145.

Fish, L. S., Busby, D., & Killian, K. (1994). Structural couple therapy in the treatment of inhibited sexual drive. *American Journal of Family Therapy, 22,* 113–125.

Friedman, J. M., & Hogan, D. R. (1985). Sexual dysfunction and low sexual desire. In D. H. Barlow (Ed.), *Clinical handbook of psychiatric disorders* (pp. 417–461). New York: Guilford Press.

Goldman, A., & Carroll, J. (1990). Educational intervention as an adjunct to treatment of erectile dysfunction in older couples. *Journal of Sex & Marital Therapy, 16,* 127–141.

Harrison, D. F. (1987). Clinical research in sexual dysfunctions: Social work contributions. *Journal of Social Service Research, 10* (2/3/4), 105–119.

Hawton, K., Catalan, J., & Fagg, J. (1991). Low sexual desire: Sex therapy results and prognostic factors. *Behaviour Research and Therapy 29,* 217–224.

Kaplan, H. S. (1979). *Disorders of sexual desire.* New York: Simon & Schuster.

Kaplan, H. S. (1990). The combined use of sex therapy and intra-penile injections in the treatment of impotence. *Journal of Sex & Marital Therapy, 16,* 195–207.

Kaplan, L., & Harder, D. W. (1991). The sexual desire conflict scale for women: Construction, internal consistency, and two initial validity tests. *Psychological Reports, 68,* 1275–1282.

Kilmann, P. R., Milan, R. J., Boland, J. P., Nankin, H. R., Davidson, E., West, M. O., Sabalis, R. F., Caid, C., & Devine, J. M. (1987). Group treatment for secondary erectile dysfunction. *Journal of Sex and Marital Therapy, 13,* 168–180.

Kinzl, J. F., Traweger, C., & Biebl, W. (1995). Sexual dysfunctions: Relationship to childhood sexual abuse and early family experiences in a nonclinical sample. *Child Abuse and Neglect, 19,* 785–792.

Knopf, J., & Seiler, M. (1990). *ISD: Inhibited sexual desire.* New York: William Morrow.

Leif, H. (1977). What's new in sex research. *Medical Aspects of Human Sexuality, 7,* 94–95.

LoPiccolo, J., Heiman, J. R., & Hogan, D. R. (1985). Effectiveness of single therapists versus cotherapy teams in sex therapy. *Journal of Consulting and Clinical Psychology, 53,* 287–294.

Macaluso, E., & Berkman, A. H. (1984). Sex counseling with groups in a general hospital. *Social Casework, 65,* 19–26.

O'Carroll, R. (1991). Sexual desire disorders: A review of controlled treatment studies. *Journal of Sex Research, 28,* 607–624.

Palace, E. M. (1995). Modification of dysfunctional patterns of sexual response through autonomic arousal and false physiological feedback. *Journal of Consulting and Clinical Psychology, 63,* 604–615.

Palace, E., & Gorzalka, B. B. (1992). Differential patterns of arousal in sexually functional and dysfunctional women: Physiological and subjective components of sexual response. *Archives of Sexual Behavior, 21,* 135–159.

Read, J. (1995). Female sexual dysfunction. *International Review of Psychiatry, 7,* 175–182.

Reece, R. (1987). Causes and treatment of sexual desire discrepancies in male couples. *Journal of Homosexuality, 14,* 157–172.

Reece, R. (1988). Special issues in the etiologies and treatments of sexual problems among gay men. *Journal of Homosexuality, 15,* 43–57.

Rosen, R. C., & Leiblum, S. R. (1987). Current approaches to the evaluation of sexual desire disorders. *Journal of Sex Research, 23,* 141–162.

Russell, L. (Summer, 1990). Sex and couple therapy: A method of treatment to enhance physical and emotional intimacy. *Journal of Sex and Marital Therapy, 16,* 111–120.

Segraves, R. T., & Segraves, K. B. (1991). Hypoactive sexual desire disorder: Prevalence and comorbidity in 906 subjects. *Journal of Sex and Marital Therapy, 17,* 55–58.

Shaw, J. (1990). Play therapy with the sexual workhorse: Successful treatment with 12 cases of inhibited ejaculation. *Journal of Sex & Marital Therapy, 16,* 159–164.

Spector, I. P., & Carey, M. P. (1990). Incidence and prevalence of sexual dysfunctions: A critical review of the literature. *Archives of Sexual Behavior, 19,* 389–408.

Stuart, F. M., Hammond, D. C., & Pett, M. A. (1987). Inhibited sexual desire in women. *Archives of Sexual Behavior, 16,* 91–106.

Stuntz, S. S., Falk, A., Hiken, M., & Carson, V. B. (1996). The journey undermined by psychosexual disorders. In V. B. Carson & E. N. Arnold (Eds.), *Mental health nursing: The nurse patient journey* (pp. 879–895). Philadelphia: W. B. Saunders.

Thyer, B. A., & Papsdorf, J. D. (1981). Relationship between irrationality and sexual arousability. *Psychological Reports, 48,* 834.

Trudel, G. (1991). Review of psychological factors in low sexual desire. *Sexual and Marital Therapy, 6,* 261–272.

Wincze, J. P., & Carey, M. P. (1991). *Sexual dysfunction: A guide for assessment and treatment.* New York: Guilford Press.

Woody, J. D., D'Souza, H. J., and Crain, D. D. (1994). Sexual functioning in clinical couples: Discriminant validity of the Sexual Interaction System Scale. *American Journal of Family Therapy, 22,* 291–303.

Chapter 21

ORGASMIC DISORDERS

Sophia F. Dziegielewski
Cheryl Resnick

OVERVIEW

Sexuality is a part of normal human growth and development. Yet sexual development and its expression is generally considered a unique and private affair. As individuals progress through the life cycle and seek to join sexually with a mate, problems can occur. Studies have illustrated that previous sexual knowledge, such as sexual abuse, parental attitudes, and sexual behaviors, as well as other environmental factors, greatly impacts the likelihood of the development of sexual disorders (Kaplan, 1995; Kaplan & Harder, 1991; Kinzl, Traweger, & Biebl, 1995; Stuart, Hammond, & Pett, 1987). Since this important aspect of development is often misunderstood, neglected, or abused within the society, individuals who suffer from sexual problems may feel at a loss as to how to address them.

According to social learning theory, individuals acquire much of their sexual behavior in large part according to socially acceptable (that is, reinforced) or unacceptable (that is, punished) codes of expression (that is, contingencies). For example, intimate sexual expression is rarely modeled. As a result, the traditional modes of education, such as parental modeling or social influence, go unlearned in this area. As a result of this privatization of sexuality, children can receive inaccurate, inappropriate, or exploitive information, on which future expectations will be modeled. Also, due to a general attempt to avoid or neglect this phase of human development, gaps in learning how to obtain this information can be created. This can lead to a lack of appropriate channels for obtaining information that is considered to be unknown, embarrassing, or forbidden. This lack of attention to the development of human sexuality can have serious long-term effects that cause adults to struggle with unrealistic expectations or to lack the proper coping skills to deal with sexual behaviors throughout their lives (Horton, 1995).

In our society, it is clear when looking at both males and females that the beliefs and cognitions that an individual holds can and do impact sexual performance and ability. Conte (1986) asserts that as many as 50% to 60% of married couples experience sexual difficulties. Thyer and Papsdorf (1981) find no evidence to support the premise that irrational beliefs inhibit one's capacity for sexual enjoyment; however, many professionals continue to argue the opposite (Eastman, 1993).

When an individual believes that he or she has encountered difficulties that cause significant disturbance in the sexual relationship, these problems are often termed *sexual dysfunctions*. In an attempt to understand problems that can develop within the human sexual response cycle, the fourth edition of the *Diagnostic and Statistical Manual of Mental Disorders* (*DSM-IV*) lists the essential feature of sexual dysfunction as having a "disturbance in the processes that characterize the sexual response cycle or by pain associated with sexual intercourse" (American Psychiatric Association [APA], 1994, p. 493).

Further, *DSM-IV* divides the sexual response cycle into the following phases: *desire phase* (desires and fantasies about sex), *excitement phase* (subjective interpretations and actual physiologic changes take place), *orgasm phase* (generalized muscular tension and contractions in the sex organs), and *resolution phase* (general sense of relaxation and release of the previously created muscular tension). The female and male orgasmic disorders are sexual difficulty disorders in which orgasm is delayed or absent following a normal excitement phase—or the opposite reaction, which results in premature ejaculation in men (Maxmen & Ward, 1995). It is important to note, however, that for a person to be diagnosed with an orgasmic disorder the following symptoms must be present: (a) the problem must be persistent and recurrent; (b) it must not occur exclusively in relation to another major clinical diagnosis (such as major depression or an adjustment disorder), and it must not be caused by substance abuse or be related to a general medical condition; and (c) it must cause marked distress or interpersonal difficulty (APA, 1994).

In assessing the orgasmic disorders, as with the other sexual disorders, it is important to note: (a) whether the condition is lifelong or acquired (with or without previously normal functioning); (b) whether it is generalized or situational (with a particular partner); (c) if it is conjunct (with or without a partner) or solitary (as in masturbation); and (d) if it is due to psychological, medical, substance, or combined factors. In clinical assessment, it is suggested that social workers obtain information on such qualities as the frequency, intensity, duration, setting, and degree of sexual impairment; the level of subjective distress; and the effects on other areas of functioning (for example, social or occupational) for each client treated in practice (Maxmen & Ward, 1995).

Orgasmic Disorders

In order to comprehend the absence of an orgasmic response, it is imperative that the existence and definition of orgasmic response be recognized. Stated simply, *orgasm* is the peak of climax or sexual excitement in sexual activity (McCary,

1973). Physiologically normal men and women are capable of achieving an orgasm. The orgasmic response generally consists of facial grimacing, generalized myotonia, carpopedal spasm, gluteal and abdominal muscle contraction, and rhythmic contractions of the orgasmic platform, which results in vaginal contractions in females and penile swelling and ejaculation in males (Anderson, 1983). Both men and women who experience orgasmic disorders often have a strong sexual drive. For example, in women the capacity to appreciate sexual foreplay, lubricate, and enjoy phallic penetration often shows no impairment (Kaplan, 1974). One of the primary problems for researchers in understanding the orgasmic response is that it can differ among individuals with regard to intensity, length, duration, and overall pleasure. Further, the response can differ in the same individual from one act of coition to another (McCary, 1973).

According to *DSM-IV,* this type of sexual dysfunction refers to "the persistent or recurrent delay in, or absence of, orgasm following a normal sexual excitement phase" (APA, 1994, p. 505). This problem may be generalized, occurring throughout all of an individual's sexual experiences, or situational, occurring with a specific partner or circumstance. The disorder is also distinguished by whether it is a lifelong or acquired condition, and by whether it is primary or secondary. Generally, Primary Orgasmic Disorder applies to individuals who have never been able to achieve orgasm through any means. Secondary Orgasmic Disorder applies to individuals who have been orgasmic in the past, but for whatever reason are currently anorgasmic.

Secondary orgasmic dysfunction may vary in degree (Milan, Kilman, & Boland, 1988). It can consist of anorgasmia with a specific partner; a prior history of orgasm with current decreased frequency; the experience of anorgasmia only in particular contexts; or recent orgasmic dysfunction with previous orgasmic capability, on all occasions of sexual activity, including masturbation (McCabe & Delaney, 1992).

Anorgasmia, which involves difficulty achieving orgasm, is generally considered to be psychogenic in nature; however, Stuntz, Falk, Hiken, and Carson (1996) warn that the consideration of a physiological factor should not be underestimated. Medical and life circumstances, such as fatigue, acute illness, medication, decreased perineal musculature, or neurological and vascular conditions, can complicate or enhance the occurrence of this difficulty. Psychological factors should also be considered essential in understanding the disorder (Fish, Busby, & Killian, 1994). Situational and environmental factors, such as societal mores as they relate to sexual roles and expectations, family attitudes, sex education or lack of it, and religious beliefs, can all affect the ability to achieve orgasm.

Among all the sexual difficulties described by women, Orgasmic Disorder is reported to be the most common (Kaplan, 1974; Wincze & Carey, 1991). Although it is difficult to calculate the exact prevalence rates of Female Orgasmic Disorder, it is estimated that approximately 30% of all women display orgasmic disturbances

(Kaplan, 1974; Kinzl et al., 1995). Morokoff and LoPiccolo (1986) suggest that 5% to 10% of American women have dealt with a lifelong inability to achieve orgasm. Palace (1995) estimates that 30% of women meet the *DSM-IV* criteria for orgasmic disorder and 20% of women meet the criteria for sexual desire disorders (about 23.5 and 15 million women, respectively).

Male Orgasmic Disorder is considered more rare when compared to the occurrence of Female Orgasmic Disorder. However, in a review of numerous studies in this area by Spector and Carey (1990), the reported occurrence rates among those who present for treatment were similar to those for females, involving approximately 4% to 10% of males. Male prevalence rates in the general population, however, remain much lower. Prevalence rates for males who suffer from inhibited orgasm are estimated to be 1% to 10% of the population (Spector & Carey, 1990). This condition remains the least common of the orgasmic disorders in males.

Premature Ejaculation

In this society, males are generally praised for their ability to perform and are chastised when they experience difficulty. Hawton, Catalan, and Fagg (1992) found various forms of "erectile dysfunction as the most frequent problem in men presenting to sexual dysfunction clinics" (p. 161). In a study conducted by Masters and Johnson (1970), 46% of the males who presented to the sexual dysfunction clinic for treatment had the presenting complaint of premature ejaculation.

The basic criteria for diagnosing premature ejaculation include: (a) persistent or recurrent ejaculation with minimal sexual stimulation before, during, or shortly after penetration (this ejaculation must also occur before the male desires it); (b) the disturbance must cause marked distress or interpersonal difficulty; and (c) the episodes of premature ejaculation must not be related to the direct effects of any substance (APA, 1994, p. 509).

A problem noted by Spector and Carey (1990) in examining previous studies in this area is that many times researchers did not clearly define the time period surrounding premature orgasm. Therefore, time periods could vary from seconds after penetration up to 10 minutes. This further complicates the definition by making the range of what could be considered normal unproblematic latency quite broad (O'Donohue, Letourneau, & Geer, 1993). Therefore, in assessing the client, it is important for the social worker to address factors that can affect the duration of the excitement phase—particularly, factors that can lead to the occurrence of too quick or unplanned orgasms. Factors that need to be considered include the age of the male, the novelty of the sexual partner or the situation surrounding the encounter, and the frequency of sexual behavior. It is important to note, however, that focusing on just one of the three criteria, such as the time from entry to orgasm, can result in an inaccurate diagnosis.

ASSESSMENT METHODS

Proper assessment requires the careful accumulation of data that are likely to affect sexual response. Age; marital status; religious beliefs; whether the couple reside together; socioeconomic status; level of education of both partners; motivation for treatment of both partners; nature of the marital relationship; functional ability of the male partner; levels of anxiety; type of anorgasmia (primary versus secondary); gynecological, physiological, and medical condition; the presence of psychosis or depression; and drug and alcohol use may all impact an individual's ability to reach orgasm.

Many medical problems can inhibit orgasmic responses, and Maxmen and Ward (1995) consider failure to address them to be one of the most common reasons for failure of sexual therapy. Medical conditions that can impede assessment and treatment include neurological disorders, such as multiple sclerosis; spinal cord and peripheral nerve damage; endocrine and metabolic disorders; diabetes; and thyroid deficiency.

Drugs (for example, sedatives and narcotics) and alcohol are also likely to inhibit an orgasmic response. Antidepressant medications and hypertensive medications can potentially suppress the orgasmic response (Knopf & Seiler, 1990). With the problem of premature ejaculation, a link to withdrawal from opioids should also be ruled out (Stuntz et al., 1996). Alcohol may retard orgasmic response in low doses, and can inhibit response entirely in higher doses (McCabe & Delaney, 1992). When alcohol abuse is linked to anorgasmia, it is important to assess which came first—the alcohol abuse or the anorgasmia (McCabe & Delaney, 1992). There is a high incidence of alcohol abuse among women who have been sexually abused as children, and these women are also more likely to display sexual disorders (Golden, 1988; Kinzl et al., 1995; Saunders, Villeponteaux, Lipovsky, & Kilpatrick, 1992).

In the assessment process, it is important to establish whether orgasmic dysfunction is primary (individual never has been able to experience orgasm) or secondary (individual formerly was able to reach orgasm). If an individual displays primary orgasmic dysfunction, the therapist must assess whether the individual in fact suffers from orgasmic inhibition, or has simply never received sufficient stimulation due to poor sexual technique or poor education or self or partner (Kaplan, 1979). The importance of a first orgasm cannot be overstated, since it marks the initial step in deconditioning inhibition. For individuals who are unable to achieve orgasm under situational circumstances, a complete evaluation of anxiety-producing factors during the situations in question may be indicated.

The level of knowledge and education regarding sexuality and sexual behavior should be assessed prior to the implementation of a treatment program. This may include the couple's comprehension regarding male and female anatomy, male and female sexual response, the possible causes of male and female dysfunction, sexual myths and misconceptions, and discussion of masturbation, oral and anal sex, and the variety of intercourse positions (McCabe & Delaney, 1992). Although research results are conflicting, it is assumed that communication skills, marital harmony, sexual anxiety, and performance anxiety may all be important factors in sexual response (McCabe & Delaney, 1992).

Therapeutic consideration of the emotional and cognitive contributing factors to the disruption of the physiological stages of sexual arousal should be made during the assessment phase. In addition, the therapist must differentiate between sexual anxiety, low sexual desire, and the ability of the individual to achieve satisfactory arousal; the functional ability and flexibility of the partner must also be taken into consideration when evaluating an individual's ability to respond sexually (Friedman & Hogan, 1985; Hawton, Catalan, & Fagg, 1991; Trudel, 1991).

In addition to self-report measures and partner evaluation measures, several authors have employed assessment scales when studying sexual response and orgasmic response. The Locke-Wallace Marital Adjustment Scale, Sexual Interaction Inventory, Sexual Interaction System Scale, Sexual History Form, Women's Sexuality Questionnaire, Sexual Arousability Inventory, Derogatis Sexual Functioning Inventory, Global Sexual Satisfaction Index, Sexual Behavior and Attitudes Questionnaire, Sex Anxiety Inventory, and a variety of other scales have been developed to assess sexual functioning (Chambless, Sultan, & Stern, 1985; Janda & O'Grady, 1980; Locke & Wallace, 1959; LoPiccolo & Steger, 1974; Morokoff & LoPiccolo, 1986; Palace, 1995; Palace & Gorzalka, 1990; Sotile & Kilmann, 1978; Woody, D'Souza & Crain, 1994). The assessment tools strive to obtain a profile of the sexual functioning of the individuals and the couple, the nature of the marital relationship (levels of marital satisfaction and happiness), levels of sexual anxiety and performance anxieties, and ratings of sexual responsiveness (orgasmic response in relation to masturbation and coitus). Generally, several assessment measures have been used in conjunction with one another.

The Sexual Interaction Inventory encompasses scales relating to frequency dissatisfaction, pleasure mean, perceptual accuracy, self acceptance, and mate acceptance (Morokoff & LoPiccolo, 1986). The Sexual History Form rates frequency of sexual intercourse, duration of foreplay, duration of intercourse, frequency of orgasm in masturbation, partner stimulation, intercourse, and stimulation during intercourse, as well as sexual relationship satisfaction and the perceived sexual relationship satisfaction of the partner (Morokoff & LoPiccolo, 1986). The Sexual Interaction System Scale (SISS) provides a viable measure designed to explore sexual interaction, sexual satisfaction, and overall marital adjustment (Woody, D'Souza & Crain, 1994).

Social work professionals recognize that the experiences, beliefs and cognitions an individual holds can and do impact sexual performance and ability. Within the treatment context, the concepts of desire and arousal are clearly different. *Desire* refers to a mental and emotional state, whereas *arousal* represents a physiological state, manifest in behavior. Distinguishing between the concepts of desire and arousal, much as making the differentiation between the treatments of the sexual arousal and desire disorders, is crucial in the provision of treatment for anorgasmic individuals or for males with premature ejaculation.

In summary, the assessment of orgasmic dysfunction requires that the social worker consider the primary versus secondary nature of the problem and take into account psychosocial factors including prior history of sexual abuse as a child; the nature of the relationship with the partner; the partner's ability to adequately perform sexually; any physiological or medical factors; and the documentation of use of substances or medications. Although not detailed in the scope of this chapter, the authors recommend Fedoroff's (1991) article as an excellent resource for conducting interviews designed to assess sexual disorders.

Special Considerations in Assessment

Female sexual dysfunction, including Orgasmic Disorder, may be particularly prevalent in women who have experienced sexual abuse or molestation in childhood (Kinzl et al., 1995; Saunders et al., 1992; Stuntz et al., 1996). In one report, women who recounted inadequate sex education reported orgasm disorders significantly more often than did either victims of a single incident of sexual abuse or nonvictims. The researchers concluded that "female orgasm requires the ability to be intimate, to confide in a partner, and to become dependent on another person without being afraid of the consequences" (Kinzl et al., 1995, pp. 790–791). Kinzl's work supports the recognition that healthy early family relationships are critical to adult sexual well-being.

EFFECTIVE INTERVENTIONS

Anorgasmic Disorders

Anderson (1983) and McCary (1973) outlined the major treatments for primary orgasmic dysfunction as a combination of: (a) sexual education and skills training, (b) Kegel exercises for women, (c) sensate focus and directed masturbation, (d) systematic desensitization, and (e) general behavioral or cognitive-behavioral approaches. In the current literature, most treatments involve a combination approach.

First, addressing sex education and skills training, individuals must have a general knowledge of human sexuality. A basic knowledge of the anatomy and physiology of self and partner is essential. Most times what knowledge the client does have was received sporadically and was not learned in a nonthreatening environment. A good basis of sex education knowledge is needed to assist in further developing skills in the ability to express individual needs and desires, intimacy, affectional touching, reciprocity of sexual needs, and general sexual functioning (O'Donohue, Letourneau, & Geer, 1993).

When dealing with sex education, more has to be provided than simply teaching body awareness. Issues regarding treatment of sexual dysfunction must take into account physiological problems that impact sexual arousal and obstacles to desire that may have emotional causes, such as stress, hidden anger, resentment, intimacy issues, and family of origin issues. Most of the treatment modalities address a multiplicity of issues pertaining to anorgasmia; however, their respective ways of addressing the problem of sexual dysfunction can vary. Some treatments concentrate on recognizing and understanding the physiological influences alone (Chambless et al., 1984); others view sexual dysfunction as a problem of faulty early sexual development that must be identified and modified (Ravart & Cote, 1992); still other treatments emphasize addressing cognitive-behavioral influences (Palace, 1995); and many treatments use a combination approach that applies physiological, developmental, and emotional components together as they relate to sexual arousal.

Second, one such treatment often utilized with women is the use of Kegel exercises. Arnold Kegel believed that orgasmic difficulty in women is related to poor tone or damage of the vaginal musculature. A treatment he originally designed to address urinary stress incontinence was adapted to increasing female orgasmic response. The type and emphasis of these exercises can vary; however, women are generally taught to control and squeeze the pubococcygeal muscle (Caird, 1988) that surrounds the vagina, urethra and anus. A simple way to start this exercise process is to instruct the woman to begin to urinate and to stop the urine several times while in midstream. To further measure this phenomena and its relation to muscle tone, Chambless et al. (1982) and other researchers utilized a perineometer. This instrument was used to measure the response while either fantasizing or imagining sexual fantasies.

Kegel exercises have been used by numerous clinicians and researchers to treat anorgasmic women, with mixed results in regard to their effectiveness. One such study that examined the physiological correlates of pubococcygeal exercise and coital orgasm was conducted by Chambless et al. (1984). No effect related to the completion of Kegel exercises upon the rate of orgasm was found. The research in regard to this issue is conflicting, however; others demonstrate a successful link between strengthening the pubococcygeal muscle and effectiveness in the treatment of anorgasmia (Graber & Kline-Graber, 1979).

Third, McCabe and Delaney (1992) describe a number of therapeutic interventions that combine physiological principles with psychoeducational ones, with the success rates of these combined treatment strategies. They found that sex education as a component of sensate focus and directed masturbation, implemented in the pioneering work of Masters and Johnson (1970), continues to be used in conjunction with other modalities. According to Kaplan (1974), the treatment of

Orgasmic Disorder involves diminishing or extinguishing the involuntary overcontrol of the orgastic response. This can occur through sensitivity teaching, where the individual learns to recognize erotic sensations associated with orgasm. This can help to inhibit the tendency to feel the need to hold back, in order to allow the orgasmic response to occur. The individual is then taught how to stimulate him- or herself intensely. If this stimulation brings a concurrent shutting off of response, the individual must simultaneously learn self-distraction.

Sensate focus and directed masturbation techniques can help individuals to become better aware of their own bodily sensations. This chapter focuses on the empirical practice of directed masturbation techniques in treating anorgasmia; for the empirical application of sensate focus exercises, see Chapter 20. Directed masturbation teaches males and females to recognize their own erotic sensations through the use of graduated masturbation exercises. Masturbation is used because: (a) it is the sexual practice most likely to result in orgasm, (b) individuals can learn to attend to their own physical sensations and sexual feelings most readily through this means, and (c) it is less anxiety-producing, in that partner evaluation is removed (Anderson, 1983).

Generally, the first step in guided masturbation involves learning to accept and identify various parts of one's own sexual anatomy. Visual exploration is highlighted. Fantasy or sexual thinking that stimulates sexual arousal is encouraged. For women, the the obvious erogenous zones, such as the clitoris, are identified (LoPiccolo & Stock, 1986). For men, direct massaging of the penis seems most beneficial. The next step generally involves direct instruction in the techniques of masturbation. Since this needs to be a very individualized process, men and women are encouraged to go slowly and to focus on the techniques that bring them the most pleasure.

Sexual fantasy and sexual imagery are highly encouraged. Clients may choose to create their own fantasies or to read sexually oriented magazines or books that can stimulate erotic thought. For some men and women who are still unable to achieve orgasm and need further assistance, electrical and vibratory stimulation can be introduced. LoPiccolo and Stock (1986) believe that, for women, it is important to begin the use of vibrators and electrical devices only at this late stage in treatment. If introduced earlier, it is believed that orgasm may become more vibrator-dependent.

In both males and females, reaching orgasm alone at first, without the partner, is encouraged. Once this has been accomplished, sensate focus exercises that involve the other partner are added. These exercises focus on the development of mutual caressing, touching, and communication. Once this is accomplished, the convergence of a reciprocal learning process is encouraged. Males are encouraged to follow the instruction of the anorgasmic female partner, helping her to achieve orgasm through direct manipulation of the genital area (LoPiccolo & Stock, 1986). Females are instructed to do the same for anorgasmic males, helping the male to reach orgasm during masturbation while pulling him closer to the vaginal area. It is recommended that combined coital and manual stimulation later be used to achieve orgasm in males (Dekker, 1993). In anorgasmic females, penile-vaginal intercourse should also include direct stimulation of the clitoris. Positions that facilitate this direct stimulation of the clitoris include those with the woman kneeling above her male partner and rear-entry intercourse, where the male can reach around her body and access the clitoris for manual stimulation.

In the treatment of orgasmic dysfunction, a combination approach of sexual education, directed masturbation, and sensate focus exercises is common. Whitehead, Mathews, and Ramage (1987) compared the effectiveness of conjoint therapy based on the work of Masters and Johnson with female-focused intervention designed by Heiman and LoPiccolo. In this work, Whitehead et al. differentiated between the two treatment models. The Heiman and LoPiccolo model (as cited in Whitehead et al., 1987) was primarily a female-focused program that allowed women to learn more about their own needs through a type of directed masturbation that encouraged self-exploration and self-stimulation. This learning was shared with the partner. In this form of treatment, the problem was identified as existing within the woman, and she was taught how to overcome deficits in sexual response. In this female-focused approach, the achievement of orgasm was a major goal.

In a second treatment group, based on the Masters and Johnson (1970) method, a couples approach was introduced and problems were assumed to reside in the relationship. The couples worked conjointly to improve sexual functioning and address sexual and marital issues, while the overall attainment of orgasm was discouraged. Whitehead et al. (1987) indicate that both forms of treatment showed evidence of being effective in increasing sexual response. However, couples therapy is referred to as the probable model of choice when addressing women who express increased anxiety, poor attitudes regarding masturbation, and problems with primary arousal and orgasm (Whitehead et al., 1987).

To further highlight this type of practice strategy, Morokoff and LoPiccolo (1986) compared minimal therapist contact sessions with a 15-session treatment program. Fourteen couples participated in minimal therapist contact (4 sessions) where as 29 couples underwent full therapist contact (15 sessions). In the minimal therapist contact group, a movie titled *Becoming Orgasmic Together* was used. This movie was shown with supportive interaction and planning on the part of the therapist. In the therapist contact group, specific techniques were also highlighted, including a guided intervention focus on education, information and systematic progression. A program originally developed by LoPiccolo and Lobitz (as cited in Morokoff & LoPiccolo, 1986) was used, and techniques similar to those described earlier in regard to direct masturbation were introduced.

Overall, both treatment programs were found to be effective in producing orgasm. Unexpectedly, the minimal treatment program produced superior results regarding the attainment of orgasm through masturbation and during coitus (with additional genital stimulation) than the full therapist contact group. The authors hypothesize that women in the minimal treatment group may have taken more responsibility for success, a factor that may have increased their motivation. The findings indicate that reduced therapist contact did not decrease effectiveness in the treatment of orgasmic dysfunction. Also, this article supports the use of education, information, feedback, and systematic progress through a program of directed masturbation in treating individuals who experience anorgasmia.

Sensate focus exercises (Masters & Johnson, 1970) and directed masturbation combine a sexual skills learning approach designed to alter behavior with educational strategies that modify communications patterns. In this form of directed masturbation, partners engage in nondemand pleasure through a series of graduated tasks ranging from sensual body massage to coitus (McCabe & Delaney, 1992). Couples are treated together, generally by a male-female cotherapy team. The couple is guided through touching techniques and focuses on open sharing and communication of feelings and sensations. There is movement from sensual touching to increased genital contact and eventual coitus (Anderson, 1983; Masters & Johnson, 1970). Although sensate focus and directed masturbation are used frequently in treatment, empirical testing of the techniques is still lacking (Anderson, 1983; McCabe & Delaney, 1992).

A fourth technique that has been used repeatedly throughout the years to treat orgasmic dysfunction is a variation of Wolpe's systematic desensitization (Anderson, 1983). Anderson cites Lazarus, Brady, Madsen, and Ullmann; Kraft and Alissa; Sotile and Kilmann; O'Gorman; and Wincze and Caird, all of whom find a correlation between positive changes in sexual functioning and the use of systematic desensitization. The underlying premise in systematic desensitization is that sexual anxiety plays a central role in the dysfunction.

It is assumed that the creation of sexual arousal, instead of the usual muscle relaxation, can prevent and help avoid the development of sexual anxiety (Dekker, 1993). In this type of in vivo desensitization, the client is trained to relax the muscles through a sequence of exercises. Anxiety-provoking stimuli are listed in hierarchical order, and the deeply relaxed client slowly confronts each of the anxiety-arousing stimuli until the stimuli fail to generate anxiety (Anderson, 1983). Empirical data relating to systematic desensitization has been mixed, with some studies showing increased orgasmic response and others demonstrating decreased sexual anxiety with increased sexual satisfaction but limited changes in orgasmic response (Anderson, 1983).

In assuming that there is a causal relationship between sexual anxiety and sexual dysfunction, systematic desensitization attempts to decrease levels of anxiety so that increased sexual responsiveness will result. Nevertheless, current research has been contradictory; Husted found an increase in orgasmic frequency with reduction in sexual anxiety, while both Dekker and Norton and Jehu found that systematic desensitization did decrease sexual anxiety yet did not effect orgasmic response (cited in McCabe & Delaney, 1992).

Last, to further address the treatment of anxiety in anorgasmic individuals, cognitive and cognitive-behavioral techniques have been employed. Palace and Gorzalka (1990) found that preexposure to anxiety-provoking stimuli enhanced both the rate and magnitude of genital arousal in both functional and dysfunctional women. However, both groups reported less subjective arousal after preexposure to anxiety-provoking stimuli. This study lends evidence to the observation that anxiety may enhance sexual physiological arousal without the concomitant cognitive recognition of arousal.

In research, several studies have been initiated that highlight the treatment of anorgasmic females from a behavioral or a cognitive-behavioral perspective. One of the most popular approaches is Barbach's (1980), which uses behavioral strategies in a group format. This approach has been tested by several researchers and has been found to be a useful technique for treating inorgasmic females (Bogat, Hamernik, & Brooks, 1987). It employs a supportive and educational group format in which individualized homework sessions are completed. Standardized measures are used and individuals are pretested and posttested throughout the studies. Results support that most of the women tested using this approach not only experience orgasm but seem to accept their own body parts and their own personal health.

Another study is that of Wilson and Wilson (1991), who selected 80 female subjects to evaluate two cognitive-behavioral sex therapy formats that were designed to alleviate inhibited female orgasm. Both group and individual sections were employed. Standardized measures were used to gather initial baseline data, and the resulting data were statistically analyzed. In general, the subjects chose individual therapy over group therapy. Women stated that they did not feel comfortable discussing such an intimate problem with a group of strangers.

Premature Ejaculation

Generally, the most common method used to treat premature ejaculation is sensate focus exercises incorporating the use of the squeeze technique discussed by Masters and Johnson (1970). This treatment starts with sensate focus exercises, where the couple are expected to touch each other with no expectation of reaching orgasm. This nondemanding touching should last for several days, and no direct genital penetration is encouraged. Once the female partner has assisted the male in reaching an erection and he reports feeling as though he will ejaculate, the squeeze technique is introduced.

At this stage in the ejaculatory response, the male feels that he cannot control the orgasmic experience, and he can feel the seminal fluid begin to flow. At that moment, the female partner is instructed to stop massaging the penis and to squeeze the glans, below the head of the penis. This means taking her thumb and placing it on the rear side of the shaft (toward the partner's body), opposite the frenulum (directly below the head of the penis); two fingers should be used to apply pressure on the top of the glans. This pressure should be applied for 3 or 4 seconds, or until the male reports that he feels uncomfortable enough to lose the urge to ejaculate. These training sessions should continue for 15 to 20 minutes, alternating between sexual stimulation and squeezing, without ejaculation.

Once control over manually stimulated erections has been achieved (approximately 2 or 3 days later), vaginal penetration is attempted. Generally, the woman assumes the top position so she can control the withdrawal of the penis from the vagina. The female is instructed to insert the penis into her vagina and to show as little movement as possible. This is to give the male time to think about other things and help distract him from the urge to ejaculate. If the male feels the urge to ejaculate, the female is instructed to withdraw the penis and implement the squeeze technique as described earlier. Eventually, thrusting and movement is added to stimulate or maintain the erection. A time span of 15 to 20 minutes is considered desirable for ejaculatory control. Masters and Johnson (1970) caution, however, that in using this technique several considerations should be weighed. First, the female partner, not the male, should be the one to add the pressure to the penis; and second, this technique should not be used as a sexual game. If it is overused, the male may become so skilled and insensitive during this process that he becomes able to avoid stimulation even when there is no desire to do so.

LoPiccolo and Stock (1986) believe there is little evidence for the efficacy of the squeeze technique when used as a solitary method. Further, Kinder and Curtiss (1988) question the use of this isolated technique and urge that before the efficacy of this treatment modality can be measured, more research is needed to compare individuals receiving this technique with a similar control group.

In general, three behavioral treatments are associated with erectile dysfunction: (a) communication technique training (to deal with social and relationship issues), (b) sexual technique training (teaching education and the practice of sexual techniques), and (c) a combination treatment that utilizes both.

Kilman et al. (1987) studied 20 couples who were tested to determine the effectiveness of current treatments on secondary erectile dysfunction. Three treatment groups (consisting of eight 2-hour sessions) were all designed to enhance the male's sexual functioning and included a *communication education group* that stressed positive communication techniques; a *sexual training group* that was designed to enhance positive sexual techniques; and a *combination treatment group* that stressed both communication and sexual training. The fourth group, referred to as the *attention-placebo control group,* implemented controls to limit the degree of treatment received, thus constituting a less powerful treatment procedure than that given the other groups. In this group, highly structured lectures were provided without any planned applicability or practice time being allotted for individual problem solving. The couples in the *no treatment control group* were pretested and waited 5 weeks for treatment to begin. After the posttest, they were provided with the combination treatment.

Several pretest measurement inventories and questionnaires were used, including the Sexual Interaction Inventory (SII), designed by LoPiccolo and Steger (1974); the Marital Adjustment Test (MAT), developed by Locke and Wallace (1959); The Sex Anxiety Inventory (SAI), developed by Janda and O'Grady (1980); and the Sexual Behavior and Attitudes Questionnaire, developed by Sotile and Kilmann (1978). The results were statistically analyzed; in summary, the study supported the view that each of the treatments for secondary erectile dysfunction has statistically significant effectiveness when compared to no treatment at all. This study served to further support the recommendation by Eastman (1993) that the importance of education, communication, and support should not be underestimated, even when a condition is organically generated.

Goldman and Carroll (1990) also highlight the importance of including education when treating secondary erectile dysfunction in older couples. In this study, 20 couples were randomly assigned to two groups; 10 completed a education workshop and 10 were used as controls. The workshop provided a structured educational format that focused on the physiological and psychological changes that occur in the sexual response cycle during aging. Sexual behavior was measured along three dimensions utilizing three standardized scales: (a) frequency of sexual behavior, (b) sexual satisfaction, and (c) knowledge and attitudes toward sex. Pretest and posttest scores were reviewed and analyzed.

Study results suggest that the couples who attended the workshop had a significant increase in knowledge levels after completion of the workshop. A slight increase in sexual behavior was noted for the experimental group, with a slight decline in this behavior for the control group. Overall, the educational workshop was considered a success, with a reported increase in knowledge and positive changes, as well as more realistic attitudes once the etiology of sexual satisfaction and erectile functioning was explained.

Although the literature has stressed the importance of education in the treatment of erectile difficulty, the addition of *play therapy* has also been considered. Shaw (1990) focused on this option in treating men who had inhibited ejaculation. The central premise of the inclusion of play therapy is the belief that sexuality should be fun and pleasureful, not performance-oriented. However, the reality for many men is that the desire to perform becomes extremely anxiety-provoking (Barlow, 1986). In play therapy, performance anxiety is addressed and males are taught to reduce the focus on performance. The focus of the intervention is on helping clients recognize and increase the spontaneous aspects of their personalities.

In Shaw's study (1990), participants were expected to create and act on fantasies, to participate in sensate focus exercises, and to take part in sexual expression board games. Fifteen males (followed over a 3-year period) were able to successfully ejaculate with their own touch, although they were unable to do so with their partners. Of the 12 men who completed the program, all reported relief within 3 to 22 months of intervention.

In general, in treatment of the orgasmic disorders there appears to be evidence and promise that supports the effectiveness of a cognitive-behavioral approach for individuals who experience orgasmic dysfunction. However, more research is needed to establish whether the group or the individual format is more successful. The limited number of professionals available to lead the sessions and the cost-effectiveness of groups increases the likelihood of the use of group modalities. Despite the emphasis on groups, it is important to note that some individuals might not be receptive to or ready for participation in a group format. The results of these studies and the current concerns within the professional climate emphasizing group work augment the need to consider such issues prior to the initiation of treatment.

CONCLUSIONS

In summary, these studies elucidate the need for more empirically based formats for both the physical and psychological treatment of sexual orgasmic disorders. Many current social work and behavioral science researchers concur with the need for the inclusion of a psychosocial component with specific measures to address the marital, social, and personal difficulties an individual may express (Goldman & Carroll, 1990; Kaplan, 1990; Shaw, 1990). The importance of the inclusion of cognitive, educational, and behavioral techniques remains a crucial element in the complete treatment of individuals experiencing any type of sexual difficulty, not just the orgasmic disorders.

Empirically based time-limited treatment modalities are believed to be the future of social work practice in this current managed care environment (Dziegielewski, 1996; Dziegielewski, 1997). However to date, empirical social work practice in the area of sexual dysfunctions, with orgasmic disorders in particular, remains very limited. More research is needed to determine exactly what types of cognitive-behavioral treatments work best and if the results remain consistent over time. This makes the social worker's role as a clinical researcher critical in helping clients.

Harrison (1987) suggested that there was a need for well-defined outcome studies in almost all topics related to human sexuality. Today, this remains a major issue in social work practice, particularly in the area of the treatment of sexual dysfunctions. Contrary to Szasz's (1980) assertion that the "so called sexual dysfunctions" (which are psychogenic in nature) are not medical diseases or problems requiring sex therapy (p. 13), social workers and other behavioral scientists have shown this belief to be outdated—and dangerous. Although the importance of including the psychosocial and psychosexual aspects in understanding sexual dysfunctions is well documented, it is frequently overlooked.

Catalan, Hawton, and Day (1990) strongly suggest that family and relationship issues be addressed in the treatment of sexual dysfunctions—prior to the discussion of other issues. The authors of this chapter support this contention, and uphold the view that increasing treatment success requires the consideration of relationship problems through a cognitive-behavioral model. If relationship problems are determined to be critical, a complete social evaluation should be conducted prior to the initiation of physical or biological treatments. A behavioral and cognitive approach to sex therapy is crucial in the treatment of sexual dysfunctions; thus, the roles of the social worker and the behavioral scientist become pivotal as well.

Consistent with the claims made by Harrison (1987), further controlled and empirically based research is needed in this area; based on our profession's demands for accountability and demonstration of practice effectiveness, there is no better time than now to continue this quest. Now researchers must ascertain which type of treatment technique works best (such as utilizing cognitive or behavioral sex therapy models), and determine how to best utilize the techniques chosen (that is, in a group, family, couples, individual, or combination format). A new need for empirical verification is taking shape, and research replication is imperative. It is yet to be determined whether these treatments and the resultant gains will actually remain consistent over time.

REFERENCES

American Psychiatric Association. (1994). *Diagnostic and Statistical Manual of Mental Disorders* (4th ed.). Washington, DC: Author.

Anderson, B. L. (1983). Primary orgasmic dysfunction: Diagnostic considerations and review of treatment. *Psychological Bulletin, 93,* 105–136.

Barbach, L. (1980). *Women discover orgasm: A therapist's guide to a new treatment approach.* New York: MacMillan.

Barlow, D. H. (1986). Causes of sexual dysfunction: The role of anxiety and cognitive interference. *Journal of Consulting and Clinical Psychology, 54,* 140–148.

Bogat, A. G., Hamernik, K., & Brooks, L. A. (1987). The influence of self-efficacy: Expectations on the treatment of preorgasmic women. *Journal of Sex & Marital Therapy, 13,* 128–136.

Caird, W. (1988). The modification of urinary urgency during sexual arousal. *Journal of Sex Research, 24,* 183–187.

Catalan, J., Hawton, K., & Day, A. (1990). Couples referred to a sexual dysfunction clinic: Psychological and physical morbidity. *British Journal of Psychiatry, 156,* 61–67.

Chambless, D. L., Stern, T., Sultan, F. E., Williams, A. J., Goldstein, A. J., Lineberger, M. H., Lifshutz, J. L., & Kelly, L. (1982). The pubococcygens and female orgasm: A correlational study with normal subjects. *Archives of Sexual Behavior, 11* (6), 479–490.

Chambless, D. L. Sultan, F. E., & Stern, T. E. (1984). Effect of pubococcygeal exercise on coital orgasm in women. *Journal of Consulting and Clinical Psychology, 52,* 114–118.

Conte, H. R. (1986). Multivariate assessment of sexual dysfunction. *Journal of Consulting and Clinical Psychology, 54,* 149–157.

Dekker, J. (1993). Inhibited male orgasm. In W. O'Donohue & J. H. Geer (Eds.), *Handbook of sexual dysfunctions: Assessment and treatment* (pp. 279–302). Boston: Allyn & Bacon.

Dziegielewski, S. F. (1996). Managed care principles: The need for social work in the health care environment. *Crisis Intervention and Time Limited Treatment, 3,* 97–111.

Dziegielewski, S. F. (1997). Time-limited brief therapy: The state of practice. *Crisis Intervention and Time Limited Treatment, 4,* 217–228.

Eastman, P. (1993, May/June). Washington report: Treating erectile dysfunction. *Geriatric Consultant,* 10–13.

Fedoroff, J. P. (1991). Interview techniques to assess sexual disorders. *Families in Society, 72,* 140–145.

Fish, L. S., Busby, D., & Killian, K. (1994). Structural couple therapy in the treatment of inhibited sexual drive. *American Journal of Family Therapy, 22,* 113–125.

Friedman, J. M., & Hogan, D. R. (1985). Sexual dysfunction and low sexual desire. In D. H. Barlow (Ed.), *Clinical handbook of psychiatric disorders* (pp. 417–461). New York: Guilford Press.

Golden, J. (1988). A second look at a case of inhibited sexual desire. *Journal of Sex Research, 25,* 304–306.

Goldman, A., & Carroll, J. (1990). Educational intervention as an adjunct to treatment of erectile dysfunction in older couples. *Journal of Sex & Marital Therapy, 16,* 127–141.

Graber, B., & Kline-Graber, G. (1979). Female orgasm: Role of the pubococcygeus muscle. *Journal of Clinical Psychology, 40* (8), 348–351.

Harrison, D. F. (1987). Clinical research in sexual dysfunctions: Social work contributions. *Journal of Social Service Research, 10* (2/3/4), 105–119.

Hawton, K., Catalan, J., & Fagg, J. (1991). Low sexual desire: Sex therapy results and prognostic factors. *Behaviour Research and Therapy, 29,* 217–224.

Hawton, K., Catalan, J., & Fagg, J. (1992) Sex therapy for erectile dysfunction: Characteristics of couples, treatment outcome, and prognostic factors. *Archives of Sexual Behavior, 21,* 161–175.

Horton, A. L. (1995). Sex related hot-line calls: Types, interventions and guidelines. In A. Roberts (Ed.), *Crisis intervention and time limited cognitive treatment* (pp. 290–312). Thousand Oaks, CA: Sage.

Janda, L. H., & O'Grady, K. E. (1980). Development of a sex anxiety inventory. *Journal of Consulting and Clinical Psychology, 48,* 169–175.

Kaplan, H. S. (1974). *The new sex therapy.* New York: Random House.

Kaplan, H. S. (1979). *Disorders of sexual desire.* New York: Simon & Schuster.

Kaplan, H. S. (1990). The combined use of sex therapy and intra-penile injections in the treatment of impotence. *Journal of Sex & Marital Therapy, 16,* 195–207.

Kaplan, H. S. (1995). *The sexual desire disorders: Dysfunctional regulation and sexual motivation.* New York: Brunner/Mazel.

Kaplan, L., & Harder, D. W. (1991). The sexual desire conflict scale for women: Construction, internal consistency, and two initial validity tests. *Psychological Reports, 68,* 1275–1282.

Kilman, P. R., Milan, R. J., Boland, J. P., Nankin, H. R., Davidson, E., West, M. O., Sabalis, R. F., Caid, C., & Devine, J. M. (1987). Group treatment for secondary erectile dysfunction. *Journal of Sex and Marital Therapy, 13,* 168–180.

Kinder, B. N., & Curtiss, G. (1988). Specific components in the etiology, assessment, and treatment of male sexual dysfunctions: Controlled outcome studies. *Journal of Sex & Marital Therapy, 14,* 40–48.

Kinzl, J. F., Traweger, C., & Biebl, W. (1995). Sexual dysfunctions: Relationship to childhood sexual abuse and early family experiences in a nonclinical sample. *Child Abuse and Neglect, 19,* 785–792.

Knopf, J., & Seiler, M. (1990). *ISD: Inhibited sexual desire.* New York: William Morrow.

Locke, H. J., & Wallace, K. M. (1959). Short marital and prediction tests: Their reliability and validity. *Journal of Marriage and Family Living. 21,* 251–255.

LoPiccolo, J., & Steger, J. C. (1974). The Sexual Interaction Inventory: A new instrument for assessment of sexual dysfunction. *Archives of Sexual Behavior, 3,* 585–595.

LoPiccolo, J., & Stock, W. E. (1986). Treatment of sexual dysfunction. *Journal of Consulting and Clinical Psychology, 54,* 158–167.

Masters, W. H., & Johnson, V. D. (1970). *Human sexual inadequacy.* Boston: Little, Brown.

Maxmen, J. S., & Ward, N. G. (1995). *Essential psychopathology and its treatment: Second edition revised for DSM-IV.* New York: W. W. Norton.

McCabe, M. P., & Delaney, S. M. (1992). An evaluation of therapeutic programs for the treatment of secondary inorgasmia in women. *Archives of Sexual Behavior, 21,* 69–89.

McCary, J. L. (1973). *Human sexuality.* New York: D. Van Nostrand.

Milan, R. J., Kilman, P., & Boland, J. (1988). Treatment outcome of secondary orgasmic dysfunction: A two to six year follow-up. *Archives of Sexual Behavior, 17,* 463–480.

Morokoff, P. J., & LoPiccolo, J. (1986). A comparative evaluation of minimal therapist contact and 15 session treatment for female orgasmic dysfunction. *Journal of Consulting and Clinical Psychology, 54,* 294–300.

O'Donohue, W., Letourneau, E., & Geer, J. H. (1993). Premature ejaculation. In W. O'Donohue & J. H. Geer (Eds.), *Handbook of sexual dysfunctions: Assessment and treatment* (pp. 303–334). Boston: Allyn & Bacon.

Palace, E. M. (1995). Modification of dysfunctional patterns of sexual response through autonomic arousal and false physiological feedback. *Journal of Consulting and Clinical Psychology, 63,* 604–615.

Palace, E., & Gorzalka, B. B. (1990). The enhancing effects of anxiety on arousal in sexually dysfunctional and functional women. *Journal of Abnormal Psychology, 99,* 403–411.

Ravart, M., & Cote, H. (1992). Sexoanalysis: A new insight-oriented treatment approach for sexual disorders. *Journal of Sex and Marital Therapy, 18,* 128–140.

Saunders, B. E., Villeponteaux, L. A., Lipovsky, J. A., & Kilpatrick, D. G. (1992). Child sexual assault as a risk factor for mental disorders among women: A community survey. *Journal Of Interpersonal Violence, 7,* 189–204.

Shaw, J. (1990). Play therapy with the sexual workhorse: Successful treatment with 12 cases of inhibited ejaculation. *Journal of Sex & Marital Therapy, 16,* 159–164.

Sotile, W. M., & Kilmann, P. R. (1978). The effects of group systematic desensitization on orgasmic dysfunction. *Archives of Sexual Behavior, 7,* 477–491.

Spector, I. P., & Carey, M. P. (1990). Incidence and prevalence of sexual dysfunctions: A critical review of the literature. *Archives of Sexual Behavior, 19,* 399–408.

Stuart, F. M., Hammond, D. C., & Pett, M. A. (1987). Inhibited sexual desire in women. *Archives of Sexual Behavior, 16,* (2), 91–106.

Stuntz, S. S., Falk, A., Hiken, M., & Carson, V. B. (1996). The journey undermined by psychosexual disorders. In V. B. Carson & E. N. Arnold (Eds.), *Mental health nursing: The nurse patient journey* (pp. 879–895). Philadelphia: W. B. Saunders.

Szasz, T. (1980). *Sex by prescription.* New York: Doubleday.

Thyer, B. A., & Papsdorf, J. D. (1981). Relationship between irrationality and sexual arousability. *Psychological Reports, 48,* 834.

Trudel, G. (1991). Review of psychological factors in low sexual desire. *Sexual and Marital Therapy, 6,* 261–272.

Whitehead, A., Mathews, A. & Ramage, M. (1987). The treatment of sexually unresponsive women: A comparative evaluation. *Behaviour Research and Therapy. 25,* 3, 195–205.

Wilson, G. L., & Wilson, L. J. (1991). Treatment acceptability of alternate sex therapies: A comparative analysis. *Journal of Sex & Marital Therapy, 17,* 35–43.

Wincze, J. P., & Carey, M. P. (1991). *Sexual dysfunction: A guide for assessment and treatment.* New York: Guilford.

Woody, J. D., D'Souza, H. J., & Crain, D. D. (1994). Sexual functioning in clinical couples: Discriminant validity of the sexual interaction scale. *American Journal of Family Therapy, 22,* 291–303.

PART VII

Eating Disorders

Chapter 22

BULIMIA NERVOSA

Laura L. Myers

OVERVIEW

Bulimia Nervosa (BN) is a widespread eating disorder characterized by bouts of overeating and subsequent inappropriate methods to lose weight (for example, self-induced vomiting, laxative abuse, and overexercise, etc.). Many people with BN are secretive about their dieting and eating behaviors, and avoid discussing them with even their closest friends. Social workers, because they work in agencies throughout our communities, including schools, churches, and counseling centers, are in a unique position to find and reach those individuals who suffer from this serious disorder (cf. Myers, 1996). This chapter summarizes contemporary ideas regarding the current operational definitions, assessment techniques, and treatment techniques to assist the social worker in treating the client with BN.

Operational Definitions

Operational definitions of BN and other eating disorders are still in a state of flux, changing significantly with each revision of the *Diagnostic and Statistical Manual of Mental Disorders,* currently in its fourth edition (*DSM-IV;* American Psychiatric Association [APA], 1994). The names of the eating disorders, the criteria, and the distinction between Anorexia Nervosa (AN) and Bulimia Nervosa have all changed in recent years. In addition, the process of operationally defining the terms used in the diagnostic criteria has also prompted numerous debates, on issues including the presence and frequency of binging, the size of the binge, the presence and frequency of purging activity, and the presence of distorted body image.

The current criteria for BN, as defined by *DSM-IV* (APA, 1994, p. 549), include: (a) recurrent episodes of binge eating; (b) recurrent inappropriate compensatory behavior to prevent weight gain, such as self-induced vomiting, misuse of laxatives, diuretics, enemas, or other medications, fasting, or excessive exercise; (c) occurrence of these behaviors, on average, at least twice a week for 3 months; (d) self-evaluation is unduly influenced by body shape and weight; and (e) occurrence of the disturbance is not exclusively during episodes of AN. If the client meets the criteria for both BN and AN, binge-eating and purging type, only the diagnosis for AN is made. The distinguishing factors between BN and AN are the presence of significant weight loss and the absence of menstrual cycles in the criteria for AN.

Binging is defined in the criteria for BN as being characterized by both of the following: (a) eating, within any 2-hour period, an amount of food that is definitely larger than most people would eat during a similar period of time and under similar circumstances; and (b) a sense of lack of control over eating during the episode, such as feeling that one cannot stop eating or control what or how much one is eating (APA, 1994). While this definition is fairly clear, there is a debate as to whether this definition does indeed describe the binging behaviors of many clients with BN.

Schlundt and Johnson (1990), believing that the classification of food intake as a binge is subjective and differs from client to client, define a binge as "the ingestion of any food substance or quantity that violates the individual's idea of dieting and thereby increases anxiety regarding weight gain" (p. 4). They argue that for different clients, a binge may involve the consumption of thousands of calories, a normal-sized meal, or even a single doughnut. The frequency of binging can also differ greatly between clients, ranging from infrequently to 15 times a day.

Purging is a required element in the diagnostic criteria of BN offered in *DSM-IV.* Purging is defined as "inappropriate compensatory behavior in order to prevent weight gain" (APA, 1994, p. 549). Self-induced vomiting is probably the most effective way to eliminate calories. Other popular methods include the use of laxatives, diuretics and diet pills, fasting, and excessive exercise. Myers (1996) offers a more complete discussion of the variations in binging and purging behaviors that occur in the client population.

Prevalence

The prevalence of BN among adolescent and young adult women is estimated to range between 1% and 3%; the corresponding figure for males ranges between 0.1% and 0.3% (APA, 1994, p. 548).

Relevance to Clinical Social Workers

BN is clearly a widespread clinical problem. Because of the prevalence of this disorder, many social workers face the challenge of working with clients with BN. It is therefore important for social workers to be informed of the available assessment and treatment techniques that have been empirically demonstrated to be effective.

ASSESSMENT METHODS

A variety of assessment methods have been developed for use in the diagnosis, treatment, and treatment evaluation of BN. Assessments usually include a structured interview, self-report measurement instruments, assessment of body image distortion, observation methods to directly measure the amount and type of food involved in the binge and purge behaviors, and a complete physical examination to discover possible medical complications, such as electrolyte disturbances, low potassium levels, or tooth decay.

Structured Clinical Interviews

Several structured interview forms have been developed to assist the social worker in gathering behavioral and psychological information pertaining to eating disorders. The Eating Disorder Examination (EDE), currently in its 12th edition, was developed by Fairburn and Cooper (1993), both leading experts in the field of eating disorders. The authors designed this instrument because they felt the interview format would provide more detailed and accurate information for the diagnosis of an eating disorder than the self-report questionnaires. The EDE offers three levels of data: (a) frequency or severity ratings on individual items indicate the presence of key behavioral and attitudinal aspects of eating disorders; (b) four subscales (restraint, eating concern, shape concern, and weight concern) assess key aspects of the eating disorder diagnoses; and (c) a global score measures the overall severity of the eating disorder psychopathology.

The EDE is an investigator-based interview, and requires that the interviewers be trained in the general technique of interviewing, the concepts discussed in the instrument, and the rules regarding the scoring of the instrument. Considerable information regarding the validity and reliability of the instrument is offered, in addition to fairly detailed instructions for administering the EDE. Guidelines for making the ratings are given for each individual question. The majority of items use a scale of 0 to 6 on which either frequency or severity is rated, 0 usually representing the absence of the feature and 6 representing its presence to an extreme degree. A code of 8 is used when it is impossible to decide upon a rating but the symptom should not be excluded, and a code of 9 is used when the behavior is not applicable to the client. The interviewer is instructed to use the less severe of two ratings when it is difficult to choose between the two. Sample questions from each of the four subscales, as well as additional diagnostic questions, are shown in Table 22.1.

Table 22.1   Sample Questions from the Eating Disorder Examination

Restraint subscale
   Over the past 4 weeks have you been *consciously trying* to restrict what you eat, whether or not you have succeeded?
   Have you gone for periods of 8 or more *waking* hours without eating anything?

Eating concern subscale
   Over the past 4 weeks have you been concerned about other people seeing you eat?
   Have you felt guilty after eating?

Weight concern subscale
   Over the past 4 weeks have you wanted to lose weight?

Shape concern subscale
   Over the past 4 weeks have you been *afraid* that you might gain weight or become fat?
   Have you felt uncomfortable seeing your body?

Diagnostic items
   Over the past 4 weeks have you made yourself sick as a means of controlling your shape or weight?
   Have you missed any menstrual periods over the past few months?

SOURCE: From Fairburn and Cooper (1993). Reprinted with permission.

In addition to the full examination with instructions, Fairburn and Cooper (1993) also include a coding sheet for use by the interviewer. It is estimated that it takes 30 to 60 minutes to complete the interview. Because of its high reliability and validity, it is a very effective instrument not only for clinical use but also for use in treatment outcome studies.

Self-Report Methods

The Eating Disorder Inventory (EDI; Garner, Olmsted, and Polivy, 1983) is a useful instrument for differentiating levels of severity as well as the subtypes of AN and BN. It has also been widely used as an outcome measure. The EDI includes 64 items, three subscales pertaining to eating disordered behaviors (drive for thinness, bulimia, and body dissatisfaction), and five subscales pertaining to the more general psychological characteristics of clients with eating disorders (ineffectiveness, perfectionism, interpersonal distrust, interoceptive awareness, and maturity fears). A revised edition, the Eating Disorder Inventory—2 (EDI-2; Garner, 1991) added 27 more items forming three additional subscales (asceticism, impulse regulation, and social insecurity). Most of the research on psychometric properties of the instrument has been completed using the first version. Each question is scored on a 6-point scale from *always* to *never,* and the EDI can be completed in about 20 minutes. Copies of the instrument can be obtained from Psychological Assessment Resources, Inc., P.O. Box 998, Odessa, FL 33556.

The Bulimia Test—Revised (BULIT-R; Thelen, Farmer, Wonderlich, & Smith, 1991) is a 28-item test that was designed to help the clinician measure the symptoms of BN as defined by *DSM-III-R* (APA, 1987). It is also useful for measuring the severity of the symptoms and treatment outcome. Each multiple choice question has five responses unique to each question, including such questions as "I feel tormented by the idea that I am fat or might gain weight," and "When I am trying to keep from gaining weight, I feel that I have to resort to vigorous exercise, strict dieting, fasting, self-induced vomiting, laxatives, or diuretics." The instrument takes approximately 10 minutes to complete. The instrument is fully described in Thelen et al. (1991) and has been reprinted in Williamson, Anderson, Jackman, and Jackson (1995).

Computerized Assessment Methods

Another method of data collection is through client self-monitoring of food intake. The Vanderbilt Food Diary involves a one-page form that allows the client to specify the food eaten at each instance, along with several other data items, such as the time, whether a meal or a snack was eaten, the place, the people involved, and the client's feelings. A booklet is created with 30 to 40 such pages, and the client completes a form each time a meal or snack is eaten. The data from the diary is then entered into a computer database using the Self-Monitoring Analysis System (SMAS; Schlundt, 1989), computer software designed to manage and analyze food intake data. SMAS can analyze the nutritional composition for grams and percentages of protein, carbohydrates, and fats, as well as summarize the compliance between a dietary plan and actual food intake. It can analyze meal frequency and timing, and can look at variables that reflect the individual's self-perception of his or her eating behavior. Statistical tests can be computed and various reports can be printed. While there are problems with self-monitoring procedures, such as difficulty in verifying the accuracy of the data and the client's failure to comply with the self-monitoring procedures, Schlundt (1995) argues that with carefully designed forms and properly trained and motivated clients, accurate data can be gathered. He further suggests that such data be supplemented by data collected through direct observation.

Another computerized system, the Body Image Testing System (Schlundt & Bell, 1993), has been developed to measure the client's perception of his or her body. Clients interact with the system to adjust the profile of a body until the chosen shape has been created. A variety of assessment tasks can be constructed using this system, including selecting one's own body shape and selecting one's ideal body shape.

Observational Methods

Standardized test meals have been used for assessment and research purposes (Rosen, 1988). Clients are asked to consume as much of a standardized meal as they feel comfortable eating. Three different meals are used: (a) a full-course dinner, (b) a spaghetti dinner, and (c) candy. The amount of food eaten at each meal is measured, as well as the client's ratings of fear, anxiety, and urge to vomit. Clients with BN are instructed not to vomit for at least 1½ hours after eating the test meal. In most cases, the clinician stays with the client throughout the process, measuring cognitions and affects.

EFFECTIVE INTERVENTIONS

Individual and Group Therapies

Cognitive-Behavioral Therapy.   Cognitive-behavioral therapy (CBT) is generally considered to be the treatment of choice for clients with BN. Components involved in CBT include self-monitoring, reducing environmental cues to binge, meal planning, introducing forbidden foods, problem-solving skills, relaxation training, education, and cognitive restructuring (Fairburn, 1988). Several CBT group and individual programs have been developed for clients with BN; in general, research studies suggest that these programs "produce substantial improvements in both eating behavior (including, in episodes of overeating, a reduction in the use of other methods of weight control and in the level of dietary restraint), as well as an improvement in attitude about body shape and weight" (Kennedy & Garfinkel, 1992, p. 311). In addition, CBT has shown to be equally or more effective in treating BN than supportive psychotherapy, focal psychotherapy, exposure with response prevention, behavior therapy, and treatment with antidepressants (Fairburn, Marcus, & Wilson, 1993).

The CBT that is probably the most widely used in practice and in research is the technique developed by Christopher Fairburn in the early 1980s. The most recent edition of the treatment manual was published in 1993 (Fairburn et al.). The treatment lasts approximately 20 weeks, and Fairburn stresses that it is important to set a time limit on treatment. He feels that improvement continues after the 20 weeks of treatment are over, and it is important for the client and the therapist to know that the improvements are no longer dependent on the therapy. The focus on the therapy is on current factors that are maintaining the eating disorder rather than on factors that occurred earlier in the client's life.

Fairburn distinguishes three stages in his CBT. The first stage lasts approximately 8 weeks or sessions. The six aims of stage one are: (a) to establish a sound therapeutic relationship; (b) to educate the patient about the cognitive view on the maintenance of BN and to explain the need for both behavior and cognitive change; (c) to establish regular weekly weighing; (d) to educate the patient about body weight regulation, the adverse effects of dieting, and the physical consequences of binge eating, self-induced vomiting, and laxative abuse; (e) to reduce the frequency of overeating by introducing a pattern of regular eating and the use of alternative behavior; and (f) to reduce secrecy and enlist the cooperation of friends and relatives (p. 366). Techniques include completing a history of the client, self-monitoring of food and liquid intake by the client (including amount, place, binge and purge activity, and context of eating), weekly weighing of the client, and psychoeducation of the client. Toward the end of this stage, Fairburn attempts to include those people who live with the client in the therapy process.

The second stage continues from the 9th to the 16th sessions. The emphasis is on continuing to replace unhealthy eating habits with healthy, stable patterns of eating. In addition, the focus broadens to address all forms of dieting, concerns about shape and weight, and more general cognitive distortions. Techniques include the introduction of forbidden foods; therapist-assisted exposure and avoidance of purging activity (in cases where the client continues to binge or to purge after forbidden foods are eaten); problem-solving skills training; and cognitive restructuring to address cognitive distortions, including dichotomous reasoning, extreme perfectionism, and low self-esteem.

The third and final stage of treatment consists of three interviews at 2-week intervals, focusing on the maintenance of change following treatment. The client is encouraged to continue weekly weighing and self-monitoring indefinitely. Plans regarding potential lapses are discussed, and a maintenance plan is written that formally sets out the plan for dealing with times when eating behaviors become problematic again. The client is encouraged to review why setbacks occur in order to prevent them from recurring. Fairburn et al. (1993) offers very detailed instructions on the individual components of the CBT, as well as ways to modify the treatment for the overweight client.

Nutrition Therapy.   Nutrition education and therapy is an extremely important component of most cognitive-behavioral treatment models. The purpose of nutrition education and management is "to educate eating-disordered patients about basic principles of good nutrition, and to help them use this information in planning healthy and appropriate patterns of food intake" (Schlundt & Johnson, 1990, p. 321). One research study suggests that nutritional counseling may be effective as a sole form of treatment for clients with BN who show little evidence of other underlying psychopathology (O'Connor, Touyz, & Beumont, 1987). A survey of 117 dietitians identified the need for more outcome research on nutrition therapy and on the effectiveness of prevention programs for clients with eating disorders (Whisenant & Smith, 1995).

The American Dietetic Association (ADA; 1994) stated its position that "nutrition education and nutrition intervention be integrated into the team treatment of patients with anorexia nervosa, bulimia nervosa, and binge eating during assessment and treatment phases of outpatient and/or inpatient therapy" (p. 902). Assessment involves measuring various aspects of the patient's eating and dieting history and his or her current nutritional status. The treatment as defined by the ADA includes two phases: the education phase and the experimental phase. There are five major objectives during the education phase: (a) collect relevant information, including a comprehensive history of weight changes, eating and exercise patterns, and purging behaviors; (b) establish a collaborative relationship between the client and the registered dietitian that will enable the client to talk about food fears and develop realistic goals for weight and behavior change; (c) define and discuss relevant principles and concepts of food, nutrition, and weight regulation, as it has been found that understanding why and how the body responds to starvation, binge eating, purging, and restriction is typically necessary before the client will risk making behavioral changes; (d) present examples of hunger patterns, typical food intake patterns, and the total caloric intake of a person who has recovered from an eating disorder, helping the client understand what recovery means; and (e) educate the family members in order to increase their understanding of the eating disorder and their support of the client (pp. 902–903).

It is during the experimental phase that the client makes changes in eating and dieting behaviors. The primary objectives of this phase are defined as follows: (a) separate food and weight-related behaviors from feelings and psychological issues; (b) change food behaviors in an incremental fashion until food intake patterns are normalized, emphasizing that changes must be gradual and setbacks are normal (self-monitoring techniques are often used during this phase, and education as to what bodily changes can be expected is usually very important); (c) slowly increase or decrease weight; (d) learn to maintain a weight that is healthful without the use of abnormal food or weight-related behaviors; and (e) learn to be comfortable in social eating situations (usually attempted in the later stages of treatment; pp. 903–904).

Pharmacological Treatment.   The outcome research on pharmacological treatment of clients with BN has shown mixed results, but most clinicians and researchers probably agree that a subgroup of clients with BN are vulnerable to depression and may require treatment with antidepressants for concurrent major depression (Kennedy & Garfinkel, 1992). Mitchell (1990) states:

> My current practice is to prescribe antidepressants as part of the initial treatment for patients who give a clear history of an affective disorder, in particular if there is evidence that the affective disorder preceded the onset of the eating disorder, for patients who remain depressed despite improvement in their eating symptoms, and for those patients who show only a partial response or a lack of response to a psychotherapy intervention, whether or not they are depressed. (p. 89)

While the social worker is not directly responsible for pharmacological treatment, it is important to be aware of the current knowledge in this area.

Group Therapies

Many of the cognitive-behavioral treatment approaches, including the one outlined in the preceding section, have been adapted for use either with the individual client or in the context of group therapy. Although both individual and group treatments have been shown to be effective in numerous research studies, there seems to be a dearth of research comparing the effectiveness of group versus individual treatment modalities. In the few studies of this type that are available, there is usually a confound based on the type of therapy that is offered to the two groups. For example, Olmsted et al. (1991) compared an 18-week individual cognitive-behavioral treatment program to a 5-week psychoeducational group program. While the individual treatment was more effective with clients with more severe eating disorder symptoms, the group program seemed to be equally as effective with clients with less severe disorders. Thus, since the group program is significantly more cost-effective, it was suggested that the therapist might use the two forms of treatment sequentially, starting with the group program. Then, only those clients needing further intervention could be enrolled in the lengthier individual treatment program. Or the therapist might choose to place the majority of the clients in the psychoeducational group program, immediately placing those clients with more severe cases into individual treatment.

Family Therapies

Several treatment approaches have been developed for use with clients with BN and their families, but Schlundt and Johnson (1990) point out that "broad empirical support for the family systems analysis of eating disorders is lacking" (p. 269). Vandereycken (1987), one of the leading researchers in the family treatment of eating disorders, suggests that the family systems approach to BN is based on clinical experience and personal belief rather than on empirical research. One exception is a study by Russell, Szmukler, Dare, and Eisler (1987) in which they compared family therapy to individual therapy. The results suggest that for younger clients, family therapy may be more effective than individual techniques. It should be noted, however, that the form of individual therapy used was a "non-specific form of individual therapy" called "individual supportive therapy," rather than the cognitive-behavioral therapy that has been empirically tested and shown to be an effective intervention.

Vanderlinden, Norre, and Vandereycken (1992) have defined and extensively utilized one family treatment program for clients with BN. The beginning phase involves the assessment of both the family and the individual family members. Assessment must consider the family structure and coalitions; the family life cycle; family functioning on behavioral, experiential, and cognitive levels; individual psychosocial functioning; the presence of individual psychopathology; and the meaning of the eating disorder on behavioral, experiential, and cognitive levels. The middle phase of family therapy focuses on promoting separation and individuation of the client from his or her family, considered a key element of treating a client with BN. The final phase emphasizes maintenance and ensuring long-term change. A number of family situations are defined that contraindicate the use of family therapy: (a) patients with a long history (more than 10 years) of eating disorders, and a significant delay in psychosocial development; (b) patients from single-parent or broken homes; (c) one or both parents display severe psychopathology; (d) history of physical or sexual abuse in family; and (e) failure of previous family therapeutic attempts (p. 151).

Prevention

Prevention is an area that has received little attention in the eating disorders field. Dickstein (1989) points out that "enough of bulimia's etiology and potential morbidity and mortality has been clarified to develop useful intervention and prevention programs" (p. 128). The Setting Conditions for Anorexia Nervosa Scale (SCANS; Slade & Dewey, 1986) was developed in an effort to recognize individuals who are at high risk for developing AN or BN. The SCANS is divided into five scales: (a) dissatisfaction and loss of control, (b) social and personal anxiety, (c) perfectionism, (d) adolescent problems, and (e) need for weight control. It includes 40 items answered on a 5-point scale anchored by different responses depending on the nature of the question (for example, 1 = very often to 5 = never or 1 = very satisfied to 5 = very dissatisfied). The instrument takes 10 to 20 minutes to complete and less than 10 minutes to score. Butler, Newton, and Slade (1988) have developed a computerized version of the SCANS. Through the use of the SCANS and the significant research that has been completed in identifying the risk factors for developing BN, it seems there is a great potential for preventive work in this area.

CONCLUSIONS

Researchers differ greatly on their estimates of the prevalence of BN in the population. Thelen, Lawrence, and Powell (1992) suggest, however, that "even if one takes the most conservative estimates of the prevalence of bulimia nervosa, it is still clear that this eating disorder is a significant problem that warrants our attention" (p. 81). The social worker is in a unique position to identify individuals who are at risk of developing this disorder or who are already experiencing its serious effects.

REFERENCES

American Dietetic Association. (1994). Position of the American Dietetic Association: Nutrition intervention in the treatment of anorexia nervosa, bulimia nervosa, and binge eating. *Journal of the American Dietetic Association, 94,* 902–907.

American Psychiatric Association. (1987). *Diagnostic and statistical manual of mental disorders* (3rd ed., rev.). Washington, DC: Author.

American Psychiatric Association. (1994). *Diagnostic and statistical manual of mental disorders* (4th ed.). Washington DC: Author.

Butler, N., Newton, T., & Slade, P. D. (1988). Validation of a computerized version of the SCANS questionnaire. *International Journal of Eating Disorders, 8,* 239–241.

Dickstein, L. J. (1989). Current college environments: Do these communities facilitate and foster bulimia in vulnerable students? In L. C. Whitaker (Ed.), *The bulimic college student: Evaluation, treatment and prevention* (pp. 107–133). New York: Haworth Press.

Fairburn, C. G. (1988). The current status of the psychological treatments for bulimia nervosa. *Journal of Psychosomatic Medicine, 32,* 635–645.

Fairburn, C. G., & Cooper, P. J. (1993). The Eating Disorder Examination (12th edition). In C. G. Fairburn & G. T. Wilson (Eds.), *Binge eating: Nature, assessment, and treatment* (pp. 317–360). New York: Guilford Press.

Fairburn, C. G., Marcus, M. D., & Wilson, G. T. (1993). Cognitive-behavioral therapy for binge eating and bulimia nervosa: A comprehensive treatment manual. In C. G. Fairburn & G. T. Wilson (Eds.), *Binge eating: Nature, assessment, and treatment* (pp. 361–404). New York: Guilford Press.

Garner, D. M. (1991). *Eating Disorder Inventory—2 manual.* Odessa, FL: Psychological Assessment Resources.

Garner, D. M., Olmsted, M. P., & Polivy, J. (1983). Development and validation of a multidimensional eating disorder inventory for anorexia and bulimia. *International Journal of Eating Disorders, 2,* 15–34.

Kennedy, S. H., & Garfinkel, P. E. (1992). Advances in diagnosis and treatment of anorexia nervosa and bulimia nervosa. *Canadian Journal of Psychiatry, 37,* 309–315.

Mitchell, J. E. (1990). *Bulimia nervosa.* Minneapolis, MN: University of Minnesota Press.

Myers, L. L. (1996). Bulimia nervosa: What social workers need to know. *Journal of Applied Social Sciences, 20,* 63–75.

O'Connor, M. A., Touyz, S. W., & Beumont, P. J. V. (1987). Nutritional management and dietary counseling in bulimia: Some preliminary observations. *International Journal of Eating Disorders, 7,* 657–662.

Olmsted, M. P., Davis, R., Rockert, W., Irvine, M. J., Eagle, M., & Garner, D. M. (1991). Efficacy of a brief group psychoeducational intervention for bulimia nervosa. *Behaviour Research and Therapy, 29,* 71–83.

Rosen, J. C. (1988). Test meals in the assessment of bulimia. In M. Hersen & A. S. Bellack (Eds.), *Dictionary of behavioral assessment* (pp. 473–474). New York: Pergamon Press.

Russell, G. F. M., Szmukler, G. I., Dare, C., & Eisler, I. (1987). An evaluation of family therapy in anorexia nervosa and bulimia nervosa. *Archives of General Psychiatry, 44,* 1047–1056.

Schlundt, D. G. (1989). Computerized behavioral assessment of eating behavior in bulimia: The self-monitoring analysis system. In W. G. Johnson (Ed.), *Advances in eating disorders: 2. Bulimia* (pp. 1–23). New York: JAI Press.

Schlundt, D. G. (1995). Assessment of specific eating behaviors and eating style. In D. B. Allison (Ed.), *Handbook of assessment methods for eating behaviors and weight-related problems: Measures, theory, and research* (pp. 241–302). Thousand Oaks, CA: Sage.

Schlundt, D. G., & Bell, C. D. (1993). The Body Image Testing System: A microcomputer program for the assessment of body image. *Journal of Behavioral Assessment and Psychopathology,* 15, 267–285.

Schlundt, D. G., & Johnson, W. G. (1990). *Eating disorders: Assessment and treatment.* Boston: Allyn & Bacon.

Slade, P. D., & Dewey, M. E. (1986). Development and preliminary validation of the SCANS: A screening instrument for identifying individuals at risk of developing anorexia and bulimia nervosa. *International Journal of Eating Disorders, 5,* 517–538.

Thelen, M. H., Farmer, J., Wonderlich, S., & Smith, M. (1991). A revision of the Bulimia Test: The BULIT-R. *Psychological Assessment, 3,* 119–124.

Thelen, M. H., Lawrence, C. M., & Powell, A. L. (1992). Body image, weight control, and eating disorders among children. In J. H. Crowther, D. L. Tennenbaum, S. E. Hobfoll, & M. A. P. Stephens (Eds.), *The etiology of bulimia nervosa: The individual and familial context* (pp. 81–101). Washington DC: Hemisphere.

Vandereycken, W. (1987). The constructive family approach to eating disorders: Critical remarks on the use of family therapy in anorexia and bulimia nervosa. *International Journal of Eating Disorders, 6,* 455–467.

Vanderlinden, J., Norre, J., & Vandereycken, W. (1992). *A practical guide to the treatment of bulimia nervosa.* New York: Brunner/Mazel.

Whisenant, S. L., & Smith, B. A. (1995). Eating disorders: Current nutrition therapy and perceived needs in dietetics education and research. *Journal of the American Dietetics Association, 95,* 1109–1112.

Williamson, D. A., Anderson, D. A., Jackman, L. P., & Jackson, S. R. (1995). Assessment of eating disordered thoughts, feelings, and behaviors. In D. B. Allison (Ed.), *Handbook of assessment methods for eating behaviors and weight-related problems: Measures, theory, and research* (pp. 347–386). Thousand Oaks, CA: Sage.

PART VIII

Personality Disorders

Chapter 23

BORDERLINE PERSONALITY DISORDER

André Ivanoff
Marsha M. Linehan
Karrie L. Recknor

OVERVIEW

According to the fourth edition of the *Diagnostic and Statistical Manual of Mental Disorders* (*DSM-IV;* American Psychiatric Association [APA], 1994), a *personality disorder* is an "enduring pattern of inner experience and behavior that differs markedly from the expectations of the individual's culture, is pervasive and inflexible, has an onset in adolescence or early adulthood, is stable over time, and leads to distress or impairment" (APA, 1994, p. 629). These patterns are not accounted for by other physical or mental disorders, and are not due to the direct effects of a substance or toxin. The ongoing tensions between psychodynamic inference and behaviorally based operationalism that guide the last two editions of the *DSM* (APA, 1987; APA, 1994) are in striking evidence in the theoretical, empirical, and classification schemas of *DSM-IV.* This creates difficulty in diagnosis, assessment, treatment, and research.

Beyond the scope of this chapter is an important debate concerning the definition and role of personality in the development of functional disorder, and, most germane to the practitioner, to what extent the longstanding behavior patterns attributed to personality may be repaired or altered sufficiently to improve functioning and quality of life. For discussions of these issues and models of personality, see the *Handbook of Personality: Theory and Research* (Pervin, 1990).

Borderline Personality Disorder (BPD) describes a disorder generally characterized by intense negative emotions, including depression, self-hatred, anger, and hopelessness. Stress-related anxiety and psychotic symptoms are also often present. In attempting to cope with these emotions, individuals meeting criteria for BPD often engage in impulsive behaviors, including alcohol or drug abuse, eating binges, self-mutilation, and, potentially, suicide. This emotional and behavioral dysregulation results in unstable and chaotic interpersonal relationships. Suicidal behavior, ranging from ideation and threats to all forms of self-harm and parasuicide, is viewed as a very common clinical characteristic of BPD. Up to 55% of inpatients diagnosed with BPD have histories of serious suicide attempts (Gunderson, 1984; Fyer, 1988), while up to 40% have histories of nonserious suicide attempts (Fyer, 1988) and up to 80% have committed self-mutilation at some time in the past.

Borderline Personality Disorder is a significant health problem, particularly among women. Approximately 11% of all mental health outpatients and 19% of psychiatric inpatients meet diagnostic criteria for BPD, and 70% to 77% of these are women (Widiger & Frances, 1991). The suicide rate of BPD clients is 5% to 10%, similar to rates of individuals diagnosed with Major Affective Disorder or Schizophrenia, the diagnostic categories with the highest suicide rates (Frances, Fyer, & Clarkin, 1986).

Borderline Personality Disorder remains a controversial and complex diagnosis. Despite the improvements made by *DSM-III-R* and *DSM-IV,* the reliability of diagnosis of BPD and other personality disorders across practitioners remains extremely problematic. Beck, Freeman, and Associates (1994) cite a nameless study in which only 40% of patients who had been diagnosed as borderline actually met DSM criteria for the disorder. Authored by social workers, *The Selling of DSM: The Rhetoric of Science in Psychiatry* (Kirk & Kutchins, 1992), describes the reliability and validity problems of *DSM.* Among some social workers, reasonable distrust of psychiatric diagnosis may originate in concern about the consequences of such labels for clients seeking treatment. Our shared position is that belief in psychiatric diagnosis is not necessary or even helpful to understanding the sets and patterns of behaviors that create this painful syndrome. We do however, believe there is an identifiable common set of behaviors that characterize individuals found among those called *borderline personality disordered* and that it is important to understand this pattern of behavior in order to help these individuals: the focus of treatment is on that identifiable set of problem behaviors.

Unfortunately, the term *borderline* has become exceedingly popular. In many respects, BPD is the diagnosis of choice to describe interpersonally difficult and difficult-to-manage clients who make practitioners feel incompetent. Aided by a long history of conceptual vagary, BPD lends itself easily to overuse as a catchall diagnosis. An example of this is a mental health staff nodding in agreement when a client is pronounced "borderline" after an incident of particularly trying interaction in which the client seems out to win over the practitioner, regardless of the presence or absence of other borderline characteristics.

Clinical Difficulty

Individuals diagnosed with BPD are high users of mental health and social services, particularly expensive emergency, acute, and crisis medical and supportive services. Obtaining needed services and assistance become sources of depression, frustration, anger, and failure (often for client and practitioner) because of the BPD client's difficulty in interpersonal functioning. Due to their interpersonally chaotic lifestyles, these individuals may be found among multiproblem clients seen in social service settings for child welfare, domestic violence, or sexual abuse issues, as well as more typically in mental health and psychiatric settings. Traditional outpatient psychotherapy has been largely ineffective with BPD patients, leaving social workers with casework expertise often working with the most severe BPD patients because of their multiple psychosocial and environmental problems.

Three hallmarks of this syndrome—client anger, threats of suicide, and suicide attempts—were identified by therapists as the three most extreme clinical stresses (Hellman, Morrison, & Abramowitz, 1986); no wonder this group is regarded as among the most frustrating to treat! Given the frustration of dealing with such difficult behavior and the often overwhelming environmental problems that result, some social workers choose to avoid working with BPD clients when possible. No single avenue of intervention is effective with BPD clients, invalidating the premise of traditional weekly session psychotherapy with traditional boundaries and limits. Social workers whose training includes tailoring interventions to individual client situations may be better able to tolerate the BPD client's needs for increased accessibility and flexibility in the therapeutic relationship.

ASSESSMENT METHODS

Several features of BPD have undergone substantial empirical investigation. These include suicidal and parasuicidal behaviors, neurological dysfunctions, cognitive deficits, psychotic symptoms, alcoholism and substance abuse, and sexual and physical abuse. Consistent with biosocial theory, findings suggest that BPD is behavioral, physiological, and environmental in nature. Further, the interrelationship of these factors paints a complicated picture that makes diagnosis, assessment, case formulation, and treatment difficult.

Given that *DSM-IV* criteria provide the most common language for diagnostic assessment, and subject to the caveats previously described above, the *DSM-IV* criteria for BPD are reprinted in Table 23.1.

Given the variance in characteristics that might be used to meet BPD criteria in any individual, diagnosis and assessment are more complex than for many other diagnostic categories. BPD is frequently comorbid with Axis I conditions, such as mood and anxiety disorders (Friedman, Shear, & Frances, 1987; Fyer, Frances, Sullivan, Hurt, & Clarkin, 1988) and psychoactive substance abuse disorders (Craig, 1988; Inman, Bascue, & Skoloda, 1985; Nace, Saxon, & Shore, 1983). As Millon (1985) suggested, the overlap may arise because BPD increases the vulnerability for various Axis I conditions. The overlap with other personality disorders is also considerable (Slodol, Rosnick, Kellman, Oldham, & Hyler, 1988; Pfohl, Coryell, Zim-

Table 23.1   *DSM-IV* Diagnostic Criteria for Borderline Personality Disorder

A pervasive pattern of instability of interpersonal relationships, self-image, and affects, and marked impulsivity beginning by early adulthood and present in a variety of contexts, as indicated by five (or more) of the following:

1. Frantic efforts to avoid real or imagined abandonment. NOTE: Do not include suicidal or self-mutilating behavior covered in Criterion 5.
2. A pattern of unstable and intense interpersonal relationships characterized by alternating between extremes of idealization and devaluation.
3. Identity disturbance: markedly and persistently unstable self-image or sense of self.
4. Impulsivity in at least two areas that are potentially self-damaging (e.g., spending, sex, substance abuse, reckless driving, and binge eating). NOTE: Do not include suicidal or self-mutilating behavior covered in Criterion 5.
5. Recurrent suicidal behavior, gestures, or threats, or self-mutilating behavior.
6. Affective instability due to a marked reactivity of mood (e.g., intense episodic dysphoria, irritability, or anxiety usually lasting a few hours and only rarely more than a few days).
7. Chronic feelings of emptiness.
8. Inappropriate, intense anger or difficulty controlling anger (e.g., frequent displays of temper, constant anger, or recurrent physical fights)
9. Transient, stress-related paranoid ideation or severe dissociative symptoms.

SOURCE: From *Diagnostic and Statistical Manual of Mental Disorders, Fourth Edition* (APA, 1994). Reprinted with permission.

merman, & Stangl, 1986). Morey (1988) found that 33.3% of 291 persons being treated for personality disorder met criteria for BPD, but also reported substantial overlaps with Histrionic, Avoidant, Dependent, Paranoid, and Negativistic Personality Disorders. There is also a high correlation between BPD and childhood sexual abuse (67% to 76% among BPD patients versus 21% in major depression patient samples) and physical abuse (Herman, Perry, & van der Kolk, 1989). While sexual abuse is a common pathway, it is definitely not the only way to generate the requisite structure for BPD; furthermore, not all individuals who have been sexually abused go on to develop BPD.

Cardinal characteristics or hallmarks of BPD are the practitioner's best guide in screening and beginning assessment. This disorder is characterized by persistent difficulties in maintaining relationships, maladaptive behavior that interferes with maintaining employment, persistent depression and misery, and repeated acts of self-harm or suicide attempts. Suicidal or parasuicidal behavior have even been described as the behavioral specialty of BPD clients (Gunderson, 1984). BPD clients are frequently seen in emergency rooms and are repeatedly hospitalized in some state of crisis or due to, or to prevent, a suicide attempt. BPD clients often suffer from Thought Disorder, Affective Disorder, Dissociative Disorder, Alcohol Abuse or Substance Abuse, eating disorders, and a variety of the anxiety disorders. They are typically high users of mental health resources while being difficult to treat and of refractory to treatment. Individuals with BPD often have difficulties with anger and other negative emotions and their expression. They often rigidly view themselves, others, and the world dichotomously, as either good or bad. They may react strongly to a therapist's lateness, absences, or changes in plans, viewing such actions as abandonment, neglect, or rejection. A discussion about therapy progress might result in the client regressing severely, which is typically viewed by practitioners as self-sabotage. Among individuals with BPD, all areas of function—cognitive, affect, and behavior—are typically affected. BPD clients present an almost unparalleled challenge to the practitioner.

Diagnostic Measures

Several self-report questionnaires, personality inventories, and structured interviews show good potential as clinical screening measures, but most require further development and validation prior to meeting standards for research use. Among self-report instruments, the Personality Diagnostic Questionnaire (PDQ-R; Hyler et al., 1989) is a brief true/false forced-choice questionnaire based on *DSM-III-R* criteria for personality disorders. The PDQ-R format is such that all questions for any single disorder appear on one page; some clinicians find this useful as a guide during the Structured Clinical Interview for *DSM-IV* (SCID-II; First, Spitzer, Gibbon, & Williams, 1995). The Millon Clinical Multiaxial Inventory (MCMI-II; Millon, 1987) is brief, true/false forced-choice, and takes about 30 minutes to complete. The MCMI-II generates three scales: (a) personality, (b) severe personality patterns, and (c) clinical syndromes. Although there are a number of self-report measures available, some tend to overdiagnose personality disorders, while several others are too long or are otherwise infeasible outside settings with large data collection capacity.

Interview instruments include the Diagnostic Interview for Borderline Personality Disorders—Revised (DIB-R; Zanarini, Gunderson, Frankenberg, & Chauncey, 1989), a semistructured interview that uses both psychodynamic and *DSM* criteria to assess for BPD; the Personality Disorder Examination (PDE; Loranger, 1996), which thematically assesses for all *DSM-IV* personality disorders; and the social work coauthored Structured Clinical Interview for *DSM-IV* (SCID-II, First et al., 1995), based on *DSM-IV* criteria. Another type of interview, the Structured Interview for *DSM* Personality Disorders (SIDP-IVP; Pfohl, Polum, & Zimmerman, 1995) addresses personality traits from the perspective of the individual experiencing them. A range of behaviors associated with a trait are included, rather than relying on a single client endorsement. Organized into topical sections rather than by disorder, the SIDP-IVP allows for more natural conversational flow, and the use of a collateral informant is possible (Pfohl et al., 1995).

Given the semistructured nature of most of these interviews, many require additional probing to clarify the client's responses. The ability to clarify with additional questions and to discriminate Axis I and Axis II disorders requires that the interviewer have some awareness of the criteria for and typical courses of major Axis I diagnoses.

Should you use a structured clinical interview in ordinary clinical practice? Yes, one can argue, because diagnosis is predictive of treatment outcomes with some interventions. This means that clients who meet criteria for BPD are likely to perform better in some treatments than in others. Do you need to use a structured clinical interview with everyone? No. Begin with a short paper-and-pencil screening scale, which is likely to identify all those who might have BPD. Structured clinical interviews administered according to protocol are generally not necessary in nonresearch clinical practice once the therapist knows the diagnostic criteria well enough to formulate questions, develop probes, and obtain the same data without using standardized questions.

Clinical Assessment

Initial and ongoing assessment serve multiple functions. Individuals entering treatment are distressed and want their lives to change, but are also generally aware that they are embedded in their life patterns and view change as frightening. Through the process of assessment, the clinician strongly affects whether an individual will return to treatment. Rarely discussed explicitly, the acceptance, understanding, and level of involvement demonstrated by the therapist during initial assessment may engage the client in treatment. Therapists should regard themselves as clinical scientists, and ward off the impulse to assume; each clinical hypothesis should be tested, and the results should be used to derive subsequent or alternative hypotheses for further testing.

It is critical to determine where an individual stands relative to prognostic indicators of treatment outcome. With BPD clients, this means that it is particularly important to know the factors related to long-term risk for suicide and parasuicide. For more discussion of these factors, see Linehan (1981; in press) and for risk assessment strategies, Bongar (1992) and Maris, Berman, Maltsberger, and Yufit (1992).

During initial assessment, a thorough history of all prior suicidal behavior must be obtained, including detailed information on the associated environment and social contingencies. This allows estimation of the short- and long-term risks of parasuicide and suicide, which is crucial for treatment planning given the 10% to 20% of BPD clients who engage in self-injurious behavior and later go on to suicide (Frances, Feyer, & Clarkin, 1986). The clinician needs to understand the specific variables that will likely be part of the management of suicidal crises with each individual client and must begin to identify the problems that may precipitate suicidal crises, for each client.

Another function of assessment involves monitoring the clients progress in treatment. It is the social worker's responsibility to keep the treatment goals in mind and to ensure that activities are clearly pointed in the direction of creating a life worth living. Ongoing assessment includes developing plans and constantly checking for the presence or absence of the resources to carry those plans through. To collect ongoing information about target problems, some forms of interventions including dialectical behavior therapy (DBT; discussed in the following section) use weekly diary cards. Targets may be individually tailored, but generally include self-harm; suicidal ideation and urges; prescription, over-the-counter, and illicit drug use; and other maladaptive behaviors. These cards are reviewed at the beginning of each individual session and help identify priorities for the session agenda.

Daily self-monitoring with the diary cards is an indispensable tool for the clinician, affording a number of advantages over the more traditional in-session narrative review of time since the last session. First, clinically, it provides a source of feedback and data to the client not available through other means, which is potentially useful as treatment progresses. Daily monitoring can also increase the accuracy of reporting since the last session, with less reliance on days-old memory. The daily nature of the diary cards provides more subtle detail of the relationship between a client's maladaptive behaviors and daily life events. Important patterns of maladaptive behavior and environmental events may become apparent only when contemporaneously monitored by the client.

A primary assessment tool used to begin treatment and to examine incidents of problem behavior that occur throughout treatment is the *chain* or *behavioral analysis*. The behavioral analysis is one of the most important aspects of assessment; errors in treatment are usually the result of errors in assessment. The purpose of behavioral analysis is to identify the problem, the cause of the problem, and the resources and obstacles that will bear on solving the problem. Behavioral analysis may be brief or may span entire sessions or longer. Table 23.2 lists the steps included in basic behavioral analysis.

EFFECTIVE INTERVENTIONS

Psychodynamic

Despite the development of a number of individual psychodynamic treatments for patients with personality disorders, including BPD (Waldinger, 1987; Kernberg,

Table 23.2   Steps in Behavioral (Chain) Analysis

1. Describe the specific problem behavior targeted in the treatment plan. Detail exactly what the client did, said, thought, and felt, including the intensity of the feelings.
2. Identify the specific precipitating event that began the chain. Start with environmental events; for example, "Why did *the problem* occur yesterday rather than the day before?"
3. Identify factors such as physical illness, poor sleeping, drug or alcohol abuse, or intense emotions that heightened the client's vulnerability to the problem chain at this time.
4. Describe the moment-by-moment chain of events. Examine thoughts, feelings, and actions, and determine whether there were any possible alternatives to these.
5. Identify the consequences of the problem behavior.
6. Generate alternative solutions; for example, what skills might the client have used to avoid the problem behavior as a solution?
7. Identify a prevention strategy to reduce future vulnerability to this problem chain.
8. Repair the significant consequences of the problem behavior.

Selzer, Koenigsberg, Carr, & Applebaum, 1989), to date no data exists on the effectiveness of these treatments. Using a 12-month group intervention based on psychodynamic theory, social workers Elsa Marziali and Heather Munroe-Blum (1994) tested Interpersonal Group Psychotherapy (IGP) for BPD against individual psychodynamic treatment as usual (TAU). IGP differs from traditional psychodynamic approaches in its inclusion of a treatment orientation phase and in therapist accessibility outside the group. Unfortunately, outcome results at 6-month, 12-month, and 24-month follow-up found no differences between the group and individual treatment.

Pharmacological

There have been approximately 15 pharmacologic treatment trials on BPD to date, 6 of which were open or uncontrolled. These trials were generally performed to investigate drug treatment of one of three symptom clusters of BPD: (a) impulsivity, including suicidal behavior and self-mutilation; (b) psychotic-schizotypal symptoms; or (c) affective lability. It is unlikely that any pharmacological agent could treat all three (Frankenberg & Zanarini, 1993; Soloff, 1994). Further, most pharmacotherapy trials of BPD are of short duration, generally 4 to 12 weeks, although BPD is a long-term disorder and acute exacerbations are episodic in nature. In sum, pharmacologic treatment studies focusing on symptom clusters suggest mixed and modest short-term efficacy of a variety of medications for acute symptoms associated with BPD. Neuroleptics—antipsychotic drugs including chlorpromazine (Thorazine), fluphenazine (Prolixin), haloperidol (Haldol), clozapine (Closaril), and risperidone (Risperidol)—seem to be most effective for treating psychotic and schizotypal symptoms. Affective disturbance responds with mixed results to monoamine oxidase inhibitors (MAOIs) and selective serotonin reuptake inhibitors (SSRIs). Impulsivity and aggression respond to varying degrees to SSRIs, such as fluoxetine (Prozac), sertraline (Zoloft), and paroxetine (Paxil); MAOIs, such as tranylcypromine (Parnate), isocarboxazid (Marplan), and phenelzine (Nardil); lithium; and antipsychotics (B. Stanley & R. Dulit, personal communication, October, 1996). For a general discussion of the use of these drugs, see *Mental Disorders, Medications, and Clinical Social Work* (Austrian, 1995).

Dialectical Behavior Therapy

Based on cognitive-behavioral and learning theories, dialectical behavior therapy, (DBT; Linehan, 1993a, 1993b) is the first psychotherapy for BPD with published empirical support based on a randomized experimental design and is designated as a "probably efficacious" treatment based on criteria for empirically validated treatments (American Psychological Association, 1993). Developed by Linehan and colleagues at the University of Washington, DBT originally began as a treatment for chronically suicidal women. Over time it became clear that most of these women also met criteria for BPD and the treatment evolved accordingly. Standard DBT is a 1-year outpatient treatment that simultaneously combines weekly individual psychotherapy with skills-training groups that run 2½ hours per week (Linehan, 1993a, 1993b). The skills-training groups teach adaptive coping skills in the areas of emotion regulation, distress tolerance, interpersonal effectiveness, and identity confusion and maladaptive cognition reduction; each of these skills areas addresses one of the four primary problem areas of BPD clients. The individual treatment addresses maladaptive behaviors while strengthening and generalizing skills. Corollary treatment components of DBT include telephone consultation, team supervision, and consultation with the therapist.

In the first clinical trial, (Linehan, Armstrong, Suarez, Allmon, & Heard, 1991) 47 chronically parasuicidal women meeting criteria for BPD were randomly assigned to either 12 months of DBT or to a community TAU. Assessments occurred every 4 months during treatment and at 12-month follow-up. Results showed that DBT clients were less likely to attempt suicide or to drop out of therapy than TAU clients. They also spent less time in psychiatric hospitals, were better adjusted interpersonally, and were less angry. DBT patients also maintained significantly higher Global Assessment Scale scores (Endicott, Spitzer, Fleiss, & Cohen, 1976) than TAU subjects (Linehan, Heard, & Armstrong, 1993). A reanalysis of the data (Linehan, Heard, & Armstrong, 1993) confirmed that the superiority of DBT was not accounted for by the fact that DBT patients had greater access to psychotherapy and to telephone consultation than did TAU patients. Since its inception, DBT has been adapted to a variety of client populations and settings. The largest application, and only other randomized clinical trial, is with substance-abusing women who also meet criteria for BPD (Linehan & Dimeff, 1995). Preliminary outcome data from this study indicate that individuals in the DBT condition appeared to decrease drug use more than did TAU subjects.

Theory and Procedures.   DBT is defined by its dialectical philosophy and biosocial theory, and by its treatment stages, goals, and strategies. *Dialectical philosophy,* as used in DBT, combines both stress-diathesis and learning models of psychopathology as the framework for synthesizing biological and environmental approaches to the etiology and maintenance of BPD. Emphasis is placed on interconnectedness and wholeness, with all things seen as inherently heterogeneous and comprised of opposing forces that synthesize to produce change. Change is, therefore, viewed as a fundamental aspect of reality.

Biosocial theory is used as the primary lens for viewing BPD behaviors. Biosocial theory views the individual dysfunction in BPD as extreme vulnerability to emotional dysregulation; BPD patterns arise from systemic dysregulation of primary emotions. This dysregulation is the result of ongoing transaction between an individual with some degree of biologically based difficulty regulating emotion and an environment that, to varying degrees, invalidates that individual's responses to the world. The transaction of this biologic vulnerability to emotion dysregulation with an invalidating environment, over time, creates and maintains BPD behavioral patterns.

Treatment Stages and Goals.   DBT is comprised of five stages: a pretreatment stage and four active treatment stages. The goals of DBT are hierarchical and function to guide the clinician in determining the agenda for treatment from session to session, as well as on a long-term basis. According to this hierarchy of treatment goals, each weekly session's agenda is based on the client's behavior since the last session. The daily diary cards described earlier provide the information for this each week.

In *pretreatment,* the therapist orients the client to the philosophy, structure, and format of treatment and obtains the client's agreement to work on the goals of treatment. Because DBT requires voluntary commitment, both therapist and client must have the option of some other form of treatment. In mandated treatment settings, voluntary commitment to DBT involves a verbal decision to pursue DBT over other treatments or over no treatment (generally no individual treatment) at all. This agreement and engagement in the treatment structure are the goals of pretreatment. The goals of DBT, listed following by stages, are clearly prescribed, with suicidal behavior and self-harm at the top of the list. For example, if a client engages in suicidal behavior, he or she must agree that reducing or eliminating suicidal behavior is a goal to work toward. Clients must also agree not to kill themselves while they are in DBT.

Stage 1 focuses on present behavior and current environmental factors, targeting life-threatening behavior and increasing clients' basic capacities (self-control and connection to therapy) to function in treatment. Stage 1 goals include: (a) decreasing suicidal or homicidal behaviors; (b) decreasing therapy interfering behaviors, such as avoidance of therapy, noncompliant behavior, and behaviors that burn out or overwhelm the therapist; (c) decreasing quality-of-life interfering behaviors, such as inability to maintain stable housing, alcohol or substance abuse, or anorexia or bulimia; and (d) increasing behavioral skills needed to make life changes, such as core mindfulness skills, distress tolerance, emotion regulation skills, and interpersonal effectiveness skills.

Stage 2 directly addresses post-traumatic stress syndrome and may include uncovering and reexperiencing prior traumatic or emotionally important events. Although clients might enter Stage 2 with suicidal ideation and strong wishes to be dead, they are not in Stage 2 if they are buying guns for suicide, hoarding pills, or making other concrete plans. If Stage 1 may be thought of as guiding the client to a state of quiet desperation (beginning from one of loud desperation), the goal of Stage 2 is to raise the client from unremitting emotional desperation (Koerner & Linehan, 1996).

Stage 3 targets increasing respect for self and achieving individual goals through synthesizing what has been learned. Developing an ongoing sense of connection to self, to others, and to life is important as clients work toward resolving problems in living.

Stage 4, a recent addition (Linehan, in press) addresses the sense of incompleteness that plagues some individuals even after the resolution of problems in living. Stage 4 goals include developing the capacity for sustained joy, through integrating the past, the present, the future, and the self and others, and accepting reality as it is.

Individual Treatment Strategies.   DBT treatment strategies are divided into four basic sets: (a) dialectical strategies, (b) core strategies (validation and problem-solving), (c) communication strategies (irreverent and reciprocal communication), and (d) case management strategies (consultation to the patient, environmental intervention, supervision, and consultation with therapists). These strategies can be divided into those most related to acceptance and those most related to change (see Table 23.3). The DBT practitioner must balance the use of these two types of strategies within each treatment interaction. One of the DBT therapist's objectives is to help the client understand that behaviors may prove both appropriate or valid and also dysfunctional or in need of change.

Dialectical Strategies.   Dialectical strategies provide the framework for the synthesis of biological and environmental approaches to the etiology and maintenance

Table 23.3   Dialectical Behavioral Therapy Primary Treatment Strategies: Acceptance and Change

Acceptance Strategies and Procedures
   1. Dialectical strategies
   2. Validation strategies
   3. Relationship strategies
   4. Environmental intervention
   5. Reciprocal communication

Change Strategies and Procedures
   1. Dialectical strategies
   2. Problem solving strategies*
   3. Contingency management
   4. Capability enhancement and skills acquisition
   5. Cognitive modification
   6. Exposure
   7. Consultation to the client
   8. Irreverent communication

*Includes behavioral analysis, insight and interpretation, solution analysis, and didactic, trouble shooting, and commitment strategies.

of BPD. The major dialectic underlying DBT is the constant struggle to balance acceptance with movement toward change. Dialectical strategies emphasize balance and helping clients find reality in shades other than black and white. Whether through stories, metaphors, or philosophizing, dialectical strategies can be used to promote change or acceptance. A favorite dialectical metaphor describes the process of therapy as climbing out of hell, but doing it with an aluminum ladder.

Validation Strategies.   Validation begins with empathy. The therapist then proceeds to analyze the client's response in relationship to its context and function. The function of validation is to make the unreasonable reasonable, and to help clients learn how and when to trust themselves. Validation can also serve as acceptance to balance change, and can function to strengthen clinical progress and the therapeutic relationship. There are three types of validation: (a) verbal (direct communication that a statement is valid; for example, "Yes, I can see that you're really upset"), (b) functional (behavioral response that indicates the therapist accepts the client's statement as valid; for example, "Let's take a look at what's upsetting you"), and (c) cheerleading (validating client's capacity, not necessarily beliefs; for example, client says "I can't do it," and therapist replies, "I know you think you can't do it, but I have complete faith that you really can do it").

Validation is further broken down into six levels: Level 1, *active observing,* is unbiased listening and observing; Level 2, *reflecting the observed,* is accurate reflection and discussion toward identification, description, and labeling of the client's behavioral patterns; Level 3, *articulating the unobserved,* is articulating thoughts, memories, assumptions, and feelings that the client is not verbalizing or expressing directly; Level 4, *validation in terms of the past or of biology,* is identifying the learning experiences and biological factors that make the client's current responses inevitable while still identifying the behavior as dysfunctional in the moment; Level 5, *validation in terms of the present,* is identifying events in the current environment that support current response patterns, highlighting those that are functional or normative and identifying those that are dysfunctional; and Level 6, *radical genuineness,* is treating the person as valid. The task is to see and respond to the client's strengths and capacities while remaining empathic toward actual difficulty and incapacity. For therapists this involves throwing off preconceptions of the client role and acting fully, completely, and spontaneously—treating the client without roles, not as fragile or invalid. Condescending responses (as felt by the client) are often invalidating at Level 6, although they may be validating at Levels 4 and 5.

Problem-Solving Strategies.   Based on a primary assumption that client's lives are currently unbearable, DBT places great emphasis on change. Problem-solving procedures, such as skills training, contingency management, cognitive modification, and exposure, are adopted directly from the cognitive-behavioral literature. Client and therapist together identify public and private problematic behaviors and the factors that are associated with the initiation and maintenance of these problem patterns. Next, the client's behavioral excesses and deficits that interfere with engaging in goal behaviors are identified, as well as what the client must learn, experience, and do to perform the goal behavior.

Suicide crisis behavior, parasuicide, self-harm, and intrusive, intense suicidal thoughts, images, and communications, as well as significant changes in suicidal ideation or urges to self-destruct, are always addressed in individual therapy immediately following their occurrence. Although nonsuicidal self-mutilation or other self-injurious behaviors may not seem as critical as actual suicide attempts to the therapist, they are never ignored in DBT; these behaviors are good predictors of future lethal acts and can also cause substantial harm.

A behavioral or chain analysis, as described in the "Assessment Methods" section of this chapter, is the standard tool used to understand problematic behavior. Using information about the event, the client's emotional and cognitive responses, overt actions that preceded the client's behavior, and the consequences of the behavior for the client and the environment, a chain analysis provides a moment-to-moment description of the problem behavior. This analysis indicates one or more of four change strategies: (a) *skills training* addresses the client's lack of capability to engage in more adaptive responses; (b) *contingency management strategies* address the reinforcement strategies that support the client's problematic behavior; (c) *cognitive modification procedures* address faulty beliefs and assumptions that interfere with the client's problem-solving capabilities; and (d) *exposure-based strategies* address anxiety, shame, or other emotional responses that interfere with the client's adaptive problem-solving attempts.

Communication and Stylistic Strategies.   *Reciprocal communication* is characterized by genuineness, warm engagement, and responsiveness. Responsiveness requires the therapist to take the client's agenda and wishes seriously and respond directly to the content of the client's communications. Therapists are encouraged to use both self-involving self-disclosures and personal self-disclosures. An example of a self-involving self-disclosure might be pointing out the effects of the client's behavior on the therapist in a nonjudgmental manner. Personal self-disclosures are used to validate and model coping and normative responses, but should only be used in the best interests of the client. *Irreverent communication* involves a direct, confrontational, matter-of-fact, or off-the-wall style. Used to knock the client from a stance of rigidity to one of uncertainty, irreverent communication is highly useful when the therapist and client are stuck or at an impasse. Often, the therapist pays closer attention to the client's indirect, rather than direct, communications. For example, when a client says, "I am going to kill myself," the therapist might irreverently respond, "But I thought you agreed not to drop out of therapy." Care is taken in observing the effects of irreverent communication to avoid misuse and potentially alienating the client.

Supervision and Consultation.   Another important mode in DBT therapy is the supervision and consultation team. DBT is regarded as a treatment system in which the therapist applies DBT to patients, while a supervisor or consultation team applies DBT to the therapist. Consultation to the therapist serves several functions. Most important, the supervisor and consultation team help ensure that the therapist stays in the therapeutic relationship and stays effective in that relationship. Without ongoing supervision or consultation, therapists can become extreme in their positions, blame the clients as much as they blame themselves, and become less open to feedback from others about the conduct of their treatment.

Telephone Consultations.   Between-session contact is an integral component of DBT. This extratherapeutic contact serves several functions: (a) to provide coaching in skills and to promote skills generalization; (b) to promote emergency crisis intervention in an contingent manner (as such, DBT clients are typically invited to call before suicidal crises, or at least before they harm themselves; once self-harm has occurred, they are told they cannot phone their therapist for 24 hours afterwards); and (c) to provide an opportunity to resolve misunderstandings and conflicts that arise during therapy sessions, instead of waiting an entire week to deal with the emotions.

Skills-training Group.   An important assumption underlying DBT is that many of the problems experienced by BPD clients are due to a combination of motivation problems and behavioral skill deficits; that is, the necessary skills to regulate painful affect were never learned. For this reason, DBT emphasizes skills building to facilitate behavior change and acceptance. In standard DBT, skills are taught weekly in 2½-hour psychoeducational skills-training groups. These skills are outlined and described in detail in the *Skills Training Manual for Borderline Personality Disorder* (Linehan, 1993b). The function of the skills group is to teach individuals specific behavioral skills necessary to ameliorate individual dysfunctional behavior patterns. The DBT group emphasizes skills-building procedures through modeling, instructions, behavioral rehearsal, feedback and coaching, and homework assignments.

Group skills training works in tandem with individual therapy. Simultaneous group and individual treatment creates a dedicated time to learn much-needed skills and a separate context for coached individual application. BPD clients frequently arrive for individual sessions in crisis; the therapist typically attends to these issues, and little time is left to learn the skills. When skills are taught in group, the individual therapist can deal with current crises and serve as a skills coach, encouraging practice of particular skills.

Group skills training has several advantages over individual skills training. Group members learn from each other and can practice skills with group members engaged in the same tasks; skills practice is coached by the skills trainer's extra set of expert eyes; and group membership often decreases isolation and increases clients' sense of feeling understood. The cotherapist role may be used and discussed as an interpersonal model. If clients are socially phobic or must begin skills training in individual sessions, moving them to group skills training becomes a focus of treatment.

The four DBT skills training modules directly target the behavioral, emotional, and cognitive instability and dysregulation of BPD: mindfulness, interpersonal effectiveness, emotion regulation, and distress tolerance. In standard DBT, the first 2 weeks of any given module are spent on mindfulness and the remaining 6 weeks are spent on the particular module.

Mindfulness. This is a psychological and behavioral translation of the meditation skills usually taught in eastern spiritual practices. The goal of this module is attentional control, awareness, and sense of true self. Three primary states of mind are presented: (a) *reasonable mind* (the logical, analytical, problem-solving state), (b) *emotion mind* (the opposite; allows creativity, passion, and drama), and (c) *wise mind* (the integration of both the reasonable and the emotion mind). Wise mind allows appropriate response—one responds as needed, given the situation.

Distress Tolerance. Distress tolerance focuses on the ability to accept both oneself and the current environmental situation in a nonevaluative manner. While implying acceptance of reality, it does not imply approval. Self-soothing, adaptive activity-oriented distraction, and consideration of the pros and cons of distress tolerance are skills within this module.

Interpersonal Effectiveness. Similar to standard interpersonal problem-solving and assertion, these skills include effective strategies for asking for what one needs and saying no to requests. Effectiveness here is defined as obtaining changes or objectives one wants, keeping the relationship, and building and maintaining self-respect.

Emotion Regulation. This is defined as the ability to: (a) increase or decrease physiological arousal associated with emotion, (b) reorient attention, (c) inhibit mood-dependent actions, (d) experience emotions without escalating or blunting, and (e) organize behavior in the service of external nonmood dependent goals. Emotion regulation begins with the identification and labeling of current emotions. This occurs through observing and describing events that prompt emotions and one's interpretations of these events and through understanding the physiological responses, emotionally expressive behaviors, and aftereffects of emotions. Reducing vulnerability to emotional reactivity is also targeted.

Marital and Family Components. In standard DBT (Linehan, 1993a), clients are offered consultation on how to handle family and friends, but others are not actively involved in DBT, except through the client. Consultation helps the client communicate effectively with the family about treatment and about what he or she needs from friends and family. Conflict resolution and problem-solving are also frequently part of consultation. Family sessions may be held if client and therapist agree they would be useful, but are never held without the client.

In response to high distress on the part of families of BPD clients and in an effort to access this important aspect of the client's environment more directly, recent adaptations of DBT have included direct family involvement. Fruzetti, Hoffman, and Linehan (in press) have extended DBT to families and significant others of BPD clients. DBT for families contains both psychoeducational didactic components and skills-building components. Families meet in multiple family groups or in individual sessions, generally with the client present. The biosocial model of BPD is explained and the characteristics of BPD are identified and normalized (for example, "Many people suffer from this disorder"). Families learn DBT skills to help support clients in their change efforts and to help themselves cope with clients' dysfunctional behavior patterns; mindfulness, distress tolerance, interpersonal effectiveness, and emotion regulation are taught in a fashion similar to their presentation in the skills manual (Linehan, 1993b).

Environmental Components: Casework and Other Consultation

Case management or environmental intervention strategies are a less developed component of standard DBT, but they provide an excellent rationale and context for many traditional advocacy and casework activities. Although these activities are familiar to many social work clinicians, DBT's strong learning theory base uses them differently and, often, for different reasons. DBT focuses on skills building and believes in the clients' ability to learn more effective ways of intervening in their own environments. Direct environmental intervention by the social worker is warranted only under certain conditions. Advocacy for its own sake is not regarded as a helpful act. Conditions requiring direct intervention include: (a) when the client is unable to act on his or her own and the outcome is very important (for example, a suicidal, depersonalizing client who cannot tell the family that he or she needs them to stay with him or her); (b) when the environment is intransigent and high in power (for example, a client applying for social services); (c) to save the life of the client or avoid substantial risk to others (for example, a client at high risk of committing suicide or child abuse); (d) when it is the humane thing to do and will cause no harm; that is, it does not substitute passive for active problem solving (for example, meeting with a client outside the ordinary setting in a crisis); (e) when the client is a minor (Linehan, 1993a).

DBT case management, as elsewhere, helps the client manage the physical and social environment to enhance overall life functioning and well-being. Case management strategies include consultation to the patient, environmental intervention, and social worker supervision and consultation. These function as guidelines for applying the DBT core strategies to the environment outside the client-therapist relationship. The social worker coaches the client on effective interaction with the environment, working to generalize skills. If the client does not possess the requisite skills for effectively intervening in the environment and the situation requires immediate resolution, the social worker acts as advocate and model and interacts with other professionals on behalf of the client, but only in the client's presence.

CONCLUSIONS

DBT is an empirically derived treatment for BPD. It is humane, client-based, and incorporates a biosocial perspective, acknowledging the powerful role of the environment in the etiology and maintenance of this longstanding behavioral disorder. It has demonstrated effectiveness in two randomized clinical trials treating women with BPD and in an inpatient program where DBT was compared to TAU (Barley, Buie, & Peterson, 1993); results were similar to those of Linehan's studies. Duke University and the Durham Veterans Administration Hospital were also funded to test DBT for women veterans diagnosed with BPD, and a fourth clinical trial with women diagnosed with eating disorders who meet criteria for BPD was recently funded at Stanford University.

Other adaptations that show excellent promise, but to date report no data, include adaptation for inpatient psychiatric settings (Swenson & Linehan, 1995), DBT for inner city suicidal adolescents (Miller, Rathus, Linehan, Wetzler, & Leigh, 1997), day treatment applications (Swenson, Sanderson, Hoffman, & Linehan, 1996), forensic psychiatric settings (including adaptations for both BPD and Antisocial Personality Disorder patients; Ball, McCann, Linehan, & Ivanoff, unpublished manuscript), and emergency psychiatric settings (McKeon, 1996, unpublished manuscript). As development and adaptation of DBT to other problems and settings occurs, it is important that those conducting these efforts remain clear about the essential need to continue empirical validation of this compassionate and scientific treatment.

REFERENCES

American Psychiatric Association. (1987). *Diagnostic and statistical manual of mental disorders* (3rd ed., rev.). Washington, DC: Author.

American Psychiatric Association. (1994). *Diagnostic and statistical manual of mental disorders* (4th ed.). Washington, DC: Author.

American Psychological Association. (1993). *Task force on promotion and dissemination of psychological procedures: A report adopted by the Division 12 Board.* Washington, DC: Author.

Austrian, S. G. (1995). *Mental disorder, medications, and clinical social work.* New York: Columbia University Press.

Ball, E., McCann, R., Linehan, M. M., & Ivanoff, A. (1996). *Dialectical behavior therapy application to an inpatient forensic unit and modifications for antisocial characteristics.* Unpublished manuscript.

Barley, W. D., Buie, S. E., & Peterson, E. W. (1993). The development of an inpatient cognitive-behavioral treatment program for borderline personality disorder. *Journal of Personality Disorders, 7,* 232–240.

Beck, A. T., Freeman, A., & Associates. (1990). Cognitive therapy of personality disorders. New York: Guilford Press.

Bongar, B. (Ed.). (1992). *Suicide: Guidelines for assessment, management, and treatment.* New York: Oxford University Press.

Craig, R. J. (1988). A psychometric study of the prevalence of DSM-III personality disorders among treated opiate addicts. *International Journal of the Addictions, 23,* 115–124.

Endicott, J., Spitzer, R. L., Fleiss, J. L., & Cohen, J. (1976). The Global Assessment Scale. *Archives of General Psychiatry, 33,* 766–771.

First, M. B., Spitzer, R. L., Gibbon, M., & Williams, J. B. (1995). Structured clinical interview for DSM-IV Axis I disorders-patient edition (SCID-I/P, Version 2.0). New York: Biometrics Research Department.

Frances, A., Fyer, M., & Clarkin, J. F. (1986). Personality and suicide. In J. J. Mann, & M. Stanley (Eds.), *Psychobiology of suicidal behavior.* New York: New York Academy of Sciences.

Frankenberg, F. R., & Zanarini, M. C. (1993). Clozapine treatment of borderline patients: A preliminary study. *Comprehensive Psychiatry, 34,* 402–405.

Friedman, C. J., Shear, M. C., & Frances, A. J. (1987). DSM-III personality disorders in panic patients. *Journal of Personality Disorders, 1,* 132–135.

Fruzetti, A. E., Hoffman, P., & Linehan, M. M. (in press). *Dialectical behavior therapy with families.* New York: Guilford Press.

Fyer, M. R. (1988). Suicide attempts in patients with borderline personality disorder. *American Journal of Psychiatry, 145,* 737–739.

Fyer, M. R., Frances, A. J., Sullivan, T., Hurt, S. W., & Clarkin, J. (1988). Comorbidity of borderline personality disorder. *Archives of General Psychiatry, 45,* 348–352.

Gunderson, J. G. (1984). *Borderline personality disorder.* Washington, DC: American Psychiatric Association Press.

Hellman, I. D., Morrison, T. L., & Abramowitz, S. I. (1986). The stresses of psychotherapeutic work: A replication and extension. *Psychological Medicine, 42,* 197–205.

Herman, J. L., Perry, J., & van der Kolk, B. (1989). Childhood trauma in borderline personality disorder. *American Journal of Psychiatry, 146,* 490–495.

Hyler, S., Reider, R., Williams, J., Spitzer, R., Lyons, M., & Hendler, J. (1989). A comparison of clinical and self-report diagnoses of DSM-III personality disorders in 552 patients. *Comprehensive Psychiatry, 30,* 170–178.

Inman, D. J., Bascue, L. O., & Skoloda, T. (1985). Identification of borderline personality disorders among substance abusing inpatients. *Journal of Substance Abuse Treatment, 2,* 229–232.

Kernberg, O., Selzer, M., Koenigsberg, H., Carr, A., & Appelbaum, A. (1989). *Psychodynamic psychotherapy of borderline patients.* New York: Basic Books.

Kirk, S. A., & Kutchins, H. (1992). *The selling of DSM: The rhetoric of science in psychiatry.* Hawthorne, NY: Aldine deGruyter.

Koerner, K., & Linehan, M. M. (1997). Case formulation in dialectical behavior therapy for borderline personality disorder. In T. Eells (Ed.), *Handbook of psychotherapy case formulation* (pp. 340–367). New York: Guilford Press.

Linehan, M. M. (1981). A social-behavioral analysis of suicide and parasuicide: Implications for clinical assessment and treatment. In H. Glazer & J. F. Clarkin (Eds.), *Depression: Behavioral and directive intervention strategies* (pp. 229–294). New York: Garland.

Linehan, M. M. (1993a). *Cognitive-behavioral treatment for borderline personality disorder.* New York: Guilford Press.

Linehan, M. M. (1993b). *Skills training manual for treating borderline personality disorder.* New York: Guilford Press.

Linehan, M. M. (in press). Dialectical behavior therapy: A model for treating the high risk, chronically suicidal patient. In A. Bohart & A. L. Greenberg (Eds.), *Empathy and psychotherapy: New directions to theory, research, and practice.* Washington, D.C.: American Psychological Association.

Linehan, M. M., Armstrong, H. E., Suarez, A., Allmon, D., & Heard, H. L. (1991). Cognitive-behavioral treatment of chronically parasuicidal borderline patients. *Archives of General Psychiatry, 48,* 1060–1064.

Linehan, M. M., & Dimeff, L. A. (1995). *Extension of standard dialectical behavior therapy to treatment of substance abusers with borderline personality disorder.* Unpublished manuscript. University of Washington.

Linehan, M. M., Heard, H. L., & Armstrong, H. E. (1993). Naturalistic follow-up of a behavioral treatment for chronically parasuicidal borderline patients. *Archives of General Psychiatry, 50,* 971–974.

Loranger, A. (1996). *Manual for the International Personality Disorder Examination.* White Plains, NY: New York Hospital–Cornell Medical Center.

Maris, R. W., Berman, A. L., Maltsberger, J. T., & Yufit, R. I. (1992). *Assessment and prediction of suicide.* New York: Guilford Press.

Marziali, E. A., & Munroe-Blum, H. (1994). *Interpersonal group psychotherapy for borderline personality disorder.* New York: Basic Books.

Miller, A. L., Rathus, J. H., Linehan, M. M., Wetzler, S., & Leigh, E. (1997). DBT adapted for suicidal adolescents. *Journal of Practical and Behavioral Psychiatry, 3,* 78–86.

Millon, T. (1987). *Manual for the MCMI-II.* Minneapolis, MN: National Computer Systems.

Morey, L. C. (1988). Personality disorders in DSM-III and DSM-IIIR: Convergence, coverage, and internal consistency. *American Journal of Psychiatry, 145,* 573–578.

Nace, E. P., Saxon, J. J., & Shore, N. (1983). A comparison of borderline and non-borderline alcoholic patients. *Archives of General Psychiatry, 50,* 157–158.

Pervin, E. A. (1990). *Handbook of personality: Theory and research.* New York: Guilford Press.

Pfohl, B., Coryell, W., Zimmerman, M., & Stangl, D. (1986). DSM-III personality disorders: Diagnostic overlap and internal consistency of individual DSM-III criteria. *Comprehensive Psychiatry, 27,* 21–34.

Pfohl, B., Polum, N., & Zimmerman, M. (1995). *The structured interview for DSM-IV personality disorders.* Unpublished manuscript. University of Iowa.

Slodol, J. H., Rosnick, L., Kellman, D., Oldham, J., & Hyler, S. (1988). Validating structure of DSM-III-R personality disorder assessments with longitudinal data. *American Journal of Psychiatry, 145,* 1297–1299.

Soloff, P. H. (1994). Is there any drug treatment of choice for the borderline patient? *Acta Psychiatrica Scandinavia, 89*(Suppl. 379), 50–55.

Swenson, C., & Linehan, M. M. (1995). *Dialectical behavior therapy in an inpatient setting.* Unpublished manuscript. University of Washington.

Swenson, C., Sanderson, C., & Linehan, M. M. (1996). *Applying dialectical behavior therapy on inpatient units.* Unpublished manuscript. University of Washington.

Waldinger, R. J. (1987). Intensive psychodynamic therapy with borderline patients: An overview. *American Journal of Psychiatry, 144,* 267–274.

Widiger, T. A., & Frances, A. J. (1989). Epidemiology, diagnosis, and comorbidity of borderline personality disorder. In A. Tasman, R. E. Hales, & A. Frances (Eds.), *American Psychiatric Press Review of Psychiatry,* Vol. 8. Washington, DC: American Psychiatric Press.

Zanarini, M. C., Gunderson, J. G., Frankenberg, F. R., & Chauncey, A. B. (1989). The revised diagnostic interview for borderlines: Discriminating BPD from other Axis II disorders. *Journal of Personality Disorder, 3,* 10–18.

Author Index

Subject Index